George Eliot

A Writer's Notebook, 1854-1879

And Uncollected Writings

George Eliot

A Writer's Notebook

1854-1879

And Uncollected Writings

Edited by

Joseph Wiesenfarth

Published for the Bibliographical Society
of the University of Virginia
by the University Press of Virginia
Charlottesville

THE UNIVERSITY PRESS OF VIRGINIA
Copyright © 1981 by the Rector and Visitors
of the University of Virginia

First published 1981

Library of Congress Cataloging in Publication Data
Eliot, George, pseud., i.e. Marian Evans, afterwards Cross, 1819-1880.
  A writer's notebook, 1854-1879, and uncollected
writings.

  Includes bibliographical references and index.
  I. Wiesenfarth, Joseph. II. Title.
PR4653.W53   1981   823'.8   80-23271
ISBN 0-8139-0887-6

Printed in the United States of America

For

William M. Gibson

Dimmi che è cagion perchè dimostri
Nel dire e nel guardar d'avermi caro?

Contents

Illustrations

Preface

A _Writer's Notebook_ prints the only manuscript in which George
Eliot recorded her research for _Adam Bede_ and _The Mill on the
Floss_. The notebook is one of two that she kept for _Felix Holt_
and one of two that are extant for _The Spanish Gypsy_. It is one
of three notebooks that she used for _Romola_, one of four that she
kept for _Middlemarch_, and one of six that she compiled for _Daniel
Deronda_. Although _Silas Marner_ seems to have been written without extensive prior study, the notebook contains at least one
entry pertinent to its composition. There are also specific
notes for poems like "Ex Oriente Lux" and "Stradivarius" and more
general notes for "The Legend of Jubal." In addition, the notebook contains information that George Eliot used in writing reviews and essays; it also shows that she was immersed in the
reading of Greek tragedy while writing _Scenes of Clerical Life_.
The earliest date that can be given with certainty for an entry
is 31 November 1854, and the latest date that can be given with
certainty is 28 December 1879.

The notebook is the longest and most comprehensive one in
George Eliot's hand, covering twenty-five years and every phase
of her career. The initial failure properly to identify its contents led to its mistitling and subsequent obscurity. The
present edition is offered to suggest its proper place in George
Eliot studies and to make available a manuscript that unedited
must remain inaccessible to most readers.

The Uncollected Writings are primarily intended to amplify
the implications of the manuscript's content. They bring together for the first time a significant number of George Eliot's
articles that have never been collected and are not readily available. The criteria for selection have been, first, an article's
relevance to entries in the notebook and, second, its relative
inaccessibility in collected editions of her works. Thus, only
one of the articles collected here has been reprinted since its
first appearance in a periodical. Articles pertinent to entries
that are easily available--"Liszt, Wagner, and Weimar" or "Woman
in France," for instance--have not been reprinted. Following the
example of Thomas Pinney in his edition of _Essays of George Eliot_
(London: Routledge and Kegan Paul, 1963), I have presented each
selection with a headnote that suggests its significance. If
evidence is not presented in a headnote to attribute an article
to George Eliot, that article will be found listed in Pinney's
Appendix A: George Eliot's Periodical Essays and Reviews (pp.
452-5). The footnotes in the Uncollected Writings are all editorial additions.

In editing the manuscript I have tried to provide an accurate clear text that is unobstructed by editorial symbols. The
one exception is the occasional use of ornamental brackets {}
that distinguish an editorial emendation from material that
George Eliot encloses within her own brackets []. Otherwise,
changes either fall under the general procedures that are out-
lined below or are recorded in the textual notes.

Entry numbers after 50 are page numbers in the manuscript;
when they appear in the middle of an entry, they are preserved
within diagonal lines separated from the text by three spaces
(thus: "My horse," he says,   /52/   "was so exceedingly lame
. . ."). Commas and periods are printed within quotation marks,
even though they are sometimes outside them in the manuscript.

The occasional double hyphen (=) is rendered as a hyphen (thus:
"cumulo-stratus," not "cumulo=stratus"). Abbreviations such as
"2d" and "wh." and "41b" are rendered in modern style (thus: "2d"
and "wh." and "41b"). The ampersand, however, is retained. So
too is George Eliot's use of "ss" instead of "ß" in German (thus:
"Dass," not "daß").

     George Eliot's inconsistent use of accents in foreign
languages is silently made consistent. Four pages of Greek quotations are reproduced in facsimile in lieu of any textual notes
in Greek.

     When George Eliot uses one of a set of quotation marks,
parentheses, or brackets, the other is silently provided.
Similarly, the editorial addition and alteration of periods and
commas for the sake of clarity is not indicated in the textual
notes. The same is true of an occasional necessary emendation
of ellipsis. Other changes are indicated.

     I have tried to preserve George Eliot's paragraphing; this
was a task, nevertheless, that sometimes required interpretation
and occasionally a decision in favor of clarity of presentation
or economy of space.

Acknowledgments

The editing of this notebook has been in process for six years, and I could not have brought the work to completion without the generosity and good will of more people than I can mention in these acknowledgments. But I would like to thank Jonathan G. Ouvry for his permission to publish the manuscript and Marjorie G. Wynne, Research Librarian of the Beinecke Rare Book and Manuscript Library at Yale University, for her unfailing support of the edition. I am also indebted to John Creasey, Head Assistant Librarian, and Janet E. Barnes of Dr. Williams's Library, London, for their courtesy during two research trips to Gordon Square. I would like to thank the Regents of the University of California for permission to publish portions of the text that appeared as "George Eliot's Notes for Adam Bede" in Nineteenth-Century Fiction in 1977. The facsimile pages of George Eliot's manuscript are reproduced by courtesy of the Beinecke Rare Book and Manuscript Library.

My principal research assistant for this project was Angela Palmisono; she invariably persisted when I gave up and inevitably found what I could not find. Her successors were Rob Watson and John Hurley. Badri N. Raina, now of the University of Delhi, India, and Susan Kahn helped me to transcribe the manuscript. Topf Wells proofread the typescript. The first full draft of the book was typed with great good will by Megan Hudson, and the camera-ready copy with skill and patience by Ardella Nelson of Quality Typing Service.

I was ably assisted in the translation of foreign languages by Frederic G. Cassidy, Matthew Hogan, and John C. McGalliard of the Dictionary of American Regional English; by Gert Loose of the University of Hamburg and by Ian Loram and Sieghardt Riegel of the University of Wisconsin-Madison; and by Romana Cortese. Priscilla Neill and Judy Touhy of the Interlibrary Loan, Memorial Library, University of Wisconsin-Madison, were unremitting in their efforts to get me every book and periodical I needed to follow George Eliot down the byways of learning. Mary Ann O'Donnell of Manhattan College, New York, traveled to the Beinecke Library for me when I could not travel there myself to check the manuscript for pencil markings and entries in purple ink. William M. Gibson, my colleague in the English Department at Wisconsin, initiated me into some of the mysteries of editing and taught me more than one lesson in proofreading.

Help from many quarters would have been to no avail, however, without the financial support of the Graduate School Research Committee and the Institute for Research in the Humanities of the University of Wisconsin-Madison. They provided me with the time and travel that I needed to carry out this work.

To my wife Louise, who worked at my side in the British Library, who translated French, German, and Italian for me when my own resources failed, who read proof, and, who in the midst of it all found time to have a baby, I owe an inexpressible debt of appreciation and affection. And to my son Adam, who neither shredded my manuscript nor ate it when opportunity inadvertently allowed, I express my infinite relief and genuine gratitude.

Introduction

On 17 April 1930, the fourth day of sale of "Valuable Printed Books, Literary . . . Manuscripts, [and] Autograph Letters," at Sotheby and Co., London, lot 913 was knocked down to Gabriel Wells, a prominent New York bookseller, for £105. The catalogue described it as follows:

GEORGE ELIOT'S BOOK OF QUOTATIONS, 311 pp. The note-book contains quotations in poetry and prose in English literature from the time of Shakespeare to Tennyson. Also quotations from Aeschylus, Euripides, Horace, Dante, Goethe and other classical writers. Also notes and extracts from works on political and ecclesiastical history, natural science, architecture, antique gems and numerous other matters, <u>bound</u> <u>in</u> <u>black</u> <u>cloth</u>. <u>8vo</u>[1]

This book of quotations had been consigned to Sotheby's by Miss Elsie Druce, the niece of John Walter Cross, Eliot's spouse from 6 May 1880 until her death on 22 December of the same year. Cross himself died 3 November 1924.

The manuscript was subsequently purchased by Yale University in 1931, with monies from the Altschul Fund, and catalogued in the Beinecke Rare Book and Manuscript Library as "COMMONPLACE BOOK: autograph manuscript notebook, with index / [307]p. 19 1/2 cm. / <u>Bound</u> <u>in</u> original cloth covers, protected by a cloth wrapper covered with black dressing." It is now listed in the register of the "George Eliot (1819-1880) and George Henry Lewes (1817-1878) Collection," prepared by Gordon S. Haight and Marjorie G. Wynne in 1975, as item IV. 6. COMMONPLACE NOTEBOOK.

In classical rhetoric the term "commonplace" is used to label a striking or notable passage that is jotted down for later reference or use; a "commonplace book" is a collection of such passages. Since the notebook in hand fits that description in very small part only, we must conclude that the designation "Commonplace Book" was given it as a convenience to catalogue what Sotheby's called a "Book of Quotations." There is certainly no indication in its provenance that George Eliot ever called her notebook by that name. Moreover, the contents of the manuscript, with few exceptions, are of a kind one would expect to find in a writer's working notebook. It contains notes which Eliot made preparatory to writing some early reviews, notes relating to all her novels (though little on <u>Silas</u> <u>Marner</u>; see entry 103, n. 5), and notes for <u>The</u> <u>Spanish</u> <u>Gypsy</u> and some shorter poems. Conservatively dated, the entries run from 1854 to 1879 and span her varied career as reviewer, essayist, novelist, and poet.[2] The misnomer "Commonplace Book" may also in part derive from Eliot's alphabetizing pages of the book from entry 49 through entry 297. It is evident, however, that only a few entries in the notebook are appropriately conjoined with these letters: the quotations from Goethe under "G" and from Horace under "H," for example. Some early entries in the book, then, do correspond to a letter-index; most, however, do not. Dante, for instance, is found under "F" and "G." And of the large body of notes taken for <u>Adam</u> <u>Bede</u>, entries 49-61 appear under "A," 62-69 under "B," 70-73 under "C," and 74-76 under "D"; but they are completely unrelated to the letters under which they appear.[3] What the notes for <u>Adam</u> <u>Bede</u> show, in short, is that a book that may originally have been designed to be a commonplace book was actually used as a writer's notebook.

    The notebook has a dark brown cloth cover that is embossed
front and back with two rectangular borders enclosing a third
border with leaf scrolls in the corners which are joined to each
other by straight fluted lines. This cover is soiled by ink
stains. The spine is embossed with five imitation hinges. The
brown cover is protected from further damage by a well-worn black
buckram jacket that seems to have been varnished. This jacket is
secured by black thread. The boards are 19.5 centimeters long
and 11.5 centimeters wide; the book's pages are, cumulatively, 2
centimeters thick. The edges of the pages are marbled, and there
are also marbled endpapers. An octagonal label pasted on the
inside of the front board reads in letterpress: Letts, Son &
Steer, / Stationers / and / Account Book Manufacturers / 8, Royal
Exchange & 24 Queen St."; and in longhand below the letterpress:
"G 721 11/11/51 / 24 Shs Post 8^V. Cloth." One white sheet of
heavy grade paper has been removed between the front endpaper and
the first page of George Eliot's index to the entries. The remaining fraction of the excised page is partially glued to the
white verso of the endpaper and covers some letters of words in
the quotations on the endpaper from Herodotus, Goethe, and Quintilian. Pages containing entries 38 and 83 to 88 are similarly
excised. The index to entries shows that 83 contained a quotation or quotations from Bunyan and that 84 (perhaps through 88)
contained "Memoranda." (Since Bunyan is alluded to in The Mill
on the Floss and since 89 begins an entry on "Inundations," these
memoranda may have applied to The Mill.) There is no entry on
the page numbered 194, though it is evident that there once were
two lines written in pencil. ("P group of M at Rome" is all that
remains visible.) And on the pages that should be numbered 233,
253, and 311 the number is missing.

    Each page contains one double brown line 1 centimeter from
the top, followed by 31 faint blue-gray ruled lines spaced 1/2
centimeter apart. Of the entries in the book, 99 percent are in
black ink, although there is some gray and purple ink to be noted,
as well as some penciled entries. The verso of the marbled front
endpaper is written on. It is followed by George Eliot's partial
index of entries. Entries 1 to 50 are numbered individually and
vary greatly in length: entry 13 is little more than a line;
entry 39 is four and a half pages. Beginning with entry 51 the
numbers no longer designate individual items but are used by
Eliot as page numbers.

    There are further variations that should also be noticed.
Beginning with entry 49 and continuing to entry 257--entries run
to 311--George Eliot has alphabetized the outer corners of pages.
The letters are in pencil. The corresponding letters and entry
numbers are as follows:

A	49–61	N	174–183
B	62–69	O	184–193
C	70–73	P	194–205
D	74–81	Q	206–213
E	82–91	R	214–223
F	92–101	S	224–235
G	102–111	T	236–245
H	112–121	U	246–255
I	122–131	V	256–263
J	132–143	W	264–273
K	144–153	X	274–279
L	154–163	Y	280–289
M	164–173	Z	290–297

The remainder of the manuscript pages are numbered 1 through 24 on the top outside edges, with the numbers 5 through 10 and 19 through 22 missing. The corresponding entry numbers (left column) and added page numbers (right column) are as follows:

298-301	1-4
302-309	11-18
310-311	23-24

Some pages also have titles that share the space above the double brown lines with entry numbers and letters:

E	89	Architecture: its History (Ruskin)
G	111	From Goethe Faust II
H	112	Goethe
H	113	Horace
H	117	Toleration
I	125	Petrarch's contempt of women.
I	129	Legendary Art
I	130	Legendary Art
I	131	Superstitions in medicine
J	135	Legendary Art
J	136	Legendary Art, contd.
J	143	Ecclesiastical Vestments
K	144	Ecclesiastical Vestments
K	145	Ecclesiastical Vestments
K	147	Legendary Art
L	154	Greek Months
O	187	Arius.
P	195	Naples
Q	212	Transmutation of Consonants
Q	213	(Grimm's Law.)
R	221	Miraculous Bushes
R	222	Worship of Apollo
S	235	Romance Languages
T	242	Study of Hebrew
V	258	Gypsies contd. from p. 221
X	279	Hebrew Alphabet
Y	282	Arguments of the Iliad
Z	296	Celtic Literature
13	304	Buddhism

This listing of titles--together with the description in Sotheby's sale catalogue--suggests the variety of subjects and sources in the notebook. But these titles are deceptive in one way. They are all in English; whereas what they designate is not. Goethe, for instance, is in German, Petrarch in Italian, Horace in Latin; the alphabet is in Hebrew, the months are in Greek, and the miraculous bushes in French. Besides English, George Eliot read Greek, Latin, French, German, Italian, and Spanish. The notebook contains entries in all these languages. For readers who prefer to read the original languages quoted, I have attempted to provide an accurate text, correcting Eliot's errors in transcription while recording them in textual notes; for readers more comfortable in English, I have striven to provide adequate translations of all quotations from foreign languages in the notes to particular entries. I also have tried to trace the sources of all entries and to suggest their pertinence to Eliot's career as reviewer, essayist, novelist, and poet. The following pages of

introduction attempt to synthesize some of this information and
to suggest the usefulness of the notebook in learning more about
George Eliot's practice of her craft.

Essays and Reviews

A significant number of entries in the notebook are related to
reviews and essays that George Eliot either wrote or projected
writing. Some entries, like 8 and 27--the story of the Flying
Dutchman and the anecdote concerning Phidias and Praxiteles--were
used verbatim or paraphrased in translation in the article "Liszt,
Wagner, and Weimar" for Fraser's Magazine[4] and the review "The
Art and Artists of Greece" for Saturday Review (see Uncollected
Writings, p. 280). Notes were also extensively taken (entries
26, 27-29, 39-40) for the first and last reviews of Adolf Stahr's
Torso: Kunst, Künstler und Kunstwerk den Alten, and the structure
of the reviews, especially "The Art of the Ancients" (Uncollected
Writings, p. 244) is indebted to these entries. The same review
contains Eliot's translation of Stahr's insistence that art and
culture, like natural products and their cultivation, developed
first in the East and then in the West:

> Modern botanical research has proved that almost everything
> which is necessary, useful, and agreeable to us in the vegetable
> kingdom came in a gradual procession from Asia, until it was
> arrested at the western coast of Europe. And now that after a
> short rest it has sprung across the Atlantic this propagation
> pursues its course through America towards the West. But the
> West receives the gifts of the East only to refine the rude, to
> develop the imperfect, to ennoble the common.

This idea was transcribed into the notebook in entry 26:

> The progress of organic nature, say the naturalists, is from East
> to West. Almost everything necessary, useful & pleasant in the
> vegetable world has gradually proceeded from Asia towards the
> West. So with human development & culture. Was it that in the
> first revolution of our globe on its axis the East was first
> towards the Sun--that it started on its course with its Eastern
> cheek on the sunny side--& so this priority, like the first move
> in chess, gave the East precedence in all things?

George Eliot found this image of cultural development so congenial
to herself that she repeated it in its original form in her
Saturday Review notice of Torso (Uncollected Writings, p. 280),
modified it to begin her Leader review of The Shaving of Shagpat
(Uncollected Writings, p. 264), and composed a poem (Uncollected
Writings, p. 285) on its theme:

> So Asia was the earliest home of light,:
> The little seeds first germinated there,
> Birds first made bridals, & the year first knew
> Autumnal ripeness.

Dating from 1866, "Ex Oriente Lux" is an instance of the lasting
seminal value of an idea that first came to Eliot in 1855.
    Another entry, 25, was similarly inspired by a book that she
was reviewing for the Leader in 1855. Saint-Marc Girardin's Cours

de Littérature Dramatique was reviewed under the title "Love in the Drama" (Uncollected Writings, p. 253). In his book Girardin asks, "Why, in ancient poetry and in the Italian novel, . . . do the women love before being loved? why do they feel the passion before inspiring it? and why, in modern poetry and romance, do we find the contrary?" When Girardin goes on to say that Shakespeare is a modern in his treatment of love--his women love only after being loved--Eliot flatly disagrees with him: "Shakespeare's women have no more decided characteristic than the frankness with which they avow their love, not only to themselves, but to the men they love." This statement complements entry 25: "It is remarkable that Shakespear's women almost always make love, in opposition to the conventional notion of what is fitting for women. Yet his pictures of women are belauded. Is it so with his contemporary dramatists?"

George Eliot's interest in the condition of women is frequently manifested in the notebook beginning with her early entries on Egyptian women (entries 2, 4-7), which suggest the superior place they held in their society. Her entries on women generally tend to give the lie to a quotation from Emilia Galotti which states that"a woman who thinks is as nauseating as a man who wears makeup" (entry 10). This bitter observation is in the same vein as one from Petrarch in entry 125: "Among the vexations of the world none is more wearisome than a woman who is insolent and incapable of silence." Eliot's belief lies more in the direction of her comment in "Woman in France: Madam de Sablé": "Women become superior in France by being admitted to a common fund of ideas; to common objects of interest with men; and this must ever be the essential condition at once of true womanly culture and true social well-being."[5] With the condition of women in mind, Eliot proposed to John Chapman that she follow her essay on "Woman in France" with one on "Woman in Germany":

The subject I now propose is "Woman in Germany"--not simply the modern German woman, who is not a very fertile subject (metaphorically speaking) but woman as she presents herself to us in all the phases of development through which the German race has run from the earliest historic twilight when it was still blended with the Scandinavian race--and its women were prophetesses, through the periods of the Volks wanderung and the romantic and bugerlich life of the Middle Ages up to our own day. There is a great deal of picturesque material on this subject and I am just in the midst of it here, so that it would suit me perhaps better than any other just now.[6]

Eliot never wrote the essay; nevertheless, she gathered material toward the writing of it in the notebook. In December 1854 she was reading Johannes Scherr's Deutsche Cultur und Sitte with a view to writing "Woman in Germany"; this was a month before she wrote Chapman. Undoubtedly Hroswitha, a nun who wrote sexually charged comedy (entry 16); Bitisia Gozzadini, who was at the University of Bologna and customarily wore men's clothes (entry 31); and Sabina von Steinbach, who worked as a sculptor on the south porch of Strassburg cathedral (entry 31) would all have found their place in the projected essay. Some space would also have been given to the heroic women of Weinsburg who were allowed to collect their valuables and flee before the surrender of their city to the enemy; they immediately determined that their husbands were more valuable than anything else and carried them away

on their backs (entry 31). And the legendary Senta, who saved the
Flying Dutchman, would also have deserved mention (entry 8). The
entries also show that Eliot would have amplified the distinction
between French and German women which she introduced in "Woman in
France":

> What were the causes of this earlier development and more abun-
> dant manifestation of womanly intellect in France? The primary
> one, perhaps, lies in the physiological characteristics of the
> Gallic race: the small brain and vivacious temperament which
> permit the fragile system of woman to sustain the superlative
> activity requisite for intellectual creativeness; while, on the
> other hand, the larger brain and slower temperament of the
> English and Germans are, in the womanly organization, generally
> dreamy and passive.[7]

Gervinus's description of the different ways that chivalry took
hold in Germany, France, and Italy would have been extremely useful in developing these distinctions (entry 30). With her notebook containing the makings of a lively essay and with the earlier
article on French women demonstrating her ability to develop a
similar subject successfully, we can only regret that Chapman did
not respond positively to George Eliot's proposal to write "Woman
in Germany."
    In addition to notes for an essay she never wrote, there are
in the notebook entries for an essay George Eliot did in fact
write but never published. Disappointed with the reception of
The Spanish Gypsy--though the reviews were, as Gordon S. Haight
says, "surprisingly laudatory"[8]--she wrote to William Blackwood
on 6 August 1868:

> It is not possible for you, without the useless pains of examin-
> ing closely, to conceive the silliness of many things that are
> said by reviewers who are in the helpless condition of judging
> without a precedent. They fling about phrases about the
> caesura etc. with a marvellous foolhardiness--very much as if a
> man were to try and make gibberish pass for Greek without in-
> quiring beforehand if any one of the company happened to know
> that ancient tongue.[9]

George Eliot set herself the task, nonetheless, of reading "Guest
on English Rhythms" during that month, and she copied notes on
"Fine pauses" and "fine appoggiatura" from him into one of her
notebooks for Middlemarch.[10] We know that she had previously
read what she described as a "good article on Blank Verse" in
Cornhill[11] while she was writing The Spanish Gypsy, and that she
subsequently read Joseph Haslewood's compendium of Ancient
Critical Essays upon English Poets and Poesy. Entries 284-293
are composed of quotations from Haslewood's edition; these form
the substance of Eliot's unpublished essay "Versification (1869),"
which she probably copied into the manuscript notebook entitled
"Poetry" (Beinecke Library) sometime after writing a first
draft.[12] It seems that she wrote a version of the essay prior
to incorporating it into "Poetry" because the manuscript contains
the essay in what must be described as fair copy and because the
opening of it seems to depend on language used in Sylvester's
Laws of Verse, which was not published until 1870.[13] Eliot, like
Sylvester, compares poetry and music and uses terms like "quaver"
and "crochet" to describe unaccented and accented syllables. The

precise passage in which this comparison is made was copied by her
into a notebook for <u>Middlemarch</u>.[14] "Versification (1869)," therefore, draws on various sources; but it moves toward one end: the
promotion of an organic theory of poetry in which "rhythmic and
tonic relations" are adjusted to "the bias of passionate experience." Because it eschews all rules imposed "for the mere
pleasure of bondage," its hero is Samuel Daniel and its villain
Thomas Campion. Although the essay is short, perhaps even a
fragment, George Eliot thought well enough of it to preserve it
with her poetry; and its close relation to entries 284-293 in
the notebook make its publication with the Uncollected Writings
appropriate (see p. 286).

<u>Adam</u> <u>Bede</u>

Entry 43 suggests another article--one on the "Opposition to New
Ideas"--that George Eliot thought about writing but never actually
wrote. Samuel Smiles's <u>The</u> <u>Life</u> <u>of</u> <u>George</u> <u>Stephenson</u>: <u>Railway</u>
<u>Engineer</u> is one of the books listed in the entry as a source to
illustrate the theme of opposition. The whole entry seems more
interesting, however, for what it can tell us about Eliot as a
novelist--the mention of Smiles's biography is particularly sig-
nificant--than for what it actually tells us about her as an
essayist. Eliot read the <u>Railway</u> <u>Engineer</u> in June 1857 and remarked that "the life of George Stephenson has been a profit and
pleasure."[15] Some of the "profit" is found in the details of
the engineer's life that contribute to the drawing of the character of a Midlands carpenter.
    Eliot made a note on Stephenson's wages while setting down
miscellaneous facts from 1800 to 1802 (entry 64). The career of
the railway engineer, therefore, was once again in her mind when
she was preoccupied with <u>Adam</u> <u>Bede</u>, and parallels between Smiles's
biography and Eliot's novel took shape. Both Adam Bede and George
Stephenson had a favorite dog. Stephenson's was "so sagacious
that he performed the office of a servant, in almost daily carrying
his dinner to him at the pit."[16] Adam's dog, Gyp, carries a
basket which "on workdays held Adam's and Seth's dinner" (<u>AB</u>, ch.
1). Stephenson, a man of "wiry muscles and practiced strength,"
beat a co-worker--who did not like "George's style of self-
assertion"[17]--in a fist fight. Adam, who, as Mr. Casson remarks,
is "a little lifted up an' peppery-like" (ch. 2), pins his co-
worker Wiry Ben to the wall (ch. 1). Stephenson did extra work
to earn enough money to marry Fanny Henderson, "a servant in a
neighboring farm-house."[18] Adam does extra work cheerfully because "his hopes were buoyant again about Hetty," the Poyser's
niece at the Hall-Farm (ch. 27). And both Stephenson and Adam
attended night school and excelled in arithmetic--one, the best
pupil of Andrew Robertson;[19] the other, the best pupil of Bartle
Massey (ch. 21). In George Stephenson, then, Eliot found not
only incidental details to supplement recollections of her
father, but a model for the temperament, intelligence, and affections of Adam Bede. George Eliot's praise of Stephenson in a
casual remark to Caroline Bray--"Geo. Stevenson is one of my
great heroes--has he not a dear old face?"[20]--makes excellent
sense to the knowledgeable reader of <u>Adam</u> <u>Bede</u>.
    Throughout the notes that she took for the novel Eliot ex-
hibits an eye for details that became immediately relevant to the
writing of it. Dinah Morris resembles John Wesley much in the

same way that Adam resembles Stephenson. Like Wesley she sometimes preaches while standing on a wall (entry 55; ch. 8); she
induces paroxysms of remorse in her hearers (53; ch. 2); she believes in divination by the drawing of lots and opening of the
Bible (51; ch. 3); she brings about jailhouse conversions (53;
ch. 45); and she rides with condemned criminals to the gallows
(52; ch. 47). The character of Dinah is drawn in a way so
strikingly reminiscent of Wesley that what Alexander Knox said of
him can also be said of her: "It will hardly be denied that even
in this frail & corrupted world, we sometimes meet persons who in
their very mien & aspect, as well as in the whole habit of life,
manifest such a signature & stamp of virtue as to make our judgment of them a matter of intuition, rather than the result of
continued examination" (entry 59).

Hetty Sorrel in her limited way is a patent card of fashion
as Eliot records it at the turn of the century. She has the
obligatory straw hat (60; ch. 22), black scarf (60; ch. 15),
white stockings (61; ch. 16), large earrings (60; ch. 15), and a
dress that "seemed a thing to be imitated by duchesses" (60; ch.
7). Whereas the coquette is à la mode, the clergyman is not. Mr.
Irwine's powdered hair is some six years out of date (60; ch.
24). Arthur Donnithorne, on the other hand, is like Hetty in being quite modern. He celebrates his coming-of-age in Book Third
very much in the manner that the Gentleman's Magazine described
the Duke of Rutland's celebrating his majority in 1799 (entry
62). For this splendid occasion, as well as for the days preceding it, Eliot was careful to draw cloud formations (69-70;
chs. 18-19) suited to the weather as it was recorded in July and
August 1799 (entry 65).

Besides being characters with a turn-of-the-century identity,
Hetty and Arthur and Adolphus Irwine also seem to be actors in a
Greek tragedy. Arthur fails to heed the advice of Mr. Irwine
and acts against the warning of the chorus of Prometheus Bound,
which Irwine refers to in chapter 16:

> Wise was the man who declared, "like is fitly coupled
>   with like, and let equal pair with equal.
> Not for grimy craftsman the hand of rich man's
>   daughter, nor must
> Simple maid plight troth with purse-proud nobleman.[21]

Hetty, who looks upon Arthur as an "olympian god" (ch. 9), is
reduced to misery by her love for him. Her face comes to resemble that of the Medusa Rondanini--"the sadder for its beauty,
like that wondrous Medusa-face, with the passionate, passionless
lips" (ch. 37)--whose tragic story of rape and punishment Eliot
records in the notebook (entry 40; see fig. 3).

The detailed notes for Adam Bede that George Eliot took and
carried with her into Germany indicate that extensive research
supplemented the recollections of her father and aunt in the
writing of the novel. The general impression that Eliot's "History of 'Adam Bede'" has long left on readers' minds is that the
character of Dinah Morris was drawn from her memory of her Methodist Aunt Samuel and the character of Adam Bede from that of her
father, Robert Evans.[22] A closer look at Eliot's notes for the
novel, however, modifies this impression considerably and recalls
Eliot's own caveat: "Adam is no more my father than Dinah is my
aunt." No "single portrait" exists in the novel, "only the suggestion of experience wrought up into new combinations."[23]

     The handful of relationships already traced are only a few
of many that exist between the notebook and novel. Others are
suggested in the notes to entries 50 to 76, but I should like to
call attention to one more here. Entry 257 is one of a series
that served Eliot in the writing of her poem "Stradivarius,"
which was published fourteen years after Adam Bede; nevertheless,
it tells us something about the novel. Lane's Modern Egyptians
contains an extended account of a magician conjuring from a drop
of ink, which is the subject of the first sentence of the novel:
"With a single drop of ink for a mirror, the Egyptian sorcerer
undertakes to reveal to any chance comer far-reaching visions of
the past." That the drop of ink is a "mirror" incontestably associates Eliot's sentence with Lane, who writes: "I asked the
magician whether objects appeared in the ink as if actually before the eyes, or as if in a glass, which makes right appear
left. He answered, that they appear as in a mirror."[24] Entry
257 demonstrates that George Eliot reread books that interested
her and that if she did not take notes from them at her first
reading she sometimes did at a subsequent reading. This practice
is relevant to the composition of The Mill on the Floss.

The Mill on the Floss

What Lane's Modern Egyptians is to Adam Bede, Anna Jameson's
Sacred and Legendary Art is to The Mill on the Floss. Between
15 August and 4 September 1862 George Eliot read and took notes
from Mrs. Jameson's two volumes as a preparation for writing
Romola. This was not her first acquaintance with Mrs. Jameson
and her work.[25] She mentions her in her letters as early as
January 1840, and she regrets having been away when Mrs. Jameson
called with Robert Noel on 23 June 1853. The two women finally
met at a dinner in February 1854.[26]
     It is reasonable to assume that George Eliot's interest in
Mrs. Jameson was stimulated by a reading of her works, the most
notable of which was Sacred and Legendary Art, published in 1848.
When Eliot composed the legend of St. Ogg in The Mill on the
Floss, she seems to have modeled it on Mrs. Jameson's version of
the legend of St. Christopher. The details of the Christopher
legend as they appear in entry 137 and those of the Ogg legend
in The Mill (I.xii), are so much alike as to suggest that Eliot
read Legendary Art prior to taking notes for Romola from it and
that Mrs. Jameson may be the "private hagiographer" whom she alludes to in that chapter. Christopher, a man of great size and
strength, carried people across a body of water. Ogg--in
rabinical legend Og, a giant--is "a boatman who gained a scanty
living by ferrying passengers across the river Floss." These
legends have a parallel structure which shows a strong man who,
for no cogent reason that is articulated in his legend, helps a
fragile and lowly but impatient wayfarer to cross a dangerous
body of water; stepping ashore, the wayfarer manifests the greatness that weakness and loneliness disguised. This episode of
each story then concludes with a blessing for future generations.
Elements of the legend of St. Ogg--sympathy and courage, an
epiphany and a raging river--are central to the development of
tragedy in The Mill on the Floss.
     The destructive flood that culminates in the death of Tom
and Maggie Tulliver was always a part of Eliot's plan for the
novel. Gordon S. Haight writes that "the flood that ends The

Mill on the Floss was not an afterthought to extricate the author
from an impossible situation, but the part of the story that
George Eliot planned first. At the British Museum in January
1859 she copied into her commonplace book accounts of inundations
from the Annual Register with details of ships driven onto
flooded fields, bridges washed away, and a family rescued from
the upper story of their house, all of which appear in the final
pages of the novel."[27] These notes comprise entries 77-81 and
show how Eliot used the minutest of details to give a realistic
character to her symbolic flood.

     A similar emphasis on specific details that configure more
general meanings of the tragic structure in the novel is found in
three other entries in the notebook; one relates to Philip Wakem,
a second to Tom, and a third to Mr. Tulliver. When George Eliot
read Wilhelm Meister's Apprenticeship in 1854, she made note of a
passage that urges men to nourish their souls with impressions
that are beautiful: "One ought, every day at least, to hear a
little song, read a good poem, see a fine picture, and, if it
were possible, to speak a few reasonable words" (entry 11). This
sentiment of Wilhelm's is shared by Philip Wakem, who says to
Maggie: "There are certain things we feel to be beautiful and
good, and we must hunger after them. How can we ever be satisfied
without them until our feelings are deadened?" (V.i). Philip's
philosophizing in the Goethean mode--a mode that Ladislaw later
adapts to Dorothea's predicament at Rome in Middlemarch--means a
great deal to Maggie, but nothing to Tom Tulliver; it only serves
to intensify the conflict between brother and sister in the novel.
Tom understands none of Philip's moral-esthetic ideas, and what
he does not understand he repudiates, whether it be poetry or
painting, man or woman. His unfortunate situation is mirrored in
another entry in the notebook. An item pertinent to The Mill
appears in entry 75 for Adam Bede where Eliot quotes Prideaux
John Selby's British Forest-Trees. Since Adam was to manage the
Donnithorne woods, Eliot had to know about trees. Among the
things she learned were the superstitions attached to the Common
Ash: "among others that of boring a hole in an ash tree & enclosing within it a living shrew-mouse; the branch of the tree
thus prepared is supposed to cure lameness & cramp in cattle,
both of which are laid to the unfortunate mouse." The shrew-
mouse appears as an image of hopelessness in The Mill on the
Floss: "At present, in relation to this demand that he should
learn Latin declensions and conjunctions, Tom was in a state of
as blank unimaginativeness concerning the cause and tendency of
his sufferings, as if he had been an innocent shrew-mouse imprisoned in the slit trunk of an ash-tree in order to cure lameness in cattle" (II.i). Tom finds himself the prisoner of ignorance and superstition more than once in the course of the
story. Not only is he forced to restore the family's honor by
working off his sick father's debts, but like Maggie he is obliged
to die that harmony might be restored to family and community.
And like his father, Tom is not intelligent enough to see his
predicament clearly. Mr. Tulliver's tragic situation, in fact,
is described in the words of Sophocles' Oedipus at Colonus,
quoted in the Greek in entry 43: "Mr. Tulliver had a destiny as
well as OEdipus, and in this case he might plead, like Oedipus,
that his deed was inflicted on him rather than committed by him"
(I.xiii). The raging flood, the irrationally trapped animal, and
the blind Oedipus remind us that George Eliot had once thought of
calling The Mill on the Floss by a title reminiscent of the

doomed House of Atreus, The House of Tulliver.[28] And her many
quotations from Greek tragedies, in entries 43 and 222-223, further remind us of the profound effect that the ancient writers
and their German editors and interpreters had on her formulation
of a theory of tragedy and her shaping of events not only in The
Mill on the Floss but also in Romola and The Spanish Gypsy.

Romola

Romola, like The Mill on the Floss, is a novel whose controversial
ending was part of its original conception; furthermore, as in
The Mill, the ending of Romola draws on George Eliot's reading of
Mrs. Jameson's Legendary Art. Romola becomes a saint and has
legends created around her: "Many legends were afterwards told in
that valley about the blessed Lady who came over the sea, but
they were legends by which all who heard might know that in times
gone by a woman had done beautiful loving deeds there, rescuing
those who were ready to perish" (ch. 68). Romola is itself a
golden legend, the story of a secular saint whose life was an affirmation of duty and fellow-feeling. Commenting on the final
chapters of that legend, Eliot wrote to Sara Hennell that "the
various strands of thought I had to work out forced me into a
more ideal treatment of Romola than I had foreseen at the outset--
though the 'Drifting Away' and the Village with the Plague belonged to my earliest vision of the story and were by deliberate
forecast adopted as romantic and symbolical elements."[29] The
notebook shows that Eliot had carefully prepared herself to
create a legend for her saintly heroine. It also shows the
origin of some of her ideas on villains.

Tito's attempt to make Romola into a pleasure-loving consort
is summed up in the epithet that describes him, "Care-Dispeller,"
and that Eliot first used in her review of Stahr's Torso in 1856
(Uncollected Writings, p. 275). The conception of Tito as a
Bacchic figure leads to the development of a mythic analogy in
Romola: Tito tries to make his wife into an Ariadne; whereas her
tragic fate is to be an Antigone.[30] She must answer the same
question that Savonarola does--"the question where the duty of
obedience ends, and the duty of resistance begins" (ch. 55)--
which Burke posed in classic terms in Reflections on the
Revolution in France: "The speculative line of demarcation where
obedience ought to end & resistance must begin, is faint, obscure, not easily definable" (entry 310, n. 6).

"Nofri" is the name of another villainous character, Tessa's
senselessly brutal stepfather, and the Delizie degli Erudite
Toscani (entry 123) shows it associated with the acts of a deranged fanatic. Dante describes a more common derangement in the
sins of men against their neighbors (entry 102). "There is he
who through his neighbor's abasement hopes to excel, and solely
for this desires that he be cast down from his greatness." This
describes Tito's attitude toward Baldassarre; while the wronged
stepfather's attitude toward his errant son is equally well
articulated by Dante: "there is he who seems to be so shamed
through being wronged, that he becomes greedy of vengeance, and
such must needs seek another's hurt." Vengeance is the subject
of entry 48 from Chichester's Naples where an aggrieved neighbor
adopts toward a constable an attitude similar to the one that
Baldassarre, a native Neopolitan, adopts toward Tito: his "only
dread was lest young limbs should escape him" (ch. 22). Looking

for bread to nourish his life of vengeance, Baldassarre's
constant watchfulness brings him the very object of his revenge,
Tito himself. The implacability of the unfortunate constable's
neighbor has become the defining mark of Baldassarre's character.

The entry Edle Rasche (48) amplifies the subject of vengeance
by providing, in capsule size, the story that was the germ of the
Tito-Baldassarre plot in Romola. Gordon S. Haight traces Eliot's
knowledge of the story to Germany in the mid-1850s: "One evening
in the winter of 1855 at Fräulein Solmar's in Berlin old General
Pfuhl told her a story of 'noble vengeance,' which impressed her
so much that she wrote it down in her Journal and later (with
slight variation) in her Commonplace Book."[31] An ungrateful
adopted son, the story goes, tries to take everything away from
his stepfather who becomes so outraged that he kills his son and
vows to continue punishing him in hell. Baldassarre, we remember,
desires "an eternity of vengeance where he, [with] undying hate,
might clutch forever an undying traitor" (ch. 30).

The notebook, which provides these insights into Romola,
contains one of three sets of notes that Eliot prepared for writing the novel. "Florentine Notes" (British Museum Add. MS. 40,
768) was compiled in May and early June 1861 in Florence and contains, among other things, clues that are followed in the present
notebook, where the notes for Romola were entered between August
1861 and January 1862. "In Florentine Notes," for example,
Tribaldo Amerigo, de' Rossi and the Delizie are mentioned as
sources to be consulted; and so too is Rock's Hierurgia. Both
works are then quoted extensively in the notebook (entries 122-124;
143-145). "Notes for Romola / 1862" (Parrish Collection, Prince-
ton University Library) comprises the last body of manuscript
material Eliot collected for the novel. It differs from the
notebook by focusing on Florentine matters: reproducing an index
of Lastri's L'Osservatore Fiorentino, for example, and a
chronology of Savonarola's life. The notebook does not have that
sharp a focus in its entries for Romola. It contains comprehensive notes on books that proved valuable to the writing of the
novel but that deal with topics that are not limited to Florence
alone. Besides Mrs. Jamesons's Legendary Art, two other such
books that are quoted extensively are Pierre Helyot's Histoire
des ordres monastiques (entries 155-168) and C. W. King's Antique
Gems (entries 169-184).

Eliot uses the notes from Helyot in several ways in Romola.
The variety of color in the garb of religious orders lends
authentic atmosphere to the great procession in chapter 43. The
differences in garb also indicate tensions in the past between
regular and reformed branches of religious orders because a
change in dress indicates a change in rule. Tensions also exist
between orders, especially between the Dominicans and Franciscans.
The variety of look and outlook within and between religious
orders, as well as the pronounced antagonism they exhibit one
with another, suggests that they are images of Florence itself:
the Bardis, for example, are split among themselves religiously
(Bardo and Dino, a reformed Bardi) and politically (Romola and
Bernardo, a Piagnone and a Medicean); the Medici are at logger-
heads with the Sforzas; the Piagnoni, Arrabiatti, and Mediceans
maneuver for power. The religious world is a metonymy for the
familial and political worlds in Romola. George Eliot used Helyot
to intensify the sense of divisiveness that pervades the novel.

Eliot learned from King's Antique Gems that one expression
of the Renaissance's passion for antiquity was the collector's

passion for ancient precious stones. Such gems were especially
valuable if they were carved as intaglios (in which a figure is
incised beneath the surface of the gem) or cameos (in which the
gem is engraved in relief so that the raised design is one color
and the background another. Tito, who has "lustrous agate-like
eyes" (R, ch. 67), tells Nello that he has "intaglios and cameos,
both curious and beautiful" which he wants to sell (ch. 3). Such
stones were bought for their monetary (entry 178) as well as for
their mystic value (entries 132-133, 175). Bernardo Rucellai
buys the best stones that Tito has; he is obviously a wealthy collector interested in the rarest items that money can buy (ch. 39).
Bernardo Scala, on the other hand, buys those gems that he thinks
will be effective against gout (ch. 6). By what they select
Rucellai and Scala highlight the opulence and the superstition
of late fifteenth-century Florence. That the invading French
buy Lorenzo de' Medici's extraordinary collection after his
death (ch. 27) and that Bardo wears prophylactic rings on pre-
scription (ch. 6) reinforce this characterization of Florence.

     Tito is provided in Romola with a valuable collection of
antique gems. He sells all but his ring for "five hundred gold
florins" (ch. 9), and he subsequently sells that for fifty or
fifty-five florins (Eliot gives one sum in chapter 16 and another
in chapter 18). None of the gems that Tito sells are in any way
ordinary. Rucellai buys "the chief rings" in Melema's collection
--"one of them is a fine sard, engraved with a subject from
Homer" (ch. 39; see fig. 10). Sards, as King notes, are extremely hard and "retain their original polish"; on them are
"found the finest works of the Greek artists"(entry 176). Scala
buys two rare stones: an agate with a lusus naturae (a trick of
nature) in it and a Jew's stone. The design of the lusus
naturae is "Cupid riding on the lion" (ch. 7); this is the same
subject that is engraved on the celebrated "Emerald signet of
Polycrates" and illustrated in King's Antique Gems (see fig. 10).
The Jew's stone was valuable in itself and yet more valuable with
an intaglio in it (see entry 184). Tito's own ring, which he
eventually sells to a Genoese, is also a remarkable gem: "This is
a curious and valuable ring, young man," says Domenico Cennini.
"This intaglio of the fish with the crested serpent above it, in
the black stratum of the onyx, or rather nicolo, is well shown by
the surrounding blue of the upper stratum" (ch. 4). "On this
gem," says King, "fine Roman intagli occur more frequently than
upon any other after the Sard."[32] The planetary figure carved in
the nicolo is that of Cetus, "a big fish with bent tail and wide
mouth," and, King explains, "if cut on a stone, with a large
crested serpent with a long mane above it, it gives good luck at
sea and restores lost things."[33] Tito also has "a fine Cleopatra
cut in sardonyx" (ch. 3), the subject suggesting its Egyptian
origin during the time of Roman domination. King describes just
such a stone in Antique Gems: "a bust of Cleopatra, given in
exact accordance with the prescribed type of the Queen, as seen
on the oldest monuments, adorned with a profusion of small curls
and many rows of necklaces, but worked out with extreme delicacy
in the black layer of an Onyx in very flat relief."[34]

     When one looks closely at these gems, it becomes clear that
George Eliot took great care to provide Tito with choice collec-
tors' items. The effect of this decision on the novel is varied
and subtle. The sale of the gems brings "a man's ransom" (the
title of chapter 9) and Tito's refusal to pay that ransom is a
straightforward indictment of his selfish conduct. Less

directly, the gems also tell us something about Baldassarre, whom
we generally see only as a beggarly, mad, and vengeful old man.
At one time he must have been otherwise; for only a scholarly,
masterful, and patient man could have put together such an extraordinary collection of gems. Tito's ring is also used like a
clue in a detective story. Bratti notices it and recognizes in
the bedraggled Tito someone worthy of his attention (ch. 1). He
takes Tito to Nello and at the barber's Melema is introduced to
Domenico Cennini, who pronounces on the merits of the ring (ch.
4). The jewels associated in the collection with the ring introduce Tito to Bardo, Scala, and Rucellai--to the men with whom he
finds his wife and fortune. The ring is so distinctive that Fra
Luca immediately recognizes it (ch. 10) and Tito feels compelled
to sell it to a merchant whom Baldassarre sees wearing it in
Genoa and who then directs him to Bratti's shop where the ring
was bought from Tito (ch. 16). Ironically, the ring that affirms
the binding relationship of Tito to Baldassarre continues to link
father and son in spite of Tito's attempt to break the tie by
selling the symbol of it. The "intaglio of the fish with the
crested serpent above it" nicely reinforces this point. Tito
claims, as King indicates, that "the stone and intaglio are of a
virtue to make the wearer fortunate, especially at sea, and also
restore to him whatever he may have lost" (ch. 4). But Baldassarre, who was literally lost at sea, returns to Tito, who
emphatically does not want him back at all. But the virtue of
the ring proves too strong for Tito to circumvent it. The use of
the ring develops into a striking illustration of how Eliot's doctrine of consequences works itself out in a circular fashion beyond the intention of the wrong-doer. The motif of jewelry in
Romola, which for George Eliot was part of the realistic background of fifteenth-century Florentine life, develops from
scholarly detail into a subtle rendering of character, value, and
theme in the novel.

The Spanish Gypsy

George Eliot's "Notes on 'The Spanish Gypsy'" show that the poem
was inspired by a Judeo-Christian subject and shaped by a sense
of Greek tragedy. Titian's "small picture" of the Annunciation
in the Scuola di San Rocco in Venice led Eliot to a Gypsy heroine
who, "as a result of foregoing hereditary conditions," says, "Behold the handmaid of the Lord." She renounces her "individual
lot" of marriage to Don Silva to embrace her "general" lot as the
daughter of the Gypsy chieftain Zarca. "Silva presents the
tragedy of entire rebellion: Fedalma of a grand submission,
which is rendered vain by the effects of Silva's rebellion:
Zarca, the struggle for a great end, rendered vain by the surrounding conditions of life."[35]
     George Eliot's reflections on her dramatic poem are so clear
and precise that they hide the agony she endured in bringing to
completion her "first serious attempt at blank verse" (Diary, 4
November 1864) which marked "an epoch for me" (Diary, 1 January
1865). The Spanish Gypsy was originally conceived as a drama and
Eliot spoke of its divisions as Acts: "I am reading about Spain
& trying a drama on a subject that fascinated me--have written
the prologue & am beginning the First Act" (Diary, 6 September
1864). Her first attempt to write this tragedy ended on 21
February 1865 with a terse note. "George has taken my drama away

<u>from</u> <u>me</u>." From September 1864 to February 1865 George Eliot's
<u>Diary</u> is a litany of ills, extending from her constant worry
about Lewes's poor health to her own "swamp of miseries": headache, depression, biliousness, dyspepsia, malaise, and feeble-
ness. She put aside the drama and wrote <u>Felix</u> <u>Holt</u>, <u>the</u> <u>Radical</u>,
which she began on 29 March 1865 and finished 31 May 1866 (Diary).

    By 30 August 1866 she had resumed work on <u>The</u> <u>Spanish</u> <u>Gypsy</u>:
"I have taken up the idea of my drama, 'The Spanish Gipsy' again,
& am reading on Spanish subjects--Bouterwek, Sismondi, Depping,
Llorente, &c." On 15 October 1866 she announces, "Recommenced
'The Spanish Gipsy,' intending to give it a new form." She had
written a part of the Introduction by 22 November, but was not to
work successfully on the poem until after a journey to Spain,
which lasted from 27 December 1866 to 16 March 1867. She
finished <u>The</u> <u>Spanish</u> <u>Gypsy</u> on 29 April 1868. Between 1 May 1867
and 29 April 1868 George Eliot pays considerably less attention
to her health in the Diary and gives instead a constant record of
the progress of the poem, the parts of which she now refers to as
Books, not Acts. What was at first meant to be a blank verse
drama, presumably written to be performed, was finished as a
dramatic poem, decidedly meant to be read. George Eliot recorded
her fatiguing struggle with <u>The</u> <u>Spanish</u> <u>Gypsy</u> in the modest headnote to the published text: "This work was originally written in
the winter of 1864-65; after a visit to Spain in 1867 it was rewritten and amplified."

    The entries that appear in the notebook were made for the
1864-65 dramatic version of <u>The</u> <u>Spanish</u> <u>Gypsy</u> and were taken from
Grellman's <u>Dissertation</u> <u>on</u> <u>the</u> <u>Gipsies</u> (entries 214-217),
Borrow's <u>The</u> <u>Zincali</u> (entries 218-220; 258), Pott's <u>Die</u> <u>Zigeuner</u>
(entries 219-220), and Dozy's <u>Histoire</u> <u>des</u> <u>Musulmans</u> <u>d'Espagne</u>
(entry 221). Subsequently, when preparing to rewrite the poem,
Eliot copied passages from "Bouterwek, Sismondi, Depping,
Liorente, &c." into the same small notebook she used as a quarry
for <u>Felix</u> <u>Holt</u> ("Notes for Felix Holt & Other," Beinecke Library).
The entries in the notebook, in short, deal with her original
conception of the poem; those in the quarry with her amplifica-
tion of it. If <u>The</u> <u>Spanish</u> <u>Gypsy</u> can be thought of as having a
"Spanish" element and a "Gypsy" element, the first is recorded in
the quarry and the second in the notebook. What this means is
that the essential plot of <u>The</u> <u>Spanish</u> <u>Gypsy</u> was shaped from the
research Eliot did on Gypsies and recorded in the notebook.

    These notes indicate that a common bond of persecution
united the Moors, Jews, and Gypsies in late fifteenth century
Spain during the reign of Ferdinand and Isabella. Like the
Moors the Gypsies were good soldiers, and like the Jews they were
a disinherited people. If the Jews were a wandering people because of the crucifixion of Christ, the Gypsies were a wandering
people because, according to legend, they refused shelter to Mary
and Joseph on their flight into Egypt. Both Jew and Gypsy,
therefore, were in search of a homeland. Certain characteristics
peculiar to Gypsies also find their way from Eliot's notes into
her poem: they excel as smiths and therefore when captured are
put to work making bullets. But they also excel as spies, which
allows them to discern the weaknesses of Bedmar. The Gypsies are
notable for the excessive love of their children, and the bond
between Zarca and Fedalma is an extraordinary instance of such
strength of kinship. Fedalma's "kidnapping" from Zarca by
"marauding Spaniards" is therefore a particularly tragic event;
at the same time, it reverses the common belief that the Gypsies

steal Christian children. The Gypsies have no religious belief
save in metempsychosis or the transmigration of souls. Zarca pro-
claims that the Gypsies believe in fidelity to one another: "Our
people's faith / Is faithfulness . . . / Each to the other, and
our common lot" (bk. III). Their nobility resides in what
amounts to a practice of fellow-feeling, an idea certainly congenial to George Eliot. One use of Gypsy religion in the poem,
therefore, is the extension of the doctrine of metempsychosis into what in Daniel Deronda is called "transmutation of self" (ch.
37). In that novel the soul of Mordecai passes into that of
Deronda, just as earlier the soul of Daniel Chrisi had passed into that of Mordecai. In The Spanish Gypsy the soul of Zarca
passes into that of Fedalma, who is "the funeral urn that bears /
The ashes of a leader" (bk. V).

     Imbedded in Eliot's readings for the poem found in the
notebook, then, are the essential elements of its structure: the
conflict of Spanish Christian with persecuted Gypsy, Jew, and
Moor; the unbreakable family bond linking Gypsy father with Gypsy
daughter; the one religious belief central to their survival; and
their seeking to find an end to their wandering Exile in a Homeland of their own. Incidental elements appear in the Gypsy occupations of smith, soldier, and spy and in their legendary rejection of Christ in the rejection of his parents. What these
essential and incidental elements of The Spanish Gypsy demanded
in order to free George Eliot's imagination for efficacious work
was reinforcement and amplification through reading the history
of Spain, through study of its geography, and, lastly, through
first-hand experience of the country itself. The last was perhaps the most important of all because Eliot was conscious, as we
saw, of doing something new--of writing blank verse seriously and
marking an epoch in her life. The technical requirements of a
task so difficult could only be alleviated by calling on a personal experience of a land and a people. Lewes and Eliot's trip
to Spain provided the necessary catalytic experience. Nevertheless, when we look back to the poem from the passages in the
notebook, it is clear that the essential plot of The Spanish
Gypsy was worked out from the first notes she took on Gypsies in
1864.

Felix Holt, the Radical

The principal manuscript containing George Eliot's research for
Felix Holt is "Notes for Felix Holt & Other," The "& Other" of
the title refers to a section of the manuscript devoted to
"Spanish Subjects. Aug. 1866," which is principally made up of
notes for The Spanish Gypsy and of a miscellany of quotations
from Richard Chenevix Trench, Max Müller, John Lubbock, and
Geoffrey Chaucer. The notes from Chaucer, Lubbock, and Müller
were subsequently reordered and transcribed in the notebook for
use in the composition of Middlemarch. So too was another body
of notes that was immediately pertinent to the composition of
Felix Holt and eventually to the writing of Middlemarch. These
notes are the statistics given in entry 270 and the quotations
from John Aryton Paris's Pharmacologia (entries 271-275). With
Felix Holt set just after the passage of the Reform Bill of 1832
and Middlemarch set just before that event, the statistics were
important to both novels; indeed, Eliot thought them so significant to Middlemarch that she entered those related to population

on the first page of a notebook for <u>Middlemarch</u> (Folger Shakespeare Library).[36] The material from the <u>Pharmacologia</u> served <u>Felix Holt</u> to the extent that the deceased Mr. Holt concocted quack remedies which Felix, trained as an apothecary, came to regard as poisonous. The same notes were rearranged for inclusion in the notebook and served as background for Lydgate and his struggle against medical superstition in Middlemarch society. One note from Paris, on Peruvian bark (entry 274), also found its way into the "Quarry for <u>Middlemarch</u>"[37] (Houghton Library, Harvard University), and Eliot used it in the novel when Lydgate deprecated the "incessant" use of "port-wine and bark" as a way for Lady Chettam to strengthen her "peculiar" constitution (ch. 10).

One thing that these notes for <u>Felix Holt</u> (which became notes for <u>Middlemarch</u>) show us is that Eliot constantly searched her quarries and transferred pertinent information from one manuscript to another. The unique contribution of the notebook to an understanding of <u>Felix Holt</u> arises from her mining the notebook itself. Six epigraphs for chapters of the novel are found in it: those for chapters 15 (entry 104, n. 5), 22 (entry 100, n. 2), 27 (entry 110, n. 9), 42 (entry 43, n. 8), 48 (entry 222, n. 2), 50 (entry 73, n. 2); the epigraph for the novel itself is from Michael Drayton's <u>Poly-Olbion</u> and is recorded in entry 107 (see n. 2). Of these seven quotations two are from Dante (entries 100, 104), and they combine with other references to <u>The Divine Comedy</u> in the novel to form a substantial body of allusion. Indeed, a significant part of the power of <u>Felix Holt</u> is Eliot's ability to make Transome Court akin to a circle of Dante's Hell.

The Introduction to <u>Felix Holt</u> presents Mr. Sampson, the coachman, as "an excellent travelling companion and commentator on the landscape; he could tell the names of sites and persons, and explained the meaning of groups, as well as the shade of Virgil in a more memorable journey." One site of that earlier and more memorable journey of Dante with Virgil is recalled in the final paragraph of the Introduction:

The poets have told us of a dolorous enchanted forest in the under world. The thorn-bushes there, and the thick barked stems, have human histories hidden in them; the power of unuttered cries dwells in the passionless-seeming branches, and the red warm blood is darkly feeding the quivering nerves and sleepless memory that watches through all dreams. These things are a parable.

George Eliot fashions this parable of sorrow from the Inferno, canto 13, which she cites to illustrate Dante's "tenderness & compassion" in entry 99. The parable is evident in the novel when Eliot presents Mrs. Transome as one of "the passionless seeming branches" living with the power of "unuttered cries" in the hell of Transome Court; there she suffers the fate of a sinful queen who has failed to achieve happiness: "Unlike the Semiraris who made laws to suit her practical licence, she loved, poor soul, in the midst of desecrated sanctities, and of honours that look tarnished in the light of monotonous and weary suns" (ch. 40; see entry 98, n. 5). Eliot creates at Transome Court an atmosphere of hopeless suffering caused by Mrs. Transome's sins. She sinned to get a lover and had a son by him, and the very things she wanted and got are hell to her.

She took Jermyn as her lover, and he fathered Harold whom she loves. Now it is Jermyn and Harold who torture her most

cruelly. Harold sits down beside her with "the unmanageable
strength of a great bird" (ch. 1), and Jermyn turns "tenderness
into "calculation": "There is heroism even in the circles of
hell for fellow-sinners who cling to each other in the fiery
whirlwind and never recriminate" (ch. 42), but Jermyn does
nothing but recriminate. Her former lover's every word severely
wounds Mrs. Transome: "Every sentence was as pleasant to her as
if it had been cut into her bared arm" (ch. 9). Her son's every
kindness tortures her even more exquisitely:

The finest threads, such as no eye sees, if bound cunningly
about the sensitive flesh, so that the movement to break them
would bring torture, make a worse bondage than any fetters.
Mrs. Transome felt the fatal threads about her, and the bitter-
ness of this helpless bondage mingled itself with the new
elegancies of the dining and drawing rooms, and all the household changes which Harold had ordered to be brought about with
magical quickness. (ch. 10)

Mrs. Transome finds herself in a state of "helpless misery" (ch.
48); indeed she is an image of "restless misery" (ch. 50): "For
more than twenty years," she says, "I have not had an hour's
happiness" (ch. 50). Consequently, she wanders about sleeplessly
at night, a "tall figure pacing slowly, with her cheek upon her
hand" (ch. 49). She assumes a Dantean posture of suffering
(entry 109, n. 5) in a hell of her own creating. The same is
true of Dorothea in Middlemarch, save that she is not in hell.
Her ardor, the energy of her affections, we might say, has led
her into a purgatorial suffering; and, consequently, she is an instance of the Dantean idea that the best suffer the most (entry
98, n. 7).

Middlemarch

The chapters of Middlemarch that are best served by a study of
the notebook and related materials are those that show Dorothea
in Rome on her wedding journey (chs. 19-22). They contain two
epigraphs from the notebook (ch. 19 from entry 98, see n. 7; ch.
21 from entry 225, see n. 6) and references to Lessing, Stahr,
King, Max Müller, and John Ruskin. If we read the original
sources that Eliot quotes in part in the notebook, more can be
learned about the novel.
     Dorothea finds herself unhappy in a marriage that she has
made against the advice of her family and friends. She is unhappy in chapter 19 because she has quarreled with her husband
about the tempo and goal of his scholarship. Ladislaw further
shakes her confidence in Casaubon, in chapters 21 and 22, by telling her that her husband's work is outdated, uninformed, and
derivative. Casaubon is shown to be different from scholars like
those Max Müller extols in his Lectures on the Science of
Language (entry 299, n. 1) whose work was original, energetic,
and daring. Casaubon is truly in the tradition of the Englishmen
mentioned by J. W. Donaldson in The New Cratylus (entry 307) who
have been idle while their continental contemporaries have been
intensely active: "Suffice it to say, that by the exertions of
the Germans alone philology has made more progress in the last
fifty years than in the preceding two hundred."[38]
     The notebook shows us that, with an unerring instinct for

scholarship that was both intellectually stimulating and pertinent
to her novels, George Eliot pursued philology by immersing herself
in the work of Grimm and Bopp (entries 199-206, 212-213, 307-309)
and their followers (entries 234-235; 240-246) as well as by reading with delight the popularizing books of Max Müller (entries
207-211, 299-305). She absorbed by her reading an accurate sense
of the methodology of comparative Indo-European grammar, which
was to affect the ways that comparative mythology would reach its
conclusions. We therefore find in the Folger notebook for
Middlemarch an outline of Grimm's law similar to that in entries
212-213 of the present notebook.[39] And she mastered this kind
of philological learning well enough to turn critic when late in
life she read T. Le Marchant Douse's Grimm's Law: A Study.[40] It
is finally relevant to remark that although Edward Casaubon did
not know German and consequently could not read the scholarship
indispensable to his work, George Eliot gave serious consideration to taking up the study of Sanskrit, the language that made
the "New Philology" possible. To what degree she finally engaged
herself with the language, we do not know; but we do know that
she read Müller's A History of Sanskrit Literature as part of her
research for Middlemarch.[41] The notebook entries on philological
study also suggest a range of methodological and scholarly exertions absent from Mr. Casaubon's fruitless investigations, which
"floated among flexible conjectures no more solid than those
etymologies which seemed strong because of likeness in sound,
until it was shown that likeness in sound made them impossible"
(ch. 48). They give point to the remark that Ladislaw makes when
he tells Dorothea that her husband is not "an Orientalist" (ch.
22; see entry 299, n. 1). They also give substance to the notion
that Will, like Goethe's poet in "Elemente" (entry 311, n. 9),
must hate the pretension that destroys beautiful things.

     Will Ladislaw, Casaubon's severest critic, finds the
scholar's sorrowing wife, cheek in hand, standing before the
statue of the Sleeping Ariadne in the Belvedere Gallery of the
Vatican Museum. Her posture duplicates that mentioned in the
epigraph of chapter 19--"guancia / Della sua palma"--and Eliot
uses the allusion to Dante to suggest Dorothea's purgatorial
existence. The posture also relates Dorothea to the statue of
Ariadne in which the reclining figure rests her forehead and
cheek on the back of her left hand (see fig. 2). This statue of
the Sleeping Ariadne is discussed at length by Stahr, who mentions that it was once thought to be a Cleopatra but eventually
was proven to be a representation of Ariadne at Naxos.[42]

     Myth relates that the faithless Theseus abandoned Ariadne
at Naxos on his way home to Athens from Crete. Bacchus found her
sleeping there, took her as his bride, and had her made a goddess; her glorious hair became a constellation. Eliot's chapter
repeats this scenario insofar as Casaubon leaves Dorothea and
Ladislaw finds her,[43] with Naumann's help, in front of the Sleeping Ariadne, "her large eyes . . . fixed dreamily on a streak of
sunlight which fell across the floor." This analogy that relates
Casaubon to Theseus, Dorothea to Ariadne, and Ladislaw to Bacchus
brings to bear the moral categories of ancient myth on a nineteenth-
century love-story.[44]

     When Ladislaw and Naumann discuss Dorothea, they disagree on
how she can best be portrayed. Naumann wants to paint her portrait; Ladislaw insists that she is a subject more apt for poetry.
He goes on to argue that the essence of Dorothea is music itself
and that painting consequently cannot touch her soul: "This woman

whom you have just seen, for example: how would you paint her
voice, pray? But her voice is much diviner than anything you
have seen of her" (ch. 19).   This discussion of the choice of an
appropriate artistic form--one that unfolds spatially, like
painting, or temporally, like music and poetry--is a replay of
Lessing's Laocoon (see entries 8a, 9), and recalls George Eliot's
summary of its argument in the Westminster Review: "Every reader
of Lessing's 'Laokoon' remembers his masterly distinction between
the methods of presentation in poetry and the plastic arts--the
acumen and aptness of illustration with which he shows how the
difference in the materials wherewith the poet and painter or
sculptor respectively work, and the difference in their mode of
appeal to the mind, properly involve a difference in their treatment of a given subject" (Uncollected Writings, p. 284).
Ladislaw's perception of Dorothea is extended to the imagery--
perhaps drawn from Horace (entry 114, n. 4)--he uses to characterize her: she has a voice like that of a "soul that had once
lived in an Aeolian harp" (ch. 9). And the whole direction of
her soul--"a soul in which knowledge passes instantaneously into
feeling, and feeling flashes back as a new organ of knowledge"--
suggests to him that Dorothea is "a poem" (ch. 22). What leads
Ladislaw toward this judgment is his observation of her as she
learns "the language of Art."
     The phrase "language of Art" is central to Ruskin's theory
of art. His argument at the beginning of Modern Painters is that
art is "nothing but a noble and expressive language, invaluable
as the vehicle of thought."[45] Both painter and critic must learn
it if they are to advance the causes of art: truth, morality,
and taste. Ruskin also discusses "the language of Art" in his
Lectures on Architecture and Painting--Eliot reviewed the book
for the Leader in 1854--where he insists that "the aim of Art, in
depicting any natural object, is to produce in the mind analogous
emotions to those produced by the object itself; but as with all
our skill and care we cannot imitate it exactly, this aim is not
attained by transcribing but by translating it into the language
of Art" (Uncollected Writings, p. 240). Only by mastering the
elements of a language can one understand the truths embodied in
its masterpieces. Mastery of the language of Art, therefore,
leads to an enlargement of the moral sensibility: "in learning
how to estimate the artistic products of a particular age according to the mental attitude and external life of that age," writes
George Eliot, "we are widening our sympathy and deepening the
basis of our tolerance and charity" (Uncollected Writings, p.
273).
     Significantly, the first thing that Dorothea says about art
when confronted with Ladislaw's sketches at Lowick is that they
are like Greek to her because she does not understand them (ch.
9). When they meet in Rome, Dorothea tells Ladislaw that she is
overcome by the art that surrounds her: "all this vast wreck of
ambitious ideals, sensuous and spiritual, mixed confusedly with
the signs of breathing forgetfulness and degradation, at first
jarred her as with an electric shock, and then urged themselves
on her with that ache belonging to a glut of confused ideas which
check the flow of emotions" (ch. 20). Ladislaw explains to
Dorothea that "Art is an old language with a great many artificial affected styles, and sometimes the chief pleasure one gets
out of knowing them is the mere sense of knowing" (ch. 21).
Under his tutelage she masters enough of the elements of the
language of Art to find that "some things which had seemed

monstrous to her were gathering intelligibility and even a natural
meaning" (ch. 22). This, among other things, eventually leads
Ladislaw to ascribe to her a moral and esthetic unity characteristic of poetry: "You are a poem--and that is to be the best part
of a poet--what makes up the poet's consciousness in his best
moods" (ch. 22). If George Eliot as narrator can go on to suggest that such a remark is not very original--"showing such
originality as we all share with the morning and the springtime
and other endless renewals"--it is simply because Ruskin had already made it an acceptable doctrine to the readers of Middlemarch.[46]
      When they are in Rome together, Ladislaw also helps Dorothea
select cameos which she presents to her sister on her return to
Lowick. Eliot once again draws on her knowledge of Antique Gems
when she has Ladislaw direct Dorothea's attention to "these little Homeric bits: they are exquisitely neat" (ch. 22). Eliot's
knowledge of King's book is also evident in chapter 1 when
Dorothea and Celia divide their mother's jewelry. Dorothea cannot finally resist taking a set of emeralds for herself:

> She was opening some ring-boxes, which disclosed a fine emerald
> with diamonds, and just then the sun passing beyond a cloud
> sent a bright gleam over the table.
>   "How very beautiful these gems are!" said Dorothea, under a
> new current of feeling, as sudden as the gleam. "It is strange
> how deeply colours seem to penetrate one, like scent. I suppose
> that is the reason why gems are used as spiritual emblems in the
> Revelation of St. John. They look like fragments of heaven. I
> think that emerald is more beautiful than any of them."

Dorothea selects the gem that is precisely suited to her needs.
Her first need, of which she is only marginally aware, is a jus-
tification of her sudden, strong feeling for the gems, and she
finds it in Scripture; undoubtedly George Eliot remembered King's
thorough discussion of "Gems of the Apocalypse" in his book.[47]
Dorothea's second need, which the emeralds also meet, is one that
she is even less aware of than the first. Her eyesight is defec-
tive: physically it is myopic (ch. 3) and spiritually it is
quixotic (ch. 2). Of all gems emeralds do the most to improve
the eyesight: like the green grass, says Pliny, "they refresh
the wearied eye."[48]
      The pattern of events in Dorothea's taking the emeralds for
herself in chapter 1 is repeated in chapter 83. Dorothea resolves not to take any jewelry; the sunlight suddenly strikes the
emeralds, her feelings are quickened, and she takes what she
thought she could not have. In chapter 83 Dorothea resolves not
to marry Ladislaw; lightning suddenly flashes, her passion is
quickened, and she decides to marry the man she thought she could
not marry.

> "Oh, I cannot bear it--my heart will break," said Dorothea,
> starting from her seat, the flood of her young passion bearing
> down all the obstructions which had kept her silent--the great
> tears rising and falling in an instant: "I don't mind about
> poverty--I hate my wealth."
>   In an instant Will was close to her and had his arms round
> her. . . .

In chapter 1 we have a "current of feeling"; in chapter 83 the

current becomes a "flood of passion." In the end Dorothea no
longer needs an apocalyptic excuse for her feelings. She accepts
the man who, like the emeralds, is described in images of brightness: "the first impression on seeing Will was one of sunny
brightness"; beside him "Mr. Casaubon stood rayless" (ch. 21).

Daniel Deronda

King was also of use in helping George Eliot develop the character
of Gwendolen in Daniel Deronda. The name Gwendolen itself came
from her reading in Charlotte Yonge's History of Christian Names,
and an account of it is given in notes taken as a proximate
preparation for writing the novel: "Gwendolen, or the Lady of
the bow, or perhaps from Gwendal, white browed, was, it seems, an
ancient British Goddess, probably the moon."[49] There are a few
hints in this sentence that Eliot used to develop the character
of Gwendolen Harleth. She rejected the identification of
Gwendolen with Venus for her identification with Diana, the moon
in classical mythology. Gwendolen Harleth in her "fierceness of
maidenhood" (ch. 7) is called "a perfect Diana" (ch. 15); she
wins an archery contest; she dresses in Greek costume; she is an
excellent horsewoman; and she is determinedly chaste and aloof:
"she objected, with a sort of physical repulsion, to being directly made love to" (ch. 7).
     What Eliot learned from Yonge, she supplemented by what she
learned from King. Gwendolen's turquoise necklace is associated
with her characterization as a horsewoman. "Turquoise," says
King, "is useful for riders. As long as one wears it his horse
will not throw him. It is also good for the eyes and averts
accidents."[50] Gwendolen repudiates the turquoise necklace--the
gems were once her father's--for Grandcourt's diamonds. These
diamonds are in the keeping of Grandcourt's estranged mistress,
Lydia Glasher, and she sends them to Gwendolen on her wedding
day. They immediately turn the once proud horsewoman into a
domestic animal: "She had been brought . . . to kneel down like
a horse under training for the arena, though she might have an objection to it all the while" (ch. 28). With Grandcourt as her
husband, Gwendolen "answered to the rein" (ch. 35). The diamonds
continuously appear as a motif of enslavement in the novel; the
turquoises as a motif of self-mastery, personal responsibility,
and moral freedom.[51]
     The notes that Eliot took specifically for Daniel Deronda in
the notebooks now at the Pforzheimer Library remind us of those
she took particularly for Romola. They are frequently highly
focused on specific items immediately applicable to the composition of the novel: notes on Celtic names and Arthurian legend
for Gwendolen's characterization; notes on the history of music
for Klesmer's characterization; notes on the Hebrew language,
Jewish history, and Talmudic wisdom for Mordecai's characterization. Often enough such notes relate to and are supplemented by
others that Eliot had taken earlier and recorded in the notebook.
As part of her philological studies, for example, she transcribed
the Hebrew alphabet (entry 279) because it was generally thought
to be the model of all known alphabets; she also read Ernest
Renan's Histoire générale et systeme comparé des langues
sémitiques (entries 240-246) to extend her knowledge of one
branch of Indo-European philology. In preparation for a trip to
Normandy and Brittany, Eliot read Renan's "La poésie des races

celtiques" (entries 296, 298) as well as Hersart de la Villemarqué's
Contes populaires des anciens Bretons (entries 296-298). She
studied the history of musical instruments (entries 236-239; 249-
255; 257) to write "The Legend of Jubal" and "Stradivarius"; and
she even recorded, from different sources in both the notebook
(entry 239) and Pforzheimer MS. 707,[52] the story of Guido
d'Arezzo's invention of the scale and his hymn to St. John which
is a mnemonic of it. These correlations and others like them
suggest that a study of the sources of Deronda entails a study of
the notebook. A brief return to Dante, by way of the jewelry
motif, illustrates the contention.

The arrival of the diamonds on Gwendolen's wedding day sig-
nals the beginning of her moral renewal through intense remorse
and emotional anguish. She becomes an image of a Pia of Maremma,
and indeed, is even more pitiable than her Medieval model:

MADONNA PIA, whose husband, feeling himself injured by her, took
her to his castle amid the swampy flats of the Maremma and got
rid of her there, makes a pathetic figure in Dante's Purgatory,
among the sinners who repented at the last and desire to be remembered compassionately by their fellow-countrymen. We know
little about the grounds of mutual discontent between the Sien-
nese couple, but we may infer with some confidence that the husband had never been a very delightful companion, and that on the
flats of the Maremma his disagreeable manners had a background
which threw them out remarkably; whence in his desire to punish
his wife to the uttermost, the nature of things was so far
against him that in relieving himself of her he could not avoid
making the relief mutual. And thus, without any hardness to the
poor Tuscan lady who had her deliverance long ago, one may feel
warranted in thinking of her with a less sympathetic interest
than of the better known Gwendolen who, instead of being delivered from her errors on earth and cleansed from their effect
in purgatory, is at the very height of her entanglement in those
fatal meshes which are woven within more closely than without,
and often make the inward torture disproportionate to what is
discernible as outward cause. (ch. 54)

So instead of our meeting Gwendolen in purgatory we meet her
yachting on the "plank-island" of her marriage, floating in
luxurious misery "between blue and blue." For the seed to bear
fruit--"Fruit and Seed" is the title of the last book of Deronda
--it must die; Gwendolen, therefore, must undergo the death of
purgation in her deliberately chosen marriage to Grandcourt.
Deronda's words and presence guide her through this suffering and
see her into a better life after she becomes "the unhappy ghost
of that Gwendolen Harleth whom Deronda had seen turning with
firm lips and proud self-possession from her losses at the
gaming-table" (ch. 56). This Gwendolen Harleth we remember as
the one who pawns her turquoise necklace.

In her misery Gwendolen seeks help from Deronda, who has himself just been made miserable by a meeting with his mother. The
Alcharisi's words have been like "arrows whose points carry the
sharpness of pity":

Lamenti saettaron me diversi
Che di pietà ferrati avean gli strali. (ch. 50)

(Lamentations pierced me, manifold, which had
their arrows barbed with pity.) (entry 100, n. 2)

As the Shakespearean epigraph of chapter 53 indicates--"My desolation does begin to make / A better life"[53]--Deronda is meant to be perfected by his sufferings. He is thus acutely sensitive to Gwendolen's harrowing ordeal when Grandcourt drowns in chapter 55. The epigraph for the chapter is once again taken from Dante, and George Eliot quoted it twice in the notebook (entries 98, 311):

>   "Ritorna a tua scienza
>   Che vuol, quanto la cosa è più perfetta
>   Piu senta il bene, e così la doglienza."
>
>   (Return to thy science
>   which has it that the more a thing is perfect,
>   the more it feels pleasure and likewise pain.)

As in Felix Holt, growth through suffering in Daniel Deronda seems peculiarly susceptible to presentation in terms of Dantean imagery.[54]

The formal structure in which the dynamics of personal development proceed, however, seems indebted to Goethe. There is a considerable body of quotation from Goethe in the notebook that testifies to Eliot's knowledge of Dichtung und Wahrheit, Wilhelm Meisters Lehrjahre and Wanderjahre, Faust, the Italiänische Reise, the West-östlicher Divan, and miscellaneous poetry (entries Endpaper, 11, 12, 13, 15, 18, 19, 24, 111-112). One of her early entries from Goethe became the epigraph of chapter 39 of Deronda:

>   'Vor den Wissenden sich stellen
>   Sicher ist's in allen Fällen!
>   Wenn du lange dich gequälet
>   Weiss er gleich wo dir es fehlet;
>   Auch auf Beifall darfst du hoffen,
>   Denn er weiss wo du's getroffen.'
>
>   (It is very satisfying in every instance
>   To place yourself before a wise man.
>   If you have tormented yourself a long while
>   He will know immediately where you are wanting;
>   And you can also hope for approbation,
>   Since he will understand your intention.)

George Eliot reached back to her reading from 1854 (entry 24) for this epigraph because it so nicely describes the action, not only of Chapter 39, where Mirah sings for Klesmer, but also of the whole novel. Gwendolen places herself before Deronda and he serves her, reluctantly, in the role of wise man; indeed, he becomes her Daniel. Deronda, in turn, places himself before Mordecai who serves him, willingly, as a wise man; he becomes his Ezra. The understanding that these wise men have of their charges leads to the regeneration of both Gwendolen and Deronda. They experience a "transmutation of self."

The phrase "transmutation of self" is used by Deronda to interpret a legend of the Buddha recorded by Max Müller in "Buddhist Pilgrims," an 1857 essay reprinted in his Chips from a German Workshop. Eliot first took note of the legend in the Felix Holt quarry and then incorporated it into the notebook as follows: "When Bouddha saw a tigress unable to feed her young, he is said to have offered his body to be devoured by them"

(entry 305). Mirah tells Daniel that Hans Meyrick had used this
legend of the Buddha to illustrate a trait in Deronda's character:
"He told us a wonderful story of Bouddha giving himself to a
famished tigress to save her and her little ones from starving.
And he said you were like Bouddha." Daniel then interprets the
story for Mirah: "It is an extreme image of what is happening
every day--the transmutation of self" (ch. 37). So just as reading King gave Eliot a way to use a turquoise necklace tellingly,
and reading Dante gave her an imagery for the presentation of
suffering, and reading Goethe gave her a strategy for personal
development, so too did reading Müller give her the Buddha as a
type of self-transcendence epitomizing the highest goal of moral
life. "Zum höchsten Dasein immerfort zu streben" ("To strive for
the highest life with all my powers")[55] is a line from _Faust_ used
in the epigraph for _Middlemarch_, chapter 81. It is another way
of saying that transmutation of self is the highest goal of human
striving. And that is what George Eliot's novels are all about.

Notes to Introduction

1. _Catalogue of Valuable Printed Books, Literary and Mediaevel Manuscripts, Autograph Letters, etc._ for auction on 14 April 1930 and three following days (Sotheby and Co.), p. 140.

2. George Eliot finished reading Goethe's _Wilhelm Meisters Lehrjahre_ on 31 November 1854; entry 11 is from that book. She finished reading Albrecht Weber's _History of Indian Literature_ on 28 December 1879; the last entry under 307 is from that book.

3. Part of the entry on Clouds (entries 70-71) falls under "C," but this seems to be an accident: the entry begins under "B" (entry 69).

4. _Essays of George Eliot_, ed. Thomas Pinney (London: Routledge and Kegan Paul, 1963), pp. 96-122; esp. p. 105.

5. Ibid., p. 80.

6. _The George Eliot Letters_, ed. Gordon S. Haight, 9 vols. (New Haven: Yale Univ. Press, 1954-55; 1978), VIII, 133-4.

7. _Essays_, p. 55.

8. Gordon S. Haight, _George Eliot: A Biography_ (New York: Oxford Univ. Press, 1968), p. 404.

9. _Letters_, IV, 466-7.

10. George Eliot quotes Edwin Guest, _A History of English Rhythms_, 2 vols. (London: William Pickering, 1838) in John C. Pratt and Victor A. Neufeldt, eds., _George Eliot's Middlemarch Notebooks: A Transcription_ (Berkeley: Univ. of California Press, 1979), pp. 73-74.

11. [J. A. Symonds], "Blank Verse," _Cornhill Magazine_, 15 (1867), 620-40, seems to be the article George Eliot refers to.

12. The Haight-Wynne register reads "copied about 1873-1876" (p. 106).

13. See James Joseph Sylvester, _The Laws of Verse or Principles of Versification Exemplified in Metrical Translations_ (London: Longmans, Green, 1870), pp. 66-67.

14. Pratt and Neufeldt, p. 88.

15. _Letters_, II, 369.

16. Samuel Smiles, _The Life of George Stephenson, Railway Engineer_ (London: John Murray, 1857), p. 20.

17. Ibid., pp. 25-26.

18. Ibid., p. 23.

19. Ibid., pp. 19, 25.

20. _Letters_, IV, 11 and n. 5.

21. Aeschylus, _The Oresteia Trilogy, Prometheus Bound_, ed. Robert W. Corrigan, trans. George Thompson (New York: Laurel Classical Drama, 1965), p. 143.

22. _Letters_, II, 502-5.

23. Ibid., p. 503.

24. Edward William Lane, _An Account of the Manners and Customs of the Modern Egyptians_, 2 vols. (London: Charles Knight, 1837), I, 373.

25. See entry 138, n. 1.

26. _Letters_, VIII, 96.

27. Introduction, _The Mill on the Floss_, Riverside Editions (Boston: Houghton Mifflin, 1962), p. v.

28. _Biography_, p. 319.

29. _Letters_, IV, 104.

30. See Joseph Wiesenfarth, _George Eliot's Mythmaking_ (Heidelberg: Carl Winter, 1977), pp. 153-62.

31. _Biography_, p. 352.

32. C. W. King, _Antique Gems_ (London: John Murray, 1860), p. 11.

33. Ibid., p. 441.

34. Ibid., p. 116.

35. _George Eliot's Life as Related in Her Letters and Journals_, ed. J. W. Cross (Edinburgh and London: William Blackwood and Sons, n.d.), III,

31-34, passim.

    36. Pratt and Neufeldt, p. 3.

    37. Anna T. Kitchel, ed., "Quarry for Middlemarch," Nineteenth-Century Fiction, 4 (1950), 34; Kitchel does not identify this entry.

    38. John William Donaldson, The New Cratylus, or Contributions towards a More Accurate Knowledge of the Greek Language (Cambridge: J. and J. J. Deighton; London: John W. Parker, 1839), p. 27. Donaldson adds another pertinent remark: "England we are sorry to say, has little to offer that will bear comparison with the performances of our continental neighbours, in regard either to comparative philology in general, or to Indian scholarship in particular" (p. 35).

    39. Pratt and Neufeldt, pp. 59, 224.

    40. Grimm's Law: A Study, or Hints towards an Explanation of the So-called "Lautverschiebung" (London: Trubner, 1876). On p. 9, the following note appears in George Eliot's hand: "This is a fallacious rule--as if ease meant the same thing for every organization--as if the broad in speech were always less easy than the narrow. Consonantal sounds which are a sort of handle to one tribe by which they lay hold of vowels are dropped or never taken by another."

    41. See Letters, VIII, 370, n. 8; 461, n. 4; George Eliot read Müller's History between August and October 1869.

    42. Adolf Stahr, Torso: Kunst, Künstler und Kunstwerk der Alten, 2 vols. (Brunswick: Friedrich Vieweg u. Sohn, 1854), II, 311-4.

    43. Ladislaw, at this point in the chapter, has just turned his back on the torso of Hercules resting after his labors, a piece of sculpture which gave Stahr the title of his book and which he discusses at length in Torso, II, 21-27; see fig. 1.

    44. See Mythmaking, pp. 193-201.

    45. Ruskin, Modern Painters, vol. 1, sec. i, ch. 2.

    46. Further discussion of Ruskin's influence on George Eliot can be found in Hugh Witemeyer, George Eliot and the Visual Arts (New Haven: Yale Univ. Press, 1979), pp. 17, 24-27, 171-3.

    47. Antique Gems, pp. 428-33.

    48. Ibid., p. 35.

    49. Quoted in William Baker, ed., Some George Eliot Notebooks (Salzburg: Institut für Englische Sprache und Literatur, 1976), I, 101.

    50. Antique Gems, p. 427.

    51. Insofar as the Grandcourt diamonds are called "poisoned gems" it is interesting to note what King records as their virtue: "Diamond has the virtue of resisting all poisons, yet if taken inwardly is itself a deadly poison. . . . It baffles magic arts, dispels vain fears, and gives success in law suits. It . . . renders the wearer bold and virtuous" (Antique Gems, p. 419). Clearly George Eliot draws on this description of the diamond, turning it around to use against Gwendolen, who is poisoned by a "sorceress" and turned into a weakling by a woman defrauded of her legal rights.

    52. See Baker, pp. 141; 265-6.

    53. Antony and Cleopatra, V.ii.1-2.

    54. "Dante," George Eliot wrote, "is at once the most precise and homely in his reproduction of actual objects, and the most soaringly at large in his imaginative combinations" (Impressions of Theophrastus Such, Works of George Eliot [Edinburgh and London: William Blackwood and Sons, 1880], p. 195).

    55. Faust, Pt. 2, 1. 4,685; see Goethe's Faust, trans. Walter Kaufmann, Anchor Books (Garden City, N.Y.: Doubleday, 1961), p. 427.

A Writer's Notebook, 1854-1879

Whatever she has done, she has studied for.

Emily Davies on George Eliot

"'I have tried pigeon-holes, but everything gets mixed in pigeon-holes: I never know whether a paper is in A or Z.'

  "'I wish you would let me sort your papers for you, uncle,' said Dorothea. 'I would letter them all, and then make a list of subjects under each letter.'"

Middlemarch

Mit Kleinen thut man kleine Thaten,
Mit Grossen wird der Kleine gross.

Goethe, Faust

Where there is much desire to learn, there of necessity will be much arguing, much writing, many opinions; for opinion in good men is but knowledge in the making.

Milton, Areopagitica

What good is like to this,
To do worthy the writing, and to write
Worthy the reading and the world's delight?

Samuel Daniel, Musophilus

{White verso of marbled front endpaper}

τὴν πεπρωμένην δὲ χρὴ
αἶσαν φέρειν ὡς ῥᾷστα γιγνώσκονθ᾽ ὅτι
τὸ τῆς ἀνάγκης ἔστ᾽ ἀδήριτον σθένος.

                                   Prom. 103[1]
                    _____

"τὰ μὲν νυν θεῖα τῶν ἀπηγημάτων οἷα ἤκουον οὐκ εἰμὶ πρόθυμος
ἐξηγέεσθαι, ἔξω ἢ τὰ οὐνόματα μοῦνον· νομίζων πάντας ἀνθρώπους
ἴσον περὶ αὐτῶν ἐπίστασθαι·"

                                   Herod. ii.2[2]

    "Ich immer vorzog von dem Menschen zu erfahren wie er dachte,
als von einem andern zu hören, wie er hätte denken sollen." Goethe,
à propos of Spinoza[3]

"Sine hâc quidem conscientiâ," says Quintilian, speaking of the
habit of written composition, "ille ipsa extempore dicendi
facultas, inanem modo loquacitatem dabit, et verba in labris
nascentia."[4]

Οἶδα παθὼν ἔλεεῖν'   (Meleager)[5]

    "To hear all naked truths
And to envisage circumstance all calm,
That is the top of sovereignty."   (Keats)[6]

    "Est enim vera lex, recta ratio, naturae congruens, diffusa
in omnes, constans, sempiterna, quae vocet ad officium jubendo,
vetando a fraude deterreat. Nec erit alia lex Romae, alia Athenis
alia nunc, alia posthac; sed et omni genti et omni tempore, una
lex et sempiterna."
                    Cicero.[7]

Spes et premia in ambiguo, certa funera et luctus.[8]

"Tönend wird für Geistes Ohren
Schon der neue Tag geboren."
                    Faust: 2d P.[9]

Οὔτοι συνέχθειν, ἀλλὰ συμφιλεῖν ἔφυν.[10]

"Clothing the palpable & the familiar
With golden exhalations of the dawn."[11]

{George Eliot's Index}

{George Eliot's Index}

1

"Il y a cela d'admirable, que le plaisir n'a pas besoin de
religion, d'appareil, ni de grands mots, il est tout par lui-
même; tandis que pour justifier les atroces combinaisons de notre
esclavage et de notre vassalité, les hommes ont accumulé les
théories et les maximes."

Mémoires de deux jeunes mariées.[1]

2

"The Egyptian women . . . appear to have enjoyed greater privilege & to have been treated with more courtesy on all occasions
than in other ancient communities." Not restricted in the use of
wine. (Wilkinson)[1]

3

Aristotle distinguishes persons intoxicated by wine & beer--"the
former lie upon their face, the latter on their backs."[1]

4

Diodorus Siculus i. 27. affirms that in Egyptian marriages an
agreement was entered into that the wife should have the control
over her husband and that no objection should be made to her
commands.[1] Probably this referred solely to household matters.--
Royal authority entrusted to women. Manetho says that the law
giving the right of regal succession to women dated as early as
the reign of Binothris, the 3d monarch of the 2d dynasty.[2]

5

Egyptian sculptures showing women weaving & using the distaff.
Sedentary occupations.[1]

6

"Diodorus informs us the Egyptians were not restricted to any
number of wives, but that every one married as many as he chose,
with the exception of the priesthood, who were by law confined to
one consort. (See Gibbon ii.xv.318, opinions of the fathers on
second marriages.)[1] It does not however appear that they generally took advantage of this privilege; & Herodotus affirms (ii.92)
that throughout Egypt it was customary to marry only one wife.
It is easy to reconcile these statements by supposing that
Diodorus Siculus speaks of a law which permitted polygamy, &
Herodotus of the usual custom of the people: & if the Egyptians
were allowed to take more than one wife we may conclude from the
numerous scenes illustrative of their domestic life, that it was
an event of rare occurrence." (No instance of two consorts given
in the sculptures). Wilkinson ii.62. Marriage between brother &
sister legal--mentioned by Diodorus & confirmed by sculptures.[2]
   "Though the Egyptians generally confined themselves to one
wife, they, like the Jews & other Eastern nations, both of ancient
& modern times, scrupled not to admit other inmates to their
hareem, most of whom appear to have been foreigners, either taken
in war, or brought to Egypt to be sold as slaves. They became
members of the family, like those in a similar situation in the
present day, & not only ranked next to the wives & children of
their lord, but probably enjoyed a share of the property at his
demise. These women were white or black slaves. . . . . but,
generally speaking, the latter were employed as domestics who
were required to wait on their mistress & her female friends. The
former likewise officiated as servants, though they of course

held a rank above the black slaves." ii.63. id.
     "The same custom prevailed among the Egyptians regarding
children, as with the Moslems & other Eastern people: no distinction being made between their offspring by a wife or any other
woman, & all equally enjoying the rights of inheritance; for
since they considered a child indebted to its father for its
existence, & the mother "little more than a nurse,"* it seemed un-
just to deny equal rights to all their progeny. And, indeed, if
Diodorus is correct, they carried this principle so far that in
dioecious plants, those which bore fruit were denominated males,
as being the cause of production & of the continuation of the
species.[3] *(This does not agree with Diodorus's account of the
superiority of the wife.)[4]

                              7
"No [Egyptian] woman can serve the holy office, either for god or
goddess. . . . . No necessity compels sons to support their
parents, unless they choose; the daughters are compelled to do so
even against their will." Herod. ii.35.[1] "Every man wears two
garments; every woman one."[2] "Like the Hellenes, every man having but one wife."[3] Nitocris, ii.100.[4] Rhodophis & Archidice,
135.[5]

                              8
Legend of the Flying Dutchman. "Ein holländisches Fahrzeug,
welches vor langer, langer Zeit das Cap der guten Hoffnung um-
segelte, wurde von einem langandauernden Sturm hingehalten. Als
die Matrosen den Capitän um Rückkehr beschworen, rief dieser aus:
'Und sollte ich in Ewigkeit auf dem Meere hausen! Nimmermehr thue
ich es.' Zur Strafe für diese Blasphemie wurde er verdammt bis
zum jüngsten Tag die Meere zu durchirren und allen Schiffen
Verderben zu bringen, die ihm auf der Fahrt begegneten. Der
Engel der Barmherzigkeit aber verkündet ihm, dass ihm alle sieben
Jahre verstattet sein solle, die Küste zu betreten und sich zu
vermählen. Würde das erwählte Weib ihm untreu, so fiele auch sie
der Hölle zur Beute, fände er aber eine Gattin, die bis in den
Tod ihn liebte,[1] so tilge ihre Treue seine Schuld und erschliesse
ihm nach leiblichem Tod die Pforten ewigen Heils. Nach Heine's
Erzählung ist es ein junges norwegisches Mädchen, welches durch
eine volksthümliche Ballade von jenem Himmelsurtheil unterrichtet,
von Jugend auf tiefes Mitgefühl für das Loos des unseligen Capitäns
empfindet. Dieser landet eines Tages auf Norwegs Küsten, um dort
ein Weib zu suchen. Sie erkennt ihn und schwört ihm Treue, fest
entschlossen, ihren Eid zu halten. Der Holländer aber, von Liebe
und Dankbarkeit für so viel Schönheit und Hingebung ergriffen,
fürchtet, sie der Gefahr eines Meineids auszusetzen, und verlässt
sie, entsagend der langersehnten Hoffnung auf endliche Erlösung
aus der Verdammniss. Das Mädchen aber, die ihn auf seinem
Fahrzeug fortsegeln sieht, stürzt sich ins Meer. Im selben Augen-
blick ist das Sühnopfer erfüllt und der fliegende Holländer ver-
sinkt in den Wogen."[2]

                              8a
     "Bei ihm (dem Griechen)[1] war der Heroismus wie die verborgenen
Funken im Kiesel, die ruhig schlafen, so lange keine äussere Gewalt
sie wecket, und dem Steine weder seine Klarheit noch seine Kälte
nehmen."
          Lessing[2]

9

"Nichts ist betrüglicher als allgemeine Gesetze für unsere Emp-
findungen. Ihr Gewebe ist so fein und verwickelt, dass es auch
der behutsamsten Speculation kaum möglich ist, einen einzelnen
Faden rein aufzufassen und durch alle Kreuzfäden zu verfolgen.
Gelingt es ihr aber auch schon, was für Nutzen hat es? Es giebt
in der Natur keine einzelne reine Empfindung; mit einer jeden
entstehen tausend andere zugleich, deren geringste die Grundemp-
findung gänzlich verändert, so dass Ausnahmen über Ausnahmen er-
wachsen, die das vermeintlich allegemeine Gesetz endlich selbst
auf eine blosse Erfahrung in wenig einzelnen Fällen einschränken."
                              Lessing. Laocoon.[1]

10

"Wie kann ein Mann ein Ding lieben, das, ihm zum Trotze, auch
denken will? Ein Frauenzimmer, das denket, ist eben so eckel als
ein Mann, der sich schminket." (Emilia Galotti)[1]

11

"Er pflegte zu sagen: Der Mensch ist so geneigt, sich mit dem
Gemeinsten abzugeben, Geist und Sinne stumpfen sich so leicht
gegen die Eindrücke des Schönen und Vollkommenen ab, dass man die
Fähigkeit, es zu empfinden, bei sich auf alle Weise erhalten
sollte. Denn einen solchen Genuss kann niemand ganz entbehren,
und nur die Ungewohnheit etwas Gutes zu geniessen ist Ursache,
dass viele Menschen schon am Albernen und Abgeschmackten, wenn es
nur neu ist, Vergnügen finden. Man sollte, sagte er, alle Tage
wenigstens ein kleines Lied hören, ein gutes Gedicht lesen, ein
treffliches Gemählde sehen, und, wenn es möglich zu machen wäre,
einige vernünftige Worte sprechen." (Goethe)[1]

12

"Die Welt ist so leer, wenn man nur Berge, Flüsse und Städte darin
denkt, aber hie und da jemand zu wissen, der mit uns übereinstimmt,
mit dem wir auch stillschweigend fortleben, das macht uns dieses
Erdenrund erst zu einem bewohnten Garten.[1]

13

Der Sinn erweitert, aber lähmt; die That belebt, aber beschränkt.
                              Wilhelm Meister.[1]

14

Tobende Eile mich treibend erfasst!
Aber wohl niemals liebten die Horen; --
Heimlich im grausamen Bunde verschworen,
Spotten sie tückisch der Liebenden Hast."

                              Heine.[1]

15

"Es is so schwer, ein grosses Talent zu fassen, geschweige denn
zwei[1] zugleich. Wir erleichtern uns dieses durch Parteilichkeit.
                              Italiänische Reise.[2]

16

Die Nonne Roswitha oder Hrosuith (weisse Rose) um 980 im Kloster
Gandersheim im Braunschweigischen lebte und schriftstellerte. Das
ist eine echte und gerechte Literatin des Mittelalters, mit einem
ziemlich bedeutenden Anflug vom dem, was die Engländer so ganz
treffend Blaustrümpfelei nennen. Frühzeitig, wie es scheint, in

das genannte Kloster getreten, widmete sie sich unter Leitung der
gelehrten Schwester Rikkardis u. der feingebildeten Aebtissin
Gerberga, der Nichte Otto's II., den classischen Studien und
machte sich durch ihr schriftstellerisches Talent bald weitum
bekannt, so dass man sie die "helltönende Stimme von Gandersheim"
nannte. Von Geberga u. deren kaiserlichem Oheim dazu ausgefordert,
erzählte sie die Thaten Otto's I. in lateinischen Hexametern.
Auch die Geschichte der Grüdung ihres Klosters, sowie mehrere
Märtyrerlegenden hat sie in lateinischen Versen geschrieben. Um
berühmtesten wurde sie jedoch durch ihre lateinischen Komödien,
in welchen sie ziemlich sklavisch den Terenz nachahmte. Von welchem
Gesichtspunkte sie bei diesen dramatischen Arbeiten ausging, setzt
sie in der Vorrede derselben auseinander, indem sie sagt: "Es
giebt viele gute Christen, die um des Vorzugs einer gebildeteren
Sprache willen den eitlen Schein der heidnischen Bücher dem Nutzen
der heiligen Schrift vorziehen, ein Fehler, wovon auch wir uns
nicht völlig freisprechen können. Dann giebt es fleissige
Bibelleser, welche, obgleich sie die übrigen Schriften der Heiden
verschmähen, dennoch die Dictungen des Terentius nur allzu häufig
lesen und, bestochen von der Anmuth der Rede, sich durch die
Bekanntschaft mit unzüchtigen Gegenständen beflecken. In Berücksichti-
gung dessen habe ich, die helltönende Stimme von Gandersheim, mich
nicht geweigert, den vielgelesenen Autor im Ausdrucke nachzuahmen,
damit in ebenderselben Weise, womit dort geiler Weiber schmuzige
Laster dargestellt sind, hier die preiswürdige Züchtigkeit
gottseliger Jungfrauen nach dem Maasse meines geringen Talentes
gerühmt werde." Der Zweck Roswitha's bei Abfassung ihrer sechs
kleinen Dramen--Lustspielen in unserem Sinne kann man dieselben
nicht nennen--war also ein moralisch-ascetischer, wie er einer
Nonne geziemte. Allein es will uns bedünken, dass wir ihrer
Nonnenhaftigkeit kaum zu nahe treten, wenn wir vermuthen, dass
sie, bevor sie ihre Komödien schrieb, sich nicht nur im Terenz,
sondern auch in der Liebe umgesehen haben müsse. Wir haben sie
uns zur Zeit, als sie die dramaturgische Feder ergriff, allerdings
nicht mehr als junges heissblütiges Mädchen zu denken, sondern
vielmehr als gesetzte Matrone mit einem säuerlich frommen Zug um
den Mund; dessenungeachtet aber hatte sie den Conflict zwischen
antikem Sensualismus und christlichem Spiritualismus, welcher in
einer classisch gebildeten Klosterschwester nothwendig entstehen
musste, noch nicht völlig überwunden. Es lodert in ihren Komödien
da und dort das Feuer der Sinnlichkeit noch ganz artig auf, und
wenn die klösterliche Dichterin nie unterlässt, ihre Stücke zu
einem höchst erbaulichen martyrologischen Schlusse zu führen, so
wählt sie doch mit Vorliebe sehr bedenkliche Situationen zur
Darstellung. Wir haben es bei ihr, wie bei ihrem Vorbilde Terenz,
meist mit Lüstlingen und Buhlerinnen zu thun und Verführung und
Bekehrung sind ihre wirksamsten Motive. Wo komische Züge vorkom-
men, sind es sehr handgreifliche, wie wenn z.B. der lüderliche
Statthalter Dulcitius Nachts in das Haus der heiligen Jungfrauen
Agape, Chionia und Irene eindringt, um sie zu entehren, bei seinem
Eintritte aber den Verstand verliert, statt der Mädchen Töpfe und
Pfannen küsst und sich so das Gesicht garstig beschmiert.
                    p. 85 Scherr, Deutsche Cultur u. Sitte[1]

                              17
"Charkteristisch ist es, dass unsern deutschen Schelmen immer
eine gewisse Sentimentalität anklebt. Sie sind keine kalten
Verstandesspitzbuben, sondern Schufte von Gefühl. (Heine's
Geständnisse. Preface)[1]

18

"Vielseitigkeit bereitet eigentlich nur das Element vor, worin
der Einseitige wirken kann, dem eben jetzt genug Raum gegeben ist.
Ja es ist jetzo die Zeit der Einseitigkeiten; wohl dem, der es
begreift, für sich und andere in diesem Sinne wirkt. Bei gewissen
Dingen versteht sich's durchaus und sogleich. Uebe dich zum
tüchtigen Violinisten und sey versichert, der Kapellmeister wird
dir deinen Platz im Orchester mit Gunst anweisen. Mache ein Organ
aus dir und erwarte, war für eine Stelle dir die Menschheit im
allgemeinen Leben wohlmeinend zugestehen werde."

Wanderjahre, Book I.[1]

19

Was kann der Mensch im Leben mehr gewinnen
Als dass sich Gott-Natur ihm offenbare?
Wie sie das Festelässt zu Geist verrinnen,
Wie sie das Geisterzeugte fest bewahre.
   --Goethe (bei Betrachtung von Schiller's Schädel)[1]

20

"Die Feinheit des Erasmus und die Milde des Melancthon hätten uns
nimmer so weit gebracht wie manchmal die göttliche Brutalität des
Bruder Martin."

Heine[1]

21

"Constatirt ist es, dass der Lebenswandel des Spinoza frei von
allem Tadel war, und rein und makellos wie das Leben seines
göttlichen Vetters, Jesu Christi. Auch wie dieser litt er für
seine Lehre, wie dieser trug er die Dornenkrone. Ueberall, wo ein
grosser Geist seinen Gedanken ausspricht, ist Golgotha . . . . Er
wurde feyerlich ausgestossen aus der Gemeinschaft Israels und
unwürdig erklärt hinfüro den Namen Jude zu tragen. Seine
christlichen Feinde waren grossmüthig genug, ihm diesen Namen zu
lassen."

Heine[1]

22

Die Sterne des Himmels erscheinen uns aber vielleicht deshalb so
schön und rein, weil wir weit von ihnen entfernt stehen & ihr
Privatleben nicht kennen. Es giebt gewiss dort oben ebenfalls
manche Sterne, welche lügen und betteln; Sterne, welche heucheln;
Sterne, welche gezwungen sind, alle möglichen Schlechtigkeiten zu
begehen; Sterne, welche sich einander küssen und verrathen; Sterne,
welche ihren Feinden und, was noch schmerzlicher ist, sogar ihren
Freunden schmeicheln, eben so gut wie wir hier unten. Jene Cometen,
die man dort oben manchmal wie Mänaden des Himmels, mit aufgelöstem
Strahlenhaar, umherschweifen sieht, das sind vielleicht lieder-
liche Sterne, die am Ende sich reuig und devot in einen obscuren
Winkel des Firmaments verkriechen und die Sonne hassen."

Ibid.[1]

23

   "Am reinsten und lieblichsten beurkundet sich dieser Goethesche
Pantheismus in seinen kleinen Liedern. Die Lehre des Spinoza hat
sich aus der mathematischen Hülle entpuppt und umflattert uns als
Goethesches Lied. Daher die Wuth unserer Orthodoxen und Pietisten
gegen das Goethesche Lied. Mit ihren frommen Bärentatzen tappen
sie nach diesem Schmetterling, der inhen beständig entflattert.

Das ist so zart aetherisch, so duftig beflügelt. . . . .
Diese Gotheschen Lieder haben einen neckischen Zauber, der un-
beschreibbar. Die harmonischen Verse umsehlingen dein Herz wie
eine zärtliche Geliebte; das Wort umarmt dich, während der Gedanke
dich küsst."
                    Heine[1]

                    24
Vor den Wissenden dich stellen
Sicher ist's in allen Fällen!
Wenn du lange dich gequälet
Weiss er gleich wo dir es fehlet;
Auch auf Beifall darfst du hoffen,
Denn er weiss wo du's getroffen.
                    West-östlicher Divan[1]

                    25
     It is remarkable that Shakespear's women almost always make
love, in opposition to the conventional notion of what is fitting
for woman. Yet his pictures of women are belauded. Is it so
with his contemporary dramatists?[1]

                    26
     The progress of organic nature, say the naturalists, is from
East to West. Almost every thing necessary, useful & pleasant in
the vegetable world has gradually proceeded from Asia towards the
West. So with human development & culture. Was it that in the
first revolution of our globe on its axis the East was first
towards the Sun--that it started on its course with its Eastern
cheek on the sunny side--& so this priority, like the first move
in chess, gave the East precedence in all things.?[1]

                    26a
"I meant the day-star should not brighter ride,
     Nor shed like influence from its lucent seat;
I meant she should be courteous, facile, sweet,
     Free from that solemn vice of greatness, pride;
I meant each softest virtue there should meet,
     Fit in that softer bosom to abide:
Only a learned & manly soul
     I purposed her, that should with even powers
The rock, the spindle, & the shears control
     Of destiny, & spin her own free hours."
                    Ben Jonson.[1]

                    27
     "Zu den Zeiten des Kaisers Tiberius," so erzählt der Verfasser
einer in barbarischem Mönchslatein des zwölften Jahrhunderts
geschriebenen Erklärung der "Wunderwerke Roms," "erschienen in
Rom zwei junge Philosophen (Wunderthäter) Phidias und Praxiteles,
welche sich öffentlich ohne alle Bekleidung zeigten. Als der
Kaiser dies erfuhr, liess er sie vor sich kommen, & fragte sie:
Weshalb geht Ihr nackt einher? Sie antworteten: "Weil Alles
nackt und offen vor unseren Blicken liegt, und weil wir die Welt
für nichts halten, darum gehen wir nackt einher und besitzen
nichts." Ob solcher Weisheit hielt sie der Kaiser hoch in seinem
Palaste. Sie rühmten sich aber solcher Wissenschaft, dass sie
Alles, was der Kaiser bei Tag und bei Nacht, ohne dass sie zugegen
wären, im Sinne führte, ihm bis auf das letzte Word zu sagen

vermöchten, und so sprachen sie zu ihm: "Herr Kaiser, wir werden
Dir Alles sagen, was Du entfernt von uns, sei es bei Tag oder bei
Nacht, in deinem Kabinette gesprochen haben wirst." "Wenn ihr
das thut, erwiderte der Kaiser, so will ich euch geben, was ihr
verlangt." Darauf jene: Wir verlangen kein Geld, sondern nur
ein Denkmal der Erinnerung (memoriam nostrorum). Am anderen
Morgen erzählten sie dem Kaiser der Reihe nach, was er in der
vergangen Nacht berathen hatte, und der Kaiser stiftete ihnen das
geforderte und versprochene Gedächtnissmal, nämlich nackte Rosse,
welche die Erde, das heisst die Mächtigen dieser Zeitlichkeit,
die über die Menschen dieser Welt herrschen, mit ihren Hufen
treten. Zum Zeichen aber, dass der mächtige König kommen wird,
der diese Rosse besteigen, das heisst, die Gewaltigen dieser
Zeitlichkeit sich unterwerfen wird, stehen neben den Rossen
halbnackte Gestalten, die mit erhobenen Armen und zusammengezogenen
Fingern dasjenige herzählen, was damals kommen sollte. Und wie sie
selbst nackt sind, so liegt alles weltliche Wissen nackt und offen
vor ihnen. Eine Frauengestalt, von Schlangen umgeben, vor sich
eine Wasserschale, sitzt zu ihren Füssen, so dass, wer ihr nahen
will, es nicht kann, bevor er sich nicht in jener Schale gebadet
hat." Stahr, Torso, p. 237.[1]

28

"The Greeks, when they conceived combinations of the human
with the brute forms, made the upper part human & the lower part
bestial; the Egyptians, the reverse." Witness, on the one hand,
the Centaurs, Satyrs, Pan, the Mermaids, &c; on the other the
dog-faced god Anubis &c.[1]

29

Praxiteles sculptured a group which represents the joyous
grace of the Hetaira in contrast with the dull sourness of the
legitimate wife. (Stahr 386)[1]

30

"Der Frauendienst der Provenzalen und Italiener, äusserlicher,
sinnlicher, neckischer, als der deutsche Minnedienst wirkte nach
meinem Geschmacke[1] auf die Liebespoesie der ersteren weit
vortheilhafter, als die tiefe heilige Versenkung der deutschen
Minnesänger auf unsere Lyrik dieser Zeit. So wahr ist es, dass
es nichts so Hehres und Hohes giebt, dem es nicht heilsam wäre,
sich seines irdischen Ursprungs zuweilen zu erinnern. Und wie
sich gerade in dem Lande der feurige religiöse Enthusiasmus zeigte,
in dem die Religiosität nie so gross war wie in Deutschland, wo
jener mangelte, so kennt man auf der anderen Seite in Deutschland,
trotz jener grossen Frauenverehrung, bis auf den heutigen Tag
nicht die französische Emporhebung und Heraushebung der Frauen
aus den Verhältnissen, die ihnen die Natur in der Gesellschaft
angewiesen hat, man entband sie nie von den Pflichten der
Häuslichkeit und der Pflege des Mannes, und selbst im Mittelalter
steht in allen rechtlichen und practischen Verhältnissen das Weib
hinter dem Manne zurück. So gut ist es, sich der Geschichte zu
erinnern, wenn man von jener gefeierten germanischen Frauenverehrung träumt. Die Deutschen haben darin allerdings einen
grossen Ruhm, dass sie vielleicht unter allen Nationen der Erde
zuerst und am vollkommensten dem Weibe eben die Stelle angewiesen
haben, welche die Natur selbst ihm bestimmt hat. Macht es ihrem
Gefühle Ehre, dass sie das Weib aus der Unterordnung emancipiren,
so ehrt es ihren verständigen Sinn nicht minder, dass sie sich

nie verleiten liessen, es aus seiner Sphäre herauszurücken und
zur Theilnahme am äusseren Bestreben der Männer zu lenken, wie in
Frankreich geschah. Jene Zeit des Frauendienstes im Mittelalter
war eine vorübergehende; sie musste eine vorübergehende sein, wie
wir uns später erklären wollen. Je höher man damals den Schwindel
trieb, desto schneller und tiefer sank man herab, und die Gemein-
heit und Unsittlichkeit, die man sobald auch in den Dichtungen in
diesem Bezuge findet, entspricht ganz der Frivolität und Ketzerei
der Franzosen nach ihrem religiösen Aufschwung.

Gervinus I, 134.[1]

31

"Belagerung von Weinsberg," ein Name, welcher mit dem Ruhm deutscher
Frauentreue für immer verbunden ist. (?)[1]
Penalty of 15 cows for stroking a woman's hand. Scherr 46[2]
Lover carrying about his mistress's letter all day unread because
his scribe was not at hand to decipher it. 105
Murner, who lived about the time of the Reformation, speaks of
the extremes to which hospitality was carried. 106[3]
Marriage a peculiarly religious ceremony first in 12 cent. 107.
Prostitution in Middle Ages. 110. 210.[4]
Bitisia Gozzadini 158.[5] Daughter of Erwin von Steinbach 167.[6]
Idea of Prophetesses gave rise to that of witch, 41.[7]

32

     Luther, in his book against the Peasants, says: "The people
must be ruled by force, the ass must have blows." He summoned all
the world "die Bauern zu zerschmeissen, zu würgen und zu stechen,
heimlich und öffentlich wie man einen tollen Hund muss tod-
schlagen. Der Pöbel will mit Gewalt regiert seyn, der Esel will
Schläge haben. Sind Unschuldige darunter, die wird Gott wohl
bewahren und retten, wie er Lott und Jeremia that. That er so
nicht so sind sie gewiss nicht unschuldig, sondern haben zum
wenigsten geschwiegen und gebilligt." Compare the words of
Armand, Abbot of Citeaux, in the Crusade against the Waldenses:
"Schlagt alles nieder, der Herr kennet die Seinen!"[1]

32{a}

     "Recreating & composing their travailed spirits with the
solemn & divine harmonies of music." Milton[1]

33

"In those vernal seasons of the year when the air is calm &
pleasant, it were an injury & a sullenness against Nature, not to
go out & see her riches & partake in her rejoicing with heaven &
earth." (Idem)[1]

34

     "When I went to the University, I was of opinion, as most
schoolboys are, that the soul was a substance distinct from the
body, & that when a man died, he, in classical phrase, animam
expiravit;[1] that it then went I knew not whither, as it had come
into the body from I knew not where, nor when; and had dwelt in
the body during life, but in what part of the body it had dwelt
I knew not. So deep-rooted was this notion of the flight of the
soul somewhither after death, as well as of its having existed
somewhere before birth, that I perfectly well remember having
much puzzled my childish apprehension, before I was twelve years
old, with asking myself this question,--Had I not been the son of

Mr. & Mrs. Watson, whose son should I have been? The question
itself was suggested in consequence of my being out of humour, at
some slight correction which I had received from my mother. This
notion of the soul was, without doubt, the offspring of prejudice
& ignorance, & I must own that my knowledge of the nature of the
soul is much the same now that it was then. I have read volumes
on the subject, but I have no scruple in saying, that I <u>know</u>
nothing about it.

Believing, as I do, in the truth of the Christian religion,
which teaches that men are accountable for their actions, I
trouble not myself with dark disquisitions concerning necessity
and liberty, matter & spirit; hoping as I do for eternal life
through Jesus Christ, I am not disturbed at my inability clearly
to convince myself that the soul is, or is not, a substance distinct from the body. The truth of the Christian religion depends
upon testimony; now man is competent to judge of the weight of
testimony, though he is not able I think fully to investigate the
nature of the soul x x x[2] I probably should never have fallen
into this scepticism on so great a point, but should have lived &
died with my school boy's faith had I not been obliged as an
opponent in the philosophical schools at Cambridge in 1758, to
find arguments against the question: Anima est suâ naturâ im-
mortalis.[3]--in turning over a great many books in search of arguments against this natural immortality of the soul, I met with an
account (I do not know in what author, but there is the same, or
a similar one mentioned in the French Encyclopédie not then published, art. <u>Mort</u>,) of a man who came to life after having been
for six weeks under water. This account, whether true or false,
suggested to me a doubt concerning the soul's being, as I had
till then without the least hesitation conceived it to be, not a
mere quality of the body, but a substance different in kind from
it. I thought one might in some measure account for the restitu-
tion of motion & life, to a body considered as a machine, whose
motions had been stopped without its fabric being destroyed; but
I could not apprehend the possibility of recalling a soul which
had left the body, with its last expiration, for the span of six
weeks.[4] I mention not this with a view of supporting the
materiality of the soul, or the contrary, but merely to show upon
what trifling circumstances our opinions are frequently formed:--
a consideration which should teach us all to speak with candour
of those who happen to differ from us, & to abate in ourselves
that dogmatizing spirit which often impels learned men to impose
on others their own inveterate prejudices as incontrovertible
truths."[5]

Bishop Watson's Anecdotes of his life.[6]

34a

"That happy breathing-place from the burthen of a perpetual moral
questioning--the sanctuary & quiet Alsatia of hunted casuistry"[1].
. . . . . "We dare not contemplate an Atlantis, a scheme, out of
which our coxcombical moral sense is for a little transitory ease
excluded. We have not the courage to imagine a state of things
for which there is neither reward nor punishment. We cling to
the painful necessities of praise[2] & blame. We would indict our
very dreams."[3]

Elia. Artificial Comedy of the Last Century.

                                   35
                           Hymn to the Infinite.
     (A squib on the occasion of the Oxford Commemoration 1852)[1]
                           "The voice of yore,
                           Which breezes bore,
                   Wailing aloud from Paxo's shore,
                   Is changed to a gladder & livelier strain,
                   For the great god Pan is alive again;
                   He lives and he reigns[2] once more.
                   With deep intuition & mystic rite
                   We worship the Absolute-Infinite
                   The Universe-Ego, the Plenary-Void,
                   The Subject-Object identified,
                   The great Nothing-Something, the Being-Thought,
                   That mouldeth the mass of Chaotic Nought,
                   Whose being[3] unended & end unbegun
                   Is the One that is All, and the All that is One.
                           Hail Light with Darkness joined!
                           Thou Potent Impotence!
                           Thou Quantitative Point
                           Of all Indifference!
                   Great Non-Existence, passing into Being,
                   Thou twofold Pole of the Electric One,
                   Thou Lawless Law, thou Seer all Unseeing,
                   Thou Process, ever doing, never done!
                           Thou Positive Negation!
                           Negative Affirmation!
                   Thou great Totality of every thing
                   That never is, but ever doth become,
                   Thee do we sing,
                   The Pantheist's King,[4]
                   With ceaseless bug, bug, bug, and endless hum, hum, hum."[5]

                                   36
                   O Mary, go & call the cattle home
                       And call the cattle home,
                     Across the sands o' Dee--
                   The western wave was wild & dark wi' foam,
                       And all alone went she.

                   The creeping tide came up along the sand,
                       And o'er & o'er the sand,
                     And round & round the land,
                     As far as eye could see;
                   The blinding mist came down & hid the land,
                       And never home came she.

                   O, is it weed, or fish or floating hair?--
                     A tress o' golden hair,
                     O' drowned maiden's hair,
                   Above the nets at sea--
                   Was never salmon yet that shone so fair
                     Among the stakes on Dee.

                   They rowed her in across the swirling foam,
                     The cruel crawling foam,[1]
                     The cruel hungry foam,
                   To the grave beside the sea:
                   But still the boatmen hear her call the cattle home
                     Across the sands o' Dee.[2]

37

"It was an ass listening to the lyre, a pig listening to the
trumpet." (Menander)[1]

{Entry 38 is missing in the manuscript.}

39

Chief Remains of Greek Sculpture (from Stahr's Torso)[1]

1

The Gate of Lions at Mycenae. This is oldest relic of Greek
sculpture and indeed so far as our knowledge extends the oldest
piece of sculpture in Europe. The walls which encircled the city
of Agamemnon are still standing, their cyclopean strength having
almost entirely defied the assaults of time and other enemies.
The Gate of Lions is the main entrance through these walls. On
the huge blocks of stone wh. form the gate posts is laid a third
crosswise, & this supports a gigantic relief showing two lionesses
with a pillar between them. The heads of the lionesses are wanting.

2

The Relief of Samothrace. Found 1790, & now deposited in the
Louvre. An inscription tells the names of the figures--Agamemnon,
accompanied by two heralds. Whether a very ancient original or
only an imitation of such, it exhibits Greek art in one of its
lowest grades. The heralds are mere repetitions of each other,
after the Egyptian abstract manner.

3

The Lycian Sculptures. Discovered by Fellows[2] at the ancient
Miletus. They are now in London. Consist of from 60 to 70
statues in a sitting posture, which formed a Temple-avenue. The
parallel position of the feet, the arms close to the body, the
straight folds of the dress, the entire absence of movement, are
all in the style of the sitting Egyptian statues.

4

The temple sculptures at Selinus. Discovered 30 years ago.
Wrought in limestone. Now in Palermo. Remains of three temples
on the fort of the old city of Selinus, which was built 608 B.C.
by Dorian Greeks on the southern coast of Sicily, & destroyed
by the Carthaginians only 200 years later. Thus the period of
these sculptures is determined as that in wh. Solon lived--a
hundred years before Phidias. These remains are reliefs which
ornamented the metope on the outside of the temple. They are at
once the only sculptures which are clearly proved to belong to
the earliest period of Grecian art. The reliefs of the oldest
temple represent incidents in the legends of Perseus and Hercules.
It is a comic situation in which Hercules here appears. According
to the myth, Hercules, having been teazed as well as amused by
the Kerkopes Passalos and Aklemon, seized them & hung them with
their heads downwards to a pole wh. he carried about on his
shoulder. Even in this position they did not cease from their
tricks and thus won him to release them. The sculpture represents
him carrying them fastened to the pole. The other represents
Perseus cutting off the head of Medusa, with an averted face.
The figures are rude & barbaric; no trace of beauty. Another relief of the same temple presents a Viga, the horses executed with
more spirit and nature. From another temple there are two reliefs
exhibiting victorious Amazons.[3]

5

The OEginetan sculptures. Discovered 1811. Now at Munich.

Struggle between the Greeks & Trojans for the body of Achilles;
Minerva forming the central figure.[4]
                    5b (After the ideal of Phidias)
Minerva statues.
  Pallas of Vellatri. Found 1797. In the Louvre. The best
adapted to give us an idea of the Parthenos of Phidias. Among
the nine Minervas in the Louvre, the one which the spectator re-
members. Strikingly like this is a Bust of Minerva in the
Glyptothek at Munich, which Anselm Feuerbach[5] says is "der reine
Gedanke in Marmor verkörpert." The Minerva Chigi in Dresden. The
Minerva of Cassel. The Minerva Giustiniani in the Braschio nuova
of the Vatican. In Wincklemann's time[6] nearly the most celebrated
statue of Pallas. It is the one of which Goethe writes to his
friend that he does not feel himself worthy to speak of it.[7] The
Pallas in Villa Albani. Wincklemann gave the palm of beauty. The
Minerva of the Hope Collection in London. Colossal statue of
Athene at Naples.[8]
                              6
Jupiters. The Jupiter of Otricoli (a bust). Jupiter Verospi.
Both at Rome. The Jupiter Verospi is seated on a throne. These
are the two sublimest Jupiters remaining.[9]
                7 (Phidias and his pupils. 490-431)
Sculptures of the Parthenon. Part of the Frise[10] representing the
Panathenea. Some of the Metopes, representing the battle between
the Centaurs and Lapithae. From the sculptures on the gable--Two
groups of women, Neptune, Ilissos, two horses of the Sun, one of
the Night. Colossal female head, found in Venice, now at Paris.[11]
                              8
The colossi of Monte Cavallo. One attributed to Phidias, the
other to Praxiteles. Probably copies from works by them.[12]
                              9
The Phigalian Sculptures. By Alkamenes, the pupil of Phidias.
Remains of a Temple of Apollo. Battle of the Amazons & Battle of
the Centaurs. In the Brit. Mus. 23 blocks of the frise.[13]
        9a (Ideal of Polykletes, contemporary of Phidias)
Juno of the Villa Ludovisi in Rome.
Mercury Belvedere[14]
        10 (Ideal of Myron, contemporary of Phidias)
Discobolus, Palace Massini alle Colonee, Rome.[15]
                              11
Period of Scopas, Praxiteles & Lysippus. 4th cent. B.C. Their
ideal the beautiful as that of Phidias the sublime.
Ideal of Scopas.
Mars Ludovisi in Rome.
Medusa Rondanini, Munich.[16]
Apollo Cithaŏdus, in the Vatican.
Apollo of Berberini, in Munich.
                    Ideal of Praxiteles.
Venus de' Medici, Florence
Capitoline Venus, Rome
  Venus Chigi, Rome.
    After Praxiteles' Venus of Cnidos:--2 in the Museo Pio
Clementino, 1 in the Villa Borghese, 1 in the Villa Ludovisi.
Venus Braschi, Rome.
Venus of Milos, in the Louvre. Clothed.
Venus of Capua, Naples. (Venus Victrix).
Venus of Arles, in the Louvre.
Venus Genitrix, Louvre.
Eros of the Vatican.

Elgin Eros, Brit. Museum.
Bacchus, Vatican (Called Sardanapolus)
Torso of Bacchus, Vatican.
Bacchus in the Louvre. (as Luaix, Release from care)
Satyr Periboëtos, numerous copies in the Vatican &c.
Silenus with the Infant Bacchus, in the Louvre.[17]
Diana Colonna, Berlin.
Diana of Versailles.
Apollo Sauroktonos. (many copies)
Ceres of the Villa Borghese.[18]
Ceres of the Vatican.
   Niobe group, Florence.
Group of Wrestlers, Florence.
   Rape of Ganymede, Vatican.

Monument of Lysicrates, certainly belonging to the period of
Praxiteles.

Lysippus, the contemporary of Alexander closes the circle of Greek
art by the perfecting of the ideal portrait.[19]

---- 40
"Die Vorstellung von ihrer ursprünglichen wunderbaren Schönheit
geht übrigens durch den ganzen Mythos von der Gorgo-Medusa hin-
durch. Es ist eine tief traurige Sage von dem herben Neide der
alten Götter gegen alle Herrlichkeit und Schönheit der Sterblichen.
Die Königstochter Medusa, so singen die alten Dichter, wagte sich
an Schönheit der Athene gleichzustellen, die dadurch zum Zorne
gereizt, sie in ein entsetzliches Ungethüm verwandelte. Nach
einer anderen Wendung der Sage, welcher der römische Dichter Ovid
folgt, war ihr Schicksal noch traurig unverdienter. Poseidon,
der wilde Gott, überwältigte die vielumworbene schöne Königstochter
in Tempel der jungfraülichen Athene, die, wie der Dichter singt,
das keusche Antlitz mit der Aegis bedeckte, um nicht den Frevel
zu schauen. Ihr Strafgericht traf die Unschuldige, da ihre Macht
gegen den Schuldigen nicht ausreichte!"[1]

41
Instances of Heroism. In the wreck of the Rothray Castle, two
men had hold of one plank at the same moment. Each wished to let
it go & save the other: one because his companion in danger was
old, the other because he was young. Both let it go at the same
moment. They had previously been strangers to each other. Both
were afterwards picked up & saved, & met again. (Told in Harriet
Martineau's History of the Thirty Years' Peace.)[1]

41a
How to find the whereabout of the Olympiads. Multiply the particular Olympiad by four, & then subtract the product from 777.
Thus, if it be the 70th Olympiad--70 x 4 yields 280; subtract 280
from 777, the remainder will be 497; & that expresses the Olympic
or Grecian period in the Christian equivalent of years B.C.[1]

41b
"Here Greece shall stay; or, if all Greece retire,
Myself will stay, till Troy or I expire;
Myself & Sthenelus will fight for fame;
God bade us fight, & 'twas with God we came"
                    Pope's Iliad, B. IX, 65.[1]

Νῶϊ δ', ἐγὼ Σθένελός τε, μαχησόμεθ' εἰς ὅ κε τέκμωρ
'Ιλίου εὕρωμεν· σὺν γὰρ θεῷ εἰλήλουθμεν.[2]

42
The Superstitions of Great Men
Materials for art. on Incompatible Opinions &c. Tycho Brahe &
Keppler.[1] Keppler's prophecy for the year 1619: Magnus Monarcha
Mundi Medio Mense Martio Morietur, applied to the weak Emperor
Matthias.[2]

=

43
    "The great matter to write well," said Pope, "is to write
naturally & from one's knowledge."[1]
=
    "Does Lord Bolingbroke understand Hebrew? No. But he under-
stands that sort of learning & what is writ about it."[2]
    "A tree is a nobler object than a prince in his coronation
robes." (This was thought a fine tribute to nature by Pope.)[3]
    "Fra Paolo est Catholique en gros, et Protestant en détail."[4]
                                        Nichol's Anecdotes.[5]

ἐν τῷ φρονεῖν γὰρ μηδὲν ἥδιστος βίος,
τὸ μὴ φρονεῖν γὰρ κάρτ' ἀνώδυνον κακόν.
                                Αἴας.[6]
                    ἀνδρί τοι χρεὼν
μνήμην προσεῖναι, τερπνὸν εἴ τί που πάθοι.
χάρις χάριν γάρ ἐστιν ἡ τίκτουσ' ἀεί·
ὅτου δ' ἀπορρεῖ μνῆστις εὖ πεπονθότος,
οὐκ ἂν γένοιτ' ἔθ' οὗτος εὐγενὴς ἀνήρ.
                                ib.[7]

τὰ δ' ἔργα τοὺς λόγους εὑρίσκεται.
                        Electra, 625[8]

                    ἐπεὶ τά γ' ἔργα μου
πεπονθότ' ἐστὶ μᾶλλον ἢ δεδρακότα
                        Œdip. Col. 266[9]

μένει τὸ θεῖον δουλίᾳ περ ἐν φρενί.
                        Agam. 1014[10]

                    τὸ μέλλον δ'
ὅπα γένοιτ' ἄν, κλύειν προχαιρέτω·
ἴσον δὲ τῷ προστένειν.
τορὸν γὰρ ἥξει ξύναρθρον ἄταις.
                        Agam. 232

[Far be it from me to know the future.
That were all as one with groaning over it
Before hand; for assuredly it will come linked with evil][11]

ἰὼ βρότεια πράγματ'· εὐτυχοῦντα μὲν
σκιά τις ἂν τρέψειεν· εἰ δὲ δυστυχῆ,
βολαῖς ὑγρώσσων σπόγγος ὤλεσεν γραφήν.
καὶ ταῦτ' ἐκείνων μᾶλλον οἰκτείρω πολύ.
                                        Agam. 1260[12]

θηλυκρατὴς ἀπέρωτος ἔρως

                        Cheoph. 576[13]

                συμπονήσατε
τῷ νῦν μογοῦντι. ταὐτά τοι πλανωμένη
πρὸς ἄλλοτ' ἄλλον πημονὴ προσιξάνει.
                                        Prom. 276[14]

Wholesome Fear, a guard of virtue
                        Eumen. 482[15]

αἰσχροῖς γὰρ αἰσχρὰ πράγματ' ἐκδιδάσκεται.
                        621 {Electra}[16]

                        43
Article on Opposition to New Ideas.
Pictorial History of England & Beckmann's History of Inventions.
    Gas Lights. State coaches (Macaulay) Post Office
Opposition Railway Surveyors. (Life of Geo. Stephenson)[17]
                        =
    In the Museum of the Royal Society at Crane Court, was a
relic said to be "Pontius Pilate's wife's grandmother's hat."[18]
                        =
    "Ich war so perfekt und vollkommen in der Unwissenheit, dass
mir unmöglich war zu wissen, dass ich sogar nichts wusste."
                        Simplicissimus. (1683)[19]
                        =
    "Je suis naturellement paresseux d'aller à la quête d'auteurs
qui disent pour moi ce que je sais bien dire sans eux."
                        Cervantes.[20]
                        =
Specimen of a critic. "The Fable is always accounted the soul of
Tragedy. And it is the Fable which is properly the poet's part.
Because the other three parts of Tragedy, to wit, the Characters,
are taken from the Moral Philosopher; the thoughts or sense from
them that teach Rhetorik; & the last part, which is the expression,
we learn from the Grammarians"
                        Rymer, Short View of Tragedy p. 86.[21]

"A noble parcel of cattle to be kept upon a wild spot, which once
maintained scare anything; & was not distinguished from the unvarying dark hue of the whole country." Arthur Young.[22]
                        =
"I lay aside the presumptuous attitude of a teacher," says Shelley
in his Dedication of "The Cenci," "& am content to paint, with such
colours as my own heart furnishes, that which has been."[23]

=
                              "When all
Is reft at once, when some surpassing spirit,
. . . . leaves
Those who remain behind nor sobs nor groans,
But pale despair, & cold tranquillity,
Nature's vast frame, the web of human things
Birth & the grave, that are not as they were."
                              Alastor.[24]

=

"We have survived a joy that fears no sorrow,
And I do feel a mighty calmness creep
Over my heart, which can no longer borrow
Its hues from chance or change, dark
Children of tomorrow."
                         Revolt of Islam.[25]

=

"And now O Lord, I take not this my sister for lust, but uprightly:
therefore mercifully ordain that we may become aged together."
                              Prayer of Tobias.[26]

44
Le Roi des Aulnes
(Translation of Goethe's Erlkönig)

Qui passe donc si tard à travers la vallée?
C'est un vieux châtelain qui, sur un coursier noir,
Un enfant dans ses bras, suit la route isolée.
Il se plaint de la nuit qui voile son manoir;
Et l'enfant (ah! pourquoi troubler ces coeurs novices?)
Se rappelle en tremblant ces récits fabuleux
Qu'aux lueurs de la lampe, au vague effroi propices
Le soir, près des foyers, racontent les nourrices.

Il croit voir. . . . . il a vu, sous les bois nébuleux,
Un de ces vains esprits, de ces antiques gnômes,
Qui, railleurs et cruels, doux et flatteurs fantômes,
Se plaisent à troubler le songe des pasteurs:
Soit qu'ils poussent leur rire à de courts intervalles,
S'attachent aux longs crins des errantes cavalles,
Ou prêtent à la nuit des rayons imposteurs.

Voilant de tous ses pas les rians artifices
Le monstre, au bord des précipices,
Marche, sans les courber, sur la cime des fleurs,
Et de sa robe aux sept couleurs
   Il a deployé les caprices,
A l'enfant qu'il attire il ouvre un frais chemin,
Fait briller sa couronne et sourit; dans sa main
Flotte le blanc troëne et les nénuphars jaunes.
"Mon père, dit l'enfant, vois-tu le roi des Aulnes?"

     "Now follows" says Börne, "the peculiarly dramatic part of
the poem, in which Goethe's bullion is duly beaten out & minted
into small coin." At last the child lies in the agonies of death
& says:
     "Mon père: il m'a saisi, je souffre . . . ah sauve-moi!"
And now the climax of absurdity. The remainder is as follows:
     "Le châtelain frissonne: et l'enfant, plein d'effroi,
Se serre sur son coeur et reste[1] immobile.

"Mais le vieux châtelain, pressant son coursier noir,
(Et l'enfant dans ses bras), regagne son manoir.
Voilà les hautes tours et la porte propice.
Le pont mouvant s'abaisse; il entre; et la nourrice
Apporte sur le seuil un vacillant flambeau.
Le père avec tendresse écarte son manteau.
"Soyez donc plus discrète, il m'a durant la route,
Isaure, entretenu des esprits qu'il redoute;
Il criait dans mes bras, mais maintenant il dort;
Reprenez votre enfant--Oh! dit elle, il est mort!"
. . . . . At the end of the poem stands this
note: "Ce beau poème élégiaque très peu
connu, est de M. H. Delatouche, un des
hommes les plus spirituels, et un des poètes
les plus distingués de notre temps."

Börne.[2]

45

"Although, as already stated, no vital actions can go on
without a reaction between the <u>solids</u> & <u>fluids</u> of the body, yet
there may be an entire loss of the latter, in certain cases without necessarily destroying life; the structure being reduced to a
state of dormant vitality in which it may remain unchanged for an
unlimited period & yet being capable of renewing all its actions
when moisture is again supplied. . . . Thus the Mosses & Liver-
worts, which inhabit situations where they are liable to occasional drought, do not suffer from being, to all appearance, completely dried up; but revive and vegetate actively, as soon as
they have been thoroughly moistened. Instances are recorded, in
which Mosses that had been for many years dried up in a Herbarium,
have been restored by moisture to active life. There is a Lyco-
podium inhabiting Peru, which, when dried up for want of moisture,
folds its leaves & contracts into a ball; & in this state, apparently quite devoid of animation, it is blown hither & thither
along the ground by the wind. As soon, however, as it reaches a
moist situation, it sends down its roots into the soil, & unfolds
to the atmosphere its leaves which from a dingy brown, speedily
change to the bright green of active vegetation. The <u>Anastatica</u>
(Rose of Jericho) is the subject of similar transformations;
contracting into a ball, when dried up by the burning sun & parch-
ing air; being detached by the wind from the spot where its slender
roots had fixed it, & rolled over the plains to indefinite distances; & then, when exposed to moisture, unfolding its leaves, &
opening its rose-like flower as if aroused from sleep. And there
is a blue Water-Lily, abounding in several of the canals at
Alexandria, which at certain seasons become so dry, that their
beds are burnt as hard as bricks by the action of the sun, so as
to be fit for use as carriage roads; yet the plants do not thereby
lose their vitality; for when the water is again admitted, they
resume their growth with redoubled vigour."

Carpenter: Comp. Phys. Vol. 1. p. 41.[1]

46

"Les existences faibles, comme était celle de Birotteau, vivent
dans les douleurs, au lieu de les changer en apophthegmes d'experience; elles s'en saturent, et s'usent en rétrogradant chaque jour
dans les malheurs consommés."

Balzac[1]

47

"Wie manches würde in der Theorie unwidersprechlich scheinen, wenn
es dem Genie nicht gelungen wäre, das Widerspiel durch die That zu
erweisen."

                    Lessing, Laokoon. p. 29.[1]

48

   "A poor man who filled the office of a kind of constable, had,
in a village south of Naples, to put in execution an unwelcome
judgment of the law against one of his neighbours. This man was
obliged to submit, but he vowed revenge, not against those who had
condemned him, but against the poor fellow who had only done his
duty, in executing the mandates of the law.
   "Woe to him," he said, "if ever he ventures to leave his
house after set of sun." The constable, who knew such words were
not uttered as a mere empty threat, took warning, & for two years
was never known to pass his threshold after the twenty-fourth
hour. It was a hot summer's night, & overcome with thirst, he
asked his wife to bring him a cup of water, as he feared to venture out himself in search of it. But when she told him that it
only stood on the outer ledge of the window, he arose, opened the
shutter, & put out his head in search of the pitcher. Before he
could reach it, a ball passed through his forehead, & he fell dead
at the feet of his wife."[1]

                    From "Naples" by Lord Bxxxxxxx

   Edle Rache. A man of wealth in Rome adopted a poor boy he
had found in the street. This boy turned out a great villain &
having previously entered the church managed by a series of arts
to possess himself of a legal title to his benefactor's property,
& finally ordered him to quit his own house telling him he was no
longer master. The outraged man killed the villain on the spot.
He was imprisoned, tried & condemned for the murder. When in
prison he refused to have a confessor. He said, "I wish to go to
Hell, for he is there, & I want to follow out my revenge."[2]

49

"The quantity of sorrow he has, does it not mean withal the quantity of sympathy he has, the quantity of faculty & victory he
shall yet have? Our sorrow is the inverted image of our noble-
ness."
                    Carlyle's Cromwell[1]

50

   "A letter written to Mr. Wesley by one of his female disciples,[1] who was employed in the Orphan House at Newcastle." "I
know not," she says, "how to agree to the not working. I am still
unwilling to take anything from any body. I work out of choice,
having never yet learned how a woman can be idle & innocent. I
have had as blessed times in my soul sitting at work as I ever had
in my life; especially in the nighttime, when I see nothing but
the light of a candle & a white cloth, hear nothing but the sound
of my own breath, with God in my sight & heaven in my soul, I
think myself one of the happiest creatures below the skies. I do
not complain that God has not made me some fine thing, to be set
up & gazed at; but I can heartily bless him that he has made me
just what I am, a creature capable of the enjoyment of himself.
If I go to the window & look out, I see the moon & stars: I medi-
tate awhile on the silence of the night, consider the world as a

beautiful structure, & the work of an almighty hand; then I sit
down to work again, and think myself one of the happiest beings
in it."

Southey's Life of Wesley[2]

51

Wesley & the Methodists. <u>Assurance</u> <u>conveyed</u> <u>by</u> <u>Visions</u>. "I
am one of many witnesses of this matter of fact," says Wesley in a
letter to his brother Samuel, "that God does now make good his
promise daily, very frequently during a representation (how made
I know not, but <u>not</u> <u>to</u> <u>the</u> <u>outward</u> <u>eye</u>) of Christ, either hanging
on the cross or standing on the right hand of God. And this I
know to be of God, because from that hour the person so affected
is a new creature, both as to his inward tempers & outward life."[1]

<u>Drawing</u> <u>of</u> <u>Lots</u>, & <u>divination</u> <u>of</u> <u>God's</u> <u>will</u> <u>by</u> <u>opening</u> <u>the</u> <u>Bible</u>
<u>at</u> <u>hazard</u> & <u>reading</u> <u>the</u> <u>first</u> <u>text</u> <u>the</u> <u>eye</u> <u>fell</u> <u>on</u>--both practiced
by Wesley.[2]

<u>Belief</u> <u>in</u> <u>present</u> <u>miracles</u>. Wesley "related cures wrought by his
faith & his prayers, which he considered & represented as posi-
tively miraculous. By thinking strongly on a text of Scripture
which promised that these signs should follow those that believe,
& by calling on Christ to increase his faith, & confirm the word
of his grace, he shook off instantaneously, he says, a fever which
had hung on him for some days, & was in a moment freed from all
pain, & restored to his former strength. He visited a believer
at night, who was not expected to live till the morning: this man
was speechless & senseless & his pulse gone. "A few of us," says
Wesley, "immediately joined in prayers. I relate the naked fact.
Before we had done, his senses & his speech returned. Now, he
that will account for this by natural causes has my free leave.
But I choose to say, this is the power of God." So too, when his
own teeth ached, he prayed & the pain left him. And this faith
was so strong, that it sufficed sometimes to cure not only himself
but his horse also. "My horse," he says, /52/ "was so exceedingly lame, that I was afraid I must have lain by. We could
not discern what was amiss, & yet he could scarce set his foot to
the ground. By riding thus seven miles I was thoroughly tired, &
my head ached more than it had done for some months. What I here
aver is the naked fact: let every man account for it as he sees
good. I then thought, 'Cannot God heal either man or beast, by
any means, or without any?' Immediately my weariness & headache
ceased, & my horse's lameness in the same instant. Nor did he
halt any more, either that day or the next."

Southey I. p. 385.[1]

<u>The</u> <u>Wesleys</u> <u>in</u> <u>the</u> <u>Prison</u> & <u>Madhouse</u>. "During John Wesley's ab-
sence in Germany, Charles had prayed with some condemned criminals
in Newgate, & accompanied them with two other clergymen to Tyburn.
[The ordinary, on these occasions, made but a sorry figure. "He
<u>would</u> read prayers," Charles Wesley says, "& he preached most
miserably." When this poor man, who seems willing enough to have
done his duty, if he had known how, would have got upon the cart
with the prisoners at the place of execution, they begged that he
would not, & the mob kept him down. What kind of machine a Newgate ordinary was in those days, may be seen in Fielding; the one
who edifies Jonathan Wild with a sermon before the punch comes
in,[2] seems to have been drawn from the life].[3] In consequence of
this, another party of poor creatures in the same dreadful

situation, implored the same assistance, & the two brothers wrought
them into a state of mind not less happy than that of Socrates when
he drank the hemlock.[4] "It was the most   /53/   glorious instance
I ever saw," says Wesley, "of faith triumphing over sin & death."
One of the sufferers was asked how he felt a few minutes only before the point of death, & he calmly answered, "I feel a peace
which I could not have believed to be possible; & I know it is the
peace of God which passeth all understanding." . . . . Even frenzy
was rebuked before him: in one of the workhouses which he visited,
was a young woman raving mad, screaming & tormenting herself continually. His countenance & manner & voice, always impressive, &
doubly so to one who had been little accustomed to looks of kindness & words of consolation, acted upon her as oil upon waves:
the moment that he began she was still & while he encouraged her
to seek relief in prayer, saying, "Jesus of Nazareth is able &
willing to deliver you," the tears ran down her cheeks. "Oh,
where is faith upon earth?" he exclaims, when he relates this
anecdote; why are these poor wretches left in the open bondage of
Satan? Jesus Master! give thou medicine to heal their sickness;
& deliver those who are now also vexed with unclean spirits."
Wesley always maintained that madness was frequently occasioned by
demoniacal possession, & in this opinion he found many to encourage
him." Ibid. I. 185.[1]

Paroxysms under Wesley's preaching. "The paroxysms of the disease
which Methodism excited, had not appeared at Bristol under White-
field's preaching; they became frequent after Wesley's arrival
there. One day, after Wesley had expounded the fourth chapter of
Acts, the persons present "called upon God to confirm his word."
"Immediately," he adds, "one that stood by, to our no small surprize, cried out   /54/   aloud, with the utmost vehemence, even
as in the agonies of death; but we continued in prayer till a new
song was put in her mouth, a thanksgiving unto our God. Soon
after two other persons in this place, well known as labouring to
live in all good conscience toward all men, were seized with strong
pain, and constrained to 'roar for the disquietude of their heart.'
But it was not long before they likewise burst forth into praise
to God their Saviour. . . . So many living witnesses hath God
given, that his hand is still stretched out to heal, & that signs
& wonders are even now wrought by his holy child Jesus." At another place, "a young man was suddenly seized with a violent trembling all over, & in a few minutes the sorrows of his heart being
enlarged, sunk down to the ground; but we ceased not calling upon
God, till he raised him up full of peace & joy in the Holy Ghost."
. . . . When these things were published, they justly gave great
offence; but they were ascribed to a wrong cause. A physician who
suspected fraud, was led by curiosity to be a spectator of these
extraordinary exhibitions, & a person whom he had known many years,
was thrown into a fit while he was present. She cried aloud &
wept violently. He who could hardly believe the evidence of his
senses, "went & stood close to her, & observed every symptom, till
great drops of sweat ran down her face, & all her bones shook."[1]

Wesley's preaching in the open air. "Sometimes when he had
finished the discourse, & pronounced the blessing, not a person
offered to move:--the charm was upon them still; and every man,
woman & child remained where they were, till he set the example
of leaving   /55/   the ground." . . . . The situation in which
he preached sometimes contributed to the impression. . . .

Sometimes, in a hot and cloudless summer day, he & his congregation
were under cover of the sycamores, which afford so deep a shade
to some of the old farm-houses in Westmoreland & Cumberland. In
such a scene, near Brough, he mentions that a bird perched in one
of the trees, & sung without intermission from the beginning of
the service till the end. . . . Sometimes, when his discourse was
not concluded till twilight, he saw that the calmness of the evening agreed with the seriousness of the people, & that "they seemed
to drink in the word of God, as a thirsty land the refreshing
showers." One of his preaching places in Cornwall was in what had
been the courtyard of a rich & honourable man; but he and all his
family were in the dust & his memory had almost perished. "At
Gwenap in the same county," he says, "I stood on the wall in the
calm still evening, with the setting sun behind me, & almost an
innumerable multitude before, behind & on either hand.[1] Many
likewise sat on the little hills, at some distance from the bulk
of the congregation. But they could all hear distinctly while I
read, 'The disciple is not above his Master,' & the rest of those
comfortable words which are every day fulfilled in our ears."
This amphitheatre was one of his favourite stations;[2] he says of
it in his old age, "I think this is one of the most magnificent
spectacles which is to be seen on this side heaven. And no music
is to be heard upon earth comparable to the sound of many thousand
voices, when they are all harmoniously joined /56/ together,
singing praises to God & the Lamb." At St. Ives, when a high
wind prevented him standing where he had intended, he found a
little enclosure near, one end of which was native rock, rising
ten or twelve feet perpendicular, from which the ground fell with
an easy descent. "A jetting out of the rock, about four feet
from the ground, gave me a very convenient pulpit. Here well
nigh the whole town, high & low, rich & poor, assembled together.
Nor was there a word to be heard nor a smile seen, from one end
of the congregation to the other. It was just the same the three
following evenings. Indeed I was afraid on Saturday, that the
roaring of the sea, raised by the north wind, would have prevented
their hearing. But God gave me so clear & strong a voice, that I
believe scarce one word was lost." "On the next day, the storm
had ceased, & the clear sky, the setting sun & the smooth still
ocean, all agreed with the state of the audience. There is a
beautiful garden at Exeter, under the ruins of the castle & of
the old city wall, in what was formerly the moat; . . . .
before the ground was thus happily appropriated, Wesley preached
there to a large assembly. . . . He says it was an awful sight!
So vast a congregation in that solemn amphitheatre & all silent
& still while I explained at large, & enforced that glorious
truth, 'Happy are they whose iniquities are forgiven, & whose sins
are covered.'"[1] In another place he says, "I rode to Blanchland,
about twenty miles from Newcastle. The rough mountains round
about were still white with snow. In the midst of them is a
small winding valley, through which the Darwent runs. On /57/
the edge of this, the little town stands which is indeed little
more than a heap of ruins. There seems to have been a large
cathedral church, by the vast walls which still remain. I stood
in the churchyard, under one side of the building, upon a large
tombstone, round which, while I was at prayers, all the congregation kneeled down on the grass. They were gathered out of the
lead mines, from all parts; many from Allandale, six miles off.
A row of children sat under the opposite wall, all quiet & still.
The whole congregation drank in every word, with such earnestness

in their looks, that I could not but hope that God will make this
wilderness sing for joy." At Gawksham, he preached "on the side
of an enormous mountain. The congregation, he says, stood & sate,
row above row, in the sylvan theatre. I believe nothing in the
postdiluvian earth can be more pleasant than the road from hence,
between huge steep mountains, clothed with wood to the top, &
watered at the bottom by a clear winding stream." . . . . . . In
the seventieth year of his age, he preached at Gwenap, to the
largest assembly that had ever collected to hear him; from the
ground which they covered he computed them to be not fewer than
thirty two thousand; & it was found, upon inquiry, that all could
hear even to the skirts of the congregation." (Ibid. I, 415)[1]

The class Wesley liked least were the farmers. The agricultural
part of the people were least susceptible of Methodism, for Methodism could be kept alive only by associations & frequent meetings;
& it is difficult, or impossible, to arrange these among a scattered /58/ population. Where converts were made, & the discipline could not be introduced among them, & the effect kept up
by constant preaching & inspection, they soon fell off."[1]

   Calumnies about Wesley. 'He had hanged himself & been cut
down just in time;--he had been fined for selling gin;--he was
not the real John Wesley, for everybody knew that Mr. Wesley was
dead. Some said he was a Quaker, others an Anabaptist; a more
sapient censor pronounced him a presbyterian papist. It was
commonly reported that he was a papist, if not a Jesuit; that he
kept Popish priests in his house;--nay it was beyond dispute that
he received large remittances from Spain, in order to make a party
among the poor, & when the Spaniards landed he was to join them
with 20,000 men. Sometimes it was reported that he was in prison
upon a charge of high treason: & there were people who confidently
affirmed that they had seen him with the Pretender in France.
Ibid. I. 386.
   After the mobs had been raised by the clergy at Wednesbury &
Walsal, for the purpose of maltreating the Methodists & their
property--after Wesley himself had been in danger of his life
from the rabble, & the magistrates had refused to interfere on his
behalf--these same magistrates issued a warrant commanding diligent search to be made after certain "disorderly persons styling
themselves Methodist preachers, who were going about raising
riots, to the great damage of his majesty's liege subjects, &
against the peace of our sovereign lord the King." This was in
1743. Ibid. I, 393-4.

                              59
Wesley believed in the immortality of animals.[1] In the agency of
evil spirits in tempting men to sin, in inflicting diseases &c.[2]
   Southey says in a note to vol. 2. "In methodistical &
mystical biography, the reader will sometimes be reminded of these
lines in Ovid:--
      In prece totus eram, caelestia numina sensi,
        Laetaque purpurea luce refulsit humus.
      Non equidem vidi (valeant mendacia vatum!)
        Te, Dea; nec fueras adspicienda viro.
      Sed quae nescieram, quorumque errore tenebar,
        Cognita sunt, nullo praecipiente, mihi."[3]

   "It will hardly be denied that even in this frail & corrupted
world, we sometimes meet persons who in their very mien & aspect,

as well as in the whole habit of life, manifest such a signature
& stamp of virtue as to make our judgment of them a matter of intuition, rather than the result of continued examination."
                    Alexander Knox, on the Character of Wesley.[4]

"Quid minuat curas, quid te tibi reddat amicum,
Quid pure tranquillet?"[5]

                              60
Costume at the end of the 18th Century.
        A gentleman in the true Parisian taste in 1793. The high
sugar-loaf hat; flowing hair[1] powdered[2] (for powder was not dis-
carded finally till some years afterwards, although the queen &
princesses abandoned it in this year) a loose cravat of white cam-
bric tied in a large bow, a frilled shirt, a white waistcoat with
red perpendicular stripes, a long green coat, with a high collar
& small cuffs, buttoned lightly over the breast, from whence it
slopes away to the hips, having very wide & long skirts--in fact
very like the "Newmarket cut" of the present day. His breeches
are tight, & reach the ankle, from whence they are buttoned at
the sides up to the middle of the thigh; he wears low top-boots.[3]
--A companion figure has a hat with a lower crown, his hair is
powdered, flows loosely, & is tied in a club behind, pigtails
having gone out of fashion with all but elderly gentlemen; his
coat is "cut away" like his companion's; he wears very small ruf-
fles at his wrist, which barely peep from the cuff; he has knee-
breeches of buckskin which were now "immense taste"; & his shoes
are tied with strings, buckles having become unfashionable.[4]
Straw bonnets worn in 1798, precisely of the shape & form still
common.[5] Printed Cotton & Calicoes superseded silks as elegant
dresses in 1796.[6]
        Scarlet leather shoes, short waists, open gowns without
hoops,[7] immense earrings & feathers showing half a yard high,
1794-1797.[8] Long black scarfs, gauze or silk.[9] Waists became
longer in 1798.[10]

                              61
Flat hat of country girl, 1773[1]

        George Lowe, one of the itinerant Methodist preachers, thus
describes his dress when he preached his first sermon in 1777:
"My dress on that occasion was not very clerical; but although it
would have offended the fastidious taste of modern times, it was
considered fashionable, & even elegant, in those days . . . . I put
on my fustian coat, a pretty red plush waistcoat, & a handsome
pair of leather breeches."[2]
Fashionable Bonnet in 1799.[3]

        "In those days (i.e. about 1760) girls of the best families
wore white stockings only on the Sundays,[4] & one week-day which
was a sort of public day:--on the other days, they wore blue Doncaster woolen stockings with white tags." (Lord Eldon)[5]
        "At a festival at Belvoir Castle in honour of the Duke of
Rutland's majority, the Prince of Wales wore at dinner a "scarlet
frock coat, black stockings, breeches & waistcoat": in the

evening at the ball "a suit of brown."[6]   The Duchess of Rutland
was attired till the ball commenced in a scarlet riding-habit.
This was in the beginning of January, 1799.[7]   (Gents. Mag. 1799)[8]

Women's preaching: decree of Conference against it, 1803.[9]

"All drink tea," says Arthur Young of the working people in
a northerly parish, 1770.[10]

62

Festivities in 1799 at Belvoir Castle, on the Duke of Rutland's
majority.[1]--Country dances, reels & hornpipes. Fire-works & il-
luminations. Transparencies--two by "that excellent artist the
Rev. W. Peters, rector of Knipton. One, Britannia trampling upon
Faction, & with her spear piercing the monster through his head.
Motto: "While Pitt[2] directs Britannia's spear, Her foes thus
prostrate shall appear." In the background, upon a pedestal,
were seen the names of Howe, St. Vincent, Duncan, Nelson of the
Nile, & Warren.[3] On the other a medallion of the Duke of Rutland.
Motto: "Hail generous youth!" at the bottom Hibernia receiving
the Leicestershire Militia, & presenting them with a wreath of
laurel. Motto: "Foremost in Hibernia's Cause." At Grantham,
eight miles distant . . . "the theatre was opened by the itinerant players belonging to Robinson's Company, for the benefit of
Messrs. Waldron and Hervetschell, with "The agreeable Surprize,"
& "All the world's a stage." The Sieur Rees, of Bartholomew Fair
notoriety, was the only puppet-show man in the marketplace.
   The worthy Rector of South Croxton[4] honoured the day by giving an entertainment to his neighbours & select friends. The
bells rang day & night: the parsonage was illuminated; & the Rev.
Philip Hackett's 'little grace cup,' which holds a gallon Winchester, was discharged upwards of 30 times, amid fireworks,
platoons firing, & other demonstrations of joy." (Gents. Mag.)[5]

"Chi vo' morir, e padron della vita del re."
                                   Italian Proverb.[6]

63

Notes of facts in 1799. Pizarro being played at the theatres.
Found fault with for its tendency to exalt Natural Religion to the
disadvantage of Xtianity. Kemble as Pizarro.[1]
   Rumour of Dr. Priestley's intention to return from America.[2]
Their Majesties at Weymouth in August. "Bold Stroke for a Wife",
"The Rivals", "Ways and Means", "The Busy Body" played before
them. Amused with country dances till 5 in the afternoon. Pur-
chasing toys for the Princess Charlotte.[3]
   Habeas Corpus Act suspended again, March 1799.[4] Jenner's
book on Vaccination review in Gent's. Mag.[5]
   Arkwright's spinning mill at Cromford built 1771. Arkwright
died 1792.[6]
   Strutt's Cotton works at Belper founded about 1776.[7]
Remarkable Persons, living in 1799.[8]
   Wordsworth, 1st. vol. of poems 1793[9]   ⎫
   Southey, made Laureate 1813[10]   ⎪ All born
   Coleridge, d. 1834[11]   ⎬ from 1770 to
   Scott, Lay of the Last Minstrel, 1805[12]   ⎪   1775
   Lamb, d. 1834[13]   ⎪
   Granville Sharp, d. 1813[14] Wilberforce[15]⎭

Horne Tooke, d. 1812[16]
Paley, d. 1805[17] Washington, died 1799, Dec. 14[18]
Duke of Bridgewater, d. 1803. His canal then in use 40
years.[19]
William Cobbett, b. 1766. Relates the early incidents of his
life in "Peter Porcupine," pub. 1796. Apparently commenced his
Weekly Register in 1800.[20]
Count Rumford in England about the end of the century.[21]
Edinburgh Review started 1802.[22]
Tom Moore b. 1780;[23]   Rogers, 1760.[24]
Elizabeth Fry b. 1780.[25]
Sir Joshua Reynolds d. 1792.[26]   "Evelina" pub. 1778.[27]

64

Notes of facts from Gents. Mag. 1800-1802.
Geo. Stephenson's wages as brakesman £1. per week.[1] A
Society existed in 1800 which offered premiums for the encourage-
ment of "Arts, Manufactures, & Commerce." Offices in the Adelphi.
It had already given away £40,000 in prizes for Inventions, Discoveries & Improvements.[2]
"Be not righteous overmuch" is the advice of a writer more
experienced in the ways of true godliness than half the ministers
of (what they call by a fashionable name) Evangelical religion."
[Gent. Mag. April, 1802.][3]
"The fashionable propensity of lake-visiting."[4] Letters
satirizing the crowding at fêtes & routs & balls, hops, masquer-
ades, pic-nics, & public breakfasts.[5]
Buxton Crescent, in 1802, "a building in this remote part of
the country that rivals the beauty of Palmyra."[6]
Encouragement of small farms advocated, as it gives the
labourer hope of becoming a farmer.[7]
Castleton in Derbyshire, centre of the mining district.
Since the Roman invasion Derbyshire has supplied the greater part
of Europe with the produce of its lead mines.[8]
Bull-baiting preached against, 1802.[9] Miss Linwood's Exhibition. Pictures added.[10] M. Garnerin, the celebrated aeronaut,
ascends from Ranelagh. "The appearance of the balloon excited
the utmost astonishment among the country people." July, 1802.
27th voyage in Europe.[11] 1800 Bill for the better observance of
Good Friday, by Dr. Porteous.[12]

65

<u>Seasons</u> in 1799. <u>July</u>. Observations made at Walton, near
Liverpool. 1. Provence rose flowers; 3. Foxglove flowers: 9.
Elder flowers: 10. gathered ripe cherries: 12. wild honey suckle
flowers: 13. Began hay-harvest, not yet general. N.B. A gentleman that was returned from Scotland observed that they were
making hay at Glasgow the first day of the month. 24. Severe
lightning in the evening. 25. Loud thunder with a heavy shower of
rain, previous to which the throstle poured fourth his song with
a degree of violence.[1]
August seems to have been a rainy month. 29. Reaping oats--
still near the sea, Liverpool.[2]
September, also rainy: "black clouds & sun." 3. Thistledown
flies. 5. Very heavy dews. 12. Housing an excellent crop of
barley. 23. Swallows congregate. The green gage & Orleans plums
much injured by the frequent rains.[3] . . . Heavy rains recorded:
an inundation in Leicestershire, September 8. "These uncommonly
heavy rains are the more alarming as the greatest part of the

wheat & barley are standing in the fields; & in this neighbourhood,
much now is not inned, some is not cut. The beans are nearly all
mown, but none carried: circumstances which the oldest person cannot remember."[4]
    Oct. 2. Lauristinus flowers. Lightning in the evening. 11.
Autumn tints conspicuous . . . leaves begin to fall. Swallows departed; 14. Thunder and lightning in the evening. 16. Gossamer
floats. 23. Gathered the winter apples: Woodcocks in the market:
26. Abundance of cobwebs. But little wheat sown. Summer fallows
drenched with wet.[5]

66

Clergy & Church affairs from 1799-1802.
    Bill to be proposed by Lord Grenville for improving the condi-
tion of the inferior clergy.[1]
    Plan ot a writer in Gent. Mag. 1802. 1. "No curates on liv-
ings amounting to £100 per ann. to have less than £50. 2. That
the curate's appointment be for life. 3. That in very small livings where not more than £20 or £30 can be given to the curate,
& also in livings under £300 per ann. a per centage should be
contributed by the Lay Impropriators, so that no clergyman should
have an income less than £150."[2]
    "Dialogues between a Churchman & a Methodist,"[3] "Rowland
Hill's Village Dialogues",[4] & "A Dialogue between a country gentleman & one of his poor neighbours who had been led away from the
church under the pretext of hearing the gospel & attending Evangelical Preachers"--all reviewed in Gent. Mag. 1802.[5] Also
"Apology for Sunday Schools" by Rowland Hill.[6]
    "The Happy Village", a poem, the scene of which is Blanchland
in Northumberland: --
        "On yonder sunny wall the pastor leans,
        "And from surrounding politicians gleans
        "News of the last & this eventful year,
         "Enough to strike the most indifferent ear."[7]
Song for a Curate, beginning: --
        "A Curate I am, & a Curate I'll be. . . .
        "All things to all men like St. Paul to become,
        "Is the only sure way to be happy
    "I have learnt throughout life to be ever at home;
    "On some days I drink port with the squire & on some
        "With the Farmer a cup of brown nappy."[8]

67

"Methodists purchasing livings." "We have heard of a clergyman
of the Church of England saying, that whoever understands a text
of Scripture is bound to explain it; & this by natural inference,
gives authority to set out preaching by an instantaneous call."[1]
    Hutton in a "Summer Tour" in 1802 speaks of his stay at
Matlock Baths. "The clery," he says, "are sometimes charged with
an unsocial behaviour, keep at a distance, preserve the rust of
the college &c. During a fortnight's stay at Matlock, we were
favoured with the company of six sons of the Church, who reversed
this charge for they were open & friendly. In one might be observed the supreme of modesty; in another, good judgment with now
& then an oath; in a third, a jolly soul contented with his glass
& his poverty; a fourth united riches, civility, & dignity; another never uttered a sentence of his own, but followed his
leader, yet possessed one of the best hearts that ever filled a
human breast; a sixth, a buck of the first magnitude, whether in
person, song, glass or joke, but all good natured."[2]

Non-residence. "Five livings, each having a good parsonage
with glebe, all contiguous to one another, & all conjointly worth
£1960, with but one resident clergyman, a curate among them for
many years. All these have been actually sold or offered for sale,
within that period; & most of them having had but single duty.
One of the above-mentioned livings, worth about £300 per ann. was
for many years under the care of a curate who kept a school, &
lived at a distance of 10 or 12 miles from the parish. (1801)[3]

68

Residence of the Clergy.
A Mr. Taylor said in the House of Commons that "the residence of
the clergy was necessary to the civilization of the people, &
particularly to keep off the tribe of canting Methodists, whose
growth was principally owing to the non-residence of the clergy."
Gent. Mag. 1801[1]

June 9, 1801. House resolved itself into committee to consider non-residence of clergy & taking of farms.[2]
A correspondent of Gent. Mag. thinks that insisting on the
residence of the clergy would do harm, because gentlemen by birth
as well as by profession who "assist towards supporting the
respectability of the cloth by the gentility & liberality of
their manners & ideas" would not take orders if "constrained to
the drudgery of parochial duty."[3]
"Many curates who now take charge of from five to ten parishes,
are actually beneficed clergymen, who reside in market towns for
the sake of company & amusements, sometimes not less than a dozen
miles from their benefices; & then they take as many curacies as
they can procure because it is 'all within a ride.'"[4]
Price of the quartern loaf in 1799, 13d; whereas in 1798 it
was 8d. Weight of penny loaf in 1799, 5 oz. 5 dr. In 1798, 8 oz.
11 dr.[5]
Morning Post founded 1782.
Morning Herald founded, 1780.[6]
1800. Royal Institution's first sitting, March.[7]
"   Russell Square & Travistock Square being built[8]
"   Bread riots at Birmingham & in London, in September &
         December[9]
"   Bill to prevent bull-baiting rejected, 3d April[10]

69

Clouds.[1] The forms of clouds in summer are very distinctly
marked. When a deposition of vapour is taking place in the highest part of the atmosphere, the Cirrus appears; & when it soon
disappears it is a sign of fine weather; but instead of disappear-
ing, it may descend a little lower, & be converted into the cirro-
cumulus,--an elegant light flocculent cloud so often seen in a
fine summer day. A farther deposition changes this small cloud
into the larger Cumulus, called the day-cloud in summer, because
it disappears in another form in the evening. It frequently takes
up its position near the horizon for the greater part of the day,
resting on the vapour plane. When a large Cumulus rises from the
horizon in the day-time with white towering heads, it is a sign
of a storm or fall of rain from that quarter; & the wind will
change to that direction in the course of the next twenty four
hours.[2] This threatening cloud is called Cumulo-Stratus. In
calm serene evenings in summer, the day-cloud descends & subsides
in the bottom of valleys, or spreads itself in hollows of the
open country, covering the ground like a lake or a sheet of snow,

as seen in moonlight, when it becomes the true <u>stratus</u> cloud.[3]
Tall objects, such as trees, steeples & even elevated ground, jut
through this cloud like rocks & islands in a lake. The air is
then perfectly calm, the temperature delightfully warm, & the in-
tenseness of the silence is broken only by the snipe drumming in
its curious summer-saults in the air--by the harsh ventriloquous
cry of the corn-craik amongst the   /70/   grass--or by the occasional bark of the watch-dog at some distant homestead. The
morning after such a night is sure to usher in the sun in bright
& peerless splendour, whose steady heat soon evaporates the sheet-
like <u>Stratus</u> from the valleys & hollows, elevating it in the form
of the beautiful compact day-cloud, above the mountain top or
vapour plane."[1]
    The <u>cirro-cumuli</u> are small cumuli high in the air--called in
Germany "<u>little sheep</u>";--
    "Scattered immensely wide from east to west,
    The beauteous semblance of a flock at rest."
<u>Cirri</u> may descend still further after forming Cirro-Cumuli & be-
come <u>cirro-stratus</u>. It consists at times of dense longitudinal
streaks . . . at other times it is like shoals of small fish,
when it is called a "herring sky," at others mottled, when it is
called a mackerel-back sky. Sometimes it is like veins of wood,
sometimes like the ripples of sand left by the retiring tide.[2]
The more mottled the cirro-stratus the higher it is in the air,
& the more dense & stratified the nearer the earth. In the last
position, it may be seen cutting off a mountain top, or stretching behind it, or cutting across the tops of large culumi. . . .
At times Cirro-Strati cut across the field of the setting sun,
where they appear in well-defined, dense striae, whose upper or
lower edges are burnished with gold, crimson, or vermilion.
Sometimes the cirro-stratus extends across the heavens in a broad
sheet, obscuring   /71/   more or less the light of the sun or
moon for days together; & in this case a halo or corona is often
seen, or a parhelion may be expected. . . . The streaked Cirro-
Strati occur frequently in Autumn, the more delicate kinds
mostly in Summer."[1]
    <u>Cumulo-stratus</u> is always a dense cloud. It spreads out its
base to the stratus form, &, in its upper part, frequently inoscu-
lates with cirri, cirro-cumuli, or cirro-strati. With all or
either of these it forms a large massive series of cumulative
clouds which hang on the horizon, displaying great mountain
shapes, raising their brilliantly illuminated silvery crests to
the sun, & presenting numerous dusky valleys between them.[2] Or
it appears in formidable white masses of variously defined
shapes, towering upwards from the horizon, ready to meet any
other form of cloud, & to conjoin with them in making the dense
dark-coloured storm-cloud. The <u>nimbus</u> or rain-cloud is the
<u>Cirro-cumulo-stratus</u>.[3]
    <u>Scud</u>. There is a form of cloud called the <u>scud</u>, not unlike
Cumuli. It is of dark or light colour according as the sun
shines on it, of varied forms floating or scudding before the
wind, & generally in front of a sombre cumulo-stratus stretching
as a background across that portion of the sky, often accompanied
by a bright streak along the horizon. It is usually the har-
binger of the rain-cloud & is therefore called "messengers,"
"carriers," or "water-wagons."[4]

                                72
<u>Signs of a high wind approaching</u>:--When cattle appear frisky &

toss their heads & jump -- when sheep leap & play, boxing each
other -- when pigs squeal, & carry straw in their mouths -- when
the cat scratches a tree or a post -- when geese attempt to fly,
or distend & clap their wings -- when pigeons clap their wings
smartly behind their backs in flying -- when crows mount in the
air & perform somersets, making at the time a garrulous noise --
when swallows fly on one side of trees, because the flies take
the leeward side for safety against the wind -- when magpies collect in small companies & make a chattering noise.

These are general indications of a storm: -- When the
missel-thrush sings long & loud -- when seagulls come in flocks
on land, & make a noise about the coast, -- and when the porpoise
comes near the shore in large numbers."[1]

"Cattle crop the high grass, sheep nibble low, while horses
bite both high & low. Thus the sheep are suited to the short
pasturage of mountainous regions;[2] whereas the ox[3] is better
suited to the plains & valleys where grass grows long."[4]

73

For now the poet cannot die,
     Nor leave his music, as of old,
     But round him ere he scarce is cold
Begins the scandal & the cry:--

"Proclaim the faults he would not show--
     Break lock & seal--betray the trust--
     Keep nothing sacred: 'tis but just
The many-headed beast should know."

Ah! Shameless! for he did but sing
     A song that pleased us from its worth;
     No public life was his on earth,
No blazoned statesman he, nor king.

He gave the people of his best:
     His worst he kept, his best he gave--
     My curse upon the clown & knave
Who will not let his ashes rest.
                    Tennyson.[1]

———

"La grande question dans la vie, c'est la douleur que l'on
cause, et la métaphysique la plus ingénieuse ne justifie pas
l'homme qui a déchiré le coeur qui l'aimait."
                    Benjamin Constant.   "Adolphe."[2]

It does repent me, words are quick & vain.
Grief for a while is blind, & so was mine--
I wish no living thing to suffer pain
                    Shelley, Prometheus Unbound[3]

74

British Forest Trees.[1] The Lime (Tilia Europaea). Not probably
indigenous in Britain, does not often ripen its seed there. Began
to be used for avenues in France in the time of Louis 14, when
people began to be tired of eternal chestnuts. Bears Topiarian
operations with impunity. Sometimes eighty or ninety feet high,
with trunk in proportion. Soil most congenial to it, a rich
clayey loam, or the alluvial deposits in low-lying meadows,
haughs, the margins of rivers &c. Also grows well in a light

gravelly loam, provided this be sufficiently retentive of
moisture. Does not flourish in retentive clays & poor tilly
soils. Propagated in England by layers chiefly.[2]

Common Ash (Fraxinus Excelsior) Virgil calls it
                              "Fraxinus in sylvis pulcherrima";
deservedly--for the beauty & lightness of its foliage,[3] & the
fine, easy, flowing line of its stems & branches. Strutt,[4] in
his "Sylva Brittanica" says, "It is in mountain scenery that the
ash appears to peculiar advantage, waving its slender branches
over some precipice which just affords it soil sufficient for its
footing, or springing between the crevices of rocks." The principal objections to it are the late period of its coming into
leaf, which in the north of England & Scotland, rarely takes
place before the beginning of June;[5] & the rapid fall of the leaf
after the first autumnal frost & this, in general without any
change of colour, or contributing to the waning beauty of the
autumn foliage. . . . . The wood of the ash surpasses all others
in toughness & elasticity of fibre. It forms the principal
material in the making of such instruments & machines as are
liable to sudden strains or shocks, & is therefore used greatly
by the maker of agricultural implements, & the coachmaker, & the
wheelwright &c. Handles of tools, pails & kitchen tables are
made from it.   /75/   From five or six years of its growth it
becomes profitable,[1] being at this age made into walking-sticks
("a good ash-plant" proverbially an excellent instrument of
castigation), for which alone its returns are considerable in
Kent & other districts not far from London, at twelve or fourteen
it will form hop-poles, hoops for casks, crates & light hurdles,
& is extensively cultivated for these purposes in Kent, Straf-
fordshire & Wiltshire: the usual mode is to grow it in holts or
coppices which are either cut over entirely at the end of a certain period, or else divided into portions, which are cut in
succession each year. . . . . . Some lingering superstitions
still attach to this tree . . . among others that of boring a
hole in an ash tree & enclosing within it a living shrew mouse;
the branch of a tree thus prepared is supposed to cure lameness
& cramp in cattle, both of which are laid to the unfortunate
mouse."[2] In glens & denes the ash grows with great luxuriance,
particularly when its roots can reach the stream which usually
flows at their bottom.[3]

Common Elm. (Ulmus Campestris). Finest in the southern & midland parts of England, north of the Trent it becomes of rarer occurrence though it is still found in great luxuriance & perfection at Doncaster, York & other parts of Yorkshire. The elm
comes into leaf in early spring & is among the very last of our
forest trees to yield to the chilling effects of the autumnal
cold & frost. When first expanded the leaves are of a pale,
though cheerful green, but they gradually become dark & glossy.
In autumn they fade to a fine clear yellow, which as Gilpin[4]
observes, "mixes kindly with the orange of the beech & the ochre
of the oak." The flowers which appear before the leaves, are in
tufts upon the shoots of the preceding year, & are of a purplish-
red colour. The Ulmus montana or Wych Elm is must less hardy,
requiring a rich alluvial soil. The wood of the /76/ common
elm is of a deep brown colour, compact & fine-grained; according
to Loudon,[1] it loses nearly two thirds of its weight in drying.
It is eminently fitted for purposes where a strong wood that will

not crack is required-- for "blocks, dead eyes & other wooden
furniture of rigging." Its durability under water, as well as
the straightness & great length of its stem, qualifies it for
making the keels of large ships, for which purpose it sells at a
very high price. It used to be employed for water pipes; & is
now used for the sleepers of railways & for wooden pavement.[2]
The Cork-barked Elm (Ulmus Suberosa) is hardier, but less picturesque & less valuable as timber. The Wych Elm is less common
in the southern than in the northern parts of England, & in
Scotland where it forms a prominent feature in the wooded scenery. There are doubts as to the Common Elm being indigenous to
Britain, but none as to the Wych Elm. The leaves are larger than
those of the Common Elm.[3]

=

"Et je veux que vous sachiez, seigneur errant, que dans ces
petits pays on parle de tout et on mord sur tout; et vous pouvez
bien vous mettre dans la tête, comme je le suis mis, qu'un curé
doit être bon hors de toute mesure, pour obliger ses paroissiens
à dire du bien de lui, surtout dans les villages."
                                        Don Quixote.[4]

-

"I claim an absolute authority in right as the freshest modern,
which gives me a despotic power over all authors before me."
                                        Swift, Tale of a Tub.[5]

77

Inundations.[1] 1771. Nov. 18. A letter from Newcastle, cited in
the Annual Register, states: "On Sat. night & early on Sunday
morning last, the greatest landflood ever remembered in the
memory of man, or any history, came pouring down the river Tyne,
& has done more damage than can be justly estimated; it swelled
over all the lower parts of the town; the Sandhill, which is a
large square, where the Exchange & the Courts of Justice stand,
was several feet under water, & shops . . . contiguous to the
banks of the river, were six feet under water; the inhabitants
were obliged to fly for security to their upper stories. The
famous quay here, noted for being the second-best in Britain for
length & breadth, was greatly damaged; several ships lying moored
at the cranes were driven from their moorings with only cabin boys
on board; those whose moorings held firm were driven upon the quay,
& there must remain till properly launched."[2] Bridges were destroyed. "The main arch of the seven which our bridge consists being a span of 75 feet was washed away; the two south arches, with
all the houses & shops on the west side, were destroyed & carried
down the flood, together with their furniture, stock, account-
books &c.[3] The owners--eight or nine of them, attempting to save
some part of their stock, were drowned by the fall of the arches &
houses; upwards of a hundred coal-lighters, that were above bridge
& treble the number below were driven down, & many went to sea &
sunk. . . . . Many thousands of deals & baulks of large timber, with household furniture, horses, cows, staiths, came floating down & almost covered the river for some hours."[4]
     A letter from Barnard Castle, Nov. 19th, says that the river
Tees (owing to an incessant rain from Friday morning to Saturday
night) swelled to such a degree /78/ as to rise upwards of 20
feet perpendicular higher than the oldest man living could remember. . . . "We have dismal accounts of what has happened below
us. At Yarum one half the town is entirely swept away & 46 persons missing.[1] We have received divers accounts of the same

accidents happening in Northumberland, Cumberland & Westmoreland,
in short, this place discovers a scene of horror & desolation too
dreadful for humanity to behold or words to express."

    Ann. Reg. under "December" says "All the letters from the
North of England are filled with the most melancholy accounts of
the late dreadful inundation. There is not one bridge standing
on either north or south Tyne, except Corbridge, three miles below Hexham, & that was damaged. At Bywell, a country village,
about six miles below, the whole village is almost destroyed, &
several families have perished there, the houses being carried
away, & wrecks of sand left instead of them. Part of one of the
churches was washed away, the graves were opened, & the living &
dead were intermixed & all floating together."

    "At Ovingham a village 8 miles below Hexham, a very tragic
misfortune happened at the ferry-boat house, the same fatal night
between the 16th & 17th of November. After the water had got into the dwelling house the family (ten in number) retired to the
upper chamber,[2] & continued there till it was two feet deep.
They then broke through the wall into the stable, thinking it a
place of greater safety both by its strength & situation. They
made themselves a temporary place to sit on by putting a deal
board & a ladder betwixt the binding balks, & there they remained
till   /79/   one o'clock in the morning, when, perceiving the
dwelling-house gone, & the stable beginning to yield to the impetuosity of the flood, three men broke out on the top of the
house, & the boatman, his wife, mother, two children, & the man
& maidservant remained as before, when in an instant the house
fell & they were all swept away by the torrent for the distance
of 257 yards into a wood where some of them climbed on trees &
remained in this situation ten hours before they were relieved.
The unhappy boatman, when he seized the tree with one hand, caught
his wife with the other; but after he had held her two or three
minutes, she was wrested from him in fifteen feet & a half depth
of water & in the midst of a rapid current. The boatman & his
brother are the only two survivors, & the boatman lives a burthen
to himself, having nothing left, without bread to eat or clothes
to put on."

    <u>Breaking of Solway Moss</u>. "Solway Moss lies on the borders
of Scotland, about ten miles north of Carlisle. A great part of
this Moss (at least above 400 acres of it) began to swell by the
inundation, & rose to such a height above the level, that at last
it rolled forward like a torrent, & continued its course above a
mile, sweeping along with it houses & trees & every other thing
in its way. It divided itself into islands of different extent,
from one to ten feet in thickness, upon which were found hares,
moor-game, &c. . . . There are about 30 what they call villages,
consisting of 4 or 5 houses together destroyed: great numbers
of cattle & sheep suffocated. It began to move on Saturday night
& continued in motion till Wednesday."[1]

80

<u>Inundations</u> (continued). 1810, November 10. This morning, about
seven o'clock, it began to rain at Boston & continued to do so
throughout the day. The wind accompanied the rain impetuously
from the E.S.E. & gradually increased in roughness; from 11
o'clock in the day till six in the evening it blew hard;[1] & from
that hour till nine a perfect hurricane. In consequence of this
continued gale for so many hours in one point the tide in the
evening came in with great rapidity, & rose, half an hour before

the expected time of full flood, to a height exceeding, by four
inches, what it is recorded to have attained on any former occasion. The consternation produced by the rise of the water several
feet above its usual level may be imagined. . . . & as it was
night & rained heavily, the situation of the inhabitants (whose
houses were inundated) was most distresssing[2]. . . . What was a
very extraordinary thing, the tide when it had flowed to its
highest, did not perceptibly subside for more than an hour. . . .
The seabanks had broken or were overflowed, & the whole neighbouring country was inundated.

"The calamity has been naturally more severe in the low districts of this country, which with difficulty find an outfall for
their drainage; & the tide having once broken into them, pursues
its course irresistibly for miles. All the fine pastures, the
pride of this neighbourhood, have in one night been laid under
water; & some thousands of sheep & other cattle have been
drowned.[3] The rain came so rapidly & unexpectedly that the
farmers had no time to save their cattle, had the thing   /81/
been practicable; but in some instances the inhabitants of farm-
houses have had difficulty in saving their own lives, & one instance is mentioned in which two persons . . . perished by the
flood, which completely swept away their dwelling-house . . . . .
Great difficulty will be experienced in supporting such cattle
as may not have perished on the inundated farms, all the ditches,
ponds & wells in many parishes being filled with salt water, which
it will take some time to get rid of. . . . The country looks
like a sea. From the hour of three on Friday morning last, till
five, it lightened as vividly & repeatedly, as is common in the
season when we most look for lightning.[1]

Places where inundations have happened.
Surrey, Yorkshire, Manchester, Derbyshire, Cheshire, Leeds, Kent,
Newcastle, Monmouthshire, Oxfordshire, Canterbury, Huddersfield.

82

Springs. The vapour which rises invisibly from the land & water
ascends in the atmosphere till it is condensed by the cold into
clouds, which restore it again to the earth in the form of rain
hail & snow; hence there is probably not a drop of water on the
globe that has not been borne on the wings of the wind. Part of
this moisture restored to the earth is reabsorbed by the air, part
supplies the wants of animal & vegetable life, a portion is carried off by the streams, & the remaining part penetrates through
porous soils till it arrives at a stratum impervious to water,
where it accumulates in subterranean lakes often of great extent.
The mountains receive the greatest portion of the aërial moisture,
&, from the many alternations of permeable & impermeable strata
they contain, a complete system of reservoirs is formed in them,
which, continually overflowing, form perennial springs at different
elevations, which unite & run down their sides in incipient rivers.
A great portion of the water at these high levels penetrates the
earth till it comes to an impermeable stratum below the plains,
where it collects in a sheet, & is forced by hydraulic pressure
to rise in springs, through cracks in the ground, to the surface.
In this manner, the water which falls on hills & mountains is
carried through highly inclined strata to great depths, & even
below the bed of the ocean, in many parts of which there are
springs of fresh water. In boring Artesian wells the water often

rushes up with such impetuosity by the hydrostatic pressure as to
form jets 40 or 50 feet high. In this operation several successive reservoirs have been met with. . . . . it consists merely in
boring a hole of small diameter & lining it with a tube.
                                     Somerville's Phys. Geography.[1]

{Entries 83 through 88 are missing in the manuscript.}

89
Architecture: its History (Ruskin)
"All European architecture, bad & good, old & new, is derived
from Greece through Rome, & coloured & perfected from the East.[1]
. . . The Doric & Corinthian orders are the roots, the one of all
Romanesque, massy capitaled buildings -- Norman, Lombard,
Byzantine, and what else you can name of the kind; & the Corinthian of all Gothic, Early English, French, German, & Tuscan. Now
observe: those old Greeks gave the shaft; Rome gave the arch; the
Arabs pointed & foliated the arch. . . . There is high probability
that the Greeks received their shaft system from Egypt; but I do
not care to keep this earlier derivation in the mind of the
reader. It is only necessary that he should be able to refer to
a fixed point of origin, when the form of the shaft was perfected. . . . . --I have said that the two orders, Doric & Corinthian, are the roots of all European architecture. . . . On one of
these orders the ornament is convex: those are Doric, Norman, &
what else you recollect of the kind. On the other the ornament
is concave: those are Corinthian, Early English, Decorated, &
what else you recollect of that kind. The transitional form, in
which the ornamental line is straight, is the centre or root of
both. All other orders are varieties of these, or phantasms &
grotesques, altogether indefinite in number & species.
     This Greek architecture, then, with its two orders, was
clumsily copied & varied by the Romans with no particular result,
until they began to bring the arch into extensive /90/ practical service; except only that the Doric capital was spoiled in
endeavours to mend it, & the Corinthian much varied & enriched
with fanciful, & often very beautiful imagery. And in this state
of things came Xtianity: seized upon the arch as her own:
decorated it, & delighted in it: invented a new Doric capital
to replace the spoiled Roman one: & all over the Roman empire
set to work, with such materials as were nearest at hand, to express & adorn herself as best she could. This Roman Christian
architecture is the exact expression of the Christianity of the
time, very fervid & beautiful--but very imperfect; in many
respects ignorant, & yet radiant with a strong, childlike light
of imagination, which flames up under Constantine, illumines all
the shores of the Bosphorus & the Aegean & the Adriatic Sea, &
then gradually, as the people give themselves up to idolatry,
becomes corpse-light. The architecture sinks into a settled
form--a strange, gilded, & embalmed repose: it, with the religion
it expressed; & so would have remained for ever,--so does remain,
where its langour has been undisturbed. But rough wakening was
ordained for it.
     This Christian art of the declining empire is divided into
two great branches, western & eastern; one centred at Rome, the
other at Byzantium, of which the one is the /91/ early Christian Romanesque, properly so called, & the other, carried to
higher imaginative perfection by Greek workmen, is distinguished
from it as Byzantine. . . . both of them a true continuance &

sequence of the art of old Rome itself, flowing uninterruptedly
down from the fountainhead & entrusted always to the best workmen
who could be found--Latins in Italy & Greeks in Greece; & thus
both branches may be ranged under the general term of Christian
Romanesque, an architecture which had lost the refinement of
Pagan art in the degradation of the empire, but which was elevated by Christianity to higher aims, & by the fancy of the Greek
workmen endowed with brighter forms. And this art the reader may
conceive as extending in its various branches over all the central provinces of the empire, taking aspects more or less refined,
according to its proximity to the seats of government. . . . . .
While in Rome & Constantinople, & in the districts under their
immediate influence, this Roman art of pure descent was practiced in all its refinement, an impure form of it--a patois of
Romanesque--was carried by inferior workmen into distant
provinces; & still ruder imitations of this patois were executed
by the barbarous nations on the skirts of the empire. But these
barbarous nations were in the strength of their youth; & while,
in the centre of Europe, a refined & purely descended art was
/92/   sinking into graceful formalism, on its confines a barbarous & borrowed art was organizing itself into strength &
consistency. The reader must therefore consider the history
of the work of the period as broadly divided into two great
heads: the one embracing the elaborately languid succession of
the Christian art of Rome; & the other, the imitations of it
executed by nations in every conceivable phase of early organization, on the edges of the empire, or included in its now merely
nominal extent.
     Some of the barbaric nations were, of course, not suscepti-
ble of this influence; &, when they burst over the Alps, appear,
like the Huns, as scourges only, or mix, as the Ostrogoths, with
the enervated Italians, & give physical strength to the mass with
which they mingle, without materially affecting its intellectual
character. But others, both south & north, of the empire, had
felt its influence, back to the beach of the Indian Ocean on the
one hand, & to the ice creeks of the North Sea on the other. On
the north & west the influence was of the Latins; on the south &
east of the Greeks. Two nations, pre-eminent above all the rest,
represent to us the force of derived mind on either side. . . . .
the Lombard & Arab. . . . .
     The work of the Lombard was to give hardihood & system to
the enervated body   /93/   & enfeebled mind of Christendom; that
of the Arab was to punish idolatry, & to proclaim the spirituality
of worship. The Lombard covered every church which he built with
the sculptured representations of bodily exercises--hunting and
war. The Arab banished all imagination of creature form from his
temples, & proclaimed from their minarets, "There is no God but
God." Opposite in their character & mission, alike in their magnificence of energy, they came from the North & from the South,
the glacier torrent & the lava stream: they met & contended over
the wreck of the Roman empire; & the very centre of the struggle,
the point of pause of both, the dead water of the opposite eddies,
charged with embayed fragments of the Roman wreck, is Venice.
     The Ducal palace of Venice contains the three elements in
exactly equal proportions--the Roman, Lombard, & Arab. . . . . .
The Xtian Roman & Byzantine work is round-arched, with single &
well-proportioned shafts; capitals imitated from classical Roman;
mouldings more or less so; & large surfaces of walls entirely
covered with imagery, mosaic, & paintings, whether of scripture

history or of sacred symbols.

The Arab school is at first the same in its principal features, the Byzantine workmen being employed by the caliphs; but the Arab rapidly introduces characters half Persepolitan, half Egyptian into the shafts & capitals: in   /94/   his intense love of excitement, he points the arch & writhes it into extravagant foliations; he banishes the animal imagery, & invents an ornamentation of his own (called Arabesque) to replace it: this not being adapted for covering large surfaces, he concentrates it on features of interest, & bars his surfaces with horizontal lines of colour, the expression of the level of the desert. He retains the dome & adds the minaret. All is done with exquisite refinement.

The changes effected by the Lombard are more curious still, for they are in the anatomy of the building, more than in its decoration. The Lombard architecture represents, as I said, the whole of that of the northern barbaric nations. And this, I believe, was at first an imitation in wood of the Xtian Roman churches or basilicas. Without staying to examine the whole structure of a basilica. . . . . it had a nave & two aisles, the nave much higher than the aisles; the nave was separated from the aisles by rows of shafts, which supported, above, large spaces of flat or dead wall, rising above the aisles, & forming the upper part of the nave, now called the clerestory, which had a gabled wooden roof.

These high dead walls were, in Roman work, built of stone, but in the wooden work of the North, they must necessarily have been   /95/   made of horizontal boards or timbers attached to uprights on the top of the nave pillars, which were themselves also of wood. Now, these uprights were necessarily thicker than the rest of the timbers & formed vertical square pilasters above the nave piers. As Christianity extended & Civilization increased these wooden structures were changed into stone. . . . The upright pilaster above the pier remains in the stone edifice, & is the first form of the great distinctive feature of Northern architecture--the vaulting shaft. In that form the Lombards brought it into Italy. . . . . .

When the vaulting shaft was introduced in the clerestory walls, additional members were added to the nave piers. Perhaps two or three pine trunks, used for a single pillar, gave the first idea of the grouped shaft. Be that as it may the arrangement of the nave pier in the form of a cross accompanies the superimposition of the vaulting shaft; together with correspondent grouping of minor shafts in doorways &c. . . . Thus, the whole body of the Northern architecture, represented by that of the Lombards, may be described as rough but majestic work, round-arched, with grouped shafts, adding vaulting shafts & endless imagery of active life & fantastic superstitions. . . .   /96/ --The glacier streams of the Lombards, & the following one of the Normans, left their erratic blocks wherever they had flowed; but without influencing, I think, the Southern nations beyond the sphere of their own presence. But the lava stream of the Arab, even after it had ceased to flow, warmed the whole of the Northern air; & the history of Gothic architecture is the history of the refinement & spiritualization of Northern work under its influence. The noblest buildings in the world, the Pisan-Romanesque, Tuscan (Giottesque) Gothic, & Veronese Gothic, are those of the Lombards schools themselves, under its close & direct influence; the various Gothics of the North are the original forms of the architecture which the Lombards brought

into Italy, changing under the less direct influence of the
Arab."

> Stones of Venice Vol. 1.

97

"Nicetas, à la prise de Constantinople voulut renoncer à écrire
l'histoire, pour venger sa patrie sur les Barbares, et afin que
jamais aucun de leurs noms ne parvint à la postérité."[1]

=

"Or se' tu quel Virgilio, e quella fonte
Che spande di parlar sì largo fiume?"[2]

> I. 79

=

"E vederai color, che son contenti
Nel fuoco, perchè speran di venire,
Quando che sia, alle beate genti."[3]   I. 118

=

"Perchè pensando consumai l'impresa,
Che fu nel cominciar cotanto tosta."[4]   II. 41

=

Fidandomi nel tuo parlare onesto,
Che onora te, e quei che udito l'hanno.[5]

> II. 113

=

"Quale i fioretti dal notturno gelo
Chinati e chiusi, poi che il Sol gl'imbianca
Si drizzan tutti aperti in loro stelo."[6]   128

=

"Questo misero modo
Tengon l'anime triste di coloro
Che visser senza infamia e senza lodo.
Mischiate sono a quel cattivo coro
Degli angeli che non furon ribelli,
Nè fur fedeli a Dio, ma per sè foro.
Cacciarli i ciel per non esser men belli,
Nè lo profondo inferno gli riceve,
Che alcuna gloria i rei avrebber d'elli"[7]

> III. 35

98

"Rispose: io era nuovo in questo stato,
Quando ci vidi venire un Possente
Con segno di vittoria incoronato"[1]   IV. 55

=

"Parlando cose, che il tacere è bello,
Sì com' era il parlar colà dov' era"[2]

> 105

=

"Genti v' eran con occhi tardi e gravi,
Di grande autorità ne' lor sembianti:
Parlavan rado, con voci soavi . . . . ."[3]
. . . .
Mi fur mostrati gli spiriti magni,
Che di vederli in me stesso m' esalto."[4]

> 112

"A vizio di lussuria fu sì rotta
Che libito fe' licito in sua legge
Per torre il biasmo, in che era condotta."[5]

> V. 55

=
"O lasso!
Quanti dolci pensier, quanto disio
Menò costoro al doloroso passo."[6]
=
"Ritorna a tua scienza,
Che vuol, quanto la cosa è più perfetta,
Più senta il bene, e così la doglienza."[7]
                         VI. 106
=
"Tristi fummo
Nell' aer dolce che dal Sol s'allegra,
Portando dentro accidioso fummo:
Or ci attristiam nella belletta negra."[8]
                        VII. 121

99

"Society always has a destructive influence on an artist:
first, by its sympathy with his meanest powers; secondly, by its
chilling want of understanding of his greatest; &, thirdly, by
its vain occupation of his time & thoughts. Of course, a painter
of man must be _among_ men; but it ought to be as a watcher, not as
a companion."
             Stones of Venice, III, 41[1]
                         =
To balance Dante's severity, there are many signs of tenderness &
compassion:[2] e.g. in the wood of suicides Canto XIII, 84, he begs
Virgil to ask questions for him of Pietro de' Vigni--"Ch' io non
potrei: tanta pietà m'accora."--Again, in C. XIV. at the beginning, he cannot go away from the Florentine transfixed as a tree
without gathering up the scattered leaves & giving them back to
the poor trunk.[3]

                              See _next_ _Page_.[4]
                         =
Fra Angelico. "The little cell was as one of the houses of
heaven prepared for him by his master. 'What need had it to be
elsewhere? Was not the Val d'Arno, with its olive woods in white
blossom, paradise enough for a poor monk? or could Christ be indeed in heaven more than here? Was He not always with him? Could
he breathe or see, but that Christ breathed beside him & looked
into his eyes?' Under every cypress avenue the angels walked; he
had seen their white robes, whiter than the dawn, at his bedside,
as he awoke in early summer. They had sung with him, one on each
side, when his voice failed for joy at sweet vesper & matin time;
his eyes were blinded by their wings at sunset, when it sank behind the hills of Luni." Ruskin[5]

100

They are very gentle words Dante uses to his old master Brunetto
Latini:
          Chè in la mente m'è fitta, ed or m'accora
          _La_ _cara_ _buona_ _imagine_ _paterna_
          Di voi, quando nel mondo ad ora ad ora
          M'insegnavate come l'uom s'eterna:
          E quant'io l'abbo in grado, mentr'io vivo
          Convien, che nella mia lingua si scerna.[1]
                              C. XV, 82.
          Lamenti saettaron me diversi,
          Che di pietà ferrati avean gli strati.[2]
                         C. XXIX. 43

    Throughout the Inferno I find only three instances of what
can be called cruelty in Dante. Everywhere else, the sufferings
of the damned fill him with pity.[3]
                              =
        Considerate la vostra semenza:
        Fatti non foste a viver come bruti,
        Ma per seguir virtute e conoscenza.[4]
                            C. XXVI. 118.
        Ella non ci diceva alcuna cosa;
        Ma lasciavane gir, solo sguardando
        A guisa di leon quando si posa.[5]
             Description of Sordello, Purgatorio, C. VI.

        Non avea pur natura ivi dipinto,
        Ma di soavità di mille odori
        Vi faceva un incognito indistinto.[6]
                          P. C. VII.
        Era già l'ora che volge 'l disio
        A' naviganti, e'ntenerisce 'l cuore,

                          101
        Lo dì ch'han detto a' dolci amici, A Dio;
        E che lo nuovo peregrin d'amore
             Punge, se ode squilla di lontano,
             Che paia 'l giorno pianger che si muore.[1]
                          Purg. C. VIII. 1-6.
        Per lei assai di lieve si comprende
             Quanto in femmina fuoco d'amor dura,
             Se l'occhio o 'l tatto spesso nol raccende.[2]
                          VIII. 76
        Lettor, tu vedi ben com'io innalzo
             La mia materia, e però, con più arte.
             Non ti maravigliar s'i' la rincalzo.[3]
                          IX. 70
        Pensa che questo dì mai non raggiorna[4]
                          XII. 84
        O gente umana, per volar su nata,
             Perchè a poco vento così cadi?[5]
                          XII. 95
        Qual di pennel fu maestro, o di stile,
             Che ritraesse l'ombre e i tratti, ch'ivi
             Mirar farieno uno 'ngegno sottile?
        Morti li morti, e i vivi parean vivi.
             Non vide me' di me chi vide 'l vero.[6]
                          XII. 64
                     "Esso
             Amor nasce in tre modi in vostro limo.
        È chi, per esser suo vicin soppresso,
             Spera eccellenza, e sol per questo brama
             Ch'el sia di sua grandezza in basso messo:
        È chi podere, grazia, onore, e fama
             Teme di perder perch' altri sormonti,

                          102
        Onde s'attrista sì che 'l contrario ama;
        Ed è chi per ingiuria par ch' adonti,
             Sì che si fa della vendetta ghiotto
             E tal convien che 'l male altrui impronti."[1]
                          C. XVII. 113

Ciacun confusamente un bene apprende,
   Nel qual si quieti l'animo, e desira:
   Perchè di giugner lui ciascun contende.[2]
                    ib. 127
O Signor mio, quando sarò io lieto
   A veder la vendetta che, nascosa,
   Fa dolce l'ira nel tuo segreto?[3]
                C. XX. 94
Parean l'occhiaje anella senza gemme.[4]
   (said of the meagre hungering spirits in purgatory
   for their gluttonous excesses) C. XXIII. 31

         Io mi son un che, quando
Amore spira, noto, e, a quel modo
Che detta dentro, vo significando.[5]
  .. ..
E qual più a gradire oltre si mette,
   Non vede più dall'uno all'altro stilo.[6]
              XXIV. 52
   Dimmi che è cagion perchè dimostri
     Nel dire e nel guardar d'avermi caro?
Ed io a lui: Li dolci detti vostri
Che, quanto durerà l'uso moderno,
Faranno cari ancora i loro inchiostri[7]
             XXVI. 110

         103
Io ritornai dalla santissim' onda,
   Rifatto sì, come piante novelle
   Rinnovellata di novella fronda,
Puro e disposto a salire alle stelle.
           End of Purgatorio.[1]
"Debili sì, che perla in bianca fronte
Non vien men tosto alle nostre pupille."[2]
           Paradiso. C. III. 14
Questa diss' io diritto alla lumiera
   Che pria m'avea parlato, ond' ella fessi
   Lucente più assai di quel ch'ell' era.
Sì come 'l Sol, che si cela egli stessi
   Per troppa luce, quando 'l caldo ha rose
   Le temperanze de' vapori spessi,
Per più letizia sì mi nascose
   Dentro al suo raggio la figura santa.[3]
             C. V. 130.
        e vien Quirino
Da sì vil padre che si rende a Marte.[4]
           C. VIII. 131
Sempre natura, se fortuna truova
   Discorde a se, come ogni altra semente
     Fuor di sua region, fa mala pruova.
E se 'l mondo laggiù ponesse mente
   Al fondamento che natura pone,
   Seguendo lui avria buona la gente.
Ma voi torcete alla religione
   Tal che fu nato a cingersi la spada,
   E fate re di tal ch'è da sermone;
Onde la traccia vostra è fuor di strada.[5]
          C. VIII. 139

104

Essa è la luce eterna di Sigieri[1]
    Che leggendo nel vico degli strami,
    <u>Sillogizzò invidiosi veri.</u>[2]
                       C. X. 136

Tin, tin sonando con sì dolce nota,
Che 'l ben disposto spirto d'amor turge.[3]
                      X. 143

Similemente operando all'artista
Ch'ha l'abito dell'arte e man che trema.[4]
                    XIII. 77

E questo ti fia sempre piombo a' piedi,
    Per farti muover lento, com' uom lasso,
    E al sì e al no, che tu non vedi;
    . . . .
    . . . .

Perch' egli incontra che più volte piega
    L'opinion corrente in falsa parte,
    E poi l'affetto lo intelletto lega.[5]
                    XIII. 112

E cieco tauro più avaccio cade
    Che cieco agnello.[6]
                    XVI. 70

Ch' avrà in te sì benigno riguardo,
    Che del fare e del chieder, tra voi due,
    Fia prima quel che tra gli altri è più tardo.[7]
                    XVII. 73

E,s'io al vero son timido amico,
    Temo di perder vita tra coloro
    Che questo tempo chiameranno antico[8]
                    XVII. 118

105

Questo tuo grido farà come vento
    Che le più alte cime più percuote;
    E ciò non fa d'onor poco argomento.[1]
                    XVII. 133.

Cuopron de' manti lor gli palafreni,
Sì che due bestie van sott' una pelle[2]
                    XXI. 133.

E come fantolin, che 'nver la mamma
    Tende le braccia poi che 'l latte prese,
    Per l'animo che 'n fin di fuor s'infiamma.[3]
                    XXIII. 21

Però salta la penna, e non lo scrivo,
    Che l'immaginar nostro a cotai pieghe,
    Non che 'l parlare, è troppo color vivo.[4]
                    XXIV. 25

Qual è colui che sognando vede,
    E dopo 'l sogno la passione impressa
    Rimane, e l'altro alla mente no riede[5]
                    XXXIII. 58

"Chè voler ciò udire è bassa voglia"[6]
                    Inferno.

"A questa tanto picciola vigilia
De' vostri sensi, ch' è del rimanente"[7]
                    ib.

Natura certo, quando lasciò l'arte

Di sì fatti animali, assai fe' bene
Per tor cotali esecutori a Marte[8]
                    ib. XXXI.
                "Ave
Maria, cantando, e cantando vanìo,
Come per acqua cupa cosa grave"[9]
                    Paradiso.   109[10]

                    106
"I have even read a eulogy on salt: there is scarcely any thing
that has not had its panegyric."[1]
                    Plato's Banquet

"N'as tu pas remarqué qu'il y a un milieu entre la science et l'i-
gnorance ? --Quel est-il?--Avoir une opinion vraie, sans pouvoir
en rendre raison: ne sais-tu pas que ce n'est là ni être savant,
puisque la science doit être fondée sur des raisons; ni être
ignorant, puisque ce qui participe du vrai ne peut s'appeler
ignorance." Ibid.[2]

"Les démons remplissent l'intervalle que sépare le ciel de la
terre: ils sont le lien qui unit le grand tout avec lui-même."
Ibid.[3]
     See in the "Banquet" an excellent account of the perpetual
death & birth of the body & mind in the individual, in the speech
of Socrates.[4]
                    =
"Heraldry, the science of those who despise every other." Hallam[5]
     "The expression [in the Paston letters] is much less formal
& quaint than that of modern Novelists, when they endeavour to
feign the familiar style of ages much later than the fifteenth
century." Hallam.[6]
                    =
"For auld stories, that men reads,
Represents to them the deeds
Of stalwart folks that livit are (lived early)
Right as they then in presence were.
And certes they suld well have prize
That in their time were wight[x] and wise."
                    Barbour[7]
          [x]valiant

                    107
"Ah! Freedom is a noble thing!
Freedom mays man to have liking; (pleasure)
Freedom all solace to man gives:
He lives at ease that freely lives"
                    "The Bruce"[1] Barbour
                    =
Knowing the heart of man is set to be
     The centre of this world about the which
These revolutions of disturbances
     Still roll; where all the aspects of misery
Predominate; whose strong effects are such
As he must bear, being powerless to redress;
And that, unless above himself he can
Erect himself, how poor a thing is man!
                    Daniel.[2]
                    =

Upon the midlands now the industrious muse doth fall
That shire wh. we the heart of England well may call.

. . . .

    My native country, then, which so brave spirits hast told,
If there be virtues yet remaining in thy earth,
Or any good of thine thou bred'st into my birth,
Accept it as thine own, whilst now I sing of thee,
Of all thy later brood the unworthiest though I be.
                              Drayton's Polyolbion[3]
                              =

"Great loobies & long
    That loath were to swink,
Clothed hem in copes
To be known from other,
And shopen him hermits
Hir case to have."   Piers Ploughman's Vision[4]

108

"It will hardly be denied that even in this frail & corrupted
world, we sometimes meet persons who, in their very mien & aspect,
as well as in the whole habit of life, manifest such a signature
& stamp of virtue, as to make our judgment of them a matter of
intuition rather than the result of continued Examination."
                    Alex. Knox on the character of John Wesley.[1]
                              =

"But I shall say no more of this at this time; for this is to be
felt & not to be talked of; & they who never touched it with
their fingers may secretly perhaps laugh at it in their hearts &
be never the wiser."
                         Jer. Taylor, on "Perfection."[2]
                              =

"In the polar regions, or on the tops of mountains, when the sun
is on the horizon, the shadow of a person is sometimes thrown on
an opposite cloud or mist, the head being surrounded by concentric
rings or circles, the number varying from one to five."
                              Somerville, Phys. Geog.[3]
                              =

"Hic depositum est corpus Jonathan Swift &c --
Ubi saeva indignatio cor lacerare nequit."[4]

109

              Dante from p. 105
                  Come gente che pensa suo cammino,
                  Che va col core, e col corpo dimora.[1]
                                      Purg. II
                  "My visage was painted with fear."[2]
                              =
                  Qui convien ch'uom voli;
              Dico con l'ali snelle e con le piume
              Del gran disio.[3]
                              =
              (Sordello)   "l'ombra tutta in se romita"[4]
                                      Purg. VI
                  L'altro vedete ch'ha fatto alla guancia
                  Della sua palma, sospirando, letto.[5] ib. VII
                              =
              Te lucis ante sì devotamente
                  Le uscì di bocca, e con sì dolce note
                  Che fece me a me uscir di mente.[6]

=
Quanto l'occhio mio potea trar d'ale.[7]
=
Rade volte risurge per li rami
L'umana probitade.[8]
Purg. VII.
Dante says to the curious who have their eyes
sewed up:
O gente sicura,
Incominciai, di veder l'alto lume,
Che 'l disio vostro solo ha 'n sua cura.[9]
Purg. C. XIII
E col suo lume se medesmo cela.
"Dark with excess of light."[10]

110
"Trassi dell'acqua non sazia la spugna."[1]
I left off asking questions before I was satisfied!
Purg. XX

Statius says to Virgil. P. XXII,
Facesti come quei che va di notte
Che porta il lume dietro, e sè non giova
Ma dopo sè fa le persone dotte.[2]
=
Disparve per lo fuoco
Come per l'acqua, il pesce andando al fondo[3]
=
Per ch' io te sopra te corono e mitrio.[4]
P. XXVII.
(Brook in the shade.)
Avvegna che si muova bruna bruna
Sotto l'ombra perpetua, che mai
Raggiar non lascia sole ivi, nè luna.[5]
=
Quando fu Giove arcanamente giusto.[6]
=
Per occulta virtù che da lei mosse
D'antico amor sentì la gran potenza.[7]

_____
_____
____
==

Hic situs est Phaeton currus auriga paterni,.
Quem si non tenuit, magnis tamen excidit avsis.[8]
Ovid. Met. ii. 327
"To hear with eyes belongs to love's rare wit."[9]
Shaks. Son.
=
The prophetic soul
Of the wide world dreaming on things to come[10]
ibid.

From Goethe   111   Faust II.
Ach! unsre Thaten selbst, so gut als unsere Leiden,
Sie hemmen unsres Lebens Gang.
Faust. 1.[1]

Und weil mein Fässchen trübe läuft
So ist die Welt auch auf der Neige.
                    Walpurgisnacht Scene[2]

Denn das Naturell der Frauen
Ist so nah mit Kunst verwandt.
                    Faust 2.[3]

Zoilo-Thersites.   Doch, wo was Rühmliches gelingt
                    Es mich sogleich in Harnisch bringt.
                    Das Tiefe hoch, das Hohe tief,
                    Das Schiefe grad, das Grade schief,
                    Das ganz allein macht mich gesund,
                    So will ich's auf dem Erdenrund.
                            Faust II.[4]

      Ich helf mir zuletzt mit Wahrheit aus.   Mephistopheles.[5]
                          =
Mit Kleinen thut man kleine Thaten,
Mit Grossen wird der Kleine gross.[6]
                          =
O weh! hinweg! & lasst mir jene Streite
Von Tyrannei und Sklaverei bei Seite.
Mich langeweilt's; denn kaum ist's abgethan,
So fangen sie von vorne wieder an;
Und keiner merkt, er ist doch nur geneckt
Von Asmodaus der dahinter steckt.
Sie streiten sich, so heisst's, um Freiheitsrechte,
Genau besehn, sind's Knechte gegen Knechte.
                            Faust II.[7]

Goethe   112
            Wenn ich auf dem Markte geh'
            Durch's Gedränge,
            Und das hübsche Mädchen seh'
            In der Menge;
            Geh' ich hier, sie kommt heran,
            Aber drüben;
            Niemand sieht uns beiden an
            Wie wir lieben.

            "Alter, hörst du noch nicht auf!
            Immer Mädchen!
            In dem jungen Lebenslauf
            Wär's ein Kätchen.
            Welche jetzt den Tag versüsst?
            Sag's mit Klarheit."
            Seht nur hin wie sie mich grüsst,
            Es ist die Wahrheit!
                        Epigrammatisch p. 264[1]

            Keinen Reimer wird man finden
            Der sich nicht den besten hielte,
            Keinen Fiedler, der nicht lieber
            Eigne Melodien spielte.
                        West-östlicher Divan 53[2]

            Mystisch heissest du ihnen,
            Weil sie närrisches bei dir denken,

Und ihren unlautern Wein
In deinem Namen verschenken.
                              Ib. 24.[3]

Horace   113
     "Absentem qui rodit amicum,
Qui non defendit alio culpante, solutos
Qui captat risus hominum famamque dicacis,
Fingere qui non visa potest, commissa tacere
Qui nequit: hic niger est, hunc tu, Romane, caveto."
                              Hor. Sat I, 4[1]
                              =

     "Ofellus
Rusticus, abnormis sapiens, crassaque Minerva"
                              Sat. I. 2[2]
(For a description of the frugal rich farmer, see this satire.)
                              =
     "Sapientem pascere barbam." II. 3.[3]
                              =
Mother praying to Jupiter for the recovery of her infant son,
& promising to make him stand naked in the Tiber.
                              See Sat. II, 3, 288
                              =
     "Genorosius
Perire quaerens" (of Cleopatra) Odes I.37.[4]
                              =
     "Deliberata morte ferocior"[5]
The fiercer from a resolve to die. ib.
                              =
     "Splendide mendax" (said of Hypermnestra)
                              Odes, III, 11[6]
                              =
(Eventide)   Sol ubi montium
Mutaret umbras, et juga demeret
Bobus fatigatis, amicum
     Tempus agens abeunte curru." Odes III.7[7]

                    114
"Virtutem incolumem odimus,
Sublatam ex oculis quaerimus invidi.
                              Odes III.21[1]

Quid leges, sine moribus
Vanae, proficiunt?   ib.[2]
                              =
     "Non secus in jugis
Exsomnis stupet Euias,
Hebrum prospiciens, et nive candidum
Thracen, ac pede barbaro
Lustratam Rhodopen." Odes, III, ?[3]

          Spirat adhuc amor
Vivuntque commissi calores
          Eoliae fidibus puellae
                              Odes I.9[4]

"Ad summam, sapiens uno minor est Jove, dives,
Liber, honoratus, pulcher, rex denique regum,
Praecipus sanus, nisi quum pituita molesta est."
                              Ep. I.1[5]

"Virtutem verba putas, et lucum ligna?"
                                        Ep. I.1[6]

     "i.e. lucum esse meram silvam, nulla
     religione sacram."[7]   (Face.)[8]
                                        =
Rustic giving away superfluous pears.   Ep. I.7[9]
                                        =
     "Rerum concordia discors."   Ep. I.12[10]

                              115
"Nam tua res agitur, paries quum proximus ardet,
Et neglecta solent incendia sumere vives"[1]
                                        =
Libera per vacuum posui vestigia princeps;
Non aliena meo pressi pede. Qui sibi fidet
Dux regit examen." Ep. I. 19[2]
                                        =
"Me libertino natum patre, et in tenui re
Majores pennas nido extendisse loqueris:
Ut, quantum generi demas, virtutibus addas."
                                        Ep. I. 20[3]
                    "Diram qui contudit hydram
Notaque fatali portenta labore subegit,
Comperit invidiam supremo fine domari."
                                        Ep. II. 1[4]
"Gemmas, marmor, ebur, Thrrhena sigilla, tabellas,
Argentum, vestes Gaetulo murice tinctas,
Sunt qui non habeant, est qui non curat habere"[5]
                                        =
     Dante, as the myth runs, when asked to go as ambassador to
the Pope, replied, "Penso, se io vo, chi rimange; e s' io rimango
chi va?"[6]
     Boccaccio, in his Life of Dante, expounds a dream of Dante's
mother during her pregnancy: She was lying under a laurel tree
when her son was born; he was nourished on the laurel berries &
became a shepherd; he was very fond of these berries, & running
eagerly one day to gather them, fell, but as she was looking to
see if he rose again, a Peacock arose in his place! This Peacock,
says Boccaccio, was the Divina Commedia, which we possess in the
place of Dante, & the resemblance is seen thus: the peacock's
/116/   flesh is incorruptible & odoriferous;[1] "la sua penna è
angelica, e in quella ha cento occhi; li suoi piedi son sozzi,
e tacita l'andatura; e oltre a ciò, ha sonora e orribile la voce.
E così, in luogo di Dante abbiamo il suo poema la Divina Commedia,
la quale ottimamente si può conformare ad un paone."[2]
                                        =
It is not long since these two eyes beheld
A mighty prince of most renowned ease
Whom England high in count of honour held
And greatest ones did sue to gaine his grace--
Of greatest ones he greatest in that place
Sat in the bosom of his Sovereinge
And Right and Loyal did his word maintain.

I saw him die, I saw him die as one
Of the meane people, & brought forth on beare,
I saw him die & no man left to moane
His doleful fate, that late him loved deare.

Scarce any left to close his eyelids neare,
Scarce any left upon his lips to lay
The sacred sod, or requiem to say.
                              Edmund Spenser, of Leicester.[3]

                         117
<u>Toleration</u>
The following acts of Parliament exhibit the history of Religious
Liberty for the last century & a half. The Toleration Act passed
in 1689 . . . It required those who availed themselves of it, to
subscribe the <u>doctrinal</u> articles of the Church of England; It excluded Roman Catholics & those who impugned the Trinity from its
benefits; & it left the Text & Corporation Acts, passed in Charles
the Second's reign, which made participation in the Lord's Supper,
according to the rites of the Church of England, a legal qualifi-
cation for civil office--in full force against Nonconformists.
Its provisions, scanty as they were, were limited by the Acts
against Occasional Conformity & Schism, which were passed in the
reign of "Anne; the former forbidding habitual Dissenters to attend worship & take the Sacrament, occasionally, in the Established Church; the latter making it illegal for any Dissenting
Teacher to undertake the education of youth. On the accession of
the House of Hanover, these two last Acts were repealed. More
than fifty years then elapsed before any further alteration was
proposed in the laws affecting liberty of conscience. . . . In
1779, profession of a belief in the Scriptures, with a declara-
tion of being a Christian & a Protestant, was substituted for
subscription to the doctrinal articles of the Church as a condition of enjoying the Toleration conceded by law. This amendment
of the Toleration Act was further enforced in 1812, by some provisions for the due regis-   /118/   tration of places of worship; but the parties before excluded, were not yet admitted to
its benefits, & the clause affecting the Unitarians was still
preserved. In the following year, Mr. William Smith, M.P. for
Norwich, procured the repeal of this last clause, by which, it
was believed, Unitarians were put on the same footing with other
classes of Dissenters. In 1828, the Sacramental Test was repealed; & in 1829 the Catholics were relieved from their dis-
abilities. The Unitarians, however, remained liable to a danger,
which was not anticipated, when the act for admitting them to a
full toleration was passed. Inheriting in regular transmission
from generation to generation, a considerable amount of property
which had been left by their Presbyterian ancestors for religious
purposes, it was argued, that their claim to it was vacated, because at the time of such endowments & foundations being created,
Unitarianism was not yet admitted to a Toleration. . . . . . . As
the trust-deeds of their forefathers rarely specified doctrines,
but were conceived in such general terms, as left room for a progressive modification--an act was introduced & passed in 1844,
which secured to Unitarians the possession of property for religious purposes, inherited from their ancestors, on the following principle--that. . . . . the usage of 25 years shall be taken
as conclusive evidence of the doctrine or worship   /119/   that
may be properly taught & observed in any Meeting house.
                              Tayler's "Retrospect."[1]
<u>Independency</u>.[2]   "The origin of Brownism is contemporaneous with
the severities of the court of High Commission directed by Whitgift.
Browne . . . was a gentleman of good family, educated at Cambridge,
& a relative of Lord Burleigh, to whom he was occasionally indebted

for protection." . . . Many who had embraced his views, withdrew
into Holland. . . . In England another gentleman, named Barrowe,
adopted them. Lord Bacon says, that Browne & Barrowe, being
gentlemen of education & good connexions, disseminated their principles by their free speaking & writing, in the Inns of Court &
other places of public resort. . . . Barrowe, Greenwood, & Penry--
all of this party--suffered death for their principles in 1593.
. . . Johnson, Ainsworth,[3] Jacob, & Robinson, were the earliest
professors of these principles in Holland, where they planted
congregations. . . . Robinson is usually regarded as the father
of Independency. . . . He was pastor of a church at Leyden during
the height of the Arminian controversy. Deeply imbued, like all
the English Puritans, with the spirit of Calvinism, he was urged
to oppose Episcopius. . . . Previous to the assembling of the
Synod of Dort, in 1618, he published in Latin an Apology for the
Independent Churches. The closing years of his ministry were
marked /120/ by an event of deep & solemn interest. The
younger members of his flock, seeing no prospect of a happy settlement in England, & disliking the tolerated condition of
exiles, determined to seek a new home on the shores of the
Atlantic. They set sail in the Mayflower 1620, & on the day of
their embarkation, the venerable man knelt down & prayed with
them on the beach.   (Ibid.)[1]

The Presbyterians fixed the foulest blow on their memory by the
ordinance which they brought into Parliament in 1648 against
blasphemy & heresy, enacting, that for certain offences of this
description which were specified--if the party on his trial
should not abjure his error, or if, having abjured, he should re-
lapse--he should suffer as in case of felony, without benefit of
clergy.[2]

The term Erastian is derived from Erastus, a German physician in
the 16th Century. The fundamental principle of the system seems
to have been this--that the church should exercise no coercive &
punitive power, except through the arm of the civil magistrate--
& especially should be restrained from inflicting, by its own
authority, the penalty of excommunication, to which, in that age,
such a fearful importance was attached. This system was taken
from the model of the Jewish polity, & recognized the Church as
only a member in the general body of the State.[3]

121
Ceremony keeps up all things: 'tis like a penny glass to a rich
spirit, or some excellent water; without it, the water were spilt,
the spirit lost.   Selden's Table Talk[1]

They talk, but blasphemously enough, that the Holy Ghost is
president of their general councils, when the truth is, the odd
man is still the Holy Ghost.
                                                            Ib.[2]

Preachers will bring anything into the text. The young master
of arts preached against non-residency in the university; whereupon the heads made an order that no man should meddle with
anything but what was in the text. The next day one preached
upon these words, "Abraham begat Isaac": when he had gone a good
way, at last he observed, that Abraham was resident; for if he

had been non-resident, he could never have begot Isaac; & so fell
foul upon the non-residents.

Ib.[3]

=

Nondum amabam, sed amare amabam.[4]

St. Augustin

=

"Fat folks (whose collops stick to their sides) are generally
lasie, whilst leaner people are of more activity." Fuller.[5]
"He had catched a great cold, had he had no other clothes to wear
than the skin of a bear not yet killed." Id.[6]
King James was wont to say, "he was a very valiant man who first
adventured on eating of oysters." id.[7]

122

Tribaldo d'Amerigo de' Rossi, Ricordanze di, Published in the
Delizie degli Eruditi Toscani.[1] ["La famiglia de' Rossi avea sue
case da S. Felicita Oltrarno, e nel Quartiere di S. Spirito, e per
la sua troppa potenza, e ricchezza, e signoria di molte Castella,
non godè assai degli Ufici maggiori della Repubblica, salvochè
dieci fiate del Priorato."][2]

"Ricordo chome di Marzo a di . . . 1493 ci vene una lettera
ala Singnioria chome el Re di Spagna cierti giovani iti chon
charovele a ciercare di paesi nuovi più là che non verito prima el
Re di Portoghalo in alto mare si misono da 3. charovele ben
fornite dongni chosa per 3. anni si dicie e chaminorono 23 dì,
e arivorono a ciertisole grandissime che mai più vi si navichò
per nazione humana popolate di huomini done assai engniudi tutti
cierte frasche intorno alla natura e non altro, e mai vidono più
christiani loro, fecionsi loro inchontro chon bastoni apuntati
chon cierte pene d'istricie suvi in schanbio di feri non áno
istechi di feri di niuna ragione, assai racholienza fu fatto
loro, dichono le lettere vè oro asai, uno fiume mena tera mischia
d'oro, grano asai, mangiolo senza far pane, chotoni assai, pini
archipresi grossi sei e dieci vingniate di uomini ispezierie
solenissime, gran cosa parve a ongniuno di quà," &c &c.[3]

Tribaldo p. 282 (1493) speaks of a certain Fra Bernardino
da Feltro, a Franciscan, much followed--è tenuto Santo
gieneralmente da tutti ' Frati /123/   loro, e dal popolo di
Firenze, beato a chi 'l tochave e chi aveva cierti brievi del
Giesù fatti di sua mane e benedetti da lui e molti sachordono abi
fatti de' miracoli, e la mattina dinanzi si partisi di qui
chandava a Perugia a far cierte pacie là nele prediche sue li
fu porto cierti libri di cierte istorie contro ala fede e molti
chape' da fanciulli li fu portato la sù, e feciene uno
chapanuccio e arseli la su ala porta del' Osservanza." . . .
[This Frate came at Easter to the Franciscan Monastery of S.
Miniato, on occasion of a general Chapter of the order][1]

Records in August 1493, that Maestro Francesco figliuolo di
Maestro Lionele Ciurmadore was fatally wounded with a partisan
"al chanto ala Paglia," by a son of Mateo Boni, a banker of
Florence, & that Boni was beheaded in the court of the Bargello.[2]
1493. Records how a certain person was stoned & torn to pieces
by the people for mutilating images. "Chonfessò avere fedito la
notte la nostra Donna a ore 4 di notte quela d' orzanmichele di

marmo dove si dichon le lalde di fuori, tuttolpopolo di Firenze
choreva a vedere, chon detto choltellino láveva dato più cholpi
in sul viso e nun ochio a Mess. dominoddio che lanbracio, e a
Santa Maria in Chanpo una piatà dipinta l'aveva guasta di poche
notte dinanzi, e quela nostra Dona chén sul chanto delo Spedale
di Santa Maria Nuova delo ricieto del Morbo di Santo Nofri si fe'
le sua chose in mano, e dipoi tutolviso e del dosso choperse di
detto istercho.[3]

Oct. 1493. Records the beheading of Mona Lisabetta   /124/   wife
of Mateo di Valore for poisoning her husband. "Detto marito pe'
sua portamenti tristi che ne dava a' chani, e porci la chaciò via
una volta, e stette parechi anni sanz' essa, tanti amici gli fu
adosso perch'era buon cristiano dasai, e bel giovane feciegliele
ritore da 3. mesi fa Fra Bernardino Frate e Predichatore deli
Osservanti di Santo Franciescho chera tenuto da tuto Firenze
santo, e quando la ritolse detto Fra Bernardino dise loro la
Mesa del chongiunto chome se navesi andare a marito allora solo
per pacificarli."[1]
1493. Records how Piero di Berto Manovelli aged 22 "che facieva
fare una bottega di cuoiaio in sulla piazza dela Stufa da
Samichele," who had been married 4 years to a daughter of Antonio
Parigi & had had a little girl already 2 years old, "e chome
piacque a Dio istimolatisi l'uno l'altro il dì di Berlinghaccio
ella si vestì monaca in S. Chiara, e lui partì subito per
vestirsi religioso nella Vernia &c."[2]
1493. Sent his little son to see a public execution. . . . Molto
bene parve a ongniuno morisi ben disposto. Idio li abi per-
donato.[3]
1494. Records the death of an abbess of the Rossi family & how a
"Predicatore del' ordine di Santa M. Novela predichò sopra 'l
corpo in Santa Filicita e fe' una bella predicha, e molto esaltò
la famiglia de' Rossi prima per chapo e memoria de S. Pier Martire
imemoria di quanto fumo credolli dela fede di Cristo quando pre-
dicava in Firenze. . . . e simile exaltò molto la detta Madonna,
la buona sua vita e governi."[4]

125
Petrarch's contempt of women

     Petrarch, out of his sonnets, is a bitter misogynist. In
his philosophical dialogue "De remidiis utriusque fortunae," he
makes Ratio denounce marriage & wives in reply to Gaudium, who
plays the part of the uxorious simpleton. E.g. "Gaudium. Non
faecunda tantum uxor, sed facunda est. Ratio. Conjugem
quaerebas, magistrum invenisti, jamque aliquid impolitum, commune
aliquid, loqui sine conjugis censura et irrisione non poteris.
Inter mundi taedia nullum importunius procaci faemina et tacere
nescia."[1]

=

     Ancient aphorisms. "We applaud many things delivered by
the ancients which are in themselves ordinary & come short of our
conceptions. Thus we usually extol & our orations cannot escape
the sayings of the wise men of Greece: Nosce teipsum of Thales,
Nihil nimis of Cleobulus; which not withstanding are but vulgar
precepts in morality, carrying with them nothing above the line
or beyond the extemporary sententiosity of common conceits with
us."[2]

=

"Il premio che si spera è che ciascuno
    Si sta da canto e ghigna
Dicendo mal di ciò che vide e sente."
                                    Machiavelli.[3]

126

Ell' ha due occhi tanto rubacuori
    Ch'ella trafigare' con essi un muro:
    Chiun che la vede convien che s'innamori;
    Ell' ha il suo cuore più ch'un cionol duro:
    E sempre ha seco un migliajo d'amadori
    Che da quegli occhi tutti presi furo:
    Ma ella guarda sempre questo e quello,
    Per modo tal che mi strugge il cervello.
                        La Nencia di Barberino.
                            By Lorenzo de' Medici[1]

                =

Negli occhi porta mia donna amore;
Perchè si fa gentil ciocch'ella mira;
Ove ella passa, ogni uom ver lei si gira;
E cui saluta, fa tremar lo core.

Sicchè sassando 'l viso tutto smuore,
Ed ogni suo difetto alor sospira:
Fuggi dinanzi a lei superbia ed ira.
Ajutatemi, donne, a farle onore.

Ogni dolcezza, ogni pensiero umile
Nasce nel core a chi parlar la sente;
Onde è laudato chi prima la vide.
Quel ch'ella par, quando un poco sorride,
Non si può dicer, nè tener a mente;
Si è nuovo miracolo e gentile.
                    Dante, La Vita Nuova, Son. XI[2]

127

Books for Historical Studies.
                =

Daunou, Cours d'Etudes Historiques. p. 98. Lon. Lib. Cat.
Milman's History of Latin Christianity. +
Ellis's "Specimens"
Maine on Ancient Law. √
Mores Catholici, by Kenelm Digby.
                =

Martin's Histoire de France √
Thierry's Histoire de Gaulois √
Haureau, Hist. du Scholasticisme. √
Geschichte des Materialismus.[1] √

Grimm, Deutsche Mythologie[2]

+Herodotus.[3]
Malcolm's Persia[4]

+Ewald's Geschichte des Volks Israel.[5] √

+Max Müller, Hist. of Sanskrit Literature.[6] √

                =

128

Luigi Pulci a un suo amico per ridere.

–

Costor, che fan sì gran disputazione
     Dell'anima, ond'ell'entri, o ond'ell'esca,
     O come il nocciol si stia nella pesca,
     Hanno studiato in su n'un gran mellone.
Aristotile allegano, e Platone,
     E voglion ch'ella in pace requisca
     Fra suoni, e canti, e fannoti una tresca,
     Che t'empie il capo di confusione.
L'anima è sol come si vede espresso
     In un pan bianco caldo un pinocchiato,
     O una carbinata in un pan fesso
E chi crede altro ha il fodero in bucato,
     E que' che per l'un cento hanno promesso
     Ci pagheran di sùcciole in mercato
          Mi dice un che v'è stato
     Nell'altra vita, e più non può tornarvi
     Che appena con la scala si può andarvi.
          Costor credon trovarvi
E'beccafichi, e gli ortolan pelati,
E'buon vin dolci, e letti spiumacciati,
          E'vanno drieto a'Frati.
Noi ce n'andrem, Pandolfo, in val di buja
Senza sentir più cantare: Alleluja.
     From a collection of poems entitled, "Sonnetti di
     Missere Matteo Franco et di Luigi Pulci jocose et faceti
     cioè da rire."[1]

129
Legendary Art[1]

Pictorial Symbols. Of the four Evangelists: the angel is the
symbol of Matthew, the lion of Mark, the ox of Luke, the eagle of
John.[2] The last frequently carries a cup from which issues a serpent; in allusion to the legend of an attempt to poison him with
the sacramental cup--when he drank & administered to the faithful
without harm, while the murderer fell down dead.[3]

     Of the Apostles:[4] Peter carries the keys, or a fish, Paul a
sword or two swords, Andrew a transverse cross, John the cup with
the serpent, James the great, the pilgrim's staff, Thomas, a
builder's rule; also a spear, St. James the less, a club, Philip
the staff or crosier surmounted by a cross, or a small cross in
his hand, Bartholomew, a knife, Matthew a purse, Simon a saw,
Thaddeus a halberd or lance, Matthias a lance.[5]

     In representations of the martyrdom of Paul, there is usually
an allusion to the legend of Plautilla who waited by the roadside
to ask his blessing. He, in return, asked for her veil to bind
his eyes, promising to give it her back again after his death.
The attendants mocked at such a promise, but Plautilla gave the
veil. After his martyrdom St Paul appeared to her & restored
the veil stained with his blood.[6]

     Authorities for Legends. Legenda Aurea, of Voragine: Flos
Sanctorum, of Ribadeneira, (French translation); the Perfetto
Legendario; the Legende delle Sante Vergini; Baillets Vie des
Saints.[7]

130 Legendary Art

According to the Spanish legend, St. James or Santiago, was an illustrious baron of Galilee, who, being the proprietor of ships,
was accustomed to fish along the shores of Gennesareth, but
solely for his good pleasure & recreation. This explains
Dante:

Ecco il Barone
Per cui laggiù si visita Galizia.[1]

The emblems of the four Latin Fathers are usually, for St.
Jerome a church, St. Augustine a book & sometimes a glowing
heart, St. Ambrose a knotted scourge, St. Gregory a book, with
pontifical robes. St. Jerome's attire is usually that of a cardinal, when he is not exhibited as a penitent. St. Gregory has
frequently the dove whispering in his ear. St. Jerome has frequently the lion for his companion.[2]

The four Greek fathers--five, if we include St. Cyril, according to the Greek practice--St. John Chrysostom, St. Basil the
Great, St. Athanasius, & St. Gregory of Nazianzen, are rarely
presented in Western art.[3] There is a curious legend of the
Penitence of Chrysostom, in which he leads a sort of Nebuchad-
nezzar life in the desert after the commission of dreadful crimes
--a legend apparently arising out of the hostile representations
of his enemies, the Egyptian monks.[4]

The patron Saints of Christendom: St. George of Cappadocia,
the patron saint of England, of Germany, of Venice--of soldiers
& armourers.[5] St. Sebastian, Patron Saint against plague &
pestilence. Both said to have lived under Diocletian.[6]

131
Superstitions in Medicine.

The words "Incantation" & "Charm" appear to be derived from the
ancient practice of curing diseases by poetry & music (Carmen).
Thus Coelius Aurelianus, "decantare loca dolentia." Democritus
says that many diseases are capable of being cured by the sound
of a flute when properly played. Marianus Capellus assures us
that fevers may be cured by appropriate songs. Asclepiades actually employed the trumpet for the relief of sciatica, & tells
us that it is to be continued until the fibres of the part begin
to palpitate, when the pain will vanish.

Paris's Pharmacologia[1]

Soranus--who was contemporary with Galen, & wrote the life
of Hippocrates, tells us that honey proved an easy remedy for the
apathae of children; but instead of at once referring the fact to
the medical qualities of the honey, he very gravely explains it,
from its having been taken from bees that hived near the tomb of
Hippocrates! And even those salutary virtues which many herbs
possess, were, in those times of superstitious delusion, attributed rather to the planet under whose ascendency they were collected or prepared, than to any natural or intrinsic properties
in the plants themselves; indeed such was the supposed importance
of planetary influence, that it was usual to prefix[2] to receipts
a symbol of the planet under whose reign the ingredients were to
be collected; & it is perhaps not generally known, that the char-
/132/   acter which we at this day place at the head of our prescriptions, & which is understood to mean nothing more than
Recipe, is in fact a relict of the astrological symbol of Jupiter,
as may be seen in many of the older works on pharmacy; although
it is at present disguised by the long down stroke which converts

it into the letter (R).[1]

   "The vervain (Verbena Officinalis), [Ib.] after libations
of honey, was to be gathered at the rising of the dog-star, when
neither sun nor moon shone, with the left hand only; when thus
prepared, it was said to vanquish fevers & other distempers, was
an antidote to the bite of serpents, & a charm to conciliate
friendship." Plin. lib. xxv. c. ix.[2]

   Every disease the origin & cause of which did not immediately strike the senses, has in all ages been attributed by the
ignorant to the wrath of heaven, to the resentment of some invisible demon, or to some malignant aspect of the stars; & hence the
introduction of a rabble of superstitious remedies, not a few of
which were rather considered as expiations at the shrine of
offended spirits, than as natural agents possessing medicinal
powers. The introduction of precious stones into the Materia
Medica arose from an Arabian superstition of this kind; indeed,
De Boot, who has written extensively on this subject, does not
pretend to account for the virtues of gems under any philosophical principles, but from their being the residence of spirits;
& he adds, that such substances, from their beauty,   /133/
splendour & value, are well adapted as receptacles for good
spirits.[1] (Note)[2] The precious stones were, at first, only used
as amulets, or external charms; but, like many other articles of
the Materia Medica, they passed, by a mistake in the mode of
their application, from the outside to the inside of the body, &
they were accordingly powdered & administered as specifics."[3]

   "Does not the fond parent still suspend the coral toy around
the neck of her infant, without being in the least aware of the
superstitious belief from which the custom originated?[4]--The sooth-
sayers attributed many mystic properties to the coral, & it was
believed to be capable of giving protection against the influence
of "evil eyes"; it was even supposed that coral would drive away
devils & evil spirits; hence arose the custom of wearing coral
amulets round the neck, & of making crowns of it. Pliny &
Dioscorides are very loud in their praises of the medicinal properties of this substance, & Paracelsus says that it should be
worn around the necks of infants as an admirable preservative
against fits, sorcery, charms, & even against poison. The bells
which are commonly suspended to it were originally intended to
frighten away evil spirits, & not to amuse the child by their
jingling sounds. . . . . . . In Sicily it is also commonly worn
as an amulet by persons of all ranks as a security against an evil
eye: a small twisted piece, resembling a horn, is worn at the
watchchain,   /134/   under the name of "Buon Fortuna," & is
occasionally pointed at those who are supposed to have evil intentions.[1]

   "It is unquestionable that certain words & ceremonies will
effectually destroy a flock of sheep, if administered with a certain quantity of arsenic."

                                                    Voltaire[2]

"St. Apollonia has been invoked against toothache; St. Avertin
against lunacy; St. Benedict against stone; St. Clara in sore
eyes; St. Herbert in hydrophobia; St. John in epilepsy; St. Mawr
in gout; St. Pernel in agues; St. Genevieve in fevers; St.
Sebastian in plague. In afflictions of the head generally, St.
Ottila was prayed to; in those of the neck, St. Blazius; in
diseases of the body, St. Lawrence & St. Erasmus; & in those of
the legs & feet, St. Rochus & St. John. St. Margaret was

supplicated for children, as well as in parturient danger; & a
long list of others may be found in Mr. Pittigrew's work on
Superstition.[3] In Brand's "Observations on Popular Antiquities"
many others may be read of.[4]   (Meryon's History of Medicine)[5]
                              =
"According to Durandas, the devil cannot endure the sound of a
consecrated bell. It is said that the wicked spirits that be in
the region of the air fear much when they hear the bells ringen;
& this is the cause why the bells be ringen when it thundereth;
to the end that the foul fiends & wicked spirits should be abashed
& flee, & cease from moving of the tempest."[6]

                            135
                        Legendary Art
Patron Saints contd. St. Roch. Patron of those who languish in
prison, of the sick in hospitals, &, especially of those who are
stricken by plague. Lived in the 13th & 14th centuries. He was
a native of Montpelier & devoted his life to tending the sick. At
last stricken himself by the plague, he left the hospital at
Piacenza & crawled into a wood that he might not disturb others
by his cries. Here his little dog went backwards & forwards to
the city each day & brought him a loaf. Hence in pictures he is
frequently accompanied by his dog. The extension of his worship
in Europe dates from the Council of Constance, where, the plague
having broken out, his image was led round the town & the pestilence ceased. The Venetians suffering frequently from the plague,
stole his relics from Montpelier & founded the Scuola di San
Rocco.[1] St. Cosmo & St. Damian, patron saints of medicine & the
medical profession--also of the Medici family. They were martyred
under Diocletian. First they were thrown into the sea, but an
angel saved them: then into the fire, but the fire refused to
burn them: then they were stoned, but the stones flew back on
those who flung them. Whence the proconsul regarding them as en-
chanters ordered them to be beheaded. They were born at AEgae in
Cilicia, where there was a famous temple of Esculapius, the scene
of miraculous cures--a temple destroyed by Constantine.[2]

                136 Legendary Art. Contd.
St. Cristopher was of the land of Canaan, of colossal stature &
terrible to behold, & being proud of his bulk & strength he determined to serve none but the most powerful king in the world. Having found this greatest king & being taken into his service, he
one day observed the said king crossing himself at the name of
the devil. Having asked the reason of this and been told it was
because the king feared the power of the devil, Cristopher set
off at once to seek the devil as the more worthy master, being
the more powerful. In crossing a desert plain he met a great
army with a terrible being at its head, & he stopped Cristopher &
asked him, "Man whither goest thou?" & Cristopher answered, "I
go to seek Satan, because he is the greatest prince in the world
& him would I serve." Then the other replied, "Seek no farther:
I am he." So Cristopher entered into the devil's service & this
lasted till they came to a cross by the wayside, whereupon the
devil was seized with fear & trembled, & turned back. Cristopher
inquiring the reason of this learns that the devil is afraid of
Jesus Christ whereupon he leaves the devil & goes to seek Jesus.
At last he came to the cell of a holy hermit, who told him that
if he would serve the great king Jesus he must fast & pray, but
Cristopher refused service of that sort. Then the hermit told

him to go to a certain river which was often swelled by the
rains, strong & wide & deep, wherein many people perished who
attempted to pass over. "Since thou wilt neither fast nor pray,"
he said, "go to that   /137/   river & use thy strength to save
those who struggle with the stream & those who are about to
perish." It may be that this good work shall prove acceptable to
Jesus Christ . . . & that he may manifest himself unto thee." To
which Cristopher replied joyfully, "This I can do. It is a service that pleaseth me well!" So he went & dwelt by the side of
the river--& having rooted up a palm tree he used it for a staff
to guide his steps, & he aided those who were about to sink, &
the weak he carried on his shoulders across the stream; & by day
& night he was always ready for his task, & failed not, & was
never wearied of helping those who needed help. And one night as
he was resting in his hut made of boughs he heard a little child's
voice crying, "Cristopher, carry me over." And after searching
twice & finding nothing & the voice calling a third time, he
sought with a lantern, & he beheld a little child, who said,
"Cristopher carry me over this night." And Cristopher lifted the
child on shoulders & took his staff & entered the stream.[1] And
the waves roared & the wind blew, & the child became heavier &
heavier till Cristopher thought he must sink; nevertheless he carried it safely to the other side. And then he said, "Who art
thou?" And the child answered that he was the maker of all
things, & in sign that Cristopher's work of charity had been accepted he bade him plant his staff in the ground & it should bear
leaves & fruit. And it was so: but the child had vanished.
Then Cristopher fell on his face & wor-   /138/   shipped Christ.
And he came to Samos in Lycia, and when the king saw him he
swooned for fear. And when he was recovered he said, "Who art
thou?" And Cristopher answered, "Formerly I was called Offero,
the bearer; but now my name is Cristopher, for I have borne
Christ." Then the king sent him to prison & sent two women to
him to tempt him. And at last when he would not be tempted he
was scourged, tortured & beheaded. And as they led him to death
he knelt down & prayed that those who looked upon him, trusting
in God, should not suffer from tempest, earthquake or fire.[1]

    (At Florence, on the facade of the ancient church of San
Miniato-tra-le-torri, Pollajuola painted a gigantic figure of St.
Cristopher, about twenty feet in height, which served during many
years as a model of form to the artists of his school: M. Angelo,
when young, copied it several times.)[2]

a.d. 326[3] St. Nicholas of Myra, sometimes called of Bari, because his relics were stolen & deposited there where a grand
church was built over them is the patron saint of children, poor
maidens, sailors, travellers & merchants. Also a protector
against thieves & losses by robbery or violence.--The first day
he was born he stood up in his bath & joined his hands together
& thanked God for bringing him into existence. He never took the
breast on Wednesdays & Fridays. He was born in Lycia. His
parents were Xtian & of illustrious birth & vast riches. They
dedicated   /139/   him to God & he became a priest. But when he
was still a youth his parents died of the plague & he inherited
their wealth. A story of him often represented in art is the
secretly furnishing a dower to the three daughters of a poor
nobleman, who were destitute of all resources. St Nicholas threw
in three purses successively through the window by night. The
most amazing of his deeds, also represented in art, was the

raising to life of three children who had been murdered & salted
down in a tub, by a wicked innkeeper who had stolen them for this
purpose. Nicholas was bishop of Myra & is always represented in
bishop's robes with three balls as his distinguishing attribute.[1]

    The four Virgin patronesses are St. Catharine, St. Barbara,
St. Margaret & St. Ursula.[2] 307. St. Catharine is the patron of
education & philosophy, theologians, students, & eloquence. She
was granddaughter of Constantine Chlorus, father of Constantine
the Great, & her mother inherited the throne of Egypt. She had
all learning, beauty & eloquence.[3] She refused to marry unless
she could have an immaculate husband, & a holy hermit was sent to
her by the Virgin Mary to tell her that Christ was the husband
she desired:[4] The hermit gave her a picture of the Virgin Mary
& her divine Son, & she hung it in her study, & that night she
dreamed that the Virgin presented her to our Lord, but he rejected her & said she was not beautiful enough. Then she awoke
in a passion of grief & told her dream to the hermit, & he taught
her the Xtian religion & /140/ baptized her. And after this
she had another dream in which Christ put a ring on her finger, &
awaking she found the ring. And the tyrant Maximin came to Alexandria & began to persecute the Christians, & Catherine resisted
him, & disputed with the philosophers whom he assembled. And the
philosophers declared themselves vanquished & converted, & the
emperor, enraged, ordered them to be consumed by fire. And they
went to death willingly, only bewailing that they were not baptized. But Catherine said to them, "Go, be of good courage, for
your blood shall be accounted to you as baptism, & the flames as
a crown of glory. The emperor Maximin, inflamed by her beauty,
wished to marry her, if she would renounce the name of Christ,
and when she refused he commanded four wheels to be made, two
turning in one direction & two in another, so that between them
she might be torn in pieces. But when she was bound to the
wheels fire came down from heaven & broke them, & the fragments
flew around so that the executioner & 3000 people perished. Then
the tyrant ordered her to be scourged & beheaded. And when she
was dead angels took her body & carried it over the desert & over
the Red Sea, till they brought it to Mount Sinai where they
buried it in a marble sepulchre.[1]

    St. Barbara is the patron saint of armourers & gunsmiths:
she is invoked against /141/   thunder & lightning, and explo-
sions of gunpowder. A.D. 303. She was the daughter of a rich
noble in Hereopolis who, fearful, from her great beauty, lest she
should be demanded in marriage & taken from him, shut her up in a
tower.[1] Here she studied, till she became convinced that her
father's gods were not the true gods. And hearing of a great
sage, named Origen of Alexandria, who taught a new religion, she
sent him a letter. And Origen sent one of his disciples disguised as a physician who taught her Christianity & baptized her.
And in her father's absence, she went to look at a building that
was being carried on according to his orders. And finding that
the workmen were making two windows she ordered them to make a
third. Her father, when he returned, was displeased at this &
asked her why she had ordered three windows instead of two. She
answered "Know, my father, that through three windows does the
soul receive light--the Father, the Son, & the Holy Ghost--&
these three are one."[2] Her father enraged at her conversion, de-
nounced her to the proconsul who had her tortured; but seeing she
would not yield, her father martyred her with his own hands.[3]

    St. Ursula, with her eleven thousand Virgins, is the

patroness of school girls & teachers. She was the daughter of a
King of Brittany, & was asked in marriage by Conon the son of the
King of England. But Ursula had made a vow of perpetual chastity.
So to avoid giving offence to a powerful monarch, she accepted
Conon on condition that he would give her as companions 11000
virgins of his country /142/   & permit her with them to visit
the sacred shrines for the space of three years. Also, that the
prince & his court should receive baptism. Such was her beauty &
wisdom, that the conditions were accepted, & Ursula with her
eleven thousand set off to Rome. Here Conon joined them, & made
a vow of perpetual chastity, & when they quitted Rome they were
accompanied by many prelates drawn towards them by their great
sanctity. And all were martyred together by the barbarians who
were besieging Cologne, where Ursula & her company arrived on
their way from Rome.[1]

St. Margaret is the patron saint of women in childbirth.
Unlike the others, she is not celebrated for learning, but meek-
ness & gentleness only. The devil appeared to her in the shape
of a dragon & tried to confound her, but she held up the cross
before him. He then swallowed her up, but immediately burst, &
she came out unharmed.[2]

The Four great Virgins of the Latin Church are St. Cecilia, St.
Agnes, St. Agatha, & St. Lucia.[3] St. Cecilia was a noble Roman
lady who lived in the reign of Alexander Severus. Her parents
were Christians & brought her up in the faith. She excelled in
music, & played on all instruments, but none sufficed to breathe
forth that flood of harmony with which her whole soul was filled:
so she invented the organ.[4] She had made V-/2-146[5]

Ecclesiastical Vestments 143

During the infancy of the Xtian religion the garments worn by the
priesthood were the same with the ordinary apparel of the period.[1]
The secular garments changed their form, but the ecclesiastical
remained the same in type only changing their materials & suffering certain modifications dependent chiefly on that change of
material.[2]

The Cassock is the ordinary every-day black garment of the
priest: with bishops it is purple, with cardinals scarlet, with
the pope white.[3] The garments used at mass by the officiating
priest are:
The Amice, from Amicire to cover: it is a piece of fine linen in
the form of an oblong square--first held over the head & then
spread on the shoulders.[4]
The Alb, is an ample linen tunic. The lower part of the alb used
anciently to be ornamented with one or several stripes of scarlet.
A remnant of the scarlet border is still retained by some of the
religious orders who trim the bottom & the sleeve cuffs with lace
under which they attach scarlet silk.[5]
The Girdle, anciently the Zone.[6]
The Maniple. Originally the maniple was a narrow strip of linen
suspended from the left arm to cleanse away the perspiration from
the face & brow. Gradually it received embellishments, till it
came to be composed of the same materials as the Chasuble.[7]
The Stole used during the first eight centuries to be called the
Orarium. It was an oblong piece of fine linen spread about the
shoulders, not unlike in shape, & worn in a fashion similar to
that of the modern female scarf. At first it was employed /144
Ecclesiastical Vestments/   to serve in place of a handkerchief &
preceded the maniple for this purpose. Then it was gradually

narrowed & enriched till it became nothing but a magnificent
scarf. The bishop, when vesting for the mass, lets his stole
hang straight down from around his neck on the right & left, the
priest crosses it over his breast; & the deacon wears it resting
on the left shoulder transversely uniting itself like a belt
under the right arm.[1]
The Chasuble. Derived from a sort of cloak called Paenula worn
by the Romans when the toga fell out of fashion. It was a nearly
circular piece of stuff with a hole in the middle to admit the
head, & was worn longer or shorter. It used to be ornamented
with Latus clavus, which in the ecclesiastical use was supplanted
by the cross. During the church ceremonies it was necessary for
the assistant deacons to elevate the sides of this mantle so as
to give freedom to the arms of the officiating priest. At length
the sides were curtailed so as to rest on the shoulders in the
present manner, leaving the arms unobstructed. This change came
about when the chasuble ceased to be made of soft stuff easily
folded & was made of rich stiff materials.--At the third council
of Toledo, 589, it was ordained that in restoring degraded
ecclesiastics: "If a bishop, he was to receive the stole, the
ring, & crosier: if a priest, the stole & chasuble; & if a
deacon, the stole & alb."[2] /Ecclesiastical Vestments 145/   The
English term chasuble is derived from casubula or casula, a small
dwelling: it was also called planeta from the Greek πλανητή.
Both names had reference to its amplitude.[1] The Dalmatic is a
vestment worn by the deacon whilst ministering at High Mass. It
derives its name from Dalmatia where it was invented. It was
originally a vest peculiar to the regal power; &, as such, became
adopted, & was used in public by several of the Roman emperors.
In the earlier ages the deacons wore a garment called colobium, a
kind of tight narrow tunic with very short sleeves. The custom
of wearing the Dalmatic under the chasuble, was anciently peculiar to the Roman pontiff. For many centuries however the bishop
has been entitled to assume this with his other vestments when he
celebrates High Mass.[2] The Tunic is worn by the sub-deacon. In
ordinary usage it resembles the dalmatic.[3] The Veil is a species
of scarf of an oblong shape, worn by the sub-deacon at High Mass,
while he holds the paten.[4] The Cope resembles a flowing & ample
cloak. Its use originally is conveyed in the name pulviale,
which is also given to it. It is now worn by bishops & priests
on various occasions particularly at vespers.[5] The Surplice,
from Superpelliceum,[6] worn not by the priest only, but by the
lowest minister who officiates at divine service.[7]

                                        Rock's Hierurgia

                            146
a vow of perpetual virginity, but having in obedience to her
parents accepted her husband Valerian, she persuaded him to
respect her vow. She told him that she had a guardian angel who
watched over her night & day, & would suffer no earthly lover to
approach her. (Chaucer has followed this legend in his "Second
Nonnes Tale").[1] She & her husband were both martyred. First the
wicked prefect, desiring her wealth which was great, ordered her
to be placed in her own bath filled with boiling water; but this
had no more effect on her body than if she had bathed in a fresh
spring. Then he sent an executioner to put her to death with the
sword; but his hand trembled so that he only gave her three
wounds which were not fatal till after three days, when she died,
singing.[2]

304 St. Agnes was also Roman. The son of the prefect fell
in love with her & asked her in marriage but she rejected him,
declaring herself betrothed to Christ. This was the origin of
her persecutions. The soldiers who carried her to a place of infamy, stripped her of her garments; but her hair immediately became like a veil covering her body. When the young Sempronius,
thinking her subdued, came into her chamber, he was struck with
blindness & fell down in convulsions. Then Agnes, seeing the
grief of his family, obtained his restoration to sight by her
prayers. Sempronius would fain have saved her then, but the
people cried against her as a sorceress, & she was thrown into
the flames. But she stood in /Legendary Art 147/ the midst
of them unharmed. Then the heathens--priests & people cried out
against her still more as a sorceress, & she was slain with the
sword. And on a certain day as her parents with many others were
praying by her sepulchre St. Agnes herself appeared before them,
all radiant of aspect; by her side was a snow-white lamb. And
she said, "Weep not; for me a throne is prepared &c."[1]

St. Agatha was of Catania in Sicily & lived in the reign of
Decius, who sent one Quintianus to reign over Sicily. Quintianus fell in love with Agatha & when she rejected his advances
& resisted all temptations & threats, he became furious, & had
her beaten with rods & her bosom torn with shears. St. Peter
came to her in prison & healed her bosom. Then Quintianus had
her cast into the flames, but an earthquake came & shook the
city, & the people thinking it had come on account of Agatha's
sufferings demanded that she should be released. She was taken
back to prison scorched & in miserable pain, & so she rendered up
her soul. The Christians took her body and buried it in a tomb of
porphyry. And a year after, the mountain Mongibello opened &
poured forth a stream of fire consuming all before it, & the
people of Catania fled for refuge to the tomb of St. Agatha &
taking her silken veil wh. lay upon it, fixed it on a lance, &
went forth in procession to meet the fire wh. had reached the
walls of the city: & the fire turned aside & the mountain ceased
to bellow, & there was calm.[2]

St. Lucia was also of Sicily & lived in the /148/ time
of Diocletian.[1] According to the oldest legend she was martyred
by a thrust in the throat with a poniard & there is no mention of
her eyes, but the later legend says that a youth being enamoured
of her, & beseeching her with letters & tender speeches, declaring it was the brightness of her eyes that inflamed him, Lucia
called for a knife, took out her eyes & sent them to her lover on
a dish. "But God would not suffer that the blessed Lucia, having
given this proof of her courage and piety should remain blind:
for one day as she knelt in prayer, behold, her eyes were restored to her more beautiful than before. . . . And this is the
reason that St. Lucia is invoked against blindness & diseases of
the eyes, & that in her effigy she bears two eyes in a dish."[2]

The Greek Bishops are distinguished from the Latin by wearing no mitre, by the planeta or chasuble being embroidered with
purple crosses, & by the staff surmounted by a cross instead of
the crozier.--In the Latin church, the pallium, worn only by
archbishops, resembles the stole: it is a white woolen band
about three fingers in breadth passed round the shoulders & from
which depend three short bands embroidered with crosses. The
infulae, two bands or lappets, depending from the mitre distinguished the bishop from the abbot.[3]

St. Sylvester was bishop of Rome under Constantine, whom

according to the legend he converted & baptized. At a contest
with philosophers & magicians, insti-   /149/   gated by the Em-
press Helena who was as yet unconverted Sylvester raised a wild
bull to life with the sign of the cross, after it had been killed
by the whisper of a magician in its ear. There is also a legend
of his having exorcised a dragon & bound up its mouth by winding
a thread 3 times around its jaws--allegorical of his overcoming
idolatry.[1]

107 St. Ignatius of Antioch was torn by lions under Trajan.[2]

St. Erasmus died under Diocletian at Mola di Gaeta. A new &
horrible death was prepared for him: he was cut open & his entrails were wound off on a sort of wheel. Such an implement is
placed in the hands of his effigy.[3]

St. Zenobio was born in the last year of the reign of Constantine, at Florence, of a noble family. He was brought up in
all the wisdom of the Gentiles, but was converted secretly by his
teachers & afterwards converted his parents. He afterwards was
secretary to Pope Damasus I, & being sent to appease the dissen-
sions in his native city was unanimously elected bishop by
Catholics & Arians. He continued to lead a life of poverty &
self-denial, honoured by the good, respected by the wicked, &
died under Honorius. A tree bursting into leaf is usually his
attribute in paintings. It is related that when his remains were
being carried to the Duomo to be deposited under the high altar,
the people crowded round on the bier in order to kiss his hands
or touch his garments. In passing through the Piazza del Duomo
the body of the saint was thrown against the trunk of a withered
elm standing near the spot where the Baptistery now stands, &
suddenly the   /150/   tree burst into fresh leaf. He also restored two children to life--one, of a French lady who had left
it in his charge while she went to Rome: represented by Masaccio;
the other, run over & trampled by oxen in the Borgo de' Albizzi.
This latter is represented in Ridolfo Ghirlandajo's picture.[1]

St. Frediano was an Irish saint who migrated to Luccia & became bishop of that city in the 6th cent. In a terrible inundation which threatened to destroy Lucca he turned the course of
the river Serchio tracing the direction in which it was to flow
by drawing a harrow along the ground, & the river obediently followed the steps of the holy man. This we find shadowed forth the
costly embankments by which the course of the Serchio was altered.[2]

San Romulo, first bishop & apostle of Fiesole. According to
the legend he was a noble Roman, a convert of St. Peter, who sent
him to Fiesole then one of the greatest Etruscan cities. He was
martyred under Nero. The cathedral is dedicated to him.[3]

St. Antony's attributes in art are the monk's cowl, the
crutch, the bell & sometimes the asperger (as a sign of his power
over evil spirits) & the pig (as the representative of sensuality,
which he subdued). This last image gave rise to the superstition
that the pig was under his special protection. The monks of the
order of St. Antony kept herds of consecrated pigs, which were
allowed to feed at the public cost, & which it was sacrilege to
kill: /151/   hence the proverb about the fatness of a "Tantony
pig." Flames of fire are often placed near St. A. or under his
feet signifying his spiritual aid against fire in all shapes.[1]

San Ranieri is the patron saint of Pisa. Some legends of
his life are represented in the Campo Santo.[2]

St. Julian, was a count who lived in his castle in great
prosperity, spending his days in hunting & his nights in feasting.

One day pursuing a deer, the poor animal turned round & said, "Thou who pursuest me shalt cause the death of thy father & mother. Julian, terrified, fled to a far country. And he became rich at a foreign court and married. And his father & mother, sad at his absence, came to seek him & presented themselves at his castle, & were welcomed & tended by their daughter-in-law, Julian himself being absent. And she put them into her own bed. And in the morning when she was gone to matins Julian returned, & seeing a bearded man in his bed he slew both the man & the woman. And when Julian learnt the truth he fled, with his wife, who refused to leave him, till they came to the bank of a great river which was often swollen by torrents so that many in attempting to pass it perished miserably. And here Julian made a cell for himself & near it a hospital for the poor; & by day & night & summer & winter, he ferried travellers across without fee. And one night a voice called him across the stream, & he found a youth who was a leper who seemed to be dying from fatigue & cold. And Julian brought him over & laid him on his own bed, & he & his wife watched him till the morning.   /152/   And at dawn the leper arose & his face was transformed & seemed that of an angel, & he said: "Julian, the Lord hath sent me to thee, for thy penitence is accepted, & thy rest is near at hand"; & then he vanished and shortly after he & his wife slept in the Lord.[1]

153

"AEquitas enim lucet ipsa per se: dubitatio cognitionem significat injuriae." (Cicero, de Officiis.)[1]

Cicero holds it an essential part of justice to punish (or avenge) a wrong: but, says he, "Sunt autem quaedam officia etiam adversus eos servanda, a quibus injuriam acceperis. Atque haud scio an satis sit, eum, qui lacessierit, injuriae suae poenitere; ut et ipse ne quid tale posthac et ceteri sint ad injuriam tardiores."[2]

"Semper autem in fide, quid senseris, non quid dixeris, cogitandum."[3]

"Totius autem injustitiae nulla capitalior quam eorum, qui, quum maxime fallunt, id agunt ut viri boni esse videantur."[4]

"Nihil est enim liberale, quod non idem justum."[5]

"Magnum est enim eadem habere monumenta majorum, eisdem uti sacris, sepulcra habere communia."[6]

"Nihil honestum esse potest, quod justitia vacat."[7]

"Sunt enim, qui in rebus contrariis parum sibi constent; voluptatem severissime contemnant, in dolore sint molliores; gloriam negligunt, frangantur infamia."[8]

"Illud (victory at Salamis) enim semel profuit, hoc (areopagus) semper proderit civitati."[9] (Comparison of Themistocles & Solon).

"Parvi enim sunt foris arma, nisi est consilium domi."[10]

Greek Months 154

1 <u>Hecatombaon</u>, first month in the Attic year, answering to the last half of our July & the first ½ of August: in it the Hecatombaea were held (festivals in wh. hecatombs were offered).[1]

2 <u>Metageitnion</u>, 2d month, answering to the Boatian Panemos & Laconian Karneios; also to the latter ½ of our August & to the first ½ of Sept. (Said to be from μετα, γείτων, because then people flitted & changed their neighbours.)

3 <u>Boedromion</u>, 3d Attic month = ½ Sept. & ½ Oct. Boedromia

celebrated, i.e. games in memory of the defeat of the Amazons
by Theseus.

4   <u>Pyanepsian</u>, 4th month = ½ Oct. & ½ Nov. Pyanepsia, feast in
    honour of Apollo said to be so called from a dish of beans,
    or peeled barley & pulse then cooled & eaten.

5   <u>Maimakterion</u>, 5th month = ½ Nov. & ½ Dec. Festival of Zeus
    Maimaktes, <u>boisterous</u>, <u>stormy</u>.

6   <u>Poseideon</u>, 6th month = ½ Dec. & ½ Jan.

7   <u>Gamelion</u>, 7th month = ½ Jan. & ½ Feb. So called because it
    was the fashionable time for weddings.

8   <u>Anthisterion</u>, 8th Attic month = ½ Feb. & ½ March. Anthisteris,
    the feast of flowers, the three days' feast of Dionysus at
    Athens.

9   <u>Elaphebolion</u> = ½ March & ½ April. Elaphebolia held; the fes-
    tival of Artemis.

10 <u>Munychion</u> = ½ April & half May. Festival of Munychia Artemis.
    Munychia harbour adjoining Piraeus.

11 <u>Thargelion</u> = ½ May & ½ June. Feast of Apollo & Artemis.

12 <u>Scirophorion</u>, 12th Attic month = ½ June & ½ July. The festi-
    val of Athena Skiros. Skiron, a white parasol, borne by the
    priestesses in this festival; thence called τὰ σκίρα, or
    σκιροφόρια.

155

<u>The Monastic Orders</u>.[1] 1. The Benedictines. St. Benedict was
the patriarch of the Monks of the West. He founded the great
monastery of Monte Cassino, in Campania & here his relics were
kept.[2] The chief Benedictine monastery of Germany was that of
Fulda: the abbot was primate & chief of all the abbots in Germany. Saint Boniface, Archbishop of Mayence & apostle of Germany,
was the founder of this monastery in 744, in order to place there
some of the numerous monks who were his coadjutors in converting
the pagans. St. Boniface obtained a "Privilege" from Pope
Zachary, submitting the monastery immediately to the jurisdiction
of the Holy See: the first instance of the kind. Previously,
monasteries were all under the jurisdiction of the Diocesan, or
the Metropolitan; or to the assemblies of Bishops frequent in
those times; or to the Patriarch [of the order] by a tacit condition. Emperors & Popes concurred in making the monasteries independent of the Bishops, sometimes, as in the case of the Mon.
of Pescara founded by Louis II, the dependence was entirely on
the temporal Sovereign, & again, the Nuns <u>delle Vergini</u> were entirely under the jurisdiction of the Doge of Venice. The riches
of Fulda increased rapidly & enormously. It had 15,000 metairies
or farms. In the 10th century, there were divisions & scandals.
Frederick, archbishop of Mayence, being banished to this monastery, attempted to commence very needful reforms, the lives of
the monks being worldly & relaxed: many in consequence renounced
the monkish habit /156/ rather than submit to a severer rule,
& some married. Again the discipline was relaxed in 1021, when
it was reformed by Abbot Richard with the aid of Irish monks. In
1063 there was a great quarrel between the Bishop of Hildesheim,
diocesan of Fulda, & the Abbot, about precedence in the church
during a ceremony, & their people came to blows. The next year
there was carnage between the soldiery & officials of the two
parties. The Abbot had to pay a large sum by way of indemnity,
& being obliged to pledge a great deal of the property of the
abbey, the monks were irritated against him, & made a procession
to offer their complaints to the emperor. But they were reduced

to submission by force of arms. The abbots were continually
accused of dissipating the property of the monastery. In 1133 a
dispute about precedence arose between the abbot & the Archbishop
of Magdeburg, which was decided by the Pope in favour of the
Abbot. In 1150 the Abbot made the village of Fulda a walled
town, but in 1331, the burghers revolted against his successor,
demolished the citadel that joined the abbey, & plundered the
valuables. The rebels were reduced to obedience by the authority
of the emperor. The peasants were in dependence on the monastery
in 1526, & ruined all the monkish establishments of Fulda
(various monasteries being clustered round the central one, in
different points of the mountains). It was not only against
their subjects that the abbots had to fortify themselves & fight,
but against their neighbours   /157/   --against troops of bandits & robbers, who had fortified themselves in various castles.
Only people of noble birth were admitted into this as into other
monasteries of Germany whose abbots were princes of the empire &
had a voice in the Diet.[1]

§The Benedictine rules & the manners of the order were reformed in 817, by St. Benedict of Aniane.[2]

§<u>Cluny</u> was founded in 910. Under St. Odon, the second
abbot, the rule of Cluny was accepted by a large number of monasteries in France; constituting a reform of these establishments.
There was great sanctity among the monks of Cluny in the commencement: the corn of which the Host was to be made was chosen
grain by grain, & washed carefully through all the processes.
One year, at the beginning of Lent, 7000 poor were relieved.
Great care was given to the education of the young. Peter the
Venerable, Abbot of Cluny in the first half of the 12th century,
forbade the use of animal fat on Fridays, an "abuse" which was
previously common among the monks. He also forbade the eating
of meat, but it was soon introduced, for certain statutes in
1204 limited the prohibition to Wednesdays & Fridays.[3]

§<u>Camaldoli</u>, founded 1012, by S. Romualdo, after he had
founded many other monasteries but could prevail on no abbot to
persevere in the severity of his own maxims. There is a dispute
about the date & origin of the name. In a "privilege" of the
emperor Henry II, the spot is called <u>Campus</u> <u>amabilis</u>. S.
Romualdo first built seven   /158/   cells on a steep height
(apparently the Sagro Eremo). He is said to have had a vision
like Jacob's, seeing the monks go up & down the ladder in white
garments, whereupon he changed the garb from black to white.
After this S. Romualdo retired to Sitria, in Umbria, where he remained 7 years, gathering penitents around him--all barefoot,
pale, neglected, some of them immersed in the solitude of their
cell as in a sepulchre. Strict silence was observed, & each administered discipline to the other. The monastery of Fontebuono
at the foot of the mountain on which the Sagro Eremo stands, was
originally a hospital for those whose health gave way under the
eremitic life. In 1105, the general of the Order made the rule
milder, & instituted the Camaldolese Nuns; & the moderating of
austerities was carried farther by subsequent generals. In 1431
the order had so lost its discipline, that an effort was made to
reform it under Pope Eugenius IV. The convents of nuns were in a
state of utter disorder; men admitted, & the nuns going in & out
at will.[1]

The Congregation of Fonte Avellana, in Umbria, in the diocese
of Faenza, were an order of barefooted hermits, whose discipline
was made yet more severe by S. Pietro[2] Damiano, especially in the

matter of self-flagellation. S. Piero Damiano was made a cardinal
in 1057. In the XVIth century, however, this order had quitted
all its severities,   /159/   lived in much licence, & had abandoned the monkish dress for one thoroughly mundane.[1]

  §La Cava is another famous centre of a congregation of the
order of S. Benedict, built in the Xth or XIth century.[2]

  §Vallombrosa was founded by S. John Gualberto in the year
1038. He inculcated the Benedictine rule with rigour. The Val-
lombrosans wore grey until in 1500 this was exchanged for brown.[3]
Pietro Ignes, who passed through the fire to prove S. John
Gualbert's accusation of sinning against the Bishop of Florence,
raised the reputation of the order. Frati Conversi were first
known as Vallombrosa.[4]

  §The abbey of Citeaux (whence the name Cistercian) not far
from Dijon was another centre of Benedictine reform. Clairvaux
was an offshoot of Citeaux, & became itself the chief of 800
monasteries. St. Bernard was its first abbot, & he gave his name
to the monks of the order of Citeaux. Clairvaux was founded in
1115.[5] The nuns of the Cistercian order were called Bernardines.[6]
The order called in France Feuillans are reformed Bernardins or
Cistertians.[7] Another order of reformed Bernardines were called
by their foundress "Filles du précieux sang," "afin que ses filles
fûssent devouées singulièrement à honorer les differentes effu-
sions de ce sang adorable."[8]

  §The abbey of Port Royal, also Cistertian, was founded 1204.
It was reformed, after falling into a state of great laxity, by
the Mère   /160/   Angélique Arnaud, in 1602, when she was only
17. In 1620 the community removed from Port Royal des Champs to
Paris, in the faubourg S. Jaques.[1] "Dans ce temps-là, il se fit
un nouvel établissement d'une maison religieuse devouée entière-
ment au culte du S.-Sacrement; de sorte que le jour et la nuit il
devait y avoir toujours quelque personne en prière devant le
Saint Sacrement."[2] The Duchess de Longueville declared herself
the foundress of this house, but dying without leaving funds for
this purpose, the new order, consisting of the Mère Angélique &
three nuns had to return to Port Royal, & the new devotion was
instituted there. The scapulary was changed from black to white
with a red cross upon it. After this, part of the community retired to P. Royal des Champs.[3] The question of Jansenism arose
for them in 1656.[4] "Tous ceux qui étaient favorables à ce livre
(de Jansenius) passaient dans le public sous le nom de Port Royal
à cause qu'effectivement la plupart avaient été composés par un
grand nombre de savants qui s'étaient rétirés à Port Royal des
Champs, lorsque les Religieuses l'avaient abandonné en 1626, et
qui après le retour de ces Religieuses, charmés de la solitude de
ce lieu. . . . avaient fait bâtir des appartements dans la cour de
ce monastère, où la plupart avaient des parentes."[5]

  §The monks of La Trappe, (dans le Perche) /161/   were
also affiliated to Citeaux. They were reformed with great austerity in the XVIIth Century by the Abbé de Rance, formerly a rich
& worldly ecclesiastic, translator of Anacreon, who retired from
the world on falling into disfavour at court.[1]

  Of the military orders under the rule of St. Benedict, the
Templars are the most famous: founded at Jerusalem 1118, with
the object of defending the Pilgrims against the cruelty of the
infidels, of keeping the roads safe & defending religion in
general; & that nothing might interfere with their devoting their
whole life to these works of charity, their foundress took the
vows of poverty, chastity & obedience. Baldwin II, King of

Jerusalem, gave them temporarily a house near the Temple of
Solomon, whence they were called Templars. Their rule was written by St. Bernard.[2] They were suppressed by Philippe le Bel in
1307.[3]

    §The Umiliati, founded in 1180-90-96-1017-or 1117?[4] They
were originally Lombard nobles taken prisoners into Germany by
Henry V., in which circumstances they adopted a grey dress, & a
life of penitence & piety. On their return to Italy they gave
themselves to the wool manufacture,[5] working with their own hands,
giving employment to a vast number of poor artisans, & distribut-
ing the superfluity of their own gains in Charity. Their wives
adopted the same life. But in 1135 St. Bernard advised them to
separate from their wives, & live in continence   /162/   & to
wear white garments. Whereupon they founded their first monastery in the quarter of Brera at Milan. Their dress consisted in
a gown & mantle of white cloth, with a large white cap.[1] (The
cap in the picture is the pudding-bag shape such as is made for
the Turks & worn by the common people of Italy.)[2] At first,
they were called Berretins from this cap; subsequently Umiliati.
But by a second change they adopted the rule of St. Benedict, &
altered the form of their dress. They were suppressed on account
of corruption after one of them had murdered S. Carlo Borromeo
(--or attempted to murder him).[3]

    The Celestines were so called when their founder became Pope
under the name of Celestin V. in the XIIIth century.[4]
                               =
II.   The Augustinians. It is matter of uncertainty & dispute how
far the Hermits of St. Augustine were derived from the African
Monks founded by the Saint himself. The regular Canons (See farther on under Prémontré) dispute this & claim that exclusively
for themselves. The various bodies of Augustinian hermits were
united under one rule by Alexander IV, 1254. They were recalci-
trant about taking to black clothes instead of brown,[5] as they
were commanded by the pope, that they might be distinguished from
the Franciscans. They multiplied marvellously: by some authors
they are said to have had 2000 monasteries & 30,000 monks,   /163/
with more than 300 convents for women. (The original rule of the
order was one written by Saint Augustine.)[1]

    The Knights of St. John, or of Rhodes or Malta, were origi-
nally hospitallers founded by the republic of Amalfi, to succour
suffering pilgrims; but as their riches increased, they embraced
the office of fighting for Christianity.[2] There are also Nuns of
this order.[3]

    The Teutonic order of Knights, founded 1190. They conquered
Prussia about 1230.[4]

    §The Sisters of the Hotel Dieu. The hospital had already
been long founded in 1097.[5] "Nous avons vu . . . en parlant de
quelques hôpitaux, qu'ils étaient desservis conjointement par des
religieux & des religieuses qui avaient leurs habitations
séparées. C'était la pratique de tout l'Occident du temps du
Cardinal Jacques de Vitry, qui mourut vers le milieu du treizième
siècle, demeuraient dans les léproseries et les Hospitaliers, dit
qu'il y avait un grand nombre de congrégations d'hommes et de
femmes qui, renonçant au siècle, demeuraient dans les léproseries
et le Hôpitaux pour servir les malades & les pauvres, vivant sous
la règle de S. Augustin sans propriété et en commun, obéissant á
un supérieur et promettant à Dieu une continence perpétuelle.
Les hommes demeuraient séparés des femmes, ne mangeant pas même
ensemble & vivant dans une grande retenue et une grande pureté."[6]

=

III.   The Dominicans.   St. Dominic was born 1170.

164
["In the Mount the Lord will appear."[1]

Thorwaldsen was just going to leave Rome when an order came for
his Jason from Hope][2]

in old Castile.   "Sa mère étant grosse de St. D. eut un songe
mystérieux, où elle s'imagina mettre au monde un petit chien, qui
d'un flambeau allumé qu'il tenait à sa gueule éclairait tout le
monde, présage evident &c. &c."[3]   He was of the noble family of
Guzman.   In 1204, accompanying the Bishop of Osma ambassador to
France, he passed through Languedoc, where his attention was
called to the heretical Albigenses.   He obtained leave from the
Pope to remain there for their conversion, & became the head of a
mission for this purpose.   For the sake of obtaining permanent
helpers he formed the plan of founding a religious order, 1215.
Pope Innocent III at first refused to confirm the order, being of
opinion that it was a more pressing business to reform those already established.   But he was at length determined to grant the
confirmation--as in the case of St. Francis, by a vision.   Having
prayed for inspiration in the choice of a rule, Dominic took that
of St. Augustine, to which he added certain statutes & constitu-
tions in usage in an ancient order--some say, that of the Carthusians, others that of the Premonstratensians.   The principal
articles were perpetual silence; almost constant fasts, at least
from the 14th September to Easter; total abstinence from meat;
the use of woollen instead of linen; a rigorous poverty; &
various other   /165/   austerities.   The renouncing of rents &
all possessions was not ordained till 1220.[1]   The order was confirmed under the title of Frati Predicatori.[2]
     §The Inquisitors--(the Holy Office was not formally founded
till 1233 by Gregory IX)--were chiefly Dominicans:[3]   also the
Master of the Sacred Palace who had the authority of inquisi-
torial censorship was a Dominican.[4]   In France, the Dominicans
were called Jacobins, because their first monastery at Paris,
founded by Matthew of Paris, was in the Rue St. Jacques.[5]
     The order of Servites or Servants of the Virgin, was founded
by seven merchants of Florence, 1233, who renounced the vanities
of the world to live in poverty.   They were of noble Tuscan
families & all belonged to a confraternity in Florence called
de' Laudesi, whose perpetual obligation it was to sing praises to
the Virgin.   They went to their oratory for this purpose the day
of the Assumption of the B.V. & were all seven divinely inspired
to renounce the world.   Seeing them in their hair shirts & chains,
& with the other marks of their vocation about them, the infants
at the breast cried, "See there the Servants of the Blessed
Virgin."   And hence they took the name of Serviti.   They built
their first monastery on M. Senario; then, to give them shelter
when they went to seek alms in Florence, which was ten miles off,
they built a small hut which afterwards grew to be the monastery
of Annunziata.[6]
     §The Theatines were so called from Theate or Chieti, the
Bishop of which place was their founder.[7]

166

§The Ursulines were founded in 1537, by Angela di Brescia, as a sort of Sisters of Charity, living, not in community but in their own families; but they subsequently formed numerous communities & finally adopted the entire monastic life.[1]

§The Padri Somaschi, were so called because the chief of their order was established at Somasche between Milan & Bergamo. They made the care & education of orphans their special function.[2]

§The Prêtres de la Doctrine Chrétienne were founded by César de Bus near the end of the XVIth century. "La lecture qu'il fit du Catéchisme du Concile de Trente lui fit concevoir le dessin d'établir une congrégation de Prêtres et de Clercs, dont la fonction fut d'enseigner la lecture Chrétienne. Ce Catechisme du Concile de Trente étant divisé en quatre parties, qui sont le Symbole, l'oraison dominicale, le décalogue et les Sacrements; le Père de Bus réduisit les quatre parties à trois différentes instructions, qu'il appelait petite, moyenne, et grande Doctrine. Cinq ou six jeunes ecclésiastiques de famille se joignirent à lui, et après les avoir instruits de la manière de faire la petite doctrine, il les envoyait dans les carrefours de la ville et à la campagne pour catéchiser tous ceux qu'ils rencontraient." Their first establishment was at Avignon.[3]

§The Barnabites, earlier in the same century, seem to have been in like manner a product of the spring-tide of religious zeal that accompanied the Reformation, their object being conversion & propaganda.[4]

167

IV. The Franciscans. St. Francis, the son of a wool-merchant at Assisi, was born in 1182.[1] He was the first founder of an order who sought a confirmation from the Pope. He feared lest it should happen to him as to the Vaudois whose institution was rejected by Popes Lucius & Innocent III.[2] The original habit was grey: The Capuchins alone have retained closely the form of this habit.[3] A reformed branch, instituted 1368 at Bruliano, between Foligno & Camerino, were called Zoccolanti because of their wooden sandals.[4]

§The Beghards, Picards, Fraticelli or Bizocchi regarded themselves as Franciscans, & had numerous religious houses all over Europe; but they were pronounced heretical. They reproached the Franciscans with their departure from the austerity of their rule. The Zoccolanti were chosen to combat them at Perugia.[5]

§The term Conventual applied to any order, implies a relaxed rule; the term Observantine, a return to strict rule.[6]

§The Capuchins arose in Spain: they were also called Barefoots (Scalzi), because they abandoned the sandals.[7]

§The Archiconfraternity of the Stigmata of St. Francis. These archiconfraternità seem to have been a sort of religious clubs, into which all ranks were admitted; the members having reciprocal duties, & certain special religious ceremonies.[8]

V. The Carthusians. Founded by St. Bruno, in the desert of Chartreux, in the diocese of Grenoble, /168/ 1086. There have been great disputes as to how St. Bruno was determined to the renunciation of the world: the miracle of his friend the Doctor being three times resuscitated during his funeral rites to declare the justice of his condemnation, was first inserted in the Breviary & then removed.[1] Silence & seclusion are their grand rules.[2] The Certosa at Pavia is one of the finest monasteries of their order.[3]

§The Beguines are the oldest of all the secular communities, whether founded by Ste. Begghe in the VIIth century, or by Lambert de Begue in the XIIth.[4]

§Amongst the Regular Canons who followed the rule of St. Augustin (being originally associated clergy, in distinction from monks, who were not necessarily clergy)[5] the Premonstratensians are the most celebrated. Their chief monastery was founded by S. Norbert in 1119, at Premontre, as a means of introducing a reform of the order.[6]

=

VI. The Carmelites, who fiercely contended that their order dated from Elijah, entered Europe in the XIIIth century. The Carmelites in Flanders had a fierce dispute on this point with the Bollandists; & it was only terminated by Papal interference.[7]

Notes made from Helyot's
Histoire des Ordres Monastiques

169

Antique Gems.[1] Homer makes no mention of signet-rings, in his minute description of works in the precious metals & of jewellery, though he particularly specifies necklaces, earrings, & head ornaments; & whenever he speaks of securing treasures it is as being effected by an artfully tied knot, not by a seal, the usual Greek & Roman substitute for a lock.[2] . . . . On the other hand as far back as records go signets appear among the Egyptians & Assyrians: witness the signet of Pharoah given to Joseph; the treasure-cell of Rhampsinitus secured by his seal; the signet of Judah given as a pledge; the temple of Belus sealed with the royal signet &c-- The Nile & the Tigris offered soft clay; & it must have suggested itself to the first individual who deposited his property in a closed vessel that it might be secured against pilferers by a plaster of clay laid on a juncture of the lid & rolled flat by a joint of a cane, & hence the first origin of the <u>perforated</u> cylinder. From the natural impressions on the cane-joint, or wood employed to stamp the clay, the transition was easy to some definite design scratched around its circumference by the owner, & appropriated to himself as his peculiar device.[3] . . . Again, if we look to Egypt, the incredible number of scarabs in clay & soft stone (of the same date as these cylinders) still remaining manifest the long-established use & the great importance of the purposes for which they were employed amongst all classes of the inhabitants of that land, the fountain-head of European civilization.[4]--Engraving on hard stones invented by the seal-engravers of Nineveh, shortly before the reign of Sargon. It was not taken up by the Egyptians until long after, since they continued their use of softer materials, gold & clay, /170/ until the time of the Ptolemies.[1] But it was speedily taken up by the Phoenicians . . . for many seals of a purely Phoenician character, yet of the earliest date, are found, bearing also legends in Semitic letters, of which they were the first inventors. They diffused the knowledge of this, together with the other arts, among the Asiatic & Insular Greeks. Homer frequently mentions the Tyrian merchant ships voyaging amongst the Islands of the Egean, & trafficking in ornaments & jewellery; & the first intagli produced among the cities of the sea-board still bear the impress of an Assyrian origin. . . . .[2]

Thence to Greece Proper the transition was rapid, & the signet, now <u>for the first time universally worn in a finger-ring</u>

came into general favour throughout all the population; a new
manner this of securing the seal, for its oriental inventors had
invariably worn their cylinder or stamp as the ornament of a
bracelet or necklace. That the invention of the finger ring is
ascribed to Prometheus, a Greek hero, and its name δακτυλιον (a
word of native origin unlike those of other ornaments, as
μανιακης & ψελλιον, from this to have been purely Greek fashion.
. . . Signet rings must have attained universal popularity in
Greece before 600 B.C., soon after which period Solon passed a
law forbidding gem-engravers to keep by them the impression of
any signet once sold. And about this time Herodotus mentions
the famous emerald of Polycrates.[3] In the Etruscan scarabs we
also discover evidences of an Asiatic origin: the subjects cut
on the early sort are exclusively animals: it was not till after
their intercourse with the Greeks had been   /171/   long established that they represented figures & scenes derived from Greek
mythology. This may be explained on the ancient theory that the
ruling Etruscan caste were a civilizing band of colonists from
Asia, who introduced among the Celtic (Pelasgian) aborigines of
Central Italy an art already flourishing in their native country.
At a later period the Hellenic settlers in Magna Grecia seem,
from their constant intercourse with the Etruscans, to have borrowed from them the form of the scarab (worshipped by the Egyptians as the symbol of the sun, by its forming the balls, deposi-
taries of its eggs, typifying the creation of the globe), but to
have imparted to the intagli engraved upon its base that elegance
& finish due to their own natural taste & advancement.[1]

     In Sicily[2] & Magna Graecia gem-engraving, like the cognate
art of die-sinking, attained to its highest perfection first.
Greece itself was ever a poor country, & distracted by perpetual
wars, whilst the colonies sent out from it were advancing, through
commerce & agriculture, to an incredible degree of prosperity.
In one Dorian colony, Cyrene, AElian notices the wonderful skill
(or numbers) of the gem-engravers; & Ismenias is reported to have
sent from Athens to Cyprus to purchase an emerald engraved with
Amymone. Most of the finest gems in our collections show, by the
identity of their style, that they proceed from the same hands
that cut the coin-dies for the mintage of these same cities.
After this the establishment of the Macedonian dynasty in Asia, &
the command of unbounded wealth, conduced greatly to the encouragement of the art. This age gives us for the first time the
portraits   /172/   of princes whose likenesses now occupy the
gem in the place of the national deity; & from many allusions of
ancient authors, it would appear that the usual signet of any
personage of importance was the likeness of himself. The example
of this substitution was probably set by Alexander, & connected
with his own assumption of divinity, which will also explain his
restriction of the privilege of engraving his sacred portrait to
Pyrgoteles, the first artist of the day in that branch; for the
numerous heads of this hero now extant are almost invariably of
much later date, & belonging to the times of the Roman empire,
when they used to be worn as amulets. With his age also begins
the series of Camei, the earliest known being the Grand Odescalchi
Sardonyx of Ptolemy & Berenice, evidently a contemporary work.[1]

     Mithridates is recorded as the founder of the first royal
cabinet of gems; we find also a work on this study dedicated to
him by the Babylonian Zachalias. Unfortunately the gem-engravers
never ventured to place their names on their works before the age
of Augustus, so that Cronius & Apollonides, mentioned by Pliny as

(after Pyrgoteles) eminent in this branch, are the only artists
of this age of perfection of whom there exists any historical
record.[2]

The Romans, following their original teachers the Etruscans,
adopted from them at first the scarab signet, & retained this
form until late in the republican period. It is impossible to
fix the date when they began to substitute signet rings for this
primitive ornament. Pliny mentions that amongst the   /173/
statues of the Kings only two, Numa & Servius Tullius, were
represented as wearing rings. These early signets also, according to Ateius Capito, were not set with engraved stones, but had
the seal cut upon the metal of the ring itself. When the use of
gold rings was introduced among them by the Greeks (those of
Sicily, no doubt), then engraved gems also began to be admired &
employed for signets. This change of fashion, which took place
in the later days of the republic, produced the numerous intagli
that are turned up in the vicinity of Rome, distinguished from
those of Greek & of imperial workmanship by the deeply-cut
intagli upon them, retaining much of the Etruscan style, & giving
nearly the same subjects as the original scarabs. Many of these
bear traces of having been set in iron rings.

But under Augustus gem-engraving reached its highest point.
Under the patronage of Maecenas flourished Dioscorides, Solon,
Aulus, Gnaeus--all the talent of Greece; either attracted to the
metropolis of the world as the most promising field for their
genius, or else originally brought there as the freed men of
those nobles whose names they assumed on manumission.[1] . . . This
also is the age, par-eminence of Camei.[2] During the two centuries
from Augustus to Severus inclusive the trade of making Pastes was
also carried to an enormous extent to meet the requirements of
the poorer classes. This business throve amazingly & has left us
innumerable relics of the extraordinary skill of the workmen in
glass until it ceases quite suddenly in the third century, together with the production, of the gem-engraver himself. . . .[3]
But Camei in   /174/   Sardonyx were also produced in large quantities, many of them extraordinary for art & material, some bearing the engraver's name . . . until the reign of Severus. In
fact, some of the finest extant belong to the times of Hadrian,
the most flourishing period of Roman art; but from the date just
mentioned gem-engraving declined & became extinct with extraordinary & unaccountable rapidity. Gold medallions & coins had
superseded the intaglio & cameo imperial portrait as personal
ornaments; the spread of Christianity acted more & more as a
check on the reproduction of other representations of the elegant
Western mythology; & those permitted by the change in religious
sentiments were only the tasteless & Barbarous symbolical figures
of the new Egyptian & Oriental creeds. At length, in the 5th
century, Roman gem-engraving, entirely vanishes, its last traces
fading away in the swarms of ill-cut & worse drawn Abraxas
Jaspers & Manichean amulets. Of the Byzantine nobles the signets
were of metal, charged with the letters of the cognomen quaintly
arranged in the form of a cross; & the few men of taste yet surviving treasured up the gems, the works of previous centuries, as
precious articles of vertù, not to be profaned by common use.[1]

Meantime the art had taken refuge in Persia, where with the
resurrection of the Achemenian dynasty & religion in the 3d century, its production came again into as general request as in the
ages preceding the Macedonian conquest. This continued down
/175/   to the Mohammedan conquest in the 7th century when it came

to an end with the dynasty whose features it had so long perpetuated.[1]

Their place is taken by the only forms permitted by the religion of the Conquerers--elegant Cuphic inscriptions arranged in cyphers wrought in a neat & precise manner upon the choicest stones. The demand for these signets throughout the East, & the taste required for the graceful combination of the flowing curves distinguishing Arabic Calligraphy, kept alive all the mechanical processes of the art until the time of its revival in Italy.

The Byzantine school of the same interval merely presents to us as evidence of its existence, a few camei of religious subjects, in which the miserable execution is on a par with the design. Throughout the West, for the same ten centuries gemengraving was unknown. The signets used were seals of metal, or else antique intagli set in rings, having their subjects interpreted in a Scriptural sense, & legends added around the bizzel to set forth this new interpretation. Official seals in the middle ages were large & elaborate designs cut on a metal matrix; but the demand for antique intagli to be set in personal signets was enormous; not regulated, however, in any degree by their beauty, but solely by the nature of the subjects on them, according to the belief in the talismanic virtue of certain sigils, determined by the rules of the various Lapidaria then so much studied.[2]

Then the art slumbered till with the first dawn of the Revival in Italy it not only woke up but within the   /176/   space of a single life-time attained to its second maturity. In the Quattro Cento the new passion for antique works was compelled at first to look for its gratification to the gems treasured up by medieval ancestors on account either of their intrinsic value or mystic virtues. To imitate was the next step, & not a difficult one; the mechanical methods, themselves of the simplest nature, were already known to the Florentines through their intercourse with the Levant, & the goldsmith who had worked from his youth on the Nelli of the same century was, as far as drawing went, quite on a level with the ancient Dioscorides or Aulus. In the Cinque Cento the possession of the wheel & magnifying glass had enabled the artist to pour forth camei with a facility unknown to the ancient engraver.[1]

=

<u>Sards</u>. The most ancient intagli are cut in cornelian chiefly but after the conquest of Asia, a finer description of this stone, came into use, called the Sard. Sards retain their original polish, whereas garnets, jacinth, & Nicoli have their surfaces scratched & roughened by wear. The dark Sard was the male, the lighter the female. The light yellow sort was in use at an earlier period, & on this are frequently found the finest works of the Greek artists. The name Sardius is derived from its being first imported into Greece from Sardis, probably brought thither from the interior of Asia.[2]

Calcedony. A semi-transparent white quartz, slightly tinted with yellow or blue. Much used at every period of antiquity. Good Greek & Roman intagli on it, but chiefly on the sappherine or bluer sort. When it   /177/   has a tinge of yellow it is called opaline. The ancient <u>Chalcedonius</u> however was a kind of Emerald. The modern or white <u>Cornelian</u>, was probably the Leucachates & Cerachates of the ancients.[1]

<u>Sardonyx</u>. Is defined by Pliny as "candor in Sarda," i.e. a white opaque layer superposed on a red transparent stratum of the

true Sard.[2]

Onyx has two layers, usually in strong contrast with each other, but of various combinations. There is a variety according to Pliny containing spots of various colours surrounded by white veins, like so many eyes. By cutting out these spots--or a blue spot with a black zone,--the so-called Nicolo (Onicolo, little onyx), is obtained.[3] In fact agate & onyx are the same substance --only in the former the layers are wavy, in the latter parallel.[4]

Plasma=the Prasius of the ancients, is a semi-transparent green stone.[5]

Jasper. Green & semi-transparent, or black, or green spotted with red (Bloodstone), or green with brown mottling, or dull yellow. The black kind presents us with many excellent intagli of every epoch. There was also a red Jasper, one kind vermilion, the other rich crimson, both valued, but the latter the rarest.[6]

Garnets, & their variety Carbuncles, much employed by the Romans & Persians.[7]

Jacinth--a stone of golden lustre, like the Topaz Lyncurium, often identified with it[8]--supposed to be the urine of the Lynx which when the beast had buried it became stone.[9] The Lychnis, classed under the genus Carbunculus by Pliny, & so called from its supposed property of lighting lamps, probably according to him included among its varieties the Jacinth, which /178/ shares in the possession of electricity in common with the diamond, the Sapphire & the Tourmaline. The Jacinth was a favourite stone with the Greek artists of the age of Theophrastus & Diocles. Head of Sappho cut on it.[1]

Beryl, of the same chemical constitution as the Emerald but much softer, & found in abundance. But in ancient times it was rare, & valued as much as the Emerald.[2]

Hyacinthus = Sapphire. The ancient Sapphire was the Lapis Lazuli.[3] A magnificent head of Jupiter, engraved on a pale sapphire nearly an inch in diameter, was discovered forming the ornament of the handle of a Turkish dagger, the intaglio being entirely concealed by the setting.[4]

Cellini gives the following table of the relative value of gems in 1560:[5] Ruby, 1 carat weight . . . . 800 gold scudi[6]

Emerald	. . . .	400
Diamond	. . . .	100
Sapphire	. . . .	10

Topaz=Chrysolite, Chrysoprax, i.e. the ancient Topaz--being of a bright greenish yellow; while the ancient Chrysolite was the modern Topaz. The Chrysoprax is an opaque apple-green stone.[7]

Magnet is a black compact hard iron ore, frequently engraved with Gnostic subjects.[8]

Obsidian, very black & sometimes semi-transparent.[9] Opals came to the Romans from India; at present the best are brought from Hungary. The Romans named it the Paederos or Cupid, as being the perfection of beauty; for the same reason in Medieval Latin & German it was called the Orphanus & the Waise.[10]

179

Subjects of Intagli. After the ring of Polycrates, the most famous signet is probably the Agate of King Pyrrhus, which is said to have been so marked naturally as to represent Apollo holding the lyre & surrounded by the nine Muses, each with her appropriate attribute. Among the Agates in the British Museum is one representing the head of Chaucer covered with the hood, as

in his well-known portrait, the resemblance of which is extraordinary; & yet the pebble is evidently in its original state,
not even polished, but merely broken in two. Among the gems at
Strawberry Hill was "a lusus naturae, a rare Egyptian pebble
representing Voltaire in his nightgown & cap, set in gold."[1]

The frequency of portraits of Alexander the Great, upon gems
of very different ages, arises from their having been worn as
amulets down to a late period.[2]

Chimerae, also called Grylli, from the Italian word signifying both a cricket & a caprice, are grotesque figures formed
of portions of various animals combined into the outline of a
monster which generally bears the shape of a bird or a horse.
Paintings of similar "capricci" were common among the ancients,
& went by the same name that they still bear in Italy. Their
first origin must have been those combinations of masks where the
engraver sought to produce effect by putting together the
strongest contrasts. A very favourite stone for these was the
red Jasper.[3]

Astrological Intagli. The signs of the Zodiac are often
seen upon gems of Roman work, either singly, combined, or as ad-
juncts to figures of deities, the representatives /180/ of
the different planets. They may be reasonably supposed to have
reference to the horoscope of the owner.[1]

Mithraic gems. The mottled green or dull yellow Jasper is
the favourite material for the extensive series of intagli connected with the worship of Mithras, the oriental equivalent for
Phoebus, whose place he took in the creeds of the second & third
centures. These works belong to the oriental doctrines so widely
diffused through the Roman world during the Middle Empire, &
which taught the exclusive worship of the sun as the fountain of
light & life. They are easily recognized by the designs they
represent: a lion (Leo is the "House of Sol") surrounded by
stars, with a bull's head between his jaws; or Mithras himself
attired as a young Persian & plunging his dagger into the throat
of a bull, above which appear the sun & moon & some signs of the
zodiac. In these compositions the lion is the type of the sun,
the bull of the earth; & the piercing of its throat with the
dagger signifies the penetration of the solar rays into the bosom
of the earth, by which all nature is nourished: which last is
expressed by the dog licking up the blood as it flows from the
wound.[2]

Serapis: To the same period belong the intagli representing
Serapis with the legend (in Greek) "there is but one God & he is
Serapis", "the one living God." A beautiful Sard of Roman Egyptian work represents Serapis seated on a throne with the triple-
headed animal described by Macrobius (B:VII) at his side; before
him stands Isis, /181/ holding the Sistrum & the wheat ears,
around the group is the legend, η κυρια Ιαις αγνη, "immaculate
is our Lady Isis." "The nature of Serapis & the Sun is one &
indivisible." Isis, so universally worshipped, is either the
earth or Nature as subjected to the sun. Hence, the body of the
goddess is covered with continuous rows of udders, to show that
the universe is maintained by the perpetual nourishment of the
earth or Nature.[1]

Gnostic gems. These are the sole glyptic monuments we possess of the last centuries of Roman dominion in the West. They
are almost without exception cut on inferior stones--on bad
Jaspers, dull Plasmas & sometimes on Loadstone or perhaps jade,
but rarely on Sards or Chalcedony. The earliest are those of

purely Egyptian types; a very frequent one being a serpent, erect, with a lion's head surrounded by seven rays, & usually accompanied by the inscription χνουφοσ or χνουιs. This is Chneph the good genius of the Egyptian religion, the type of life & of the sun. Sometimes we find this idea more fully developed in the form of a lion-headed man, bearing a wand entwined with a serpent, the head of which is directed towards his face. A common inscription round the figure is the Hebrew Greek CEMEC EIΛAM, "the eternal sun," alluding to the appearance of Christ "the sun of righteous-ness"; to whom also refers the legend Anathanabla, "thou art our Father," a corruption of the Hebrew "Lanu atha ab."[2]

The figure which has given its name to this entire class is the god Abraxas, or as the name　/182/　reads on the gems Abrasax. The letters of this word, when employed as Greek numerals, make up the number 365; the successive emanations of the Great Creative Principle, which embraces all within itself & hence is styled the Pleroma. The numerical value of Abrasax is equivalent to that of Mithras, the representative of Christ; hence the figure of this god is a combination of various attri-butes. He is therefore depicted with the head of a cock, sacred to the sun; or of a Lion; the type of Mithras, with a human body clad in a cuirass, whilst his legs are serpents, emblems of the good genius; in his hands he wields the scourge--the Egyptian badge of sovereignty; & a shield to denote his office of guardian to the faithful. On one side of him, or in the exergue is the word IAW, the Jehovah of the Hebrews, a malignant spirit, whose influence Abraxas was thus intreated to avert--at least this is Matter's explanation. --Most of the Gnostic gems appear to have been designed for amulets, or periapta, being too large for ring stones. --It was the Gnostic belief that the soul when released from the body, & on its way to be absorbed into the infinite of the Godhead, was obliged to pass through the regions of the planets, each of which was ruled by its own presiding genius, & only obtained permission to do this by means of a formula of prayer addressed to each genius, & preserved in Origen. These /183/　spirits were, Adonai, of the Sun; Iao, of the Moon; Elio, of Jupiter; Sabao, of Mars; Orai, of Venus; Astaphai, of Mercury; & Ildabaoth, of Saturn.

Curious that the Freemasons have retained many of the Gnostic emblems. It must be remembered that they claim descent from the Templars who were suppressed on the charge of Manicheism & on grounds similar to those that led to the extirpation of the Albigenses.[1]

Christian intagli are very rare.[2]
King maintains that Abraxas, Adonai, & Sabao are merely titles & synonyms of Iao[3] = the Greek name for Jehovah of the Jews--Iao was the Sun i.e. in the philosophic explanation of the old reli-gion, Bacchus.[4] (Bacchus is often called Sabazius from the cry Sabaoi raised by his votaries during the orgies, a word clearly the same as the Hebrew Sabi, glory.)[5]

Last come the Isiac symbols, or those used in the worship of Isis.[6] From the extreme rudeness of many of these intagli, there can be little doubt that the manufacture of them was carried on long after the date usually assigned for the total extinction of the glyptic art in Europe. The mechanical proceedings of this art are so simple, that the sole cause of its being discontinued must have been the cessation of demand. But we actually have many Byzantine Camei of the Middle Ages, & as the Manichean branch of the great Gnostic heresy flourished down to the XIIIth century under the names of Paulicians, Bulgarians, Albigenses, & Cathari, some of the barbarous   /184/   engravings in which the last trace of ancient art has disappeared may justly be referred to a period long subsequent to the fall of the Western empire.[1] --When the art had expired, the Gnostic amulets were ascribed to the ancient Hebrews, & thence called Jew's stones.[2]

For information on Antique gems, see Winkelmann's Catalogue of Stosch's Gems, & Lessing's Antiquarische Briefe.[3] For information as to the state of knowledge on the subject in the XVth century, see Camillo Leonardi's Speculum Lapidum.[4]

=

"Est deformitatis et corporis vitiorum satis bella materies ad jocandum", says Cicero. De Orat. II.22[5]

185

Greek the native language of Christianity

For some considerable time (it cannot but be an indefinable part of the three first centuries), the church of Rome, & most, if not all the churches of the West, were if we may so speak, Greek religious colonies. Their language was Greek, their organization Greek, their writers Greek, their Scriptures Greek; & many vestiges & traditions show that their ritual, their Liturgy was Greek. Through Greek the communication of the churches of Rome & of the West was constantly kept up with the East; & through Greek, every heresiarch, or his disciples, having found his way to Rome, propagated, with more or less success, his peculiar doctrines. Greek was the commercial language throughout the empire; by which the Jews, before the destruction of their city, already so widely disseminated through the world, & altogether engaged in commerce, carried on their affairs. The Greek Old Testament was read in the Synagogues of the foreign Jews. The churches, formed sometimes on the foundation, to a certain extent on the model, of the synagogues, would adhere for some time, no doubt, to their language. The Gospels & the Apostolic writings, so soon as they became part of the public worship, would be read, as the Septuagint was, in their original tongue. All the Christian writings which appeared in Rome & in the West are Greek or were originally Greek: the Epistles of Clement, the Shepherd of Hermas, the Clementine Recognitions and   /186/   Homilies; the works of Justin Martyr, down to Caius & Hippolytus, the author of the Refutation of all Heresies. The Octavius of Minicius Felix, & the Treatise of Novation on the Trinity, are the earliest known works of Latin Xtian literature which came from Rome. So was it too in Gaul: there the first Christians were settled, chiefly in the Greek cities, which owned Marseilles as their parent, & which retained the use of Greek as their vernacular tongue. Irenaeus wrote in Greek; the account of the Martyrs of Lyons & Vienne is in Greek. Vestiges of the old Greek ritual long survived not only in Rome, but also in some of the Gallic churches. The Kyrie eleison still lingers in the Latin service. The singular fact, related by the historian Sozomen, that there was no public preaching in Rome, here finds an explanation.[1]

Arius.   187
"It was now, apparently, that the Council (of Nicea) first heard the songs which Arius had written under the name of Thalia, for the sake of popularizing his speculations with the lower orders. The songs were set to tunes, or written in metres, which

had acquired a questionable reputation from their use in the
licentious verses of the heathen poet Sotades, ordinarily used in
the low revels or dances of Alexandria; & the grave Arius himself
is said, in moments of wild excitement, to have danced like an
Eastern dervish, whilst he sang these abstract statements in long
straggling lines, of which about twenty are preserved to us. To
us the chief surprise is that any enthusiasm should have been excited by sentences such as these:--'God was not always Father;
once he was not Father; afterwards he became Father.' But in
proportion to the attraction which they possessed for the partisans of Arius, was the dismay which they roused in the minds of
those by whom the expressions which Arius thus lightly set aside
were regarded as the watchwords of the Christian faith. The
Bishops, on hearing the song, raised their hands in horror, &
after the manner of Orientals, when wishing to express their disgust at blasphemous words, kept their ears fast closed, & their
eyes fast shut."
                    Stanley, Eastern Church[1]

                              188
The Divisions of the Eastern Church. "Look for a moment at the
countries included within the range of the Oriental churches.
What they lose in historical, they gain in geographical grandeur.
Their barbarism & their degradation have bound them to the local
peculiarities from which the more progressive Church of the West
has shaken itself free. It is a church, in fact, not of cities &
villages, but of mountains, & rivers, & caves, & dens of the
earth. The eye passes from height to height, & rests on the successive sanctuaries in which the religion of the East has in-
trenched itself, as within large natural fortresses, against its
oppressors--Athos in Turkey, Cinai in Arabia, Arat in Armenia,
the Cedars of Lebanon, the catacombs of Kieff, the cavern of
Megaspelion, the cliffs of Meteora. Or we see it advancing up &
down the streams, or clinging to the banks, of the mighty rivers
which form the highways & arteries of the wide plains of the
East. . . . . In this natural framework--with that strong
identity of religion & race so familiar to the east, so difficult
to be understood in the west,--may be traced three main groups
of Churches, which we will proceed to distinguish.[1]
     I. The first group contains those isolated fragments of an
earlier Christendom   /189/   which emerge here & there from the
midst of Mahometanism & heathenism in Africa & Further Asia. In
the strict language of ancient theology, they must be called
heretical sects. But they are, in fact, the Natural Churches of
their respective countries protesting against the supposed inno-
vations of the See of Constantinople, & holding with desperate
fidelity to forms & doctrines of earlier date. (a) The "Chal-
daean Xtians" called by their opponents "Nestorians" are the most
remote of these old Separatists. . . . . . living in the selected
fastnesses of Kurdistan, they represent the persecuted remnant of
the Ancient Church of Central Asia. . . . . Their sacred city of
Edessa is identical with . . . the traditional birth-place of
Abraham. . . . . . One colony alone remains. . . . The Xtians of
St. Thomas, as they are called, are still clustered round the
tomb of S. Thomas, whether the Apostle or the Nestorian merchant
of the same name who restored if he did not found the settlement."[1] (b) The Armenians. Their home is the mountain tract
that encircles Ararat. But though distinct from all surrounding
nations, they yet are scattered far & wide among them, extending

their episcopate, & carrying on at the same time the chief trade
of Asia. A race, a church of merchant princes . . . divided from
the Constantinopolitan Church /190/ by an almost impercepti-
ble difference, arising, it is said from the accidental absence
of the Armenian bishops from the Council of Chalcedon, whose decrees were therefore never understood, & therefore never received.[1] (c) The Church of Syria is the oldest of all the Gentile Churches. . . . . The purely national church of Syria is
represented by two very different communions. The first is the
Jacobite or Monophysite Church, of which the Patriarch resides at
Diarbekir. The patriarch, doubtless after the first illustrious
Bishop of Antioch, is always called Ignatius. The other communion of Syria is, in like manner, the representative both of a
sect & a nation. The Maronites, so called from their founder
Maro in the fifth century, comprise at once the only relics of
the old Monothelite heretics, & the whole Christian population of
Mount Lebanon, where the cedar grove & its neighbouring convent
of Kanobin form their chief sanctuary. But their main peculiarity
is this, that alone of all the Eastern Churches, they have retained the close communion with the Latin Church wh. they adopted
in the twelfth century through the Crusaders. Their allegiance
is given to Rome, & their learning has borne fruit in the west
through the labours /191/ of the two Assemans.[1] (d) In the
times of the early councils the Churches of Syria & Egypt were
usually opposed: now they are united under the common theological name of Monophysite. . . . But the Church of Egypt is much
more than the relic of an ancient sect. . . . Within its narrow
limits have now shrunk the learning & the lineage of Ancient
Egypt. The language of the Coptic Services understood neither by
priests nor people, is the language, although debased, of the ancient Pharaohs. . . . . But there is a daughter of the Coptic
Church still farther South, which is the extremest type of what
may be called Oriental Ultramontanism--the Church of Abyssinia.
. . . Whatever there is of Jewish or old Egyptian ritual preserved in the Coptic Church, is carried to excess in the Abyssinian. The likeness of the Sacred Ark, called the Ark of Zion,
is the centre of Abyssinian devotion. . . . There alone the
Jewish Sabbath is observed as well as the Christian Sunday. The
"Sinew that shrank", no less than the flesh of swine, hare, &
aquatic fowl, is still forbidden to be eaten. Dancing still
forms part of their ritual, as it did in the Jewish temple. The
wild shriek which goes up at Abyssinian funerals is the exact
counterpart of that which Herodotus heard in Ancient Egypt. The
polygamy /192/ of the Jewish Church still lingers here.[1]
II. The next group in Eastern Xtendom is that which gives its
name to the whole. It is, in fact, the Orthodox Imperial Church.
The "Greek Church" . . . includes the wide-spread race that
speaks the Greek language, from the desert of Sinai through all
the islands & coasts of the Archipelago, having its centre in
Greece & Constantinople. . . . . The Greek Church is thus the
only living representative of the Hellenic race, & speaks in the
only living voice which has come down to us from the Apostolic
age. But its main characteristic is its lineal descent from the
first Christian empire. "Romaic" not Hellenic is the name by
which (till quite recently) a Greek would have distinguished himself from the Mussulman population around him.[2] III. The third
group of the Eastern Ch. consists of those barbarian tribes of
the North, whose conversion by the Byzantine Church corresponds
with the conversion of the Teutonic tribes by the Latin Church.

(a)   The tribes on the Lower Danube:--The Sclavonic Bulgaria &
Servia on the South: the Latin or Romanic Wallachia & Moldavia
on the North. . . . . . . The   /193/   Church of Moldavia &
Wallachia is remarkable as being of Latin origin, yet Greek in
doctrine & ritual: a counterpoise to the two churches of Bohemia
& Poland, which being Sclavonic by race, are Latin by religion.
To these national communities should be added the extensive
colony of Greek Christians who under the name of "Raitzen" occupy
large districts in Hungary. (b) There remains the far wider
field of the Church of Russia.[1]

194
{A blank page.}

195

Naples
"On the 23d March 1821, the German army entered the city, took
possession of the forts, encamped in the squares, & placed guards
there as if they had been in the midst of enemies. There was no
demonstration of public rejoicing either as a form or by the popu-
lace; nor was there any appearance of sorrow, as those who mourned
over the present state of things feared to show their regret, or
because every other feeling was absorbed in that of wonder."[1]
. . . . "Canosa rejoiced at thus being relieved from all
restraints upon his tyranny, & laid down the following maxims by
which the government was to be guided:--To punish every crime, &
take vengeance for every offence committed during the long reign
of Ferdinand: to draw up a list of the late delinquencies, of
all committed during the five previous years, or during the ten
years of the reigns of the French Kings, or under the Constitution of Sicily, or during the Neapolitan republic; or at the time
of the first rebellion in the year 1793; to punish with death,
prison & exile, all opposed to an absolute government: the form
of a trial to be set aside, as too slow, & the punishments to be
summarily executed: & left to the arbitrement of the judge; the
treaty of Casalanza to be annulled as well as all previous com-
pacts, whether in the   /196/   form of treaties or pardons; &
to seize this opportunity to deliver the Kingdom from the enemies
of thrones."[1]
    "Generals Rossaroll & Pepe were condemned to death without
trial, simply by a proclamation of the police; a large reward
was promised for the arrest of the most noted of the revolutionary
leaders at Monteforte. . . . Several Juntas were formed, composed
of the vehement partisans of absolutism, called Juntas of Scru-
tiny, because intended to scrutinize the lives of all the officials of the state, & of the highest & most influential citizens.
The judges & their verdicts struck all with terror." Not a day
passed without the bell of justice being heard, & the public being invited to solemn prayers; a signal, & a melancholy act of
solemn devotion, used with us to denote that a sufferer is about
to be led out to execution. Those accused of bearing arms, or
who concealed any badge of a society, were tried by courts martial. In the midst of these scenes the Prince of Canosa, minister of police, arrived in the city: he had resolved before any
edicts or reports could acquaint the people with his presence to
announce himself, & therefore ordered the revival of an atrocious
exhibition long forgotten by the old & unknown to the young,
called the Frusta.[2] At midday, in the populous Via di Toledo, a
large   /197/   detachment of German soldiers were seen, drawn up

in military array; next to them stood the assistant of the
executioner, who at intervals blew a trumpet, & a little behind
him more Germans, & several officers of police, who surrounded a
man naked from the waist upwards, his feet bare, his wrists
tightly bound, & with all the badges of the Carbonari hung round
his neck; he wore a tri-coloured cap, on which was inscribed in
large letters "Carbonaro." This unhappy man was mounted on an
ass, & followed by the executioner who at every blast of the
trumpet scourged his shoulders with a whip made of ropes & nails,
until his flesh was stained with his blood, & his agony was shown
by his pallor, while his head sank upon his breast. The mob followed this procession in silent horror.[1] . . . . . If any asked
the meaning of the punishment, they were told the person flogged
was a Carbonaro, a gentleman from the provinces (& a gentleman he
appeared to be both in face & person) who after being scourged,
was to suffer the penalty of the galleys for fifteen years; &
this not by the sentence of a magistrate, but by the order of the
Prince of Canosa, minister of Police, who had just arrived in the
city. On the following two days, two more scourgings were wit-
nessed, as terrible   /198/   as the first, though the Austrian
soldiers did not attend, either from horror or shame at the
scene. No other took place in Metropolis."[1]

199
Synopsis of Languages   } Smith's Gibbon[1]
                              1854
=
Aryan Class (Inflected)[2]

Indian Family		Slavic Family	
Sanscrit	Zend	Lithuanian	
Bengalee	Pehlvi	Old Slavian[3]	Slavakish
Malabar	Modern	Russian	Servian
(this side	Persian	Polish	Bulgarian
the Ganges)		Bohemian	Croatian
		Wendish	

Celtic Family

Gaelic	Iberian	Irish	Welsh	Breton
	or			
	Euscarra[4]			

=
Semitic Class. (Inflected)

Hebrew	Aramaic	Arabic.	Ethiopic.
	Chaldaic		
	Syriac		

? Coptic: Sabidic, Rashmudian[5]
=
Tartar Class (agglutinative)

Tungusian	Finnish.	Magyar.	Turkish.	Mongholic.
Mandschou	Lappish			
	Esthonian			
	Lettish (Now know to be Indo-European)			

Malayan Class (agglutinative)
=
Monosyllabic Class
Chinese, Anamish, Laos, Burmese

                    Isolated Languages
   Basque   Kaukasian   Japanese
   Albanian*   Tibetian,* Armenian,† Georgian
        *Now known to be Aryan   *Turanian   †Indo-Europ.[6]

                           200
        The Indo-European Languages. (Bopp) Clark.
                            -

I Indic or
Sanskrit.[1]   The heroic poems in Sanskrit, the Mahabharata &
Ramayana, supposed by Wilson to date 300 B.C.: the Laws of Manu
600 B.C: the prose Brahmanas or commentaries on the Vedas, 800
B.C: the Vedas, 1300 B.C.[2]
     The related Indian languages are 1. The Prakrit or popular
dialects assigned to subordinate characters in Hindoo dramas.
2. The Pali, which was conveyed by banished Buddhists to Ceylon.
It became, like Sanskrit, from which it differed principally in
the loss of grammatical forms, a learned language. It contains
theological works on the Buddhist religion as early as the 5th
century A.C.[3] 3. The Kawi which was preserved in the islands of
Java & Bali as a literary & poetic language. Its grammatical
forms became mutilated, very much like those of the Pali, by contact with a strange people. 4. The Gypsy language: this is the
old Sanskrit very much corrupted & mixed with foreign elements.[4]
     The modern languages of India, reckoned by Pott[5] as 24 in
number, bear the relation of daughters to Sanskrit, not that of
sisters like the 4 just mentioned. The principal is Hindostanee.[6]

                      II. Iranic
So-called from Iran = Aryan, applied to the regions between the
Hindoo Koosh & the Persian gulf.

                           201
1. Zend. Language of the Zend-Avesta. Its elucidation has been
assisted by the discovery of the arrow-headed inscriptions belonging to the time of the Achemenidae. The age of Darius, to whom
some of these inscriptions owe their existence, lends some help
in conjecturing the age of the Zend-Avesta. The latter appears
to have the older grammatical forms, hence the language of the
Zend-Avesta is referred to before 500 B.C.[1] Pott is inclined to
fix its locality in Bactria.[2]
2. The next Iranian language is that of the arrow-headed inscriptions, belonging to the reign of the Achemenidae--the fifth century B.C.--& to the land of Media
3. The Modern Persian
4. The Pashtoo, in Afghanistan, the Beloochee spoken at the mouth
of the Indus, & the Parsee by the Parsees in Guzerat & elsewhere.
These lie to the East of Iran.[3]
5. To the West of Iran are the language of the Koords; the
Ossetic, spoken by a small mountain tribe on the Caucasus; & the
Armenian.[4]

                   III. Letto-Slavic
1. The Lettic includes the Lettish, the Lithuanian, & the Old
Prussian.
     The Lithuanian is now spoken only by a small population in
the northeast of Prussia & in the neighbouring districts of
Russia. It has great philological value on account of its almost
perfect preservation of some of the original grammatical forms.

The Old Prussian bore   /202/   a very close resemblance to it.
The Lettish is spoken in Kurland & Livonia, but has been much corrupted by the influence of other languages.[1]

2.   The Second Slavic branch includes a large number of languages
stretching from the Adriatic to the Gulf of Finland, & from the
coast of the North Sea to the Ural mountains; but principally
condensed in Russia & Austria. History cannot trace the Slavs
back to Asia, but it finds them at an early period in the extreme
East of Europe. They are believed to have been the Bondivoi mentioned by Herodotus as at the northern shore of the Caspian in
the fifth cent. B.C. They appear in Dacia n.w. of the Black Sea
in collision with the Romans under Trajan. We find the evidence
of their presence later in Pannonia, for Buda is one of the names
of Pesth, the capital of Hungary. The Slavonians began to attain
political consolidation after the death of Attila who had held
them in subjection. The Bohemian nation appears as early as 650;
the Bulgarian about the same time, but in greater power under
Boris in 850; the Moravian under Rastislaw & Swatoplak during the
9th century; the Polish in the 7th; the Russian under Rurik in
862; & the Servian in the eleventh century. The literature of
the Slavonians is modern; the earliest remains go no farther back
than the 9th century. Methodius & Cyrillus, Christian mission-
aries from Constan-   /203/   tinople translated the Gospels into
the language of the people among whom they dwelt, probably Bulgarians, making an alphabet founded on the Greek which is still
used in Servia & Russia. The language is therefore sometimes
called Old Bulgarian as well as Old Slavic & Church Slavic. The
last name is used in consequence of the language being still employed in the services of the Greek Church.
    No less than <u>fifteen</u> languages are counted as belonging to
this class. Those which contain the most important literature
are--1. the Bohemian, which begins with national poems of the
13th century. 2. The Polish, beginning with the Psalter of
Florian 13th or 14th century; 3. the Russian.[1]

IV. Graeco-Italic

    The Hellenic & Italic races seem to have parted company in
the neighbourhood of the Danube & to have taken a southerly direction previously to the approach of the Slavic race.[2]
1 The <u>Greek</u>. Dialects, AEolic, Doric, Ionic.
    The oldest Ionic is seen in the poems of Homer & Hesiod.
Next is the New Ionic of Herodotus. But its richest productions
are in the Attic.
    The AEolic was spoken chiefly in Asia Minor, Boeotia &
Thessaly, & includes Alceus, Sappho & Corinna--The Doric was
spoken chiefly in the north of Greece, in the Peloponnese, Crete
& Sicily. Principal representatives Pindar & Theocritus.[3]

    2 The Italic branch. Latin was not the only language
spoken by the Indo-European people who   /204/   entered the
Peninsula from the north. Their speech was marked by varieties
as distinct as the Greek dialects.[1] Italy seems to have been in-
vaded in succession by distinct races, some of them perhaps not
Indo-European. But several of the tribes of which remains have
been preserved evidently belong to the same family as the Latin.
In the extreme S.E. of the country inscriptions have been discovered composed in a language which for want of a better name
has been called <u>Iapygian</u>. It seems at one time to have prevailed

more or less throughout Apulia & Calabria. The language has not
been sufficiently deciphered to determine the ethnological position of the tribe who spoke it. Clearer evidence is supplied
about the <u>Latin</u> & <u>Umbrian</u> branches. The latter, including the
Marsians & Samnites, comprised a considerable population. The
dialects among them have a close resemblance to one another but
in many points they form a contrast to the Latin. Distinctions
appear which are also found in other classes of the Indo-European
languages. Thus, where the Latins use q, the Samnite & Umbrian
used p, sounds wh. also distinguish the Ionic from the Attic, &
the Celtic of Bretagne & Wales from the Gaelic & Irish. The Latin
has on the whole, some such relation to the Umbro-Samnite as the
Ionic to the Doric; while the Oscan, Umbrian & other Italic dialects differ as the Doric of Sicily from that of Sparta.[2]

205
V. Celtic

This name appears, variously modified, in application to the
Galatians of Asia Minor, the Gauls (Galli) of N. Italy & France,
the Celt-Iberi of Spain, & the Gael of Scotland. The earliest
notices of the people represent them in the S.W. of Europe & in
the British Isles, but we have no historical evidence to connect
them with their original abode in Asia. The settlement in Asia
Minor was apparently a migration eastward from Europe. Bohemia
owes its name to them, for the Boii were one of their tribes.
The Celtic languages are now spoken in Ireland, the Isle of Man,
the Highlands of Scotland, Wales & Bretagne. Some remains are
also preserved of the language of Cornwall & of the ancient
Gauls.[1]

VI. Teutonic

This includes three principal branches, the Gothic, the Low
German, & the Scandinavian. It is distinguished from the Germanic which comprises the High German language.[2]
1. <u>Gothic</u> is represented by the Meso-Gothic translation of the
Scriptures by Ulfilas 360-380.[3]
2. <u>Low German</u>. This includes: α. the old Saxon, spoken on the
continent, & supplying a valuable poem of the 9th century, called
the Heljand (Saviour): β. the Frisian, spoken by a numerous people who occupied the coasts of the North Sea /206/   from
Flanders to Jutland in the 13th century. It contains some remains of the 13th & 14th centuries which strikingly resemble the
language of the Angles; γ. the Dutch. δ. the Flemish; & ε. the
Anglo-Saxon. This last is the most important of the Low German
branch, both in regard to the compass of its literature. The
poem of Beowulf exhibits the ante-Christian ideas of the 6th &
7th centuries, & contains many reminiscences brought over from
the continent, although in its present form it is of a much later
date & greatly Christianised.[1]
3. The <u>Scandinavian</u> branch includes α. The Icelandic, which pos-
sesses an extensive & valuable literature, some of it dating as
far back as the 9th century. β. the Swedish, which, especially
in the earliest periods, nearly resembles the Icelandic. Its
literary remains begin about the 10th century. γ. The Danish,
whose literature begins the latter part of the 12th c.[2]

VII. Germanic

The High German forms the last class. Its literary remains date
from the 9th century. As they thus begin 500 years later than

the Gothic translation they naturally exhibit a still greater
falling off in the grammatical forms.[3]

207
The Semitic Family. (M. Müller)

Divided into three Branches, the <u>Aramaic</u>, the <u>Hebraic</u>, & the
<u>Arabic</u>.[1]

    1. The Aramaic occupies the north, including Syria, Meso-
potamia, & part of the ancient Kingdoms of Babylonia & Assyria.
It is known to us chiefly in two dialects, the <u>Syriac</u> & <u>Chaldee</u>.
The former has been preserved to us in a translation of the Bible
(the Peshito = simple) ascribed to the second century, & in the
rich Xtian literature dating from the fourth. The Old Testament
was translated from Hebrew, the New Testament from Greek, about
200. It is still spoken, corruptly by the Nestorians of Kurdistan & by some Christian tribes in Mesopotamia.[2]

    The <u>Chaldee</u> is the name given to the language adopted by the
Jews during the Babylonian captivity. The book of Ezra contains
fragments in Chaldee, contemporaneous with the cuneiform inscriptions of Darius & Xerxes. The so-called Targums {Arabic, tarjam,
to explain}, or translations & paraphrases of the O.T. written
during the centuries immediately after the Xtian era (the most
ancient are those of Onkelos & Jonathan in the 2d century) give
us another specimen of the Aramaic, or the language of Babylonia
as transplanted to Palestine. This Aramaic was the language
spoken by Christ. After the destruction of Jerusalem, the literature of the Jews continued to be written in this dialect.[3] The
Talmud (instruction) of Jerusalem was finished /208/   towards
the end of the 4th, that of Babylon towards the end of the 5th
century. They exhibit the Aramean as spoken by the educated Jews
settled in these two localities, though greatly spoiled by an admixture of strange elements. The <u>Masora</u> & the traditional commentary of the O.T. was written in this dialect in the tenth century. Soon after the Jews adopted Arabic as their literary
language, & retained it to the 13th century. They then returned
to a kind of modernized Hebrew which they still continue to em-
ploy for learned discussions.[1]

    II. The second branch of the Semitic family is the <u>Hebraic</u>,
chiefly represented by the ancient language of Palestine, where
Hebrew was spoken & written from the days of Moses to the times
of the Maccabees. The ancient language of Phoenicia, to judge
from inscriptions, was most closely allied to Hebrew, & the language of the Carthaginians too must be referred to the same
branch. Hebrew was first encroached upon by Aramaic dialects,
through the political ascendancy of Babylon, & still more of
Syria; & was at last swept away by Arabic which since the conquest
of Syria & Palestine in 636, has monopolized nearly the whole area
formerly occupied by the two elder branches, Hebraic & Aramaic.[2]

    III. The Arabic branch sprang from the Arabian peninsula
where it is still spoken by a compact mass of aboriginal inhabi-
/209/   tants. Its most ancient documents are the <u>Himyaritic</u> inscriptions. In very early times this Arabic branch was transplanted to Africa where, south of Egypt & Nubia, an ancient
Semitic dialect has maintained itself to this day. This is the
Ghez, Ethiopic or Abyssinian.[1] Though no longer spoken in its
purity by the people of Habesh, it is still preserved in their
sacred writings, translations of the Bible & similar works which
date from the 3d & 4th centuries. The modern language of

Abyssinia is called <u>Amharic</u>.[2] [i.e. Ebkili--v. Renan][3]

_____

    "What applies to Sanscrit & the Aryan family applies to the
whole realm of speech. Every language, without a single exception, that has yet been cast into the crucible of comparative
grammar, has been found to contain these two substantial elements,
<u>predicative & demonstrative roots</u>."[4]
    As all languages, so far as we can judge at present, can be
reduced in the end to roots, predicative & demonstrative, it is
clear that, according to the manner in which roots are put together, we may expect to find three kinds of languages, or three
stages in the gradual formation of speech
    1. Roots may be used as words, each root preserving its
full independence.
    2. Two roots may be joined together to form words, & in
these compounds one root may   /210/   lose its independence.[1]
    3. Two roots may be joined together to form words, & in
these compounds both roots may lose their independence.
    These are the 1. Radical Stage, represented by ancient
Chinese. 2. The Terminational or agglutinative stage represented by the Turanian languages & 3. the Inflectional stage,
represented by the Aryan & Semitic languages. These last have
been called organic or amalgamating. The first stage excludes
phonetic corruption altogether. The second stage excludes corruption in the principal root & in the termination.[2]
    By far the largest number of languages belong to the second
or terminational stage. The whole of what is called the Turanian
family consists of such languages. The name Turanian is used in
opposition to Aryan, (<u>toros</u> means swift horseman), & is applied
to the nomadic races of Asia as opposed to the agricultural or
Aryan races.[3]

                    The Turanian Family
consists of two great divisions, the <u>Northern</u> & the <u>Southern</u>.
    The northern is sometimes called the Ural-Altaic or Ugro-
Tataric, & it is divided into five sections, viz.

                    211
1. The Tungusic. 2. Mongolic. 3. Turkic. 4. Finnic. 5.
Samoyedic.
    The Southern, which occupies the South of Asia, is divided
into four classes, viz.
    1. the Tamulic, or the languages of the Dekhan: 2. the
Bhotya, or the dialects of Tibet & Bhotan. 3. the Taic, or the
dialects of Siam, 4. the Malaic, or the Malay & Polynesian dialects.
    The most characteristic feature of the Turanian languages
is what has been called agglutination, or "gluing together."
This means not only that, in their grammar, pronouns are <u>glued</u>
to the verbs in order to form the conjugation, or prepositions to
substantives in order to form declension. <u>That</u> would not be a
distinguishing characteristic of the Turanian or nomad languages;
for in Hebrew as well as in Sanscrit, conjugation & declension
were originally formed on the same principle. What distinguishes
the Turanian languages is, that in them the conjugation & declension can still be taken to pieces; & although the terminations have by no means always retained their significative power
as independent words, they are felt as modificatory syllables, &
as distinct from the roots to which they are appended.[1]

212   Transmutation of Consonants   (Grimm's Law.)[1]   213

§1. Sanskrit, Greek, Latin §2. Gothic, Anglo-Saxon, English §3. Old High German

§1	Labial (B, P, F. Ph)	Guttural (G, K, Ch)	Dental (D, T, Th)
	§B __ P _____ F. Ph_____	G _____ K _____ Ch_____	D _____ T ____ Th duhitar?
	pitri_____1 Bhar	1 γονυ 1 καλαμος 1 χορτος	1 Dasan__twam___ θυγατηρ__
	pater_____ φερω	genu___calamus hortus_	decem_____
	πατῆρ 2 φυλλον	2 γιγνωσκειν 2 cannabis ___	δεκα
	__folium_	noscere_____	2 duco

§2			
	§P __ F _____ B_____	K _____ H(Ch)	G_____ T ____ Th ___ D
	fadar____ 1 baira, bear	1 knui,knee___	gards_ 1 taihun thu___dauhtar
	2 blad__	2 kunnan_____	ten __ ____(dag)
	(blade?)__	know_____	2 tuila_ _____

§3			
	§Ph__ F _____ P_____	Ch_____ H(g) K_____	Z(th)__ D ___ T
	fatar____ 1 piru_	1 chniu_1 Halm Karts_	1 zehan__du___tohtar
	2 plat_	2chunan__2 Hanf guirdan_	2 ziuhn__ ___(tochter)
		(cingere)_	(ziehen)_ ___(tag)

The law is: a Media of each of the three organs becomes a tenuis; a tenuis becomes an aspirata; an aspirata becomes a media &c.

Grimm's System. The consonantismus presents three trilogies; its sounds being

I.   Spirantes: H, S, J, V.
II. Liquidae: L, M, N, R
III. Mutae: B, D, G. (Medial)
     P, T, K (tenues)
     Ph, Th, Ch (aspirates)

V. p. 280

214
Gipseys

Working in iron is the most usual occupation of the Gipseys.
In Spain very few follow any regular business; but among these
few some are smiths: in Hungary this trade is so common among
them, that there is a proverb "So many Gipseys, so many smiths."
The same might be said of those in Translyvania, Wallachia, Moldavia, & all Turkey in Europe. There is an old record of a Hungarian King Uladislaus, in the year 1496, wherein it is ordered,
that every officer & subject of whatsoever rank or condition, do
allow to Thos. Polgar, leader of five-and-twenty tents of wandering Gipseys, free residence everywhere, & on no account to molest
him & his people; because they had prepared musket bullets, &
other military stores, for the Bishop Sigismund, at Fünfkirchen.
Another instance occurred in the year 1565, when Mustapha, Turkish
regent of Bosnia, besieged Crupa; the Turks having expended their
powder & cannon balls, Gipseys were employed to make the latter,
part of iron, the rest of stone, cased with lead. (Grellman).[1]

Their Cheiromancy. During the seventeenth & beginning of
the 18th centuries the Gipseys were considered as only a super-
numerary party; there being men of great learning, who not only
read lectures in college on the divine art of cheiromancy, but
wrote many books, vilifying these /215/ people & endeavouring
to spoil their market by exposing their ignorance.[1]

The more common Gipsey occupations wherein the men & women
take an equal share are--in Spain, keeping inns; in Hungary &
Turkey principally music; & goldwashing in Transylvania, the
Banat, Moldavia & Wallachia. Formerly the Gipseys were concerned
in smuggling.[2] (They are also extensive horse dealers).[3]

Their excessive fondness for their children has been made
use of to recover debts. When, as is frequently the case in
Hungary & Transylvania, they are in debt, the creditor seizes a
child, & by that means obtains a settlement of his demand.[4]

When the Gipseys first arrived in Europe they had leaders
and chiefs, to conduct the various tribes in their migrations.
Krantz & Munster mention counts & knights; Crusius cites a duke
Michael; Muratori, a Duke Andreas; Aventinus {Annalibus Briorum}[5]
records a King Zindelo; not to speak of inscriptions or monuments
erected in different places to the memories of Duke Panuel, &
Count Johannes; & a noble Knight Petrus in the 15th century.[6]

About the end of the 15th century their persecution commenced in Spain. King Ferdinand, who esteemed it a good work to
expatriate useful & profitable subjects--Jews & even Moorish
families--could /216/ much less have any scruple in laying
hands on the Gipseys.[1] The edict for their extermination was
published in the year 1492. But, instead of passing the bound-
aries, they slunk into hiding-places, & shortly after appeared
everywhere in as great numbers as before. The Emperor Charles V.
persecuted them afresh, as did Philip II. also. In France,
Francis I. passed an edict for their expulsion & at the assembly
of the States of Orleans in 1561, all governors of cities received
orders to drive them away with fire & sword. Nevertheless, in
1612 they had collected again & increased to such a degree that a
new order came out for their extermination.

In Italy, their situation has been equally precarious. In
1572 they were driven from Milan & Parma, & somewhat earlier from
the Venetian territory.

The greatest number of sentences of exile have been issued
against them in Germany--as well imperial decrees as those of particular princes.[2] The beginning was made under Maximilian I. in

1500 at the Augsburg diet "there being authentic evidence of
their being spies, betraying the Xtians to the Turks."[3]
    First appearance in Europe. Mention is made of them in Ger-
many so early as   /217/   1417, when they appeared in the vicinity of the North Sea: 1418, in Switzerland & the Grisons: 1422,
in Italy: 17 August 1427, straggling about Paris.[1] (Pasquier,
Recherches de la France)[2]
    The Bologna chronicle ascertains the time of their appearance
in Italy. The horde there mentioned, arrived in that city July,
1422, & consisted of about a hundred men, whose leader's name was
Andreas. They travelled from Bologna to Forli, intending to proceed to pay the Pope a visit at Rome.
    Hungary is certainly the country whence they came into Ger-
many. Not only the time confirms this, as we find them in Hungary in 1417, but Aventin says Hungary was one of the countries
he supposed them to come from. Their original place of rendezvous
was most probably Turkey.[3]
    One story (said to be told by the Gypseys themselves) was
that their wandering from Egypt was inflicted on them as a punishment for the sin of their ancestors in refusing an asylum to the
Infant Jesus when carried by his mother & Joseph to Egypt.[4]
    Others asserted that the King of Hungary had seized their
country, & imposed on them this penance of wandering.[5] Enough to
say, they chose to be considered as pilgrims & this profession
met with the more ready belief, as it coincided with the infatua-
tion of the times.[6] Crusius, Wurstisen & /218/ Guler, mention papal permissions which these people acquired, for wandering
unmolested, through all Christian countries, so long as the time
of their pilgrimage lasted.[1]
    Quiñones 1632 observes: "The Moors with whom they hold cor-
respondence let them go & come without any obstacle: an instance
of this was seen in the year 1627, when two galleys from Spain
were carrying assistance to Mamora, which was then besieged by
the Moors. These galleys struck on a shoal, when the Moors seized
all the people on board, making captives of the Christians &
setting at liberty all the Moors who were chained to the oar; as
for the Gypsy galley-slaves whom they found amongst these last,
they did not make them slaves, but received them as people friendly to them, & at their devotions which matter was public &
notorious."[2]
    The Gypsies designate water by the Sanscrit name "Pani," a
word brought by the race from the sunny Ind, & esteemed so holy
that they have never presumed to modify it. Borrow, I. 112.
    Names of the Gypsies. Zincalo = the black men (of Sind or
Ind!), Romano = the husbands: & Chal = the Indians, are the
three words by which the Gypsies themselves distinguish their
race in general.[3]

                         219
The Names of the Gypsies. Borrow says, among themselves, they
have three words to distinguish themselves & their race in
general: Zincalo, Romano, & Chal. They likewise call themselves
"Cales" by which appellation indeed they are tolerably well known
by the Spaniards, & which is merely the plural termination of the
compound word Zincalo, & signifies "the black men."[1]
    In Germany, says Pott, the common people call them Tatars &
Saracens; & he conjectures that the English word "tatter" may have
come from their ragged clothing. Thinks the Coolies a robber
tribe in India who had a Polygar or chief, are not to come into

the question, although a gypsey chief in Hungary was named
Polgar: but this name probably was no more than the Hungarian
word for <u>Bürger</u>. In Turkey they are called Färäwni, i.e. Pharaoh's
sons--& formerly in Hungary, Pharaoh Nepek = Pharaoh's people. In
Spain they have been called New Castilians, <u>Gitáno</u> being regarded
as a term of infamy: & in the official papers of Maria Theresa
they are called UjMagyar, new Magyars.[2]

 <u>Sinde</u>. Not far from Hanau Difenbach saw two gypsey women
who called themselves "Arme Schwarze," & explained that Sinti
(or Sindh) meant "people, their people."[3] "They spoke their own
language /220/ sometimes pure, sometimes mixed with German according as they supposed themselves to be understood."[1]

 "Chai," says Borrow, "is a modification of the word Chal,
which by the Gitanos of Estremadura is applied to Egypt & in many
parts of Spain is equivalent to Heaven . . . Thus, Chai may mean,
The Men of Egypt, or The Sons of Heaven."[2]

 "In the English dialect Chab; e.g Rommany Chab, whence the
cant expression, Rum Chap."[3]

 Rommany is of Sanscrit origin & signifies, the Husbands.
(Pott admits that this is doubtful, & that it may merely mean
<u>man</u>.)[4]

 "When the Gypsies wish to praise the proficiency of any individual in their tongue, they are in the habit of saying that,
'He understands the seven jargons.'"[5]

 Costume: silver rings in the ears. Kerchief on the head.
Loose garment.[6]

 Origin: The supposition that Timour's invasion of Hindostan
caused the emigration of a multitude of Hindoos i.e. gypsies, is
opposed by the fact that in <u>1422</u> the Bishop of Forli spoke of
them as "gentes non multum morigeratae, Sed quasi bruta animalia
et furentes."[7] This was only 16 years after the invasion of
Hindostan. Also, less weightily, by a story of their existence
in great numbers at Samarcand & a plan

221

Miraculous Bushes.
"Nul, peut-être, ne représentait aussi bien le vieux temps et le
principe païen, que ce borgne, Moslim, fils d'Ocba. En lui il n'y
avait pas même l'ombre de la foi mahométane. . . . Cependant . . .
il n'en croyait que plus fermement aux préjugés superstitieux du
paganisme, aux songes prophétiques, aux mystérieuses paroles qui
sortaient des <u>gharcads</u>, espèces de ronces épineuses qui, pendant
le paganisme et dans certaines contrées de l'Arabie, passaient
pour des oracles." Dozy. 1. 98[1]

(<u>Gypsies</u> <u>contd</u>.) of Timour's to get rid of them prior to that invasion.[2]--Their native place, say the learned, was Moultan.[3]

 <u>Soldiers</u>. There were a number of Chingarri or Hungarian
gypsies in Napoleon's army when he entered Spain. They were
recognized with enthusiasm by their Spanish brethren.[4]

 <u>Religion</u>. The gypsies are believers in metempsychosis--
their sole article of faith.[5]

 Borrow knew a Zingarro or Turkish gypsy who was a great
vendor of precious stones & poisons, travelling everywhere.[6]

 Martin del Rio, in his "tractatus de Magia" says, "When, in
the year 1584 I was marching in Spain with the regiment, a multitude of these wretches (Gypsies) were infesting the fields.[7] . .
. . . . . . at this time they had a Count, a fellow who spoke the
Castilian see p. 258[8]

222

Worship of Apollo
"We may select. . . . as proofs of the influence of this worship
on political concerns, the armistice connected with the festivals
of Apollo, the truce observed in the sacred places & roads, the
soothing influence of the purifications for homicide, together
with the idea of the punishing & avenging god, & the great influence of the Oracles in the regulations of public affairs. It
has, moreover, been frequently remarked how by its sanctity, by
the dignified & severe character of its music, by all its symbols
& rites, the worship endeavoured to lull the minds of individuals
into a state of composure & security, consistently, however, with
an occasional elevation to a state of ecstatic delight."

Müller's Dorians 1 369[1]

μίμνει δὲ μίμνοντος ἐν θρόνῳ Διὸς

παθεῖν τὸν ἔρξαντα.

Agam. 1494[2]

χερῶν ἄκρους κτένας

Agam. AEgisthus' speech[3]

(Exiles)

οἶδ' ἐγὼ φεύγοντας ἄνδρας ἐλπίδας σιτουμένους.[4]

οὓς μὲν γάρ τις ἔπεμψεν

οἶδεν· ἀντὶ δὲ φωτῶν

τεύχη καὶ σποδὸς εἰς ἑκάστου δόμους ἀφικνεῖται.[5]

223

οὔτοι σ' Ἀπόλλων οὐδ' Ἀθηναίας σθένος

ῥύσαιτ' ἂν ὥστε μὴ οὐ παρημελημένον

ἔρρειν, τὸ χαίρειν μὴ μαθόνθ' ὅπου φρενῶν

ἀναίματον βόσκημα, δαιμόνων σκιάν

Eumen. 289[1]

χρόνος καθαιρεῖ πάντα γηράσκων ὁμοῦ.

Ibid. 274[2]

Ἴσον φέρει νύξ - τοῖς δὲ τολμῶσιν πλέον

Euripides Phonissae[3]

=

"δύναμιν οὐ σέβουσα πλούτου παράσημον αἴνῳ--"

not honouring the power of wealth falsely stamped with praise.

Agamemnon.[4]

οὐκ ἄλλων πάρα

μαθοῦσ', ἐμαυτῆς δύσφορον λέξω βίον

Agam. 832.[5]

"τελεσσίφρων μῆνις"

684[6]

"Her soft eyes yet shot arrows, making wounds of compassion."
Vid Ag. 222

=

Δυσέρωτες δὴ φαινόμεθ' ὄντες.

τοῦδ', ὅτι τοῦτο στίλβει κατὰ γῆν,

Δι' ἀπειροσύνην ἄλλου βιότου,

κοὐκ ἀπόδειξιν τῶν ὑπὸ γαίας.   Eurip. Hipp. 193[7]

οὐδείς μ' ἀρέσκει νυκτὶ θαυμαστὸς θεῶν.
                                       Hipp.[8]

224

<u>Salutations</u>. The Thibetans put out their tongues & scratch their right ear.

Certain savages throw themselves on their backs, as small dogs do.[1]

A chief who met Petherick spat in his face. Petherick had presence of mind enough to spit in return. It was exactly "the thing." Petherick was at once pronounced to be "a great chief."[2]

The Tongans & many other Polynesians always sit down when speaking to a superior.[3]

At Vatavulu it is respectful to turn one's back on a superior, especially in addressing him.[4]

Some of the Esquimaux pull noses as a token of respect.[5]

Kissing was entirely unknown to the Tahitians, the New Zealanders, the Papouans, & the Aborigines of Australia, nor was it in use among the Esquimaux.[6]

In the Navigation Isles the word <u>hongi</u> means to salute by pressing noses.[7]

225
Contents of Comte's Politique Positive[1]
Vol. I

Discours préliminaire pp. 1 321
Introduction Fondamentale à la fois scientifique et logique.
Appréciation générale de cette Introduction.
Introduction indirecte, essentiellement analytique, ou Cosmologie.
Introduction directe, naturellement synthétique, ou Biologie
Appendice. Discours funèbre sur Blainville.
=
Vol. II

c. 1. Théorie générale de la religion, ou théorie positive de l'unité humaine
2. Appréciation sociologique du problème humain; d'où théorie positive de la propriété matérielle.
3. Théorie positive de la famille humaine
4. Théorie positive du langage humain
5. Théorie positive de l'organisme social
6. Théorie positive de l'Existence sociale systématisée par le sacerdoce.
7. Théorie positive des limites générales de variation propre à l'ordre humain.
Vol. III

c. 1. Théorie positive de l'évolution humaine, ou lois générales du mouvement intellectuel et social.
2. Théorie positive de l'âge fétichique, ou appréciation générale du régime spontané de l'humanité.
3. Théorie positive de l'état Théocratique; ou appréciation générale du polythéisme conservateur.

226
Vol. III. continued

c. 4. Théorie positive de l'élaboration grecque, ou appréciation

générale du polythéisme intellectuel.
    5. Théorie positive de l'incorporation romaine, ou apprécia-
tion générale du polythéisme social.
    6. Théorie positive de la transition catholic-féodale, ou
appréciation générale du monothéisme défensif.
    7. Théorie positive de la révolution occidentale, ou apprécia-
tion générale du double mouvement moderne.

Tableau synthétique de l'avenir humain
c. 1 Théorie fondamentale du Grand-Etre; d'où tableau simultané
de la religion universelle et de l'existence normale.
    2 Tableau générale de l'existence affective, ou systématisa-
tion finale du culte positif.
    3 Tableau général de l'existence théorique, ou systématisation
finale du dogme positif.
    4 Tableau général de l'existence active, ou systématisation
finale du régime positif.
    5 Appréciation systématique du présent, d'après la combinai-
son de l'avenir avec le passé; d'où tableau général de la transition extrème.
        Conclusion général du Tome Quatrième
        Conclusion totale du Système de politique positive
        Invocation finale
        Appendice. Bibliothèque positiviste au dix-neuvième siècle.

227
    "Chacun de nous, sans doute, subit directement toutes les
fatalités extérieures, qui ne peuvent atteindre l'espèce qu'en
affectant les individus. Néanmoins, leur principale pression ne
s'applique personnellement que d'une manière indirecte, par
l'entremise de l'humanité. C'est surtout à travers l'ordre social
que chaque homme supporte le joug de l'ordre matériel et de
l'ordre vital, dont le poids individuel s'accroît ainsi de toute
l'influence exercée sur l'ensemble des contemporains et même des
prédécesseurs. D'ailleurs, l'action providentielle de l'humanité
protège chacun de ses serviteurs contre les ascendants moins
nobles, qu'elle modifie de plus en plus." (Pol. pos. II.
55)[1]

=
    Chronology of Auguste Comte's Life
Born, January 19, 1798
Beginning of relations with Saint-Simon, 1818.
Rupture with Saint-Simon, 1824. (Death of SS. 1825)
Marriage, 1825. Beginning of the "Cours", Ap. 1. 1826
Interrupted by mania after 3 leçons: resumed 1828.
Cours de Phil. Pos. 6 vols. 1830-1842. Loss of property 1843
Discours préliminaire, 1848. Separation, 1842.
Relations with Madame de Vaux, 1845
Politique Positive, 1851-1854. Synthèse, 1856.
Death, September 5, 1857.

228
    Translations of the Bible into English.
=
The N.T. was first translated by Wickliffe from the Vulgate,
about 1380.[1]
    The next translation was by William Tyndal, printed at
Antwerp 1528, in 8vo without a name, & without either calendar,
references in the margin, or table at the end; it was corrected

by the author, & printed in 1534 & 1536, having had 5 editions in
Holland.

In the meantime Tyndal was translating several books of the
Old Testament, as the Pentateuch, & the book of Jonah, printed
1531; the books of Joshua, Judges, Ruth, the 4 books of Kings,
the 2 books of Chronicles, & Nehemiah. About the same time
George Joy, sometime fellow of Peter-college Cam. translated the
Psalter, the prophecy of Jeremiah, & the song of Moses, & printed
them beyond Sea.

In the year 1535, the whole Bible was printed the first time
in folio, adorned with wooden cuts, & Scripture references; it
was done by several hands, & dedicated to King Henry VIII by
Miles Coverdale. In the last page it is said to be printed in
the year of our Lord 1535, & finished the fourth day of October.
This Bible was reprinted in 4to 1550, & again with a new title
1553.

Two years after the Bible was reprinted in English, with
this title, "The Holy Bible, /239/ which is all the Holy
Scripture, in which are contagned the Olde & Newe Testament truly
& purely translated into English by (a fictitious name) Thomas
Matthew, 1537." It has a calendar with an almanac; & an exhorta-
tion to the study of the Scripture, signed by J.R. John Rogers; a
table of contents & marriages; marginal notes & a prologue; & in
the Apocalypse some wooden cuts. At the beginning of the prophets
are printed on the top of the page R.G. Richard Grafton; & at the
bottom E.W. Edward Whitchurch, who were the printers. This translation, to the end of the Book of Chronicles, & the book of Jonah,
with all the N. Testament was Tyndal's; the rest was Miles Coverdale's & John Rogers's.

In the year 1539 the above-named translation having been revised & corrected by Archbp. Cranmer was reprinted. And again,
in 1541 with a preface by Cranmer, having been revised by Tonstal
& Heath, Bishop of Durham & Rochester.

Soon after King Edward's accession 1548-9 the Bible of 1541
was reprinted, with Cranmer's prologue; & the liturgy of the
Church of England, being first composed & established, the translation of the Psalter, commonly called the old translation, in use
at this day, was taken from it. Next year, Coverdale's Testament
of 1535 was reprinted, with Erasmus's paraphrase; but there was
no new translation.

In the reign of Queen Mary 1555, the   /230/   Exiles at
Geneva undertook a new translation, commonly called the Geneva
Bible; the names of the translators were: Coverdale, Goodman,
Gilby, Whittingham, Sampson, Cole, Knox, Bodleigh & Pullam, who
published the N.T. first in small 12mo. by Conrad Badius. The
whole Bible was published with marginal notes 1559, dedicated to
Queen Elizabeth. It went through 20 or 30 editions in her reign.

Cranmer's Bible had been reprinted in 1562 & 66 for the use
of the churches. But complaints being made of its incorrectness,
archbishop Parker projected a new translation & assigned the
several books of the O. & N.T. to about fourteen dignitaries of
the church, most of whom being bishops, it was from them called
the Bishops' Bible: printed 1568 with maps & cuts. Reprinted
1572 with alterations. In 1582 the Roman Catholic exiles translated the New Testament-- "In the English College at Rheims.
Printed by John Togny." The O.T. of this translation was first
published at Douay in 2 volumes, the first 1609, the second 1610,
"by Lawrence Kellam at the sign of the Holy Lamb."

At the request of the Puritans in the Hampton Court Conference,

King James appointed a new translation to be executed, which was
to be as close as possible to the Bishops' Bible. It was begun
1606; finished 1611 by 47 divines, divided into six companies.

231

Thus, the Translations are:--
1 Wickliffe's New Testament, 1380
2 Tyndal's N.T.   .   . 1526
3 Coverdale's Bible .   . 1535
4 Matthew's Bible . . .   1537
5 Cranmer's Bible   .   . 1539
6 The Geneva Bible . . .   1555
7 The Bishops' Bible . . . 1568
8 The Rheims N.T.   .   . 1589
9 The Douay O.T.. . . .   1610
10 Authorized Translation.. 1611
                         = (Neale's Hist. of the Puritans)[1]

232

     For Books are not absolutely dead things, but doe contain a
potencie of life in them to be as active as that soul whose
progeny they are; nay they do preserve as in a violl the purest
efficacie & extraction of that living intellect that bred them.
. . . . . As good almost a man as kill a good book. . . . Many
a man lives a burthen to the earth; but a good book is the pre-
tious life-blood of a master spirit, imbalmed & treasured up
on purpose to a life beyond life. 'Tis true, no age can restore
a life, whereof perhaps there is no great losse; & revolutions
of ages doe not oft recover the loss of a rejected truth, for
the want of which whole Nations fare the worse. We should be
wary therefore what persecution we raise against the living
labours of public men, how we spill that seasoned life of man
preservèd & storèd up in Books; since we see a kind of homicide may be thus committed, sometimes a martyrdome, & if it
extend to the whole impression, a kind of massacre, whereof
the execution ends not in the slaying of an elementall life,
but strikes at that ethereall & fift essence, the breath of
reason it selfe, <u>slaies</u> <u>an</u> <u>immortality</u> <u>rather</u> <u>than</u> <u>a</u> <u>life</u>.
                                   Milton: Areopagitica[1]

{233}

     "I am not able to unfold how this cautelous enterprise of
licensing can be exempted from the number of vain & impossible
attempts. And he who were pleasantly disposed could not well
avoid to lik'n it to the exploit of that gallant man who thought
to pound up the crows by shutting his parkgate."[1]
     "To knaw out the choicest periods of exquisitest books, &
to commit such a treacherous fraud against <u>the</u> <u>orphan</u> <u>remainders</u>
<u>of</u> <u>worthiest</u> <u>men</u> <u>after</u> <u>death</u>."[2]
     "Where there is much desire to learn, there of necessity
will be much arguing, much writing, many opinions; for opinion in
good men is but knowledge in the making."[3]
     "When the new light which we beg for shines in upon us,
there be who envy & oppose, if it come not first in at their
casements."[4]
     "If it come to prohibiting there is not ought more likely to
be prohibited than truth itself; whose first appearance to our
eyes blear'd & dimm'd with prejudice & custom, is more unsightly
& unplausible than many errors, ev'n as the person is of many a

great man slight & contemptible to see to."

Areopagitica.

234   The Romance Languages

Perticari, <u>Scrittori</u> <u>del</u> <u>Trecento</u>, mentions the names of
some writers of little note who first put forward the theory that
Italian was originally a dialect of the old Roman population,
Latin being only the language of the upper classes, of law, & of
literature. This theory is fully treated by Maffei, <u>Verona</u>
<u>illustrata</u>. Perticari holds that the ancient Provençal was that
ancient dialect of Italy.[1] [The historians of the Crusades apply
the term <u>Provincia</u> to all the South of France, distinguishing the
inhabitants of the northern & southern parts of that country by
the name Francigenae & Provinciales: an ancient grammar of the
Langue d'Oc is called Donatus Provincialis.][2]

Raynouard's theory is that the Latin by the influence of the
German, was corrupted into an uniform language, called the Romance,
spoken for some centuries, & at least as late as the reign of
Charlemagne over the whole of Western Europe: that this language
is preserved unchanged in the Troubadour poetry & the early literature of Provence; & that it was gradually modified into the
Italian, Spanish, Portuguese, French, modern Provençal & their
various dialects, wh. are all derived indirectly indeed from the
Latin, but directly from the Romance.[3]

"All we know is, that the Latin language disappeared as a
living language from Western Europe soon after the sixth century,
& that a new form of speech appeared in its place,   /235/   which
as far as we can learn from the earliest monuments of it, had a
different character in Spain, in Italy, & in N. & S. France: in
these several Latin dialects we find numerous forms, idioms &
words not borrowed from the Latin but corresponding or identical
with each other."

G.C. Lewis. Rom. Lang.[1]

The Moravians have translated the Bible into the Negro Talkee-
talkee, of which they have composed a grammar. This negro patois
includes many African words, but has for its basis English pared
of inflexions & softened by a multitude of vowel terminations.

Ibid. Note.[2]

"It is a curious fact that the hills of King's Seat & Craigy
Barns, which form the lower boundary of Dowally, a parish in
Perthshire, have been <u>for</u> <u>centuries</u> the separatory barrier of the
English & Gaelic. In the first house below them, the English is
& has been spoken, & in the first house not a mile distant above
them, the Gaelic."   Ib.[3]

236

<u>The Organ</u>. The hydraulic organs of the ancients, described by
Vitruvius & Athenaeus, are not now to be understood. Those of
the middle ages are equally obscure as to their structure. As to
the pneumatic organ, Fétis says: "Je ne veux point élever de
doute sur l'existence de l'orgue pneumatic au 4me siècle, car un
passage du commentaire de St. Augustus sur le 56th psaume ne
laisse aucun doute sur la connaissance qu'on avait alors de cet
instrument: 'Organa dicuntur omnia instrumenta musicorum; <u>non</u>
<u>solum</u> <u>illud</u> <u>organum</u> <u>dicitur</u>, <u>quod</u> <u>grande</u> <u>est</u> <u>et</u> <u>inflatur</u> <u>follibus</u>,
sed etiam quidquid aptatur ad cantilenam et corporeum est.' . . .
. . . Les annales d'Eginhart, Sécrétaire de Charlemagne, nous
fournissent l'indication précise de l'époque où parut en Europe
le premier orgue pneumatique qui fut entendu dans les Gaules; ce

fut en 757 que l'empereur Constantin Copronyme envoya cet
instrument à Pépin, qui le fit placer, dit on, dans l'église de
Saint Corneille à Compiègne."[1]

"Nul doute que les premières orgues à vent n'aient été de
petites boîtes portatives, comme on en voit dans quelques peintures
anciennes et dans des manuscrits des douzième et treizième siècles
. . . . [2] . . . . Quant aux petites orgues portatives que les
musiciens s'attachaient au corps par des courroies, pour les jouer
d'une main tandis qu'ils faisaient mouvoir le soufflet de l'autre,
les dimensions de leur clavier étaient beaucoup plus petites, et
la main étendue /237/ pouvait embrasser l'espace d'une quinte.
On donnait à cet instrument le nom de nimfali."[1]

"Le plus ancien orgue construit dans l'Europe méridional, et
dont on a conservé le souvenir, est celui que Georges, prêtre
Vénitien, a fait en l'année 826 pour le palais d'Aix la Chapelle
par ordre de Louis le Débonnaire. Ce Georges paraît avoir été
Grec d'origine; ce qui a peut-être contribué à établir l'opinion
que les orgues ont passé de la Grèce dans l'Occident. Mais il
avait voyagé en Allemagne et il ne serait pas impossible qu'il y
eût appris les principes de la construction de ces instruments.
Il est certain qu'au neuvième siècle il y avait en Allemagne, de
plus habiles facteurs d'orgues et des organistes plus instruits
qu'ailleurs, car le pape Jean VIII (élu en 872) écrivait à Anno,
évêque de Freising (en Bavière), pour le prier d'envoyer en Italie
un orgue avec un artiste capable d'en construire et d'en jouer."

"Rien n'était plus difficile que de faire des accords sur le
clavier de cet instrument. D'abord composé d'un seul jeu d'anches
appelé régal, il n'avait point de registre, et ses touches étaient
d'une telle dimension en largeur, qu'on ne pouvait faire résonner
les notes qu'en les frappant à coups de poing." . . . "Il y avait
. . . des orgues dont le clavier, composé d'un petit nombre de
touches plus larges que la main, et concaves à leur partie
supérieure, n'avait pu être joué que par les points ou les coudes."

Fétis, Résumé phil. de l'Histoire de la Musique[2]

238

Method of Guido d'Arezzo. "Le son le plus grave d'un chant étant
trouvé par le monocorde, il y aurait eu trop de lenteur à chercher
sur cet instrument toutes les autres notes de ce chant; Gui conseilla donc de prendre pour modèle une mélodie connue, quelle
qu'elle fût, pourvu qu'on la sût bien, et de comparer les intonations des notes de cette mélodie avec celles des notes semblables
du chant qu'on voulait apprendre. Bientôt ces comparaisons
répétées devaient imprimer dans la mémoire le souvenir des intonations. Dans une lettre qu'il écrivait à ce sujet à un moine de
ses amis, il dit qu'il avait l'habitude de se servir, dans l'école
qu'il dirigeait, du chant de l'hymne de St. Jean-Baptiste:

Ut queant laxis, Resonare fibris,
Mira gestorum, Famuli tuorum,
Solve polluti, Labii reatum
Sancte Joannes.

Les enfants de choeur chantaient cet hymne au commencement et à la
fin de la leçon qu'il leur donnait. Or, remarquez que dans la
mélodie que Gui avait choisi pour ses élèves, l'intonation de la
note s'élève d'un degré sur chacune des syllabes ut re &c; les
successeurs de ce moine en ont conclu qu'il avait voulu désigner
par ces syllabes les notes de l'échelle, bien qu'il ne se soit
servi de ces noms en aucun endroit des traités de musique qui
nous restent de lui. . . . . . l'honneur d'une invention à laquelle

/239/   Gui n'a point pensé lui est restée, tandis que personne
n'a songé à revendiquer pour lui la gloire d'avoir inventé la
méthode d'enseignement par l'analogie, qui lui appartient réellement, et qui naguère a été donnée comme une chose nouvelle par M.
Jacotot, sous le nom d'enseignement universel."
Fétis, Resumé &c.[1]

240

Coptic Language. "M. Lepsius fit paraître en 1836, deux opuscules
[Zwei sprachvergleichende Abhandlungen: I. Über die Anordnung
und Verwandtschaft des Semitischen, Indischen, Altpersischen und
Alt-AEgyptischen Alphabets. II. Ueber den Ursprung und die
Verwandschaft der Zahlwörter in der Indogermanischen, Semitischen,
und Koptischen Sprache] où par la comparaison des noms des nombres
et des alphabets, il cherche à établir l'identité originelle des
trois familles indo-européenne, sémitique et copte. Toutefois,
il reconnaissait que le copte formait un rameau distinct et presque
aussi différent du rameau sémitique que celui-ci l'est du rameau
indo-européen. M. Schwarze (Das alte AEgypten, 1843) a soutenu
la même thèse. Le copte, suivant ce philologue, forme à lui seul
une famille, analogue aux langues sémitiques par sa grammaire et
aux langues indo-germaniques par ses racines, mais, en général,
plus rapprochée des langues Sémitiques par un caractère de simpli-
cité, par la marque de structure logique et le degré de culture
auquel elle est parvenue. M. Theodore Benfey (Ueber das Verhältniss der AEgyptischen Sprache zum Semitischen Sprachstamm) a repris
le parallèle. . . . . La conclusion de son livre c'est que la
famille sémitique doit se diviser en deux branches séparées par
l'isthme de Suez: la branche asiatique, renfermant toutes les
langues qu'on est convenu d'appeler Sémitiques   /241/   et la
branche Africaine, renfermant le Copte et toutes les langues de
l'Afrique Septentrionale jusqu'à l'Atlantique.[1] . . . . . M.
Bunsen a adopté les mêmes conclusions. . . . M. Ernest Meier et M.
Paul Bötticher ont essayé d'appuyer la même thèse par des arguments empruntés à la comparaison des radicaux. . . . .
    Ajoutons, toutefois, que ces divers travaux n'ont point
passé sans de vives contradictions. MM. Pott, Ewald, Wenrich
protestèrent à diverses reprises contre l'abus de la méthode comparative appliquée à des langues aussi dissemblables. M. Ewald
surtout, à propos du livre de M. Benfey, insista vivement sur le
tort que de pareils ouvrages faisaient à la philologie, en
répandant sur la méthode de cette science une teinte de vague et
d'arbitraire.[2] . . . . .
    L'élément le plus essentiel sur lequel on puisse instituer
la comparaison des langues, ce sont assurément les flexions du
nom et du verbe; or, c'est précisément par ce côté que le système
de la langue égyptienne diffère du système sémitique. La langue
égyptienne mérite à peine de prendre rang parmi les langues à
flexions. Plus on remonte vers son état primitif, plus on trouve
une langue analogue au chinois, une langue monosyllabique, sans
ciment, si j'ose le dire, exprimant les modalités par des ex-
posants groupés, mais non agglutinés autour de la racine. . . . .
Il faut donc former pour la langue et la civilisation de l'Egypte
une famille à part qu'on appellera, si l'on veut, chamitique."[3]
Renan, Hist. Lang. Sém.

242

<u>Study</u> <u>of</u> <u>Hebrew</u>
"Ce fut surtout dans le Magreb que le mouvement grammatical fondé

par l'école juive d'Orient porta ses fruits. Menahem ben-Serouk
de Tortose, et Dounasch ben Lébrât, de Fez (960 ou 970) composè-
rent les plus anciens travaux de lexicographie hébraïque."[1] . . .
. . .

     Les travaux de cette première école sont presque tous écrits
en arabe. Lorsque, vers la fin du XIIme siècle, cette langue
cessa d'être parlée des juifs, on se porta de préférence vers des
travaux écrits en hébreu. . . . Les Kimchis de Narbonne, sont les
réprésentants les plus célèbres de cette nouvelle série de
travaux. . . . Ce ne fut qu'au XVIe siècle, au moment où la science
de l'hébreu allait passer entre les mains des Chrétiens, qu'on
vit la renommée des Kimchis effacée par celle d'Elias Levita (mort
à Venise en 1549), qui porta la méthode rabinnique au dernier
degré de perfection dont elle était susceptible, et fut le maître
d'un grand nombre d'hébraïsants Chrétiens." . . . Jusqu'ici, en
effet, la science de l'hébreu a été la possession exclusive des
juifs. Le très petit nombre de Chrétiens qui surent l'hébreu
. . . étaient des juifs convertis ou fils de convertis.[2] . . . Les
efforts de Raymond Lully et les décrets du Concile de Vienne en
1311 ne réussirent point à créer une étude sérieuse de l'hébreu.
Seul, l'ordre de Saint Dominique, en vue des besoins de la
polémique contre les juifs, posséda quelques hommes initiés à la
science des rabbins."[3]

                              243
"Vers la fin du XVe siècle et au commencement du XVIe, un vif
attrait de curiosité entraîne de ce côté toute l'opinion savante.
. . . Les juifs furent naturellement les maîtres de cette nouvelle
génération d'hébraïsants. Il fallait à cette époque, pour savoir
l'hébreu faire de longs voyages, s'attacher à un rabbin dont on
écoutait les paroles comme des oracles, et dont on achetait les
leçons à prix d'or.[1] . . . L'homme dont le nom mérite le plus de
rester attaché à cette révolution, qui devait avoir des consé-
quences si graves dans l'histoire de l'esprit humain, c'est Reuchlin.
Les trois livres De rudimentis hebraicis (1506) furent la première
grammaire hébraïque régulière, composée pour l'usage des chrétiens,
et fixèrent les termes techniques employés depuis dans les écoles
européennes."[2] . . . .
     Elias Levita s'était attiré les anathèmes de la synagogue,
en élevant des doutes sur l'ancienneté des points-voyelles.[3]
                                        Renan, Lang. Sem.

[Sur la littérature carthaginoise, voir Salluste, Bellum Jugurth.
C. XVII; Pline, Hist. Nat. XVIII, v; Columelle, I, i, 6 et suiv.;
XII, iv, 2.][4]
                              =
"Quant à langue vulgaire, on peut dire que les Juifs, depuis la
captivité de Babylone, en ont adopté quatre principales: le
chaldéen, l'arabe, l'espagnol et l'allemand. L'Arabe est encore
parlé par les Juifs d'Afrique. L'espagnol et   /244/   l'allemand
devinrent réellement au moyen âge des langues nationales pour les
deux grandes factions du peuple Juif, qui les portèrent avec eux
dans leurs diverses migrations. Ainsi, la plupart des Juifs de
l'Europe Centrale étant originaires de l'Alsace et de l'Allemagne
du Sud, ont parlé presque jusqu'à nos jours un jargon allemand
mêlé d'hébreu (Judenteutsch) plein d'archaïsmes et même d'altéra-
tions artificielles. (Jost: dans l'Encycl. d'Ersch et Gruber,
art. Judenteutsch) au contraire, la langue des Juifs de Constantinople, qui sont venus d'Espagne, est encore aujourd'hui

l'espagnol du XVe siècle. Par un de ces caprices qui ne se
recontrent que dans l'histoire du peuple juif, les deux langues
susdites sont devenues à leur tour pour les Israélites deux
langues mortes et respectées. Ainsi, parmi les Israélites
français qui n'ont pas reçu d'instruction, plusieurs savent encore, pour les avoir entendu répéter à leurs pères, quelques mots
espagnols et allemands; ces mots se présentent à eux comme des
souvenirs d'une langue nationale, ils les prennent pour de
l'hébreu. L'habitude où sont les juifs allemands et polonais
d'écrire et d'imprimer le Judenteutsch en charactères hébreux a
donné lieu à une méprise analogue, en faisant croire que l'usage
de la langue hébraïque leur est encore familier."[1]

245

Assyrian civilization. "Cette civilization est pour nous le
résultat du mélange des Chamites ou Couschites avec les Sémites
et les Ariens, sur les bords du Tigre, comme la civilisation
Phénicienne est le résultat du mélange des Sémites et des
Chamites sur les côtes de la mer rouge et de la Méditerranée. Il
y a, en effet, dans ces deux civilisations, une foule de traits
qui ne se laissent expliquer ni par le caractère sémitique ni par
le caractère arien pris isolément. Nulle part nous ne voyons les
Sémites arriver d'eux-mêmes à un développement d'art, de commerce,
et de vie politique. Le paganisme Sémitique, qui a son siège à
Babylone, se laisse rattacher presque tout entier à la mythologie
soit des Couschites, soit de l'Iran. L'idée d'une grande
monarchie absolue, se résumant en un seul homme servi par une
vaste hiérarchie de fonctionnaires, idée qui fut d'abord réalisée
dans l'Asie occidentale par l'Assyrie, est profondément opposée à
l'esprit des Sémites. La royauté ne s'établit chez les Juifs qu'à
l'imitation des étrangers, et fut incessamment combattue par les
prophètes, vrais représentants de l'esprit sémitique, également
hostiles à la royauté laïque, à la civilisation matérielle et aux
influences de l'Assyrie. D'un autre côté, le caractère colossal
scientifique, industriel de la civilisation assyrienne ne
convient pas aux Ariens,   /246/   qui nous apparaissent, dans
les temps anciens, comme peu constructeurs et peu portés vers
l'études des sciences physiques. On est donc amené à placer, sur
le Tigre, un premier fond de population analogue à celle d'Egypte,
puis une couche sémitique, qui fit de sa langue la langue vulgaire
de ces contrées; puis enfin une classe guerrière et politique,
sans doute peu nombreuse et d'origine iranienne. Ces derniers
sont les vrais Chaldiens, dont le nom s'est appliqué à un pays et
à une langue sémitique, à peu près comme les noms de France, de
Bourgogne, &c. d'origine germanique, désignent de nos jours des
pays qui n'ont rien de germain.[1]

                                        Renan, p. 198.

Arabic Literature. "Il résulte des textes cités par M. de Sacy:
1e. que l'écriture n'a pas été comme des Arabes de l'Hedjaz et du
Nedjad plus d'un siècle avant l'hégire; 2e. que l'alphabet fut
transmis aux Arabes par les Syriens; 3e. que l'écriture resta,
avant l'islamisme, et même assez long temps après, l'apanage
presque exclusif des juifs et des chrétiens."[2]

247

"Time & the fruitful hour are more than we,
And these lay hold upon us"   (Swinburne, Atalanta)[1]
                        =

"For what lies light on many & they forget,
Small things & transitory as a wind o' the sea,
I forget never; I have seen thee all thine years
A man in arms, strong & a joy to men
Seeing thine head glitter & thine hand burn its way
Through a heavy & iron furrow of sundering spears;
But always also a flower of three suns old,
The small one thing that lying drew down my life
To lie with thee & feed thee; a child & weak,
Mine, a delight to no man, sweet to me."

Ibid.[2]

=

"For is it a grief to you that I have part,
Being woman merely, in your male might & deeds
Done by main strength? yet in my body is throned
As great a heart, & in my spirit, O men,
I have not less of godlike."   Ibid.[3]

=

Thine eyes that are quiet, thine hands that are tender,
          thy lips that are loving,
Comfort & cool me as dew in the dawn of a moon
          like a dream;
And my heart yearns baffled & blind, moved vainly
          toward thee, & moving
As the refluent seaweed moves in the languid
          exuberant stream,
Fair as a rose is on earth, as a rose under water in prison,
          That stretches & swings to the slow passionate
pulse of the sea--

Swinburne. Hesperia.[4]

248

In the month of the long decline of roses
I, beholding the summer dead before me,
Set my face to the sea & journeyed silent,
Gazing eagerly where above the sea-mark
Flame as fierce as the fervid eyes of lions
Half divided the eyelids of the sunset;
Till I heard as it were a noise of waters
Moving tremulous under feet of angels
Multitudinous, out of all the heavens;
Knew the fluttering wind, the fluttered foliage,
Shaken fitfully, full of sound & shadow;
And saw, trodden upon by noiseless angels,
Long mysterious reaches fed with moonlight,
Sweet sad straits in a soft subsiding channel,
Blown about by the lips of winds I knew not.

Swinburne: "Hendecasyllabics"[1]

=

Saw the Lesbians. . . . .
          . . . .   beheld among them
Soar, as a bird soars

"Newly fledged, her visible song, a marvel,
Made of perfect sound and exceeding passion,
Sweetly shapen, terrible, full of thunders,
          Clothed with the wind's wings."

"Sapphics."[2]

"Clothed about with flame & with tears, and singing
Songs that move the heart of the shaken heaven,
Songs that break the heart of the earth with pity,
       Hearing, to hear them."

Ib.[3]

249

Musical Instruments. The Violin. Some have supposed that the
Greeks & Romans had a musical instrument resembling the Viol, in
the magadis (from μαγας, a chevalet). But this supposition is
supported neither by authors nor sculpture. They show nothing in
proof or evidence that the Greeks possessed an instrument with a
neck and a bridge. India is the country in which the instruments
played with a bow had their origin. There the primitive violin
still exists in the ravanastron, which consists of a wooden cylinder (sycamore) hollow from one end to the other. On one side is
stretched the skin of a serpent, & this is the "table d'harmonie."
This cylinder is traversed a third of its length by a stem of wood,
carved beneath, flat above, wh. serves as a handle, being 55 centimeters in length while the body is 11 cent. The instrument
has two strings of gazelle-gut, fastened by two large pegs in the
handle; there is a little bridge, sloped at its summit, hollowed
below, so as to form two little legs. The bow is a thin bamboo,
with a mesh of hair. This instrument is now abandoned to the
poor Buddhist monks who go begging. According to Hindoo tradition, it was invented by Ravana, King of Ceylon, 5000 years B.C.
There is another instrument called the Rouana, which may be regarded as the Bass of the Ravanastron.[1]

     Posterior to this is the Omerti, also an   /250/   instru-
ment with a bow, & with two strings, the body of which is made of
a cocoa nut of which a third has been cut off, & the shell
thinned & polished. In some the table d'harmonie is made of
skin, in others of fine-grained wood. On comparing this instrument with the Kemangeb of the Arabs, the Indian is seen to be the
original. Villoteau in the Descr. d'Egypte t. xiii, remarks that
this word Kemangeb is Persian. In the Kemangeb the strings are
made of meshes of black hair firmly stretched.[1]

     The Arabian rebâb is much ruder--serving only to guide the
voice of the poet or tale-teller. The body is made of two pieces
of parchment stretched on five pieces of wood. One kind has only
one string; another has two.[2]

     The Russian goudok, with its three strings, its finger board
on the handle, its regularly constructed sonorous case, its open-
ings in the table d'harmonie, its bridge proportioned to the
length of the strings, its "Cordier" like that of our violins is
a perfect viol & not like a primitive essay.[3]

     No traces of bow instruments appear on the European conti-
nent before the end of the VIIIth century or beginning of the
IXth. But Venantius Fortunatus bishop of Poietiers who died
about 609, & is supposed to have produced his elegiac poems about
570, tells us that the crwth or crouth of the Gaelic bards
/251/   was then known & that it apparently existed long before
in England. The poet renders this barbarian word by chrotta:
        "Romanus lyra plaudat tibi, barbarus harpa,
     Graecus Achilliaca, chrotta Britanna canat."[1]
     The crwth is not a primitive but a developed instrument; for
the idea of a sonorous case composed of an anterior & posterior
table with sides & a handle, several strings lifted by a bridge &
attached by iron pegs to the back of the head, cannot have been a

primitive idea. A MS. of the XIth century represents a crowned
personage holding in his left hand a crwth with 3 strings which
he plays with a bow. Also at Melrose, built at the beginning of
the XIVth century, there is a like representation.[2] A bard of
the XVth cent. says that the crwth with 6 strings was ingeniously
contrived to render 100 sounds.[3]

The MS. of St. Martial of Limoges, already mentioned, proves
that the crwth had reached the south of France in the XIth cent.[4]

The Rotta, rota, rothe, was the old psaltery with 10 strings,
in the form of a triangle. St. Boniface (VIIIth cent.) says
"delectat me quoque cytharistam habere, qui possit cytharizare in
cythara, quam nos appellamus rottae (sic)."[5] A Provençal poet of
the XIIth century speaks of the rota with 17 strings.[6]

The rebeck (the rubèbe or rebelle of the middle ages, wh.
had at first only one or two strings like the Arabian rebâs) was
not, /252/   as Villemarqué supposes (Barzaz Breiz) equivalent

to the crwth. The rebeck was narrow towards the handle ;

the crwth was this shape . The rubèbe, according to a

Dominican of the XIIIth cent. had 2 strings tuned ; the

soprano instrument of the same sort had 3 strings; in France
called the gigue, during the 12, 13, & 14th centuries; it is in
the 15th century that this name seems to have been exchanged for
rebec. The Germans called it the Geige ohne Bunde.[1] "La rubèbe,
la gigue, les quatre classes enfin du genre rebec, qu'on trouve
déjà établies dès le quinzième siècle, à savoir, dessus, alto,
ténor, et basse, sont des instruments populaires placés entre les
mains des ménétriers et qui servent en général pour la danse et
pour les chanteurs des rues."[2]

The other class of instruments, having the sonorous case, of
two tables united by sides at right angles with them, & curving
inwards at the centre, which were called vielle or viole (the
        ⎧trithant
crwth   ⎩three-corded was the type of them) belong to a more developed form of art.[3]

By the beginning of the XIth century we see the vielle or
viole on monuments. Some of them are without bridges; but this
must be the mistake of the artist or his negligence, for the
bridge is the correlate of the bow.[4]

It was near the end of the XVth century that three musicians
superior to their   /{253}[1]/   age, Dufay, Binchois, & Dunstaple,
conceived the improvement of having for every genus of instruments
a complete family, soprano, alto, tenor & bass--sometimes even
double bass. This division was established in the XVth century.[2]
When was the violin born? In 1556, was printed the Pratica di
Musica of Louis Zacconi: he gives the compass of the violin as

that of our own time . No viol had this compass. The

first certain instance of the violin being used orchestrally is
in the Orfeo of Monteverde, at Mantua 1607.[3]

Musical Instrument Makers of Celebrity.
Kerlino, of Brescia, about 1450, the first celebrated maker of
viols & rebecs.[4] Giovanni Paolo Magini, 1590-1640, made violins:
a pupil of Gasparo de Sala, some of whose violins remain--one

dated 1566. Mariani of Pesaro also made Violins, from 1570-1620:
they are not valued. Whereas Magini's have been made celebrated
by De Beriot, who played with success on one at Paris & London.
This Magini must not be confounded with Santo Magini, in the 17th
century, who made double basses.[5]

Andrea Amati, founder of the great School of Cremona, was
born within the first 20 years of the 16th century, since a rebec
made by him is dated 1546. "Lorsqu'il travaillait, personne ne
recherchait la puissance et /254/   l'éclat du son qu'on demande
aujourd'hui; loin de là l'instrument qui aurait en cette grande
sonorité aurait blessé l'oreille d'un auditoire accoutumé à la
musique douce dont nous voyons encore les monuments."[1] Niccolo
Amati, 1596-1684, the most famous of the name. His pupils were
his son Geronimo, Andrea Garneri, Paolo Grancino & Antonio
Stradivari.[2] (Violins are made of maple & deal). The maple used
by the old masters came from Croatia, Dalmatia & even Turkey. It
was sent to Venice prepared for the oars of galleys, & the Turks,
they say, took care to choose the most undulated wood that it
might break more quickly. In this the Violin makers found the
wood most suitable for their violins. The deal came from the
southern side of the Twin Tyrolese mountains).[3]

Stradivarius was born 1644.[4] From 1700, when he was fifty
six, till 1725, his violins are in perfection.[5] Everything is
perfect except "la barre," which is too weak "par suite de
l'élévation progressive du diapason depuis le commencement du
dix-huitème siècle, laquelle a eu pour résultat une augmentation
considérable de tension et une pression plus grande exercée sur
la table. De là, la nécessité de rebarrer tous les anciens
violons et violoncelles."[6]

Stradivarius lived till he was 93. "Sa vie s'écoula tout
entière dans un paisible /255/   atelier, en face d'un établi,
le compas ou l'outil à la main."[1] The instruments made by him
are multitudinous. He finished one when he was 92. He had secured his tomb in 1729; he was buried in 1737. His life was
peaceful save that in 1702 during the war of the Succession,
Cremona was taken by the Marshal Villeroi, retaken by Prince
Eugène, & again by the French; but after this Italy enjoyed a
long tranquillity.[2]

Polledro, Violinist of Turin, chapel royal, heard his master
speak of Stradivari: he was tall & thin--wore a white woollen
cap in winter & a cotton one in summer--an apron of white leather
when he worked, & as he was always working, there was little
change of costume. He had gained a good deal of money, for it
was a saying at Cremona, "as rich as Stradivari." The price he
fixed for his violins was 4 louis d'or.[3]

Joseph Guarnerius (Garneri) a contemporary of Stradivarius
(Giuseppe Antonio Guarneri) called Giuseppe del Jesu because many
of his violins bear the mark   IHS .[4] Born at Cremona 1683.
Some of his instruments equal to the best of Stradiv: Immediately
after this best epoch, his instruments became terribly inferior.
He was idle & disorderly; his wife, a Tyrolese woman, was unhappy
with him, though she often helped him in his work. He died in
prison, where he had been confined several years, in 1745.[5] He
made violins in prison, assisted by his

see p. 257

256

"Vielseitigkeit bereitet eigentlich nur das Element vor, worin
der Einseitige wirken kann, dem eben jetzt genug Raum gegeben ist.

Ja, es ist jetzo die Zeit der Einseitigkeiten; wohl dem, der es
begreift, für sich und andere in diesem Sinne wirkt. Bei
gewissen Dingen versteht sich's durchaus und sogleich. Uebe dich
zum tüchtigen Violinist und sey versichert, der Capellmeister
wird dir deinen Platz im Orchester mit Gunst anweisen. Mache ein
Organ aus dir und erwarte, was für seine Stelle dir die Menschheit
im allgemeinen Leben wohlmeinend zugestehen werde." (Goethe)[1]

257

jailor's daughter, who sold them for him, got his varnish &c.
Paganini played on one of his violins.[1]

=

Egyptian musical instruments. Lane (Mod. Egyptians) mentions:
1. the Kemangeb, a Persian word meaning bowed instrument, or
"place of the bow": like the Indian Omerti, the body being a
cocoa-nut shell.[2]
2. The Kanoon, a kind of Dulcimer, with numerous strings & a
bridge. Played with plectra.[3]
3. The 'ood--meaning wood, el 'ood, says Lane, being the origin
of lute--is a lute played with a plectrum, & has been for many
centuries the favourite instrument of the best Arab musicians.[4]
4. The Nay, a kind of flute. Then there are also the tambourine,
the rabab; a hautboy called "zemr" & various kinds of drums including the kettle drum; cymbals, brass castanets, & double reed
pipes which, with an earthen drum or darabbkkel is much used by
the boatmen of Nile.[5]
     The "brass castanets" were small cymbals for the fingers, &
were introduced into Spain by the Moors(?)--altered then in form
& made of chestnut wood.[6]

=

258
Gypsies contd. from p. 221

idiom with as much purity as if he had been a native of Toledo;
he was acquainted with all the ports of Spain & all the difficult
& broken ground of the provinces. He knew the exact strength of
every city, & who were the principal people in each, & the exact
amount of their property; there was nothing relating to the state,
however secret, that he was not acquainted with."[1]
     The patteran or Trail, to mark out for brethren the direc-
tion in which they will find their race--grass plucked & strewn
along the way. A cross drawn at the opening of a lane, with the
stem pointing along it.[2]
     The Edict of Charles III., 1783, concerning the Spanish
gypsies, rejected entirely the persecuting acts enjoined by previous laws, & encouraged the Gypsies to mingle themselves with
the Spanish population.[3]

259
"The untimely Music of neglected lays."
                              Daniel: Musophilus[1]

=

     Be it that my unseasonable Song
     Come out of time, that Fault is in the time;
     And I must not do Virtue so much wrong
     As love her ought the worse for others Crime:--
     And yet I find some Blessed spirits among
     That cherish me, & like & grace my Rhime.

A gain that I do more in Soul esteem,
Than all the gain of Dust the world doth Crave:
And if I may attain but to redeem
My Name from desolation & the Grave;
I shall have done enough, & better deem
T' have lived to be, than to have dy'd to have.[2]

. . . .

Besides some vip'rous Critick may bereave
The opinion of thy worth by some defect;
And get more reputation of his wit,
By but controlling of some Word or Sense,
Than thou shalt Honour by contriving it.[3]

. . . .

Besides, so many so confus'dly sing,
Whose diverse discords have the Music marr'd,
And in contempt that Mystery doth bring,
That he must Sing aloud that will be heard,
And the received Opinion of the Thing,
For some unhallow'd string that vilely jarr'd
Hath so unseason'd now the Ears of men
That who doth touch the tenor of that vein,
Is held but vain; and his unreckon'd Pen,
The title but of Levity doth gain.[4]

260

And therefore leave the left & outworn Course
Of unregarded ways, & labour how
To fit the times & what is most in force;
Be new with Men's affections that are new,
Strive not to run an idle Counter-course,
Out from the Secret Humours men allow.
        For not discreetly to compose our Parts
Unto the Frame of Men (which we must be)
Is to put off ourselves, & make our arts
Rebels to Nature & Society,
Whereby we come to bury our Deserts
In th'obscure grave of Singularity.[1]

. . . .

        Well were it with mankind, if what the most
Did like were best, but Ignorance will live
By others square, as by Example lost.
And Man to Man must th' Hand of Error give,
That none can fall alone at their own cost;
And all because Men judge not, but believe[2]

. . . .

When as (perhaps) the words thou scornest now
May live, the speaking picture of the Mind;
The Extract of the Soul, that labour'd how
To leave the Image of herself behind.[3]
        For these lines are the Veins, the Arteries,
And undecaying lifestrings of those Hearts,

That still shall pant, & still shall exercise
The Motion, Spirit & Nature both imparts,
And shall with those alive so sympathize
As nourished with their Powers, enjoy their Parts.
    O blessed Letters that combine in one
All ages past, & make one live with all.[4]

261

By you we do confer with who are gone
And the Dead-living into Council call:
By you th' unborn shall have Communion
Of what we feel & what doth us befal.
    Soul of the World, Knowledge, without Thee,
What hath the Earth that truly glorious is?
Why should our Pride make such a stir to be,
To be forgot? What good is like to this
To do worthy the writing, & to write
Worthy the Reading & the world's Delight?[1]

.   .   .   .   .   = ...

Critics

Prodigious wits! that study to confound
The Life of Wit, to seem to know aright;
As if themselves had fortunately found
Some stand from off the Earth beyond our sight;
Whence overlooking all as from above,
Their grace is not to work, but to reprove.
    But how came they placed in so high degree
Above the reach & compass of the rest?
Who hath admitted them only to be
Free denizens of skill, to judge the best?
From whom the world as yet could never see
The Warrant of their Wit soundly exprest.[2]

.   .   .   .

Sacred Religion! Mother of Form & Fear!
How gorgeously sometimes dost thou sit deck'd?
What pompous Vestures do we make thee wear
What stately piles we prodigal erect.[3]

.   .   .   .

Another Time all plain, all quite thread bare

262

Thou must have all within & nought without;
Sit poorly without light, disrob'd: No Care
Of outward Grace, t' amuse the poor Devout;
Pow'rless, unfollow'd; Scarcely then can spare
The necessary rites to set them out.[1]
    =
Philosophus.[2]
How can your promise of the time to come
Whenas the present is so negligent?[3]
    =
How many Thousands acres heard the name
Of Sidney or of Spencer; or their Books?

And yet brave Fellows & presume of Fame
And seem to bear down all the world with Looks.[4]
                              =
Whilst tim'rous knowledge stands considering
Audacious ignorance has done the deed.
For who knows most, the more he knows to doubt;
The least discourse is commonly most stout.[5]
                              =
The unmaterial swellings of your Pen,
Touch not the Spirit that action doth import.[6]
                              =
And for my part if only one allow
The Care my lab'ring Spirits take in this;
He is to me a The'tre large enow,
And his applause only sufficient is:
All my Respect is bent but to his brow;
That is my All, & all I am is his.
        And if some worthy spirits be pleased too
It shall more comfort breed, but not more Will.
But what if none? It cannot yet undo

                    263
The Love I bear unto this Holy skill.
This is the thing that I was born to do:
This is my Scene, this Part I must fulfil.[1]
                              =
O Scatt'ring Gath'rers! That without Regard
Of Times to come, will (to be made) undo;
As if you were the last of men, prepared
To bury in your graves all other too.
Dare you prophane that Holy Portion,
Which never Sacrilegious Hand durst do?[2]
                              =
What suit of Grace hath Virtue to put on,
If Vice shall wear as good, & do as well?
If Wrong, if Craft, if Indiscretion,
Act as fair Parts with Ends as laudable?
        Which all this mighty volume of Events
The World, the universal Map of Deeds,
Strongly controls; & proves from all Descents,
That the Directest Courses best succeeds,
When Craft (wrapt still in many Comberments)
With all her Cunning thrives not, tho' it speeds.
        For should not grave & learn'd Experience
That looks with the Eyes of all the world beside,
And with all Ages holds Intelligence
Go safer than Deceit without a Guide?
Which in the By-Paths of her Diffidence,
Crossing the ways of Right, still runs more wide.[3]

        .   .   .   .

Pow'r above Pow'rs! O Heavenly Eloquence!
That with the Strong Run of commanding Words,
Dost manage, guide & master th' Eminence

                    264
Of Men's Affections more than all their Swords!
Shall we not offer to thy Excellence

The richest Treasure that our Wit affords?
　　　Thou that Canst do much more with one poor Pen,
Than all the Pow'rs of Princes can effect;
And draw, divert, dispose & fashion Men,
Better than Force or Rigor can direct!
Should we this Ornament of Glory then,
As th' unmaterial Fruits of Shades neglect?[1]

　　　.　　.　　.　　.　　.　　.　　.　　.

When all that ever hotter Spirits exprest,
Comes bettered by the patience of the North,
And who (in Time) knows whither we may Vent
The Treasure of our Tongue?　To what strange Shores
This gain of our best glory shall be sent,
T' enrich unknowing nations with our Stores?
What worlds in th' yet unformed Occident
May come refined with th' Accents that are ours?
Or who can tell for what great Work in Hand
The greatness of our Stile is now ordain'd?
What pow'rs it shall bring in, what Spirits command?
What Thoughts let out, what Humours keep restrain'd?
What Mischief it may pow'rfully withstand;
And what fair ends may thereby be attain'd?
　　　And as for Poesy (Mother of this Force)
That breeds, brings forth, & nourishes this might;
Teaching it in a loose, yet measured Course
With comely Motions how to go upright;
And fost'ring it with bountiful Discourse
Adorns it thus in Fashions of Delight.
　　　What should I say?　Since it is well approved

　　　　　　265
The Speech of Heaven, with whom they have Commerce
That only seem out of themselves removed,
And do with more than Human Skills converse:
Those numbers wherewith Heaven & Earth are moved
Shew Weakness speaks in Prose but Pow'r in Verse.[1]
　　　　　　　　　　　　Musophilus.
　　　　　　=
He who hath never warr'd with Misery
Nor ever tugged with danger & distress
Hath had n' Occasion nor no field to try
The Strength & Forces of his Worthiness.

　　　.　　.　　.　　.　　.　　.　　.　　.　　.

Not to b' unhappy is unhappiness
And Mis'ry not to have known Misery.

　　　.　　.　　.　　.　　.　　.　　.　　.

　　　He that endures for what his conscience knows
Not to be ill, doth from a patience high
Look, only on the Cause whereto he owes
Those Sufferings, not on his Misery:
The more h' endures, the more his Glory grows.
　　　.　　.　　.　　.　　.　　.　　.   Epistle to Wriothesly[2]

266

Now sleeps the crimson petal, now the white;
Nor waves the cypress in the palace walk;
Nor winks the gold fin in the porphyry font:
The fire-fly wakens: waken thou with me.

Now droops the milk-white peacock like a ghost,
And like a ghost she glimmers on to me.

Now lies the Earth all Danäe to the stars,
And all thy heart lies open unto me.

Now slides the silent meteor on, and leaves
A shining furrow, as thy thoughts in me.

Now folds the lily all her sweetness up,
And slips into the bosom of the lake:
So fold thyself, my dearest, thou, & slip
Into my bosom and be lost in me.

                    The Princess, p. 150[1]

267

Buddha's Cave. "Our traveller, as we have said, entered India by
way of Kabul. Shortly after he arrived at . . . Peshawer, Hiouen-
thsang heard of an Extraordinary Cave, where Buddha had formerly
converted a dragon, & had promised his new pupil to leave him his
shadow, in order that, whenever the evil passions of his dragon-
nature should revive, the aspect of his master's shadowy features
might remind him of his former vows. This promise was fulfilled,
& the dragon-cave became a famous place of pilgrimage. Our Traveller was told that the roads leading to the cave were extremely
dangerous, & infested by robbers--that for three years none of the
pilgrims had ever returned from the cave. But he replied, 'It
would be difficult during a hundred thousand Kalpas to meet one
single time with the true shadow of Buddha; how could I, having
come so near, pass on without going to adore it?' He left his
companions behind & after asking in vain for a guide, he met at
last with a boy who showed him to a farm belonging to a convent.
Here he found an old man who undertook to act as his guide. They
had hardly proceeded a few miles when they were attacked by robbers five. The monk took off his cap & displayed his Ecclesiastical robes. 'Master,' said one of the robbers, 'where are you
going?' Hiouen-thsang replied, 'I desire to adore the shadow of
Buddha.' 'Master', said the robber, 'have you not heard that
these roads are full of bandits?' 'Robbers are men,' Hiouen-
thsang exclaimed, 'and at present   /268/   when I am going to
adore the shadow of Buddha, even though the roads were full of
wild beasts, I should walk on without fear. Surely, then, I
ought not to fear you, as you are men whose heart is possessed of
pity.' The robbers were moved by these words, & opened their
hearts to the true faith. After this little incident, Hiouen-
thsang proceeded with his guide. He passed a stream rushing down
between two precipitous walls of rock. In the rock itself there
was a door which opened. All was dark. But Hiouen-thsang entered, advanced towards the East, then moved fifty steps backwards & began his devotions. He made one hundred salutations,
but he saw nothing. He reproached himself bitterly with his
former sins, he cried, & abandoned himself to utter despair, because the shadow of Buddha would not appear before him. At last,

after many prayers & invocations, he saw on the eastern wall a dim
light, of the size of a saucepan, such as the Buddhist monks carry
in their hands. But it disappeared. He continued praying full of
joy & pain, & again he saw a light, which vanished like lightning.
Then he vowed, full of devotion & love, that he would never leave
the place till he had seen the shadow of the 'Venerable of the
age.' After two hundred prayers, the cave was suddenly bathed in
light, & the shadow of Buddha, of a brilliant white colour, rose
majestically on the wall, as when the clouds suddenly open and,
all at once, display the marvellous /269/   image of the 'Mountain of Light.' A dazzling splendour lighted up the features of
the divine countenance. Hiouen-thsang was lost in contemplation
& wonder, & would not turn his eyes away from the sublime & in-
comparable object. . . . After he awoke from his trance, he called
in six men & commanded them to light a fire in the cave in order
to burn incense; but, as the approach of the light made the shadow
of Buddha disappear, the fire was extinguished. Then five of the
men saw the shadow but the sixth saw nothing. The old man who
had acted as a guide was astonished when Hiouen-thsang told him
the Vision. 'Master,' he said, 'without the sincerity of your
faith, & the energy of your vows, you could not have seen such a
miracle.'
     This is the account given by Hiouen-thsang's biographers.
. . . But in the 'Si-Yu-Ki', which contains his diary, he tells
the story in a different way. The Cave is described with almost
the same words. But afterwards, the writer continues: 'Formerly,
the shadow of Buddha was seen in the cave, bright, like his natural appearance, & with all the marks of his divine beauty. One
might have said, it was Buddha himself. For some centuries, however, it can no longer be seen completely. Though one does see
something, it is only a feeble & doubtful resemblance. If a man
prays with sincere faith, & if he has received from above a hidden impression, he sees the shadow clearly, but he cannot enjoy
the sight for any length of time.'"

                              Max Müller, Buddhist Pilgrims[1]

                              270
Population.   1861. Total population of Great Britain about
30,000,000. About 570,000 majority of Women. 105 boys born to
100 girls. Under 17 years males preponderate; above, females.

Population of England & Wales only 20,000,000. Increase in 10
years, 6 per cent.[1]

(Popu. of Engd. & Wales in 1832: 14,105,645.)[2]

     1 quarter of corn per head annually needed for sustenance.
12 million qrs. produced annually in England & Wales.
Rate of production 30 bushels per acre on an average[3]
[63 lbs per imperial Bushel of Wheat selling at 40s. per qr. 32s.
per sack=280 lbs net][4]

Agricultural Report 1833. Lancashire bushel = 70 lbs. Rent paid
for some arable land--40 to 60s per acre. Grazing land from 35
to 45s. Labourers 10s. per week in Leicestershire.
     Stiff, unkind soil, well-farmed, from 25 to 28 bushels per
acre--of wheat. Labourer's wages; 1 bushel per week; then
$1\frac{1}{8}$, then $1\frac{1}{2}$. Some land yielding 4 to 5 qrs. per acre, near

Doncaster.   3 grs. on an average, the best land--average rent
25s.[5]

                              271
     Notes from Paris's Pharmacologia.   (1866)[1]
Sympathetic powder of Sir Kenelm Digby.   "Anoint the sword that
has made the wound & dress it (the sword) two or three times a
day.   Let the wound in the mean time be drawn together, & carefully bound with linen rags, but above all be let alone for seven
days." See Sir K. Digby's Discourse on the cure by sympathy pron.
at Montpelier, translated by R. White, Gent. 1658.   The powder,
as we learn from contemporary physicians, was calcined green
vitriol.[2]
     So the rust of the spear of Telephus in Homer cures the
wounds inflicted by the weapon, (probably verdigris, says Paris,
rationalizing.)[3]
     "Who can doubt that a drink in which the ring of Saint
Remigius had been immersed was a very useful febrifuge diluent?"[4]
     Boyle recommended the thigh-bone of an executed criminal as
a powerful remedy in dysentery.[5]
     Paralytic to whom Davy was about to give nitrous oxide cured
by the putting of the thermometer under his tongue--which he fan-
cied was the curative process.[6]
     Theory that every natural poison carried within itself its
own antidote--hair or blood of a mad dog to cure its bite.   Evil
effects of witchcraft prevented by 3 scruples of the ashes of a
witch well & carefully burnt at a stake.[7]
     Soranus attributes the effects of honey in curing the aphthae
of children to the fact that the bees from whom it was taken hived
near the tomb of Hippocrates.[8]   /272/   "The doses," said the
mathematical school, "are as the squares of the constitution."[1]
     Medical Theories: Galen's--the four humours, hot, cold,
moist & dry. Methodic Sect--Solids the seat of disease: relax-
ing & bracing remedies. Iatro-mathematical school--lentor or
morbid viscidity of the blood the cause of disease: remedies
attenuant & diluent. Chemical school--no source of diseases but
the presence of some morbid acid or alkali, some untoward fer-
mentation of the fluids or some diseased condition in the chemical combinations in the body:--all remedies must act by producing
some chemical change. (Stahl)[2]
     The doctrine of Signatures--principally adopted by Paracel-
sus, Baptista Porta & Crollius, though traces of it may be found
in ancient authors. Did not exist as a regular theory till the
end of the XIVth cent. Tumeric, because of its yellow colour,
would relieve jaundice: the Euphrasia (eye bright) good for the
eyes, because of the black spot in its corolla.[3]
     An extensive list of animal substances has been discarded
from the Materia Medica, since it has been known that they owe
their properties to one & the same principle, as to gelatine,
albumen, carbonate of lime: & again, every animal substance containing nitrogen yields ammonia. Such discoveries have banished
Earthworms; vipers skinned & deprived of their entrails; human
skulls; dried blood; elk's hoof; urine of a child; of a healthy
young man &c. In like manner, the fixed alkaline salt produced
by the incineration of   /273/   different vegetables has been
found to be potass, except marine plants which yield soda, & perhaps some of the Tetradynamia which yield Ammonia. Before this,
every vegetable was supposed to hold & yield a different salt--
salt of wormwood, salt of broom, salt of bean-stalks.[1]

Theriaka Andromachi, otherwise called Antidotum Mithridatium contains 72 ingredients.[2]

Difficulty of identifying plants in the ancient Pharmacopeia because general names become particular, as, Cicuta meant not hemlock only but vegetable poisons in general. Opium meant juice in general. Alkali meant that particular residuum which was obtained by lixiviating the ashes of the plant named Kali.[3]

For the botanical history of the middle ages see Macer's Herbal. For the 17th century, see Turnos, Culpepper, Lovel.[4]

"Those medicines alone are practically similar whose operations have been found by experience to continue the same through every condition of the human body. Arsenic & bark would appear medicinally similar in certain states of the body, as in ague; but in other conditions no two substances can be more dissimilar in their operations."[5]

Of Plants it may be said as a general rule, that "Quae genue convenient, virtute convenient."[6] Thus the Umbelliferae, which grow on dry ground, are aromatic; while the aquatic species are among the most deadly poisons. /274/ The Cruciferae are aromatic & acrid in their nature, containing essential oils, which are obtainable by distillation; & Linnaeus asserts (not accurately however) that "among all the leguminous or papillionaceous tribe there is no deleterious plant to be found." Individuals in these natural orders although very nearly related, do nevertheless possess various & even opposite qualities. In the subdivision even of a genus there is often a remarkable difference in the properties of the species: there are e.g. Solanmus {Strychnos, Nightshade}, lettuces, cucumbers & mushrooms, both esculent & poisonous. The same individual will vary from culture or other circumstances, as much as plants which have no botanic affinity: the Camomile, e.g. may have its whole disk changed by cultivation to ligulate white florets, destitute of medicinal properties.[1]

Relation between the Linnaean system & the natural properties of plants, e.g. a plant whose flower has 5 stamina, 1 pistil, 1 petal, & whose fruit is of the berry kind may be at once pronounced poisonous.[2]

Bark first ministered in 1639.[3] In 1799 it fell into total discredit from its inability to cure the ague: it was afterwards discovered that the bark had been adulterated with an inferior species.[4]

Bezoar, from Pa-hazar (Persian) a destroyer of poison. A morbid concretion in the bodies of land animals. Some of them held powerful /275/ alexipharmics, so much so that other medicines having alexipharmic powers were called Bezoardic. Sometimes bought for their weight in gold. First recommended by Avenzoar. A composition of Bezoar with absorbent powers had been much used under the name of Gascoigne powders; but the real Benzoar was rarely used; Gypsum or pipeclay tinged with ox-gall provides less expensive ingredient.[1]

Countess of Chinchona in 1639 brought from Peru into Spain a certain quantity of quinine, but it was not put into general circulation till ten years afterwards by the Jesuits of Rome, who had received a considerable mass.[2]

276
Chaucer. Canterbury Tales[1]
1 Knight's Tale: Palamon & Arcite.
2 Miller's Tale. Carpenter & Deluge (Boccaccio)
3 Reve's Tale. The Miller & Students (Boccaccio)

```
    4 Coke's Tale.  (Broken Off.)
   +5 Man of Lawes Tale.  Constance, the Emperor's daughter
    6 Wife of Bathes Tale.  What women like best:  The Lothely
             Wife.
    7 Freres Tale.  The Sompnour & the Devil
    8 Sompnours Tale.  The tricked Frere.
   +9 Clerkes Tale.  Griselda
  +10 Marchantes Tale.  January & May.
   11 Squier's Tale.  Cambuscan  (unfinished)
  +12 Frankelein's Tale.  The Knight of Bretagne
   13 The Doctour's Tale.  Virginia.
   14 Pardoneres Tale.  The three ribalds who plot to kill each
             other
   15 Shipmanns Tale.  The Monk & Merchant  (Boccaccio)
   16 Prioresses Tale.  The Boy Martyr.
   17 Chaucer himself.  Sir Thopas and
   18        "          the Tale of Melibeus
   19²The Monkes Tale.  Stories of Fallen Greatness
   20³The Second Nonnes Tale.  Saint Cecilia
   21¹Nonnes Preestes Tale.  The Cock & the Fox
   22 Chanones Yemannes Tale.  Transmuter of Metals
   23 Manciples Tale.  Apollo & the Crow.
   24 The Persones Tale.  A Sermon.
```

277

"He had more tow on his distaffe
Than Gerveis knew."[1]
                  =   Canterbury Tales
"We list not of the chaff ne of the stre
Maken so long a tale as of the corn"[2]
                  =   ib
One of us two must bowen douteless
And, sith a man is more reasonable
Than woman is, ye moste be suffrable.
                  =   Wife of Bath's Prologue[3]
"As lewed people demen comunly
Of thinges that be made more subtilly,
Than they can in hir lewedness comprehend
They demen gladly to the badder end."[4]
                  =
"Janus sits by the fire with doble berd
And drinketh of his bugle horn the wine
Before him stant brawne of the tusked swine
And Nowel cried every lusty man."[5]
                  =
"Hire facounde eke full womanly & plain,
No contrefeted termes hadde she
To semen wise; but after hire degree
She spake, & all hire wordes more or less
Souning in vertue & in gentlenesse."
                           Griselda[6]

278

Hieroglyphic writing is either
1 Iconographic (otherwise ideographic) in which the symbol is a
   direct imitation, as a circle for the Sun, a male fig. for a
   man, a female fig. for a woman, & the two together for mankind.
   (Also a part is taken for the whole)
2 Anaglyphic or tropical, in which the meaning is conveyed

figuratively, <u>as</u> <u>a</u> <u>leg</u> <u>in</u> <u>a</u> <u>trap</u> for <u>deceit</u>. <u>A</u> <u>youth</u> <u>with</u> <u>a</u> <u>finger</u> <u>in</u> <u>his</u> <u>mouth</u> for an <u>infant</u>.

3 The allegorical or enigmatic, in which the object intended is represented by a conventional emblem as two water-plants of slightly different forms for Upper & Lower Egypt.

4 Kyriologic or phonetic, in which the initial letter (sound) of the hieroglyph's primitive meaning stands for the initial letters of other words, & for the words themselves having the same initial letters.[1]

279 Hebrew Alphabet[1]

Aleph	א	gutturale très faible
Beth	ב	B
Gimel	ג	GH
Daleth	ד	D
He	ה	H doux
Vau	ו	OU (W)
Zain	ז	Z
Cheth	ח	Orig. power proby. syllabic <u>che</u> reduced in Greek to he--e
Theth	ט	Considered by modern Hebraists a mere t.
Iod	׳ ׳	Held by some a nasal consonant, by others a guttural, by others O, I or Y.
Caph	כ	K, as a terminal ך
Lamed	ל ל	L
Mem	מ	M: terminal, ם
Nun	נ	N: terminal ן
Samech	ס	S
Ayin	ע	Gutturale forte
Pe	פ	P: terminal, ף
Tsadi	צ *	Ç: terminal ץ
Koph	ק ק	Khh
Resh	ר	R
Shin	שׁ	S or sch
Sin	שׂ	s
Tau	ת	TH or T

* Never included in the Greek alphabet

280[1]

	Medial	Tenues	aspirata
Guttural & palatal	g	k (c, g)	gh, ch, h with perhaps ng, y, wh
Dental	d	t	dh (as th in this) th (as in thing) z, s zh (ch in church) sh, j (Eng.) j (French)
Labials	b	p	v, f, w

Perhaps the four last placed among the dentals partake equally of the palatal character.

The vowels should be written in the following order (with their continental pronunciation) i, e, a, o, u.

The liquids, r, l, n, m -- beginning from the throat & advancing along the palate & teeth to the lips.

The gradations of consonantal sounds are infinite, so to speak. There may be as many t's as can represent the possible varieties of contact between the palate at the line of the teeth, to an inch beyond it. The Arabs have two t's.

sibilants

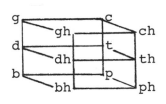

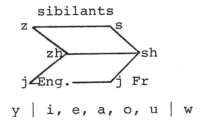

y | i, e, a, o, u | w

Saxon Letters in addition to the Roman
  ð dh; þ th; (thorn)   ƿ w. (wên)
These are runic letters   Supra. 212

281

From Pausanias ch. XVII.

Near the altar of Minerva Chalcioecos are two statues of Pausanias who commanded the Lacedemonians at Plataea. . . . . I shall content myself with adding what I heard from a private person of Byzantium, namely, that if Pausanias saw all his projects discovered, & if among all those who took refuge in the Chalceioecos, he was the only one who was not protected by that asylum, the reason was that he could never purify himself from the murder of which I am about to tell. When in the neighbourhood of the Hellespont with the vessels of the Lacedemonians & of the other Greeks, Pausanias became enamoured of a young girl of Byzantium named Cleonice, who was brought to him at the beginning of the night by those who had charge of this commission. In approaching him she involuntarily overturned the lamp which was burning in his chamber: Pausanias, who was already asleep, was awakened by the noise, & being in perpetual fear & agitation on account of the project he had already formed of betraying Greece, he rose, struck the girl with his sabre & killed her. He could never get purified from this crime. In vain he had recourse to all sorts of expiations: in vain he ranged himself among the supplicants of Jupiter Physius; & went to Phigalia in Arcadia to those who evoke spirits. He justly endured the punishment of the crime he had committed against Cleonice & the gods.[1]

Arguments of   282   the Iliad[1]

α. B.   I.   The contention of Agamemnon & Achilles.
β.   II.   The Trial of the army & catalogue of the Forces.
γ.   III.   The duel of Menelaus & Paris.
δ.   IV.   Breach of the truce by Pandarus aiming an arrow at Menelaus, who is wounded, but cured by Machaon. The first Battle; Agamemnon having reviewed the troops.
ε.   V.   The acts of Diomed.
ζ.   VI.   The episodes of Glaucus & Diomed, & of Hector & Andromache.
η.   VII.   Single combat between Hector & Ajax. Truce, that the Trojans may bury their dead. Greek camp fortified.
θ.   VIII.   Second battle & distress of the Greeks. The Trojans watch all night under arms.
ι.   IX.   The embassy to Achilles
κ.   X.   Night adventure of Diomed & Ulysses in which they seize the horses of Rhesus.
λ.   XI.   Third Battle: acts of Agamemnon. Hector makes great slaughter, & opposes Ajax: Machaon wounded & carried to the tent of Nestor; Achilles sends Patroclus to inquire who is thus wounded.
μ.   XII.   The Battle at the Grecian wall.
ν.   XIII.   Fourth Battle continued, in which Neptune assists the Greeks: the acts of Idomeneus.
ξ.   XIV.   Juno deceives Jupiter by the girdle of Venus.
ο.   XV.   The fifth battle at the ships & the acts of Ajax.
π.   XVI.   Sixth battle: acts & death of Patroclus.
ρ.   XVII.   Seventh Battle, for the body of Patroclus. The acts of Menelaus.
σ.   XVIII.   Grief of Achilles at the death of Patroclus. Thetis comforts him & goes to Vulcan to obtain Achilles' shield.

283

τ.   XIX.   Reconciliation of Achilles & Agamemnon. Achilles arms for the fight & addresses his horses.
υ.   XX.   Battle of the Gods, & the acts of Achilles.
φ.   XXI.   Battle in the river Scadamder.
χ.   XXII.   Death of Hector.
ψ.   XXIII.   Funeral games in honour of Patroclus.
ω.   XXIV.   The redemption of the body of Hector.

Odyssey.[1]

α.   I.   Minerva's descent to Ithaca.
β.   II.   Council of Ithaca. Telemachus embarks.
γ.   III.   The interview of Telemachus & Nestor at Pylus.
δ.   IV.   The conference with Menelaus.
ε.   V.   Departure of Ulysses from Calypso: his shipwreck.
ζ.   VI.   Nausicaa discovers Ulysses.

η.   VII.   The palace & gardens of Alcinoüs.
θ. VIII.   Demodocus sings: Games.
ι.   IX.   Ulysses tells his adventures among the Cicons, Lotaphagi,
            & Cyclopes.
κ.   X.   Adventures with AEolos, the Laestrygons & Circe.
λ.   XI.   The descent into hell.
μ.   XII.   The Sirens: Scylla & Charybdis: Oxen of Helios.
ν. XIII.   Arrival of Ulysses in Ithaca.
ξ.   XIV.   Conversation with Eumaeus.
ο.   XV.   The return of Telemachus.
π.   XVI.   The discovery of Ulysses to Telemachus.
ρ. XVII.   Ulysses goes to his palace: the dog Argus.
σ. XVIII.   The fight of Irus & Ulysses.
τ.   XIX.   Discovery of Ulysses to Euryclea.
υ.   XX.   Banquet of the Suitors.
φ.   XXI.   The bending of Ulysses' bow.
χ. XXII.   Death of the Suitors.
ψ. XXIII.   Recognition of Ulysses by Penelope.
ω. XXIV.   The shades of the suitors: Laertes.

284

"The first & most necessary poynt that ever I found meete to be
considered in making of a delectable poeme is this, to ground it
upon some fine invention. For it is not inough to roll in pleasant wordes, nor yet to thunder in Rym, Ram, Ruff, by letter (quoth
my Master Chaucer) nor yet to abound in apt vocables, or epythetes,
unlesse the Invention have in it also aliquid salis. . . . And
again many Inventions are good, & yet not finely handled. And
for a general forewarning: what Theame soever you do take in
hande, if you do handle it but tanquam in oratione perpetua, &
never studie for some depth of devise in ye Invention, & some
figures also in the handlying thereof: it will appeare to the
skilful Reader but a tale of a tubbe. . . . If I should undertake
to wryte in praise of a gentlewoman, I would neither praise hir
christal eye nor her cherry lippe &c. For these things are trita
& obvia. . . . To conclude therein, I would have you stand most
upon the excellencie of your Invention, & sticke not to studie
deeply for some fine devise. For that being founde, pleasant
woordes will follow well inough & fast inough."
        Gascoigne, "Certayne Notes of Instruction concerning
the making of verse or ryme in English." 1575[1]

"This brutish poetry"-- "I mean this tynkerly verse which we call
ryme"--Webbe, Discourse of Eng. Poetry 1586[2]
The first beginning of Ryme (as we nowe terme it) though it be
something auncient, yet nothing famous.
                                        ib.[3]

285

"Yet is there such a natural force or quantity in eche word, that
it will not abide any place but one without some foule disgrace".
ib.[1]

                           =

"Ze man also be warre with composing ony thing in the same manner,
as hes bene ower oft usit of before. As in speciall, gif ze speik
of love, be warre ze descryve zour Loves makdome, or her fairnes.
And siclyke that ze descryve not the morning, & rysing of the
Sunne, in the Preface of zour verse: for thir thingis are sa oft
& dyverslie writtin upon be Poetis already that gif ze do the

lyke, it will appeare, ze bot imitate, & that it cummis not of
zour zwin Inventioun, quhilk is ane of the chief properties of
ane poete &c."
          1584. King James, Reulis and Cautely of Scottis Poems[2]
                              =
"Whatsoever forme of words doth mouve, delight & sway the affections of men, in what Scythian sort soever it be disposed or uttered, that is true number, measure eloquence, & the perfection
of speech: which .˙. hath as many shapes as there be tongues or
nations in the world, nor can with all the tyrannical Rules of
Idle Rhetoric be governed otherwise than Custome, & present observation will allow."[1]
                    Samuel Daniel, Defence of Ryme, 1603[3]
                              =
     So that their (the Greeks' & Latins') plenty seems to have
bred the same wast & contempt as ours doth now, though it had not
power to disvalew what was worthy of posterity, nor keepe back
the repu-   /286/   tation of excellences, destined to continue
for many ages. . . . . . To delight an exterior sense we smoth up
a weake confused sense, affecting sound to be unsound, & all to
seem Servum pecus, onely to imitate the Greeks & Latines whose
felicity in this kinde, might be something to themselves, to whom
their own idioma was naturall, but to us it can yield no other
commodity than a sound. We admire them not for their smoth-
gliding words, but for their inventions: which treasure, if it
were to be found in Welch & Irish we should hold those languages
in the same estimation, & they may thank their swords that made
their tongues so famous & universall as they are. For to say
truth, their verse is many times but a confused deliverer of
their excellent conceits, whose scattered limbs we are fain to
look out & joine together, to discerne the image of what they
represent unto us. . . . . & then aganine, when you finde them
disobedient to their own laws, you must hold it to be licentia
poetica, & so dispensable." Daniel. ibid[1]

     "Sure in an Eminent Spirite whom nature hath fitted for that
mystery, Ryme is no impediment to his conceits, but rather gives
him winges to mount & carries him not out of his course, but as
it were beyonde his power to a farre happyer flight." ib.[2]

     "The body of our imagination, being as an unformed Chaos
without fashion, without day, if by the divine power of the
spirit it be   /287/   wrought into an Orbe of order & forme, is
it not more pleasing to nature that desires a certainty & com-
ports not with that which is infinite &c."[1]

     "Wrong to England . . . to turne the faire streame & full
course of her accents, into the shallow current of a loose uncertainty, cleane out of the way of her knowne delight."[2]
     "We see some fantasticke put on a fashion which afterward
gravitie it selfe is faine to put on, because it will not be out
of the weare of other men, & Recti apud nos locum tenet error ubi
publicus factus est."[3]
                              =
     "I must confesse, that to mine own eare, those continuall
cadences of couplets used in long & continued Poems, are very
tyresome & unpleasing, by reason that still, me thinks they runne
on, with a sound of one nature, & a kinde of certaintie which
stuffs the delight rather than intertaines it. But, yet

notwithstanding, I must not out of mine own daintinesse, condemn
this kind of writing, which peradventure to another may seeme
most delightfulle: and many worthy compositions wee see to have
passed with commendation in that kinde. Besides, me thinkes sometimes, to beguile the care with a running out & passing over the
Ryme, as no bound to stay us in the line where the violence of
the matter will break thorow, is rather graceful than otherwise.[*]
. . . And I must confesse my Adversarie hath wrought this much
upon me, that I think a Tragedie   /288/   would indeed best com-
porte with a blancke Verse, & dispense with Ryme, saving in the
Chorus or where a sentence shall require a couplet. And to
avoyde this over-glutting the eare with that always certaine, &
full incounter of Ryme, I have assaide in some of my Epistles to
alter the usuall place of meeting & to set it further off by one
verse, to trie how I could disuse my owne eare, & to ease it of
this continuall burthen, which indeed seems to surcharge it a
little too much, but as yet I cannot come to please myselfe therein."[1]

"But in these things, I say; I dare not take upon me to teach
that they ought to be so, in respect my selfe holds them to be so,
or that I thinke it right; for indeed there is no right in these
things that are continually in a wandering motion, carried with
the violence of our uncertaine likings, being but only the time
that gives them their power."   Daniel, ibid[2]

"You shall never have my subscription or consent (though you
should charge me with the authoritie of five hundreth Maister
Drants,) to make your Carpēnter our Carpĕnter: an inch longer or
bigger than God & his Englishe people have made him."   Gabriel
Harvey to Spencer.[3]

"Say you suddāinly if you list; by my certaĭnly & certaĭnty
I will not." id.[4]

"I like your late English hexameters so exceedingly well,
that I also enure my Penne   /289/   sometime in that kinde;
which I fynd indeede, as I have heard you often defende in worde,
neither so harde, nor so harshe, that it will easily & fairely
yeeld itself to our Moother tongue. For the onely, or chiefest
hardnesse, whych seemeth, is in the Accent: whyche sometime
gapeth, and as it were yawneth ilfavouredly, comming shorte of
that it should, & sometime exceeding the measure of the Number,
as in Carpenter, the middle syllable being used short in speache,
when it shall be read long in Verse, seemeth like a lame gosling,
that draweth one legge after hir: & Heaven, beeing used short as
one syllable, when it is in verse, stretched out with a Diastole,
is like a lame dog that holds up one legge. But it is to be
wonne with Custome & rough words must be subdued with use. For
why, in god's name, may not we, as else the Greekes, have the
kingdome of oure owne language, & measure our Accentes by the
sounde, reserving the Quantitie to the Verse?"
                    Edmund Spencer to Gabriel Harvey   1580[1]
                              =
"I have observed, & so may any one that is either practiced
in singing or hath a natural ear able to time a song, that the
Latine verses of six feete, as the Heroick & Iambick, or of five
feet, as the Trochaick, are in nature all of the same length of
sound with our English verses of five feete; for either of them

being timed with the hand, <u>quinque perficiunt tempora</u>, they fill
up the quantity (as it were) of five

v. p. 291.

290

> I cannot eat but little meat
>   My stomach is not good,
> But sure I think, that I can drink
>   With him that wears a hood.
> Though I go bare, take ye no care
>   I nothing am acold,
> I stuff my skin so full within
>   With jolly good ale & old.

Chorus

> Back & side go bare, go bare,
>   Both foot & hand go colde!
> But, belly, God send thee good ale enough,
>   Whether it be new or olde!

> I love no roast but a nut-brown toast,
>   And a crab laid in the fire;
> A little bread shall do me stead,
>   Moche Bread I nought desire;
> No frost, no snowe, no winde I trow,
>   Can hurt me if I wolde,
> I am so wrapt, & throwly lapt
>   In jolly good ale & old.

Chorus.

=   Gammer Gurton's Needle.[1]

> Mihi est propositum in taberna mori,
> Vinum sit appositum morientis ori,
> Ut dicant cum venerint angelorum chori
> Deus sit propitius huic potatori.

Walter Map.[2]

291

of five sem'briefs; as for example if any man will prove to time
these verses with his hand:
  A pure Iambick: <u>Suis et ipsa viribus Roma ruit.</u>[1]
  A licentiate Iambick: <u>Ducent volentes fata, nolentes trahunt.</u>[2]
  An Heroick Verse: <u>Tytere tu patulae recubans sub tegmine fagi.</u>[3]
  A Trochaic Verse: <u>Nox est perpetua una dormienda.</u>[4]
  Eng. Iambicks pure: The more secure the more the stroke we feele
                       Of unprevented harms; so gloomy stormes
                       Appear the sterner if the day be cleere.

English Iamb. licentiate: Hārke hōw thĕse winds do murmur at thy
                          flight.
The Eng. Trochee: Still where Envy leaves, remorse doth enter.

   The cause why these verses differing in feete yeeld the same
length of sound, is by reason of some rests, which either the
necessity of the numbers, or the heaviness of the syllables do
beget. For we find in musick, that oftentimes the straines of a
song can not be reduct to true number without some rests prefixed
in the beginning & middle, as also at the close if need requires.

Besides, our English monosyllables require many breathings which
no doubt lengthen a verse: so that it is no wonder if for these
reasons our English verses of five feet hold pace with the latins
of sixe. The pure Iambick in English needs small demonstration,
because it consists simply of Iambick feete; but our Iambick licentiate offers itself to a farther consideration; for in the
third & fifth place we must of force hold the Iambick foote; in
the first, second, & fourth place we may use a Spondee or Iambick
& sometime a Tribrach or dactyl, but rarely an Anapaestick foote,
& that in the second or fourth place.

292
But why an Iambick in the third place? I answer, that the fore-
part of the verse may the gentlier slide into his Dimeter: as
for example sake, divide this verse: Harke how these winds do
murmure at thy flight. 'Harke how these winds': there the voice
doth naturally affect a rest[1]. . . . .
Though as I said before, the naturall breathing place of our
English Iambic verse is in the last syllable of the second foot,
as our Trochee, after the manner of the Latine heroick & Iambick,
rests naturally in the first of the third foot; yet no man is
tyed altogether to observe this rule, but he may alter it, after
the judgment of his eare, which Poets, Orators & Musicians ought
of all men to have most excellent. Again, though I said pre-
emptorily before, that the third & fift place of our licentiate
Iambic must always hold an Iambic foot, yet I will show for example in both places where a Tribrack may be very formally taken:
& first in the third place: 'Some trade in Barbary, some in
Turky trade.'
                 'Men that do fall to misery, quickly fall.'
    . . . . Tribrack in the fifth place . . .
             'Renown'd in every art there lives not any.'
To proceede farther, I see no reason why the English Iambick in
his first place, may not as well borrow a foot of the Trochy, as
our Trochy, or the Latine hendicasillable, may in the like case
make bold with the Iambick: but it must be done ever with this
Caveat, which is, that a Spondee, Dactile, or Tribrack do supply
the next places: for an Iambick beginning with a single short
syllable /293/   & the other ending before with the like, would
too much drink up the verse if they came immediately together.
. . . . . . Though I have set downe these second licenses as good
& agreable enough, yet for the most part, my first rules are
generall."
        Campion, Observations in the Art of Eng. Poesie 1602[1]

(Campion is styled in the margin of the Polimanteia 1595 "Sweet
master Campion":[2] in the Theatrum Poetarum 1675 by Edward Phil-
lips, "a writer of no extraordinary fame.")[3]

     The Defence of Ryme by Samuel Daniel . . . has proved one of
the few pieces of poetical criticism from time to time reprinted,
& has always accompanied the poems of the author. Born 1562;
died 1619.[4]

                       . . . . .
The hexameter, says Webbe in his "Discourse of English Poetrie"
will stand more orderlye in our English speech than any of the
other kindes (!), untill we have some tolleration of words made
by speciall rule.[5]
        V. Haslewood's collection of Essays.[6]

294

Religion & Superstition. Cicero (de Natura Deor. II, 28) derives
the word religious from relĕgere. "Qui autem omnia, quae ad cul-
tum deorum pertinerent, diligenter retracterent et tanquam rele-
gerent, sunt dicti religiosi, ex relĕgendo, ut elegantes ex
eligendo, tanquam a deligendo diligentes, ex intelligendo intelli-
gentes. His enim in verbis omnibus inest vis legendi eadem, quae
in religioso."[1] In Smith's Dict. Sub.v. I find that Lactantius &
St. Augustine (in Retract. I. 13) assume religare as the primitive, Lact. citing Lucretius "religionum nodis animos exsolvere"
in support of this etymology.[2] Cicero's derivation is supported
by the word religens, pious, religious--"religentem esse oportet,
religiosum nefas."[3] But certainly Cicero seems unfortunate in
the derivation he gives just before for superstitious: "Nam qui
totos dies precabantur et immolabant, ut sui sibi liberi superstites essent, superstitiosi sunt appellati; quod nomen postea
latius patet."[4] Lactantius (v. note in Pankoncke) ridicules him
for this derivation & himself gives the following explanation:
"Superstitiosi sunt ii qui superstitem memoriam defunctorum
colunt, aut qui parentibus suis superstites, colebant imagines
corum domi, tanquam deos Penates."[5] [Perhaps, says the lexicon,
the force of the word lies in the prefix, the root Sta having
little more than the meaning of the substantive verb. If so, the
etymological signification is, "a being Excessive."] The Greek
words used with the same general function as religion are
ετσέβεια & θρησκεία.

295

The former implies the more moral element--reverence, dutiful-
ness; the latter, worship, observance. The latter word is the
one used in the New Testament, as, e.g. in the Epistle of James.
One derivation is from θρηξ, because of the Thracian mysteries;
another from τρέω, as implying fear; another, from θρέω, from the
muttering of prayers.
     See, in Grote, quoted a propos of Epimenides, called to
Athens from Crete to allay the religious terrors of the Athenians[1]
(δειοιδαιμονίας):[2] "θεοφιλὴs καὶ σοφὸs περὶ τὰ θεῖα τὴν
ενθουσιαστικὴν καὶ τελεστικὴν σοφίαν."[3]
                              =
     In relation to the function of the poet see the effect pro-
duced by Tyrtaeus at Sparta during the Messenian war.[4] "So frequent were the aggressions of the Messenians upon the Spartan
territory, that a large portion of the border land was left un-
cultivated: scarcity ensued, & the proprietors of the deserted
farms, driven to despair, pressed for a redivision of the landed
property of the State. It was in appeasing these discontents
that the poem of Tyrtaeus called Eunomia, "Legal Order," was
found signally beneficial."[5] V. Aristotle, Pol. V.7,1. Pausan.
IV.18,2.[6]
          Tyrtaeus qui mares animos in martia bella
          Versibus exacuit.
                              Hors. Ars Poet. 402[7]

Celtic Literature   296

"Les Gallois possèdent deux poèmes historiques, du VIme siècle,
où il est question d'un chef cambrien du nom d'Arthur, qui a
réellement existé. . . . il n'a rien de merveilleux. . . . . Les
Triades me paraissent avoir voulu faire un personnage réel de

l'Arthur mythologique; c'est bien encore le héro des anciens
bardes, mais dépouillé de son auréole. . . . .[1] Contes des
anciens Bretons: ils ont été rédigés dans les premières années
du XIIe siècle[2] --Siècle d'Auguste de la littérature Gauloise.
4. Walter of Oxford, Geoffrey of Monmouth & Maître Wace
remanièrent, l'un en Gaulois, l'autre en Latin, et le troisième
en Français d'après eux, la vieille chronique Bretonne, source de
tous les romans du Brut.[3] [Brut en langue Celtique signifie
tradition vulgaire]"[4] The source of this chronique, or rather the
voices of which it is the complex echo, was the popular Breton
songs transmitted orally up to the first half of the XIIth century. Villemarqué. Barzas-Breiz.[5]
     Lancelot, more anciently written Ancelot. In the Romance
language Ancel is servant, & Ancelot is its diminutive. Ancelot
is a translation of the Celtic Mael, servant, & under this name
there is in the Welsh traditions a chief whose characteristics &
adventures correspond to those of Lancelot.[6]
     (Renan's Poésie de la Race Celtique.)[7] Les monuments de la
littérature bretonne sont:
I. Poésie. Les poèmes Gallois.   §1 Les plus anciennes poésies
galloises venues jusqu'à nous sont celles des Kenverz ou Bardes
primitifs, parmi /297/   lesquels se placent au premier rang
Taliessin, Merzin, Aneurin et Lywa'h-Hen, qui vivaient au VIme
siècle, et plusieurs autres moins connus, qui ont fleuri de l'an 664
époque de la chute de la monarchie Bretonne, à l'an 1066. Elles
occupent les 180 first pages of Owen Myvyr's Archaeology of
Wales.[1] [The MSS. usually cited for their antiquity are: "1 Le
Livre Noir, commencé au Xe siècle, et fini au XIIe. 2 Les livres
de Taliessin et d'Aneurin, vers la fin du XI siècle. 3 Le livre
rouge de Hengest, XIVe siècle."][2] §2. Les Chants populaires
Armoricaines.[3]
II. Prose. §1 Les Triades ou traditions bardiques.[4] §2. Les
Chroniques nationales: e.g. le Brut y Brenhined ou Histoire des
Rois, écrite en 950 par un Breton du Continent.[5] §3. Contes
populaires des anciens Bretons. The Mabinoghion.[6] "Ils forment
deux classes très distinctes: dans les uns Arthur figure comme
principe d'unité, dans les autres il ne paraît pas." They were
collected in the first half of the 12th century.[7]

     Celtic care for the Dead. "Nulle part la condition des
morts n'a été meilleure que chez les peuples bretons; nulle part
le tombeau ne recueille autant de souvenirs et de prières. C'est
que la vie n'est pas pour ces peuples une aventure personnelle
que chacun court pour son propre compte à ses risques et périls:
c'est un anneau dans une longue tradition, un don reçu et transmis,
une dette payée et un devoir accompli."[8]
     "La race Celtique s'est usée à résister au temps et à dé-
fendre les causes désespérées".[9] "Le Messianisme Celtique.
Presque tous les grands appels au surnaturel /298/   sont dus
à des peuples espérant contre toute espérance. . . . Israel
humilié rêva la conquête spirituelle du monde et y réussit."[1]
     "La pierre à aiguiser de Tudwal n'aiguisait que l'épée des
braves."[2]
     "Les peuples Celtiques ont eu pitié même de Judas. Saint
Brandan le rencontra sur un rocher au milieu des mers polaires:
il passe là un jour par semaine pour se refraîchir des feux de
l'enfer, un drap qu'il avait donné en aumône à un lépreux est
suspendu devant lui et tempère ses souffrances."[3]
     "Un jour Saint Keivin s'endormit en priant à sa fenêtre les

bras étendus; une hirondelle, apercevant la main ouverte du vieux
moine, trouva la place excellente pour y faire son nid; le saint
à son réveil, voyant la mère qui couvait ses oeufs, ne voulait
pas la déranger, et attendit pour se relever que les petits fus-
sent éclos."[4]

"Joan of Arc, on her trial, when asked if she heard supernatural voices-- dixit, quod si esset in uno nemore, bene audiret
voces venientes ad eam."[5]

According to a bardic tradition, the young bard, Taliessin,
oppressed by heat, drank of the potion of knowledge prepared by
some mother for her child: immediately his Soul is filled with
knowledge, but at the same time he is exposed to all the labours
& sorrows entailed by the potion.[6]

299

Antiquity of the Vedas.[1]   Veda = οῖδα.[2]   Rig-Veda means the Veda
of hymns of Praise.[3] Rig is from a root meaning, to celebrate.
In the Rig Veda we must distinguish between the original collection of the hymns or Mantras called the Sanhitâ or collection, &
a number of prose works called Brâhmanas & Sutras, the substance
of which turns on the proper use of the hymns at sacrifices,
their sacred meanings, supposed authors & other topics. These
are of a much later period.[4]

The Rigveda contains 1028 hymns. As early as 600 B.C. every
syllable had been counted. All manuscripts are modern; but just
as there is no MS. of the O.T. in Hebrew older than the Xth century A.C., yet the Septuagint is proof that the O.T. existed in
MS. in the 3d century B.C.; so the fact of the aforesaid counting
proves the Veda to have existed 600 B.C. Moreover, at that time
its language had ceased to be intelligible generally. Learned
commentaries were needed.[5] In the contemporary Sutras, not only
the hymns, but the Brâhmanas which stand midway, are regarded as
of divine authority. Such illustrative treatises as the Brâhmanas
could only spring up when explanation was wanted, & we find that
the authors of the Brâhmanas had already lost the power of understanding the text of the ancient hymns. Thus two strata of intellectual & literary growth are wanted between the date 600
B.C. & the time of the Vedas. These must be each two or three
hundred years, & we are thus carried to 1100 or 1200 B.C. at the
latest time when the Vedic hymns may be supposed to have been
collectively finished. The collection /300/ again contains
ancient & modern hymns, the hymns of the sons together with the
hymns of the fathers, & earlier ancestors; so that we cannot well
assign a date more recent than 1200 to 1500 B.C.[1]

Max Müller, Chips from a German Workshop.

=

The word for Revelation in Sanskrit is Sruti = hearing. This is
applied only to the Vedic hymns & the Brâhmanas. The laws of
Manu are only Smriti--recollection or tradition.[2]

Deva, bright, is in the Veda used for the Gods. In the
Zendavesta daêva means evil spirits. Many of the Vedic gods with
Indra at their head have been degraded to the position of daêvas
to make room for Ahura mazda the Wise Spirit. In Buddhism again,
these ancient devas are mere legendary beings, carried about in
shows, as servants of Buddha, goblins, or fabulous heroes.[3]

Agni, fire; Surya the Sun; Ushas, the dawn; Maruts, the
storms; Prithivi, the Earth; Âp, the waters; Nadi, the rivers;
Varuna, the sky; Mitra, the sun; Indra, day.[4]

Max Müller, ibid.

301

Study of Zendavesta. (Avesta means sacred or authorized text;
according to the Parsis Zend is the Pehlevi translation of the
same word. Dr. Martin Haug holds that Zend means interpretation.)[1] Anquetil du Perron, his enthusiasm being kindled by a
facsimile of a page of the Zendavesta, enlisted as a private
soldier in order to secure a passage to India, & spent six years,
1754-1761, in different parts of Western India, trying to collect
MSS. of the Zoroastrian writings, & to acquire from the Dustoors
a knowledge of their contents. His example was followed by Rask,
a learned Dane, who after collecting at Bombay many valuable MSS
for the Danish govt. wrote in 1826 his essay on the age & genuineness of the Zend language. Another Dane, at present one of the
most learned Zend scholars in Europe, Westergaard, has published
an edition of the Zendavesta (1852) first having been to India.
All this time, while French & German scholars such as Burnouf,
Bopp & Spiegel were hard at work deciphering the remains of the
Magian religion, hardly anything was contributed by English students living in the very heart of Parsiism at Bombay & Poona. Dr.
Martin Haug, the author of "Essays on the Sacred Language, writ-
ings, & religion of the Parsis," is Professor of Sanskrit at
Poona.[2]

The results of Rask's labour, as presented by himself, were:
1. That Zend is a brother of Sanskrit. 2. That modern Persian is
derived from Zend. 3. That the Zendavesta of the works of Zoroaster must have been reduced to writing at least   /302/   previously to the conquest of Alexander.[1] [Elsewhere M.M. says "there are
no facts that prove the text of the Avesta in the state in which
the Parsis of Bombay & Yezd now possess it (a translation of the
original) to have been committed to writing previous to the Sassanian dynasty"(226 A.D.)][2]

The first edition of the Zend texts, the outlines of a Zend
grammar with the translation & philological anatomy of considerable portions of the Zoroastrian writings were the work of the
late Eugène Burnouf. Zend is nearer to Sanskrit than any other
Indo-European language.[3] But it is probable that the Zoroastrians
had been settled in India before they immigrated into Persia.[4]

"Altogether", says Spiegel, "it is interesting to trace the
progress of religion in the Persian writings. It is a significant fact that in the oldest, i.e. the 2d part of the Yasna,
nothing is formed in the doctrine regarding God. In the writings
of the second period, i.e. in the Vendidad, we trace the advance
to a theological & in its way mild & scientific system. Out of
this, in the last place, i.e. in the first part of the Yasna & in
the whole of the Yeshts, there springs the stern & intolerant
religion of the Sassanian epoch."[5]

Pehlevi, now more commonly known as Huzvaresh. The legends
of Sassanian coins, the bi-lingual inscription of the Sassanian
emperors, & the translation of the Avesta by Sassanian reformers
represent the Persian language in its third phase.[6] The two previous phases are the Zend of the Avesta & that of Achaemenian inscriptions.[7] Parsi followed Pehlevi, & their period ended   /303/
with the downfall of the Sassanians. "The Arab conquest quenched
the last sparks of Persian nationality; & the fire-altars of the
Zoroastrians were never to be lighted again, except in the oasis
of Yezd & on the soil of the country which the Zoroastrians had
quitted as the disinherited sons of Manu."[1]

Some of the Parsis who are unable to read or write, still
mutter hymns & prayers in their temples, which though to them

mere sound, disclose to the experienced ear of a European scholar
the time-honoured accents of Zoroaster's speech.[2]
                              =
Burnouf showed that three of the most famous names in the Shah-
nameh, Jemschid, Feridun, & Garshasp, can be traced back to three
heroes mentioned in the Zendavesta as the representatives of the
three earliest generations of mankind, Yima Kshaêta, Thrâetaona &
Keresâspa; & that the prototypes of these Zoroastrian heroes
could be found again in the Yama-Trita & Krishasva of the Veda.[3]

> "The work of heaven performing, Feridun
> First purified the world from Sin & Crime.
> Yet Feridun was not an angel, nor
> Composed of musk & ambergris."
>   Atkinson's Shahnameh.[4]

Buddhism   304
Alexander Csoma de Körös, a Hungarian, made his way from Hungary
to Thibet, on foot, without any means of his own, & with the sole
object of discovering somewhere in Central Asia the native home
of the Hungarians. Arrived at Thibet his enthusiasm found a new
vent in acquiring a language which no European before his time
had mastered, & in exploring the vast collection of the Canonical
books of the Buddhists, preserved in that language. He arrived
at Calcutta without a penny, but was heartily welcomed by the
Asiatic Society & enabled to publish the results of his researches.
     The Sacred Canon of the Tibetans consists of two collections
commonly called the Kanjur & Tanjur: the former 108 vols. folio,
the latter 225.[1] Csoma de Körös gave a most valuable analysis of
this immense Bible, sufficient to show that the principal portions of it were a translation from the Sanskrit original discovered in Nepal by Mr. Hodgson. Csoma de Körös died soon after.[2]
About the same time Schmidt discovered the Mongolian version, &
Turnour presented to the world the Buddhist literature of Ceylon,
composed in the sacred language of that island, the ancient Pâli.[3]
At the beginning of the 16th century the Tamul conquerors of Ceylon are reported to have burnt every Buddhist book they could discover; but Buddhism remained the religion of the country, & in the
18th century regained its ascendancy.[4]
     The sacred canon of the Buddhists is /305/ called the
Tripitaka or, the Three Baskets. The 1st contains the morality &
is called Vinaya. The 2d Sûtras or discourses of Buddha. The 3d
all relating to philosophy & metaphysics.[1]
     "The most important element of the Buddhist reform has al-
ways been its social & moral code, not its metaphysical theories.
That moral code, taken by itself, is one of the most perfect which
the world has ever known."[2] (vide Spence Hardy, Legends & Theories
of the Buddhists)[3] "All virtues we are told spring from Maitrî--
i.e. charity or universal love."[4]
     When Bouddha saw a tigress unable to feed her young, he is
said to have offered his body to be devoured by them.[5]
     Proselytism began in Buddhism.[6] Bouddha means enlightened.[7]
     There are 455,000,000 Buddhists.[8]
     Buddhism became the state religion of India in the time of
Asoka; & Asoka was the grandson of Chandragypta, the contemporary
of Seleucus Nicator.[9]
     In 65 A.D. Buddhism was officially recognized as the third
state religion of China.[10]
                              =

In Buddhism among the laity, the Indian castes still continue to
exist wherever they existed in the past; it is only the Brahman
caste, or priesthood by birth, that has been abolished, & in its
place a clergy by choice of vocation substituted. (Weber)[11]

306

"The Fegeeans looked with horror on the Samoans because they had
no religion--no belief in cruel gods, nor any sanguinary rites."
                                                Lubbock, p. 357.[1]
"The New Zealanders. . . . tattooed with great dexterity & elegance. The process is extremely painful--could not be supported
all at once--sometimes spread over months or even years. To have
shrunk from it would have been a great disgrace." ibid.[2]

"The Dacotahs (N.A. Indians) believe that the Great Spirit made
all things except thunder & rice." ibid.[3]
(vide Tylor's Early History of Mankind.)[4]

307

Grimm's Law. According to this law High German uses tenues,
where the Gothic has medials, & the Sanscrit, Latin, & Zend, have
aspirates; it has aspirates where the Gothic has tenues, & the
last three languages medials; & medials where there are aspirates
in Gothic, & tenues in the rest. (Donaldson, New Cratyl. 89)[1]
     The Zend sometimes corresponds to the Gothic, the Lithuanian
entirely with the Latin & Sanscrit, except that it has no aspirates. The Greek sometimes agrees with the Sanscrit, Latin &c at
other times with the Old High German. Besides the Greek & High
German have prefixes where the other languages have the same word
without a prefix. (Ibid)[2]
                              =
Lautverschiebung. "Auf zwei regelrechten stufen nemlich tritt das
genau in einander gefügte verhältniss der stummen consonanten
jener urverwandten sprachen ( )[3] einer abweichung, einmal
sämmtlicher deutscher, und dann wiederum der hochdeutschen
entgegen; so dass, gerade wie die deutschen sprachen hierin
ueberhaupt von den urverwandten verschieden sind, auch die hochdeutsche von allen übrigen deutschen verschieden ist. Die be-
gonnene bewegung hat nicht eingehalten, sondern ihren kreis erst
in der hochdeutschen mundart erfüllt. Wenn folglich, z.b. ein
lateinisches, griechisches oder indisches wort die erste stufe
einnimmt, so findet sich das ihm entsprechende gothische auf der
zweiten, das hochdeutsche auf der dritten; ein vierter standpunct
wäre unmöglich, weil er nothwendig /308/ auf den ersten
zurückkehren müste.
     Dieses characteristische und für die erforschung unserer
sprache willkommene merkmal scheint gleichwohl keinen ursprünglichen, nur einen historischen unterschied zu liefern, von dem in
früheren zeiten der hochdeutsche, in noch früheren alle übrigen
deutschen stämme nicht betroffen wurden. Er zeigt bloss eine im
verlauf der jahrhunderte eingetretne richtung an, durch welche der
eigentlichen und nahen gemeinschaft des gesammten deutschen volks
kein eintrag geschieht. Hiervon zeugen uns merkwürdige ausnahmen
und unterbrechungen, denen die regel der lautverschiebung einzeln
und sogar reihenweise unterliegt, ohne dadurch überhaupt aufgeho-
ben zu werden."
                    Grimm, Einleitung Deutsche Grammatik[1]
"Vaterländische alte sagen, wie es mir scheint, haben ihren eignen
Reiz in einer gewissen mangelhaftigkeit, ja der glaube beruht mit

darauf, weil das Gefühl einem sagt, dass die lüge alles ausspinnen
möchte. . . Jede zu grosse fülle lässt wieder leer. Die rechte
Poesie gleicht einem menschen, der sich tausendfältig freuen kann,
wo er laub und gras wachsen, die sonne auf- und nieder gehen sieht;
die falsche einem der in fremde länder fährt, und sich an   /309/
den bergen der Schweiz, dem himmel und meer Italiens zu erheben
wähnt. Steht er nun mitten darin, so wird sein vergnügen
vielleicht lange nicht reichen an das mass des daheimbebliebnen,
dem sein apfelbaum im hausgarten jährlich blüht und die finken
darauf schlagen. . . . . Es giebt auch keinen rechten Unterschied
zwischen antiker un romantischer poesie. Die geschichte der
mahlerei, poesie und sprache lehret viele abwege meiden, denn sie
zeigt uns, dass jederzeit die wahrheit denen erschienen ist,
welche auf die spur der natur, fern von menschlicher schulweisheit
getreten sind." (Grimm, Deutsch Grammatik, Dedication to Savigny.)
1819.[1]

The word Deutsch. Gothic þiudiskô ἐθνικῶς in Galatians 2, 14.
Hence þiuda inferred to be = Ἔθνος: consequently the old High
German diutisc is derived from diot, the old Anglo-Saxon þeódisc
from þeod.[2] "der sinn des Wortes ist gentilis, gentilitius,
popularis, vulgaris, was vom gesammten Volk im gegensatz zu den
einzelnen stämmen gilt, heimatlich, allgemein verständlich. Aber
auch das nebensinn von heidnisch, barbarisch, den þiudisks wie
ἐθνικῶς, ebenso Ἔθνος, þiuda, vulgus, im munde der geistlichen
schriftsteller an sich tragen, darf man nicht verwiesen. Hierin
stimmt es zu germanicus: beide ausdrücke auf die sprache gezogen
bezeichnen die germeine, rohe vulgarsprache gegenüber die
gebildeten."[3]

Goths = gutþiuda.

310

"Since I can do no good because a woman
Reach constantly at something that is near it"
                              Maid's Tragedy.[1]
Pues ne podemos haber aquello que
queremos, queramos aquello que podremos.[2]
                    =
"Quoniam Delphis oracula cessant
Et genus humanum damnat caligo futuri."
                              Juv. VI.555[3]
                    =
The moving Finger writes, & having writ,
    Moves on: nor all thy Pity & Wit
Shall lure it back to cancel half a line
    Nor all thy tears wash out a word of it.[4]
                    =
"I also could speak as ye do: if your soul were in my soul's
stead, I could heap up words against you, & shake mine head at
you."   Job, XVI.[5]

"The speculative line of demarcation where obedience ought to end
& resistance must begin is faint, & obscure, not easily definable."
Burke, Reflections.[6]
                    =
"Partout la pensée morale des hommes s'élève et aspire fort au-
dessus de leur vie. Et gardez vous de croire que parce qu'elle ne
gouvernait pas immédiatement les actions, parce que la pratique

démentait sans cesse et étrangement la théorie, l'influence de la
théorie fut nulle et sans valeur. C'est beaucoup que le jugement
des hommes sur les actions humaines; tôt ou tart il devient
efficace."

Guizot, Hist de la Civiln.[7]

{311}

And now we fight the battle,
  But then we wear the crown
Of full & everlasting
  And passionless renown.[1]

              "Nil sine magno
Vita labore dedit mortalibus."[2]
                  =
"Moriar; mors ultima linea rerum est."[3]
                  =
"The souls by nature pitched too high
  By suffering plunged too low?"   Keble?[4]
                  =
              "Ritorna a tua scienza
Che vuol, quanto la cosa è più perfetta
Pui senta il bene, e così la doglienza."[5]
                  =
Was kann der Mensch in Leben mehr gewinnen
Als dass sich Gott-Natur ihm offenbare,
Wie sie das Feste lässt zu Geist verrinnen
Wie sie das Geisterzeugte fest bewahre. [6]
                  =
"If thou has heard a word, let it die with
thee; & be bold, it will not burst thee."

Ecclesiasticus.[7]

                  =
Dann zuletzt ist unerlässlich,
Dass der Dichter manches hasse;
Was unleidlich ist und hässlich
Nicht wie schönes Leben lasse.

Westöstliche Divan[8]

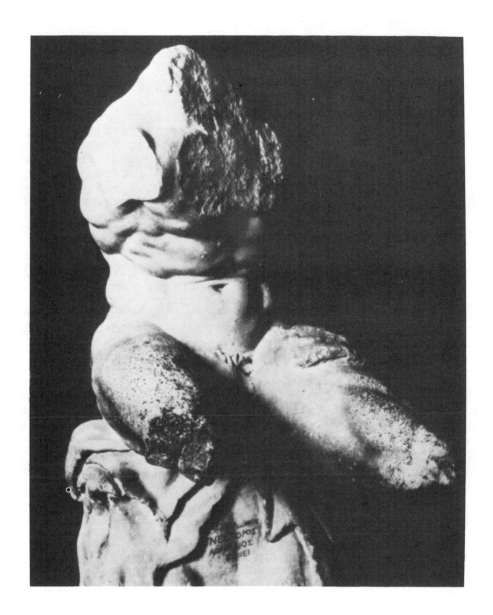

1.   Torso of Hercules (Vatican Museum)

2. Sleeping Ariadne (Vatican Museum)

3. Medusa Rondanini (Glyptothek, Munich)

The Superstitions of Great men

Materials for art: on Incompatible Opinions &c.
Tycho Brahe & Keppler. Keppler's prophecy for the
year 1619: ... May nus Monarcha Mundi
Medio Mense Martio Morietur, applied to
the weak Emperor Matthias.

43

"The great matter to write well," said Pope, "is to
write naturally & from one's knowledge."

"Does Lord Bolingbroke understand Hebrew? No.
But he understands that sort of learning & what is
writ about it."
"A bee is a nobler object than a prince in his
coronation robes." (This was thought a fine tribute
to nature by Pope.)
"Fra Paolo est Catholique en gros, et Protestant
en détail."

Nichols' anecdotes.

Ἐν τῷ φρονεῖν γὰρ μηδὲν ἥδιστος βίος,
τὸ μὴ φρονεῖν γὰρ κάρτ' ἀνώδυνον κακόν.
Αἴας.

ἀνδρί τοι χρεὼν
μνήμην προσεῖναι, τερπνὸν εἴ τί που πάθοι.
χάρις χάριν γάρ ἐστιν ἡ τίκτουσ' ἀεί.
ὅτου δ' ἀπορρεῖ μνῆστις εὖ πεπονθότος,
οὐκ ἂν γένοιτ' ἔθ' οὗτος εὐγενὴς ἀνήρ.
ib. 5

τὰ δ' ἔργα τοὺς λόγους εὑρίσκεται
Electra, 625.

4. Greek Quotations in George Eliot's Hand
(Notebook, entry 43; courtesy of The Beinecke
Rare Book and Manuscript Library, Yale University)

5. Greek Quotations in George Eliot's Hand
(Notebook, entry 43; courtesy of The Beinecke
Rare Book and Manuscript Library, Yale University)

6. Gentleman's Costume in 1793

    (F. W. Fairholt's Costume in England)

Flat hat of a country girl, 1773

George Lowe, one of the itinerant methodist preachers, thus
describes his dress when he preached his first sermon in 1777:
"My dress on that occasion was not very clerical; but
although it would have offended the fastidious taste of modern
times, it was considered fashionable, & even elegant, in
those days.... I put on my fustian coat, a pretty
red plush waistcoat, & a handsome pair of leather
breeches."
Fashionable Bonnet in 1799.

"In those days (i.e. about 1760) girls of the best families
wore white stockings only on the Sundays, & one week day, which
was a sort of public day:— on the other days, they wore blue
Doncaster woollen stockings with white tops". (Lord Eldon)

"At a festival at Belvoir Castle in honour of the Duke
of Rutland's majority, the Prince of Wales wore at
dinner a "scarlet-frock coat, black stockings, breeches &
waistcoat": in the evening at the ball "a suit of brown".
The Duchess of Rutland was attired till the ball commenced
in a scarlet riding-habit. This was in the beginning
of January, 1799. (Gent. Mag. 1799)

Women's preaching: decree of Conference against it, 1803.

"All drink tea", says Arthur Young of the working
people in a northerly parish, 1770

7. George Eliot's Drawings of Fashionable Hats

    (Notebook, entry 61; courtesy of The Beinecke

Rare Book and Manuscript Library, Yale University)

actor which we at this day place at the head of our prescriptions, & which is understood to mean nothing more than Recipe, is in fact a relief of the astrological symbol of Jupiter, as may be seen in many of the older works on pharmacy; although it is at present disguised by the long down stroke which converts it into the letter (R).

"The vervain (Vabena officinalis), [Ib.] after libations of honey, was to be gathered at the rising of the dog-star, when neither sun nor moon shone, with the left hand only; when thus prepared, it was said to vanquish fevers & other distempers, was an antidote to the bite of serpents, & a charm to conciliate friendship. Plin. lib. xxv. c. IX.

Every disease the origin & cause of which did not immediately strike the senses, has in all ages been attributed by the ignorant to the wrath of heaven, to the resentment of some invisible demon, or to some malignant aspect of the stars; & hence the introduction of a rabble of superstitious remedies, not a few of which were rather considered as expiations at the shrine of offended spirits, than as natural agents possessing medicinal powers. The introduction of precious stones into the Materia Medica arose from an Arabian superstition of this kind; indeed, De Boot, who has written extensively on this subject, does not pretend to account for the virtues of gems upon any philosophical principle, but upon their being the residence of spirits; & he adds, that such substances, from their beauty

8. Manuscript Page with Astrological Symbol (Notebook, entry 132; courtesy of The Beinecke Rare Book and Manuscript Library, Yale University)

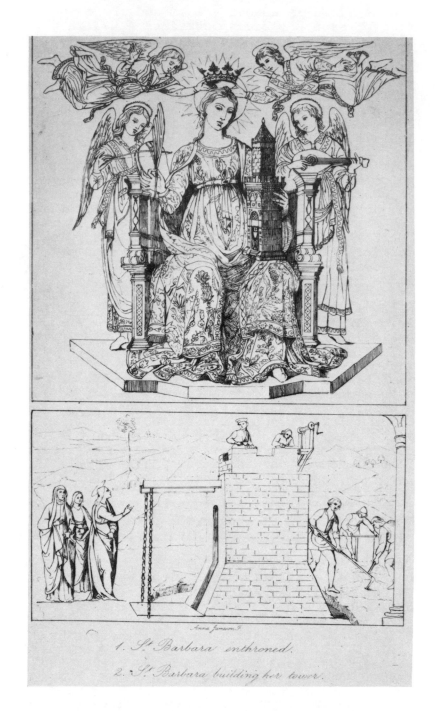

1. St. Barbara enthroned.

2. St. Barbara building her tower.

9. St. Barbara Holding a Tower

(Mrs. Jameson's Legendary Art)

Hercules and Antæus: Cinque-Cento Sard.

Horses of Achilles mourning over the slain Patroclus: Greek. Yellow Sard.

Antique Gem, with forged name of artist Mycon: Greek. Sard.

" Graved on the gem the god of Love I see,
    Whose mighty force no mortal heart can flee;
    With dext'rous rein he guides the lion's might,
    Unnumber'd graces spring around to light;
    In one hand grasped aloft the whip he rears
    O'er the rough neck, in one the bridle bears.
    The murd'rous god that tames the monster dire,
    How few of mortals shall escape his ire!"
                    MARCUS ARGENTARIUS, *Anthol.* IX. 221.

10.   Sards Engraved with Homeric Subjects

(C. W. King's <u>Antique</u> <u>Gems</u>)

11. Table of Grimm's Law

(Notebook, entries 212, 213; courtesy of The Beinecke Rare Book and Manuscript Library, Yale University)

Worship of Apollo

"We may select .... a proof of the influence
of this worship on political concerns, the
armistices connected with the festivals of Apollo,
the truce observed in the sacred places & roads,
the soothing influence of the purifications
for homicide, together with the idea of the
punishing & avenging god, & the great influence
of the oracles in the regulation of public
affairs. It has, moreover, been frequently remarked how by its sanctity, by the dignified &
severe character of its music, by all its
symbols & rites, this worship endeavoured to
lull the minds of individuals into a
state of composure & security, consistently,
however, with an occasional elevation to a
a state of ecstatic delight."

— Müller's Dorians I. 369.

μίμνει δὲ μίμνοντος ἐν θρόνῳ Διὸς
παθεῖν τὸν ἔρξαντα.

Agam. 1494

χερῶν ἄκρους κτένας.

Agam. [...]

(Exiles)
οἶδ' ἐγὼ φεύγοντας ἄνδρας ἐλπίδας
σιτουμένας.

 οὓς μὲν γὰρ εἰς ἔπεμψεν
οἶδεν, ἀντὶ δὲ φωτῶν
τεύχη καὶ σποδὸς εἰς ἑκάστου δόμους ἀφικνεῖται.

Agam. 4[...]

12. Greek Quotations in George Eliot's Hand
(Notebook, entry 222; courtesy of The Beinecke
Rare Book and Manuscript Library, Yale University)

13. Greek Quotations in George Eliot's Hand (Notebook, entry 223; courtesy of The Beinecke Rare Book and Manuscript Library, Yale University)

as Villemarqué supposes (Bargaz-Breiz) equivalent to the crwth. The rebeck was narrow towards the handle 𝄢; the crwth was this shape 𝄫. The rubibe, according to a Dominican of the XIIIᵗʰ cent. had 2 strings tuned 𝄢; the soprano instrument of the same sort had 3 strings; in France called the gigue, during the 12, 13, & 14ᵗʰ centuries; it is in the 15ᵗʰ century that this name seems to have been exchanged for rebec. The Germans called it the Geige ohne Bunde. "La rubébe la gigue, les quatre classes enfin du genre rebec, qu'on trouve déjà établies, dès le quinzième siècle, à savoir, Dessus, alto, ténor, et basses, sont des instrumens populaire placés entre les mains des ménétriers et qui servent en général pour la danse et pour les chanteurs des rues."

The other class of instruments, having the sonorous case, of two tables united by sides at right angles with them, & curving inwards at the centre, which were called vielle or viole (the crwth (three-corded was the type of them) belong to a more developed form of art.

By the beginning of the XIᵗʰ century we see the Vielle or Viole on monuments. Some of them are without bridges; but this must be the mistake of the artist or his negligence, for the bridge is the correlate of the bow.

It was near the end of the XVᵗʰ century that three musicians superior to their

Aleph	א	Guttural très faible
Beth	ב	B
Gimel	ג	GH
Daleth	ד	D
He	ה	H doux
Vau	ו	OU (W)
Zain	ז	Z
Cheth	ח	Orig. power probl. syllabic *che* reduced, in Greek, to *he* — *e*
Theth	ט	Considered by modern Hebraists a mere T. or Y.
Iod	י	Held by some a nasal consonant, by others a *jude*, by others Q.
Caph	כ	K. M a terminal ך
Lamed	ל	L
Mem	מ	M : terminal, ם
Nun	נ	N : terminal ן
Samech	ס	S
Ayin	ע	Guttural forte
Pe	פ	P : terminal ף
Tsadi	צ *	C : terminal ץ
Koph	ק P	Khh
Resh	ר	R
Shin	ש	S or sch
Sin	שׂ	S
Tau	ת	TH or T

* Never included in the Greek alphabet.

15.   Hebrew Alphabet (Notebook, entry 279)

(Notebook, entry 279; courtesy of The Beinecke

Rare Book and Manuscript Library, Yale University)

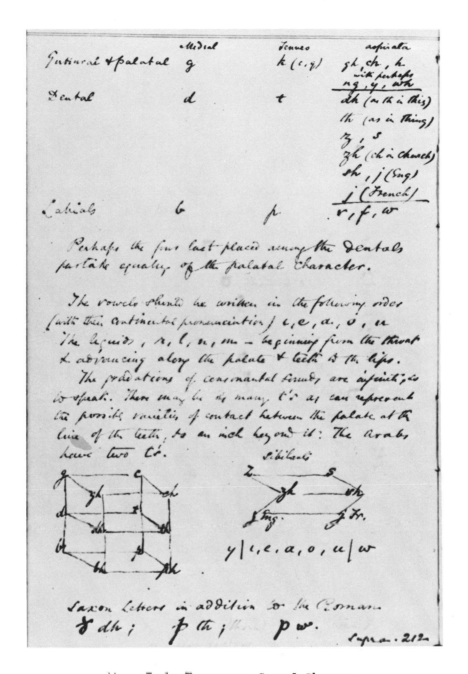

	Medial	Tenues	aspirata
Guttural & palatal	g	k (c, q)	gh, ch, h with perhaps ng, y, wh
Dental	d	t	dh (as th in this) th (as in thing) z, s zh (ch in church) sh, j (Eng) j (French)
Labials	b	p	v, f, w

Perhaps the first last placed among the Dentals partake equally of the palatal character.

The vowels should be written in the following order (with their continental pronunciation) i, e, a, o, u The liquids, r, l, n, m — beginning from the throat & advancing along the palate & teeth to the lips.

The gradations of consonantal sounds, are infinite; so to speak. There may be as many t's as can represent the possible varieties of contact between the palate at the line of the teeth, to an inch beyond it: The Arabs have two t's.

Saxon Letters in addition to the Roman ð dh; þ th; p w.

Supra. 212.

16.   Indo-European Sound Changes

(Notebook, entry 280; courtesy of The Beinecke

Rare Book and Manuscript Library, Yale University)

Abbreviations

Notes

Textual Notes

Abbreviations

AB	Adam Bede
Biography	Gordon S. Haight. *George Eliot: A Biography*. New York: Oxford University Press, 1968.
DD	*Daniel Deronda*
Diary	George Eliot's MS. diary of July 1861 to December 1877 (Beinecke Library).
Essays	Thomas Pinney, ed. *Essays of George Eliot*. New York: Columbia University Press, 1963.
Extracts Interesting	MS. notebook "Extracts made by G. H. Lewes (Interesting)" (Beinecke Library).
FH	*Felix Holt, The Radical*
GE	George Eliot
GHL	George Henry Lewes
GHL Journal	Lewes's MS. journals: X. 24 July 1856 to 31 March 1859; XI. 1 April 1858 to January 1866 (Beinecke Library).
Goethe	George Henry Lewes. *The Life and Works of Goethe*. 2 vols. Boston: Ticknor and Fields, 1856.
Interesting Extracts	George Eliot's MS. notebook labelled "Interesting Extracts" (Folger Shakespeare Library).
Journal	George Eliot's MS. journal of 1849 to 1861 (Beinecke Library).
Letters	Gordon S. Haight, ed. *The George Eliot Letters*. 9 vols. New Haven: Yale University Press, 1954-55, 1978.
Library	William Baker. *The George Eliot - George Henry Lewes Library: An Annotated Catalogue of Their Books at Dr. Williams's Library*, London. New York: Garland, 1977.
Life	J. W. Cross, ed. *George Eliot's Life as Related in Her Letters and Journals*. 3 vols. Edinburgh and London: William Blackwood and Sons, n.d.
LJOP	*The Legend of Jubal and Other Poems*
M	*Middlemarch*
MF	*The Mill on the Floss*
MS. Goethe	Lewes's MS. labelled "Goethe" (Beinecke Library).
Mythmaking	Joseph Wiesenfarth. *George Eliot's Mythmaking*. Heidelberg: Carl Winter Universitätsverlag, 1977.
Ouvry Inventory	A list of family books made by Lewes's granddaughter, Mrs. Carrington Ouvry, some of which were Eliot's and Lewes's (courtesy of Gordon S. Haight).
Pforzheimer MSS. 707-11	MS. notebooks for *Daniel Deronda* (Carl H. Pforzheimer Library). These are being edited by William Baker, who has published MS. 707 as *Some George Eliot Notebooks*. Vol. 1. Salzburg, Austria: Institue für Englische Sprache und Literatur, 1976.
Pratt and Neufeldt	John C. Pratt and Victor A. Neufeldt, eds., *George Eliot's Middlemarch Notebooks: A Transcription*. Berkeley: University of California Press, 1979.
Quarry for FH	MS. notebook labelled "Notes for Felix Holt & Other" (Beinecke Library)
R	*Romola*
SCL	*Scenes of Clerical Life*
SM	*Silas Marner*
TSG	*The Spanish Gypsy*
WR	*Westminster Review*

Notes

Endpaper

1. _Prometheus Bound_, ll. 103-5. _Translation_: "My allotted doom I needs must bear as lightly as I may, knowing the might of Necessity brooketh no resistance" (_Aeschylus_, Herbert Weir Smyth, trans., Loeb Classical Library, 2 vols. [Cambridge, Mass.: Harvard Univ. Press; London: William Heinemann, 1956], I, 227). The text GE used was G. F. Schoemann, _Des Aeschylos Gefesselter Prometheus, Griechisch und Deutsch mit Einleitung, Anmerkungen und dem Gelösten Prometheus_ (Greifswald: A. Koch, 1844). This book, now in Dr. Williams's Library, has l. 105 marked; it was included by GHL in his review of "German and English Translations from the Greek," _Foreign Quarterly Review_, USA ed. 33 (1844), 248-58. GE writes in her Journal for 10 February 1858 that she is reading "the 'Prometheus' in the morning." At this time she had just finished writing _AB_, ch. 9. Mr. Irwine refers to "the chorus in the Prometheus," which cautions against "imprudent marriage," in _AB_, ch. 16. See also entry 43, n. 14.

2. _Herodotus_, II, 2-3. _Translation_: "Now, for the stories which I heard about the gods, I am not desirous to relate them, saving only the names of the deities; for I hold that no man knows about the gods more than another; and I will say no more about them than what I am constrained to say by the course of my history" (_Herodotus_, trans. A. D. Godley, Loeb Classical Library, 4 vols. [Cambridge, Mass.: Harvard Univ. Press; London: William Heinemann, 1957-63], I, 277-9). GE annotated the Greek text of P. Wesseling and F. V. Reiz, 7 vols. (Edinburgh, 1807); see _Library_, p. 95, no. 1012. See also entry 7 and nn. below. "Herodotus, which she was learning to read with Mr. Casaubon," is mentioned as among Dorothea's "favourite books" in _M_, ch. 48.

3. _Dichtung und Wahrheit_, pt. 4, bk. 16, _Goethe's sämmtliche Werke_, 40 vols. (Stuttgart und Tübingen: J. G. Cotta'scher, 1840), XXII, 174. _Translation_: "I always preferred to learn from an author himself how he did think than to hear from someone else how he should have thought." GE and GHL read Goethe in the German edition cited above. It corresponds to the description given in the Ouvry Inventory and the pagination agrees with that cited in GHL's MS. "Goethe" and in GE's entry 112 below. GE writes in her Journal, 23 December 1854, "Turned over the _Dichtung u. Wahrheit_." Goethe's remarks were made in defense of Spinoza, whose _Ethics_ GE translated and who she said spoke "from his own soul" (_Letters_, I, 321).

4. _The Institutes of Oratory_, X.iii.2-5. _Translation_: "Without the consciousness of . . . preliminary study our powers of speaking extempore will give us nothing but an empty flow of words" (_The Institutio Oratorio of Quintilian_, trans. H. E. Butler, Loeb Classical Library, 4 vols. [Cambridge, Mass.: Harvard Univ. Press; London: William Heinemann, 1970], IV, 93).

5. A. S. F. Gow and D. L. Page, eds., _The Greek Anthology: Hellenistic Epigrams_, 2 vols. (London: Cambridge Univ. Press, 1968), I, 243, entry CII. _Translation_: "I have learned to pity."

6. _Hyperion_, II, 203-5.

7. _De Re Publica_, III.xxii.33. _Translation_: "True law is right reason in agreement with nature; it is of universal application, unchanging and everlasting; it summons to duty by its commands, and averts from wrongdoing by its prohibitions. . . . And there will not be different laws at Rome and at Athens, or different laws now and in the future, but one eternal and unchangeable law" (_Cicero_, trans. Clinton Walker Keyes, Loeb Classical Library, 28 vols. [Cambridge, Mass.: Harvard Univ. Press; London: William Heinemann, 1970], XVI, 211. GE has written in the "i" in _omni_ and _genti_ heavily in black ink.

8. C. Cornelius Taciti, _Historiarum_, bk. 2, ch. 45. _Translation_: "Whereas hope and reward are uncertain, tragedy and grief are inevitable."

9. _Faust, Der Zweite Teil Der Tragodie_, I: 4667-68, _Goethe's sämmtliche Werke_, XII, 5. _Translation_: "Thundering for the spirit's ear / We can feel the day appear" (_Goethe's Faust_, trans. Walter Kaufmann, Anchor Books [Garden City, New York: Doubleday, 1961], p. 427). GE notes in her Journal: "Tried reading the 2d part of Faust aloud, but gave it up, as it was too difficult for G[eorge] to follow it rapidly enough" (19 January 1855).

10. Sophocles, _Antigone_, l. 523. _Translation_: "My nature is for mutual love, not hate" (_Sophocles_, trans. F. Storr, Loeb Classical Library, 2 vols. [Cambridge, Mass.: Harvard Univ. Press; London: William Heinemann, 1956], I, 354). This passage appears slightly transformed in _DD_, ch. 32, when Mirah tells Deronda, "It is much easier to me to share in love than in hatred. I remember a play I read in German . . . where the heroine says something like that." Deronda names the _Antigone_, and Mirah replies, "Ah, you know it." The German edition that GE knew best was August Böckh's _Des Sophokles Antigone_, which GHL reviewed in "The Antigone and Its Critics," _Foreign Quarterly Review_, USA ed. 35 (1845), 31-40, and which GE mentions in "The Antigone and Its Moral," _Leader_, 7 (1856), 306; rpt. _Essays_, pp. 261-5.

11. "The Death of Wallenstein," _The Complete Works of Samuel Taylor Coleridge_, ed. W. G. T. Shedd, 7 vols. (New York: Harper, 1956), VII, 682. A phrase from this quotation appears in _FH_, ch. 16: Some "speakers at Reform banquets . . . dwelt on the abolition of all abuses, and on millenial blessedness generally, others, whose imaginations were less suffused with exhalations of the dawn, insisted chiefly on the ballot-box."

Entry 1

1. "Mémoires de deux jeunes mariées," ch. 27, _Scènes de la vie privée_, _Oeuvres complètes de M. de Balzac_, _La Comédie humaine_ (Paris: Béthune et Plon, n.d.), II, 106. _Translation_: "It is to be wondered at that pleasure has need of neither religion nor contrivance nor fine words, but stands on its own; whereas, to justify the cruel artifices of our slavery and servitude men have acquired theories and maxims." "Memoirs of Two Young Married Women." GHL wrote that only some half-dozen works of Balzac "are perfectly unexceptionable on the point of morality. The rest are all dangerous, insidious" ("Balzac and George Sand," _Foreign Quarterly Review_, USA ed. 33 [1844], 149). _Père Goriot_, for instance, is "extremely clever but extremely disagreeable." Passion in _Goriot_ is petty, "and creates no sympathy. . . . The man himself excites no sympathy" (157). On the other hand, "Balzac's knowledge of character is immense, his penetration of motive is astonishing; his works are experiences of life, psychological studies" (154). GE's evaluation of Balzac is similar: he creates the effect of "walking among . . . human carrion" and causes "moral nausea" because he does not "call forth our best sympathies" (_Essays_, p. 146). His _Père Goriot_ is a "hateful book" (_Life_, II, 115). Nevertheless he has a "magic force" and "is perhaps the most wonderful writer of fiction the world has ever seen" (_Essays_, p. 146).

Entry 2

1. John Gardner Wilkinson, _Manners and Customs of the Ancient Egyptians, including Their Private Life, Government, Laws, Art, Manufactures, Religion, and Early History_, 3 vols. (London: John Murray, 1837), II, 167.

Entry 3

1. Ibid., 172.

Entry 4

1. History here provides an early instance of the problem of mastery in marriage (the problem Chaucer's Wife of Bath gave literary currency), which is a central preoccupation of GE in _R_, _FH_, _M_, and _DD_. See also entry 6, n. 4.

2. Wilkinson, II, 58-59.

Entry 5

1. Ibid., 59-60.

Entry 6

1. The parenthetical reference to Gibbon's _Decline and Fall_ is typical of GE's practice of interpolating footnotes into her text.

2. Wilkinson, II, 63.

3. Ibid., 64-65.

4. Wilkinson's note, not GE's. GE recalled these entries from Wilkinson and Herodotus, bk. 2, when working up DD. She mentions both authors in a notebook for DD (Pforzheimer MS. 711, p. [2]). The rights of Grandcourt's children by Lydia Glasher preoccupy Gwendolen Harleth.

Entry 7

1. Herodotus, II, 35-36. The Nine Books of the History of Herodotus, ed. Peter Edmund Laurent and trans. Thomas Gaisford, 2 vols. (Oxford: Henry Slatter, 1837), I, 123; less well known than that of Rawlinson, this was the translation GE used. Entry 7 shows GE, not uncharacteristically, going from a secondary to a primary source, in this case from Wilkinson to Herodotus. See Endpaper, n. 2, for GE's reading of Herodotus in the Greek.

2. Herodotus, II, 36 (Laurent I, 124).

3. Ibid., II, 94 (I, 146).

4. Ibid., II, 100 (I, 152). Nitocris, an Egyptian queen, avenged the death of her brother, who ruled before her, by contriving to drown all who had been involved in his murder; then she killed herself. See also Library, p. 95, no. 1012, for another GE reference to Nitocris.

5. Herodotus, II, 134-5 (I, 171-2). Rhodopis and Archidice were famous courtesans; Rhodopis gave a tenth part of her possessions to have a memorial dedicated to herself; Archidice was the theme of song throughout Greece.

Entry 8

1. GE's italics.

2. Franz Liszt, "Wagner's Fliegender Holländer," Neue Zeitschrift für Musik, 41 (1854), 122. Translation: "A Dutch vessel, which a long time ago sailed round the Cape of Good Hope, was greatly delayed by an unrelenting storm. When the sailors begged their captain to turn back, he shouted, "Even if I have to sail the sea for all eternity, I'll never turn back!" As a punishment for this blasphemy, he was condemned to wander about the ocean until the last day, and bring destruction to all ships which met him on their way. The angel of mercy, however, announced to him that he should be permitted to go on shore every seven years and marry: if the wife he chose proved untrue to him, she too would become the prey of the Evil One; but if he found a wife who would love him till death, her truth would expiate his guilt, and would open to him the gates of salvation. According to Heine's story, a Norwegian maiden, who learns in a folk song of heaven's judgment on the captain, feels from her youth a deep sympathy for the wretched man's fate. When the Hollander lands on Norway's coast to seek a wife, the maiden recognizes him, pledges herself to him, completely determined to keep her oath. The Hollander, however, stirred by love and gratitude at so much beauty and devotion, fears the danger of perjury and leaves her, renouncing his long-awaited hope of delivery from damnation. The maiden, nevertheless, who sees him sailing away, throws herself into the sea and drowns. That very moment atonement is made and the Flying Dutchman sinks into the waves."

GE and GHL attended three of Wagner's operas in Weimar in September 1854. GE did not like "Lohengrin": "one may venture to say that it fails in one grand requisite of art, based on an unchangeable element in human nature--the need for contrast. With the 'Fliegender Holländer' I was delighted; the poem and the music were alike charming. The 'Tannhäuser,' too, created in me a great desire to hear it again" (Life, I, 274). At Weimar, GE and GHL heard Liszt conduct "Ernani"--"Liszt looked splendid as he conducted the opera" (Life, I, 274)--breakfasted with him, and listened to his playing: "For the first time in my life I beheld real inspiration--for the first time I heard the true tones of the piano" (Life, I, 281). For GE's further account of Liszt, Wagner, and Der Fliegende Holländer see "Liszt, Wagner, and Weimar," Frazer's Magazine, 52 (July 1855), 48-62; rpt. Essays, pp. 96-122. In the

translation above, the words from "As a punishment" to "gates of salvation"
are from GE's rendering of Heine's story in this article; see Essays, p. 105.
Philip Wakem alludes to the Flying Dutchman and Senta in MF when he says that
Maggie "will be selling her soul to that ghostly boatsman who haunts the Floss
--only for the sake of being drifted in a boat forever" (VI. 13). Gwendolen
alludes to the Flying Dutchman in DD, ch. 54, when she says to Grandcourt, "I
think we shall go on always, like the Flying Dutchman."

Entry 8a
    1. GE's insertion.
    2. Gotthold Ephraim Lessing, Laokoon, oder über die gränzen der Malerei
und Poesie (1766), Ch. 1; see Lessings Werke (Donaueschingen: im Verlage
deutscher Classiker, 1822), III, 14-15. Translation: "With him (the Greek)
heroism was like a spark buried in flint, which slept undisturbed as long as
no outside force awakened it or took from it either its clarity or coldness."
    We know from an entry in her Journal of 11 November 1854--"I began read-
ing Lessing's Laocoon in bed"--that GE first read the book in Berlin. (She
finished reading it on 19 November.) A copy had been lent to her by O. F.
Gruppe, whom she very much admired (and whose Gegenwart und Zukunft der
Philosophie in Deutschland she reviewed in Leader, 6 [28 July 1855], 723-4, and
whose Adriadne: Die tragische Kunst der Griechen she praised as "one of the
best books, if not the very best, we have on the Greek drama" [Essays, p.
149]). "He lent me 'Lessing,'" wrote GE, "and that is an additional circumstance to remember with pleasure in connection with the Laocoon" (Life, I,
288). Following GHL, who called Lessing "the least German" of "all Germans"
("Lessing," Edinburgh Review, 82 [1845], 453) and "that most British of
Germans" ("Emilia Galotti," Leader, 3 [26 June 1852], p. 617), GE called the
Laocoon "the most un-German of all . . . German books" (Life, I, 303). GE
again refers to the Laocoon at the opening of "Belles Lettres" in the Contemporary Literature section of WR, 66 (October 1856), USA ed. 311: "Every reader
of Lessing's 'Laocoon' remembers his masterly distinction between the methods
of presentation in poetry and the plastic arts--the acumen and the aptness of
illustration with which he shows how the difference in the materials wherewith
the poet and painter or sculptor respectively work, and the difference in
their mode of appeal to the mind, properly involve a difference in their treatment of a given subject." She continues this analysis of the "Laocoon" for a
paragraph (see Uncollected Writings) showing how thoroughly she has mastered
the principles. Some fifteen years later, in ch. 19 of M, Will Ladislaw calls
Lessing's distinctions to the attention of Adolf Naumann (a reincarnation of
Friedrich Overbeck) when he wants to paint Dorothea Brooke into one of his
historical canvases: "'No, nonsense, Naumann! English ladies are not at
everybody's service as models. And you want to express too much with your
painting. . . . Your painting and Plastik are poor stuff after all. They per-
turb and dull conceptions instead of raising them. Language is a finer
medium. . . . --This woman whom you have just seen, for example: how would you
paint her voice, pray? But her voice is much diviner than anything you have
seen of her." On GE and Lessing, see Hugh Witemeyer, George Eliot and the
Visual Arts (New Haven: Yale Univ. Press, 1979), pp. 40-43.

Entry 9
    1. Laokoon, ch. 4. See Lessing's Werke, III, 42. Translation: "Noth-
ing is more deceptive than to set down general laws for our feelings. Their
web is so fine and entangled that even the most wary speculation is hardly
able to take hold of a single thread and follow it past those that cross it.
But if such speculation does succeed, what is the good of it? We find in
nature no single pure feeling: with each one a thousand others stand together and the slightest of these changes the first feeling, so that exception
grows upon exception until the supposed general law becomes merely the experience of a few isolated cases."
    GE may have been referring to this passage when in her MS. notebook

entitled "Interesting Extracts" (Folger Shakespeare Library) she remarks:
"Lessing, Laokoon . . . . See excellent statement how no mental act is simple"
(p. 62). Two pages later, following Lessing, she coins a motto of her own:
"Seeking to cause emotion by a new general term is like trying to measure
without a unit of measure" ("Interesting Extracts," p. 64). Lessing's analysis
of the nature of feeling is also relevant to GE's dramatization of its com-
plexity in M, where the central image is the web and feelings are forever at
"their weaving work" (M, ch. 42). See also Reva Stump, Movement and Vision
in George Eliot's Novels (Seattle: University of Washington Press, 1959), pp.
172-214, for an analysis of the web imagery in M.

Entry 10
    1. Gotthold Ephraim Lessing, Emilia Galotti, Ein Trauerspiel in fünf
Aufzugen (1772), IV. iii, Gesammelte Werke, Neue rechtmaßige Ausgabe (Leipzig:
G.F. Göschen'sche Verlagshandlung, 1853), II, 335. Translation: "How can a
man love a creature who, to spite him, thinks. A woman who thinks is as
nauseating as a man who wears makeup." GE and GHL saw Emilia Galotti per-
formed in Berlin on 21 November 1854 and GE remarked in her Journal that "the
Roman myth of Virginius is grand, but the situation transported to modern
times and divested of its political bearing is simply shocking" (see also Life,
I, 303). This observation closely follows that of GHL on Lessing's tragedy:
"There is a radical error in conception. . . . He has selected the story of
Virginius; but he has placed it in modern times, and made the scene a petty
Italian Princedom. The story is essentially a Roman story: to transplant it
to another land is to make it no longer probable" ("Lessing," Edinburgh
Review, 82 [1845], 462). There is a similar criticism in GHL's "Emilia
Galotti," Leader 3 (26 June 1852), 617.

Entry 11
    1. Wilhelm Meisters Lehrjahre, bk. 5, ch. 1, Goethe's sämmtliche Werke,
XVII, 3. Translation: "He was wont to say, 'Men are so inclined to content
themselves with what is commonest; the spirit and the senses so easily grow
dead to the impressions of the beautiful and perfect,--that every one should
study, by all methods, to nourish in his mind the faculty of feeling these
things. For no man can bear to be entirely deprived of such enjoyments: it
is only because they are not used to taste of what is excellent that the
generality of people take delight in silly and insipid things, provided they
be new. For this reason,' he would add, 'one ought, every day at least, to
hear a little song, read a good poem, see a fine picture, and, if it were possible, to speak a few reasonable words'" (The Works of F.W. von Goethe, with
his Life by George Henry Lewes, ed. Nathan Haskell Dole, trans. Sir Walter
Scott, Sir Theodore Martin, John Oxenford, Thomas Carlyle et al., 14 vols.
[London and Boston: Francis A. Niccolls & Co., n.d.], Wilhelm Meister's
Apprenticeship, II, 5.)
    GE finished reading the Lehrjahre on 31 November 1854 (Journal). What
Wilhelm says in this passage becomes an element of Philip Wakem's philosophy,
which he explains to Maggie Tulliver in the Red Deeps: "It seems to me we can
never give up longing and wishing while we are thoroughly alive. There are
certain things we feel to be beautiful and good, and we must hunger after them.
How can we ever be satisfied without them until our feelings are deadened? I
delight in fine pictures--I long to be able to paint such. I strive and
strive, and can't produce what I want. This is pain to me, and always will be
pain, until my faculties lose their keenness, like aged eyes" (MF, V. i). GE's
interest in the Apprenticeship is demonstrated in her essay "The Morality of
Wilhelm Meister," Leader, 6 (21 July 1855), 703 (rpt. Essays, pp. 143-7) which
builds on GHL's discussion of the novel in his Goethe, I, 215-8. GE's essay
is specific in the illustration of general principles of the kind GHL lays
down in his chapter.

Entry 12
   1. _Lehrjahre_, bk. 7, ch. 5, _Goethe's sämmliche Werke_, XVII,200.
Translation: "The world is so waste and empty, when we figure only towns and
hills and rivers in it; but to know of some one here and there whom we accord
with, who is living on with us, even in silence,--this makes our earthly ball a
peopled garden" (_The Works of F.W. von Goethe_, _Wilhelm Meister_, II, 196).

Entry 13
   1. _Lehrjahre_, bk. 8, ch. 5, _Goethe's sämmtliche Werke_, XVII, 331. This
same quotation appears in GHL's notebook "Extracts Interesting." He quotes
the sentence in context and translates it as follows: "Thought expands but
lames: Action animates but narrows" (p. [30]).

Entry 14
   1. "Lieder" 2, "Es treibt mich hin, es treibt mich her!" from "Junge
Leiden" (1817-1821) in "Buch der Lieder," _Heinrich Heine's sämmtliche Werke_,
6 vols. (3rd ed. Philadelphia: John Weik, 1856), II, 24. GE read the earlier
1855 printing of this edition; see _Essays_, p. 216. _Translation_: "Now I am
seized with the madness of speed. / Oh, but they never were lovers, these
hours; / Banded together with hideous powers / They mock at the lover's unrest
and his need" (_Poems of Heinrich Heine_, trans. Louis Untermeyer, Revised Edition [New York: Harcourt, Brace and Company, 1923], p. 22). GE reviewed John
E. Wallis's _Heinrich Heine's Book of Songs_ in the _Saturday Review_, 1 (26 April
1856), 523-4, and sharply differed with his translations of Heine; see Uncollected Writings.

Entry 15
   1. GE's italics.
   2. "Bericht, August," _Zweiter Römischer Aufenthalt vom Juni 1787 bis April
1788_, _Werke_, XXIV, 92. GHL translates and comments on this passage in his MS.
"Goethe": "He says of the disputes in Rome about Raphael & Michel Ang--. 'It
is difficult to appreciate one such genius, still more to appreciate two.
Hence people lighten the task by _partizanship_'" (p. [10], paging from back).
GE read the _Italiänische Reise_ between 1 and 10 December 1854 (Journal).

Entry 16
   1. Johannes Scherr, _Deutsche Cultur und Sitte_ (Leipzig: Otto Wigand,
1854), pp. 84-86. The copy of Scherr which GE used is now in Dr. Williams's
Library; it contains marked passages and notes in GE's hand on pp. 626-[7].
GE mentions reading Scherr in December 1854 and March 1855 (Journal). This
long entry on Hroswitha is a capsule biography of a successful Medieval woman.
It is one instance of many in the notebook that GE was interested in the condition of women throughout the history of civilization. Entries 2, 4, 5, 6, 7
deal with Egyptian women; entry 8 presents the legendary Senta, whose heroic
death saves the Flying Dutchman; entry 25 treats of the freedom of Shakespeare's heroines; entry 30 contrasts German concepts of women with French and
Italian; entry 31 returns to Scherr and singles out, among others, two successful women: Bitisia Gozzadini and Sabina von Steinbach. It is interesting to
note, further, that GE read and heavily marked Mary Wollstonecraft's _A Vindi-
cation of the Rights of Woman_; see _Library_, p. 214, no. 2309.
   Translation: "The nun Roswitha or Hrosuith (white rose) lived and wrote
in Gandersheim Cloister, Brunswick, about the year 980. She is a genuine
Medieval author and had a significant influence on those whom the English so
appropriately call bluestockings. She entered the Cloister, so it seems, when
she was young and placed herself under the direction of the learned Sister
Rikkardis and the cultured abbess, Gerberga, the niece of Otto II, for classical studies and made herself widely enough known through her talent as a writer
to be called "The Ringing Voice of Gandersheim." With the encouragement of

Gerberga and her imperial uncle, Roswitha told the story of the exploits of
Otto I in Latin hexameter. She also wrote the history of the founding of the
Cloister and retold many saints legends in Latin verse. She made her greatest
fame, however, with her Latin comedies in which she imitated Terence in a
rather servile manner. She tells us in the preface what her point of view is
in these dramatic works: 'Many good Christians prefer the vanities of pagan
writings to Holy Scripture because they like a refined style--a mistake from
which I cannot fully acquit myself. There are also diligent readers of the
Bible, who, though they despise the writings of the saints, nevertheless read
the poetry of Terence, seduced by the grace of his style; they thereby disgrace themselves by coming to know immodest things. With these facts in mind,
I, the Ringing Voice of Gandersheim, have not refused to imitate the much appreciated Terence in expression, so that in the very style that the despicable
vices of voluptuous women are presented, the praiseworthy discipline of devout
young women may be praised to the degree that my limited skill allows.
Roswitha's intention in her six short plays--they cannot be called comedies to
our way of thinking--was accordingly moral-aesthetic, as befits a nun. It
seems that we are hardly impugning her religious profession when we conjecture
that before she wrote her comedies she must have looked not only into Terence
but also into love itself. We imagine her at the time that she took up the
dramatic pen certainly not as a young passionate girl but much more as a confirmed matron with a sourly pious turn to her mouth; nevertheless, she had not
yet completely resolved the conflict, which must inevitably arise in a nun
trained in the classics, between pagan sensuality and Christian spirituality.
The fire of sensuality still arose here and there in very polite fashion: if
the cloistered poet never failed to bring her plays to an edifying conclusion
in martyrdom, she had a predilection for questionable situations in their
plotting. We have with Roswitha, as with her master Terence, mostly to deal
with characters who are libertines and prostitutes, and seduction and conversion are her most important themes. Where comical scenes appear, they are very
obvious; for example, when the dissolute governor Dulcitius forces his way into the house of the holy women Agape, Chionia, and Irene to ravish them, he
goes mad as he enters, kisses pots and pancakes instead of the maidens and
gets himself a dirty face." (Translated with Louise Halpin Wiesenfarth.)

Entry 17
    1. <u>Vermischte Schriften von Heinrich Heine</u>, 3 vols. (Hamburg: Hoffman
und Campe, 1854), I, 5. <u>Translation</u>: "It is quite typical that our German
troublemakers cling to a true sentimentality. They are not cold calculating
scoundrels but emotional rascals." GE read the <u>Geständnisse</u> (<u>Confessions</u>) on
20-21 December 1854 (Journal). She gave particular attention to it--the Fore-
word of which Heine wrote in March 1854--in her essay "German Wit: Heinrich
Heine," <u>WR</u>, 65 (January 1856), 1-33; rpt. <u>Essays</u>, pp. 216-54. "Heine's
'Geständnisse,'" GE remarks, "immensely amused with the wit of it in the first
fifty pages, but afterwards it burns low, and the want of principle and purpose make it wearisome" (<u>Life</u>, I, 304).

Entry 18
    1. <u>Wilhelm Meisters Wanderjahre oder die Entsagenden</u>, bk. 1, ch. 4,
<u>Goethe's sämmtliche Werke</u>, XVIII, 38-39. This same passage appears as entry
256. <u>Translation</u>: "Many-sidedness really only prepares the element in which
the one-sided man can work, for whom there is then sufficient room. Yes, it
is now the time for one-sidedness; it is good for him who comprehends it and
works in this sense for himself and others! In certain things it is completely and at once obvious. Practise yourself to be a capable violinist, and
be assured the director of an orchestra will offer you your place with favour.
Make an organ of yourself, and await the kind of position mankind, in general
well meaning, will grant you" (<u>Wilhelm Meister</u>: <u>Apprenticeship and Travels</u>
trans. R.O. Moon, 2 vols. [London: G.T. Foulis & Co. Ltd., 1947], II, 35).

GHL's MS. "Goethe" contains an entry under the title Vielseitigkeit; it makes reference to another passage in Goethe on D'Alembert which gives instances of "many-sidedness" (p. [3], paging from back). Whatever he may have thought of Vielseitigkeit, GHL held a low opinion of the Wanderjahre as a whole: "I find in it almost every fault a work can have: it is unintelligible, it is tiresome, it is fragmentary, it is dull, and it is often ill-written" (Goethe, II, 418). GE's reaction was the same: "Read Wanderjahre-- à mourir d'ennui (Journal, 23 December 1854).

Entry 19

1. "Im ernsten Beinhaus," Goethe's Werke, Vollständige Ausgabe letzter Hand (Stuttgart and Tübingen: J.G. Cotta'schen, 1830), XXIII, 284. Translation: "What more can man achieve in life / Than that God-Nature be revealed to him? / How it dissolves the steadfast into spirit, / How it steadfastly preserves what issues from the spirit." (Meditation on Schiller's Skull.)

Entry 20

1. Heinrich Heine, "Zur Geschichte der Religion und Philosophie in Deutschland," Sämmtliche Werke (4th ed., Philadelphia: John Weik, 1857), III, 141. Translation: "The subtlety of Erasmus and the gentleness of Melancthon would never have brought us as far as the occasional godlike brutality of Brother Martin." Brother Martin is, of course, Luther. For further remarks on Luther's brutality, see entry 32.

Entry 21

1. "Zur Geschichte," p. 158. Translation: "It is perfectly clear that Spinoza's life was beyond reproach and as pure and spotless as the life of his divine cousin Jesus Christ. Like Jesus, Spinoza also suffered for his teachings; like him, he wore a crown of thorns. Wherever a great soul utters its thoughts, there is Golgotha. . . . He was solemnly expelled from the community of Israel and pronounced unworthy to call himself a Jew. His Christian enemies, however, were generous enough to allow him that name." GE used the third sentence (which I give in her translation) in "German Wit: Heinrich Heine" to illustrate Heine's prose style: "He continually throws out those finely-chiselled sayings which stamp themselves on the memory, and become familiar by quotation" (Essays, p. 251). The meaning and construction of this "Wherever . . . there" sentence of Heine's was so thoroughly stamped on GE's memory that she reproduced them three months later in a "finely chiselled" sentence of her own: "Wherever the strength of a man's intellect, or moral sense, or affection brings him into opposition with the rules which society sanctioned, there is renewed the conflict between Antigone and Creon" (Essays, p. 265).

Entry 22

1. "Die Romantische Schule," bk. 2, ch. 3, Sämmtliche Werke, V, 194. Translation: "Perhaps the stars of heaven appear to us so pure and lovely because we are at a great distance from them, and are not familiar with their private lives. Doubtless, in the realms above, there are stars that lie and beg; stars that play the hypocrite; stars that are forced to do all manner of evil deeds; stars that kiss one another, and then betray; stars that flatter their enemies, and, what is more painful yet, even their friends, just as we do here below. Perhaps those comets that we sometimes behold above, sweeping past our vision with flaming, radiant hair, like maenads of the firmament, are dissolute stars, that eventually, repentant and devout, creep into some dark corner of the sky, and hate the sun" (The Romantic School, trans. S.L. Gleishman [New York: Henry Holt and Company, 1882], p. 125). This work, GE remarks in "German Wit," is a delightful introduction to that phase of German literature known as the Romantic School" (Essays, p. 238).

Entry 23

1."Zur Geschichte," Sämmtliche Werke, III, 102. Translation: "It is in
his songs that Goethe's pantheism reveals itself with greater purity and
charm. The doctrine of Spinoza has escaped from its chrysalid mathematical
form, and flutters about us as a lyric of Goethe. Hence the wrath displayed
by our orthodox believers and pietists against Goethe's song. With their
pious bears' paws they make clumsy efforts to seize this butterfly that constantly eludes their grasp; so delicately ethereal, so lightly winged is
Goethe's song. . . . These songs of Goethe's have a coquettish charm that is
indescribable: the harmonious verses entwine themselves about the heart like
a tenderly loved one; the word embraces whilst the thought kisses thee" (Religion and Philosophy in Germany: A Fragment, trans. John Snodgrass, The
English and Foreign Philosophical Library, Vol. XXVIII [Boston: Houghton,
Mifflin and Company, 1882], pp. 137-8). GE discusses Heine's own pantheism in
"German Wit" (Essays, p. 243). For GE's ability to see a comic side to pantheism, see entry 35.

Entry 24

1. "Tefkir Namch, Buch der Betrachtungen," West-östlicher Divan, Goethe's
sämmtliche Werke, IV, 46. Translation: "It is very satisfying in every instance / To place yourself before a wise man / If you have tormented yourself
for a long while / He will know immediately where you are wanting; / And you
can also hope for approbation / Since he will understand your intention."
Quoted in German, this entry serves as the epigraph of DD, ch. 39. Deronda
serves as wise man for Gwendolen, just as Mordecai serves as wise man for
Deronda. GHL remarked in his Goethe that the West-östlicher Divan "is West-
Eastern: the images are Eastern; the feeling is Western" (p. 403). GE, in
reviewing George Meredith's The Shaving of Shagpat, repeats GHL's analysis almost verbatim (see Uncollected Writings). In a second review of Shagpat, her
opinion is that it "will be the thousand and second night" ("Belles Lettres,"
WR, 65 [April 1856], USA ed. 350); earlier, writing of Goethe's Roman Elegies,
as part of his discussion of the Divan, GHL remarked that Goethe "had thrown
himself into the classical past, reproducing its forms with unsurpassed ease
and witchery, yet never for a moment ceasing to be original" (Goethe, p. 403).
He also reviewed Shagpat in Saturday Review, 1 (19 January 1856), 216.

Entry 25

1. GE's observation on Shakespeare's women found its way into her review
of Saint-Marc Girardin's Cours de littérature dramatique, vol. 3, in Leader, 6
(25 August 1855), 820-21. Girardin argued that, unlike the heroines of antiquity ("ancient poetry was accustomed to represent its heroines as making
the first avowals of love"), Shakespeare's heroines do not "feel the passion
before inspiring it." GE flatly contradicted Girardin: "Shakespeare's women
have no more decided characteristic than the frankness with which they avow
their love, not only to themselves, but to the men they love." See Uncollected
Writings for her review "Love in the Drama." Girardin's vol. 3 was reviewed
again in WR, 64 (October 1855), USA ed. 316-8. GHL had reviewed vol. 1 in
"St. Marc Girardin's Lectures on the Drama," Foreign Quarterly Review, 33 (1844),
USA ed. 59-78.

Entry 26

1. This idea derives from GE's reading of Vol. I of Adolf Stahr, Torso:
Kunst, Künstler und Kunstwerk der Alten, 2 vols. (Brunswick: Friedrich Vieweg
u. Sohn, 1854). She changes the wording and uses it in the second paragraph
of her review of Torso I, "The Art of the Ancients," Leader 6 (17 March 1855),
15. The same idea, modified once again, appears in the opening paragraph of
GE's review of George Meredith's The Shaving of Shagpat, Leader 7 (5 January
1856), 15. GE uses it a third time in the first paragraph of "The Art and
Artists of Greece," Saturday Review, 2 (31 May 1856), 109-10, where she reviews

Torso I and II. GE's poem "Ex Oriente Lux" also develops this idea. For the
reviews and the poem, see Uncollected Writings.

Entry 26a
    1. "On Lucy, Countess of Bedford," Epigrams, LXXVI. GE's transcription
differs widely from the standard text of this poem. See Ben Jonson, Vol. 8:
The Poems, The Prose Works, ed. C. H. Hereford and Percy and Evelyn Simpson
(Oxford: Clarendon Press, 1947), pp. 52-53. GE refers to this poem in a
letter to Mrs. Frederick Lehmann on 2 April 1877: "You remember what old Ben
Jonson wished for his perfect woman. Besides 'each softest virtue' she was to
have 'a manly soul'" (Letters, VI, 360).

Entry 27
    1. Torso, I, 237. GE translated this passage in "The Art and Artists of
Greece," Saturday Review, 2 (1856), 110; see Uncollected Writings. GE met
Stahr in Berlin and was reading Torso when she wrote to Sara Hennell on 9
January 1855. "Professor Stahr is a very erudite man, and, what is very much
rarer amongst Germans, a good writer, who knows how to select his materials
and has above all a charming talent for description" (Letters, I, 192). In
her Journal, however, her enthusiasm is more moderate: "Read Stahr's 'Torso'--
too long-winded a style for reading aloud" (Life, I, 304). GE's reading and
reviewing of Stahr's two volumes was continuously valuable to her as a source
for allusions in her novels. From Captain Wybrow as an Antinous in "Mr.
Gilfil's Love-Story" to Gwendolen as the Leubronn Diana in DD, we see GE's
memory returning to Stahr. The picturesque scene in ch. 19 of M, which opens
with Dorothea standing in front of the Sleeping Ariadne in the Belvedere Gallery of the Vatican Museum, is indebted to Torso, II, 311-4. For GE's reviews
of Stahr's book, see Uncollected Writings.

Entry 28
    1. Torso, I, 263.

Entry 29
    1. Ibid., p. 386.

Entry 30
    1.Georg Gottfried Gervinus, Geschichte der poetischen National-literatur
der Deutschen, 5 vols. (Leipzig: Wilhelm Engelmann, 1840), I, 173-4. "Nach
meinem Gesmacke" does not appear in this text of Gervinus. Translation: "The
courtly love of the Provençal and Italian troubadours--more superficial, sen-
sual, and playful than that of German poets--had a happier effect on their
love poetry than the depth, piety, and seriousness of the minnesingers had on
ours. There is nothing so sublime and elevated, certainly, that it will not
profit from remembering its earthy origin from time to time. And just as a
fiery religious enthusiasm was evident in France--though religiosity was always stronger here even while such enthusiasm was lacking--so, in spite of our
tremendous reverence for women even to this very day, we cannot find in Germany the French manner of raising women above their circumstances and of making
them stand out from the conditions which nature and society imposed on them.
Women in Germany were never freed from domestic duties and the care of their
husbands; even in the Middle Ages woman is far behind man in all the legal and
practical aspects of life. It is therefore important to remember history when
we talk dreamily of the celebrated Germanic adoration of women. To be sure,
Germany is justly famous for being perhaps the first nation to assign to woman
the place she was destined by nature to have. If it is a credit to the country's life of feeling that woman was emancipated from an inferior position,
its common sense is likewise to be honored for never allowing woman to remove
herself from her sphere and take part in the affairs of men, as was the case
in France. That remote time of courtly love in the Middle Ages was necessarily

transitory, as we shall explain later. The more, consequently, that one
indulged in its ephemeral fraudulence, the more quickly and deeply one was
taken in; and the nastiness and immorality that are found in the relevant
writings of the period correspond exactly to the frivolity and heresy of the
French after their religious reawakening. (Translated with Gert Loose and
Ian Loram.)

Entry 31

1. Johannes Scherr, _Deutsche Cultur und Sitte_, p. 93. _Translation_:
"'The siege of Weinsberg,' a name with which the glorious constancy of German
womanhood is associated for all time." In 1140, before the surrender of
Weinsberg, the women were allowed to rescue their valuables and flee; forth-
with, they carried their husbands away on their backs.

2. Ibid., p. 46. This and the remainder of the page citations which GE
gives from Scherr are correct.

3. Murner indicates that a guest could expect to sleep with his host's
wife.

4. GE's interest in courtesans is seen earlier in entries 7 and 29.

5. Bitisia Gozzadini was, according to Scherr, the thirteenth century's
version of an emancipated woman: she was at the University of Bologna in 1236
and customarily dressed in men's clothes.

6. Sabina, a sculptor, the daughter of Erwin von Steinbach, presumably
carved a relief, in classical style, which she signed; it is on the south
porch of Strasburg cathedral.

7. Each of these entries from Scherr indicates GE's interest in the condition of women in the Middle Ages and Reformation: woman is seen as heroic,
protected, literate, prostituted, and married in a church; she is seen as a
scholar, man's equal, a sculptor, and a victim. GE's heroines will find the
same range of experience in their lives, from the seduced and outcast Hetty to
the scholarly Romola and Dorothea.

Entry 32

1. I am uncertain of the exact source of this entry. _Translation_:
"(He summoned all the world) to smash, choke, and stab the farmers, secretly
and in the open, the way a mad dog must be killed. The people must be ruled
by force, the ass must have blows. The innocent among them God will protect
and save, as he did Lot and Jeremiah. If he does not, then they are not guilt-
less, but have at the very least said nothing and acquiesced . . . . Strike
down all; the Lord knows his own." Scherr discusses Luther and the farmers in
his chapter on the Reformation, and some of the quotations that appear above
appear in _Deutsche Cultur und Sitte_ (see p. 273); but beginning with Scherr,
GE has gone beyond this first source to explore Luther's brutality further.
In Dr. Williams's Library the copy of Luther, _Memoirs_, ed. and trans. J.
Michelet, 2 vols. (Brussels: Cattoir and Co., 1837), I, 210, has a passage
concerning Luther's cruelty to the peasants marked, presumably by GE. What
Heine called "the godlike brutality of Brother Martin" (entry 20) represents
to GE a spirit of doctrine destroying fellow-feeling. Luther aptly illustrates a sentence in _M_, ch. 61: "There is no general doctrine which is not
capable of eating out our morality if unchecked by the deep-seated habit of
direct fellow-feeling with individual fellow-men."

Entry 32a

1. "Of Education. To Master Samuel Hartlib" (1644). GE, however, did
not take this quotation directly from Milton's treatise but from Thomas
Keightley, _An Account of the Life, Opinions, and Writings of John Milton.
With an Introduction to Paradise Lost_ (London: Chapman and Hall, 1855), p.
238. She reviewed Keightley's book twice, once for _Leader_, 6 (4 August 1855),
750, rpt. _Essays_, pp. 154-7; once for _WR_, 65 (October 1855), USA ed. 314-6.
In the _Westminster_ article, GE devoted a paragraph to Milton on education.
See Uncollected Writings.

Entry 33

   1. Milton, "Of Education," in Keightley, p. 239.

Entry 34

   1. "Breathed out his soul," in Watson's own translation.

   2. GE's ellipsis indicates the omission of the following passage: "and I consider the testimony concerning the resurrection of Jesus (and that fact is the corner-stone of the Christian church) to be worthy of entire credit."

   3. <u>Translation</u>: The soul is by its own nature immortal.

   4. The notion of reanimation was used by GE in <u>The Lifted Veil</u>. See also entry 45 for another approach to the same subject.

   5. GE opposed dogmatic religion from <u>SCL</u> to <u>DD</u>. Amos Barton's "dogmatizing spirit" leads to his unpopularity among his flock. Too narrow a doctrine is a fault in the otherwise admirable Mr. Tryan. The popular Mr. Irwin in <u>AB</u> avoids doctrinal disputes and preaches short moral sermons. As Adam Bede himself says, religion is feelings, not ideas. GE opposes a "dogmatizing spirit" precisely because it tends to destroy religious feeling; see entry 32, n. 1.

   6. Richard Watson, <u>Anecdotes of the Life of Richard Watson, Bishop of Landaff, Written by Himself at Different Intervals and Revised in 1814</u> (London: T. Cadell and W. Davis, 1817), pp. 14-16.

Entry 34a

   1. [Charles Lamb], "On the Artificial Comedy of the Last Century," <u>Elia, Essays Which Have Appeared under that Signature in the London Magazine</u> (London: Taylor and Hessey, 1823), p. 325. "Began to read Charles Lamb after dinner" (Journal, 28 November 1855). GHL wrote of Lamb: "How fine and subtle the criticisms on poets and painters. How pregnant the many observations carelessly thrown in, leading the mind to muse upon the perplexities of our nature!" "Charles Lamb--His Genius and Writings," <u>British Quarterly Review</u>, 7 (1848), USA ed. 311. An entry in GHL's Journal X (Beinecke Library, VI. 1) indicates that GE was reading Lamb again on 3 August 1858: "M. read Charles Lamb's <u>Elia</u>."

   2. Lamb's text reads "shame."

   3. <u>Elia</u>, pp. 329-30. Lamb's observations recall those of GE in a letter to Francis Watts, 3 August 1842: "I could shed tears of joy to believe that in this lovely world I may lie on the grass and ruminate on possibilities without dreading lest my conclusions should be everlastingly fatal," <u>Letters</u>, I, 143. GE mentions the <u>Elia</u> essays in a letter to John Blackwood, 11 December 1857; see <u>Letters</u>, II, 411. GHL remarked, "It is on the 'Essays of Elia' that Lamb's fame must rest. The foundation is strong enough to last for ever. There all moods are reflected; every chord is touched, and by a master spirit" (p. 310).

Entry 35

   1. Henry Longueville Mansel, "Scenes from an Unfinished Drama, entitled <u>Phrontisterion</u>, or Oxford in the 19th Century" (Oxford: J. Vincent, 1851); rpt. <u>The Oxford Ironies</u>, ed. George Gordon (London: H. Milford, 1927), pp. 92-93.

   2. Mansel's text reads "breathes."

   3. Mansel's text reads "beginning."

   4. In GE's entry given as same line as "Thee do we sing."

   5. The epigraph of <u>M</u>, ch. 51, seems to derive from this entry:

          Party is Nature too, and you shall see
          By force of Logic how they both agree:
          The Many in the One, the One in Many
          All is not Some, nor Some the same as Any:
          Genus holds species, both are great or small:
          One genus highest, one not high at all;

> Each species has its differentia too,
> This is not That, and He was never You,
> Though this and that are AYES, and you and he
> Are like as one to one, or three to three.

Entry 36

1.   Ruskin quotes this line in Modern Painters, vol. III, pt. 4, ch. 12,
"On the Pathetic Fallacy," and remarks: "The foam is not cruel, neither does
it crawl.   The state of mind which attributes to it these characters of a living creature is one in which reason is unhinged by grief.   All violent feelings have the same effect.   They produce in us a falseness in all our impressions of external things, which I would generally characterize as the 'pathetic
fallacy.'"   GE reviewed Modern Painters III in April 1856, quoting this passage from Ruskin along with Kingsley's line; see WR, 65 (1856), USA ed. 346.
2.   Charles Kingsley, Alton Locke, 2 vols. (London: Chapman and Hall,
1850), II, 55-56.   GE's rendering of this poem differs from the version in
Alton Locke: Kingsley repeats "And call the cattle home" in st. 1; also, GE's
"western wave" is "dark"; whereas, Kingsley's "western wind" is "dank"; his st.
2, l. 3 ends with "sand"; his st. 4, l. 4 reads "her grave"; his st. 1, ll.
1-4 are in quotation marks, so too is all of his st. 3.   (I can find no prece-
dent for GE's version, but, according to the Ouvry Inventory, the GE-GHL
library did contain a copy of Alton Locke.)   When GE reviewed Westward Ho!
she quoted st. 1, l. 2, substituting "Along" for "Across"; WR, 64 (1855), USA
ed. 151; see also Essays, p. 125 and n. 7.

Entry 37

1.   "The Hated Man," l. 18; Menander, The Principal Fragments, trans.
Francis G. Allinson (1921; Cambridge, Mass.:   Harvard Univ. Press, 1951), pp.
409, 461.   GE twice reviewed Guillaume Guizot, Ménandre: Etude historique et
littéraire sur la Comédie et la Société Grecques (Paris: Didier, 1855):
"Menander and the Greek Comedy," Leader, 6 (16 June 1855), 478-9; "Belles
Lettres," WR, 64 (1855), USA ed. 158-60.   The Leader review, the more interesting of the two, is reprinted in Uncollected Writings.

Entry 39

1.   See entry 26 for GE's first entry from Torso.   These notes from Vol. I
are preparatory to GE's reviews mentioned in entry 26, n. 1.
2.   Charles Fellows (1799-1860), who discovered the ancient city of
Xanthus.
3.   Entries 1-4 from ch. 5 "Aelteste erhaltene Hauptwerk der griechischen
Skulptur," Stahr, Torso, I, 85-94.   See entry for GE's first quotation from
Stahr.
4.   Ch. 7, "Die äginetischen Bildwerke," Torso, I, 109-34.
5.   Anselm Feuerbach (1798-1851), a German archeologist, whose Der vati-
kanische Apollo (1833) made him famous.   He speaks of the Minerva as "pure
thought embodied in marble."
6.   Johann Joachim Wincklemann (1717-68), who wrote Geschichte der Kunst
des Altertums (1764), which gave method to the study of ancient art.
7.   See Torso, I, 157.
8.   Ch. 8, "Phidias und seine Werke," subsection A.   Das Atheneideal--
Erhaltene Athenebilder, Torso, I, 155-9.
9.   Ch. 8, subsection B.   Das Jupiterideal--Erhaltene Nachbildungen,
Torso, I, 165-6.
10.   Here and elsewhere GE uses the French word frise instead of the
English frieze.
11.   Ch. 9, "Die Parthenonskulpturen," Torso, I, 177-222, but especially
pp. 218-22.
12.   Ch. 10, "Die Kolosse von Monte Cavallo," Torso, I, 225-48.
13.   Ch. 11, "Alkamenis und die Skulpturen des Apollotempels zu Bossä,"

<u>Torso</u>, I, 249-74. The 23 blocks are in the British Museum.

14. Ch. 12, "Polyklet und die Juno Ludovisi," <u>Torso</u>, I, 277-83.

15. Ch. 13, "Myron und der Diskobol," <u>Torso</u>, I, 291-302.

16. Hetty is compared to the Medusa Rondanini in bk. 5, ch. 37, of <u>Adam Bede</u>. See entry 40, n. 1, and fig. 3.

17. An allusion to a copy of this statue appears in a humorous context in <u>FH</u>, ch. 43. "Mrs. Holt's attention, having been directed to the squirrel which had scampered on to the head of the Silenus carrying the infant Bacchus, had been drawn downward to the tiny baby looked at with so much affection by the rather ugly and hairy gentleman, of whom she nevertheless spoke with reserve as of one who possibly belonged to the Transome family."

18. Mrs. Irwine appears "as erect in her comely <u>embonpoint</u> as a statue of Ceres" in <u>AB</u>, ch. 5.

19. Ch. 14, "Skopas und Praxiteles," <u>Torso</u>, I, 305-93.

Entry 40

1. <u>Torso</u> I, 314-5. <u>Translation</u>: "The evidence of Medusa's astonishing beauty everywhere permeates her myth. Her story is a tragic account of the acute jealousy of the ancient gods directed against all splendor and beauty in mankind. The poets of antiquity tell how Medusa, a king's daughter, dared to compare herself in beauty to Athena, and the goddess, thereby enraged, changed the girl into a horrible monster. According to another version of the story--one which the Roman poet Ovid followed--Medusa's fate was yet more undeserved. The wild god Poseidon raped the incomparably beautiful princess in Athena's temple, and the goddess, according to the poet, covered her chaste countenance so as not to witness the crime. Athena's punishment, moreover, fell on the innocent victim, because she was powerless to punish the guilty god." In her <u>Leader</u> review of <u>Torso</u>, GE refers to "the terrible beauty of the Medusa Rondanini," having the description quoted in entry 40 in mind. When Hetty is on "The Journey in Despair" (<u>AB</u>, ch. 37), the narrator tries to catch a semblance of that "terrible beauty" in Hetty's face, "the sadder for its beauty, like that wondrous Medusa-face, with the passionate, passionless lips" (see fig. 3).

Entry 41

1. Harriet Martineau, <u>The History of England during the Thirty Years Peace: 1816-1846</u>. 2 vols. (London: Charles Knight, 1850), II, 187. GE was reading the <u>History</u> in 1858 and remarked of Martineau in her Journal (2 and 3 February 1858) that "She has a sentimental style in this history which is fatiguing and not instructive. But her history of the Reform Movement is very interesting." GHL reviewed Martineau's <u>History</u> and found that "considerable portions are mere surplusage"; whereas, the Catholic Emancipation and the Reform Bill "are treated with great vigour" ("The Thirty Years Peace," <u>British Quarterly Review</u>, II [1850], 371).

Entry 41a

1. I am uncertain of the exact source of this entry. Similar information was available in numerous classical handbooks in both English and German as well as in editions of Pindar. Usually, however, the chronology is computed from 776, not 777. One English source that uses 777 is Sir Harris Nicholas, <u>The Chronology of History</u> (London: Longman, Rees, Orme, Brown, Green, & Longman, 1833), p. 2.

Entry 41b

1. <u>Homer</u>, trans. Alexander Pope, 3 vols. (London: A. J. Valpy, 1833). These lines serve as a translation of the Greek that follows them.

2. <u>Homer Ilias Graece et Latine</u>, ed. Samuel Clarke, 2 vols. (London: J. Cuthell et al., 1815), I, 354; IX, 48-49. This passage is marked in the GE-GHL copy in Dr. Williams's Library. The endpages in the volume also contain

annotations in GE's hand along with the date "Aug. 15. 79." GE's most extensive quotations from the Iliad in Greek appear in "Interesting Extracts," pp. 57-61. See also entry 282, n. 1.

Entry 42

1. Tycho Brahe (1546-1601), a Danish astronomer, the discoverer of the "new star" (see his De Nova Stella, 1573), and the originator of the Tychonic system, which sought a middle ground between Ptolemy and Copernicus.

2. Johannes Kepler (1571-1630), a German astronomer, whose work laid the foundations of modern dynamical astronomy. He was a colleague of Brahe's at Prague. His prophecy is that "A great monarch of the world will die in the middle of the month of March." Mathias, born the son of Maximillian II in 1557, ruled the Holy Roman Empire from 1612-19, dying in the year mentioned in the prophecy attributed to Kepler. I have been unable to find this quotation in Kepler's works.

Entry 43

1. Joseph Spence, Anecdotes, Observations, and Characters, of Books and Men. Collected from the Conversation of Mr. Pope and Other Eminent Persons of His Time, ed. Samuel Weller Singer (London: W.H. Carpenter, 1820), p. 291.

2. Ibid., p. 178.

3. Ibid., p. 11.

4. Ibid., pp. 185-6 and 186n. Translation: "Father Paul is on the whole Catholic, but Protestant in particulars." Fra Paolo is Paolo Sarpi, author of The History of the Council of Trent.

5. John Nichols, Literary Anecdotes of the Eighteenth Century (London: John Nichols, 1812). A thorough check of Nichols shows that GE's ascription of these anecdotes to him is erroneous. Her source is Spence.

6. Translation: "Life without thought is the sweetest life / Because ignorance is bliss" (Sophocles, Ajax, ll. 554-5). GE began reading Ajax on 22 September 1856. This was the same day she began to write "Amos Barton." GHL reviewed Sophokles Tragodien, ed. F. W. G. Stäger (Halle, 1842) in "German and English Translations from the Greek," Foreign Quarterly Review, 33 (1844), USA ed. 248-58. It is certain that GE used the Boeckh ed. of Antigone and the Schoemann ed, of Prometheus, which GHL reviewed in this same article; it is probable, therefore, that she used the Stäger edition for Ajax, Electra, and Oedipus at Colonus.

7. Ajax, ll. 520-24. GE provides a translation of these lines in the second epigraph to FH, ch. 42: "Yea, it becomes a man. / To cherish memory, where he had delight. / For kindness is the natural birth of kindness. / Whose soul records not the great debt of joy, / Is stamped for ever an ignoble man."

8. Sophocles, Electra, l. 625. GE offers a translation of this line in the second line of the first epigraph to FH, ch. 42: "Thou sayst it, and not I; for thou has done / The ugly deed that made these ugly words." GE finished reading Electra on 12 August 1857, while she was writing "Janet's Repentance," which was finished on 9 October (Journal). Line 621 of Electra is quoted below; see n. 16.

9. Sophocles, Oedipus at Colonus, ll. 266-7. Translation: "My deeds 'were rather suffered by me than performed'" (The Tragedies of Sophocles [Boston: D.C. Heath, 1865], p. 68). GE quoted these lines in the first two editions of MF, I.xiii. They are applied to the unfortunate Mr. Tulliver: "Mr. Tulliver had a destiny as well as OEdipus, and in this case he might plead, like OEdipus, that his deed was inflicted upon him rather than committed by him." On 22 April 1857, GE noted in her Journal, "Reading the OEdipus Colonus & Shelley." GHL translated approximately the first 230 lines of the Colonus; see "Extracts Interesting," back to front.

10. Aeschylus, Agamemnon, l. 1014. Translation: "The gift divine still abides even in the soul of one enslaved" (Aeschylus, trans. Smyth, II, 91). Des Aeschylos Oresteia, Griechisch und Deutsch, ed. Johannes Franz (Leipzig:

Hahn'schen, 1846) is the text of the Oresteia which GE used; it is now in Dr. Williams's Library. GE, according to her Journal, began reading the Agamemnon on 12 August 1857 and finished it on 6 December. This reading overlaps her writing the last pages of "Janet's Repentance" (concluded 9 October) and AB (begun 22 October 1857).

11. Agamemnon, 11. 232-5. The translation (as well as the brackets) is GE's rendering of "Franz's German: "Voraus zu wissen / den Gang der Zukunft, das bleibe fern von mir. / Dem wär' voraus trauern gleich. / Denn sicher kommt sie gepaart mit Unheil" (p. 21).

12. Agamemnon, 1259-62. Translation: "Alas for human fortune! When prosperous, a mere shadow can overturn it; if calamitous, the dash of a wet sponge blots out the drawing. And this last I deem far more pitiable than that" (Aeschylus, trans. Herbert Weir Smyth, Loeb Classical Library, 2 vols. [Cambridge: Harvard University Press; London: William Heinemann, 1957], II, 119). This passage is marked in the Franz edition in Dr. Williams's Library.

13. Aeschylus, Choephorae, 1. 576; this passage is marked in the Franz edition in Dr. Williams's Library. Mr. Irwine comments on the unhappy relation-ship between Arthur Donnithorne and his grandfather, the Squire, saying, "Ah, my boy, it is not only woman's love that is ἀπέρωτος ἔρος, as old Aeschylus calls it. There's plenty of 'unloving love' in the world of a masculine kind" (AB, ch. 22). What Franz translates "entsetzlicher Liebe" (p. 176) becomes Irwine's "unloving love." In the Journal, 17 December 1857, GE remarks, "I am in the Choephorae now." Between entries for 13 and 20 January, she notes, "Enjoying the writing of my 5th chapter [of AB] . . . . having finished Choephorae."

14. Aeschylus, Prometheus Bound, 11. 274-6. Translation: "Consent, I pray you, oh consent. Take part in the trouble of him who is now in sore dis-tress. Of a truth, afflication wandereth impartially abroad and alighteth upon all in turn" (Smyth, trans., Aeschylus, I, 241). For the text GE used, see Endpaper, n. 1.

15. Aeschylus, Eumenides, 1. 482; trans. by Franz as "Oft zum Heile dient die Furcht." This passage is marked in Dr. Williams's Library copy of Des Aeschylus Oresteia. Mr. Irwine translates this sentiment in a homely way to Arthur Donnithorne when he compares a dangerous love to smallpox: "There are certain alterative doses which a man may administer to himself by keeping un-pleasant consequences before his mind. . . " (AB, ch. 16). Deronda invokes a similar moral sentiment when he advises Gwendolen to "Turn your fear into a safeguard" (DD, ch. 36). GE began reading the Eumenides between 13 and 20 January 1858; she concluded her reading of it on 3 February. By 10 February, she had finished writing ch. 9 of AB, according to her Journal.

16. Sophocles, Electra, 1. 621. Translation: "Baseness is from base-ness learnt" (Storr, trans., Sophocles, II, 173).

17. GE here projects an article that she never published and indicates the sources which she intends to draw on: G. L. Craik, Knight's Pictorial History of England to George III, 8 vols. (London: Charles Knight, 1838-44); once part of the GE-GHL library, this book was sold at auction by Sotheby's 17 June 1923 (see Library, p. 229); John Beckmann, A History of Inventions, Discoveries and Origins, trans. William Johnston and ed. William Francis and J. W. Griffith, 2 vols. (London: Henry G. Bohn, 1846); Thomas Babington Macaulay, The History of England from the Accession of James II, 5 vols. (Philadelphia: E.H. Butler, 1856), I, 380-81, 278-99. Samuel Smiles, The Life of George Stephenson, Railway Engineer (London: J. Murray, 1857). Macaulay deals with the opposition to the "Flying Coach," to London street-lighting, and to the London penny-post in "The State of England in 1685" (vol. I, ch. 3); stage-coach days are vividly recalled in the Introduction to FH. Beckmann treats of the problems of lighting streets in European cities (II, 178-85), as well as of opposition to a variety of inventions. Smiles deals with the opposition to railway surveyors subsequent to Stephenson's perfecting the locomotive (ch. 15, pp. 174-8); this last is dramatized in M

when Caleb Garth rescues the hapless railway surveyors from "six or seven men
in smock-frocks with hayforks in their hands" (ch. 56). Opposition to the
railway is also seen in the Introduction to FH where the coachman, "now, as in
a perpetual vision saw the ruined country strewn with shattered limbs, and regarded Mr. Huskisson's death as a proof of God's anger against Stephenson."
William Huskisson (1770-1830) was accidently killed at the opening of the
Manchester to Liverpool railway on 15 September 1830. This accident is mentioned again in M, where the railroad is considered "pretty well seasoned now
it had done for Huskisson" (ch. 41). For Stephenson, see entry 64, n. 1.

18. This tidbit of millinery hearsay cannot be documented from the last
manuscript catalogue of the repository of the museum dated 1764. The
Royal Society moved from Crane Court to Somerset House in 1780 and all items
in the museum, except a few scientific ones, were transferred to the British
Museum.

19. Simplicissimus, bk. 1, ch. 1. Translation: "I was so complete and
at ease in my ignorance that it was even impossible for me to know what I
didn't know." See Hans Jakob Christoph von Grimmelshausen, Der abenteüerliche
Simplicissimus und andere Schriften, ed. Adelbert Keller, Bibliothek des
literarischen Vereins (Stuttgart: Literarischer Verein, 1854), vol. 33, p.
29. GE made a note on p. 626 of her copy of Deutsche Cultur und Sitte (see
entry 31, n. 1) that Scherr discussed Simplicissimus on p. 295. The usual date
for the publication of Simplicissimus is given as 1668, not 1683.

20. Miguel de Cervantes Saavedra, L'Ingenieux Hidalgo Don Quichotte de
la Manche, trans., Louis Viardot, 2 vols. (Paris: J.-J. Dubochet, 1836), I,
53. Translation: "I am naturally slow to seek out authors who say for me what
I can very well say for myself." GE first read Don Quixote in 1840. On 23
June 1840 she writes to Maria Lewis, whose copy of Cervantes she borrowed, "I
soon hope to finish." On 20 July she writes, "I have quite finished" (see
Letters, I, 55, 60). In September 1864 GE was reading Don Quixote (sometimes
aloud to GHL) while she was learning Spanish (Letters, IV, 163-5). Shortly
before her death, in December 1880, GE once again indicates that she is reading an English translation of Cervantes (see Letters, VII, 342).

21. Ch. 7, par. 1, "A Short View of Tragedy; Its Original Excellency,
and Corruption, With Some Reflections on Shakespear, and Other Practitioners
for the Stage," The Critical Works of Thomas Rymer, ed. Curt A. Zimansky (New
Haven: Yale Univ. Press, 1956), p. 131. GE's 1693 edition of Rymer is in
Dr. Williams's Library.

22. Arthur Young, A Six Months Tour through the North of England, 4
vols. (London: W. Strahan, 1770), II, 195. The "noble parcel" Young mentions consists of 20 horses, 40 cows, 1200 sheep, and 300 "beasts in summer."

23. "Dedication to Leigh Hunt, Esq." from The Cenci. Dr. Williams's
Library has Percy Bysshe Shelley, The Cenci. A Tragedy in Five Acts (London:
C. & J. Ollier, 1821). This passage is on p.[v]. Shelley's words suggest
GE's program for realism in AB: "My strongest effort is . . . . to give a
faithful account of men and things as they have mirrored themselves in my
mind" (ch. 17). GHL reviewed The Poetical Works of Percy Bysshe Shelley
(London: Moxon, 1839) in "Percy Bysshe Shelley," WR, 35 (April 1841), USA
ed. 154-75. The works GHL reviews are The Cenci, "Alastor," "Revolt of
Islam"--the three works GE quotes here; he regrets that he can only mention
Prometheus Unbound--GE's only other quotation from Shelley is from the
Prometheus (see entry 73). The Cenci, wrote GHL, is the "most magnificent
tragedy of modern times" (p. 165). GE quotes The Cenci, II.ii.482-7, in the
epigraph to DD, ch. 54.

24. "Alastor," ll. 713-20. GE read "the greater part of Shelley's poems"
in the Scilly Isles between 15 March and 28 June 1857 (Letters, II, 354-8).
"Alastor, or the Spirit of Solitude," wrote GHL in his review of Shelley,
"is perhaps, of all his poems, that which pleases the generality of people
most, because it contains nothing of his peculiar views" (p. 165).

25. "Laon and Cyntha," IX.xix.169-72. "This poem is the inspiration of

liberty" (p. 165), wrote GHL in his review of Shelley.

26. Book of Tobit (VIII, 7), Apocrypha. The passage from "mercifully" to "together" was used by GE as the epigraph for M, ch. 74, where Mrs. Bulstrode learns of her husband's guilt. There are two Greek quotations from Tobit in "Interesting Abstracts," pp. 28 [75].

Entry 44

1. Text has demeure, not reste.

2. "Le Roi des Aulnes," Gesammelte Schriften von Ludwig Börne (Hamburg: Hoffmann and Campe, 1840), V, 62-69. Translation: "The King of the Elves. Who is crossing the valley so late at night? It is an old lord who, riding his black charger and carrying a child in his arms, follows a remote road. He complains of the dark night that engulfs his manor; and the child (ah! why trouble young hearts?) tremblingly recalls those incredible stories that, to the glimmering of the lamp and with welcome fright in the night, nurses told by the fireside.

"He thinks he sees . . . he saw, beneath the misty woods, one of those foolish spirits, one of those ancient elves, which, jeering and cruel, sweet and obsequious phantoms, delight in disturbing shepherds' dreams: they may shout their laughs at short intervals, they may fasten themselves to the manes of wandering horses, or fill the night with false lights.

"Glimmering fantasies concealing his every step, the monster, at the edge of chasms, walks atop flowers without bending them, and from his cloak of seven colors he has brought forth his tricks; to the child who is fascinated he shows a fresh path, makes his crown gleam and smiles; in his hand floats a white privet and yellow waterlilies. 'Father,' asks the child, 'Do you see the Elfking?'

. . . .

"'Father, he's grabbed me, I suffer . . . oh save me!' The lord shivers: and the child full of fright hugs himself and remains still.

"But the old lord, urging on his black charger (and the child in his arms), arrives at the manor. There are the high towers and the hospitable door. The drawbridge is lowered; he enters; and the nurse carries a flickering torch to the threshold. The father tenderly opens his cloak. 'Be more careful, Isaure, he's been troubled along the way by spirits whom he fears; he was crying in my arms, but now he's asleep. Take your child.' 'Oh!' she cries, 'he's dead!'

"This beautiful elegiac poem, little known, was written by Mr. H. Delatouche, one of the most spiritual men and one of the most distinguished poets of his time."

The poem in GE's notebook is by M. H. Delatouche, and Börne quotes it as an illustration of the inability of the French to understand the Romanticism of Germany in general and here of Goethe in particular. GE describes Börne in "German Wit: Heinrich Heine" as "a remarkable political writer of the ultra liberal party in Germany, who resided in Paris at the same time with Heine: a man of stern, uncompromising partisanship and bitter humour" (Essays, p. 238). GE considers Börne in the context of Heine's unpleasant book on him and also in the context of the characterization of Heine as a Hellene and of Börne as a "Nazarene--ascetic, spiritualistic, despising the pure artist as destitute of earnestness" (ibid.).

Entry 45

1. William Benjamin Carpenter, Principles of Physiology: General and Comparative (3rd ed. London: John Churchill, 1851), I, 41. Herbert Spencer reviewed this book for WR, 61 (January 1852), USA ed. 146-7, when GE was editor of WR. See also entry 34, n. 4.

Entry 46

1. Honoré de Balzac, "Histoire de la grandeur et de la décadence de

César Birotteau," Scènes de la vie parisienne, II, La Comédie humaine (Paris:
Béthune et Plon, 1844), X, 426. Translation: "Weak men like Birotteau live
in their sorrows, instead of changing them into instructive experiences; they
wallow in misery and wear themselves out with past woes." This sentence expresses GE's idea that sorrow, which is unavoidable, should make one's life
richer rather than poorer. In his essay "Balzac and George Sand" GHL excepted
César Birotteau from those books of Balzac that were "dangerous, insidious"
(p. 149). "In César Birroteau he has exhibited the heroic greatness of in-
tegrity side by side with the most childish vanity and simplicity. It is a
fine lesson" (p. 156). See Foreign Quarterly Review, 33 (1844), USA ed.
145-63. In her Journal, 18 August 1856, GE writes, "Finished César Birroteau
aloud."

Entry 47
    1. Laokoon, ch. 4; see entry 8a, n. 2. Translation: "How many things
would in theory appear incontestable if genius had not in actuality disproved
them."

Entry 48
    1. Lord B******** [F. R. Chichester, Earl of Belfast], Naples; Political,
Social, and Religious, 2 vols. (London: T. Cautley Newby, 1856), I, 247-8.
The implacability of character found in Baldassarre Calvo in R--"Baldassarre's only dread was lest the young limbs should escape him" (ch. 22)--is
anticipated in the character of the vengeful neighbor. Tito is as surely
marked for death as is the constable.
    2. "Edle Rache" means noble vengeance. This is the germ for the Tito-
Baldassarre plot in R. Haight comments on it as follows: "One evening in the
winter of 1855 at Fräulein Solmar's in Berlin old General Pfuhl told her [GE]
a story of 'noble vengeance,' which impressed her so much that she wrote it
down in her Journal and later (with slight variation) in her Commonplace
Book" (Biography, p. 352). In R, Baldassarre's desire for vengeance is so hot
that "unending fire" would be "coolness to his burning hatred" (ch. 24). He
desires an "eternity of vengeance where he, [with] undying hate, might clutch
for ever an undying traitor" (ch. 30).

Entry 49
    1. Oliver Cromwell's Letters and Speeches: With Elucidations by Thomas
Carlyle, 2 vols. (London: Chapman and Hall, 1845), I, 75. GE was reading
Carlyle's Cromwell, according to the Autograph Journal on 22 May 1857; see
also Letters, II, 330, n. 6. This passage bears directly on the central psychological development of the hero in AB: Adam must have his hardness shattered by suffering and then in his sorrow achieve sympathy with others: "And
there is but one way in which a strong determined soul can learn it [fellow-
feeling]--by getting his heartstrings bound round the weak and erring, so that
he must share not only the outward consequence of their error, but their inward suffering" (ch. 19). Returning to this theme in ch. 42, the narrator remarks, "Deep, unspeakable suffering may well be called a baptism, a regeneration, the initiation into a new state."

Entry 50
    1. Jenny Keith.
    2. Robert Southey, The Life of Wesley; and Rise and Progress of Methodism,
3d ed., 2 vols. (London: Longman, Brown, Green, Longmans, 1846), II, 376-7n.
Dinah Morris echoes the sentiment of Jenny Keith's letter when she says: "I
am poor, like you: I have to get my living with my hands; but no lord nor
lady can be so happy as me, if they haven't got the love of God in their
souls (AB, ch. 2).

Entry 51

1. Ibid., p. 221. In "The Preaching" Dinah tries to make her hearers "see Thee hanging on the cross and . . . see Thee as Thou wilt come again in Thy glory to judge them at the last." Also "she made them feel that he [Christ] was among them bodily, and might at any moment show himself to them in some way that would strike anguish and penitence into their hearts" (AB, ch. 2).

2. Ibid., pp. 205-6. Speaking of Dinah and Seth, the narrator remarks: "They believed in present miracles, in instantaneous conversions, in revelations by dreams and visions; they drew lots, and sought for Divine guidance by opening the Bible at hazard. . ." (AB, ch. 3). See David Leon Higdon, "Sortes Biblicae in Adam Bede," Papers on Language and Literature, 9 (1973), 396-405.

Entry 52

1. Life of Wesley, I, 384-5.

2. Henry Fielding, The History of the Life of the Late Jonathan Wild the Great (1743), bk. 4, ch. 13.

3. GE's brackets here enclose a footnote from the Life of Wesley, I, 185-6.

4. Plato, Phaedo, 117C.

Entry 53

1. Life of Wesley, I, 185-7. "Methodists are great folks for going into prisons," says Adam, when wondering whether Dinah had gone to see Hetty in Stoniton jail (AB, ch. 41). Ch. 45 finds Dinah, in imitation of the Wesleys, consoling Hetty, a condemned criminal, in jail.

Entry 54

1. Ibid., pp. 209-10. In "The Preaching" the stranger "wondered whether she [Dinah] could have that power of rousing their [her hearers'] more violent emotions, which must surely be a necessary seal of her vocation as a Methodist preacher. . ." (AB, ch. 2). Bessy Cranage, with "a great terror . . . upon her" comes close to a paroxysm in ch. 2. Hetty's confession--"I will speak . . . I will tell . . . I won't hide it any more"--with its subsequent overtones of psychodrama, also confirms Dinah's efficacy as a Methodist preacher (ch. 45).

Entry 55

1. Dinah Morris began her ministry of preaching in a similar situation. She tells Mr. Irwine: "I went to where the little flock of people was gathered together, and stepped on the low wall that was built against the green hillside, and I spoke the words that were given to me abundantly" (AB, ch. 8).

2. The narrator in AB associates the early days of Methodism with "an amphitheatre of green hills" (ch. 3).

Entry 56

1. Though she does not cite this text, its message is the burden of Dinah's preaching in AB, ch. 2.

Entry 57

1. Life of Wesley, I, 415-8.

Entry 58

1. Ibid., pp. 419-21. The stranger remarks to Mr. Casson: "But you've not got many Methodists about here, surely--in this agricultural spot? I should have thought there would hardly be such a thing as a Methodist to be found about here. You're all farmers, aren't you? The Methodists can seldom lay much hold on them" (AB, ch. 2).

Entry 59

   1. Life of Wesley, II, 90-91. Dorothea, walking with her St. Bernard
dog, Monk, rejects the gift of a Maltese puppy from Sir James Chettam, saying,
"I like to think that animals have souls something like our own, and either
carry on their own little affairs or can be companions to us, like Monk here"
(M, ch. 3).

   2. Ibid., p. 89.

   3. Ibid., p. 515. Southey quotes Fasti, vi. 251-6, which, in translation,
reads: "I was wrapt up in prayer; I felt the heavenly deity, and the glad
ground gleamed with a purple light. Not indeed that I saw thee, O goddess (far
from me be the lies of poets!), nor was it meet that men should look upon thee;
but my ignorance was enlightened and my errors corrected without the help of
an instructor" (Ovid's Fasti, trans. Sir James George Frazer, Loeb Classical
Library [Cambridge, Mass.: Harvard Univ. Press; London: William Heinemann,
1967], p. 339).

   4. Life of Wesley, II, 417. Dinah tells her congregation of her hearing
Wesley, "that man of God," preach when she was a little girl: "I thought he
had perhaps come down from the sky to preach to us . . . ." When Dinah herself preaches, the words of Knox on Wesley are recalled: "the quiet depth of
conviction with which she spoke seemed in itself as evidence for the truth of
her message" (AB, ch. 2). This same passage, with slightly altered punctua-
tion, also appears in entry 108. It is used as the epigraph of DD, ch. 20,
where it suggests the way that Mrs. Meyrick, in support of Deronda, comes to
affirm Mirah's "goodness."

   5. Ibid., p. 498. Horace, Epistles, I.xviii.101-2. Translation: "What
will lessen care? What will make you a friend to yourself? What gives you
unruffled calm . . .?" (Horace: Satires, Epistles, and Ars Poetica, trans.
H. Rushton Fairclough, Loeb Classical Library [Cambridge, Mass.: Harvard Univ.
Press; London: William Heinemann, 1966], p. 377).

Entry 60

   1. Dinah describes John Wesley, whom she saw as a girl, as "a very old
man" with "very long white hair" (AB, ch. 2).

   2. Mr. Irwine is described as having "powdered hair, all thrown backward
and tied behind with a black ribbon--a bit of conservatism in costume which
tells you that he is not a young man" (AB, ch. 5). His "conservatism" is suggested by his carrying the style of 1793 into 1799. In "The Health-Drinking"
Arthur's modern dress is distinguished from "Mr. Irwin's powder, and well-
brushed but well-worn black" (ch. 24).

   3. "Mr. Poyser had no reason to be ashamed of his leg, and suspected
that the growing abuse of top-boots and other fashions tending to disguise the
nether limbs, had their origin in a pitiable degeneracy of the human calf" (AB,
ch. 18).

   4. F. W. Fairholt, Costume in England: A History of Dress from the
Earliest Period till the Close of the Eighteenth Century (London: Chapman and
Hall, 1846), pp. 398-9. See also fig. 6, from Fairholt, p. 298.

   5. Fairholt, pp. 402, 546. Dinah creates a mild sensation by not wearing
a hat. Wiry Ben remarks, "My eye, she's got her bonnet off. I mun go a bit
nearer" (AB, ch. 2). Hetty, on the other hand, wears "her straw hat trimmed
white" (ch. 22).

   6. Fairholt, pp. 401-2. Hetty's dress "seemed a thing to be imitated in
silk by duchesses" (AB, ch. 7), her stays were of "a dark greenish cotton texture" (ch. 15), and Mary Burge's "new print dress looks very contemptible by
the side of Hetty's resplendent toilette" (ch. 15).

   7. Fairholt, p. 401. "While Arthur gazed into Hetty's dark beseeching
eyes, it made no difference to him what sort of English she spoke; and even
if hoops and powder had been in fashion, he would very likely not have been
sensible just then that Hetty wanted those signs of high breeding" (AB, ch. 12).

   8. Fairholt, p. 402. Dinah speaks against earrings and gets Bessy Cranage

to throw hers away during "The Preaching" (AB, ch. 2). Hetty dreams of having "large beautiful earrings" (ch. 9); shortly after, she is seen with "a pair of large earrings," with "great glass earrings in her ears" (ch. 15). Feathers are mentioned in connection with Hetty's desire to dress up "with feathers in her hair . . . like Miss Lydia and Lady Dacey" (ch. 15).

9. Fairholt, p. 402. Hetty's vanity is ridiculed by her having nothing but "an old lace scarf"--"an old old scarf, full of rents, but it would make a becoming border round her shoulders, and set off the whiteness of her upper arm" (AB, ch. 15).

10. Fairholt, p. 403.

Entry 61

1. Fairholt, p. 385. GE reproduced Fairholt's rendering of this hat in the notebook; see fig. 7. Fairholt's drawing is reproduced here from p. 385, fig. 1.

2. Alexander Strachan, Recollections of the Life and Times of the Late Rev. George Lowe (London: John Mason, 1848), p. 61.

3. Fairholt, p. 546. GE reproduced Fairholt's rendering of this hat in the notebook; see fig. 7. Fairholt's drawing is reproduced here from p. 546, fig. 264.

4. One of Hetty's dreams was "always [to] wear white stockings" (AB, ch. 9), not on Sundays and public days only. White stockings also appear in her recollection of Arthur's having kissed her: "He would like to see her in nice clothes, and thin shoes and white stockings, perhaps with silk clocks to them" (ch. 15). Hetty also goes to Arthur's "Birthday Feast" wearing "white cotton stockings" (ch. 22).

5. Horace Twiss, The Public and Private Life of Lord Chancellor Eldon, with Selections from His Correspondence, 3 vols. (London: John Murray, 1844), I, 43.

6. At the celebration of his own majority, Arthur Donnithorne wears "a bright-blue frock-coat, the highest mode" (AB, ch. 22).

7. AB begins on 18 June 1799.

8. "Interesting intelligence from Various Parts of the Country," Gentleman's Magazine, 69 (January 1799), 73.

9. Adam tells Dinah what he told Arthur when Donnithorne spoke of hearing her preach out of doors: "And I said, 'Nay, sir, you can't do that, for Conference has forbid women preaching, and she's given it up, all but talking to the people a bit in their houses'" (Epilogue). Neither GE nor Adam give exactly correct information. It was the "opinion" of the conference (Manchester, 25 July 1803) that women "in general" ought not to preach. "But if any woman among us think she has an extraordinary call from God to speak in public . . . we are of the opinion she should, in general, address her own sex, and those only." See Minutes of the Methodist Conferences, from the first, held in London, by the late Rev. John Wesley, A.M. in the year 1744 (London: Conference Office, 1813), II, 188.

10. Arthur Young, A Six Months Tour Through the North of England, 4 vols. (see entry 43, n. 10). Young makes this remark in relation to Scorton (II, 159), Ruth and Fremington, (II, 190), Severiton (II, 255), and Morpeth (III, 22).

Entry 62

1. In general, the events surrounding the celebration of John Henry Duke of Rutland's majority are the historical source GE drew on to create Arthur Donnithorne's more modest coming-of-age birthday celebration in Book Third of AB.

2. William Pitt (the Younger), 1759-1806; Prime Minister 1783-1801, 1804-06.

3. All are names of distinguished British naval commanders in the wars with France. Richard Howe (1726-99) was made admiral of the fleet and general

of marines in 1796. John Jervis (1735-1823), Earl of St. Vincent (1797), defeated the Spanish fleet off Cape St. Vincent on 14 February 1797. Adam Duncan (1731-1804), Viscount Duncan of Camperdown (1797), defeated the Dutch off Camperdown in 1797. Horatio Nelson (1758-1805), Baron Nelson of the Nile (1798), demolished the French fleet in Aboukir Bay in August 1798. John Borlase Warren (1753-1822) intercepted and destroyed the French fleet off the northwest coast of Ireland in October 1798.

4. The "Worthy Rector of South Croxton" becomes in AB the Rev. Adolphus Irwine, Rector of Broxton.

5. "Interesting Intelligence from various Parts of the Country," Gentleman's Magazine, 69 (January 1799), 73-75.

6. Translation: "He who is willing to die is master of the life of the king." A proverb proven true in R, as Baldassarre's murder of Tito shows.

Entry 63

1. Gentleman's Magazine, 69 (October 1799), 833-4; a play by Kotzebue appearing in translation.

2. Ibid., pp. 841-3. Joseph Priestley (1733-1804), scientist and theologian, emigrated from England to America in 1794 because of the intolerance shown his religious opinions.

3. "The Royal Excursion," Gentleman's Magazine, 69 (September 1799), 803-4.

4. "Domestic Occurrences," Gentleman's Magazine, 69 (February 1799), 160. GE seems to have gotten the date incorrectly insofar as Lord Holland protested against the Habeas Corpus Suspension Act on 15 February 1799.

5. Gentleman's Magazine, 69 (October 1899), 876. Edward Jenner, An Inquiry into the Causes and Effects of Variolae Vaccinae, a Disease discovered in some Western Counties of England, particularly Gloucestershire, and known by the Name of Cow-Pox.

6. Sir Richard Arkwright (1732-92), inventor of spinning machinery, set up a mill run by water power and designed for the manufacture of ribbed stockings at Cromford, Derbyshire, in 1771. Adam cautions Seth against "being over-speritial" by pointing to "Arkwright's mills there at Cromford" (AB, ch. 1).

7. Jedidiah Strutt (1726-97), improver of the stocking frame and sometime partner of Arkwright.

8. AB begins on 18 June 1799 (ch. 1) and ends "near the end of June, in 1807" (Epilogue).

9. William Wordsworth (1770-1850) published The Evening Walk and Descriptive Sketches of a Pedestrian Tour of the Alps in 1793.

10. Robert Southey (1774-1843). GE read his Life of Wesley in preparation for writing AB; see entries 50-59.

11. Samuel Taylor Coleridge (1772-1834). Arthur recommends "The Ancient Mariner" to his godmother, Mrs. Irwine, as a "queer wizard-like" story (AB, ch. 5).

12. Sir Walter Scott (1771-1832); The Lay of the Last Minstrel (1805) was his first full-length narrative poem.

13. Charles Lamb (1775-1834). GE quotes Lamb's "On the Artificial Comedy of the Last Century," in entry 34a.

14. Granville Sharp (1735-1813), a philanthropist, fought for the liberation of slaves in England and advocated the cause of the American colonies.

15. Samuel Wilberforce (1805-73), Anglican bishop, first of Oxford and then of Winchester; noted for his support of conservative causes.

16. John Horne Tooke (1763-1812), a clergyman, who, as a politician, supported John Wilkes and opposed Charles James Fox; as a philologist he established his reputation by publishing The Diversions of Purley (1786, 1798).

17. William Paley (1743-1805), Archdeacon of Carlisle, published, among other books, Evidences of Christianity (1794) and Natural Theology (1802).

18. George Washington (1732-99).

19. Francis Egerton (1736-1803), third Duke of Bridgewater, began construction of a canal from Worsley to Manchester in 1760 and constructed one
from Liverpool to Manchester from 1762-72. There is an indirect allusion to
the work of Bridgewater in AB, ch. 52: "Surely all other leisure is hurry
compared with a sunny walk through the fields from 'afternoon church,'--as such
walks used to be in those old leisurely times, when the boat, gliding sleepily
along the canal, was the newest locomotive wonder."

20. William Cobbett (1763-1835). GE gives, as does Cobbett himself, the
wrong date (1766) for his birth. Cobbett's Weekly Political Register began
publication in January 1802.

21. Sir Benjamin Thompson, Count von Rumford (1753-1814), noted scientist
and inventor, devised a system for curing smokey chimneys ("Rumfordizing") and
thereby made English domestic life more pleasant. He founded The Royal Institution (mentioned in entry 68) in 1800.

22. Francis Jeffrey, Henry Brougham, Sydney Smith and other Whigs founded
The Edinburgh Review in October 1802.

23. Thomas Moore (1779-1852). GE gives the wrong birth date.

24. Thomas Rogers (1760-1821), headmaster of Wakefield grammar school
(1795-1814), was noted for his evening lectures and his work for prison reform;
published Lectures on the Liturgy of the Church of England in 1804.

25. Elizabeth Fry (1780-1845), Quaker minister, famous for her work in
reforming prisons.

26. Sir Joshua Reynolds (1723-92).

27. Fanny Burney's Evelina, or, the History of a Young Lady's Entrance
into the World was published in January 1788.

Entry 64

1. "Stephenson's wages, while working as a brakeman at the Dolly pit,
Black Callerton, amounted from 1£. 15s to 2£ in the fortnight." Samuel
Smiles, The Life of George Stephenson, p. 22. Aspects of the character of
Adam Bede are modeled on that of George Stephenson. Each had a favorite dog.
Stephenson's was "so sagacious that he performed the office of a servant, in
almost daily carrying his dinner to him at the pit" (Life, p. 20). Adam's
dog, Gyp, carries a basket which "on workdays held Adam's and Seth's dinner"
(AB, ch. 1). Stephenson, a man of "wiry muscles and practiced strength," beat
a co-worker--who did not like "George's style of self-assertion"--in a fist-
fight (Life, pp. 25-26). Adam, who--as Mr. Casson remarks--is "a little
lifted up an' peppery-like" (ch. 2), pins his co-worker Wiry Ben to the wall
(ch. 1). Stephenson did extra work to earn enough money to marry Fanny Henderson, "a servant in a neighboring farmhouse" (Life, p. 23). Adam does extra
work cheerfully because "his hopes were buoyant again about Hetty" (ch. 27).
And both Stephenson and Adam attended night-school and excelled in arithmetic
--one, the best student of Andrew Robertson (Life, pp. 19, 25); the other, the
best student of Bartle Massey (AB, ch. 21). GHL records GE's reading of the
Railway Engineer in his journal on 26 June 1857: "Marian read aloud the Life
of George Stephenson" (GHL Journal X, p. [68]).

2. "The chief objects of the Society are to promote the Arts, Manufac-
tures, and Commerce, of this kingdom, by giving rewards for all such useful
Inventions, Discoveries, or Improvements . . . as tend to that purpose"
(Gentleman's Magazine, 70 [April 1800], 361).

3. GE's parenthesis. From a review of Memories of John Bacon, Esq.
R.A., with Reflections drawn from a View of his moral and religious Character,
by Richard Cecil, in Gentleman's Magazine, 72 (April 1802}, 336.

4. From a review of The Lakers; a Comic Opera of Three Acts, reviewed in
ibid., p. 337.

5. Gentleman's Magazine, 72 (June 1802), 504.

6. Ibid., p. 536.

7. Ibid., p. 532.

8. Ibid., p. 535.
9. Gentleman's Magazine, 72 (October 1802), 953-4.
10. From a review of Catalogue of Miss Linwood's Exhibition of Pictures in Hanover Square in Gentleman's Magazine, 72 (July 1802), 652. Mary Linwood (1755-1845) imitated famous paintings in worsted embroidery. In 1798 she opened an exhibition of her work at the Hanover Square Rooms, which contained one hundred copies of pictures by old and modern masters. "Salvator Mundi," in imitation of Carlo Dolci's painting, was considered her masterpiece.
11. "Aeronautic Expeditions of M. Garnerin," Gentleman's Magazine, 72 (July 1802), 663-8.
12. Dr. Beilby Porteus, the Bishop of London, presented this bill on 21 April 1800; it passed without any opposition. The Annual Register or View of the History, Politics, and Literature for the Year 1800 (London: Otridge and Son, et al., 1802), p. 146.

Entry 65
1. J. Holt, "Meteorological Diaries for July and August, 1799," Gentleman's Magazine, 69 (August 1799), 634. GE calls on these observations in the opening paragraph of AB, ch. 22, which is set on 30 July 1799--a day Holt lists as a "fine day"--Arthur Donnithorne's 21st birthday.
2. J. Holt, "Meteorological Diaries for August and September, 1799," Gentleman's Magazine, 69 (September 1799), 730. The generally rainy weather of August 1799 is recalled in the opening paragraph of AB, ch. 27: "The reaping of the wheat had begun in our north midland county of Loamshire, but the harvest was likely still to be retarded by the heavy rains, which were causing inundations and much damage throughout the country. From this last trouble the Broxton and Hayslope farmers . . . had not suffered . . . ." Some indications of the trouble caused by heavy rains is given by Holt under 18 August, the day on which ch. 27 is set: "The low lands are laid under water with the rain of yesterday and the day before. Cattle have in some places been in danger of perishing; families have been obliged to remove; the hay has floated, and removed great quantities into the sea, some of which has been cast on shore again. A field of wheat was covered with hay, which however, was removed without much injury."
3. J. Holt, "Meteorological Diaries for September and October, 1799," Gentleman's Magazine, 69 (October 1799), 826. Mrs. Poyser mentions the barley crop in AB, ch. 32, and the narrator alludes to it again at the beginning of ch. 33.
4. "Country News, Sept. 8," ibid., p. 898. "The Barley was all carried at last, and the harvest suppers went by without waiting for the dismal crop of beans" (AB, ch. 33).
5. J. Holt, "Meteorological Diaries for October and November," Gentleman's Magazine, 69 (November 1799), 914. "The apples and nuts were gathered and stored" (AB, ch. 33).

Entry 66
1. Gentleman's Magazine, 72 (June 1802), 502.
2. Ibid., pp. 502-3.
3. The title of a book reviewed in ibid., p. 529. This title may have suggested to GE ch. 8 of AB in which Mr. Irwine is the Churchman and Dinah the Methodist.
4. Reviewed in ibid., pp. 528-9.
5. Reviewed in ibid., p. 529. The book argues that "to despise the ministers and ordinances of God" is to despise God himself. Joshua Rann assaults Mr. Irwine with a similar argument when he complains that Will Maskery has called the rector a "dumb dog" and an "idle shepherd" (AB, ch. 5).
6. Reviewed in ibid., p. 532.
7. Richard Wallis, "The Happy Village," reviewed in ibid., pp. 536-7.
8. "To the Author of 'The Rector and the Curate,'" published in ibid., p. 544.

Entry 67

1. Gentleman's Magazine, 72 (July 1802), 643.

2. "A Midsummer Tour," Gentleman's Magazine, 72 (August 1802), 707. AB uses this picture of the clergy in defense of Adolphus Irwine: "Sixty years ago . . . all clergymen were not zealous; indeed there is reason to believe that the number of zealous clergymen was small, and it is probable that if one among the small minority had owned the livings of Broxton and Hayslope in the year 1799, you would have liked him no better than you like Mr. Irwine" (ch. 17). The religion of the Dodsons in MF is of "a simple, semi-pagan kind," and they seem to take after their clergyman: "The vicar of their pleasant rural parish was not a controversialist, but a good hand at whist, and one who had a joke always ready for a blooming female parishioner" (IV.i).

3. Gentleman's Magazine, 71 (April 1801), 307. The Rev. Adolphus Irwine holds three livings: "Rector of Broxton, Vicar of Hayslope, and Vicar of Blythe," but he is "a pluralist at whom the severest Church-reformer would have found it difficult to look sour." Mr. Irwine, "with all his three livings," has "no more than seven hundred a-year," with which he supports himself, "his splendid mother," "his sickly sister," and "a second sister, who was usually spoken of without any adjective" (AB, ch. 5).

Entry 68

1. "Proceedings in Parliament, 1801," Gentleman's Magazine, 71 (July 1801), 649. The subject of residency comes up between Mr. Casson and the stranger: "Parson Irwine, sir, doesn't live here; he lives at Brox'on, over the hill there. The parsonage here's a tumble-down place, sir, not fit for gentry to live in" (AB, ch. 2).

2. "Proceedings in the last Session of Parliament," Gentleman's Magazine, 71 (September 1801), 84.

3. A Southern Faunist, "Residence of Clergy," Gentleman's Magazine, 71 (October 1801), 897. Mr. Irwine, who does not reside at Hayslope is one of these "gentlemen by birth as well as by profession."

4. Philoepiscopos, "Dignity of Clergy," Gentleman's Magazine, 71 (December 1801), 1089. Philoepiscopos writes in answer to A Southern Faunist (see n. 3) and maintains the need for residency while, at the same time, admitting that "if a curate has nothing more to maintain a wife and family than the mere profits arising from curatizing, he must be, of all men, the most miserable."

5. "Appendix to the Chronicle," Annual Register, 1799, p. 187. "Those were dear times when wheaten bread and fresh meat were delicacies to working people" (AB, ch. 4). The "rapid rise of the price of bread" is mentioned again in "A Crisis" (ch. 27).

6. Gentleman's Magazine, 50 (November 1780), [497], lists The Morning Herald for the first time; but the Morning Post is listed earlier than the date GE gives: see Gentleman's Magazine 49 (March 1779), [105].

7. "A society, under the title of 'The Royal Institution of Great Britain,' and under the patronage of his majesty, commencing its sittings, for the first time, this day [11 March 1800]. Its professed object is to direct the public attention to the arts, by an establishment for diffusing the knowledge and facilitating the general introduction of useful mechanical inventions and improvements" (Annual Register, 1800, p. 6).

8. Annual Register, 1800, p. 31.

9. Ibid., p. 212.

10. Ibid., p. 148.

Entry 69

1. Clouds were first classified by Luke Howard, Essay on the Modifications of Clouds (London: John Churchill, 1803). GE's source, however, is Henry Stephens, The Book of the Farm, detailing the Labours of the Farmer, Farm-Steward, Ploughman, Shepherd, Hedger, Cattleman, Field-Worker and Dairy-Maid, 3 vols. (Edinburgh and London: William Blackwood and Sons, 1844). In AB, Mr. Craig, anticipating Howard, tells Martin Poyser, "It's a great thing

to ha' studied the look o' the clouds. Lord bless you! th' met'orological almanecks can learn me nothing, but there's a pretty sight o' things I could let <u>them</u> up to, if they'd just come to me" (ch. 18). GE found it necessary to know about clouds to re-create the rainy weather that prevailed in the midlands in July and August of 1799 (see entry 65) and to describe the occasional exception to that weather, like Arthur's birthday, 30 July, or the day Adam finds him kissing Hetty, 18 August.

2. A cloud on the horizon arouses Mr. Craig to instruct Martin Poyser: "Ye see that darkish blue cloud there upo' the 'rizon--ye know what I mean by the 'rizon, where the land and sky seems to meet? . . . . Well, you mark my words, as that cloud 'ull spread o'er the sky pretty nigh as quick as you'd spread a tarpaulin over one o'er your hay-ricks." Craig predicts a "downfall afore twenty-four hours is past" (<u>AB</u>, ch. 18), but, as a matter of fact, it does not rain (ch. 19).

3. Dinah may be referring to a stratus cloud while talking in the evening to Seth about her premonition of sister Allen's needing her: "I saw her as plain as we see that bit of thin white cloud, lifting up her poor thin hand and beckoning to me" (<u>AB</u>, ch. 3).

Entry 70

1. The <u>Book</u> of the <u>Farm</u>, II, 738. Stephens classifies the above under summer weather in the 1844 edition.

2. Although Stephens classifies the cirro-stratus under "Of the Weather in Winter," GE seems to refer to such a cloud on Arthur's birthday (30 July): "there was no cloud but a long dash of light, downy ripple, high, high up in the far-off blue sky" (<u>AB</u>, ch. 22).

Entry 71

1. The <u>Book</u> of the <u>Farm</u>, I, 248-9. The wording of this particular entry (but not of any other) more closely approximates that of an American edition by Stephens and John P. Norton, The <u>Farmer's</u> <u>Guide</u> to <u>Practical</u> <u>Agriculture</u>, 2 vols. (New York: Leonard Scott, 1858), I, 68.

2. ". . . There had been heavy showers in the morning, though now the clouds had rolled off and lay in towering silvery masses on the horizon" (<u>AB</u>, ch. 18). This is the day of Thias Bede's funeral.

3. The <u>Book</u> of the <u>Farm</u>, I, 249-50. Seth says to Adam, "But see what clouds have gathered since we set out. I'm thinking we shall have more rain" (<u>AB</u>, ch. 4). This is 18 August 1800--"a day on which a blighting sorrow may fall upon a man"--the day that Adam sees Arthur kissing Hetty in the Grove.

4. The <u>Book</u> of the <u>Farm</u>, I, 251.

Entry 72

1. Henry Stephens, The <u>Book</u> of the <u>Farm</u>, 2 vols. (Edinburgh and London: William Blackwood and Sons, 1851), I, 83.

2. Adam, waiting to meet Dinah on her return from Sloman's End, chooses a spot "almost at the top of a hill" where there are "no cattle, not even a nibbling sheep near" (<u>AB</u>, ch. 54).

3. "The ox is . . . suited to the plains and valleys, where grass grows long, and may be cropped by the scythe-like operation of its tongue and teeth . . . . the pasture will be eaten barer by the horse and sheep than the ox left it." GE had this passage from Henry Stephens in mind when she wrote: "The ox--we may venture to assert it on the authority of a great classic--is not given to use his teeth as an instrument of attack" (<u>MF</u>, II.v).

4. The <u>Book</u> of the <u>Farm</u> (1851 ed), II, 171.

Entry 73

1. Alfred Lord Tennyson, "To--, <u>After</u> <u>Reading</u> a <u>Life</u> and <u>Letters</u>," 11. 13-28. GE does not indent line 19 in her MS. It is debated whether Tennyson was objecting to the revelation of Keats's love-letters in Lord Houghton's

Life and Literary Remains of Keats (1848) or to the notorious private life of Byron as seen in Thomas Medwin's Journal of the Conversations of Byron (1824) (The Poems of Tennyson, ed. Christopher Ricks [London: Longmans, 1969], pp. 846-7). Whatever inspired Tennyson's poem, GE was clear as to its meaning--a writer's work cannot stand by itself once "the scandal and the cry" of his private life are known. GE certainly copied this poem after her life as "George Eliot" was threatened by her life as "Mrs. Lewes." Joseph Liggins had already claimed to be the author of Scenes of Clerical Life and the Evans family had cast off its sister by 13 June 1857 (Haight, A Biography, pp. 230-33). Should Liggins force GE to reveal her identity, she knew her success as an author would suffer from her "notorious" union with GHL.

2. Benjamin Constant de Rebecque, Adolphe: anecdote trouvée dans les papiers d'un inconnu (1815), Réponse. Translation: "The great question in life is the suffering we cause; and the utmost ingenuity of metaphysics cannot justify the man who has pierced the heart that loved him." This is GE's translation and appears as the epigraph of FH, ch. 50.

3. Percy Bysshe Shelley, Prometheus Unbound, I. 303-5. Adam essentially interprets these lines in his own words when he meets Arthur a second time in the wood: "But feeling overmuch about her [Hetty] has perhaps made me unfair to you . . . . I've no right to be hard towards them as have done wrong and repent" (AB, ch. 48).

Entry 74

1. Prideaux John Selby, A History of British Forest-Trees, Indigenous and Introduced (London: John Van Voorst, 1842). The countryside in AB and Adam's position as manager of the woods on the Donnithorne estate explain GE's interest in Selby on trees.

2. British Forest-Trees, pp. 2-8. Below the hills of Hayslope, a "hanging woods, divided by bright patches of pasture or furrowed crops," shows "the warm tints of the young oak and the tender green of the ash and lime" (AB, ch. 12).

3. Translation: "Fairest is the ash in the woods" (Eclogues vii. 65, Virgil, trans. H. Rushton Fairclough, Loeb Classical Library [Cambridge, Mass., Harvard Univ. Press; London: William Heinemann, 1967], p. 54).

4. Jacob George Strutt (1790-1864), Sylva Britannica, or Portraits of Forest Trees, Distinguished for their Antiquity, Magnitude, or Beauty (London: Bohn, 1826).

5. The passage quoted in n. 2 above shows the ash coming into leaf on 18 June.

Entry 75

1. The ash and sycamore are found on the Donnithorne estate near the Home Close (AB, ch. 18).

2. The shrew-mouse appears as an image of hopelessness in MF, II.i: "At present, in relation to this demand that he should learn Latin declensions and conjugations, Tom was in a state of as blank unimaginativeness concerning the cause and tendency of his sufferings, as if he had been an innocent shrew-mouse imprisoned in the slit trunk of an ash-tree in order to cure lameness in cattle."

3. British Forest-Trees, pp. 87-98.

4. William Gilpin (1724-1804), Remarks on Forest Scenery, and Other Woodland Views, 2 vols. (London: R. Blamire, 1791).

Entry 76

1. John Claudius Loudon (1785-1843), Aboretum et fruticetum Britannicum; or, The Trees and Shrubs of Britain (London: the Author, 1838).

2. British Forest-Trees, pp. 104-14.

3. Ibid., pp. 120-26.

4. L'Ingenieux Hidalgo Don Quichotte de la Manche, I, 64. Translation:

"I want you to know, sir, that in small areas like this everything is spoken about and everything criticized; and it is well to understand, as I see it, that a priest should be good beyond measure so that his parishioners can speak well of him, especially in town." See entry 43, n. 20.

5. "A Digression in the Modern Kind," A Tale of a Tub, ed. A. C. Guthkelch and David Nichol Smith (Oxford: Oxford Univ. Press, 1920), p. 130.

Entry 77

1. Gordon S. Haight writes, "The flood that ends The Mill on the Floss was not an afterthought to extricate the author from an impossible situation, but the part of the story that George Eliot planned first. At the British Museum in January 1859 she copied into her commonplace book accounts of inundations from the Annual Register. . . ." Introduction, The Mill on the Floss, Riverside Editions (Boston: Houghton Mifflin Company, 1961), p. v. A letter from Emily Davies to Jane Crow, 21 August 1869, adds further testimony of the same kind: "Whatever she has done she has studied for. Before she began to write the Mill on the Floss, she had it all in her mind, and she read about the Trent to make sure that the physical conditions of some English rivers were such as to make the inundation possible, and assured herself that the population in its neighbourhood was such as to justify her picture" (Letters, VIII, 466). GE used entries 77-81 when writing MF, VII.v. The inundations of November 1771 are probably those referred to by "old men" who "had shaken their heads and talked of sixty years ago, when the same sort of weather, happening about the equinox, brought on the great floods, which swept the bridge away, and reduced the town to great misery." Since the flood in MF takes place in September 1839, sixty-eight "years ago" would be a more precise figure.

2. Bob Jakin remarks on seeing his boats secure, "It's wonderful this fastening isn't broke too, as well as the mooring."

3. "She [Maggie] could see now that the bridge was broken down. . . ."

4. "Great God! there were floating masses in it [the river], that might dash against her boat as she passed, and cause her to perish too soon." "Huge fragments," of course, swamp Maggie and Tom's boat.

Entry 78

1. Maggie and Tom are the only casualties: "And every man and woman mentioned in this history was still living--except those whose end we know" (MF, Conclusion).

2. Maggie "could hear shouts from the windows overlooking the river" on her way over the flooded fields to rescue Tom from "the attic in the central gable."

Entry 79

1. Annual Register, 1771, pp. 155-60.

Entry 80

1. GE gives a sense of the wind's violence when she describes Maggie in the boat, "her streaming hair dashed about by the wind."

2. The flood comes at night in MF, and Maggie, carrying a candle, has to wake Bob Jakin from sleep.

3. Maggie notices "the poor dumb beasts on a mound where they had taken refuge."

Entry 81

1. Annual Register, 1810, pp. 286-7.

Entry 82

1. Mary Somerville, Physical Geography (1st ed. London 1848; 3rd ed. Philadelphia: Blanchard and Lea, 1857), pp. 221-2.

Entry 89

1. John Ruskin, <u>Stones of Venice</u>, <u>Volume One</u>, <u>The Foundations</u>, <u>The Works of John Ruskin</u>, ed. E. T. Cook and Alexander Wedderburn, Library Edition (London: George Allen, 1903), IX, 34-40. <u>Stones of Venice</u> was first published in 3 vols. in London by Smith, Elder, & Co. in 1847 (vol. 1) and 1853 (vols. 2 and 3). Vols. 2 (<u>The Sea-Stories</u>) and 3 (<u>The Fall</u>) passed through GE's hands as editor of <u>WR</u> and were reviewed in <u>WR</u>, 37 (October 1853), 308-9 and 38 (January 1854) 166-7. GHL also reviewed <u>Stones</u>, vols. 2 and 3, for the <u>Leader</u>, 4 (17 September 1853), 905-7, and (15 October 1853), 1001-03. That GE knew GHL's reviews seems evident from a later entry; see entry 99, n. 1.

These notes from <u>Stones of Venice</u> were probably written in preparation for GE and GHL's trip to Italy, which began in March 1860, immediately following the completion of <u>MF</u>. When in Venice itself, GE wrote, "I am glad to find Ruskin calling the Palace of Doges one of the two most perfect buildings in the world. . . . This spot is a focus of architectural wonders: but the palace is the crown of them all" (<u>Life</u>, II, 200). GE's admiration for Ruskin was immense, as she indicated in a letter to Sophia Hennell, 17 September 1858: "I venerate him as one of the great teachers of the day . . . he teaches with the inspiration of a Hebrew prophet . . ." (<u>Letters</u>, II, 422). Her most extended appreciation of him appeared in the form of a review of <u>Modern Painters</u> III in <u>WR</u>, 64 (April 1856), USA ed. 343-7; the evaluative portion of that essay is given in Uncollected Writings. GE wrote a less memorable review of <u>Modern Painters</u> IV for <u>WR</u>, 65 (July 1856), USA ed. 150-52. An earlier review of <u>Lectures on Architecture and Painting</u>, which appeared as "Ruskin's Lectures," <u>Leader</u>, 5 (10 June 1854), 545-6, is significant for <u>M</u>, chs. 9 and 21-22, and is given in Uncollected Writings.

Entry 97

1. Nicetas Acominatus (d. 1206) was a Byzantine historian whose annals of the Byzantine empire cover the years 1118 to 1206. I am unable to identify the source of this entry. <u>Translation</u>: "In order to avenge his country against the Barbarians Nicetas wanted to give up writing history when Constantinople fell so that none of their names would be known to posterity."

2. Dante Alighieri, <u>La Divina Commedia</u>, Inferno, I, 79-80. <u>Translation</u>: "Art thou then that Virgil, and that fountain which pours abroad so rich a stream of speech?" This translation--and the translation of all GE's entries from the Inferno--is that of John A. Carlyle, <u>Dante's Divine Comedy</u>: <u>The Inferno</u> (London: Chapman & Hall, 1849). GHL reviewed this volume in <u>The Athenaeum</u>, No. 1115 (10 March 1849), 246-7: "As an edition of 'The Inferno' the book is valuable,--as a translation it is very useful" (247). Carlyle's translation is still held to be important: "Carlyle's Inferno was one of the most valuable and influential translations ever published in English" (Gilbert F. Cunningham, <u>The Divine Comedy in English</u>: <u>A Critical Bibliography</u> 1782-1900, 2 vols. [Edinburgh and London: Oliver and Boyd, 1965], I, 48). Carlyle's translation is listed in the Ouvry Inventory.

GHL had earlier reviewed Leigh Hunt, <u>Stories from the Italian Poets with the Lives of the Writers</u>, 2 vols. (London: Chapman and Hall, 1846), for the <u>Foreign Quarterly Review</u> 36 (1846), USA ed. 179-90. GE certainly knew Hunt's book (see entry 99, n. 2); indeed, she seems to have used it as a <u>vade mecum</u>: many of the passages she quotes from Dante were singled out by Hunt. These are indicated in each case by a reference to Hunt's <u>Stories</u>. For Inferno, I, 79-80, see <u>Stories</u>, I, 85.

3. Inferno, I, 118-20. <u>Translation</u>: "And then thou shalt see those who are contented in the fire: for they hope to come, whensoever it be, amongst the blessed."

4. Inferno, II, 41-42. <u>Translation</u>: "For with thinking I wasted the enterprise, that had been so quick in its commencement."

5. Inferno, II, 113-4. <u>Translation</u>: "Confiding in thy noble speech, which honours thee, and them who have heard it."

6. Inferno II, 127-9. <u>Translation</u>: As flowerets, by the nightly chillness bended down and closed, erect themselves all open on their stems when the sun whitens them." See also Hunt, <u>Stories</u>, I, 86.

7. Inferno, III, 34-42. <u>Translation</u>: "This miserable mode the dreary souls of those sustain, who lived without blame, and without praise. / They are mixed with that caitiff choir of angels, who were not rebellious, nor were faithful to God; but were for themselves. / Heaven chased them forth to keep its beauty from impair; and the deep Hell receives them not, for the wicked would have some glory over them." See also Hunt, <u>Stories</u>, I, 88.

Entry 98

1. Inferno, IV, 52-54. <u>Translation</u>: "Replied: 'I was new in this condition, when I saw a Mighty One [Jesus Christ] come to us, crowned with sign of victory.'"

2. Inferno, IV, 104-5. <u>Translation</u>: "Speaking things which it is well to pass in silence, as it was well to speak there where I was."

3. Inferno, IV, 112-4. <u>Translation</u>: "In it were people with eyes slow and grave, of great authority in their appearance; they spoke seldom, with mild voices."

4. Inferno, IV, 119-20. <u>Translation</u>: "There . . . were shown to me the great spirits, so that I glory within myself for having seen them." See also Hunt, <u>Stories</u>, I, 93. "Eyes slow and grave" from l. 112 is joined to "great spirits" from l. 119 in <u>DD</u>, ch. 36: Deronda "had a wonderful power of standing perfectly still, and in that position reminded one sometimes of Dante's <u>spiriti</u> <u>magni</u> <u>con</u> <u>occhi</u> <u>tardi</u> <u>e</u> <u>gravi</u>."

5. Inferno, V, 55-57. <u>Translation</u>: "With the vice of luxury she was so broken, that she made lust and law alike in her decree, to take away the blame she had incurred." This is a reference to Semiramis, ruler of Assyria (9th c. B.C.), who was noted for her licentious character. GE suggests in <u>FH</u> that Mrs. Transome had sinned but had no power to make "lust and law alike": "Unlike that Semiramis who made laws to suit her practical licence, she [Mrs. Transome] lived, poor soul, in the midst of desecrated sanctities, and of honours that looked tarnished in the light of monotonous and weary suns" (ch. 40). See Hunt, <u>Stories</u>, I, 95.

6. Inferno, V, 112-4. <u>Translation</u>: "Ah me! what sweet thoughts, what longing led them to the woeful pass!" This is a reference to Paolo and Francesca, lovers who sinned and went to hell; yet they still are "two that go together, and seem so light upon the wind" (V, 75). In comparison with Jermyn and Mrs. Transome in <u>FH</u>, sinners who blame each other, they are an ideal: "There is heroism even in the circles of hell for fellow-sinners who cling to each other in the fiery whirlwind and never recriminate" (ch. 42). See also Hunt, <u>Stories</u>, I, 98.

7. Inferno, VI, 106-8. <u>Translation</u>: "Return to thy science, which has it, that the more a thing is perfect, the more it feels pleasure and likewise pain." GE uses this as the epigraph for <u>DD</u>, ch. 55, which follows Deronda's final interview with his mother. Deronda is described as having "a quivering imaginative sense," a "quick, responsive fibre," and, in his suffering over a mother lost, "he allowed himself in his solitude to sob."

8. Inferno, VII, 121-4. <u>Translation</u>: "Sullen were we in the sweet air, that is gladdened by the Sun, carrying lazy smoke within our hearts; / now lie we sullen here in the black mire." The "we" here are the souls of those who were gloomy, silent and ill-humored. See also Hunt, <u>Stories</u>, I, 103.

Entry 99

1. Cook and Wedderburn, eds., <u>Works</u>, XI, 53. This passage appears as a footnote in GHL's review of <u>Stones</u> <u>of</u> <u>Venice</u>, vol. 3, in <u>Leader</u>, 4 (15 October 1853), 1002. In "Interesting Extracts" GE quotes two passages from Plato's <u>Republic</u> on the tyranny of society, calling "Society . . . itself the greatest Sophist, educating and moulding young & old. What Sophist or private

instructor could withstand the powerful voice of the world?" (p. 15).

2. Leigh Hunt had accused Dante of inhuman severity in the Commedia: "Such a vision as that of his poem . . . seems no better than the dream of a hypochondriacal savage, and his nutshell a rottenness to be spit out of the mouth" (Stories, I, 60). "Where he is sweet-natured once, he is bitter a hundred times (I, 55). GHL took Hunt to task for his naivete in "Leigh Hunt on the Italian Poets," Foreign Quarterly Review, 36 (1846), USA ed. 179-90. GHL especially chides Hunt for lacking in historical sense in his criticism: "the whole poem is never looked upon as a product of the middle ages" (183). John A. Carlyle, in the introduction to Dante's Divine Comedy: The Inferno also took issue with Hunt in the strongest terms: "His [Dante's] ideas of Mercy, and Humanity, and Christian Freedom, and the means of attaining them, are not the same as yours: not the same but unspeakably larger and sounder." Carlyle was thus quoted by GHL in the Athenaeum (No. 1115 [1849], 247) as refuting "the criticism one of our poets recently put forth respecting Dante's intolerance and fierceness" (ibid.). GE's entry on "Dante's severity" seems to be her contribution to the controversy. It is a nice irony that the passages she quotes (translation: I "could not speak for pity") and alludes to concerning Pietro are specifically referred to by Hunt, Stories, I, 114-5.

3. This episode in the wood of the suicides begins in XIII, 27, and is concluded at XIV, 3. GE alluded to it in the final paragraph of the Introduction of FH: "The poets have told us of a dolorous enchanted forest in the underworld. The thorn-bushes there, and the thick-barked stems, have human histories hidden in them; the power of unuttered cries dwells in the passionless seeming branches, and the red warm blood is darkly feeding the quivering nerves of a sleepless memory that watches through all dreams." Mrs. Transome turns out to be one of "the passionless seeming branches" with the power of "unuttered cries" living in the hell of Transome Court.

4. GE's direction.

5. John Ruskin, Modern Painters V (1860); Cook and Wedderburn, eds., Works, VIII, 370-71. GE and GHL saw a significant number of Fra Angelico's paintings in Florence on 22 May 1860. Their enthusiasm for him is suggested by GHL's journal entry for that date: "After dinner drove to a print shop and bought engravings of Fra Angelico." See Letters III, 295-6.

Entry 100

1. Inferno, XV, 82-87. Translation: "For in my memory is fixed and now goes to my heart the dear and kind, paternal image of you, when in the world, hour by hour, / you taught me how man makes himself eternal; and whilst I live, beseems my tongue should show what gratitude I have for it."

2. Inferno, XXIX, 43-44. Translation: "Lamentations pierced me, manifold, which had their arrows barbed with pity; whereat I covered my ears with my hands." See also Hunt, Stories, I, 134. GE quotes these lines in DD, ch. 50, and loosely translates them for the epigraph of FH, ch. 22: "Her gentle looks shot arrows, piercing him / As gods are pierced, with poison of sweet pity."

3. See 99, n. 3. The entry under 99 beginning "To balance Dante's severity" should be considered as ending here, its thesis having been illustrated by the two quotations coming between GE's commentary.

4. Inferno, XXVI, 118-20. Translation: "Consider your origin: ye were not formed to live like brutes, but to follow virtue and knowledge." This is the voice of Ulysses exhorting his mariners. GE quotes from this canto again in entry 105; see 105, n. 7. See also Hunt, Stories, I, 127-8.

5. Purgatorio, VI, 64-66. Translation: "Naught it said to us, but allowed us to go on, watching only after the fashion of a lion when he couches." For translation of the Purgatorio I have followed Thomas Okey, The Purgatorio of Dante Alighieri (London: J.M. Dent & Sons Ltd., 1901), except where otherwise indicated. Leigh Hunt renders this particular passage on Sordello with a noteworthy freshness: "eyeing them like a lion on the watch," Stories, I, 167.

Sordello is described again in an entry under 109; see entry 109, n. 4.

    6. Purgatorio, VII, 79-81. Translation: "Not only had Nature painted there, but of the sweetness of a thousand scents made there one, unknown and indefinable." See also Hunt, Stories, I, 168.

Entry 101

    1. Purgatorio, VIII, 1-6. Translation: "It was now the hour when men at sea think longingly of home, and feel their hearts melt within them to remember the day on which they bade adieu to beloved friends; and now, too, was the hour when the pilgrim, new to his journey, is thrilled with the like tenderness, when he hears the vesper-bell in the distance, which seems to mourn for the expiring day" (trans. Hunt, Stories, I, 170).

    2. Purgatorio, VIII, 76-78. Translation: "By her [the remarried wife of Sordello, the Provençal poet] right easily may be known, how long the fire of love doth last in a woman, if eye and touch do not oft rekindle it."

    3. Purgatorio, IX, 70-72. Translation: "Reader, well thou seest how I exalt my subject, therefore marvel thou not if with greater art I sustain it."

    4. Purgatorio, XII, 84. Translation: "Think that this day never dawns again."

    5. Purgatorio, XII, 95-96. Translation: "O human folk, born to fly upward, why at a breath of wind thus fall ye down?"

    6. Purgatorio, XII, 64-68. Translation: "What master were he of brush or of graver, who drew the shades and the lineaments, which there would make every subtle wit stare? / Dead seemed the dead, and the living, living. He saw not better than I who saw the reality of all that I trod upon while I was going bent down."

Entry 102

    1. Purgatorio, XVII, 113-23. Translation: "The evil we love is our neighbours', and this love arises in three ways in your clay. / There is he who his neighbour's abasement hopes to excel, and solely for this desires that he be cast down from his greatness; / there is he who fears to lose power, favour, honour and fame because another is exalted, wherefore he groweth sad so that he loves the contrary; / and there is he who seems to be so shamed through being wronged, that he becomes greedy of vengeance, and such must needs seek another's hurt." Tito Melema exemplifies the first of these evils and Baldassarre the third in R; Edward Casaubon exemplifies the second in M.

    2. Purgatorio, XVII, 127-9. Translation: "Each one apprehends vaguely a good wherein the mind may find rest, and desires it; wherefore each one strives to attain thereto."

    3. Purgatorio, XX, 94-96. Translation: "O Lord, how shall I rejoice to see the vengeance which even now thou huggest in delight to thy bosom" (trans. Hunt, Stories, I, 195). Hunt was deeply offended by these lines: Dante suggests that "the reason why God prohibited revenge to mankind was its being 'too delicate a morsel for any but himself'. . . . God hugs revenge to his bosom with delight! The supreme Being confounded with a poor grinning Florentine" (ibid., n. 2).

    4. Purgatorio, XXIII, 31. Translation: "The sockets of their eyes looked like rings from which gems had dropped" (trans. Hunt, Stories, I, 199).

    5. Purgatorio, XXIV, 52-54. Translation: "I am one . . . who writes as Love would have him, heeding no manner but his dictator's, and uttering simply what he suggests" (trans. Hunt, Stories, I, 203). Dante here speaks to the poet Buonaggiunta of Lucca, describing the "sweet new style" (dolce stil nuovo).

    6. Purgatorio, XXIV, 61-62. Translation: "And he who sets himself to search farther [and writes other than "Love would have him"], has lost all sense of difference between the one style and the other."

    7. Purgatorio, XXVI, 110-14. Translation: "'Tell me, what is the cause wherefore thou showest in speech and look that thou holdest me so dear'

[demands the poet Guido Guinicelli of Dante]. / And I to him: 'Your sweet ditties, which so long as modern use shall last, will make their very ink precious.'" See also Hunt, Stories, I, 207.

Entry 103

1. Purgatorio, XXXIII, 142-5. Translation: "I came back from the most holy waves, born again, even as new trees renewed with new foliage, pure and ready to mount to the stars." See also Hunt, Stories, I, 218.

2. Paradiso, III, 14-15. Translation: "Not more distinct from the surrounding whiteness than pearls themselves are from the forehead they adorn" (trans. Hunt, Stories, I, 221-2). "A curious and happy image," says Hunt (p. 222, n. 1).

3. Paradiso, V, 130-37. Translation: "This I said, turned towards the light which first had spoken to me; whereat it glowed far brighter yet than what it was before. / Like as the sun which hideth him by excess of light when the heat hath gnawed away the tempering of the thick vapours, / so by access of joy the sacred figure hid him in his own rays." For the translation of the Paradiso I have followed Philip Henry Wicksteed, The Paradiso of Dante Alighieri (London: J.M. Dent & Sons Ltd., 1899), except where otherwise indicated. Hunt also notices this passage in Stories, I, 224.

4. Paradiso, VIII, 131-2. Translation: "And Quirinus cometh of so base father that he is assigned to Mars."

5. Paradiso, VIII, 139-48. Translation: "Ever doth nature, if she find fortune unharmonious with herself, like any other seed out of its proper region, make an ill essay. / And if the world down there took heed to the foundation nature layeth, and followed it, it would have satisfaction in its folk. / But ye wrench to a religious order him born to gird the sword, and make a king of him who should be for discourse; wherefore your track runneth abroad the road." See Hunt, Stories, I, 226. GE transforms this passage into a portion of her argument against Favourable Chance in SM, ch. 9: "Let him [a man] forsake a decent craft that he may pursue the gentilities of a profession to which nature never called him, and his religion will infallibly be the worship of blessed Chance, which he will believe in as the mighty creator of success."

Entry 104

1. The entry, which reads "de Sigieri eterna," contains a transposition mark to indicate that GE wanted "eterna" moved forward.

2. Paradiso, X, 136-8. Translation: "It is the light eternal of Sigier who, lecturing in the Vicus Straminis, syllogized truths that brought him into hate."

3. Paradiso, X, 143-4. Translation: "A chiming sound of so sweet note, that the well-ordered spirit with love swelleth." See also Hunt, Stories, I, 228-9.

4. Paradiso, XIII, 77-78. Translation: Working "as doth the artist who hath the knack of the art and a trembling hand."

5. Paradiso, XVIII, 112-4. Translation: "And let this ever be lead to thy feet, to make thee move slow, like a weary man; both to the yea and the nay thou seest not; . . . . wherefore it chanceth many times swift-formed opinion leaneth the wrong way, and then conceit bindeth the intellect." See also Hunt, Stories, I, 231, and n. 1. GE loosely translates ll. 112-4 in the epigraph of FH, ch. 15: "And doubt shall be as lead upon the feet / Of thy most anxious will." The MS. of FH (British Library) shows that the epigraph was quoted first in Italian, then crossed out, and finally translated.

6. Paradiso, XVI, 70-71. Translation: "And a blind bull falls with more headlong dive Than a blind lamb" (trans. Laurence Binyon, The Portable Dante, ed. Paolo Milano [New York: The Viking Press, 1947], p. 451).

7. Paradiso, XVII, 73-75. Translation: "So benignly shall he regard thee, that in the matter of asking and receiving, the customary order of things shall be reversed between you two, and the gift anticipate the request"

(trans. Hunt, Stories, I, 241).

8. Paradiso, XVII, 118-20. Translation: "If I prove but a timid friend to truth, I fear I shall not survive with the generations by whom the present times will be called times of old" (trans. Hunt, Stories, I, 243).

Entry 105

1. Paradiso, XVII, 133-5. Translation: "Thy voice, as the wind does, shall smite loudest the loftiest summits; and no little shall that redound to thy praise" (trans. Hunt, Stories, I, 243-4).

2. Paradiso, XXI, 133-4. Translation: The cardinals of the Church "ride upon palfreys covered with their spreading mantles, so that two beasts go under one skin" (trans. Hunt, Stories, I, 255-6).

3. Paradiso, XXIII, 121-3. Translation: "And as the infant who toward his mother stretcheth up his arms when he hath had the milk, because his mind flameth forth even into outward gesture." See also Hunt, Stories, I, 263.

4. Paradiso, XXIV, 25-27. Translation: "Therefore my pen must skip, and I resign: Imagination, and our speech much more, Is of too vivid hue for shades so fine" (trans. Binyon, The Portable Dante, p. 491). See also Hunt, Stories, I, 263: "Mortal imagination cannot unfold such wonder."

5. Paradiso, XXXIII, 58-60. Translation: "As he who dreams sees, and when disappears the dream, the passion of its print remains, and naught else to the memory adheres" (trans. Binyon, The Portable Dante, p. 541). See also Hunt, Stories, I, 277.

6. Inferno, XXX, 148. Translation: "For the wish to hear it is a vulgar wish." See also Hunt, Stories, I, 135 and n. 1. Caleb Garth is remarkably free of such vulgarity: "If there was anything discreditable to be found out concerning another man, Caleb preferred not to know it" (M, ch. 53). See also 311, n. 8.

7. Inferno, XXVI, 114-5. Translation: "To this brief vigil of your senses that remains." GE had already quoted from Ulysses' speech in entry 100.

8. Inferno, XXXI, 49-51. Translation: "Nature certainly, when she left off the art of making animals like these, did very well, in taking away such executioners from Mars."

9. Paradiso, III, 121-3. Translation: "She . . . began to sing Ave Maria, and vanished as she sang, like . . . a heavy thing through the deep water." See also Hunt, Stories, I, 223 and 223-4, n. 1.

10. This number does not identify a line of poetry; it indicates that entries from Dante continue in 109.

Entry 106

1. Symposium, 177B. For the French translation of André Dacier and Jean Nicholas Grow (which GE followed) see the revised edition of Oeuvres Completes de Platon, ed. Emile Saisset 10 vols. (Paris: Bibliotheque-Charpentier, 1869), V, 349.

2. Symposium, 202; see Saisset, ed., Platon, V, 389. Translation: "Haven't you noticed that there's something halfway between knowledge and ig-norance?" -- "What is it?" -- "To have a correct opinion without being able to support it: don't you know that this is neither knowledge (for knowledge de-pends on reasons) nor ignorance (for what touches truth is not ignorance)."

3. Symposium, 202E; see Saisset, ed., Platon, V, 391. Translation: "Spirits fill the space that separates heaven from earth; they are the force which makes everything one.

4. See Symposium, 207D-208; see Saisset, ed., Platon, V, 400-402.

5. Henry Hallam, Introduction to the Literature of Europe, 4 vols. (London: John Murray, 1837-39), I, 184. A copy of this edition, with this passage marked, and with marginalia by Leigh Hunt, is in Dr. Williams's Library. In writing to Maria Lewis on 3 September 1851, GE says, "I strongly recommend Hallam to you. I shall read it again if I live" (Letters, I, 107).

The place of the quotation from Hallam in the manuscript suggests that GE reread him sometime in 1860. GE alludes to Hallam's Introduction in her review "The Influence of Rationalism," Fortnightly Review, I (15 May 1865), 43-55; see Essays, p. 405 and n. 9.

    6. Hallam, Introduction, I, 119.

    7. John Barbour, The Bruce; or, The History of Robert I, King of Scotland, ll. 17-22. The poem, according to Hallam, "seems to have been completed in 1373." GE may have been led to the poem by Hallam, who called it "the earliest historical or epic narrative" in the English language (Introduction, I, 62). For a text of the poem, see the edition of J. Pinkerton from the 1489 MS. (London: C. Nicol, 1790).

Entry 107

    1. The Bruce, ll. 225-8.

    2. Samuel Daniel, "To the Lady Margaret Countess of Cumberland," ll. 92-99, Poems and A Defense of Ryme, ed. Arthur Colby Sprague (Cambridge, Mass.: Harvard Univ. Press, 1930), pp. 113-4.

    3. Michael Drayton, Poly-Olbion, The Thirteenth Song, ll. 1-2, 8-12, Michael Drayton Tercentenary Edition, ed. J. William Hebel, et al., 5 vols. (Oxford: Shakespeare Head Press, 1961), IV, 275. Both Drayton and GE were natives of Warwickshire, and his lines had an irresistable appeal for her. She uses them as the epigraph for FH, and, in John Blackwood's opinion, they gave "the key note beautifully" (Letters, IV, 246). GE may have been led to the Poly-Olbion by Hallam's praise of it: "There is probably no poem of this kind in any other language, comparable together in extent and excellence to the Polyolbion; nor can any one read a portion of it without admiration for its learned and highly gifted author" (Introduction, III, 497). GE's 1610 ed. of Drayton's Poems is now at Yale; see Library, p. 255.

    4. Piers Plowman, B. Prologue, ll. 55-57, The Vision of William concerning Piers the Plowman in Three Parallel Texts, ed. W. W. Skeat (London: Oxford Univ. Press, 1886), p. 6. The unusual word "loobies" (country bumpkins) appears in M, ch. 35 when the narrator talks about the method of writing parables, "where you might put a monkey for a margrave": "Thus while I tell the truth about loobies, my reader's imagination need not be entirely excluded from an occupation with lords."

Entry 108

    1. This same passage, with slightly altered punctuation, appears in entry 59 (see entry 59, n. 4). It may be repeated here to reinforce the following quotation from Jeremy Taylor. Both emphasize the importance of non-rational knowledge, and Knox also suggests that Wesley is the kind of "perfect" servant of God whom Taylor touches on in his sermon.

    2. Jeremy Taylor, "A Sermon Preached to the University of Dublin," The Worthy Communicant, ed. Charles Page Eden (London: Longman, Brown, Green, and Longmans, 1850), p. 381. This passage serves as one of two epigraphs to DD, ch. 60.

    3. Mary Somerville, Physical Geography, p. 302.

    4. This is, in part, the epitaph on Jonathan Swift's tombstone. GE quotes the italicized portion of it in "The Lifted Veil," which was published in Blackwood's Magazine, 1 July 1859 (and the entry probably preceded its appearance in the story, as the italicized line suggests); see The Works of George Eliot: Silas Marner, The Lifted Veil, Brother Jacob (Edinburgh and London: William Blackwood and Sons, 1879), p. 279. GE refers to the epitaph again in a letter from Rome to Mrs. Richard Congreve, 4-6 April 1860: "Poor Keats's tombstone, with that despairing bitter inscription ["Here lies one whose name was writ in water"], is almost as painful to think of as Swift's" (Letters, III, 288 and n. 9).

Entry 109

   1. Purgatorio, II, 11-12. Translation: "Like folk who ponder o'er their road, who in heart do go and in body stay." See also Hunt, Stories, I, 158.

   2. Purgatorio, II, 82: "Di meraviglia, credo, mi dipinsi." See Hunt, Stories, I, 160. "Wonder" translates meraviglia more appropriately than "fear." GE uses her translation in R, ch. 45: "I remember Piero di Cosimo said . . . he believed there was something in it [the story that Tito had stolen Baldassarre's gems], for he saw Melema's face when the man laid hold of him, and he never saw a visage so 'painted with fear,' as our sour old Dante says."

   3. Purgatorio, IV, 27-29. Translation: "But here a man must fly, / I mean with swift wings and with the plumes of great desire."

   4. Purgatorio, VI, 72. Translation: "A soul which, placed alone, solitary." See also Hunt, Stories, I, 167; Sordello had already been depicted in entry 100.

   5. Purgatorio, VII, 107-8. Translation: "The other see, who sighing, hath made a bed for his cheek with the palm of his hand." See also Hunt, Stories, I, 169. The "other" here is Henry of Navarre. These two lines, with "L'altro" changed to "L'altra," serve as the epigraph to M, ch. 19. Dorothea, in the same chapter, assumes the pose of Henry--her hand making a bed for her cheek--as she stands before the statue of the Sleeping Ariadne (who rests her cheek on the back of her hand) in the Vatican Museum (see fig. 2). In M, ch. 55, Dorothea places the miniature of Aunt Julia--Ladislaw's grandmother, whom he resembles--in her hand and lays her cheek on it. Mrs. Transome is found in the same pose in FH, ch. 49: Esther sees "Mrs. Transome's tall figure pacing slowly, with her cheek upon her hand." In each scene this striking pose is an indication of suffering.

   6. Purgatorio, VIII, 13-15. Translation: "'Te lucis ante' so devoutly proceeded from its mouth, and with such sweet music, that it rapt me from my very sense of self." See Hunt, Stories, I, 171, where the evening hymn, "Te lucis ante terminum," is rendered, "Thee before the closing light."

   7. Purgatorio, X, 25. Translation: "And so far as mine eye could wing its flight." See Hunt, Stories, I, 175.

   8. Purgatorio, VII, 121-2. Translation: "Rarely doth human probity rise through the branches."

   9. Purgatorio, XIII, 85-87. Translation: "I . . . began" 'O people assured of seeing the Light above, which alone your desire hath in its care.'" See also Hunt, Stories, I, 183.

   10. Purgatorio, XVII, 57. Okey renders this line: "And conceals itself with its own light."

Entry 110

   1. Purgatorio, XX, 3. Okey renders this line: "I drew the sponge from the water unfilled."

   2. Purgatorio, XXII, 67-69. Translation: "Thou didst like one who goes by night, and carries the light behind him, and profits not himself, but maketh persons wise that follow him."

   3. Purgatorio, XXVI, 134-5. Translation: "He [Arnauld Daniel] vanished away through the fire as a fish does in water" (trans. Hunt, Stories, I, 207).

   4. Purgatorio, XXVII, 142. Translation: "Wherefore I [Virgil] do crown and mitre thee [Dante] over thyself." In Hunt's words, Virgil makes Dante "the tried and purified lord over himself" (Stories, I, 209).

   5. Purgatorio, XXVIII, 31-33. Translation: "Full darkly it [the stream] flows beneath the everlasting shade, which never lets sun, nor moon, beam there." See also Hunt, Stories, I, 211.

   6. Purgatorio, XXIX, 120. Translation: "When Jove was mysteriously just."

   7. Purgatorio, XXX, 38-39. Translation: "Through the hidden virtue which went out from her, [I] felt the mighty power of ancient love." See

also Hunt, Stories, I, 213.

    8. Metamorphosis II. 327-8. Translation: "Here lies Phaeton who drove his father's (Phoebus's) chariot; although his failure was great, his daring was even greater."

    9. Shakespeare, Sonnets, No. 23, l. 14. This line is also cited in the Berg M notebook as a "fine ending" (Pratt and Neufeldt, p. 212). It serves as one of the epigraphs of FH, ch. 27. GE uses it again in M to describe Mrs. Vincy as she watches the convalescent Fred, who longs to hear a word about Mary Garth: "No word passed his lip; but 'to hear with eyes belongs to love's rare wit,' and the mother in the fulness of her heart not only divined Fred's longing, but felt ready for any sacrifice in order to satisfy him" (M, ch. 27).

    10. Ibid., No. 107, ll. 1-2.

Entry 111

    1. Goethe's sämmtliche Werke, XI, 29. Translation: "Alas! our actions equally with our sufferings, clog the course of our lives" (Faust: A Dramatic Poem by Goethe, trans. A. Hayward [Boston: Ticknor, Reed, and Fields, 1853], p. 47). GHL commended this translation in The Life and Works of Goethe, II, 313. Hayward translated the First Part of Faust only. These entries from Goethe, among the few that correspond with a letter (this quotation is on the last MS page lettered "G") were probably made between August 1854 and January 1856. GE first quotes Faust in a letter to John Chapman dated 30 August 1854. She comments on the West-östlicher Divan in a review of Meredith's Shagpat in January 1856; see Uncollected Writings.

    2. Ibid., XI, 179. Translation: "And because my own cask runs thick, the world also is come to the dregs" (trans. Hayward, p. 188).

    3. Ibid., XII, 22. Translation: "What is natural in women is closely related to art."

    4. Ibid., p. 37. Translation: "But, once something famous is achieved, I immediately appear ready for battle. High is low and low high, the twisted is straight and the straight twisted: only such things make me strong. That's how I want it on this earthly round."

    5. Ibid., p. 73. Translation: "I help myself out, in the end, with the truth."

    6. Ibid., p. 137. Translation: "With small men a man does small deeds, with great men the small man grows." This same quotation appears in the "Quarry for Middlemarch," Nineteenth-Century Fiction, 4 (1950), 32.

    7. Ibid., p. 99. Translation: "Alas! Away! Let me forever sidestep those wars of tyranny and slavery. They bore me: as soon as they are over with, they straight away begin again. And no one notices that Asmodeus, who hangs behind, is toying with him. Men fight with each other, so it's said, for the rights of freedom; but clearly, it is slave who fights against slave."

Entry 112

    1. "Stets derselbe," Epigrammatisch, Goethe's sämmtliche Werke, II, 264-5. Translation: "When I go through the throng to the market and see a pretty girl in the crowd, I stand right here and she comes along, but on the other side; no one notices that we two are in love. / 'Pay no attention to age just yet! There's always a girl! Earlier in life perhaps a kitten. Which one now sweetens the day? Tell me clearly.' Only look how she greets me; it's the truth!"

    2. "Buch des Unmuths" in "Rendsch Nameh," West-östlicher Divan, Goethe's sämmtliche Werke, IV, 51 (GE gives the wrong page number). Translation: "You can't find a hack who doesn't think himself the best poet or a fiddle-scraper who wouldn't rather play his own compositions." See entry 24, n. 1.

    3. "Offenbar Geheimnis" in "Hafis Nameh," ibid., p. 24. Translation: "You call them mystical because, to your thinking, they are foolish and make a present of their cloudy wine in your name."

Entry 113

1. _Satires_ I.iv.81-85. _Translation_: "The man who backbites an absent friend; who fails to defend him when another finds fault; the man who courts the loud laughter of others and the reputation of a wit; who can invent what he never saw, who cannot keep a secret--that man is black of heart; of him beware, good Roman" (Horace, _Satires_, _Epistles_ and _Ars_ _Poetica_, trans. H. Rushton Fairclough [1929; Cambridge, Mass.: Harvard Univ. Press; London: William Heinemann, 1966], p. 55). In her Journal for 25 December 1858, GE remarks: "Christmas Day . . . . I am reading through Horace in this pause." These notes probably come from this period.

2. _Satires_ II.ii.2-3. "Ofellus, a peasant, a philosopher unschooled and of mother-wit" (Fairclough, p. 137).

3. _Satires_ II.iii.35. _Translation_: "To grow a wise man's beard" (Fairclough, p. 155).

4. _Odes_ I.xxxvii.21-22. _Translation_: "Seeking to die a nobler death" (Horace, _The_ _Odes_ _and_ _Epodes_, trans. C. E. Bennett [1914; Cambridge, Mass.: Harvard Univ. Press; London: William Heinemann, 1960], p. 101).

5. _Odes_ I.xxxvii.30.

6. _Odes_ III.ix.35. Confusing "ix" with "xi," GE gives an incorrect reference. _Translation_: "Brilliant liar."

7. Odes III.vi.41-44. _Translation_: "When the sun shifted the shadows of the mountain sides and lifted the yoke from weary steers, bringing the welcome time of rest with his departing car" (Bennett, p. 203).

Entry 114

1. _Odes_ III.xxiv.31-32. _Translation_: We "hate virtue while it lives and mourn it only when snatched from sight" (Bennett, p. 225).

2. _Odes_ III.xxiv.35-36. _Translation_: "Of what avail are empty laws, if we lack principle?" (Bennett, p. 255).

3. _Odes_ III.xxv.8-12. _Translation_: "Just so upon the mountain-tops does the sleepless Bacchanal stand rapt, looking out o'er Hebrus and o'er Thrace glistening with snow, and Rhodope trodden by barbarian feet" (Bennett, p. 259).

4. _Odes_ IV.ix.10-12. _Translation_: "Still breathes the love of the Aeolian maid, and lives her passion confided to the lyre" (Bennett, p. 319).

5. _Epistles_ I.i.106-8. _Translation_: "To sum up: the wise man is less than Jove alone. He is rich, free, honoured, beautiful, nay a king of kings; above all, sound--save when troubled by the 'flu'" (Fairclough, p. 259).

6. _Epistles_ I.vi.31-32. _Translation_: "Do you think Virtue but words, and a forest but firewood?" (Fairclough, p. 289).

7. _Translation_: "Merely a wood, not a sacred wood."

8. "Face." may be an abbreviation for _facetia_, a witticism.

9. _Epistles_, I.vii.15-19.

10. _Epistles_ I.xii.19. _Translation_: "The discordant harmony of things."

Entry 115

1. _Epistles_ I.xviii.84-85. _Translation_: "'Tis your own safety that's at stake, when your neighbour's wall is in flames, and fires neglected are wont to gather strength" (Fairclough, p. 375).

2. _Epistles_ I.xix.21-23. _Translation_: "I was the first to plant free footsteps on a virgin soil; I walked not where others trod. Who trusts himself will lead and rule the swarm" (Fairclough, p. 383).

3. _Epistles_ I.xx.20-22. _Translation_: "I was a freedman's son, and amid slender means spread wings too wide for my nest, thus adding to my merits what you take from my birth" (Fairclough, p. 391).

4. _Epistles_ II.i.10-12. _Translation_: "He who crushed the fell Hydra and laid low with fated toil the monsters of story found that Envy is quelled only by death that comes at last" (Fairclough, p. 115). The "He" referred to here is Hercules. Mr. Fairbrother reminds Tertius Lydgate that Hercules "at last wore the Nessus shirt" (_M_, ch. 18), which is what relates directly to

envy and death. In <u>M</u>, ch. 19, Will Ladislaw is found standing before the Belvedere Torso (see fig. 1) which, according to Stahr (<u>Torso</u>, II, 20-27), represents Hercules resting after slaying the Nemean lion, one of the "monsters of story."

    5. <u>Epistles</u> II.ii.180-81. <u>Translation</u>: "Gems, marble, ivory, Tuscan vases, paintings, plate, robes dyed in Gaetulian purple--there are those who have not; there is one who cares not to have" (Fairclough, p. 439).

    6. <u>Translation</u>: "I ask myself, if I go, who will stay; and if I stay, who will go?" See also Hunt, <u>Stories</u>, I, 37, n. 1.

Entry 116

    1. Boccaccio, <u>Trattatello in Laude di Dante</u> (ca. 1348); see "Life of Dante," <u>The Early Lives of Dante</u>, ed. and trans. Philip H. Wicksteed (London: Alexander Moring Ltd., 1904), pp. 9-10; 101-7. This vision is first mentioned in sec. 2 of the "Life," but it is explicated in sec. 17.

    2. <u>Translation</u>: "Its quill is angelic and has a hundred eyes; its feet are filthy, and its gait stately; moreover, its voice is sour and loud and horrible. And so in Dante's place we have his poem the Divine Comedy, which can very well be compared to a peacock." (Translated with Romana Cortese.)

    3. Edmund Spenser, "The Ruins of Time," 11. 183-91, in <u>Complaints</u> (1591) <u>Spenser's Minor Poems</u>, ed. Ernest De Selincourt (Oxford: Clarendon Press, 1960), p. 133.

Entry 119

    1. John James Tayler, <u>Retrospect of the Religious Life of England or the Church, Puritanism, and Free Inquiry</u> (London: John Chapman, 1845), pp. 532-4n. What Tayler says about Toleration provides the historical circumstances connected with the emergence of such Dissenting congregations as those of Lantern Yard in <u>SM</u> and Malthouse Yard in <u>FH</u>.

    2. Tayler's discussion is entitled "Independency, and the More Extreme Forms of Puritanism." Independency regards "every association of Christians for worship and edification, as a Church complete in itself, competent to the exercise of every ecclesiastical function" (pp. 179-80). Yesterday's Independents are today's Congregationists. The Rev. Rufus Lyon in <u>FH</u> is described as "an Independent preacher" (ch. 6) and the "minister of the Independent Chapel" of Malthouse Yard (ch. 3).

    3. Mr. Lyon, asking for a debate with the Rev. Augustus Debarry as a reward for returning a pocket-book and note-book, sets up Ainsworth as a model: "He [Mr. Ainsworth] had thought of nothing but the glory of the highest cause, and had converted the offer of recompense [for returning a valuable diamond] into a public debate with a Jew of the chief mysteries of the faith" (<u>FH</u>, ch. 15). GE has a note on this incident in her "Quarry for <u>FH</u>."

Entry 120

    1. Taylor, pp. 179-84.
    2. Ibid., pp. 207-8.
    3. Ibid., pp. 487-8.

Entry 121

    1. The <u>Table-Talk of John Selden</u>, ed. S. W. Swinger (2nd ed.; London: John Russell Smith, 1856), p. 24. Selden first published <u>Table-Talk</u> in London in 1689. Reading Tayler's <u>Retrospect</u> (see entries 117-9) may have led GE to Selden and Fuller (see below), both of whom Tayler refers to in notes.

    2. <u>Table-Talk</u> (1856), p. 42; this entry is headed "Councils" in Selden.
    3. Ibid., p. 126.
    4. St. Augustine's <u>Confessions</u>, ed. and trans. W. H. D. Rouse, Loeb Classical Library (London: William Heinemann; New York: MacMillan, 1912), III, i, 99-100. <u>Translation</u>: "I was not in love as yet, yet I loved to be in love." Augustine's Latin also served Shelley in the epigraph to "Alastor; or,

The Spirit of Solitude." GE quotes "Alastor" in entry 44.

   5.   Thomas Fuller, The History of the Worthies of England (1st ed. 1662;
London: Thomas Tegg, 1840), p. 166; Fuller is speaking here of "The Manufacturers" of Bedfordshire.

   6.   Ibid., p. 304.   Fuller is speaking of the "duke of Medina Sidonia, admiral of the Spanish fleet in the year eighty-eight" (1588, the defeat of the
Spanish Armada), who, seeing Sir Richard Edgecombe's stately house in Cornwall
from his ship, promised it to himself once the English were defeated.   GE
used this sentence as the epigraph of M, ch. 10.

   7.   Ibid., p. 493.

Entry 122

   1.   Tribaldo's memoirs appear in "Istoria di Giovanni Cambi Cittadino
Fiorentino con alcune operette di Donato Giannoti, di Marco Foscari, e di
Tribaldo de' Rossi," ed. Fr. Ildefonso di San Luigi, Delizi degli Erudite
Toscani (Firenze: Gaet. Cambiagi Stampador Granducale, 1786), XXIII, 236-303.
The Delizie and Tribaldo are referred to in GE's MS. notebook "Florentine Notes,"
but they are not quoted there.   In transcribing Tribaldo's Italian in the
present notebook, GE sometimes substitutes the modern form of a word for
Tribaldo's older form (e.g., Spagna for Spangnia) and at other times she uses
both forms alternately (ala and alla).

   2.   Ibid., p. xxi.   Translation: "The de' Rossi family had its homes in
St. Felicita Oltrarno and in the district of the Holy Spirit.   Because of the
family's excessive power, wealth, and rule over many castles, it never held
many of the Republic's major offices except for the Priorate."   (This and the
following translations were adapted from a translation by Romana Cortese.)

   3.   Delizie, p. 281.   Translation: "I remember how in March, 1493, the
Signoria received a letter which said that some young men, under the sponsor-
ship of the King of Spain and with three galleys, went in search of new countries, beyond those already discovered by the King of Portugal.   It is said
that they set out to sea on three galleys well-stocked with provisions for
three years.   After twenty-three days of navigation, they arrived at some huge
islands which were never again explored by a civilized country.   These islands
were inhabited by semi-naked men who wore a few leafy boughs around their loins
and nothing else.   These natives were never again seen by Christian men.   They
advanced toward the explorers with pointed sticks.   The points of these sticks
were made of porcupine needles, instead of iron, because the natives did not
have iron weapons of any kind.   The natives received the explorers very well.
The letters say that there was much gold on those islands (a river carried soil
mixed with gold), wheat (which the natives did not eat in bread form), cotton,
pines, and cypresses as thick as the circle formed by sixteen men with their
arms spread out.   Truly indeed!   It was a great marvel to everyone of us, etc."

   R begins "in the mid spring-time of 1492" in Florence, "which has hardly
changed its outline since the days of Columbus."   Columbus is mentioned again
as "waiting and arguing for the three poor vessels with which he was to set
sail from the port of Palos" (Proem).

Entry 123

   1.   Delizie, p. 282.   Translation: "He was considered a saint by all the
Friars and the people of Florence.   Blessed were those who touched him as well
as those who received breviaries of Christ made and blessed by him.   Many
agreed that he performed miracles.   He left this place to go to Perugia to
bring peace there with his sermons.   Books against the faith and many children's locks of hair were brought to him.   He piled them up in a little mound
and set fire to them in front of the door of the Osservanza."

   2.   Delizie, p. 283.   "Francesco, son of Lionele, was attacked at the
corner of the Puglia."

   3.   Delizie, p. 284.   Translation: "He confessed to having damaged Our
Lady at 4 o'clock at night--the marble Lady of St. Michael on the outside of

the church and in front of whom lauds were said. All the people of Florence
ran to see. They say that he hit her on the face with a knife several times
and that he hit Jesus Christ, who was in the arms of the Virgin, in the eye.
A few nights before he also damaged St. Mary of Champo, a painted pieta, and
Our Lady who is at the corner of the Hospital of Santa Maria Novella, the
hospital belonging to the Refuge of St. Nofri. He moved his bowels in his
hands and then smeared the whole face and body of the image with the said
excrement."

GE associates the name Nofri with a kind of deranged violence by giving
it to Tessa's brutal guardian: "Her obedience had been a little helped by
her own dread lest the alarming stepfather Nofri should turn up even in this
quarter . . . and beat her at least, if he did not drag her back to work for
him" (R, ch. 33).

Entry 124

1. Delizie, p. 286. Translation: "The said husband threw her out of
the house once because of her whoring. Thereafter he remained alone for many
years. Several friends interceded in her behalf; because he was a good Christian and because a handsome young man convinced him, he took her back three
months ago. When she returned, Fra Bernardino, Friar and Preacher of the Osservanti of St. Francis, who was held to be a saint by all Florence, said a
wedding Mass for them, as if they were going through a marriage again, only to
pacify them."

2. Delizie, p. 287. Translation: "Manovelli, who had a leather shop on
the Stufa of St. Michael, and his wife agreed to enter religious orders: as
it pleased God to incline them, on the day of Berlinghaccio, she became a nun
in St. Chiara and he left immediately after to put on a religious habit in
the Vernia, etc."

3. Delizie, p. 288. Translation: "Everyone approved of dying well disposed. God had forgiven him."

4. Delizie, p. 290. Translation: "A preacher of the order of Santa
Maria Novella preached over the body at St. Felicita, and it was a nice sermon.
He praised the family de' Rossi very much, in memory of St. Peter, Martyr; and,
when he preached in Florence, for our devotion to the Christian faith. . . .
He also greatly praised the said Madonna, her good life and conduct."

Entry 125

1. Francesco Petrarca, De remediis utriusque fortune (Bern, 1595), pp.
198-9. This passage from Remedies against Fortune appears in bk. 2, ch. 67.
Translation: "Joy: 'A wife is not only fertile but eloquent.' Reason:
'You sought a mate, you found a master; moreover, something unpolished, something common. You will not be able to speak without the censure and derision
of a wife. Among the vexations of the world none is more wearisome than a
woman who is insolent and incapable of silence.'" (Translated with John C.
McGalliard.)

2. Pseudodoxia Epidemica, bk. 1, ch. 6, The Works of Sir Thomas Browne,
ed. Simon Wilkin, 3 vols. (London: Bohn, 1852), I, 49. This passage is marked
in the copy in Dr. Williams's Library. This passage also was copied by GHL
into his notebook "Extracts Interesting," p. 63, under the heading, "Aphoristic
commonplaces"; moreover, neither the words "aphorism" nor "aphoristic" appear
on Browne's page and both GHL and GE omit between the words "Thales" and
"Nihil" the phrase 'Nosce tempus, of Pittarcus" and between the words "withstanding" and "are" the phrase "to speak indifferently"; finally, GE's punctua-
tion follows GHL's, not Browne's. It seems, then, that GE copied the passage
from GHL's notebook and not from Browne's text.

3. Prologueto "Mandragola," Opere Minori di Niccolo Machiavelli, ed. F.-L.
Polidori (Florence: Felice Le Monnier, 1852), p. 254. Translation: "The reward one hopes for is that each may stand and grin, bad-mouthing what he sees
and hears." (Translated with Romana Cortese.) In her diary, 26 January 1862,

GE remarks: "Finished La Mandragola, 2d time reading for sake of Florentine expressions."

Entry 126

1. Lorenzo de' Medici, "La Nencia da Barberino," I Maggiori Autori Della Letteratura Italiana, ed. Giuseppe Prezzolini (Milan: Mondadori, 1925), II, 314. Translation: "She has those eyes peculiar to thieves of the heart that can pierce a wall. Whomever she fixes on it is better for him to fall in love with her at once, even though her heart is like a stone. She is always followed by a thousand lovers who are taken with those eyes. She turns and looks at this one and that, and I am at my wit's end to have her to myself." (Translated with Romana Cortese.) In R, ch. 13, Tito sings the "Carnival Song" of Lorenzo de' Medici.

2. Opere Minori di Dante Alighieri, ed. Pietro Fraticelli, 3 vols. (Florence: Barbera, Bianchi e Comp., 1856-57), II, 87-88. This edition of Dante is in the GE-GHL collection in Dr. Williams's Library (see Library, no. 531) and is marked. The sonnet is from section XXI of the Vita; not section XI, as GE indicates. It is quoted in full as the epigraph to M, ch. 54, in which Ladislaw takes leave of Dorothea and has to save "himself from falling down at her feet." Translation: "My lady carries love within her eyes; All that she looks on is made pleasanter; Upon her path men turn to gaze at her; He whom she greeteth feels his heart to rise, And droops his troubled visage, full of sighs, And of his evil heart is then aware; Hate loves, and pride becomes a worshipper. O women, help to praise her in somewise. Humbleness, and the hope that hopeth well, By speech of hers into the mind are brought, And who beholds is blessed oftenwhiles. The look she hath when she a little smiles Cannot be said, nor holden in the thought; 'Tis such a new and gracious miracle." (Dante Gabriel Rossetti, "The New Life," The Portable Dante, p. 579; see entry 104, n. 6).

Entry 127

1. The books that GE lists are the following: Pierre Claude François Daunon, Cours d'études historiques, 20 vols. (Paris: Firmin Didot Frères, 1842-49); Henry Hart Milman, History of Latin Christianity, including that of the Popes to the Pontificate of Nicholas V, 6 vols. (London: John Murray, 1854-55); George Ellis, Specimens of Early English Metrical Romances, 3 vols. (London: Longman et al., 1805); Sir Henry James Sumner Maine, Ancient Law, its Connection with the Early History of Society and its Relation to Modern Ideas (London: John Murray, 1861); Kenelm Henry Digby, More's Catholici or Ages of Faith (London: J. Booker, 1831-41); Henri Martin, Martin's History of France: the Age of Louis XIV, trans. Mary L. Booth, 2 vols. (Boston: Walker, Wise and Co., 1865); Amédée Simon Dominique Thierry, Histoire des Gaulois, depuis les temps plus reculés jusqu'à l'entière soumission de la Gaule à la domination romaine, 8 vols. (Paris: A. Sautelet, 1828); Barthélémy Haureau, Histoire de la philosophie scolastique, 2 vols. (1850; Paris: Durand et Pedone-Laurel, 1872-80); Friedrich Albert Lange, Geschichte des Materialismus und Kritik seiner Bedeutung in der Gegenwart, 2 vols. (Iserlohn: J. Baedeker, 1866).

2. Jakob Grimm, Deutsche Mythologie, 2 vols. (1835; Göttingen: Dietrich, 1844). For GE's later interest in the work of Jakob Grimm, see entries 212-3 and 307-8.

3. GE's interest in Herodotus is reflected above in Endpaper, n. 2, and entry 7, n. 2.

4. Sir John Malcolm, History of Persia from the Most Early Period to the Present Time, 2 vols. (London: John Murray, 1829).

5. Georg Heinrich August Ewald, Geschichte des volkes Israel bis Christus, 7 vols. (Göttingen: Dietrich, 1843-59).

6. Friedrich Max Müller, A History of Sanskrit Literature, so far as it illustrates the primitive religion of the Brahmans (London: Williams and

Norgate, 1859). GE took extensive notes from various books by Max Müller:
see entries 207-11, 212-3, 267-9, 299-300, 301-5. The principal body of notes
taken from Sanskrit Literature is in Pratt and Neufeldt, pp. 28-30, and
passim.

Entry 128
    1. Luigi Pulci and Matteo Franco, Il "Libro dei Sonetti," ed. Giulio
Dolci, Biblioteca Rara, 4th series, vol. 82 (Milan, Genoa, Rome, Naples:
Società Anonima Editrici Dante Alighieri, 1933), pp. 124-5. Translation:
"Luigi Pulci to a friend for a good laugh. These people who make such a fuss
about the soul--where it comes in, where it goes out--or try to determine how
a pit is set in a peach are in fact experts in melons only. They throw Plato
together with Aristotle and want the soul to be at peace amid noise and song.
They make such a mess of things that they give you a headache. As anyone can
clearly see the soul is best found in a warm white bread or pistachio cake or
in a grilled pork cutlet sandwich. Whoever believes otherwise sends his scab-
bard to the laundry, and those who for one promised hard cash pay up with
chestnuts at the market. Someone tells me that he's gone to the life beyond
and now can't return to it because he barely made it the first time with a
ladder. These people think that they can find fig-pickers, bald-headed
vegetable-gardeners, good sweet wines, and fluffed-up beds and at the same
time run with the Friars. You and I, Pandolfo, will be better off walking in
the dark and not hearing them sing Alleluia." (Translated with Romana Cortese
and Louise Halpin Wiesenfarth.) Pulci's friend here is Pandolfo Rucellai and
the object of his scorn the philosophy of Marsilio Ficino. Pulci's poetry is
quoted three times in R (chs. 6, 8, and 57) as a kind of sharp, common-sense,
hometown wisdom. But the most extensive commentary on Pulci comes in ch. 39
where Niccolò Ridolfi quotes a conversation with the poet: "Luigi was in
his rattling vein, he was maintaining that nothing perverted the palate like
opinion. 'Opinion,' he said, 'corrupts the saliva--that's why men took to
pepper. Scepticism is the only philosophy that doesn't bring a taste in the
mouth.'" Pulci's attack on Ficino suggests that Neoplatonism does bring such
a taste. GE's entry in her Diary for 9 January 1862 indicates that she was
then reading Pulci along with Juvenal and Machiavelli (see entry 125, n. 3).

Entry 129
    1. Entries 129-30, 135-42, 146-52 are taken from Mrs. [Anna] Jameson,
Sacred and Legendary Art, 2 vols. (London: Longman, Brown, Green and Longmans,
1848). In her Diary, GE made the following entry on 15 August 1861: "Discussed the plot of my novel [Romola] with G[HL] & in the course of our conversation I struck out an idea with which he was thoroughly satisfied as a "back-
bone" for the work. After lunch we went to the London Library & looked over
some books. In the evening Dr. Bodichon came in, & afterwards I began Mrs.
Jameson's Sacred & Legendary Art." She read this book for the next fortnight
and on 31 August 1861 wrote that she "copied out the Lives of some saints from
Mrs. Jameson." She was reading it again on 2 September, and on 4 September she
notes, "Read Legendary Art & wrote from it this morning." The Ouvry Inventory
lists Mrs. Jameson's "Legendary Art" in 2 vols. as an item in the Leweses'
library.
    2. Legendary Art, I, 99-100.
    3. Ibid., I, 128-9.
    4. GE indents this entire paragraph.
    5. Legendary Art, I, 146-7.
    6. Ibid., I, 193-4.
    7. Ibid., I, xii. "'Talk not of monks and their legends, young man!'
said Bardo, interrupting Tito," who had been telling him that when he was
briefly in Athens a monk "insisted . . . on showing us the spot where St
Philip baptised the Ethiopian eunuch, or some such legend" (R, ch. 6). Here
the Renaissance humanist objects to the Medieval mind that believes such

stories as those the Legenda Aurea contains and the monk relates to Tito. The
irony is that Bardo's son, Dino, becomes a monk and his daughter, Romola, is
made into a "blessed Lady" and has legends created around her: "Many legends
were afterwards told in that valley about the blessed Lady who came over the
sea, but they were legends by which all who heard might know that in times gone
by a woman had done beautiful loving deeds there, rescuing those who were ready
to perish" (ch. 68). R is itself a golden legend, the story of a secular saint
whose life was an affirmation of duty and fellow-feeling. Commenting on the
final chapters of R, GE wrote to Sara Hennell as follows: "The various strands
of thought I had to work out forced me into a more ideal treatment of Romola
than I had foreseen at the outset--though the 'Drifting away' and the Village
with the Plague belonged to my earliest vision of the story and were by deliberate forecast adopted as romantic and symbolical elements" (Letters, IV,
104). That Romola was to be saintly enough to have a legend of her own, therefore, was central to GE's conception of the novel.

Entry 130
     1. Ibid., I, 208. St. James is mentioned under this title in TSG, bk.
II, when Arias sings: "Straight out-flushing like the rainbow, / See him come,
celestial Baron, / Mounted knight, with red-crossed banner, / Plunging earth-
ward to the battle, / Glorious Santiago!" GE also appends a note to this song
as a gloss on the title "Celestial Baron": "The Spaniards conceived their
patron Santiago (St. James), the great captain of their armies, as a knight
and baron: to them, the incongruity would have lain in conceiving him simply
as a Galilean fisherman." Six lines from Dante, including those used by Mrs.
Jameson (translation: There is that baron / Whose shrine men visit in Galicia),
are also cited.
     2. Ibid., I, 263-4; Mrs. Jameson discusses these saints as "The Four
Latin Fathers." St. Jerome's lion is used as an allusion in TSG, bk. I, when
Zarca is referred to: "His look might chase / A herd of monks, and make them
fly more swift / Than from St Jerome's lion."
     3. Legendary Art, I, 310.
     4. Ibid., I, 320.
     5. Ibid., II, 4.
     6. Ibid., II, 21. Nello suggests that Piero di Casimo paint Tito as the
saint: "Ask him . . . to turn his eyes upward, and thou mayst make a Saint
Sebastian of him that will draw troops of devout women . . ." (R, ch. 4).

Entry 131
     1. John Ayrton Paris, Pharmacologia, Being an Extended Inquiry into the
Operations of Medicinal Bodies upon Which are Founded the Theory and Art of
Prescribing (1st ed. 1812; London: Samuel Highley, 9th ed. 1843), p. 7 n. In
her Diary, GE remarks on 24 August 1861 that she "copied extracts on medical
superstitions & read Mrs. Jameson."
     2. Paris writes "prefer," not "prefix."

Entry 132
     1. Pharmacologia, pp. 20-21; Paris writes, ". . . converts it into the
letter R, that, were it not for its cloven foot, we might be led to question
its superstitious origin" (p. 21). GE draws the R with its "cloven foot,"
which Paris reproduces. Although SM was published 2 April 1861, before this
entry was made on 24 August 1861, GE may have read Paris earlier and found him
useful in developing the character of Silas, who is skilled enough in the
preparation of medicine from herbs to cure Sally Oates and become suspected of
communicating with the devil: "When Doctor Kimble gave physic, it was natural
that it should have an effect; but when a weaver, who came from nobody knew
where, worked wonders with a bottle of brown waters, the occult character of
the process was evident" (SM, ch. 2). Silas is presently seen to be as powerful a healer as the Wise Woman of Tarley, who "tied a thread" around a child's

toe to "keep off the water in the head" (<u>SM</u>, ch. 2). See fig. 8.
    2. <u>Pharmacologia</u>, p. 20n.

Entry 133
    1. Ibid., pp. 18-19.
    2. What follows is from a footnote.
    3. <u>Pharmacologia</u>, p. 19n.
    4. Ibid., p. 23.

Entry 134
    1. Ibid., p. 23n.
    2. Quoted in <u>Pharmacologia</u>, p. 31. With reference to Bulstrode's piety,
Lydgate caustically uses the last part of this quotation: "As to his religious
notions--why, as Voltaire said, incantations will destroy a flock of sheep if
administered with a certain quantity of arsenic" (<u>M</u>, ch. 17).
    3. Thomas Joseph Pettigrew, <u>On Superstitions connected with the History</u>
<u>and Practice of Medicine</u> (London: John Churchill, 1844), pp. 37-38. The
GE - GHL library contains a copy of Pettigrew; see <u>Library</u>, p. 156, no. 1673.
On 28 August 1861 GE notes in her Diary, "In the evening read Pettigrew on
Medical Superstitions."
    4. John Brand, <u>Observations on Popular Antiquities</u> (Newcastle-upon-Tyne,
1777).
    5. Edward Meryon, <u>The History of Medicine comprising a Narrative of its</u>
<u>Progress from the Earliest Ages to the Present Time and of the Delusions</u>
<u>Incidental to its Advance from Empiricism to the Dignity of a Science</u> (London:
Longman, Green, Longman, and Roberts, 1861), pp. 104-5.
    6. Mrs. [Anna] Jameson, <u>Sacred and Legendary Art</u>, 2 vols. (London:
Longman, Brown, Green and Longmans, 1848), II, 378. Durandus is mentioned in
Jameson's account of the bell as a symbol in representations of St. Anthony
the Hermit. GE probably made this note on 4 September 1861 (see 129, n. 1
above). William Durandus wrote <u>Rationale Divinorum Officiorum</u> in the late 13th
century; see bk. 1, ch. 5, for bells.

Entry 135
    1. <u>Legendary Art</u>, II, 33-38.
    2. Ibid., 41.

Entry 137
    1. Tessa alludes to the legend of St. Christopher during "The Peasants'
Fair" when she sees dancers on stilts and asks Tito, "Do you think Saint Christopher helps them?" "Because Saint Christopher is so very tall; and he is
very good: if anybody looks at him he takes care of them all day. He is on
the wall of the church--too tall to stand up there--but I saw him walking
through the streets one San Giovanni, carrying the little Gesù" (<u>R</u>, ch. 14).

Entry 138
    1. Ibid., 48-53. Although GE did not copy these legends from Mrs. Jame-
son into her notebook until August-September 1861 (Diary), she modeled the
Legend of St. Ogg in <u>MF</u> on that portion of the legend of St. Christopher beginning, "So he went" (entry 137) and ending, "& worshipped Christ" (entries
137-8); see <u>Mythmaking</u>, pp. 106-7. GE mentions Mrs. Jameson in her letters as
early as 14 January 1840 and regrets having been away when Mrs. Jameson called
with Robert Noel on 23 June 1853. They dined together in February 1854
(<u>Letters</u>, VIII, 96), and Mrs. Jameson wrote to Ottilie von Goethe that "the
lady who is with him [GHL] I have seen before her (known) liaison with him"
(<u>Letters</u>, II, 231); the liaison became known in July 1854. Long acquaintance
with Mrs. Jameson's writings, meeting her personally, and having her
<u>Legendary Art</u> available on her library shelves (Ouvry Inventory) suggest that
GE had read in the book prior to taking notes from it. The closeness in

pattern of the St. Ogg legend to Mrs. Jameson's version of the Christopher legend substantiates this inference. And GE's acknowledgement of a debt to a "private hagiographer" may even be an oblique reference to Mrs. Jameson, whose Christopher served as a model for Ogg.

    2. <u>Legendary Art</u>, II, 53. Tessa alludes to this painting in <u>R</u>, ch. 14; see entry 137, n. 1.

    3. This entry begins in the left margin in the MS.

Entry 139

    1. <u>Legendary Art</u>, II, 60-69 passim.

    2. Ibid., 76.

    3. Piero di Casimo tells Romola, "You . . . are fit to be a model for a wise Saint Catherine of Egypt," (<u>R</u>, ch. 49).

    4. Dinah Morris, who is beautiful and eloquent and devoted to Jesus, is referred to as St. Catherine by Arthur Donnithorne: "She looked like St. Catherine in a Quaker dress" (<u>AB</u>, ch. 5).

Entry 140

    1. <u>Legendary Art</u>, II, 78-86 passim.

Entry 141

    1. "From the summit of her tower she contemplated the stars of heaven and their courses," writes Mrs. Jameson. GE invokes this image in <u>M</u>, ch. 10, when describing Dorothea: "Sometimes when Dorothea was in company, there seemed to be as complete an air of repose about her as if she had been a picture of Santa Barbara looking out from her tower into the clear air." Later, when Lowick becomes her prison, Dorothea characteristically gazes out of the window of her boudoir.

    2. Mrs. Jameson prints her own etching of "St. Barbara, enthroned," which copies Matteo di Siena's picture in the Church of San Domenico at Siena, dated 1479; see <u>Legendary Art</u>, II, 105 and fig. 9. St. Barbara is shown holding an architectural model of her tower. She is one of those "saints with architectural models in their hands" whom Dorothea has seen in Italian paintings (<u>M</u>, ch. 22). As Ladislaw teaches Dorothea the language of art—"Art is an old language with a great many artificial affected styles, and sometimes the chief pleasure one gets out of knowing them is the mere sense of knowing" (ch. 21)—some things "which had seemed monstrous to her were gathering intelligibility and even a natural meaning" (ch. 22). Mrs. Jameson's <u>Legendary Art</u> serves as a grammar for learning such an "old language." (The only other saint depicted with an architectural model in his hands is St. Petronius, who holds a replica of the city of Bologna; see <u>Legendary Art</u>, II, 338.)

    3. <u>Legendary Art</u>, II, 103-5 passim.

Entry 142

    1. Ibid., 112-22 passim. St. Ursula is mentioned in GE's poem "Agatha" (1868): "The walls had little pictures hung a-row / Telling the stories of St. Ursula / And Saint Elizabeth the lowly queen," <u>TLJ</u>, pp. 52-53.

    2. <u>Legendary Art</u>, II, 130-32.

    3. Ibid., 201 passim.

    4. Ibid., 202. Gwendolen aspires to be a St. Cecilia in <u>DD</u>, ch. 3.

    5. St. Cecilia's legend continues under entry 146.

Entry 143

    1. Daniel Rock, <u>Hierurgia; or the Holy Sacrifice of the Mass</u>, 2 vols. (London: Joseph Booker, 1833); GE took her notes from vol. II, pt. ii, ch. 12. GE's Journal has the following entries: 2 September 1861: "Read on Vestments in Rock's Hierurgia"; 3 September: "Wrote out Ecclesiastical Vestments from Rock." GE anticipated the need of such information for <u>R</u>; in fact, however, she used little of it. In the MS. "Florentine Notes" GE mentions

"Rock's Hierurgia for church ceremonies (?)" under "Hints and Queries." These
entries in the Notebook show that she pursued her original query and read in
Rock's book.

    2. Hierurgia, 599-600.

    3. Ibid., p. 611. Tito says to Nello, after examining "a symbolical pic-
ture": "And the Golden Age can always come back as long as men are born in the
form of babies, and don't come into the world in cassock or furred mantle" (R,
ch. 3).

    4. Ibid., pp. 611-2.

    5. Ibid., pp. 613-5.

    6. Ibid., p. 618.

    7. Ibid., pp. 619-20.

Entry 144

    1. Ibid., pp. 622-30 passim.

    2. Ibid., pp. 630-45 passim.

Entry 145

    1. Ibid., p. 644.

    2. Ibid., pp. 647-8.

    3. Ibid., pp. 651-2.

    4. Ibid., p. 653.

    5. Ibid., pp. 655-7 passim.

    6. Ibid., p. 661.

    7. Ibid., p. 659.

Entry 146

    1. Legendary Art, II, 203n.

    2. Ibid., 204-5.

Entry 147

    1. Ibid., 220-23 passim.

    2. Ibid., 229-32 passim.

Entry 148

    1. Ibid., 234. Santa Lucia's eyes appear as a laboratory specimen in
M, ch. 36: "the inspection of macerated muscle or of eyes presented in a
dish (like Santa Lucia's), and other incidents of scientific inquiry, are observed to be less incompatible with poetic love than a native dulness or a
lively addiction to the lowest prose."

    2. Ibid., 236-7.

    3. Ibid., 309-10.

Entry 149

    1. Ibid., 313-7 passim.

    2. Ibid., 321-2.

    3. Ibid., 327.

Entry 150

    1. Ibid., 331-2. In the great procession of 30 October 1496 (R, chs.
42-43) the "Canons of the Duomo" carry "a sacred relic--the very head, en-
closed in silver, of San Zenobio, immortal bishop of Florence, whose virtues
were held to have saved the city perhaps a thousand years before" (R, ch. 43).

    2. Ibid., 334-5.

    3. Ibid., 339-40.

Entry 151

    1. Ibid., 378-80. Savonarola is maliciously compared with St. Anthony:
"The Frate has been preaching to the birds, like Saint Anthony, and he's been

telling the hawks they were made to feed the sparrows, as every good Florentine citizen was made to feed six starving beggarmen from Arezzo or Bologna" (R, ch. 42).   St. Anthony's pig appears in TSG, bk. 1, in a passage comparing Jews and animals: "Jews are not fit for heaven, but on earth / They are most useful. 'Tis the same with mules, / Horses, or oxen, or with any pig / Except Saint Anthony's."

    2. Legendary Art, II, 391.

Entry 152

    1. Ibid., 393-5.

Entry 153

    1. Cicero, De Officiis, trans. Walter Miller, Loeb Classical Library (1913; Cambridge, Mass.: Harvard Univ. Press; London: William Heinemann, 1961), I.ix.30. Translation: "For righteousness shines with a brilliance of its own, but doubt is a sign that we are thinking of a possible wrong" (p. 31). GE's Diary indicates that she was reading the De Officiis on 5 November and again between 25 and 29 November 1861.

    2. Ibid. I.xi.33. Translation: "There are certain duties that we owe even to those who have wronged us. . . ; or rather, I am inclined to think, it is sufficient that the agressor should be brought to repent of his wrong-doing, in order that he may not repeat the offence and that others may be deterred from doing wrong" (pp. 35-37).

    3. Ibid. I.xiii.40. Translation: "In the matter of a promise one must always consider the meaning and not the mere words" (p. 45).

    4. Ibid. I.xiii.41. Translation: "Of all forms of injustice, none is more flagrant than that of the hypocrite who, at the very moment when he is most false, makes it his business to appear virtuous" (p. 47).

    5. Ibid. I.xiv.43. Translation: "Nothing is generous, if it is not at the same time just" (p. 49).

    6. Ibid. I.xvii.55. Translation: "It means much to share in common the same family traditions, the same forms of domestic worship, and the same ancestral tombs" (p. 59).

    7. Ibid. I.xviii.62. Translation: "Nothing that lacks justice can be morally right" (p. 65).

    8. Ibid. I.xxi.71. Translation: "There are people who in opposite circumstances do not act consistently: they have the utmost contempt for pleasure, but in pain they are too sensitive; they are indifferent to glory, but they are crushed by disgrace" (p. 73).

    9. Ibid. I.xxii.75. Translation: "The victory at Salamis served the state only once; the Areopagus will serve it forever."   Themistocles won the battle of Salamis; Solon created the Areopagus (p. 77.)

    10. Ibid. I.xxii.76. Translation: "Arms are of little value in the field unless there is wise counsel at home" (p. 77).

Entry 154

    1. There is no external evidence to indicate GE's source for this entry. The kind of information found here, however, could have been summarized from Karl Friedrich Hermann, Lehrbuch der Gottesdienstlichen Alterthümer der Griechen (Heidelberg: Akademische Verlagsbuchhandlung von J. C. B. Mohr, 1858), pp. 358-426. This particular ordering of the Greek months was first established by Joseph Scaliger (1540-1609).

Entry 155

    1. Pierre Helyot, Histoire des ordres monastiques, religieux et militaires, et des congrégations séculières, 8 vols. (Paris: Jean Baptiste Coignard, 1718). On 29 December 1861, GE writes in the Diary, "Wrote out notes on the monastic orders." GE uses her notes from Helyot in R in several ways. The variety of color in the garb of religious orders lends authentic

local color to the great procession in ch. 43. The variety of garb also
indicates tensions in the past between regular and reformed branches of religious orders because a change in dress indicates a change in rule. Tensions
also exist between orders, especially between the Dominicans and Franciscans.
The variety of look and outlook within and between religious orders, as well
as the pronounced tensions they exhibit one with another, suggests that they
are images of Florence itself: the Bardis, for example, are split among
themselves religiously (Bardo and Dino, a reformed Bardi) and politically
(Romola and Bernardo, a Piagnone and a Medicean); the Medici are at logger-
heads with the Sforzas; the Piagnoni, Arrabiatti, and Mediceans maneuver for
power. The religious world is a metonymy for the familial and political
worlds in R. This structure suggests the importance of one theme of the
novel: reform must begin with the individual.
    2. Histoire, V, 1-7 passim. Dino compares himself to St. Benedict when
he says to Romola, "I was ready, like the blessed Saint Benedict, to roll myself among thorns, and court smarting wounds as a deliverance from temptation" (R, ch. 15).

Entry 157
    1. Ibid., pp. 125-36 passim.
    2. Ibid., p. 145. "A white stream of reformed Benedictines" appears
in the procession supplicating the aid of the Madonna dell' Impruneta (R, ch.
43).
    3. Ibid., pp. 186-201 passim.

Entry 158
    1. Ibid., pp. 245-59 passim.
    2. Helyot speaks of "Saint Pierre Damien." GE seems unsure whether to
translate Pierre as Pietro or Piero.

Entry 159
    1. Histoire, V, 281-6 passim.
    2. Ibid., pp. 287-8 passim; two dates are given for the founding of La
Cava: 980 and 1025.
    3. "Monks again . . . Vallombrosan and other varieties of Benedictines,
reminding the instructed eye by niceties of form and colour that in ages of
abuse, long ago, reformers had arisen who had marked a change of spirit by a
change of garb" (R, ch. 43).
    4. Ibid., pp. 298-311 passim. Procrastination, followed by rain, allows
Fra Domenico, as well as Savonarola, to avoid a similar trial by fire in R,
ch. 65.
    5. Ibid., pp. 341-70 passim.
    6. Ibid., p. 373. (GE's spelling of "Cistertian" and "Bernardine" varies.)
    7. Ibid., p. 401.
    8. Ibid., pp. 450-51.

Entry 160
    1. Ibid., pp. 456-7.
    2. Ibid., p. 457. Translation: "From that time forward it became a new
kind of religious house, devoted entirely to the worship of the Blessed Sacrament; so that night and day someone was at prayer before the Blessed Sacrament."
    3. Ibid., p. 458.
    4. Ibid., p. 461.
    5. Ibid., p. 465. Translation: "Those who espoused Jansenius's book
were known generally as 'Port Royalists' because the greater number of them,
intellectuals at that, had gone to Port Royal in the Fields when the nuns left
there in 1626; and after that the nuns returned, the 'Port Royalists,' many
of whom were parents of the religious, charmed by the peace and quiet of the
place, built apartments attached to the monastery."

Entry 161
    1. *Histoire*, VI, 3-5.
    2. Ibid., pp. 21-22.
    3. Ibid., p. 26.
    4. Ibid., p. 152; the date of the founding is disputed by historians,
according to Helyot.
    5. "Frati Umiliati, or Humbled Brethren, from Ognissanti, with a glori-
ous tradition of being the earliest workers in the wool trade" walk in procession in R, ch. 43.

Entry 162
    1. *Histoire*, VI, 153-6.
    2. See ibid., p. [157] for picture.
    3. Ibid., 160-61.
    4. Ibid., p. 180; this sentence is not indented in the manuscript.
    5. "The black of the Augustinians of San Spirito" is mentioned in R, ch.
43. An Augustinian monk is Bernardo del Nero's confessor. Romola meets him
at Parto on her way back to Florence: "Of Savonarola the monk told her, in
that tone of unfavorable prejudice which was usual in the Black Brethren
(Frati Neri) towards the brother who showed white under his black, that he had
confessed himself a deceiver of the people" (R, ch. 70).

Entry 163
    1. *Histoire*, III, 6-17 passim.
    2. Ibid., pp. 72-76 passim.
    3. Ibid., p. 121.
    4. Ibid., pp. 140, 143.
    5. Ibid., p. 186.
    6. Ibid., pp. 184-5. _Translation_: "We have seen when speaking of hos-
pitals that they were run by both men and women religious who kept separate
places of residence. This had been the practice in the West since the days of
Cardinal Jacques de Vitry, who died toward the middle of the thirteenth century and who, speaking of the Hospitalers, said that there were many congregations of men and women who, renouncing the world—and living in leprosaria and
hospitals to assist the sick and the poor—followed the rule of Saint Augustine,
owned no property, shared what they had in common, obeyed a superior, and took
a promise of perpetual chastity. The men dwelt apart from the women; indeed,
the men and women did not even eat together but lived circumspectly and in
exemplary purity."

Entry 164
    1. Genesis 22.14.
    2. Just Matthias Thiele, _Thorwaldsen's_ _Leben_, 3 vols. (Lepizig: Carl B.
Lorck, 1852), I, 78-79. GE reviewed vol. 2 of this book for "Contemporary
Literature," _Westminster_ _Review_, 65 (1856), USA ed. 149. On 8 March 1803, the
day that the Danish sculptor Thorwaldsen postponed leaving Rome until the following morning, the English collector Hope came to his studio and agreed to pay
him £300 for a statue of the Jason in marble. This last minute episode allowed
Thorwaldsen to remain in Rome. See Thiele, _The_ _Life_ _of_ _Thorwaldsen_, trans. M. R.
Barnard (London: Chapman and Hall, 1865), pp. 45-59. In M, ch. 22, "Will
could not omit [a visit to] Thorwaldsen" when giving Dorothea and Casaubon a
tour of artists' ateliers in Rome.
    3. *Histoire*, III, 198. _Translation_: "Late in her pregnancy St. Dominic's
mother had a mysterious dream in which she imagined giving birth to a small
dog that carried a lighted torch in its muzzle and gave light everywhere,
clearly a sign _et_ _cetera_."

Entry 165
    1. Ibid. 201-4 passim.

2. Savonarola is a Dominican and the order has a prominent place in R. The Dominicans are known as the Order of Preachers in English or Frati Predicatori in Italian.

3. *Histoire*, III, 220-21.

4. Ibid., pp. 212-3.

5. Ibid., p. 224.

6. Ibid., pp. 298-301. "The unmixed black of the Servites, the famous Florentine order founded by seven merchants who forsook their gains to adore the Divine Mother" is seen in procession in R, ch. 43.

7. *Histoire*, IV, 72.

Entry 166

1. Ibid., p. 150.

2. Ibid., pp. 227-8.

3. Ibid., p. 236. <u>Translation</u>: "His reading of the Catechism of the Council of Trent led Cesar de Bus to think of establishing a congregation of priests and clerics dedicated to the teaching of Christian reading. The Catechism of the Council of Trent was divided into four sections (Symbolism, The Lord's Prayer, The Ten Commandments, and the Sacraments), and Father de Bus reduced these to three levels of instruction, which he called elementary, middle, and advanced doctrine. Five or six young ecclesiastics of good family joined him, and after learning how to instruct others in elementary doctrine, they went into the town streets and into the countryside to catechize all whom they met."

4. Ibid., 102-6 passim.

Entry 167

1. *Histoire*, VII, 2.

2. Ibid., p. 12.

3. Ibid., p. 35.

4. Ibid., pp. 71-74. Franciscans wearing "<u>zoccoli</u>, or wooden shoes" appear in R, ch. 43.

5. Ibid., pp. 75-78 passim.

6. Ibid., p. 78.

7. Ibid., p. 120.

8. Ibid., pp. 363-5 passim.

Entry 168

1. Ibid., p. 366.

2. Ibid., p. 375. With silence and seclusion as his rules, it is interesting to note that "Fra Michele, a Carthusian lay brother [is] in the service of the Mediceans" (R, ch. 45).

3. Ibid., p. 400.

4. *Histoire*, VIII, 1-2.

5. *Histoire*, II, 13.

6. Ibid., 156-8.

7. *Histoire*, I, 282. "The white over dark of the Carmelites" appears in the procession in R, ch. 43.

Entry 169

1. Entries 169 through 184 are taken from Charles William King, <u>Antique Gems: Their Origin, Uses, and Value as Interpreters of Ancient History; and as Illustrative of Ancient Art: with Hints to Gem Collectors</u> (London: John Murray, 1860). GE read King as part of her preparation for writing R, in which gems are frequently referred to. The phrase "antique gems" appears in R, ch. 3, when Tito asks Nello if there is any "wealthy Florentine addicted to purchasing antique gems?" and in ch. 27, when we are told that "French agents had already begun to see that such very fine antique gems as Lorenzo had collected belonged by right to the first nation in Europe."

    2. <u>Antique</u> <u>Gems</u>, p. xxxiv. This entry begins GE's notes on the history of gem-engraving.
    3. Ibid., pp. xxxiv-v.
    4. Ibid., pp. xxxv-vi.

Entry 170
    1. Ibid., pp. xxxvi-vii.
    2. Ibid., p. xxxvii.
    3. Ibid., pp. xxxvii-viii.

Entry 171
    1. Ibid., pp. xxxviii-ix.
    2. Tito's ring "was found in Sicily" (<u>R</u>, ch. 4).

Entry 172
    1. <u>Antique</u> <u>Gems</u>, pp. xxxix-xi.
    2. Ibid., pp. xl-xli.

Entry 173
    1. Ibid., pp. xli-ii.
    2. In <u>M</u>, ch. 22, Dorothea asks Ladislaw's advice on cameos she is buying. He remarks, "I am not particularly knowing, but there can be no mistake about these Homeric bits: they are exquisitely neat."
    3. <u>Antique</u> <u>Gems</u>, pp. xlii-iii.

Entry 174
    1. Ibid., xliii.

Entry 175
    1. Ibid., xlii-iv.
    2. Ibid., xliv-v.

Entry 176
    1. Ibid., pp. xlv-vi. <u>R</u> begins in the year 1492. Tito is easily able to sell the gems that Baldassarre had acquired to Florentine collectors like Bartolomeo Scala and Bernardo Rucellai. Rucellai is presented as a collector pure and simple: he buys Tito's best gems. Scala buys two that he thinks will help him against the gout. Bardo, a collector who cannot buy any, wears prophylactic rings that were prescribed for him. In short, <u>R</u> is set in a century that made gem-collecting a passion both for the intrinsic and mystic value of gems.
    2. Ibid., pp. 5-7. When Baldassarre challenges Tito at "A Supper in the Rucellai Gardens" (<u>R</u>, ch. 39), Bernardo Rucellai puts him to the test, saying, "If you are the person you claim to be, you can doubtless give some description of the gems which were your property. I myself was the purchaser of more than one gem from Messer Tito--the chief rings, I believe, in his collection. One of them is a fine sard, engraved with a subject from Homer." Here the sard is mentioned as a prize antique gem in the Baldassarre-Tito collection--a description borne out by King's high valuation of the stone. See fig. 10.

Entry 177
    1. Ibid., pp. 7-8.
    2. Ibid., pp. 8-9. Among Tito's gems is "a fine Cleopatra cut in sardonyx, and one or two other intaglios and cameos, both curious and beautiful, worthy of being added to the cabinet of a prince" (<u>R</u>, ch. 3).
    3. Ibid., p. 11. Tito's signet ring contains a nicolo: Domenico Cennini calls it "curious and valuable" and describes it as follows: "This intaglio of the fish with the crested serpent above it, in the black stratum

of the onyx, or rather nicolo, is well shown by the surrounding blue of the upper stratum" (R, ch. 4). This design is described by King as a planetary figure: Cetus, "a big fish with bent tail and wide mouth" and "if cut on a stone, with a large crested serpent with a long mane above it, it gives good luck at sea and restores lost things" (King, p. 441).

4. Ibid., p. 11, n. 6. Bartolomeo Scala buys an agate with a "lusus naturae in it--a most wonderful semblance of Cupid riding on the lion"(R, ch. 7). See fig. 10.

5. Ibid., p. 14.

6. Ibid., pp. 16-18.

7. Ibid., p. 20.

8. Ibid., p. 24.

9. Ibid., p. 25, n. 3.

Entry 178

1. Ibid., pp. 24-26 passim.

2. Ibid., pp. 38-39.

3. Ibid., p. 44.

4. Ibid., p. 49. Baldassarre in desperation tears open the breve his mother gave him and finds a sapphire: "There was an amulet. It was very small, but it was as blue as those far-off waters; it was an engraved sapphire, which must be worth some gold ducats" (R, ch. 30).

5. King provides this table to show that "at the Renaissance the price of coloured gems of perfect quality far exceeded that of the Diamond" (p. 51). When Tito is fleeing Florence in R, ch. 67, he flings diamonds to his pursuers: "There are diamonds, gold."

6. A ruby, valued as the most precious of stones, was given by Dolfo Spini to Tito; see R, ch. 66. Spini consequently feels especially double-crossed by Melema: "And he's got that fine ruby of mine, I was fool enough to give him yesterday. Malediction!"

7. Antique Gems, pp. 56-59 passim.

8. Ibid., p. 60.

9. Ibid., p. 63.

10. Ibid., pp. 55-56.

Entry 179

1. Ibid., pp. 316-7. Scala buys an agate from Tito with a lusus naturae in it (R, ch. 6).

2. Ibid., p. 322.

3. Ibid., pp. 327-8.

Entry 180

1. Ibid., pp. 331-2.

2. Ibid., pp. 338-9.

Entry 181

1. Ibid., pp. 340-42.

2. Ibid., pp. 342-4.

Entry 183

1. Ibid., pp. 347-51.

2. Ibid., p. 352.

3. Ibid., p. 354.

4. Ibid., p. 357.

5. Ibid., p. 365.

6. Ibid., p. 366.

Entry 184

1. Ibid., p. 369.

2. Ibid., p. 370. Tito sells a "'Jew's stone,' with the lion-headed serpent enchased in it" to Bartolomeo Scala (R, ch. 7). The engraved subject and the antiquity of such a stone were believed to give a "mystic potency" (King, p. 370). Scala buys it to protect himself against the gout.

3. Ibid., pp. 467-8.

4. Ibid., p. 434.

5. De Oratore II.lix.239; if GE's reference is to book and paragraph, it is incorrect. Translation: "In deformity and physical ugliness there is a good enough butt for joking."

Entry 186

1. This entry, which does not appear in quotation marks, seems to be GE's summary of facts from Stanley's Eastern Church, which she quotes directly in the next entry. See 187, n. 1.

Entry 187

1. Arthur Penrhyn Stanley, Lectures on the History of the Eastern Church (3d ed. London: John Murray, 1864), pp. 131-2.

Entry 188

1. Ibid., pp. 3-4.

Entry 189

1. Ibid., pp. 4-6.

Entry 190

1. Ibid., pp. 6-7.

Entry 191

1. Ibid., pp. 7-8.

Entry 192

1. Ibid., pp. 8-12.

2. Ibid., pp. 13-16.

Entry 193

1. Ibid., pp. 16-17.

Entry 195

1. General Pietro Colletta, History of the Kingdom of Naples, trans. S. Horner, 2 vols. (Edinburgh: T. Constable, 1858), II, 424. GE may have read Colletta while she was still writing R. There is no indication in her Diary that she read him between 9 June 1863, when she finished R, and 19 July 1864, when she began reading Gibbon, from whose Decline and Fall she takes entry 199 in the notebook. Colletta's account of events in Naples in the 1820s recalls GE's account of similar events in Florence in the 1490s. In both decades a populist revolution is overthrown by an absolutist tyranny. In the scourging of the Carbonaro in Naples the suffering of Christ's passion is recalled; in the sufferings of Savonarola the recollection of the Passion is even more pointed: he is tortured during Holy Week, he suffers on a gibbet that looks like a cross, and he dies because of his virtues--he was too great "a molesta-tion to vicious citizens and greedy foreign tyrants" to live (R, ch. 71). Both men, but especially Savonarola, recall the sentence of Heine, which GE quoted in her essay on him, that "Wherever a great soul utters its thoughts, there is Golgotha" (Essays, p. 251).

Entry 196

1. Colletta, II, 436.

2. The Scourge.

Entry 197
    1. Colletta, II, 440-41.

Entry 198
    1. Ibid., p. 441.

Entry 199
    1. Edward Gibbon, The History of the Decline and Fall of the Roman Empire, notes by Dean Milman and M. Guizot, ed. William Smith, 8 vols. (London: John Murray, 1854), II, map: "The Migrations of the Barbarians" containing an inset: "Synopsis of Languages according to their Internal & External Relationship." GE's outline follows Smith's inset, but she modifies his classifications with details gathered from other philologists, such as Thomas Clark and Max Müller, whose works she quotes below. According to her Diary, GE was reading volume two of Gibbon on 6 August 1864 and she had already begun reading philology: "I am nearly at an end of Gibbon vol. II, & am reading a little on Philology, much interrupted by visitors &c."
    2. All parenthetical remarks are GE's additions.
    3. Smith lists the Old Slavian languages (Russian through Croatian) under the "German Class of Languages," which is a heading equal to "Slavic Family" and "Indian Family." Only Lithuanian falls under the "Slavic Family."
    4. Smith does not mention Euscarra.
    5. Smith lists these as a separate class after Malayan.
    6. These footnoted entries are GE's additions.

Entry 200
    1. Entries 201 to 206 are taken from Thomas Clark, The Student's Handbook of Comparative Grammar, Applied to the Sanskrit, Zend, Greek, Latin, Gothic, Anglo-Saxon, and English Language (London: Longman, Green, Longman, Roberts, & Green, 1862); Clark's handbook is based on the work of Franz Bopp, Vergleichende Grammatik des Sanskrit, Zend, Griechischen, Lateinischen, Litthauischen, Altslawischen, Gothischen und Deutschen, 1833-37; see Clark, p. vii. Clark's classification of Indo-European languages amplifies portions of the diagram from Smith's Gibbon given in entry 199. Clark omits a discussion of the Semitic family, but GE supplements this omission in entries 207-10 with the work of Max Müller.
    2. Clark, pp. 6-7, 9.
    3. Ibid., p. 10.
    4. Ibid., pp. 10-11.
    5. August Friedrich Pott, Etymologische Forschungen auf dem Gebiete der Indo-Germanischen Sprachen, 1833-36.
    6. Clark, p. 11.

Entry 201
    1. Ibid., pp. 11-12.
    2. Ibid., p. 13.
    3. Ibid., p. 14.
    4. Ibid., pp. 14-15.

Entry 202
    1. Ibid., pp. 15-16.

Entry 203
    1. Ibid., pp. 16-18.
    2. Ibid., p. 19.
    3. Ibid., pp. 20-21.

Entry 204
    1. Ibid., p. 22.

    2. Ibid., pp. 23-24.

Entry 205
    1. Ibid., p. 25.
    2. Ibid., p. 27.
    3. Ibid., pp. 29-30.

Entry 206
    1. Ibid., p. 30.
    2. Ibid., p. 31.
    3. Ibid.

Entry 207
    1. Max Müller, Lectures on the Science of Language, 2 vols. (London: Longman, Green, Longman, Roberts, & Green, 4th ed. 1864). Entries 207-11 are drawn from vol. 1, Lecture VIII, "Morphological Classification." GE records reading "Müller's book on Language" on 13 January 1862 (Diary). A few months later, in "A Box of Books," Blackwood's Magazine, 91 (April 1862), 434-51, GHL reviewed this First Series of lectures, interesting himself in the question of the scientific aspect of the study of language and, while praising Müller, taking issue (1) with his exposition of the "phonetic decay" (GHL suggests that phonetic metamorphosis would be a better term) and (2) with his discussion of the origin of language from primal roots ("It is not that no new roots are formed, or are no longer capable of being formed, but that the existing roots prevent the continuance of the new"). Müller's theory of the origin of language from a single source (discussed in Lecture VIII) is analogous to Casaubon's theory of the origin of myth in a single culture. Müller has therefore occasionally been proposed as a prototype of Casaubon in M. Although GE read the First Series of Lectures in January 1862, these notes probably were written subsequent to July 1864, when she was reading Gibbon's Decline and Fall, which provides entry 199, and possibly in August 1864, when she was "reading a little in Philology" (Diary, 6 August 1864). Also, entries 212-3 draw on Müller's discussion of Grimm's Law which appeared in Lectures, Second Series, first published in 1864; the First Series was first published in 1861.
    2. Müller, I, 287.
    3. Ibid., p. 288.

Entry 208
    1. Ibid., p. 289.
    2. Ibid., p. 292.

Entry 209
    1. Müller adds, "Or, as it is called by the people themselves, the Gees language." GE tried to incorporate the substance of this sentence by inventing a cognate of Gees, which seems to be "Ghez," a word illegibly inserted above the line before "Ethiopic."
    2. Müller, I, 292-3.
    3. Ernest Renan, Histoire générale et système comparé des langues sémitiques (Paris: Calman Levy, n.d.); see entries 240-46 below.
    4. Müller, I, 283-4.

Entry 210
    1. Ibid., p. 298.
    2. Ibid., p. 299.
    3. Ibid., p. 300.

Entry 211
    1. Ibid., pp. 301-3.

Entries 212-3

1. This diagram suggests that GE continued her study of Comparative Philology by reading and summarizing parts of Jacob Grimm, Geschichte der Deutschen Sprache (1848; Leipzig: S. Hirzel, 1853). Max Müller, Lectures, II (see 207, n. 1) devotes his fifth lecture to "Grimm's Law," and Clark, Student's Handbook (see 200, n. 1) discusses "The Transmutation of Consonants." From Müller and Clark, therefore, GE may have gotten her titles for entries 212-3. But her tables on these pages do not correspond to theirs; rather they reflect Grimm's own in the Geschichte, secs. 392-434. Clark, at the end of his discussion of Transmutation, refers precisely to these sections in Grimm's History. Moreover, GE's statement of "The Law" (212) is an exact translation of Grimm's German: "die media jedes der drei organe geht über in tenuis, die tenuis in aspirata und die aspirata wieder in media" (sec. 393). Finally, the outline of "Grimm's system" derives from the Geschichte: spirantes, sec. 294; liquids, sec. 309; mutes, sec. 344. Some dozen years after making the present notes, GE read and annotated T. Le Marchant Douse, Grimm's Law: A Study (London: Trübner, 1876). Her marginalia on pp. 9 and 53 show her contradicting Douse; a note on p. 231, "Fundamental principle, 55," refers to Douse's sec. 26, pp. 55-57, which is a discussion of mutes, tenues, and aspirates.

In GE's diagram the vertical lines separate three columns which are first column, Labials; second, Gutturals; third, Dentals. The numbers followed by brackets represent a horizontal arrangement: #1 Medial consonants in Sanscrit, Greek, and Latin; #2 Tenuis consonants in Gothic and Anglo-Saxon; #3 Aspirated consonants in Old High German. It is important to note that there is no relation between the three vertical columns and the language-families written above them.

Similar, but not the same, diagrams appear in Pratt and Neufeldt, pp. 59, 224; these can with certainty be traced to Max Müller's Lectures; that is not the case, however, with entries 212-3 here.

Entry 214

1. Henrich M. G. Grellman, Dissertation on the Gipsies, Being an Historical Enquiry, Concerning the Manner of Life, OEconomy, Customs and Conditions of these People in Europe, and their Origin, trans. Matthew Roper (London: G. Brigg, 1787), p. 28. In TSG, bk. I, the Host remarks of the Gypsies taken prisoner by the Duke: "He needed smiths, and doubtless the brave Moor / Has missed some useful scouts and archers too" (TSG, p. 50). Zarca amplifies this statement in bk. IV: "I was prisoner here, / Forging the bullets meant for Moorish hearts" (p. 331). He also remarks, in bk. III, with Gypsy pride: "A blacksmith once / Founded a dynasty, and raised on high / The leathern apron over armies spread / Between the mountains like a lake of steel" (p. 267). GE reports on 6 September 1864 that she is "trying a drama on a subject that has fascinated me" (Diary). That subject, inspired by Titian's Annunciation, is renunciation; and it could be worked out, in GE's estimation, only by having a Gypsy as heroine (see Life, III, 34-35). These entries, presumably, were made prior to 6 September 1864 when TSG was begun.

Entry 215

1. Grellman, p. 35. Cheiromancy is another name for palmistry, which Grellman denounces as a "deception of the Gipsey women."

2. Ibid., p. 37.

3. Ibid., p. 30.

4. Ibid., p. 49. This practice is obviously a reversal of the common lore that Gypsies steal children. GE uses it significantly in TSG where Fedalma, the daughter of the Zincalo chief, Zarca, is "stolen" by "marauding Spaniards" (bk. I, p. 139). The reunion of father and daughter is the inciting event of TSG.

5. Ibid., p. 196, n. 5; GE has this reference at the bottom of the page

as a footnote.
    6. Ibid., p. 53.

Entry 216
    1. In TSG the Moors, Jews, and Gypsies are in league against their common persecutors, the Spanish Catholics. Zarca, the Gypsy chieftain, fights along-side El Zagal, the king of the Moors, and both are served by Sephardo, who tells Don Silva: "I am a Jew; / And while the Christian persecutes my race, / I'll turn at need even the Christian's trust / Into a weapon and a shield for Jews" (bk. II, p. 200). The historical situation is a precedent for the dramatic events in TSG. The poem is set during the reign of Ferdinand and Isabella. Ferdinand is spoken of as "shrunken as a relic" and as one whom gold, gems, and brocade make look like a king (bk. I, p. 52). "Queen Isabel" is also mentioned (bk. I, p. 4). The "roaring bigotry" of Ferdinand and Isa-bella and their persecution of the Jews is denounced by Don Silva as "the cup / Filled with besotting venom, half infused / By avarice and half by priests" (bk. II, p. 200).
    2. This litany of expulsions, which emphasizes the wandering character of the Gypsies gave GE the theme for TSG: the need of a wandering people to find a homeland; thus, Zarca is presented as a Zincali Moses ("the saviour of his tribe," bk. I, p. 146) who intends "To lead his people over Bahr el Scham / And plant them on the shore of Africa" (bk. III, p. 233).
    3. Precisely what Zarca does is betray the Christians to the Moors: "I learned the secrets of the town's defence, . . . And so could serve the purpose of the Moor" (bk. IV, p. 331).

Entry 217
    1. Grellman, pp. 93-94.
    2. Ibid., p. 209, n. 5.
    3. Ibid., pp. 94-95.
    4. Ibid., p. 100. This version of the origin of the Gypsies' wandering is repeated in TSG by Blasco: God "sent the Gypsies wandering / In punishment because they sheltered not / Our Lady and Saint Joseph (and no doubt / Stole the small ass they fled with into Egypt)" bk. I, p. 49.
    5. Ibid., pp. 99-100.
    6. Ibid., pp. 100-101.

Entry 218
    1. Ibid., pp. 101-2.
    2. George Borrow, The Zincali; or, An Account of the Gypsies of Spain, 2 vols. (London: John Murray, 3d ed. 1843), I, 100-101. This is the edition GE consulted; whereas, Pott, whom she quotes, cites the 1841 ed. Borrow is alluded to in M, ch. 32, when young Cranch squinted at Mary Garth, "like the gypsies when Borrow read the New Testament to them."
    3. Borrow, I, 2-3; 50-51.

Entry 219
    1. GE is here quoting the 1841 ed. of Borrow as it is cited in August Friedrich Pott, Die Zigeuner in Europa und Asien, 2 vols. (Halle, 1845-46; rpt. Leipzig, 1964), I, 27.
    2. Borrow quoted in Pott, I, 31-32.
    3. Pott, I, 33.

Entry 220
    1. Ibid.
    2. Borrow quoted in Pott, I, 35.
    3. Borrow, II, *34; the asterisk indicates a special section of Borrow's book.
    4. Pott, I, 38.

5. Borrow, II, 125.

6. Ibid., I, 296-7.

7. Borrow's translation: "raging rabble, of brutal and animal propensities," Zincali, I, 45. Zarca's sense of his people includes but transcends this description: "My vagabonds are a seed more generous, / Quick as the serpent, loving as the hound, / And beautiful as disinherited gods" (bk. I, p. 160).

Entry 221

1. R. Dozy, Histoire des Musulmans d'Espagne, jusqu'à la conquête de l'Andalousie par les Almoravides (711-1110), 4 vols. (Leyden: E.J. Brill, 1861), I, 97-98. Translation: "Perhaps no one represents old times and paganism better than Moslim, the one-eyed son of Ocba. There wasn't even a trace of the Mohametan religion in him; nevertheless, he believed all the more strongly in the superstitious prejudices of paganism, in prophetic dreams, in mysterious words that issued from gharcads, a kind of thorn bush, which, in certain regions of Arabia during pagan times, took the place of oracles."

2. Borrow, I, 44-45.

3. Borrow, II, 114-5.

4. Borrow, I, 13-14; Borrow writes "Chingany," not "Chingarri," which is unmistakably what GE records.

5. Borrow, II, 91-93. Zarca makes it a point of pride that "Our people's faith / Is faithfulness," that "we will be true Each to the Other, and our common lot" (bk. III, p. 288). The idea of metempsychosis is hinted at once in a speech by Zarca and once in a speech of Fedalma's. Zarca says: "The Zincali have no god / Who speaks to them and calls them his, unless / I, Zarca, carry living in my frame/ The power divine that chooses them and saves" (bk. IV, p. 325). After his death, Fedalma becomes Zarca's female counterpart: "I am but as the funeral urn that bears / The ashes of a leader" (bk. V, p. 369); the suggestion being that in some way Zarca's soul has entered her body. In DD this idea, which Borrow shows as deriving from Buddhism, is more explicitly enunciated. The myth of the Buddha, who gave himself as a meal to a hungry tigress, says Deronda, is the myth of "the transmutation of self" (ch. 37). In the novel Daniel Charisi lives on in Mordecai, and Mordecai lives on in Daniel Deronda.

6. Borrow, I, 41.

7. Ibid., p. 69.

8. Entry 221 continues in entry 258 on p. 110.

Entry 222

1. C. O. Müller, The History and Antiquities of the Doric Race, trans. Henry Tufnell and George Cornewall Lewis (London: John Murray, 1830), vol. I, bk. ii, ch. 8, pp. 382-3.

2. Aeschylus, Agamemnon, ll. 1494-95; Franz, Des Aeschylos Oresteia, p. 116. Translation: "'Tis law as steadfast as the throne of Zeus-- / Our days are heritors of days gone by": epigraph to FH, ch. 48. According to her Diary GE was reading the Agamemnon for a second time in the spring and summer of 1865 (see entries for 10 May and 29 July). For her first reading of Aeschylus see 43, n. 10. Along with Aeschylus, GE indicates that she is reading "Theatre of the Greeks, Klein's Hist. of the Drama &c." This immersion in classical tragedy just at the moment that she is beginning a new novel (Diary, 29 March 1865: "I have begun a Novel") has suggested to Fred C. Thomson that FH was meant to be a tragedy with the fall of the House of Transome modeled on that of the House of Atreus; see "Felix Holt as Classic Tragedy," Nineteenth-Century Fiction, 16 (1961-62), 47-58. In FH, ch. 48, Harold Transome, having been told by Jermyn that he is his son, seeks confirmation of this statement from his mother and gets it. The epigraph is thus a statement of the law of Nemesis--of what GE calls the "hard entail of suffering" (FH, Author's Introduction).

3. Agamemnon, l. 1526; Franz, p. 118. Translation: "the very finger

tips."

4. _Agamemnon_, l. 1600; Franz, p. 124. _Translation_: "I myself know that exiles feed on hope."

5. _Agamemnon_, ll. 407-9; Franz, p. 32. _Translation_: "For whom each sent forth, them he knows; but to the home of each come urns and ashes, not living men" (_Aeschylus_, trans. Herbert Weir Smyth, II, 39). Something of this sentiment is expressed by Sephardo in _TSG_ when the young "Spaniards he knows by name are returned as corpses (bk. IV, pp. 327, 328-9).

Entry 223

1. _Eumenides_, ll. 287-90; Franz, pp. 242, 244. _Translation_: "Nay, be sure, not Apollo nor Athena's might can save thee from perishing, spurned and neglected, knowing not where in thy soul is joy--a bloodless victim of the powers below, a shadow of thyself" (_Aeschylus_, II, 301). The sentiment of these lines seems to be embodied in Mrs. Transome, who tells Esther, "For more than twenty years I have not had an hour's happiness. Harold knows it, and yet he is hard to me" (_FH_, ch. 50).

2. Franz, p. 242. _Translation_: "Time does away with all things, aging with them" (Aeschylus, _The Oresteia_, trans. David Young [Norman: University of Oklahoma Press, 1974], p. 109).

3. _The Phonecian Women_, l. 726. _Translation_: "Night, which gives cover to both sides, especially favors the agressor." GE wrote Mrs. Richard Congreve, 28 November 1863, that prior to "the 5th of November" she was "swimming in . . . Euripides" (_Letters_ IV, 116). I have found no direct reference to GE's reading of this tragedy in 1865; she was, nevertheless, still reading Euripides in the 70s (see _Letters_ V, 372, 391).

4. _Agamemnon_, ll. 718-9; Franz, p. 54.

5. _Agamemnon_, ll. 796-7; Franz, p. 60. GE gives an alternate line number used by Franz in the right margin rather than the standard number in the left margin. _Translation_: "Untaught by others, I can tell of my own weary life" (_Aeschylus_, II, 71).

6. _Agamemnon_, ll. 658-9; Franz, p. 50. GE again gives the alternate line number from the right margin. _Translation_: "Wrath working its will."

7. Euripides, _Hippolytos_, ll. 193-6. _Translation_: "We have an intense attachment to the present life because it has a bright appearance and because we have no experience of an afterlife; we have no word from the world below." See _Library_, p. 60, no. 676, describing an edition of Euripides in the GE - GHL library.

8. _Hippolytos_, l. 106. _Translation_: "A god who is worshipped in the night is an alien god."

Entry 224

1. Unidentified.

2. John Petherick, _Egypt, the Soudan, and Central Africa_ (Edinburgh and London: William Blackwood and Sons, 1861), p. 364; GHL reviewed this book for _Blackwood's Magazine_, 89 (1861), 440-53; he records Petherick's encounter with the spitting chief on p. 447.

3. John Lubbock, _Pre-Historic Times_ (London: Williams and Norgate, 1865), p. 458. GE indicates that she is "reading Lubbock's Prehistoric Ages" on 6 March 1868 (Diary); see also _Letters_, IV, 424, where GE tells Sara Hennell, "I am reading about savages and semi-savages." GE and GHL later read Lubbock's _Origin of Civilization_ (1870) in 1877 (_Letters_, VI, 364); see also entries 306 and 360, n. 1.

4. Ibid.

5. Ibid.

6. Ibid.

7. Max Müller, _Lectures on the Science of Language_, II, 164; a similar note on _hongi_ appears in Pratt and Neufeldt, p. 57.

Entry 225

1. Auguste Comte, Système de Politique Positive, ou Traité de Sociologie, Instituant la Religion de l'Humanité, 4 vols. (Paris, 1851-54). GE records reading the Politique Positive in a letter to Mrs. Richard Congreve in October 1863 (Letters, IV, 111) and in a letter to Mme. Bodichon on 4 December 1863 (Letters, IV, 119); GHL records his and GE's reading of it in his Journal, 10-11 January 1867 (Letters, IV, 331). GE quotes the Politique Positive in the quarry for FH. Her most extensive quotations from Comte's work are in a MS. notebook in the Nuneaton Public Libraries collection (GE 890 ELI-8), catalogued as "George Eliot's Commonplace Book," pp. 25-42. This notebook has been studied by Valerie Dodd, who has kindly allowed me to read a preliminary statement of her findings prior to their anticipated publication in Studies in Bibliography. An argument for the influence of Comte's Politique Positive on FH is made by W. F. T. Myers, "Politics and Personality in Felix Holt," Renaissance and Modern Studies, 10 (1966), 5-33.

Entry 227

1. Translation: "Each of us, without doubt, is directly subject to external necessity, which affects the race only through the individual. Furthermore, the pressure of such necessity does not affect us personally but only indirectly through the intervention of humanity. It is through the social order that each man carries the yoke of the material order and the vital order, the weight of which consequently increases with the influence exercised by one's contemporaries and one's predecessors. But the providential action of humanity protects its servants against less noble propensities, which it modifies more and more." (Translated with Louise Halpin Wiesenfarth.)

Entry 228

1. Daniel Neal, The History of the Puritans; or, Protestant Nonconformists; from the Reformation in 1517 to the Revolution in 1688: Comprising an Account of Their Principles; Their Attempts for a Farther Reformation in the Church; Their Sufferings; and the Lives and Characters of Their Most Considerable Divines, 5 vols. (1732-38; London: William Baynes & Son, 1822), II, 78-83. GE read Neal's Puritans as an aid to writing FH. The "Quarry for FH" contains a considerable body of notes from Neal. The notes in that MS. and the one in hand helped GE to shape the character of the Rev. Rufus Lyon (nicknamed "Revelations"), who in his actions bears a resemblance to the reverend Mr. Ainsworth; Neal's discussion of Ainsworth (II, 42) is quoted by GE in the quarry. She records that she is reading Neal in her diary for 23 July 1865; on 15 November she writes, "I have reached the fourth volume." This reading of Neal overlapped GE's rereading of the Bible: "Writing Mr. Lyon's story, which I have determined to insert as a narrative. Reading the Bible" (Diary, 16 August 1865).

Entry 231

1. GE always spells the name Neal with a final e.

Entry 232

1. Complete Prose Works of John Milton, Volume II: 1643-1648, ed. Ernest Sirluck, (New Haven: Yale Univ. Press, 1959), 492-3; see entry 32, no. 1, for GE on Milton.

Entry [233]

1. Ibid., p. 520. This is the first entry on a page without a number; sequentially the page would be [233].
    2. Ibid., pp. 534-5.
    3. Ibid., p. 554.
    4. Ibid., p. 562.
    5. Ibid., pp. 565-6.

Entry 234
  1. George Cornewall Lewis, An Essay on the Origin and Formation of the
Romance Languages (Oxford: D. A. Talboys, 1835), p. 11. Insofar as this book
contains "an examination of M. Raynouard's theory of the relation of the
Italian, Spanish, Provençal, and French to the Latin," GE may have read it as
an aid to taking up her work on TSG once again, which she did on 30 August
1866 (Diary). On 6 December 1866, in the midst of her revision of TSG, she
was reading Lewis's Astronomy of the Ancients (Diary).
  2. Ibid., p. 58.
  3. Ibid., pp. 35-36.

Entry 235
  1. Ibid., p. 40.
  2. Ibid., pp. 23-24n.
  3. Ibid., p. 40n.

Entry 236
  1. F. J. Fétis, "Résume philosophique de l'histoire de la musique,"
Bibliographie universelle des musiciens et biographie générale de la musique
(Meline, Brussels: Cans et Cie, 1837), I, cliii-vii passim. Translation: "I
do not wish to raise a doubt about the existence of a wind organ in the 4th
century because a passage of commentary by St. Augustine on the 56th psalm
leaves no doubt about the organ being known that early: 'All musical instruments are called organs, not only the one with the specific name "organ,"
which is large and has inflatable bellows, but whatever instrument is of a certain size and is used in song is also called an organ.' . . . The chronicles of
Eginhart, secretary to Charlemagne, give us a precise indication of the time
when the first wind organ appeared in Europe among the Gauls. In 757 Emperor
Constantine Corpronyme sent such an instrument to Pepin, who, it is said, had
it installed in the church of St. Cornelius of Compiegne."
  2. Ibid., p. clvii. Translation: "Without a doubt the first wind organs
were simply small portable boxes like those seen in some old paintings and in
manuscripts dating from the twelfth and thirteenth centuries."

Entry 237
  1. Ibid., p. clix. Translation: "As to small portable organs which
musicians carry attached to their bodies by straps and play with one hand while
pumping air with the other, the size of their keyboards is very small indeed,
with the hand able only to extend the space of a fifth. Such an instrument is
called a nimfali."
  2. Ibid., pp. clvii-viii. Translation: "The oldest organ built in central Europe of which there is a record is the one which George, a Venetian
priest, made in 826 for the palace of Aix-la-Chapelle by the order of Louis
the Debonnaire. This George seems to have been born a Greek, a fact, perhaps,
that strengthened the opinion that organs came to the West from Greece. But
he had travelled in Germany and it is quite possible that it was there that he
mastered the principles for building these instruments. Without a doubt Germany in the ninth century was the place where the most gifted organ-makers and
the most accomplished organists dwelt, because Pope John VIII (who was elected
in 872) wrote to Anno, bishop of Freising in Bavaria, asking him to send to
Italy an organ and along with it a musician who could assemble it as well as
play it.
  "Nothing could be more difficult than tuning an organ. Having only a
single reed-stop called royal, there was no register; and the keys were so
wide that they could only be sounded by banging them with the fist. . . .
There were organs whose keyboards, composed of a small number of keys as wide
as the hand and with a concave surface, could only be played with the fists or
the elbows."

Entry 239

1. Ibid., pp. clxvii-viii. <u>Translation</u>: "Even though the lowest note of a melody could be located on a single string, it would take too long to find all the other notes of the song on the same string. Guido suggested, therefore, that a melody which was familiar (whatever it might be), provided it was well known, be used as a model--its notes being compared to those of the melody one wanted to learn. Soon such repeated comparisons would imprint the intonations on the memory. In a letter which he wrote on this subject to a monk who was a friend of his, he said that he habitually availed himself in his own school of the melody of a hymn to St. John the Baptist:

> <u>Ut</u> gulant laxis,
> <u>Re</u>sonare fibris,
> <u>Mi</u>ra gestorum,
> <u>Fa</u>muli tuorum,
> <u>Sol</u>ve polluti,
> <u>La</u>bii reatum
> Sancte Johannes.

The children in the choir sang this hymn at the beginning and the end of the lesson he gave them. Note that in the melody Guido chose for his pupils, the pitch of the note is raised a degree for each of the syllables: <u>ut</u>, <u>re</u>, &c. Those who followed this monk concluded that he wanted to design a scale of notes with these syllables, even though he never used these names in any of his writings on music that survive him. . . . The honor of an invention to which Guido gave no thought, curiously enough, is his; whereas, no one dreamed of crediting him with the honor of devising a method of teaching by analogy, which he actually did, and which only recently has been presented as something new by Mr. Jacotot under the name of <u>universal</u> <u>teaching</u>." GE quotes the same hymn in Pforzheimer MS. 707, p. 141.

Entry 240

1. Ernest Renan, <u>Histoire</u> <u>générale</u> <u>et</u> <u>systeme</u> <u>comparé</u> <u>des</u> <u>langues</u> <u>sémitiques</u> (Paris: Calman Levy, 3rd ed. 1863), pp. 80-81; Dr. Williams's Library contains this edition with GE's pencilled markings; see <u>Library</u>, p. 168, no. 1796. GE indicates that she was reading this book on 20 November 1866 (Diary). This reading of Renan is related to different projects in GE's career: one is her study of philology; another is her composition of <u>TSG</u> in which a learned Jewish astrologer named Sephardo appears; and a third in her eventual composition of <u>DD</u>.

<u>Translation</u>. "Lepsius published two short treatises in 1836 [<u>Two</u> <u>Essays</u> <u>on</u> <u>Comparative</u> <u>Philology</u>: I. <u>On</u> <u>the</u> <u>Structure</u> <u>and</u> <u>Relationship</u> <u>of</u> <u>the</u> <u>Semitic</u>, <u>Indian</u>, <u>Ethiopian</u>, <u>Old</u> <u>Persian</u>, <u>and</u> <u>Old</u> <u>Egyptian</u> <u>Alphabets</u>; II. <u>On</u> <u>the</u> <u>Origin</u> <u>and</u> <u>Relationship</u> <u>of</u> <u>Numerals</u> <u>in</u> <u>the</u> <u>Indo-Germanic</u>, <u>Semitic</u> <u>and</u> <u>Coptic</u> <u>Languages</u>] wherein, by comparing the names of numbers and alphabets, he tried to establish the original unity of the Indo-European, Semitic, and Coptic language-families. Nevertheless, he recognized that Coptic formed a perfectly distinct and also almost different branch from Semitic, which itself was a branch of Indo-European. Schwarze [<u>The</u> <u>Ancient</u> <u>Egyptians</u>, 1843] held the same view. Coptic, according to this scholar, was a separate family by itself, analogous to Semitic languages in its grammar and to Indo-Germanic languages in its roots, but, generally, closer to the Semitic languages in its simplicity, its lack of logical structure, and in the degree of development it had attained. Theodore Benfey [<u>On</u> <u>the</u> <u>Relationship</u> <u>of</u> <u>the</u> <u>Egyptian</u> <u>Language</u> <u>to</u> <u>the</u> <u>Semitic</u> <u>Family</u>] took up the parallel once again."

Entry 241

1. Ibid., p. 81. <u>Translation</u>: "Benfey's conclusion is that the Semitic family should be divided into two branches separated by the isthmus of Suez: the Asiatic branch taking in all the languages usually called Semitic, and the

African encompassing the Coptic and the North African languages as far west
as the Atlantic Ocean."

    2. Ibid., pp. 82-83. <u>Translation</u>: "Bunsen adopted the same conclu-
sions. . . . Ernest Meier and Paul Boetticher sustained the same thesis with
arguments borrowed from the comparative study of roots. . . . Let us add, however, that these various studies were not lacking in contradictions. Pott,
Ewald, and Wenrich protested at different times the abuse of applying a comparative methodology to dissimilar languages. Ewald especially, commenting
on Benfey's book, vehemently insisted on the wrong that weak similarities did
to philology by pouring over the rigor of this science the taint of a vague
and arbitrary methodology."

    3. Ibid., pp. 87-88, 89. <u>Translation</u>: "Without a doubt the indispen-
sable element needed for the comparative study of languages is a knowledge of
the inflection of nouns and verbs. Now it is precisely on this point that the
Egyptian language differs from the Semitic. Egyptian can hardly claim a place
among inflected languages. The more one traces its primitive condition, the
more one finds a language similar to Chinese, a monosyllabic language without
cement, so to speak, expressing modalities by a grouping of exponents, but not
by variations on the same root. . . . It is, consequently, necessary to create
for the language and civilization of Egypt a family all by itself, which we
can call, if we choose, <u>Hamitic</u>."

Entry 242

    1. Ibid., p. 173. <u>Translation</u>: "It was principally in the Magreb that
the grammatical movement inaugurated by the Jewish school in the East was most
successful. Menahem ben-Serouk, of Tortose, and Dounasch ben Lebrat, of Fez
(960 or 970) composed the oldest Hebrew dictionary."

    2. Ibid., p. 174. <u>Translation</u>: "The works of this early school are
nearly all written in Arabic. When, towards the end of the twelfth century,
the Jews no longer spoke this language, preference was given to books written
in Hebrew. . . . The Kimchis of Narbonne wrote the best known works of this
new school. . . . It was only in the sixteenth century, at the moment when the
study of Hebrew was passing into the hands of the Christians, that the fame of
the Kimchis was superseded by that of Elias Levita (d. Venice, 1549), who developed the rabbinical method to the highest degree of perfection that it could
attain and who became the teacher of Christian Hebraists. . . . Prior to this
time the study of Hebrew had been exclusively the domain of Jews. The small
number of Christians who knew the language had either been Jews or the sons
of converts from Judaism."

    3. Ibid., p. 175. <u>Translation</u>: "The efforts of Raymond Lulle and the
decrees of the Council of Vienna in 1311 did not succeed in making Hebrew a
serious course of study. Only the Dominicans, to sharpen their polemic against
the Jews, trained a few scholars in rabbinical wisdom."

Entry 243

    1. Ibid., p. 175. <u>Translation</u>: "[Study in the Scriptures] at the end
of the fifteenth and the beginning of the sixteenth century created a lively
interest among scholars [in the study of Hebrew]. . . . Jews were, naturally,
the teachers of this new generation of Hebraists. In order to study Hebrew
at this time one had to travel great distances, place oneself under the guidance of a rabbi (whose words were oracles), and pay for lessons in gold."

    2. Ibid., p. 176. <u>Translation</u>: "Reuchlin is the man whose name stands
above all others in this revolution of learning, which brought about changes
that significantly modified the history of mankind. His three volumes <u>On the
Rudiments of Hebrew</u> (1506) was the first grammar composed for the use of
Christians, and it established the technical terms that were used everywhere
in European schools."

    3. Ibid., p. 177. <u>Translation</u>: "Elias Levita called down upon himself
the hostility of the synagogue because he raised doubts about the antiquity of

vowel-points."
    4. Ibid., p. 188, n. 1.

Entry 244
    1. Ibid., pp. 166-7. <u>Translation</u>: "As to an everyday speech, it can be said that the Jews adopted four different languages during the Babylonian captivity: Chaldean, Arabic, Spanish, and German. Arabic is still spoken by Jews in Africa. Spanish and German actually became the national language for two large fractions of the Jewish race, and they carried these languages with them in their migrations. So that the majority of Central European Jews, originating in Alsace and southern Germany, spoke, almost up until the present, a jargon of German blended with Hebrew (Jewishgerman), full of archaisms and artificial changes. (Jost, in the Encyclopaedia of Ersch and Gruber, article on <u>Judenteutsch</u>.) On the other hand, the language of the Jews of Constantinople, who emigrated to Spain, remains to this day the Spanish of the fifteenth century. By one of those caprices that is found only in the history of the Jews, the aforementioned languages became in their turn two dead and respected languages. So, among French Jews who were uneducated, many still knew some words of Spanish and German because they heard them spoken by their fathers; these words, presenting themselves as the remnants of a national language, were taken to be Hebrew. The custom among German and Polish Jews of writing and printing Jewishgerman in Hebrew characters has given rise to a similar misunderstanding--the notion that the use of the Hebrew language is still common."

Entry 246
    1. Ibid., pp. 214-5. <u>Translation</u>: "This civilization is for us the result of the mingling of the Hamites with the Semites and Aryans on the banks of the Tigris, just as the Phonecian civilization is the result of the mingling of Semites and Hamites along the shores of the Red and Mediterranean Seas. There is, indeed, in these two civilizations a body of traits which cannot be explained by either the Semitic or Aryan character taken by itself. Nowhere do we find the Semitic people by themselves achieving a developed art, commerce, or political life. Semitic paganism, situated in Babylon, is bound up in part with a mythology that may be Aryan. The idea of an absolute monarchy centered on a single great individual who is served by a vast hierarchy of functionaries--an idea that was first brought to life in western Asia by Assyria--is profoundly opposed to the spirit of the Semitic people. Royalty established itself among the Jews only in imitation of foreign powers, and it was incessantly combatted by the prophets, who were the true representatives of the Semitic spirit and were equally enemies of a secular kingship, of a materialistic civilization, and of the influence of Assyria. On the other hand, the great scientific and industrial achievements of Assyrian civilization do not arise from the Aryan character, which in antiquity seemed not to interest itself in applied science. Consequently, one is led to fix on the banks of the Tigris as the first center of a population (analogous to that of Egypt) at that time basically Semitic, which made its language the popular language of these regions and then created political and military classes, which, though not numerous, were Aryan in origin. These last were the true Chaldeans, who gave their name to a nation and language, somewhat in the way that the names of France, of Burgundy, and like names of Germanic origin are given in our own time to countries that are in no way Teutonic."
    The Chaldean plains are mentioned by Sephardo in <u>TSG</u>, bk. 2, when he is speaking with Don Silva: "I hold less / Than Aben-Ezra, of that aged lore / Brought by long centuries from Chaldaean plains." Moslems and Jews are also associated together in the poem by virtue of their common origin (as well as their common enemy). Zarca calls out in bk. 4: "Now hear me, Moors and Hebrews of Bedmar, / Our kindred by the warmth of Eastern blood!"
    2. Ibid., p. 351. <u>Translation</u>: "DeSacy's conclusions were: 1) that

writing was not known to the Arabs of Hedjag and Nedjed more than a century before the Hegira; 2) that the alphabet was transmitted to the Arabs by the Syrians; 3) that writing, before the founding of Islam and even a long time after it, was known almost exclusively to Jews and Christians."

Entry 247

1. Algernon Charles Swinburne, *Atalanta in Calydon. A Tragedy.* (London: Edward Moxon, 1865), p. 40. GE probably read Swinburne in the autumn of 1866. Her entry comes between one from Renan (whom she was reading on 6 November 1866) and one on musical instruments (about which she was reading 15 September 1866); her reading of Fétis (see entries 236-9) seems to be the beginning of her study of this subject. The *Atalanta* was reviewed in the *Fortnightly Review*, I (1865), 75-80, by J. Leicester Warren; this was the first issue of this new journal edited by GHL. Exercising editorial prerogative, GHL altered Warren's text on p. 75 to call Swinburne one of "our contemporaneous minor poets" (see *Letters*, VIII, 356 n. 6). GHL and Swinburne met in December 1865, shortly after the review appeared, at a party given by Moxon (*Swinburne Letters*, ed. Cecil Y. Lang, 6 vols. [New Haven: Yale Univ. Press, 1962], I, 143, 149). Swinburne recalled that meeting to Clement K. Shorter, describing GHL as "a hideous smirking scribbler," in 1896: "I only met him once, but I remember not only that he was the ugliest of human beings I ever saw except perhaps his consort George Eliot, but that it was such a mean and vulgar ugliness as suggested nothing but the idea of a smart, pert, impudent counter-jumper" (ibid., VI, 117).

2. *Atalanta in Calydon*, pp. 37-38.

3. Ibid., p. 54.

4. Algernon Charles Swinburne, *Poems and Ballads* (London: Edward Moxon, 1866), p. 202.

Entry 248

1. Ibid., p. 233; the scansion of the first two lines quoted anticipates GE's thorough study of prosody in entries 284-93.

2. *Poems and Ballads*, p. 237.

3. Ibid., p. 238.

Entry 249

1. François Joseph Fétis, *Antoine Stradivari* (Paris: Vuillaume, Luthier, 1856), pp. 3-6 passim. This book served as the inspiration of "Stradivarius" (1873), a poem in praise of simple fact and good workmanship: "'Tis God gives skill, / But not without men's hands: He could not make / Antonio Stradivari's violins / Without Antonio," says Stradivarius as the poem ends (*LJOP*, p. 218).

Entry 250

1. Ibid., pp. 7-8.

2. Ibid., p. 10.

3. Ibid., pp. 11-12.

Entry 251

1. Ibid., p. 12. *Translation*: "The Roman praises you with the lyre; the Barbarian sings with the harp, the Greek with the cithara, and the Briton with the crouth."

2. Ibid., pp. 15-18 passim.

3. Ibid., pp. 19-20n.

4. Ibid., p. 19.

5. Ibid., pp. 27-28.

6. Ibid., p. 30.

Entry 252

1. Ibid., pp. 31-34 passim. *Translation*: "viols without sides."

2. Ibid., pp. 33-34. <u>Translation</u>: "The <u>rubebe</u>, the <u>gigue</u>--in short, the four classes of the <u>rebec</u> kind which we have already found established from the fifteenth century, namely, treble, alto, tenor, and bass, were the popular instruments in the hands of minstrels, and served in general for dancing and for street singers" (F. J. Fétis, <u>Notice of Anthony Stradivari</u>, trans. John Bishop [London: Robert Cocks, 1864], p. 31).

3. Fétis, <u>Antoine Stradivari</u>, p. 35.

4. Ibid., p. 39.

Entry [253]

1. GE did not number this page.

2. Fétis, p. 41.

3. Ibid., pp. 46-47.

4. Ibid., pp. 49-50.

5. Ibid., pp. 52-54 passim.

Entry 254

1. Ibid., p. 55. <u>Translation</u>: "When he worked, no one demanded a tone of that power and brilliance which is now required. So far from it, an instrument which should have possessed such a degree of sonority would have offended the ears of an audience accustomed to the tranquil music of which we still possess specimens" (Bishop, p. 51).

2. Ibid., p. 59.

3. Ibid., p. 63. "I am one best / Here in Cremona, using sunlight well / To fashion finest maple till it serves / More cunningly than throats, for harmony," says Stradivarius in GE's poem (<u>LJOP</u>, p. 216).

4. Ibid., p. 67.

5. "Antonio / At sixty-nine wrought placidly his best," writes GE in "Stradivarius" (<u>LJOP</u>, p. 212).

6. Fétis, pp. 68-69. <u>Translation</u>: "The bar alone is too weak, in consequence of the gradual rise in the pitch, from the beginning of the eighteenth century; the inevitable result of which has been a considerable increase of tension and a much greater pressure exercised on the belly. Hence the necessity has arisen for re-barring all the old violins and violon-cellos" (Bishop, p. 65).

Entry 255

1. Ibid., p. 72. <u>Translation</u>: His life "was entirely passed away in a quiet workshop, before a bench, with compass or tool in hand" (Bishop, p. 68).

2. Fétis, p. 75.

3. Ibid., p. 76. GE uses this information in "Stradivarius": "That plain white-aproned man . . . stood at work / Patient and accurate full fourscore years" (<u>LJOP</u>, p. 212). "Naldo, a painter of eclectic school" finds Stradivarius dull and tries to find hidden motives in the master's work: "Perhaps thou hast some pleasant vice to feed-- / The love of louis d'ors in heaps of four, / Each violin a heap . . ." (<u>LJOP</u>, pp. 213-4).

4. Ibid., pp. 106-7.

5. Ibid., pp. 108-9; GE has Stradivarius remark on Guarnerius: "His quality declines: he spoils his hand / With over-drinking" (<u>LJOP</u>, p. 216).

Entry 256

1. <u>Wilhelm Meisters Wanderjahre oder die Entsagenden</u>, bk. 1, ch. 4; <u>Goethe's sämmtliche Werke</u>, XVIII, 38-39. This same passage was quoted earlier in entry 18 with slight variations.

Entry 257

1. Fétis, pp. 109-10.

2. Edward William Lane, <u>An Account of the Manners and Customs of the</u>

<u>Modern</u> <u>Egyptians</u>, 2 vols. (London: Charles Knight, 1836), II, 66-67; "place
of the bow" comes from Fétis's "<u>lieu</u> <u>de</u> <u>l'archet</u>," p. 8.
    3. Ibid., pp. 69-72 passim.
    4. Ibid., p. 74.
    5. Ibid., pp. 75-81 passim.
    6. Unidentified.

Entry 258
    1. George Borrow, <u>The</u> <u>Zincali</u>, I, 69-70; see entry 218, n. 2.
    2. Ibid., pp. 37-38.
    3. Ibid., pp. 200-208 passim.

Entry 259
    1. Samuel Daniel, <u>Musophilus</u>: <u>Containing</u> <u>a</u> <u>generall</u> <u>defence</u> <u>of</u> <u>learning</u>
(London: Simon Waterson, 1599), l. 11. The quotations from Daniel in entries
259 to 265 reflect a good many of GE's sentiments on the value of knowledge,
the importance of poetry, the limitations of critics, and the vagaries of
fame. These same sentiments are rendered dramatically in her poem on artistic
creation, "The Legend of Jubal," which she began writing on 5 October 1869
(Diary). GE had certainly read Daniel and made these entries in her notebook
before that date. The dating of entries 267-9 (see 269, n. 1) from January
1868 establishes this fact.
    2. <u>Musophilus</u>, ll. 21-32.
    3. Ibid., ll. 54-58.
    4. Ibid., ll. 62-71.

Entry 260
    1. Ibid., ll. 74-85.
    2. Ibid., ll. 99-104.
    3. Ibid., ll. 177-80.

Entry 261
    1. Ibid., ll. 191-200.
    2. Ibid., ll. 209-20.
    3. Ibid., ll. 295-8.

Entry 262
    1. Ibid., ll. 301-6.
    2. Daniel writes <u>Philocosmus</u>.
    3. <u>Musophilus</u>, ll. 424-5.
    4. Ibid., ll. 440-43.
    5. Ibid., ll. 490-93.
    6. Ibid., ll. 504-5.

Entry 263
    1. Ibid., ll. 567-78.
    2. Ibid., ll. 767-72.
    3. Ibid., ll. 905-20; ll. 905-12 and 915-8 are used as the epigraph of
<u>M</u>, ch. 68. This epigraph works two ways in the chapter, suggesting, first,
how Bulstrode thinks himself very different from Raffles, an obvious profli-
gate; and, second, how, from the narrator's point of view, the straightforward
Caleb Garth deserves to be distinguished from the devious Bulstrode.

Entry 264
    1. Ibid., ll. 939-50.

Entry 265
    1. Ibid., ll. 955-80.
    2. "To Henry Wriothesly Earle of Southampton," ll. 1-4, 29-30, 53-57.

GE quotes ll. 1-4 in a letter of 9 November 1871 to Alexander Main and affectionately calls the poet "old Daniel" and compares his lines to "Goethe's famous--'Wie nie sein Brod mit Tränen ass'" (Letters, V, 213).

Entry 266

1. Alfred Tennyson, The Princess: A Medley, 2nd ed. (London: Moxon, 1848), pp. 150-51; pt. VII, ll. 161-74. In GE's review of Maud (WR, 64 [1855], 596-601), which she did not like, she called Tennyson "the highest order of poet" and praised The Princess: "The 'Princess', too, with all that criticism has to say against it, has passages of inspiration and lyrical gems imbedded in it, which make a fresh claim on our gratitude" (Essays, p. 191). Her liking for the poem is also expressed in her scattered quotations from it: see Essays, pp. 200, 205; Letters, VI, 311.

Entry 269

1. Max Müller, "Buddhist Pilgrims, 1857," Chips from a German Workshop (1st ed. 1867; New York: Charles Scribners, 1869), I, 267-70. GE has a brief note in her Diary for 21 January 1868: "Fin[ished] Max Müller's Essays." In her "Quarry for FH" GE refers to Chips as "Max Müller's Essays" in the table of contents. A number of entries that were first made in the quarry were later transferred to this notebook; see, e.g., entries 270-75, 299-305. The notes on Buddha's Cave do not appear in the "Quarry for FH" but they are a continuation of the material GE was copying from Chips. When she ran out of space in the quarry she continued her entries in the notebook. This entry therefore can be confidently dated 1868.

Entry 270

1. These figures, with some slight variations, dated "Aug. 1868," appear in Pratt and Neufeldt, p. 94, n. 2; the editors suggest that they originate in the census material for 1861.
2. This note first appears in "Quarry for FH," [p. 4]; see also Pratt and Neufeldt, p. 94, n. 2. For the pertinence of these notes to FH, see Fred C. Thomson, "The Genesis of Felix Holt," PMLA, 74 (1959), 578.
3. "Quarry for FH," [p. 43].
4. Ibid., [p. 3].
5. Ibid. The inspiration behind these notes seems to be the "Parliamentary Committee Report on Agriculture of 1833"; rpt. as "Report of the Select Committee on Agriculture," Annual Register 1833, vol. 75, pp. 341-54.

Entry 271

1. John Ayrton Paris, Pharmacologia; Being an Extended Inquiry into the Operations of Medicinal Bodies upon Which Are Founded the Theory and Art of Prescribing (9th ed. London: Samuel Highley, 1843); see entries 131-3 for GE's earlier use of Paris. GE's occasional citation of page numbers from the Pharmacologia in the "Quarry for FH" suggests that she used Paris's 9th ed. GE wrote these notes for background information on the quack remedies that are discussed by Mrs. Holt, Felix, and Rufus Lyon in FH, chs. 5 and 6. Mrs. Holt believes in the efficacy of the medicines her deceased husband once concocted; Felix, who was an apothecary's apprentice for five years, does not. He says to Mr. Lyon, "I know that the Cathartic Pills are a drastic compound which may be as bad as poison to half the people who swallow them; that the Elixir is an absurd farrago of a dozen incompatible things; and that the Cancer Cure might as well be bottled ditch-water" (FH, ch. 6).

These entries from Paris appear in a different arrangement in "Quarry for FH," [pp. 13-21]. In citing sources I will give the pages from both Pharmacologia and the quarry to suggest the extent of rearrangement from one notebook to the other. The date 1866 (the year FH was published) which GE gives in parentheses does not refer either to the time these notes were first taken in the summer of 1865 (see Fred C. Thomson, "Genesis of Felix Holt,"

PMLA, 74 [1959], 576-84), or to the time they were transcribed into the notebook, which entry 270 demonstrates to have been after "Aug. 1868." They were probably rewritten "soon after September 1868," the date that Anna T. Kitchel gives for GE's beginning the "Quarry for Middlemarch" (see Nineteenth-Century Fiction, 4 [1950], 2). These transcribed notes can be seen as supplementing those on the medical background of M found in the "Quarry for Middlemarch," which shows that Kitchel was not aware of GE's reading in Paris's Pharmacologia (see entry 274, n. 4).

    2. Paris, pp. 24-25 and p. 24n; "Quarry for FH" [p. 13].
    3. Paris, p. 25; "Quarry" [p. 15].
    4. Paris, p. 26; "Quarry" [p. 15].
    5. Paris, p. 35; "Quarry" [p. 15].
    6. Paris, p. 28; "Quarry" [p. 13].
    7. Paris, pp. 50-51 and 51n; "Quarry" [p. 16].
    8. Paris, p. 20; "Quarry" [p. 14].

Entry 272
    1. Paris, p. 41n; "Quarry" [p. 13].
    2. Paris, pp. 42-46 passim; "Quarry" [pp. 15-16].
    3. Paris, pp. 47-49 passim; "Quarry" [p. 16].

Entry 273
    1. Paris, pp. 75-77; "Quarry" [pp. 17-18].
    2. Paris, p. 78n.; "Quarry" [p. 18]. Paris calls this concoction a "heterogeneous farrago"; in like manner, Felix Holt calls his father's Elixir an "absurd farrago" (FH, ch. 6).
    3. Paris, pp. 94-97 passim; "Quarry" [p. 18].
    4. Paris, p. 22; "Quarry" [p. 14].
    5. Paris, p. 163; "Quarry" [p. 14].
    6. Translation: "Things that are alike have like powers."

Entry 274
    1. Paris, pp. 107-09; "Quarry" [pp. 21-22].
    2. Paris, p. 110; "Quarry" [p. 22].
    3. Paris, p. 83; "Quarry" [p. 23].
    4. Paris, p. 127; "Quarry" [p. 23]. This entry appears in GE's "Quarry for Middlemarch," p. 34; its source is listed as "unidentified," p. 41, n. 88.

Entry 275
    1. Paris, pp. 129n-30n; "Quarry" [p. 23].
    2. "Cinchona," Chambers Encyclopaedia (London: W. & R. Chambers, 1862), III, 35-36.

Entry 276
    1. GE reviewed Robert Bell's 1854 ed. of the Poetical Works of Geoffrey Chaucer, vols. 1-4, in Westminster Review, 64 (1855), USA ed. 156-7. Her one quotation from Chaucer emphasized the importance of his language:

> And for there is so great diversity
> In English, and in writing of our tongue,
> So I pray God that none miswrite thee
> Ne thee mismetre for defaut of tongue.

On 15 September 1866 GE returns to this same theme when she writes in her Diary that she is "reading Chaucer to study English." For this purpose she did not read Bell but probably a current printing of Thomas Tyrwhitt's edition, for instance, The Poetical Works of Geoffrey Chaucer (London: E. Moxon, 1851). She cites "Tyrwhitt, essay on Lang. & Versifn. of Chaucer" in her Folger notebook for M (see Pratt and Neufeldt, p. 4), and she gives a similar list of the tales in the Berg notebook (ibid., pp. 178-9).

Nearly the same order of tales that appears here appears in the "Quarry for FH"; all the quotations in entry 277 below also appear there. GE's use of superscripts--19[1], 20[2], 21[3]--shows that she wants the order of the tales to be: "Nonnes Priestes," "Monkes," "Second Nonnes." In the "Quarry for FH" (where 23, not 24, numbered tales are given, the order is: "Monkes," "Nonnes Priestes," "Second Nonnes"; this is also the order in the Berg notebook.

Entry 277

1. "The Miller's Tale," ll. 3774-75; see Works of Geoffrey Chaucer, ed. F. N. Robinson (Boston: Houghton Mifflin Co., 1957), p. 54. This quotation serves as epigraph to M, ch. 12. Like Absalon before him, Fred Vincy goes to pay suit and finds a Nicholas in his way. His suit is to the mean-spirited Peter Featherstone, who sends him to Nicholas Bulstrode for a letter of certification before giving him any money.

2. "The Man of Law's Tale," ll. 701-2; see Robinson, p. 69.

3. "The Wife of Bath's Prologue," ll. 440-42; see Robinson, p. 80. This quotation serves as epigraph to M, ch. 65. Lydgate scolds Rosamond for having written to his uncle Godwin; her response is tears. "Nevertheless," reads the chapter's last sentence, "she had mastered him."

4. "The Squire's Tale," ll. 221-4; see Robinson, p. 130.

5. "The Franklin's Tale," ll. 1252-55; see Robinson, p. 141.

6. "The Physician's Tale," ll. 50-54; see Robinson, p. 145. The first two and one-half lines serve as epigraph to M, ch. 21. Dorothea leaves off crying (Casaubon had reprimanded her for criticizing his scholarship) to receive Ladislaw, who tells her how worthless Casaubon's work is. Her surprise gives way to a defence of her husband. When she and Casaubon are alone, Dorothea apologizes for having criticized him earlier. In the chapter her instinct is confirmed by Ladislaw's knowledge, but her response is pity, not triumph.

Entry 278

1. Philip Smith, A History of the World from the Earliest Records to the Present Time, vol. I. Ancient History (London: Walton and Maberly, 1864), p. 79.

Entry 279

1. This entry appears in different colored inks. The names of the Hebrew letters, the letters themselves, the commentary to the right of Cheth, Theth, and Iod, and the footnote are in black ink. All other commentary, beginning with "gutturale très faible" is in purple ink. The source of and purpose of this entry is uncertain. The alphabet most closely resembles one reproduced in Nouveau Larousse Illustre, 7 vols. (Paris: Librairie Larousse [1898]), V, 57, which includes such annotations as "gutturale très faible" and "gutt. forte." The recording of the alphabet may have been supplemented by GE's reading of a work like J. W. Donaldson's The New Cratylus (see entry 307, n. 1), which develops a relationship between the Hebrew and Greek alphabet (pp. 96-107) that clearly interests GE on this page. Following an entry on hieroglyphic writing, this one on the Hebrew alphabet seems to be part of her study of philology generally, rather than of Hebrew specifically. GE later reproduced part of this alphabet in her Hebrew grammar; see Library, p. 72, no. 799, and my review of it in Literary Research Newsletter, 3 (1978), 131-4. For a commentary on GE's study of Hebrew, see William Baker, Studies in Bibliography and Booklore, 11 (1976), 75-84.

Entry 280

1. In her index for the notebook, under the letter "L," GE describes this entry as "Letters or vocal sounds." Max Müller treats "The Physiological Alphabet" in Lectures on the Science of Language (see 207, n. 1), II, 95-159; this may be one source of this entry. Another seems to be F. Baudry,

Grammaire comparée des langues classiques: 1re Partie: Phonétique (Paris: A. Durand et Pedone Lauriel, 1868), p. 32, where an arrangement of vowels suggests the one in GE's text. GE was also interested in the work of Alexander J. Ellis (see Letters, VI, 5) whom Müller cites extensively, pp. 97-98n. The words "(thorn)," "(wen)," and "These are runic letters" are written in pencil. The word "thorn" was originally placed before "ᚧ," but erased; "wen" was originally before "Þ" and was also erased.

Entry 281
    1. Pausanias, Description of Greece, Bk. III. "Laconia," XVII, 7-9.

Entry 282
    1. GE's letters indicate that she read and studied the Iliad in 1868. She writes to Sara Hennell on 22 March, saying that "I am studying that semi-savage poem, the Iliad. How enviable it is to be a classic. When a verse in the Iliad bears six different meanings and nobody knows which is right, a commentator finds this equivocalness in itself admirable!" (Letters, IV, 424). (GE is here referring to a remark of Samuel Clarke, editor of Homer [see entry 41b, n. 2], which she records in "Quarry for FH": "IL. V.150. There are half a dozen ways of interpreting this. Ab Eustathio laudatur haec ambiguitas, says Clarke.") GE's interest in Homer and Homeric scholarship is evident earlier and later as well. She quotes Homer extensively in "Interesting Extracts," pp. 57-61. She read Mark Pattison's article on the Homeric scholar Friedrich August Wolf in the North British Review, 42 (June 1865), 245-99 (see Letters, V, 124, n. 6), and Wolf's own book Prolegomena ad Homerum in December 1870 (see Letters, V, 124, and n. 6). She discussed Homer with John Fiske in November 1873, and he reports in a letter to his wife that "I found her thoroughly acquainted with the whole literature of the Homeric question; and she seems to have read all of Homer in Greek, too, and could meet me everywhere. She didn't talk like a blue-stocking . . . but like a plain woman, who talked of Homer as simply as she would of flat-irons" (Letters, V, 464). Pforzheimer MS. 711 contains a page and a third of bibliography on the "Homeric Question," pp. 15-[16]. GE continued reading Homer, practically speaking, until the end of her life. In her Diary for 1879 (Berg Collection, New York Public Library) GE made the following entries on her reading of Homer from 31 March to 20 December 1879: 31 March: "Iliad in Monro's ed." 12, 15, 18 April: "Homer." 21 April: "Homer III." 22 April: "Homer IV." 25 April: "Finished Iliad IV." 6 May: "Homer," 1 June: "Finished Iliad VI." 20 December: "Finished the Iliad." See also Pratt and Neufeldt, passim. The summary of the arguments of the Iliad in this entry is taken from Alexander Pope's translation of it from 1715-20. See entry 41b, n. 1, for GE's earlier use of Pope.

Entry 283
    1. GE first read the Odyssey in Greek in 1855 (see Letters II, 202 n. 9). She began reading it again in January 1880 (see Letters VII, 242). The summary of the arguments of the Odyssey is taken from Pope's translation of 1725-26.

Entry 284
    1. This quotation from George Gascoigne's essay and the quotations from other essays that follow it are taken from Joseph Haslewood, ed., Ancient Critical Essays upon English Poets and Poesy, 2 vols. (London: Robert Triphook, 1815); the passage from Gascoigne is from Haslewood, II, 3-4. In 1869 GE wrote the draft of an essay entitled "Versification" based on the notes set down in entries 284-93, supplemented by [J. A. Symonds] "Blank Verse," Cornhill Magazine, 15 (1867), 620-40 (see Diary, 30 May 1867, where GE mentions a "good article on Blank Verse in an old Cornhill"), Edwin Guest, A History of English Rhythms, 2 vols. (London: W. Pickering, 1838), and, some time later, by James J. Sylvester, The Laws of Verse; or, Principles of

<u>Versification</u> (London: Longmans, Green, 1870). "Versification" was never published by GE; it is printed below in the Uncollected Writings. GE's interest in the technical aspects of versification intensified with her writing of <u>TSG</u>, <u>TLJ</u>, a variety of shorter poems, and epigraphs ("mottoes") for <u>M</u> and <u>DD</u>.

    2. William Webbe, "A Discussion of English Poetrie," Haslewood, II, 32.

    3. Ibid., p. 55.

Entry 285

    1. Ibid., p. 61.

    2. K. James, "A Treatise of the Airt of Scottis Poesie," Haslewood, II, 112-3. GE changed the phrase "makdome, or her fairnes" first to "makdom and her fairnesse" and then to "makdom and fairness" in <u>M</u>., ch. 15, when alluding to woman's form and beauty, as referred to in King James's essay.

    3. Haslewood, II, 200. This entire passage is quoted in GE's essay "Versification." Daniel expresses GE's view that "power over the minds of men is . . . the measure of perfection." Daniel's "A Defence of Ryme" was a successful rebuttal of Thomas Campion's attempt to introduce classical versification into English poetry in "Observations in the Art of English Poesie." GE quotes Campion below in entries 289, 291-3.

Entry 286

    1. Haslewood, II, 200-201.

    2. Ibid., p. 202.

Entry 287

    1. Ibid., pp. 202-3.

    2. Ibid., pp. 214-5.

    3. Ibid., p. 216. <u>Translation</u>: "Error, when made fashionable, is believed as truth among us."

    4. Ibid., p. 217.

Entry 288

    1. Ibid., pp. 217-8.

    2. Ibid., p. 218.

    3. Ibid., p. 278; GE seems to have spelled the poet's name "Spenser" in a mistaken attribution of this passage, which she crossed out; otherwise, she spells it "Spencer."

    4. Ibid., p. 280.

Entry 289

    1. Ibid., p. 260. GE insists in "Versification" that "English verse" was written by "poets and not by carpenters." Harvey's and Spenser's discussion of the use of the word <u>carpenter</u> may have contributed to GE's choice of a foil to the poet.

Entry 290

    1. II. 11. 1-24. The play is dated 1575; its author is unknown, though it has been attributed both to J. Still and to William Stevenson. In Pratt and Neufeldt, p. 7, GE has a note on the play: "Gammer Gurton's Needle, 1551, acted first in Christ's College, Cambridge, written by Stite, afterwards Bishop of Bath and Wells." (The editors mistakenly transcribe "Stite" for "Still.") GE is quoting Thomas Warton, <u>The History of English Poetry</u>, 3 vols. (London, 1840), III, 180.

    2. "Confessio Goliae," 11. 45-48. <u>Translation</u>: "In the tavern I intend to die; / Let the wine be at my dying lips, / That the angels' choirs, when they come, may say: / 'To this tippler, O God, be kind'" (translated by Matthew Hogan). See Thomas Wright, ed., <u>The Latin Poems Commonly Attributed to Walter Mapes</u> (Hildesheim: Georg Olms, 1968), p. 73.

Entry 291

    1. Campion has "Roma viribus," not "viribus Roma." Horace, Epodes XVI. 2. Translation: "And Rome by her own strength is falling."

    2. Seneca, Epistles CVII.ii. Translation: "The Fates lead the willing but pull along the unwilling."

    3. Virgil, Eclogues I.1. Translation: "You, Tityrus, lying refreshed beneath the shady beech-tree."

    4. Catullus, Carmina V.6. Translation: "We must sleep one eternal night."

Entry 292

    1. Thomas Campion, "Observations in the Art of English Poesie. Wherein it is demonstratively prooved, and by example confirmed, that the English toong will receive eight severall kinds of numbers, proper to it selfe, which are all in this booke set forth, and were never before this time by any man attempted" (1602), Haslewood, II, 168-9.

Entry 293

    1. Ibid., pp. 170-72. This long passage from Campion (running from entry 289 to 291-3) became the object of attack in GE's essay "Versification" where she summarizes it and quotes from it to suggest the absurdity of its rules and logic.

    2. Haslewood, II, vin. GE uses this epithet in "Versification."

    3. Ibid., p. xviiin. GE uses and confirms this judgment in "Versification."

    4. Ibid., p. xv and n.

    5. Ibid., p. 69.

    6. See entry 284, n. 1 above.

Entry 294

    1. De Natura Deorum II.xxxviii.72. Translation: "Those . . . who carefully reviewed and so to speak retraced all the lore of ritual were called 'religious' from relegere (to retrace or re-read), like 'elegant from eligere (to select), 'diligent' from diligere (to care for), 'intelligent' from intellegere (to understand); for all these words contain the same sense of 'picking out' (legere) that is present in 'religious'" (Cicero, De Rerum Natura; Academica, trans. H. Rackham, Loeb Classical Library [1933; Cambridge, Mass.: Harvard Univ. Press, and London: William Heinemann, 1961], p. 193). This same passage is quoted in William Smith, Latin-English Dictionary (London: John Murray, 1855), p. 947. GE draws mainly on Smith's entries for religio (pp. 947-8) and superstitio (p. 1091) for the contents of entries 294-5.

    2. Translation: "To free minds from the bonds of religious scruples" (translated by Matthew Hogan).

    3. Translation: "To be religious is a duty; superstitious, a sin" (translated by Matthew Hogan).

    4. De Natura Deorum II.xxviii.72. Translation: "Persons who spent their days in prayer and sacrifice to ensure that their children should outlive them were termed 'superstitious' (from superstes, a survivor), and the word later acquired a wider application" (Rackham, p. 193).

    5. Translation: "The superstitious are those who preserve the abiding memory of the deceased; or who, as surviving their parents, preserve their portraits at home, like the household gods" (translated by Matthew Hogan).

Entry 295

    1. George Grote, History of Greece, 12 vols. (New York: Harper and Brothers, 1857), III, 85. Epimenedes was called to Athens "to heal both the epidemic and the mental affliction prevalent among the Athenian people. . . . The favor of Epimenedes with the gods, his knowledge of propitiatory ceremonies, and his power of working on religious feeling, was completely

successful in restoring both health and mental tranquillity to Athens" (ibid).
On 1 March 1868, while writing TSG, GE made the following entry in her Diary:
"Finished . . . 4th B. of the Iliad. I shall now read Grote." GE's Journal
also shows that she was reading Grote's Greece in 1869-70 (Letters, V, 156
n. 8). See also Pratt and Neufeldt, pp. xxxiii-v and passim.

   2. Grote, III, 84, n. 2. This word appears in a quotation from
Plutarch's Lives, "Solon," ch. 12. Translation: "superstitious fears"
(Bernadotte Perrin, trans., Plutarch's Lives, Loeb Classical Library, 10 vols.
(London: William Heinemann; New York: Macmillan, 1914), I, 433.

   3. Grote, III, 85, n. 2. See Plutarch, "Solon," ch. 12. Translation:
"He was reputed to be a man beloved of the gods, and endowed with a mystical
and heaven-sent wisdom in religious matters" (Perrin, Plutarch's Lives, I, 433).

   4. Grote says that Tyrtaeus "was an impressive and efficacious minstrel"
and that he was able "not merely to reanimate the languishing courage of the
baffled warrior, but also to soothe the discontents of the mutinous. That his
strains, which long maintained undiminished popularity among the Spartans,
contributed to determine the ultimate issue of the war, there is no reason to
doubt" (Grote, II, 432).

   5. Grote, II, 434.

   6. Ibid., n. 1.

   7. Horace, Ars Poetica, 1. 402. Translation: "Tyrtaeus with his poetry
steeled gallant hearts for battle."

Entry 296

   1. Th. de la Villemarqué, Contes populaires des anciens Bretons, 2 vols.
(Paris: W. Coquebert, 1842), I, 24-25. Translation: "The Welsh have two
historical poems from the sixth century which concern themselves with a Cambrian
leader named Arthur, who really existed. . . . There is nothing marvellous
about him. . . . I think The Triades wanted to turn the mythological Arthur
into a real person; he is still the hero of the ancient poets but quite without
his halo. . . ." GE mentions Villemarqué in a letter to Mme. Bodichon, 3
August 1865: "It is settled now that we are to go for a month's holiday in
Normandy and Brittany starting next Thursday. So I am reading Villemarqué and
setting my mind towards Celtic legends, that I may people the land with great
shadows when there are no solid Bretons in sight"(Letters, VIII, 349).

   2. Villemarqué, I, 28. Translation: "Stories of the ancient Bretons:
they were edited in the early years of the twelfth century--the golden age of
Gaulish literature."

   3. Ibid., I, 32. Translation: "Walter of Oxford, Geoffrey of Monmouth,
and Wace are, the one in Gaulish, the other in Latin, and the third in French
following them, the old Breton chronicle, the source of all the romans du Brut
or popular romances."

   4. Ibid., I, 16. Translation: "Brut in the Celtic language signifies
the vernacular tradition."

   5. Barzaz Breiz; Chants populaires de la Bretagne (Paris, 1839) is an
earlier book by Villemarqué. GE copied a story from it in her notes for TSG
in "Quarry for FH."

   6. Villemarqué, I, 65.

   7. Ernest Renan, "La poésie des races celtiques," Reveu des deux Mondes,
5 (1854), 473-506; rpt. in vol. 2 of Oeuvres complètes de Ernest Renan, ed.
Henriette Psichari, 10 vols. (Paris: Calmann-Lévy, n.d.). GE quotes this
essay in entries 296-7.

Entry 297

   1. Villemarqué, II, 306. Translation: "The monuments of Breton
literature are: I. Poetry. Welch poems. (1) The oldest Welch poetry that
has come down to us is that of Kenverz or the primitive bards, among whom the
most notable are Taliessin, Merzin, Aneurin, and Lywarc'h-Henn, who lived in
the sixth century, and many others less well known, who flourished from 664,

the period of the fall of the Breton monarchy, to 1066. They fill the first
180 pages of Owen Myvyr's Archaeology of Wales."

   2. Ibid., pp. 306-7. <u>Translation</u>: "The manuscripts are: 1 The Black
Book, begun in the tenth and finished in the twelfth century. 2 The books of
Taliessin and of Aneurin, toward the end of the eleventh century. 3 The Red
Book of Hengest, fourteenth century."

   3. Ibid., p. 314. <u>Translation</u>: "Popular Armorican songs."

   4. Ibid., p. 318. <u>Translation</u>: "The Triads or bardic traditions."

   5. Ibid., p. 321. <u>Translation</u>: "The National Chronicles: e.g., <u>Brut y
Brenhined</u> or History of Kings, written in 950 by a Breton from the continent."

   6. Ibid., p. 323. <u>Translation</u>: "Popular stories of the ancient Bretons.
The Mabinoghion."

   7. Ibid., p. 325. <u>Translation</u>: "They form two separate categories: in
the one the figure of Arthur is a unifying principle; in the other he does not
appear."

   8. Renan, <u>Oeuvres</u>, II, 256. <u>Translation</u>: "Nowhere has reverence for
the dead been greater than among the Breton peoples; nowhere have so many
memories and prayers clustered about the tomb. This is because life is not
for these people a personal adventure, undertaken by each man on his own account, and at his own risks and perils; it is a link in a long chain, a gift
received and handed on, a debt paid and a duty done" (<u>The Poetry of the Celtic
Races, and Other Studies by Ernest Renan</u>, trans. William G. Hutchison [London:
Walter Scott, n.d.], p. 6).

   9. Renan, <u>Oeuvres</u>, II, 257. <u>Translation</u>: "Thus the Celtic race has worn
itself out in resistance to its time, and in the defence of desperate causes"
(Hutchinson, p. 7).

Entry 298

   1. Ibid., pp. 259-60. <u>Translation</u>: "Celtic Messianism. 'Nearly all
great appeals to the supernatural are due to peoples hoping against all hope.
. . . Israel in humiliation dreamed of the spiritual conquest of the world,
and the dream has come to pass'" (Hutchison, p. 10).

   2. Ibid., p. 261. <u>Translation</u>: "The grindstone of Tudwal . . . would
only sharpen brave men's swords" (Hutchison, p. 13).

   3. Ibid., p. 264. <u>Translation</u>: "Even Judas is not denied a share of
their pity. St. Brandan found him upon a rock in the midst of the Polar seas;
once a week he passes a day there to refresh himself from the fires of hell.
A cloak that he had given to a beggar is hung before him, and tempers his sufferings" (Hutchison, p. 15).

   4. Ibid., p. 269. <u>Translation</u>: "One day St. Kevin fell asleep, while
he was praying at his window with outstretched arms; and a swallow preceiving
the open hand of the venerable monk, considered it an excellent place wherein
to make her nest. The saint on awaking saw the mother sitting upon her eggs,
and, loth to disturb her, waited for the little ones to be hatched before he
arose from his knees" (Hutchison, pp. 21-22).

   5. Ibid., p. 271n. <u>Translation</u>: "Take me to the woods . . . and I
shall hear them clearly" (Hutchison, p. 24).

   6. Villemarqué, I, 92.

Entry 299

   1. Entries 299-305 are from vol. one of Max Müller, <u>Chips from a German
Workshop</u>; see entry 269 n. 1 above. All the notes that appear here were first
transcribed in the "Quarry for <u>FH</u>." GE has culled her earlier notes and or-
ganized them differently for <u>A Writer's Notebook</u>, grouping related items scattered through <u>Chips</u> into unified segments; consequently the page references
are frequently non-sequential. Some of this material appears again in Pratt
and Neufeldt, pp. 219-23.

   These notes constitute a summary of the significance of the findings of
landmark European scholarship on Asian religions that were made possible

through the mastery of Oriental languages by a handful of dedicated scholars. They are the impetus behind an exchange between Dorothea and Ladislaw, which they also make completely intelligible. Dorothea remarks, "It seems to me that with Mr. Casaubon's learning he must have before him the same materials as German scholars--has he not?" "'Not exactly the same materials,' said Will, thinking that he would be duly reserved. 'He is not an Orientalist, you know. He does not profess to have more than second-hand knowledge there'" (M, ch. 22). Furthermore, the extraordinary vitality, originality, and productivity of such scholars as de Perron, Rask, Westergaard, Burnouf, Bopp, Spiegel, Haug, and Csoma de Körös are a comment on the moribund, imitative, and unproductive Edward Casaubon, who wandered in "accustomed vaults . . . taper in hand" (M, ch. 63). Casaubon is like the English students in Bombay and Poona whom Müller chided for learning nothing of Parsiism while the Germans and French learned everything. GE further supplemented these notes on the study of Oriental languages by reading Max Müller's History of Ancient Sanscrit Literature (see entry 127, n. 6); see also Pratt and Neufeldt, pp. xlviii-ix.

2. "Lecture on the Vedas, or the Sacred Books of the Brahmans, Delivered at Leeds, 1865," Chips, p. 8. "Veda is the same word which appears in the Greek οἶδα, I know, and in the English, wise, wisdom, to wit" (ibid.).

3. Ibid., pp. 9-10.

4. Ibid., p. 10.

5. Ibid., pp. 10-11.

Entry 300

1. Ibid., pp. 12-13.

2. Ibid., p. 17.

3. Ibid., pp. 24-25. In Pratt and Neufeldt GE has two further notes on Deva: "Sanskrit alphabet called Deva. negâre--the writing of the Gods" (p. 12). "In the language of the gypsies devel meaning God, is connected with Sanskrit deva" (p. 58).

4. Chips, p. 27.

Entry 301

1. "On the Study of the Zend-Avesta in India" (1862), Chips, p. 120.

2. Ibid., p. 117.

Entry 302

1. "The Veda and Zend-Avesta" (1853), Chips, p. 80.

2. "Genesis and the Zend-Avesta," Chips, p. 148.

3. "The Veda and Zend-Avesta," Chips, p. 80.

4. Ibid., pp. 83-84.

5. Ibid., p. 86n.

6. Ibid., p. 89.

7. Ibid., pp. 84-88 summarized.

Entry 303

1. Ibid., p. 92.

2. Ibid., p. 88.

3. Ibid., p. 96.

4. Ibid., p. 100.

Entry 304

1. "Buddhism" (1862), Chips, p. 189.

2. Ibid., p. 190.

3. Ibid., pp. 190-91.

4. Ibid., p. 193.

Entry 305

1. Ibid., p. 193.

2. Ibid., p. 217.

3. Ibid.

4. Ibid., p. 218.

5. "Buddhist Pilgrims" (1857), <u>Chips</u>, p. 245. In <u>DD</u>, ch. 37, Mirah
tells Daniel that Hans Meyrick had used this legend of the Buddha to illustrate
a trait of his character: "He told us a wonderful story of Bouddha giving
himself to a famished tigress to save her and her little ones from starving.
And he said you were like Bouddha." Deronda then interprets the story for
her: "It is an extreme image of what is happening every day--the transmutation of self." Such a transmutation is central to Gwendolen's change of
character and Deronda's becoming the deliverer of his people by absorbing into
himself the Jewish identity of Daniel Charisi and the Zionism of Mordecai.
(See also entry 221, n. 5.)

6. <u>Chips</u>, p. 252. "No Jew, no Greek, no Roman, no Brahman ever thought
of converting people to his own national form of worship" (ibid.).

7. "Buddhism," <u>Chips</u>, p. 211.

8. Ibid.

9. Ibid., p. 220.

10. "Buddhist Pilgrims," <u>Chips</u>, p. 254.

11. Albrecht Weber, <u>The History of Indian Literature</u> (Boston: Houghton,
Osgood, & Co., 1878), p. 306. In her Diary for 1879 (Berg Collection, New York
Public Library) GE makes the following entry for 28 December 1879: "Finished
Weber's Indian Literature." This entry is in purple ink; whereas, all quotations from Müller are in black ink. Consequently, it must be taken as an addition to the original notes. Indeed, it may be the last entry she made in the
notebook.

Entry 306

1. John Lubbock, <u>Pre-Historic Times</u>, p. 357; see entry 224 n. 1. All
the entries on this page also appear in "Quarry for <u>FH</u>" where they were first
made while GE was writing <u>TSG</u>: "Finished the description of Silva's watch.
Part IV. p. 15. Reading Lubbock's Prehistoric Ages" (Diary, 6 March 1868).
These notes certainly were transcribed into <u>A Writer's Notebook</u> at a later
date. Although they appear in the "Quarry for <u>FH</u>" before GE's entries from
Tyrwhitt's ed. of <u>The Canterbury Tales</u> (see entry 276 n. 1), they appear here
after them. In the light of her earlier remark to Sara Hennell--"I am reading
about savages and semi-savages, and I think that our religious oracles would
do well to study savage ideas by a method of comparison with their own"
(<u>Letters</u>, IV, 424)--GE may have been thinking of the character of Bulstrode
when she transferred them to the present notebook. Bulstrode, in fear of ex-
posure, wonders "by what sacrifice he could stay the rod. His belief in these
moments of dread was, that if he spontaneously did something right, God would
save him from the consequences of wrong-doing. For religion can only change
when the emotions which fill it are changed; and the religion of personal fear
remains nearly at the level of the savage" (<u>M</u>, ch. 61). The suggestion is
that Bulstrode still believes in something like "cruel gods" and "sanguinary
rites."

2. Lubbock, p. 367.

3. Ibid., p. 416.

4. Edward B. Tylor, <u>Researches into the Early History of Mankind and the
Development of Civilization</u> (1865). In "Quarry for <u>FH</u>" GE's entry is more extensive, adding, after <u>Mankind</u>, "for savage customs and ideas." GE finished
reading Tylor's <u>Early History</u> on 18 August 1874 (<u>Letters</u>, VI, 90, n. 7a).
Earlier, 4 July 1872, she told Mrs. Congreve that she was "in the middle" of
another of Tylor's books, <u>Primitive Culture: Researches into the Development
of Mythology, Philosophy, Religion, Art and Custom</u> (1871) (<u>Letters</u>, V, 288 and
n. 3).

Entry 307

    1. John William Donaldson, The New Cratylus, or Contributions towards a More Accurate Knowledge of the Greek Language (Cambridge: J.J. Deighton, 1839), pp. 89-90. This law is illustrated diagramatically in entries 212-3.

    2. Donaldson, p. 90.

    3. The parentheses suggest that the unrelated languages could be listed.

Entry 308

    1. Jacob Grimm, Deutsche Grammatik (1819-37; Göttingen: Dieterische Buchhandlung, 1840), p. 8. This entry is written in black ink, but the "e" in Deutsche has been added in purple ink. Translation: "Sound-shift. A precisely patterned relationship exists on two levels between mute consonants in languages unrelated to German and a change that occurred at one time in all the Germanic languages and High German; consequently, just as the Germanic languages are different in this way from the unrelated languages so is High German different from other Germanic languages. Once underway the change did not halt but was first completed in the High German dialect. If, for example, a Latin, Greek, or Indian word reaches the first level of change, it is found to correspond with a Gothic word on the second level and a High German word on the third level. A fourth position is an impossibility, because it would necessarily have to return to the first level.

    "This significant and, for research in German, very welcome characteristic seems likewise not to be an indigenous difference but rather a historical one which, in early times, did not affect High German or, in even earlier times, the Germanic languages generally. It simply designates a certain direction through which, in the course of centuries, the actual and immediate relationship of Germanic peoples developed. There are of course some exceptions and interruptions, individually and serially, that have the sound-shift underlying them without being cancelled by them." (Translated with Sieghardt Riegel.)

Entry 309

    1. Deutsche Grammatik, Dedication, par. [4]. Translation: "It seems to me that the old sayings of the Fatherland have their very charm in a certain incompleteness: we take them on faith because our feelings tell us that what is missing might explain everything. . . . Too great a fulness leaves one empty. True poetry is like a man who can be endlessly happy watching the leaves and grass grow and the sun rise and set. False poetry is like a man who travels to a foreign country and fancies himself exalted by the mountains of Switzerland and the sea and sky of Italy. Standing in the midst of these things the traveler's pleasure is not as thoroughgoing as that of a man who stays at home with his apple tree, which blooms every year, and the finches that sing in its branches. . . . There is no real difference between classic and romantic poetry. The history of painting, poetry, and language teaches us to avoid many byways, because it shows us that truth is always revealed to those who, far from the wisdom of the schoolroom, walk the path of nature." (Translated with Sieghardt Riegel.)

    2. GE added a cryptic note relating to these words to the "Contents" page of the "Quarry for FH": "Theotistic language = Anglo-Saxon word[x]"; "[x]theodisc þeodisc from þeód = old High German diutisc from diot? x Theodiscus = Deutsch."

    3. Deutsche Grammatik, p. 12. Translation: "The meaning of the word is gentilis, gentilitius, popularis, vulgaris, which is valid among all the people in contrast to individual tribes, where it is generally understood as homely, inherited. But it cannot be denied that it also has the secondary connotation of heathen, barbarian, the þiudisks like ἐθνικῶς, just as ἔθνος, þiuda, vulgus do in the mouths of Church writers. In this way it is like Germanicus: both expressions in relation to language designate a common raw vulgar speech in contrast to educated usage." (Translated with Sieghardt Riegel.)

Entry 310

 1. Francis Beaumont and John Fletcher, The Maid's Tragedy IV.i.253-4.
This entry became the epigraph to M, ch. 1. It defines the social condition
in which "later-born Theresas" are prevented from achieving a "far-resonant
action" (Prelude). The antithesis of this attitude is expressed by Swinburne
in the third section of entry 247.

 2. Spanish proverb. It serves as the epigraph of M, ch. 46, where GE
translates it: "Since we cannot get what we like, let us like what we can
get." In this chapter, Ladislaw makes the best of his position as editor of
the "Pioneer" and exile from Lowick.

 3. Juvenal, Satires VI.555-6. Translation: "[Greater faith is placed
in Ammon] because the oracles from Delphi cease and the obscurity of the future
damns the human race" (translated with Matthew Hogan). GE records reading
Juvenal on 2 April 1862 (Letters, IV, 24).

 4. Rubáiyát of Omar Khayyám, The Astronomer--Poet of Persia, trans.
Edward FitzGerald (1859; Waterville, Maine: Colby College Press, 1959), p.
87, st. LI; in the 1868 ed., this is st. LXXVI; in the 1872 ed. and thereafter, st. LXXI.

 5. Book of Job, XVI, 4. GE used this quotation as the epigraph of FH,
ch. 37, in which Mr. Lyon finds that many things are being said against Felix,
who is in jail awaiting trial for the murder of Tucker.

 6. Edmund Burke, Reflections on the Revolution in France (1790; New
York: Liberal Arts Press, 1955), p. 34. This quotation from Burke expresses
the central moral problem that Savonarola and Romola must solve for themselves. GE rephrases it in R, ch. 55: "The question where the duty of obedience ends, and the duty of resistance begins, could in no case be an easy
one."

 7. François Guizot, Histoire de la civilization en France, 4 vols. (Paris,
Didier, 1846), III, 363-4. Translation: "The moral thought of men is everywhere above and strives to be above their actual lives. You must avoid believing that because it does not immediately govern actions, because actual
practice struggles ceaselessly and oddly with theory that theory has no influence and is without value. The judgment of men upon their actions is very
important indeed; sooner or later it becomes efficacious." GE entered this
same quotation in "Quarry for FH" after quotations from Henry Hallam's Middle
Ages, which, according to her Diary, she began reading on 24 November 1865.
Guizot's statement represents GE's own moral perspective exactly and suggests
why her novels are peopled with moral idealists like Romola, Felix, Dorothea,
and Deronda. Guizot's last sentence serves as the epigraph for M, ch. 38.

Entry 311

 1. "Hic breve vivitur" ("Brief life is here our portion," trans. J. M.
Neale) from Bernard of Cluny, Hora novissima in The English Hymnal (London:
Geoffrey Cumberlege, Oxford University Press and A. R. Mowbray & Co., 1933),
General Hymns No. 371, p. 514.

 2. Horace, Satires I.ix.59-60. Translation: "The prizes of life are
not to be had without great labor."

 3. Horace, Epistles I.xvi.79. Translation: "I will die; death is the
final limit for everything." GE uses this sentiment of Horace when Mr.
Casaubon faces death as a personal event for the first time: "When the commonplace 'We must all die' transforms itself suddenly into the acute consciousness 'I must die--and soon,' then death grapples us, and his fingers are
cruel" (M, ch. 42.)

 4. John Keble, "St. Philip and St. James," The Christian Year (London:
Humphrey Milford, Oxford University Press, 1914), p. 164.

 5. Inferno, VI, 106-8; see entry 98 for the same passage and 98, n. 7,
for its application to Deronda in DD, ch. 55. Keble's lines may have reminded
GE of this passage.

 6. Goethe, "In ernsten Beinhaus"; see entry 19 for the same passage and

19, n. 1.

    7. Ecclesiasticus XIX.10. GE uses the first part of this passage ("If
. . . thee") as the epigraph of <u>M</u>, ch. 69, in which Caleb Garth says to
Bulstrode, after hearing Raffles's story about the banker, "Such tales as that
will never tempt my tongue." See entry 105 for a similar sentiment and 105,
n. 6, for its application to Caleb in <u>M</u>, ch. 53.

    8. Goethe, "Elemente," 11. 17-20, <u>Goethe's sämmtliche Werke</u>, IV, 7.
<u>Translation</u>: "In the end it is necessary / that the poet hate many things; /
it is intolerable and hateful / not to allow beautiful things to live." GE
recalls these lines in <u>M</u>, ch. 22, when Dorothea asks Ladislaw to promise not
to criticize Casaubon's work on the Key to all Mythologies again. He agrees,
with a silent reservation: "If he never said a cutting word about Mr Casaubon
again and left off receiving favours from him, it would clearly be permissible
to hate him the more. The poet must know how to hate, says Goethe; and Will
was at least ready with that accomplishment." Ladislaw hates Casaubon for his
unsympathetic treatment of Dorothea, whose beauty he considers so complete
that he says to her, "You <u>are</u> a poem."

Textual Notes

A single bracket encloses the emended text and is followed by the original text. The symbols used in the textual notes are angle brackets around a letter or word to indicate that it is crossed out, written over, or smudged (thus, in entry 39: The Gate] The <Lions> Gate); angle brackets around a question mark to indicate that a word or letter is irrecoverable (thus, in entry 39, an obliterated word: hugh blocks] hugh <?> blocks; in entry 137, an obliterated letter: blew] blew<?>); arrows surrounding a word to indicate that it is inserted above the line (thus, in entry 39: Parthenos] ↑Parthenos↓). After the textual notes for the Endpaper and Index, the subsequent notes are introduced by entry (not page) numbers.

Endpaper.　vetando a fraude] vetando, et grande
Index.　　 76. Costume] ↑76↓. Costume
Entry 4.　 control over] control <of> ↑over↓　　monarch of] monr. of
　　　6.　 not however appear] not ↑however↓ appear　　the people:] the <?>
　　　　　 ↑people↓:　　to one wife] to <with> one wife　　ranked next]
　　　　　 ranked <?> next　　Egyptians regarding] Egyptns. regarding
　　　　　 *(This] (*This
　　　8.　 holländisches] Holländisches　　auch sie der] auch <die> ↑sie der↓
　　　　　 Mädchen, welches] Mädchen, <?> welches　　durch eine] durch ein
　　　8a.　verborgenen] verborgene
　　　15.　zu fassen] zu <?> fassen　　Parteilichkeit] Parteylichkeit
　　　16.　Aebtissin Gerberga, der] Aebtessin der　　dass man] das man
　　　　　 hat sie] hat <sich> sie　　nachahmte] nachamte　　bei Abfassung]
　　　　　 bei <?> Abfassung　　war also] war als　　im Terenz] in Terenz
　　　　　 den Mund] den <?> Mund　　christlichem] Christlichem
　　　18.　versteht sich's] versteht's sich
　　　19.　offenbare?] offenbare,
　　　21.　frei von] frei <?> von　　Golgotha. . . .] Golgotha x x x x
　　　　　 christlichen] kristliche
　　　22.　dort oben] dort <?> ↑oben↓　　wir hir unten] wir unten
　　　　　 Firmaments] Firmamenter
　　　25.　love, in] love, <to> in
　　　27.　zwölften] Zwölften　　Ihr nackt] ihr nackt　　Alles nackt] alles
　　　　　 nackt　　Alles, was] alles was　　wir werden dir Alles] wir wir
　　　　　 werden Dir alles　　anderen Morgen] andern Morgen　　geforderte]
　　　　　 gefordete　　namlich nackte] namlich, <?> nackte　　weltliche]
　　　　　 Weltliche
　　　30.　deutschen Minnesänger] Deutscher Minnesänger　　französische]
　　　　　 Französische　　darin allerdings] ↑darin↓ allerdings
　　　　　 emancipiren] emanciperten　　verständigen Sinn nicht] verständigen
　　　　　 nicht　　aus seiner Sphäre] aus<ser> seiner Sphäre
　　　　　 den Schwindel] den <?> Schwindel
　　　31.　deutscher Frauentreue] Deutscher Frauentreue　　Bitisia] Bitizia
　　　32.　todschlagen] todtschlagen
　　　32a.　their travailed] their <troubled> ↑travailed↓
　　　34.　somewhither] some<where>↑whither↓　　having been for] having for
　　　　　 impels learned] impels <?> learned
　　　35.　Paxo's] Paxos'　　god Pan] God Pan　　Indifference] indifference
　　　　　 being] Being　　Process] process　　every thing] everything
　　　39.　§1. The Gate] The <Lions> Gate　　hugh blocks] hugh <?> blocks
　　　　　 §4. Discovered 30 years ago] ↑Discovered 30 years ago↓
　　　　　 city] town ↑city↓　　determined as] determined <?> as
　　　　　 Amazons] amazons　　§5. at Munich] at <?> Munich
　　　　　 §5b. Parthenos] ↑Parthenos↓　　time nearly the most celebrated
　　　　　 statue] time <?> ↑nearly the most celebrated↓ statue　　§6. (a bust]
　　　　　 ↑(a bust)↓　　§7. Lapithae. From] Lapithae. <?> From
　　　　　 women, Neptune] women, <?> ↑Neptune↓　　9a: contemporary] cot:
　　　　　 §10. contemporary] cot.　　§11. of Scopas] of <?> Scopas

Luaix, Release from care] Luaix, <?> ↑Release from care↓

40.   ihrer ürsprunglichen wunderbaren] ihrer wunderbaren   anderen
      Wendung] andern Wendung   Sage, welcher] Sage, welche
      ihre Macht] ihr Macht

42.   1619: Magnus] 1619: <?> Magnus

43.   For Greek see figs. 4 and 5.   Ideas] ideas   perfekt] perfect

44.   aux lueurs] au <?> ↑lueurs↓   Goethe's bullion] Goethe's <sterling>
      bullion   entretenu] m'entretenu

47.   wurde] ↑wurde↓

48.   twenty-fourth] twenty fourth

49.   quantity of] ↑quantity of↓

50.   the light] the <flame> light

54.   'roar] "roar   heart.'] heart."

55.   farm-houses] farm houses   'The] "The   Master,'] Master,"

56.   "I rode] 'I rode

58.   persons styling] persons <calling> styling

59.   prece] praece   praecipiente] parcipiente

61.   his dress] his ↑dress↓

62.   Hackett's] Hackit's   Italian] Ital.

63.   Wife"] wife"   afternoon] aftern.   century] centy.

67.   dignity; another] dignity another

68.   September & December] Sepr. & Decr.

70.   cut across] cut <off> across

72.   when the cat] ↑when the cat↓

73.   Benjamin] Benj.   Prometheus Unbound] Prom. Unb.

74.   the first autumnal] the ↑first↓ autumnal   Handles] Handes

76.   seigneur errant] ↑seigneur errant↓   dans la tête] dans <l'esprit>
      la tête

77.   & treble the number below] ↑& treble the number below↓

78.   November] Novr.

79.   moor-game, &c. . . . There] moore game & c . . . There

80.   at <Boston> Boston

82.   hail & snow] hail<?> ↑&↓ snow   from the many] from ↑the↓ many
      a tube] a <?> tube

94.   his intense] his <extravagant> ↑intense↓   at first] ↑at first↓
      was separated] was <supported above by> separated

95.   superstitions. . . . /96/] superstitions--<The history of Gothic
      architecture is the history of this refinement & spiritualization
      of Northern work and of its influence -- the noble buildings> 96.

98.   com' era] come<e> era

100. accora] accoura   sguardando] guardando   faceva] facea

101. giorno pianger che] giorno che   parean] paren   messo] misso
      perder] perdere

102. Signor] signor   Parean] paren   stilo] stile   inchiostri]
      inchiostro

104. Che leggendo] Che <sillogezzando> ↑leggendo↓   strami] Strami
      com'] com<e>'

105. due] duo   sott'] sott<a>]   'nver] '<m>nver   troppo color]
      troppo <celor> ↑color↓   bassa] basso   tor] tor'

106. account] ↑account↓

107. disturbances still] disturbances <still roll> still

108. of life] of <their lives> life   continued Examination] continued
      <observation> Examination   surrounded] <r>surrounded

109. core] cuor   snelle] snelli   tutta] tutto   ale] ali
      cela] cele

110. dell'] dall'   corono] corona   muova] muove

111. unsre Thaten] unsere Thaten   unsres Lebens] unseres Lebens
      Doch, wo] Denn wo   Mephistopheles] Meph.   O weh] O <w?h> ↑weh↓
      sind's] sinds

112.   Melodien] melodien
114.   molesta est] molesta <sit> ↑est↓
115.   Dux] <Rex>   laurel berries] laurel ↑berries↓
121.   clothes to] clothes <?> to
122.   sue case] su<a>e cas<a>↑e↓   Singnioria] Singnoria   chon
        charovele] chon charevole   charovele ben] charevole ben
        chaminorono] ch<?>am↑in↓orono   (1493)] ↑1493↓
123.   beato a chi'l tochava e chi aveua] beati a chi'l toccava e chi avea
        Francesco figliuolo] Francesco <?> figliuolo   a son of Mateo]
        ↑a son of↓ Mateo   a certain] ↑a↓ certain   ore 4] ora 4
        domineddio] domeniddo
124.   dasai] assai   feciegliele] fecigliele   fa Fra] ↑fa↓ Fra
        santo] Santo   del' ordine] del ordine   prima] primo
125.   loqui sine] loqui <sinte> sine   nullum] nullam   Machiavelli]
        Macehiavelli
127.   Studies. Daunou] Studies. <?> Daunou
128.   Aristotile] Aristotele   espresso] espress<a>↑o↓
        E'beccafichi] E beccafichi
129.   or a fish] ↑or a fish↓   knife, Matthew] knife, Mathew
        veil] <scarf> ↑veil↓
132.   relict] reli<ef>ct   such substances] such <?> substances
134.   Herbert] He↑u↓bert   In afflictions] In affections
135.   St. Cosmo] St. <Christopher> Cosmo
136.   & Christopher answered] & C. answered
137.   blew] blew<?>   said, "Who] said, "who
138.   to Samos] to <Ly> Samos
140.   brought it to] brought to
141.   who taught a new religion] ↑who taught a new religion↓   does the
        soul] does <light> the soul   by Conon the] by ↑Conon↓ the
        would give] would <?>give
142.   & when] & <?> when   Cologne, where Ursula & her company] Cologne,
        <?>↑where Ursula & her company↓
143.   black] ↑black↓
145.   casula] casula   sub-deadon] sub deacon
148.   chasuble being] chasuble ↑being↓   archbishops, resembles]
        archbishops <& patriarchs,> resembles
149.   Gentiles, but] Gentiles, <& because distinguished> ↑but↓
151.   shalt cause the] shalt <murder> ↑cause the↓
153.   (aeropagus)] ↑(aeropagus)↓   enim sunt] enim <est> sunt
154.   Elaphebolion] Elaphebolion
155.   I. The Benedictines.] ↑I. The Benedictines↓   archbishop] archbp.
156.   The Abbot] The abbot
157.   12th] the ↑XII↓ 1<2>th
158.   Romualdo] Romuldo
160.   savants] savans   appartements] appartemens
161.   were also] was also   Henry V., in] Henry V., ↑in↓
162.   Augustinians.] ↑Augustinians↓ <Dominicans>
163.   et en] ↑et↓ en
164.   September] Sep.
165.   Laudesi] Laudesi
166.   quatre] quatre<s>   Sacrements] Sacremens
170.   Greeks had] Greeks <that> had
171.   to the intagli] to the <m> intagli   Cyrene, AElian] Cyrene, <?>
        Aelian
174.   centuries gem-engraving] centuries gem engraving
177.   Leucachates] Leuc<h>achates   Prasius of] ↑Prasius↓ <?> of
        Lychnis, classed] Lychnis, <were> classed   according to him]
        ↑according to him↓
181.   Chneph] ↑Chneph↓ <C<h>neph>

183. Greek name for] ↑Greek name for↓
185. considerable time (it] considerable (it
187. abstract] ab<?>stract
188. first group] first groupe
189. (b)] (b)
190. communions] communi<ties>↑ons↓
191. (d)] (d)
192. next group] next groupe   third group] third groupe
193. the extensive] the <?> extensive
195. 23d.] 23.
197. of Canosa] ↑of↓ Canosa
201. Zend-Avesta] Zendavesta   hence the language] hence ↑the language↓
      of some of] of ↑some of↓
202. Slavs back] Slaves back   the Bulgarian] The Bulgarian   century;
      the Polish] centy.' the Polish
203. the most] ↑the↓ most   13th century] 13 centy.   14th century]
      14 centy.
204. determine] ↑determine↓   Ionic from the Attic, &] Ionic ↑from↓ &
      the Attic, &
205. Asia.] Asia <Minor>.
206. begin about] begin abt.   century. γ. The] century. T.γ. The
207. language adopted] language <of the> adopted   finished /208]
      finished †Arabic, tarjam, to explain 208
208. whole area] wholly area
209. Ghez,] ↑Ghez↓
211. Tibet] <Thibet>
212. See fig. 11.
213. See fig. 11.
214. Europe] Eur:
215. could /216/] could *Annalibus Briorum 216
216. expulsion] ex<termination>↑pulsion↓
219. Diefenbach] Di<?>enbach
222. to lull] to <?> lull   For Greek: see fig. 12.
223. For Greek: see fig. 13.
224. right ear] e$\overset{2}{a}$r (right)
226. continued] contind.   Appréciation systématique] Appreciation
      <finale> systématique   dix-neuvième] dix-neuv↑e↓.
228. Byble] B<i>yble
229. truly] tryly
230. were: Coverdale] were, Coverdale   assigned] assign
231. Puritans) 232] Puritans 232
232. almost kill] almost <kill many> kill   fift] sift
236. Gaules] G<allois>↑aules↓
237. peut-être] peut être   instruments] instrumens   étaient] était
238. conseilla donc] conseilla donc<?>   répétées] répétéa   qu'il
      leur] qu'il ↑leur↓   désigner] <diriger?> désigner
240. I. Über] I. übe<?>   analogue] analogues
241. et toutes les langues de l'Afrique] ↑et toutes les langues de
      l'Afrique↓
244. ne se] ne <sont> se   du peuple juif] d<es> peuple<s> juif<s>
      reçu] reçu<s>   hébraique leur est] hébraique est]
245. arriver d'eux-mêmes] arriver <?> d'eux-mêmes   l'Iran] l'Iran<?>
      par une] par<?> une
247. Atlanta) For] Atlanta. For
248. were a] were <the> a   bird] bird<?>
249. a bow had their origin] a <?> ↑bow had their↓ origin
      According] Accordg.
250. goudok] Goudok   609, & is] 609, ↑&↓ is
251. psaltery with] psaltery <?> with

252.   <u>basse</u>] basses   instruments] instrumens   servent] serv<on>t
253.   have been made] have ↑been↓ made
254.   monuments] monumens   violons] violins
256.   eigentlich nur] eigentlich ↑nur↓   Sinne] sinne
261.   with who are gone] with <ages> ↑who are↓ gone
264.   command?] com↑[mand?↓
273.   Mithridatium] Mithridatum   identifying] identify   not hemlock]
       ↑not↓ hemlock   in general] in <which> general
274.   Solanmus] Solanmus*   powerful /275/] powerful *Strychnos,
       Nightshade. 275
278.   (sound)] ↑(sound)↓
279.   gutturale très] guttural très   in Greek] ↑in Greek↓   a guttural,
       by others O, I or Y.] a gutt, by oth. O ↑I or Y.↓   gutturale forte]
       gutturale forte
281.   person] ↑person↓   he was] <t>he was   she involuntarily]
       she she involuntarily
282.   obtain Achilles'] obtain <?> Achilles'
284.   are good] are <fine> good   Theame] The↑a↓me   To conclude]
       to conclude
285.   force or] ↑force or↓   Daniel, Defence of] Daniel, <Apologie for>
       ↑Defence of↓
286.   Greeks &] ↑Greeks &↓
287.   gravitie it selfe] gravitie selfe
288.   Spencer to Gabriel] <Spenser to> ↑Gabriel↓
289.   a natural] ↑a natural↓
290.   wrapt] <lapt> ↑wrapt↓
291.   any man will] any man man will   to a farther] to ↑a↓ farther
292.   Again, though I] Again, ↑though↓ I
293.   says Webbe] says <John Harrington> ↑Webbe↓
296.   Les monuments] Les monumens
297.   fleuri de] fleuridé   grands appels] grands ↑appels↓
298.   passe] passu
299.   to have existed] to have to have existed   intelligible]
       intelligble
300.   Manu] Menou   Ahura mazda] Ahuramazda
302.   (a translation of the original)] ↑(a translation of the original)↓
       formed] ↑formed↓   followed] foll<u>owed</u>
303.   Jemschid] Jemshid   Yima Kshaêta, Thrâetaona] Yima, = Ksharta,
       Thrâetona   Yama-Trita] Yama, Trita
304.   Nepal] Nepaul
307.   gefügte] <verfugten> ↑gefügte↓
308.   weil er nothwendig /308/ auf] weil er nothwendig 308 will er
       nothwendig auf   an, durch] an, <durch welche> durch
       zeugen] ze<?>↑ū↓gen
309.   old Anglo-Saxon] ↑old↓ Anglo-Saxon   þiudisks] þiud<ikcs>↑isks↓
310.   podemos haber] podemos aver
311.   magno] magna

Uncollected Writings

THE CREED OF CHRISTENDOM

Leader, 2 (20 September 1851), 897-9

In February 1851 George Eliot proposed writing a review of William Rathbone Greg's The Creed of Christendom (London: John Chapman, 1851), for the Westminster Review and relating Greg's book to Charles Christian Hennell's An Inquiry concerning the Origin of Christianity (1838; 2nd ed. London: Allman, 1841), but the editors were not interested: "Mr. Hickson referred the matter to Slack again and he writes that he shall not have room for it and that the subject will not suit on this occasion, so you see I am obliged to be idle and I like it best" (Letters, I, 346). When John Chapman bought the Westminster, he offered to publish the article and George Eliot agreed to write it. He did not, in fact, publish it because an article by James Martineau supplanted it (Letters, I, 349, n. 7); however, he convinced Thornton Leigh Hunt to publish it. In this way "The Creed of Christendom" became the first article that George Eliot published in the Leader, which was founded by Hunt and George Henry Lewes in 1850. In writing to Sarah Hennell, 13 October 1851, George Eliot says that "Mr. Greg thought the Review 'well done and in a kindly spirit'--but thought there was not much in it--dreadful true, since there was only all his book" (Letters, I, 369). The mention of Hennell's Inquiry toward the end of the review allows her to pay tribute to the book that precipitated her break with orthodoxy in November 1841 (Letters, I, 120-21 and n. 9). "Mr. Hennell," she writes in September 1847 after rereading the book, "ought to be one of the happiest of men that he has done such life's work" (Letters, I, 237). This review is also notable for its clear statement of a doctrine of consequences, quoted from Greg, that was to inform all of George Eliot's fiction.

English Protestantism, effete as it seems in its ecclesiastical and sectarian forms, is manifesting the vitality of its roots in the vigorous and rapid growth of free religious inquiry among earnest men. The writers who are heading the present movement against dogmatic theology, are not mere speculators enamoured of theory, and careless of its practical results. Still less are they anti-religious zealots, who identify all faith with superstition. They are men at once devout and practical, who have been driven into antagonism with the dominant belief by the force of their moral, no less than of their intellectual nature, and who have been led to the avowal of that antagonism, not simply by the impulse of candour, but by an interest in the spiritual well-being of society. They know that to call dogmatic Christianity the popular creed is a misnomer; that the doctrines taught in our pulpits neither have, nor can have, any hold on the masses; and that if our population is to be Christianized, religious teaching must be conducted in a new spirit and on new principles. They protest against the current faith, because they would substitute for it one purer and more influential; they lay the axe to the old, only that there may be freer play for the energies which are ever tending to the development of the new and more perfect.

  Among these pioneers of the New Reformation, Mr. Greg is likely to be one of the most effective. Without any pretension to striking originality or extensive learning, his work perhaps all the more exhibits that sound, practical judgment which discerns at once the hinge of a question, and it bears throughout the impress of an honesty, geniality, and refinement which imply a moral nature of a very high order. The absence of any very profound critical erudition, far from disqualifying Mr. Greg for

the task he has undertaken, is essential to the aim of his book--
namely, to show at what conclusions concerning the Bible and
Christianity a sensible, educated layman is likely to arrive,
with such an amount of critical attainment as is compatible with
the work that lies before him in daily life. If such conclusions
must necessarily be unsound because they are formed in ignorance
of the last new edition of every Biblical critic, orthodox or
heterodox, the right of private judgment is a nullity, and the un-
clerical mind must either dismiss the subject altogether, or surrender itself to a more consistent spiritual despotism than that
of Protestant divines. The Creed of Christendom claims the attention of the theologian, not that it may teach him Biblical criticism, but that it may render him more familiar with the impression
made by the vexed questions of his science on an earnest, cultivated mind, cut off by no barrier of caste or prejudice from full
sympathy and acquaintance with the spirit and wants of the age.
Another class of readers to whom it is adapted, are those strug-
gling towards free religious thought amidst the impediments of
critical ignorance and early artificial associations. To such,
Mr. Greg's book will be valuable, both as an introductory manual
of Biblical criticism and as a help in the consideration of certain moral questions.
     In stating the reasons which urged him to publication, Mr.
Greg says:--

"Much observation of the conversation and controversy of the religious world had brought the conviction that the evil resulting
from the received notions as to scriptural authority has been
immensely under-estimated. I was compelled to see that there is
scarcely a low and dishonouring conception of God current among
men, scarcely a narrow and malignant passion of the human heart,
scarcely a moral obliquity, scarcely a political error or mis-
deed, which Biblical texts are not, and may not be, without any
violence to their obvious signification, adduced to countenance
and justify. On the other hand I was compelled to see how many
clear, honest, and aspiring minds have been hampered and baffled
in their struggles after truth and light, how many tender, pure,
and loving hearts have been hardened, perverted, and forced to a
denial of their nobler nature and their better instincts, by the
ruthless influence of some passages of Scripture which seemed in
the clearest language to condemn the good and to denounce the
true. No work contributed more than Mr. Newman's Phases of
Faith, to force upon me the conviction that little progress can
be hoped, either for religious science or charitable feeling,
till the question of Biblical authority shall have been placed
upon a sounder footing, and viewed in a very different light."

Mr. Greg sets out by examining the dogma of Scriptural inspiration,
which he justly regards as the keystone of Protestant orthodoxy.
After considering separately each of the grounds on which it
rests, he concludes that there is no valid foundation for believing the Hebrew and Christian canonical writings to be inspired,
in the ordinary acceptation of the word--that is, dictated or suggested by God; that hence we must regard them "as records, not
revelations; as histories, to be investigated like other histories; documents, of which the date, the authorship, the
genuineness, the accuracy of the text, are to be ascertained by
the same principles as we apply to other documents." Having thus
cleared away the dazzling haze with which the inspiration dogma

invests the Biblical writings, he proceeds to investigate the
genuineness and authenticity of the Old Testament canon, and
traces briefly but forcibly the chief results of modern criticism
in relation to this subject; indicating such of the reasons on
which they are founded as are readily appreciable by the general
reader. According to these results, no longer held debatable by
critics of high standing, the Pentateuch, instead of being, as is
popularly supposed, the production of Moses, is a compilation from
separate documents, the earliest of which must have been written
as late as the time of Saul; while the whole book of Deuteronomy,
and many parts of the preceding books, are irrefragably proved by
the subsequent history of the Hebrews to have had no existence
prior to the reign of Josiah. Mr. Greg instances some of the
straits to which English divines have been driven, in the effort
to maintain the authority of the Old Testament in the face of
scientific discovery; and dwells on the advantage which would ac-
crue, not only to the truthfulness of divines, but to the real
instructiveness of the Hebrew writings, if the latter were regarded as merely human narratives, traditions, and speculations.
He next discusses the prophecies, and adduces many considerations
tending to prove how far we are from possessing that clear knowledge concerning them which alone could warrant the conclusions of
orthodoxy. In his opinion,--

"The Hebrew prophets were wise, gifted, earnest men, deeply
conversant with the Past--looking far into the Future--shocked
with the unrighteousness around them--sagacious to see impending
evil--bold to denounce wickedness in high places--imbued, above
all, with an unfailing faith, peculiarly strong among their
people, that national delinquency and national virtue would
alike meet with a temporal and inevitable retribution--and
gifted 'with the glorious faculty of poetic hope, exerted on
human prospects, and presenting its results with the vividness
of prophecy'--but prophets in no stricter sense than this."

The Theism of the Hebrews, Mr. Greg maintains, was impure and progressive; they arrived at their mono-theism by the same stages
that characterize the development of the human race in general,
the Old Testament exhibiting strong evidence that the Hebrew deity
was originally a family god, elevated by Moses to the dignity
of a national god, and ultimately, owing to the influence of
prophets and sages, and yet more to the contact of the Hebrews
with other Oriental nations, expanded into the God of the Universe.
     The claims of the New Testament on our credence are next con-
sidered. The chapters on the Origin of the Gospels and the
Fidelity of the Gospel History contain no fresh contributions to
Biblical criticism, nor anything new to persons conversant with
this class of subjects; but they are a well arranged summary of
salient facts and arguments, gathered chiefly from Strauss, Hug,
Schleiermacher, and Hennell. The conclusions to which the writer
is led are, that we have no certitude as to the Gospels conveying
the testimony of eyewitnesses, while, on the other hand, there is
the strongest evidence of their containing a large admixture of
legend, and that we can trust them no further than as giving an
outline of Christ's life and teaching. Hence Mr. Greg holds that
dogmas founded on sayings attributed to Jesus, but discordant
with the impression of his character conveyed by the general
tenor of the Gospels, must be rejected; for example, the dogmas

of the necessity of belief to salvation, the proper Deity of
Christ, and the Atonement. We quote some of his reflections on
these results:--

"In fine, then, we arrive at this irresistible conclusion, that,
knowing many passages in the Evangelists to be unauthentic, and
having reason to suspect the authenticity of many others, and
not being able with absolute certainty to point to any which are
perfectly and indubitably authentic--the probability in favour
of the fidelity of any of the texts relied on to prove the peculiar and perplexing doctrines of modern orthodoxy, is far inferior to the probability against the truth of those doctrines.
A doctrine perplexing to our reason, and painful to our feelings,
may be from God; but in this case the proof of its being from
God must be proportionately clear and irrefragable; the assertion of it in a narrative, which does not scruple to attribute to
God's messenger words which he never uttered, is not only no
proof, but does not even amount to a presumption. There is no
text in the Evangelists, the Divine (or Christian) origin of
which is sufficiently unquestionable to enable it to serve as
the foundation of doctrines repugnant to natural feeling or to
common sense.

     "But it will be objected, if these conclusions are sound,
absolute uncertainty is thrown over the whole Gospel history, and
over all Christ's teaching. To this we reply, in limine, in the
language of Algernon Sydney, 'No consequences can destroy a
truth'; the sole matter for consideration is, Are our arguments
correct?--not, Do they lead to a result which is embarrassing
and unwelcome?

     "But the inference is excessive; the premises do not reach
so far. The uncertainty thrown is not over the main points of
Christ's history, which, after all retrenchments, still stands
out an intelligible, though a skeleton account--not over the
grand features, the pervading tone of his doctrines or his character, which still present to us a clear, consistent and splendid
delineation; but over those individual statements, passages, and
discourses which mar this delineation--which break its unity--
which destroy its consistency--which cloud its clearness--which
tarnish its beauty. The gain to us seems immense.

     "It is true we have no longer absolute certainty with regard
to any one especial text or scene; such is neither necessary nor
attainable; it is true that, instead of passively accepting the
whole heterogeneous and indigestible mass, we must, by the careful and conscientious exercise of those faculties with which we
are endowed, by ratiocination and moral tact, separate what
Christ did, from what he did not teach, as best we may. But the
task will be difficult to those only who look in the Gospels for
a minute, dogmatic, and sententious creed; not to those who seek
only to learn Christ's spirit that they may imbibe it, and to
comprehend his views of virtue and of God, that they may draw
strength and consolation from those fountains of living water."

In discussing the limits of Apostolic wisdom and authority, Mr.
Greg's prepossessions, perhaps, lead him to heighten the difference between the spirit and teaching of the Apostles and those of
their Master; but for much that he maintains under this head, he
had strictly critical grounds. His observations on the misappre-
hension of the Apostles and the early Church concerning the "gift
of tongues" are especially just and pointed. In the chapter on

Miracles, he treats the subject chiefly on a priori grounds, and only cursorily touches on the question whether the miraculous narratives in the Gospels bear the marks of credibility. He argues for the position, long ago strenuously maintained by Locke, and admitted by many even of our orthodox divines, that a miracle can never authenticate a doctrine; and he further shows, that miracles are not a safe foundation on which to rest the claims of Christianity, inasmuch as they are not susceptible of proof by documentary evidence. The crowning miracle of the Resurrection he considers separately, giving a condensed analysis of the evidence on which it rests. The conclusion that this evidence is insufficient is, he thinks, rendered needlessly painful by the undue doctrinal value assigned by theologians to the Resurrection of Christ, whether as a sanction of his doctrines, or as a type and pledge of our own resurrection; for, viewed in the one light it is superfluous, while in the other, it utterly fails of the supposed end, since a bodily resurrection after three days' interment, can bear no resemblance to anything that awaits ourselves.

Even after the renunciation of implicit credence in the Gospel narratives and Apostolic writings, and the rejection of all miraculous evidence, the question remains--Is Christianity a revealed religion? Since, however, the lustre of Christ's life and teaching may have been obscured by the errors and limitations of his biographers and immediate disciples, it is still possible that he may have had a special divine mission. In seeking for an answer to this question, Mr. Greg "finds no adequate reason for believing Jesus to be the son of God, nor his doctrines to be a direct and special revelation." The following is his conception of Jesus:--

"We do not believe that Christianity contains anything which a genius like Christ's, brought up and nourished as his had been, might not have disentangled for itself. We hold that God has so arranged matters in this beautiful and well-ordered but mysteriously governed universe, that one great mind after another will arise from time to time, as such as needed, to discover and flash forth before the eyes of men the truths that are wanted, and the amount of truth that can be borne. We conceive that this is effected by endowing them--or (for we pretend to no scholastic nicety of expression) by having arranged that nature and the course of events shall send them into the world endowed with that superior mental and moral organization, in which grand truths, sublime gleams of spiritual light, will spontaneously and inevitably arise. Such a one we believe was Jesus of Nazareth-- the most exalted genius whom God ever sent upon earth; in himself an embodied revelation; humanity in its divinest phase-- "God manifest in the flesh," according to Eastern hyperbole; an exemplar vouch-safed, in an early age of the world, of what man may and should become, in the course of ages, in his progress towards the realization of his destiny; an individual gifted with a glorious intellect, a noble soul, a fine organization, and a perfectly balanced moral being; and who, by virtue of these endowments, saw further than all other men--

            "Beyond the verge of that blue sky,
            Where God's sublimest secrets lie;"

an earnest, not only of what humanity may be, but of what it will

be, when the most perfected races shall bear the same relation
to the finest minds of existing times, as these now bear to the
Bushmen and the Esquimaux. He was, as Parker beautifully expresses it, 'the possibility of the rare made real.' He was a
sublime poet, prophet, hero, and philosopher; and had the usual
fate of such--misrepresented by his enemies, misconstrued by his
friends; unhappy in this, that his nearest intimates and followers were not of a calibre to understand him; happy in this,
that his words contained such undying seeds of truth as could
survive even the media through which they passed. Like the wheat
found in the Egyptian catacombs, they retain the power of germi-
nating undiminished, whenever their appropriate soil is found.
They have been preserved almost pure, notwithstanding the Judaic
narrowness of Peter, the orthodox passions of John, and the metaphysical subtleties of Paul. Everything seems to us to confirm
the conclusion that we have in the Christianity of Scripture a
code of beautiful, simple, sublime, profound, but not perfect
truth, obscured by having come down to us by the intervention of
minds far inferior to that of its Author; narrowed by their
uncultivation; marred by their misapprehensions; and tarnished
by their foreign admixtures. It is a collection of grand truths
transmitted to us by men who only half comprehended their
grandeur, and imperfectly grasped their truth."

If Christianity be no longer regarded as a revelation, but as the
conception of a fallible though transcendently gifted mind, it
follows that only so much of it is to be accepted as harmonizes
with the reason and conscience: Christianity becomes "Christian
Ecleticism." Mr. Greg unhesitatingly receives many of Christ's
precepts as unsurpassable and unimprovable: for example, those
which inculcate the worthlessness of ceremonial observance and the
necessity of active virtue, purity of heart as the security for
purity of life, universal philanthropy, forgiveness of injuries,
self-sacrifice in the cause of duty, humility, and genuine sincerity. He regards as next in perfection the views which Christianity unfolds of God as a Father.

"In the two great points essential to our practical life, viz.,
our feelings towards God and our conduct towards man, the Gospels
contain little about which men can differ--little from which they
can dissent. He is our Father, we are all brethren. This much
lies open to the most ignorant and busy, as fully as to the most
leisurely and learned. This needs no priest to teach it, no
authority to endorse it. The rest is speculation; intensely
interesting, indeed, but of no practical necessity."

Other tenets taught in the Christian Scriptures, however, Mr. Greg
thinks open to grave objections. He urges, for example, that the
New Testament assigns an efficacy to prayer incompatible with any
elevated conception of Deity; that it inculcates resignation, not
as the result of a self-reasoning faith in the wisdom and justice
of the supreme will, but on the narrow ground that sufferings are
specially ordained for the benefit of the individual; and that it
appeals to the selfish motives--the desire for recompense, rather
than to the highest--the love of the good for its own sake. He
holds that the conception of the pardon of sin, or repentance and
conversion, tends to contravene the system on which man is trained
and disciplined, and the entire scheme of God's government--the
conviction that every breach of the Divine law is attended with

inexorable consequences, being essential to a healthy condition
of the conscience and a just theory of Providence:--

"Let any one look back upon his past career, look inward on his
daily life, and then say what effect would be produced upon him,
were the conviction once fixedly embedded in his soul, that everything done is done irrevocably, that even the omnipotence of God
cannot <u>uncommit</u> a deed, cannot make that undone which has been
done; that every act of his <u>must</u> bear its allotted fruit according to the everlasting laws--must remain for ever ineffaceably
inscribed on the tablets of universal Nature. And, then, let him
consider what would have been the result upon the moral condition
of our race, had all men ever held this conviction.
    "Perhaps you have led a youth of dissipation and excess
which has undermined and enfeebled your constitution, and you
have transmitted this injured and enfeebled constitution to your
children. They suffer, in consequence, through life; suffering
is entailed upon them; your repentance, were it in sackcloth and
ashes, cannot help you or them. Your punishment is tremendous,
but it is legitimate and inevitable. You have broken Nature's
laws, or you have ignored them, and no one violates or neglects
them with impunity. What a lesson for timely reflection and
obedience is here!
    "Again--you have broken the seventh commandment. You
grieve--you repent--you resolutely determine against any such
weakness in future. It is well; but 'you know that God is mer-
ciful--you feel that he will forgive you.' You are comforted.
But no--there is no forgiveness of sins--the injured party may
forgive you--your accomplice or victim may forgive you, according to the meaning of human language; but <u>the deed is done</u>, and
all the powers of Nature, were they to conspire in your behalf,
could not make it undone; the consequences to the body--the consequences to the soul--though no man may perceive them, are
there--are written in the annals of the past, and must reverberate
through all time.
    "But all this, let it be understood, in no degree militates
against the value or the necessity of repentance. Repentance,
contrition of soul, bears, like every other act, its own fruit--
the fruit of purifying the heart, of amending the future: not
as man has hitherto conceived--of effacing the past. The commission of sin is an irrevocable act, but it does not incapaci-
tate the soul for virtue. Its consequences cannot be expunged,
but the course need not be pursued. Sin, though it is inefface-
able, calls for no despair, but for efforts more energetic than
before. Repentance is still as valid as ever; but it is valid
to secure the future, not to obliterate the past.
    "The moral to be drawn from these reflections is this:--God
has placed the lot of man--not, perhaps, altogether of the individuals, but certainly of the race--in his own hands, by surrounding him with <u>laws</u>, on knowledge of which, and on conformity
to which, his well-being depends. The study of these, and the
principle of obedience to them, forms, therefore, the great aim
of education, both of men and nations. They must be taught:--
    "1. The <u>physical</u> <u>laws</u>, on which God has made <u>health</u> to
depend.
    "2. The <u>moral</u> <u>laws</u>, on which He has made <u>happiness</u> to
depend.
    "3. The <u>intellectual</u> <u>laws</u>, on which He has made <u>knowledge</u>
to depend.

"4. The <u>social</u> <u>and</u> <u>political</u> <u>laws</u>, on which He has made
<u>national</u> <u>prosperity</u> to depend.
      "5. The <u>economic</u> <u>laws</u>, on which He has made <u>wealth</u> to
depend.
      "A true comprehension of all these, <u>and</u> <u>of</u> <u>their</u> <u>unexcep-</u>
<u>tional</u> <u>and</u> <u>unalterable</u> <u>nature</u>, would ultimately rescue mankind
from all their vice and nearly all their suffering, save
casualties and sorrows."

Mr. Greg also shows that Christianity teaches an ascetic and
depreciating view of life, incompatible with that energetic devotion to the improvement of our races, and with that delight in
the innocent adornment of our existence in this world, which are
essential to a noble and well-balanced soul.
      In the concluding chapter we have the author's reflections
on "the great enigma--the question of man's future existence." He
applies himself, evidently with his utmost strength, to prove the
invalidity and even futility of a conclusion which, after all, he
himself holds. He labours to make clear that the belief in a
future state is not demanded by any process of our intellect or
any tendency of our moral nature, in order that he may fall back
with the greater confidence on the assertion of his belief in it
as an intuition on a par with our belief in the reality of an external world.
      We have endeavoured to give our readers a faithful idea of
Mr. Greg's work. Though far from setting our seal to all his
opinions, we think that the <u>Creed</u> <u>of</u> <u>Christendom</u> sets forth very
powerfully much truth of which society is in urgent need, while
it opens to us an acquaintance with an individual mind possessing
a strong moral and intellectual charm.
      The deservedly respectful reception of Mr. Greg's work by
the periodical press, compared with that given twelve years ago
to a work of kindred character--Hennell's <u>Inquiry</u> <u>concerning</u> <u>the</u>
<u>Origin</u> <u>of</u> <u>Christianity</u>--is no slight indication of advancement,
either in plain speaking or in liberality of religious views.
Though too distinct in their method, and to a considerable extent
in their matter, for one to be regarded as superseding the other,
both these works have the same object, to ascertain how far the
popular idea of Christianity will sustain the test of impartial
criticism; they are alike animated by a spirit of candour and
reverence, and they have substantially the same result. Hennell,
it is true, holds that Jesus shared the common theocratic hope of
his nation, and thinks there is strong evidence that, at the commencement of his career, he expected the Divine attestation to
his Messiahship to be given in such a general adhesion of the
people to his cause as would enable him to free his nation from
the Roman yoke by insurrection, and effect the political as well
as the spiritual regeneration of Israel. He regards the character of Jesus as less exceptional than it appears under Mr. Greg's
view; but he estimates very highly the power and beauty in his
nature and the value of his moral teaching. The <u>Inquiry</u> <u>concern-</u>
<u>ing</u> <u>the</u> <u>Origin</u> <u>of</u> <u>Christianity</u> is evidently the production of a
mind which has brought to the independent study of the New Testa-
ment the rare combination of analytic acumen with breadth of conception. Its merit was at once recognized in Germany, where it
was speedily translated. While in our own country it was welcomed by many distinguished minds, and has had an extensive,
though latent, influence in promoting the intelligent study of
the Christian Scriptures. That Mr. Greg has found it a valu-

able aid is not only evidenced in his text, but avowed by frequent
references in his notes, though, doubtless through a temporary
forgetfulness, he speaks in his preface as if he had no predeces-
sor among laymen in the path of free but reverent inquiry into
the claims of Christianity.

Nevertheless, when Hennell's work first appeared, the Reviews dared not acknowledge the merit which it was privately admitted to possess, and four years after the appearance of the
second edition, it received, from a periodical which has recently
bestowed elaborate praise on the Creed of Christendom, a rather
contemptuous critique, the object of which was, obviously, to put
down the book by no fairer means than that of presenting details,
adduced by Hennell merely in the light of cumulative evidence, as
if they formed the sole basis of his argument.

In this annus mirabilis of 1851, however, our reviewers have
attained a higher standard of courage and fairness than could be
ascribed to them in 1838, or even in 1845. "La terre tourne,"
says Pascal, "malgré qu'on le nie; et vous aussi, mes révérends
pères, vous tournez avec elle--The earth turns in spite of all
denials; and you also, my reverend fathers, turn with it."

RUSKIN'S LECTURES

Leader, 5 (10 June 1854), 545-6

Gordon S. Haight identified this article on John Ruskin's Lectures on
Architecture and Painting (London: Smith, Elder and Co., 1854) as one which
George Henry Lewes was supposed to write but that in fact George Eliot wrote
when Lewes was taken ill in the late spring of 1854 (see Biography, p. 144).
This seems to have been fortuitous for the author of Middlemarch because a
phrase from this review became important to the novel. The discussion
of "the language of Art" is pertinent at two points in Middlemarch. When Mr.
Brooke shows Dorothea the sketches done by Will Ladislaw in chapter 9, she
remarks, "They are a language I do not understand. I suppose there is some
relation between pictures and nature which I am too ignorant to feel--just as
you see what a Greek sentence stands for which means nothing to me." And in
chapter 21 Ladislaw tells Dorothea that "Art is an old language with a great
many artificial affected styles, and sometimes the chief pleasure one gets out
of knowing them is the mere sense of knowing." When in chapter 22 we are told
that "some things which had seemed monstrous" to Dorothea--like "saints with
architectural models in their hands [see fig. 9] or knives accidently wedged
in their skulls"--were "gathering intelligibility and even a natural meaning,"
we are to understand that she is learning the vocabulary of the difficult
"language of Art," which, as George Eliot says in her later review of Modern
Painters III, is also a language of morality: "in learning how to estimate
the artistic products of a particular age according to the mental attitude and
external life of that age we are widening our sympathy and deepening the basis
of our tolerance and charity." George Eliot quotes Ruskin in entries 83-89.

It is reserved for writers like Mr. Ruskin to treat perpetually
the same subjects, and to be ever new and ever interesting. And
this is due partly to the intrinsic interest of these subjects,
and perhaps mainly to a command of language and illustration, and
a charm of style unsurpassed by any living writer, but in part
also to his earnest belief in the doctrines he advocates, and
genuine worship of truth wherever he recognises its existence.
In this sense, at least, his bitterest opponents cannot deny that
he has done good service. He may be called the great Protestant
of Modern Art; he first exhorted us to think for ourselves, to
examine the worth of the old traditional opinions whereby our
minds were fettered, and to adopt no creed till we have submitted
it to the test of private judgment. Further, he has preached un-
ceasingly to us the great doctrine that no one has a right to be
indifferent to these things, and that it is a duty we owe to ourselves no less than to one another, to cultivate that love and
knowledge of Nature, and that appreciation of Art, which are so
conducive to the perfecting of our higher attributes, to the refinement of our baser instincts, and to the development of all
gentle and holy sympathies between us.
     The lectures now printed were delivered at Edinburgh last
winter. They are four. The two first are on the subject of improvement in our domestic architecture, strongly insisting, as
ever, on the superiority of the Gothic to the Greek type. The
third is dedicated to another cause, for which Mr. Ruskin has
often before laid lance in rest,--the supremacy of Turner as a
landscape painter; and the fourth to the latest "mission" of the
author,--the interpretation of the Pre-Raphaelite principles.
The interest of the book is greatly enhanced by the addition of
engravings of the drawings used by Mr. Ruskin, principally to

illustrate the two first lectures.

The grounds on which Mr. Ruskin asserts the inferiority of Greek architecture have been already set forth in his former works. We have not space to follow him into its technical deficiencies. But we do most heartily symphathise with his desire to free men's minds from that Greek (worse than Egyptian bondage),--from the theory that a building or an ornament, however ill-adapted to our age, to our climate, to our manners, must be beautiful, must be classical, because it is Greek. Whatever is true in its own time is classical. The art of an era should be the outward and visible expression of the spirit of that era. When the Greek type was classical it was true, vital, the offspring of its age. Nothing is more pitiable than that want of noble self-reliance in a people which neglects the treasures of their own hearts and minds, in order to recur to a lifeless imitation of extinct form and spirit, and calling incessantly on the heroic Past, is obstinately blind to the heroic Present.

> "The forms
> Of the heroic alter in all ages;
> The Spirit in the forms remains the same."

Mr. Ruskin says that the delivery of these lectures "excited, as may be imagined, considerable indignation and controversy." It certainly may be imagined! We can conceive that persons who had never in their lives entertained a doubt that a straight, lofty, uniform frontage, such as constitutes what is generally called "a handsome street," was the ne plus ultra of desirable town archi- tecture,--may have been rather indignant at hearing their city's chief glory held up as a model--to be avoided--may have been un- able at first fully to appreciate advice such as the following:--

> "You must expect at first that there will be difficulties and in- consistencies in carrying out the new style; but they will soon be conquered if you attempt not too much at once. Do not be afraid of incongruities,--do not think of unities of effect. In- troduce your Gothic line by line and stone by stone; never mind mixing it with your present architecture; your existing houses will be none the worse for having little bits of better work fitted to them; build a porch, or point a window, if you can do nothing else; and remember it is the glory of Gothic architec- ture that it can do anything. Whatever you really and seriously want, Gothic will do for you; but it must be an earnest want. It is its pride to accommodate itself to your needs; and the one general law under which it acts is simply this,--find out what will make you comfortable, build that in the strongest and boldest way, and then set your fancy free in the decoration of it. Don't do anything to imitate this cathedral or that, how- ever beautiful. Do what is convenient; and if the form be a new one, so much the better; then set your mason's wits to work, to find out some new way of treating it. Only be steadily de- termined that, even if you cannot get the best Gothic, at least you will have no Greek; and in a few years' time,--in less time than you could learn a new science or a new language thoroughly, --the whole art of your native country will be reanimated."

These lectures will in some degree answer the charge of inconsis- tency, which has been so often brought against Mr. Ruskin by some of his critics, who, perceiving that the Pre-Raphaelites paint

every object within view, even to the middle distances, with a
clearness of outline and a minute attention to detail which is
almost microscopic, while in many of Turner's pictures, a totally
opposite treatment is carried to such a length, that even the immediate foreground is vague and undistinguishable--have concluded
that it is impossible both can be right, and that in admiring
Turner and lauding the Pre-Raphaelites, Mr. Ruskin pledges himself at once to two opposite decisions on the same subject. But
apparent differences and discrepancies often strike the eye near
the surface, while essential resemblances lie deep; and it is
possible that in this case Mr. Ruskin may have looked deeper than
his critics. The one common principle recognised by him in the
system of Turner and in that of the Pre-Raphaelites, is the anxious pursuit of truth, as seen through their own eyes, not accepted in the traditionary conventionalisms which during a long
era of decadence have grown up around Art, impeding its growth,
checking the free and vivifying influence of nature upon it, and
rendering its inspired message to men a mere parrot-cry. We are
reminded of the saying of a contemporary French author, who, writing of the successive schools through which art has been handed
down to us, and quoting the ever quoted image of Lucretius,

"Et, quasi cursores, vitai lampada tradunt,"[1]

adds, with bitter, "Quelques uns l'ont porté comme un cierge,
mais d'autres comme un cigare."[2] And the illustration, though
somewhat beneath the dignity of the subject, aptly expresses the
different tone of feeling regarding Art in the 13th and 19th
centuries,--the severe and reverent earnestness of the one, the
faithless indifference of the other.
     The growth of conventionalism in Art is not difficult to
comprehend. To a certain degree, all artistic interpretation of
Nature is conventional. The aim of Art, in depicting any natural
object, is to produce in the mind analogous emotions to those
produced by the object itself; but as with all our skill and care
we cannot imitate it exactly, this aim is not attained by transcribing, but by translating it into the language of Art. And
here arises the danger to inferior workmen; for here begins what
Mr. Ruskin calls "the distinction between noble conventionalism
and false conventionalism." "Noble conventionalism," he says,
"is not an agreement between the artist and spectator that the
one shall misrepresent nature sixty times over, and the other believe the misrepresentation sixty times over, but it is an agreement that certain means and limitations being prescribed, only
that kind of truth is to be expected which is consistent with
those means." And he adds, "Its conditions always consist in
stopping short of nature, not in falsifying nature." But no one
can translate properly from a language without thoroughly understanding that language; and hence the presumption that the Pre-
Raphaelites are in the right road to successful translation of
nature, by studying her in her minutest details with unwearying
care and fidelity, before they attempt to reproduce her by art.
That is an apprenticeship through which all great artists must
pass--must have passed. That Turner did so, the history of his
most arduous student life testifies; he mastered detail, before
he ventured to rise above detail. And that the Pre-Raphaelites,
at present swathed and stiff in the swaddling clothes of their
artistic infancy, will one day rise as he rose, become men, and
put away from them childish things, is the hope and belief of

Mr. Ruskin--a belief founded less on the individual artists than on the eternal principles, whereon they have taken their stand.

At the risk of injuring the force of Mr. Ruskin's interesting defence of Pre-Raphaelite peculiarities, we must present the reader with one extract:--

"You perceive that the principal resistance they have to make is to that spurious beauty, whose attractiveness had tempted men to forget, or to despise, the more noble quality of sincerity: and in order at once to put them beyond the power of temptation from this beauty, they are, as a body, characterised by a total absence of sensibility to the ordinary and popular forms of artistic gracefulness; while, to all that still lower kind of prettiness, which regulates the disposition of our scenes upon the stage, and which appears in our lower art, as in our annuals, our commonplace portraits, and statuary, the Pre-Raphaelites are not only dead, but they regard it with a contempt and aversion approaching to disgust. This character is absolutely necessary to them in the present time; but it, of course, occasionally renders their work comparatively unpleasing. As the school becomes less aggressive, and more authoritative--which it will do --they will enlist into their ranks men who will work, mainly, upon their principles, and yet embrace more of those characters which are generally attractive, and this great ground of offence will be removed.

"Again, you observe that, as landscape painters, their principles must, in great part, confine them to mere foreground work; and singularly enough, that they may not be tempted away from this work, they have been born with comparatively little enjoyment of those evanescent effects and distant sublimities which nothing but the memory can arrest, and nothing but a daring conventionalism portray. But for this work they are not needed. Turner had done it before them; he, though his capacity embraced everything, and though he would sometimes, in his foregrounds, paint the spots upon a dead trout, and the dyes upon a butterfly's wing, yet for the most part delighting to begin at that very point where Pre-Raphaelitism becomes powerless.

"Lastly. The habit of constantly carrying everything up to the utmost point of completion deadens the Pre-Raphaelites in general to the merits of men who, with an equal love of truth up to a certain point, yet express themselves habitually with speed and power, rather than with finish, and give abstracts of truth rather than total truth. Probably to the end of time artists will more or less be divided into these classes, and it will be impossible to make men like Millais understand the merits of men like Tintoret; but this is more to be regretted because the Pre-Raphaelites have enormous powers of imagination, as well as of realisation, and do not yet themselves know of how much they would be capable, if they sometimes worked on a larger scale, and with a less laborious finish."

The lecture on Turner has a peculiar interest, an interest which is excited less by Turner the artist, than by Turner the man. We have seldom been more affected than by Mr. Ruskin's touching picture of a deep large heart, crushed and chilled by early repression into reserve and gloom, and concealing its treasures of tender and generous feeling beneath an outward antagonism, which reacted painfully on himself. That Turner was a great artist, we hope and believe few will now be found to question. That a really

great artist cannot be other than a great man, is a principle that
some of us at least hold with all our faith. But how great a man
Turner was may be judged from two or three of the anecdotes it
has been a labour of love to Mr. Ruskin to record:--

"You have, perhaps not many of you, heard of a painter of the
name of Bird: I do not myself know his works, but Turner saw
some merit in them: and when Bird first sent a picture to the
Academy for exhibition, Turner was on the hanging committee.
Bird's picture had great merit; but no place for it could be
found. Turner pleaded hard for it. No, the thing was impossible. Turner sat down and looked at Bird's picture for a long
time; then insisted that a place must be found for it. He was
still met by the assertion of impracticability. He said no more,
but took down one of his own pictures, sent it out of the
Academy, and hung Bird's in its place.
    "Match that if you can, among the annals of hanging com-
mittees. But he could do nobler things than this.
    "When Turner's picture of Cologne was exhibited in the year
1826, it was hung between two portraits, by Sir Thomas Lawrence,
of Lady Wallscourt, and Lady Robert Manners.
    "The sky of Turner's picture was exceedingly bright, and it
had a most injurious effect on the colour of the two portraits.
Lawrence naturally felt mortified, and complained openly of the
position of his pictures. You are aware that artists were at
that time permitted to retouch their pictures on the walls of
the Academy. On the morning of the opening of the exhibition,
at the private view, a friend of Turner's who had seen the
Cologne in all its splendour, led a group of expectant critics
up to the picture. He started back from it in consternation.
The golden sky had changed to a dun colour. He ran up to Turner,
who was in another part of the room. 'Turner, what have you
been doing to your picture?' 'Oh,' muttered Turner, in a low
voice, 'poor Lawrence was so unhappy. It's only lamp black.
It'll all wash off after the exhibition!' He had actually
passed a wash of lamp black in water-colour over the whole sky,
and utterly spoiled his picture for the time, and so left it
through the exhibition, lest it should hurt Lawrence's."

We cannot deny ourselves the pleasure of making one more extract,
the concluding passage of the lecture on Turner. As a specimen
of Mr. Ruskin's magical style, it is charming; but even that gives
way before the deeper interest excited by the life-struggle of a
great soul, sharing the destiny of its fellows in all ages, the
lonely life, the long withheld sympathy, the tardy appreciation,
the crown of thorns--living, the crown of laurel--dead.

"Imagine what it was for a man to live seventy years in this
hard world, with the kindest heart, and the noblest intellect of
his time, and never to meet with a single word or ray of sympathy, until he felt himself sinking into the grave. From the
time he knew his true greatness all the world was turned against
him; he held his own; but it could not be without roughness of
bearing, and hardening of the temper, if not of the heart. No
one understood him, no one trusted him, and every one cried out
against him. Imagine, any of you, the effect upon your own
minds, if every voice you heard from the human beings around you
were raised, year after year, through all your lives, only in
condemnation of your efforts, and denial of your success. This

may be borne, and borne easily, by men who have fixed religious
principles, or supporting domestic ties. But Turner had no one
to teach him in his youth, and no one to love him in his old age.
Respect and affection, if they came at all, came unbelieved, or
came too late. Naturally irritable, though kind,--naturally sus-
picious, though generous,--the gold gradually became dim, and the
most fine gold changed, or if not changed, overcast and clouded.
The deep heart was still beating, but it was beneath a dark and
melancholy mail, between whose joints, however, sometimes the
slightest arrows found entrance, and power of giving pain. He
received no consolation in his last years, nor in his death.
Cut off in great part from all society--first, by labour, and at
last by sickness--hunted to his grave by the malignities of small
critics, and the jealousies of hopeless rivalry, he died in the
house of a stranger,--one companion of his life, and one only,
staying with him to the last. The window of his death-chamber
was turned towards the west, and the sun shone upon his face in
its setting, and rested there, as he expired."

                              Notes

1. And like runners they carry the lamp of life. De Rerum Natura 2.79.
2. Some carry it like a taper, others like a cigar.

THE ART OF THE ANCIENTS

Leader, 6 (17 March 1855), 257-8

George Eliot's notes for this review are found in entries 39-40. For her comments on Stahr's style see entry 27, n. 1. Adolf Wilhelm Theodor Stahr, says Gordon S. Haight, "shared Lewes's interest in Goethe and Spinoza and wrote on the history of art and philosophy. Marian described him as 'pale, nervous, sickly looking, with scarcely any moral radiation, so to speak'; his literary egotism was ludicrously prominent" (Biography, p. 170). Nevertheless, his Torso: Kunst, Künstler und Kunstwerk der Alten (Brunswick: Friedrich Vieweg, 1854), was a valuable source for classical allusions that appeared in George Eliot's novels. The Medusa Rondanini (see fig. 3), for instance, mentioned in this review of Torso, served her in a description of Hetty in Adam Bede (see entry 40, n. 1). And the idea that civilization moved from East to West was one to which she returned again and again (see entry 26, n. 1). George Eliot's two subsequent reviews of Stahr also appear below.

The books of which a reviewer can say that he has read every word, and has laid them down wishing for more, are far from being as plentiful as blackberries, especially in German literature. Professor Stahr's Torso, however, is one of these exceptional books: we have read it from beginning to end with delight, and are eager for the second part, which is yet to appear. The name of Adolf Stahr is well known in Germany, and not unknown in England, as that of a writer who has that rare mastery of the unwieldy German language which makes his works charm by their form as well as their matter. There is not a trace of pedantry in his books; you perceive his knowledge as you perceive the daylight, by the clearness with which objects are presented to you. He has written a work on Aristotle, to which scholars give a high rank; but his Weimar und Jena may be read with pleasure by the idlest young lady, and his Jahr in Italien is a favourite companion of artistic travellers. His preeminent talent lies in description both of natural scenery and works of art; he has not only an intense susceptibility to the beautiful, but he is in possession of the magic word which will convey his impression to the mind of the reader. These excellent qualities are remarkably exhibited in his latest and yet uncompleted work, the title of which we have given above. It is more historical and descriptive than disquisitional; condensed enough to serve as an introductory manual for those who have the opportunity of immediately studying ancient sculpture, and yet so full and vivid in its descriptions, and so philosophic in its mode of considering the development of art, that it may be read with lively interest in a country town, far away from all casts and museums. To any one who is not already very wise on Greek art, and who is so happy as to have time and opportunity to study its original remains, or, what is next best, to go to the Crystal Palace, we recommend Professor Stahr's book. It will not tell him everything, but it will do him the greater service of creating a thirst for more knowledge than it conveys.

The early chapters are occupied with the consideration of the physical geography of Greece and the characteristics of the Greek races, their religion and political institutions, as bearing on the development of art. A chapter on Daedalus, the mythic father of Greek art, whom tradition connects with Egypt, leads us naturally to the question how far Hellenic art is to be regarded as a purely indigenous, independent product of Greece, or simply

as a higher development of oriental art. It is well known that
Winckelmann espoused the former opinion, and his authority prevailed among German critics in maintaining a view which is opposed to all analogy and to the direct evidence furnished by
oriental and Greek remains, long after it had been given up by
English, French, and Italian investigators of the highest rank.
It is a fact characteristic of our good friends the Germans (who,
something like those Fakirs that seek for the divine light by
perpetually contemplating the end of their noses, generally pre-
determine what things must be in their studies, and think it an
idle business to inquire what things are), that when Ludwig Ross,
a distinguished traveller and critic, after diligently investigat-
ing the remains of art in the countries round the Levant, enunciated the opinion that the social, religious, and artistic culture of Greece could not be understood apart from the supposition
that the Greeks had been influenced by the culture of earlier
peoples, he was contemptuously decried as a "Tourist." Of course,
a man who had looked at the fact must be incapacitated for forming the reine Idee. But a truer spirit of investigation has
arisen among the German critics of the last thirty years, and men
such as Creuzer, Thiersch, Böckh, Schorn, and Anselm Feuerbach
have recognised the influence of oriental, and especially of
Egyptian, art on Greece. "The process of development, in culture
and art," says Professor Stahr, "is the same as that of natural
products and their cultivation by man. Modern botanical research
has proved that almost everything which is necessary, useful, and
agreeable to us in the vegetable kingdom came in a gradual procession from Asia, until it was arrested at the western coast of
Europe. And now that after a short rest it has sprung across the
Atlantic this propagation pursues its course through America
towards the West. But the West receives the gifts of the East
only to refine the rude, to develop the imperfect, to ennoble the
common."

After general considerations on the progress of Greek art
from Daedalus to Phidias, and from Phidias to Hadrian, and on the
criteria of relative antiquity, the author commences his descriptive survey of the principal remains of Hellenic sculpture--those
remains which best illustrate the ideals of the successive epochs.
The Gate of Lions at Mycenae, and the reliefs at Samothrace representing Agamemnon seated on a throne accompanied by two heralds,
bear strong traces of the abstract Egyptian manner; the one
herald, for example, being the repetition of the other. So do the
Lycian sculptures, consisting of from sixty to seventy statues in
a sitting posture, which formed the avenue to a temple; the perfect parallelism of the stiff posture of the arms, the straight
lines of the drapery, everything is Egyptian in style. A yet more
important specimen of Greek art, discovered in Sicily about
thirty years ago, are the remains of a temple on the citadel of
Selinus, a city which was built by Dorian Greeks 608 B.C., and
destroyed by the Carthaginians only 200 years later, so that the
period of these sculptures is absolutely determined. Here we have
an ill-proportioned Hercules carrying a couple of his tormentors
slung on a pole over his shoulder, and Perseus, protected by
Minerva, slaying Medusa. The upper part of all the figures is
de face, the legs de profil--again an Egyptian fashion. The
Medusa is a hideous caricature; how far from the terrible beauty
of the Medusa Rondanini!

A chapter on temple pediments and their sculptural ornaments
introduces the OEginetan sculptures, the originals of which are

at Munich, and a cast of which may be seen at the Crystal Palace.
They doubtless adorned the temple erected by the wealthy OEginetans
to Minerva--a temple belonging to the earliest works of Doric
architecture, and probably built in the time of Solon, for they
were found in the accumulations of rubbish overblown with brush-
wood which surrounded its ruins. The remarkable point in these
sculptures is the high degree of truthfulness and beauty in the
limbs, and the uniformity and utter unmeaningness of the faces.
This inequality Stahr regards as the remains of the earlier
hieratic influence, the tendency of which was to keep up traditional and conventional forms; but perhaps he is nearer the true
reason when he says, that on comparing the OEginetan sculptures
with the works of the early Italian masters, Giotto and Pietro
Perugino, we observe a striking difference between them in this
respect: the early Italian masters were animated by the spiritualistic idea that the body was but an unworthy dwelling for the
immortal soul, and hence they threw all their power into the
face, where the soul might be said to look out from its taber-
nacle; whereas in the conception of the Greeks, a fine body was
the primary condition of a fine mind--<u>first</u> <u>the</u> <u>body</u>, <u>and</u> <u>then</u> <u>the</u>
<u>soul</u> <u>by</u> <u>and</u> <u>through</u> <u>the</u> <u>body</u>, was the order of their ideas. Hence,
in Greek art, the expression of the face would naturally be the
last in the order of development.

The chapters on Phidias and his works, include a survey of
the sculptures of the Parthenon (by us modern barbarians called
the Elgin marbles), which, alas! are the only works immediately
and unquestionably his now remaining; a description of what the
Parthenon was in its glory; and the history of its sad fate. It
is exasperating to think that after surviving the bigotry of
early Christianity, the inroads of northern barbarians, the cru-
sading adventurers of the middle ages, who as Dukes of Athens
made the Acropolis their citadel, nay, the Turkish conquest under
Omar, the Parthenon was at last, nearly at the end of the seventeenth century, blown into fragments in a siege conducted by
Königsmark, the German general of the Venetian army. The Turkish
Pacha had deposited all his treasures and ammunition in the
Parthenon, which had hitherto served him as a mosque; a bomb fell
into the powder magazine, and the temple, which had stood in its
beauty 2000 years, was a heap of ruins! Besides the fragmentary
relics of the Parthenon, we possess, as we have said, nothing that
can be regarded as the immediate work of Phidias; but we know that
the glorious ideals of the Zeus and Athene were of his creation,
and the descriptions of his works, which are preserved to us,
assure us that, on looking at the Jupiter Otricoli or the Pallas
Velletri, we are really looking at a product of the mind of
Phidias, even though these may not be direct copies from his
works. With Phidias are connected the Colossi on the Monte
Cavallo--two groups representing Castor and Pollux, each controlling a restive horse--from the fact that one of them is inscribed
with his name, and that Pliny speaks of one of the two naked
Colossi "as having been the work of Phidias." The result of the
scanty evidence on the subject seems to be, that one of the
colossal groups is a copy of an original work of Phidias in bronze.
The other is inscribed with the name of Praxiteles.

Next in interest to the remains of the Parthenon are those
of the temple of Apollo, in the city of Phigalia, in Arcadia
(the Phigalian marbles in the British Museum), the work of
Alkamenes, the pupil of Phidias, and discovered in 1811. The
temple itself, with its six-and-thirty marble pillars gleaming

through the dark green of the mountain forests, had been long known, but a startled fox first revealed to a company of English and German artists, and connoisseurs, the only aperture in the heap of ruins and accumulated rubbish which filled the interior to the height of sixteen feet. On looking in, they found that the little animal had made its bed on a splendid relief, and after immense labour, twenty-three compartments of the frieze were brought forth to the light: an invaluable addition to the small amount of Greek sculpture, the locality, date, and originality of which are beyond all doubt.

The two greatest contemporaries of Phidias were Polycletos and Myron. To the former we owe the Juno-ideal, of which the Juno Ludovisi is the highest presentation, and the conception of Mercury as the Greek youth in the culmination of blended beauty and strength, the Hermes Enagonios, presiding over Paloestra. Myron's genius was more realistic, and was chiefly directed to the reproduction of athletic and gymnastic subjects, and of animal life. The well-known Discobolus is, in all probability, a copy from a bronze original by him.

To this great triad of sculptors who adorned the age of Pericles, succeeded in the following age, the fourth century B.C., another triad, Scopas, Praxiteles, and Lysippus, whose style Winckelmann characterises as the beautiful in distinction from that of Phidias, which was the sublime. In the second period, the severe bronze which had hitherto been the favourite material, gave way to the more life-like marble. To this fact, that the artists of the Phidian age wrought principally in bronze, we must attribute our almost total loss of their productions, metal in every form having been an object of Barbarian greediness. Scopas was one of the most fertile of the ancient masters; he created whole species of ideal beings, as attendants on Bacchus, Neptune, Apollo, and Venus; yet not a single original work of his remains, not even one of the seven which were dragged away to Rome in the days of Greek humiliation. The Mars Ludovisi is probably a copy from an original of his, and he transformed the ideal of the Eumenides, the personified terror of conscience, from the hideousness assigned to it in the earlier poetry and art, into an appalling beauty. Praxiteles, "The Master of Beauty," is the one among all the artists of this age who has been brought nearest to us by the remains of his creations. To him we owe the Venus-ideal of which the Aphrodite of Gnidos was the culmination, the conception of Eros as the lovely youth, the voluptuous beauty of the Bacchus, the graceful strength and freedom of the Diana, the benignant repose of the Ceres, and the famous Satyr which an ancient art legend describes him as valuing together with his Eros, above all his other works. Even so early as the time of Pliny, it was doubted whether the great Niobe group, discovered at Rome in 1583, and now at Florence, were the work of Scopas or of Praxiteles. But we at last know that the statue of Niobe was one of the finest works of Praxiteles, for Greek poetry, which has proved less perishable than Greek sculpture, makes Niobe say: "Me living the Gods turned to stone, but in stone Praxiteles has made me breathe again."

To the chapter on Praxiteles follows a long and valuable one on the Social Position of the Artist in Greece, and another on the relation between Art and Freedom. Then comes a highly interesting survey of ancient Portrait-sculpture; and finally, this first part of the work closes with the consideration of the Colouring and Nudity of Greek statues. We are glad to find

Professor Stahr insisting, that in the highest period of Greek
art the colouring of statues was not guided by the barbaric idea
of producing illusion, but by a fine sense of relief in colours,
an opinion which we have advocated in these columns.[1]

Our space will not allow us to dwell longer on the contents
of this delightful work. Let the readers of German, and the
lovers of art, procure it for themselves.

Note

1. I have not located this opinion with certainty in the Leader. There
is, however, a discussion of the coloring of Greek statues in "Contemporary
Literature," Westminster Review, 64 (April 1855) USA ed., 319-20. Eliot refers
to this review in her later notice of Torso II in Westminster Review, 65
(April 1856), USA ed. 347. If indeed the reference is to the Leader, it might
be to "Owen Jones on Decorative Art," a review of "An Attempt to Define the
Principles which Should Regulate the Employment of Colours in the Decorative
Arts: With a Few Words on the Present Necessity of an Architectural Education
on the Part of the Public. Read before the Society of Arts, April 28th, 1862,
By Owen Jones." See Leader, 2 (8 May 1852), 445-6.

MENANDER AND THE GREEK COMEDY

<u>Leader</u>, 6 (16 June 1855), 578-9

George Eliot mentions this review of Guillaume Guizot's <u>Ménandre</u>: <u>Etude historique et littéraire sur la Comédie et la Société Grecque</u> (Paris: Didier, 1855) in a letter to Sara Hennell, 17 June 1855 (<u>Letters</u>, II, 203). The article is especially interesting for the two instances in which she speaks of the 'highest comedy': first, as "a picture of real domestic life and manners," and, second, as "tragedy in the disguise of mirth." The one suggests a theory of realism she was soon to state in her review of Julia Kavanaugh's novel <u>Rachel Gray</u> (<u>Leader</u>, 7 [5 January 1856], 19):

<u>Rachel Gray</u> is not a story of a fine lady's sorrows wept into embroidered pocket-handkerchiefs, or of genius thrust into the background by toad-eating stupidity. It does not harrow us with the sufferings and temptations of a destitute needlewoman, or abash us by the refined sentiments and heroic deeds of naavies and ratcatchers. It tells the trials of a dressmaker who <u>could</u> get work, and of a small grocer, very vulgar, and not at all heroic, whose business was gradually swallowed up by a large shop over the way. Thus far <u>Rachel Gray</u> is commendable: it occupies ground which is very far from being exhausted, and it undertakes to impress us with the every-day sorrows of our commonplace fellow-men, and so to widen our sympathies, as Browning beautifully says--

> Art was given for that
> God uses us to help each other so,
> Lending our minds out.

The other suggests George Eliot's theory of comedy. <u>Silas Marner</u>, she says, is not "at all a sad story as a whole," though some critics misread it as a tragedy; indeed, she wrote it in prose, she said, because "in poetry there could be no equal play of humour" (<u>Letters</u>, III, 382). George Eliot quotes Menander in entry 37.

Those are pleasant epochs in our lives when what has hitherto been a mere name for us becomes the centre for a group of pleasant and fertile ideas--when, for instance, our travels bring us to some southern village which we have only known before as a mark in our map, and from that day forth the once barren word suggests to us a charming picture of houses lit up by a glowing sun, a cluster of tall trees with tame goats browsing on the patch of grass beneath them, and a large stone fountain where dark-complexioned women are filling their pitchers--or when Mr. A.B., whose name we have seen in the visiting-book of an hotel, becomes the definite image of a capital fellow, whose pleasant talk has beguiled us a five hours' journey in a diligence, and who turns out to be a man very much like ourselves, with dubious theories, still more dubious hopes, and quite indubitable sorrows. And there is the same sort of pleasure in getting something like a clear conception of an ancient author, whose name has all our life belonged to that inventory of unknown things which so much of our youth is taken up in learning. If we may suppose that to any of our readers Menander has hitherto thus remained a mere <u>nominis umbra</u>, let such readers go to M. Guillaume Guizot's very agreeable volume, and they will learn, without the least trouble to themselves, all that scholarly research has hitherto been able to discover of Menander and his writings. It is true that all

the preliminary hard work had been done by Meineke, for what hard
work in the way of historical research and criticism has <u>not</u> been
done by Germans? They are the purveyors of the raw material of
learning for all Europe; but, as Mr. Toots suggests, raw materials
require to be cooked, and in this kind of cookery, as well as in
the other, the French are supreme.[1] To have the Latin work of a
German writer <u>boiled</u> <u>down</u> to a portable bulk and served up in that
delicate crystal vessel, the French language, is a benefit that
will be appreciated by those who are at all acquainted with the
works of Germans, and still more by those who are not acquainted
with Latin. This is the service rendered by M. Guillaume Guizot,
and the way in which he has performed it quite merits, as it has
won, the prize of the French Academy. It is a double pleasure to
welcome a young author when he is an exception to that rather
melancholy generalisation, that great fathers have insignificant
sons; and we think this book on Menander gives some promise that
we may one day have to speak familiarly of Guizot the Elder, lest
our hearers should confound an illustrious father with an illustrious son.

      In the first chapter of this work, which is only an octavo
of about 450 pages, we have the history of Menander's reputation
and writings:--the abundant jealousy and the sparing justice
awarded him by his contemporaries, his long reign as a "dead but
sceptred monarch" over the comic stage, first of Athens and then
of Rome, the almost total destruction of his works, first through
the bigotry of Byzantine priests and subsequently through the
oblivion of Greek literature in the middle ages, and lastly the
awakened interest about his works on the revival of learning, when
scholars, amongst whom it is interesting to know that Grotius was
one, began to collect the fragments--the <u>disjecti</u> <u>membra</u> <u>poëtœ</u>.
In the second chapter M. Guizot presents all the accessible de-
tails concerning Menander's life and character, details which may
be summed up under his early but not unquestioned success as a
dramatist, his friendship for Epicurus and Theophrastus, his addiction to pleasure in general, and to the pleasure of loving
Glycera in particular. Indeed, if we accept the rather dubious
authority of Phaedrus, neither Menander's wisdom nor his wit saved
him from being something of a fop; for that fabulist says of him,
we hope calumniously,

              Unguento delibutus, vestitu adfluens,
              Veniebat gressu delicato et languido;[2]

which is as much as to say of a man in these days that he scents
himself with otto of roses, is fastidious about the cut of his
trousers, and walks--like a "walking gentleman." This description is strangely at variance with the calm, massive dignity of
his fine statue in the Vatican, of which M. Guizot gives us an
excellent engraving at the beginning of his volume. But then,
dear reader, Menander squinted, and where relentless destiny has
inflicted a personal defect of that sort, poor human nature is
rarely great enough to keep between the two extremes of an attempt to dazzle beholders into oblivion of the defect by finery,
and a despairing self-neglect. So, for our parts, we think
Menander's foppery belonged to the pathos of his life; and, indeed, what weakness of a great man is not pathetic? . . . The
third chapter discusses the Subjects of the Drama in the three
periods of Greek comedy: the ancient period, when its main object was political satire, a form of comedy peculiar to Greece,

and made immortal by the genius of Aristophanes; the middle
period, when its subjects ceased to be political, and became
purely social, but when the manners were chiefly caricature and
the characters conventional types, corresponding in many respects
to the early comedies of Molière; and the new period, when it became what the highest modern comedy is, a picture of real domestic
life and manners. Of this last species of comedy, Menander was,
by the common consent of critics subsequent to his own age, the
greatest master Greece ever produced; and the simple statement
of this fact is enough to indicate how great a loss is the
destruction of his comedies to those who care about a knowledge
of Greek life; for Terence, while appropriating the plots and
characters and poetry of Menander, threw away all that was
specifically Greek and substituted what was specifically Roman.
The succeeding chapters on the plot, the characters, the sentiments, and the passions in the Greek drama of the three periods
are really fascinating, from the skill with which M. Guizot weaves
together his materials and the judgment with which he chooses his
illustrative extracts. The fragments of Menander--mere "dust
of broken marble" as they are--afford us some interesting
glimpses into the Greek intérieur of his time. Amongst other
things, we gather that the married woman in Greece had then
ceased to be a mere piece of furniture, or live stock, too insignificant to determine in any degree a man's happiness or
misery. The bitter invectives against women and marriage in the
New Comedy are the best--or the worst--proofs of the domestic
ascendancy women had acquired. Here is a fragment in which a
female emancipationist of that day asserts the rights of woman,
according to the moderate views of 300 B.C.:--"Above all if a man
is wise, he will not keep his wife too much a prisoner in the re-
cesses of his house. For our eyes take delight in outdoor pleasures. Let a woman have as much as she likes of these pleasures,
see everything, and go everywhere. This sight-seeing will of itself satisfy her, and keep her out of mischief; whereas all of
us, men, women, and children alike, ardently desire what is
hidden from us. But the husband who shuts up his wife under lock
and seal, fancying that he shows his prudence in this way, loses
his labour, and is a wiseacre for his pains; for if one of us has
placed her heart out of the conjugal home, she flies away more
swiftly than an arrow or a bird; she would deceive the hundred
eyes of Argus! . . ."

It is amusing also to see how despotic a personage the cook
had become in the establishment, giving himself the airs common
to people who are conscious of being indispensable. "He who in-
sults one of us," said these mighty functionaries, "never escapes
the punishment he deserves: so sacred is our art." They piqued
themselves immensely on their skill. Here is a story of one who
seems to have been the prototype of that famous French chef who
prepared a multifarious dinner tout en boeuf. "I was the pupil
of Soterides. One day the King Nicomedes wished to eat some
sardines. It was the depth of winter, and twelve days march from
the sea. Nevertheless Soterides satisfied the king so completely,
that there was a general cry of admiration. Pray how was that
possible? He took a radish, cut it into long thin slices, which
he shaped like sardines; then, while they were frying, he basted
them with oil, sprinkled them with salt very cleverly, threw over
them a dozen black poppy seeds, and presented this ragout to the
Bythinian appetite of his master. Nicomedes ate the radish, and
praised the sardines. You see, cooks differ in nothing from

poets: the art of both is equally an art of intelligence."

In his last two chapters, M. Guizot considers the style and the imitators of Menander, and in an appendix he presents a translation of all the fragments that have an other than a philological interest. Among these there are no fewer than seven hundred and fifty-seven aphorisms, which are preserved to us in greater abundance than other fragments, because they were collected as "beauties" by ancient scholars. Very grave and very melancholy some of these moral sentences are, but probably an equal number of sad and serious sayings might be culled from Molière. We may say of the highest comedy what Demetrius said in another sense of the satiric drama--that it is παιζουσα τραγωδια, "tragedy in the disguise of mirth." Indeed it may be likened to those choicest of all fruits, the flavour of which is so cunningly mixed by Nature that we know not whether to call them sweet or acid, and in this wonderful equivoque lies their very exquisiteness.

Among the fragments of Menander there are some passages of elegiac sadness; for example: "O Parmene, I call him a happy man, nay, the happiest of all men, who soon returns to the place whence he came, after having contemplated, without sorrow, the magnificence of this world, the sun that everywhere diffuses its beams, the stars, the ocean, the clouds and fire: whether he lives an age or only a few short years, this spectacle will always be the same: never will he see one more sublime. Think of life as a fair, where man arrives like a wayfarer: tumult, market, thieves, games of chance and amusements! If thou set out first for the place of halting and repose, thou wilt be the better provided for the end of the journey, and thou wilt go without having made enemies. But he who late in the day falls into poverty--a wretched old man, weary, disenchanted, and ruined--loses his way, and meets nothing but hatred and snares: a long life leads not to a gentle death."

But perhaps we are dwelling a little too long on this subject of Menander and Greek Comedy--we should rather say flitting about it a little too long. Let us hope, however, that we have dwelt enough on it to persuade the reader that he will find in M. Guizot's book a masterly treatment of a subject which has a really human and not merely a scholarly interest.

Notes

1. Mr. Toots appears in Dickens's Dombey and Son.
2. Dripping ointment, in raiment flowing,
         He minced his languid way along.
              (Translated by Matthew Hogan)

LOVE IN THE DRAMA

Leader, 6 (25 August 1855), 820-21

George Eliot's review of Saint-Marc Girardin's Cours de Littérature Dramatique (Paris: Charpentier, 1855), exemplifies a sentence from her reflection "Judgment on Authors" (in "Leaves from a Note-Book") which posits the two sides of critical practice: "We should learn nothing without the tendency to implicit acceptance; but there must clearly be a limit to such mental submission, else we should come to a stand-still" (Essays, p. 443). She finds the limit of implicit acceptance when Girardin's investigation of love touches Shakespeare's women. Her commentary demonstrates a wide and ready knowledge of the Shakespearean canon and an understanding of the frank actions of his heroines. Item 25 is directly related to her commentary on Shakespeare's women in this essay. She reviewed this same volume with a slightly different emphasis in Westminster Review, 63 (October 1855), USA ed. 316-7.

M. SAINT-MARC GIRARDIN is a writer who makes the public not only desire his volumes, but wait for them. The reason of this, in the case of the Cours de Littérature Dramatique, is that it consists of lectures given by him at the Sorbonne, so that the volumes can only appear after their contents have been delivered in "winged words." The first volume was published in 1843, the second in 1849, and it is only now, after the lapse of another six years, that we obtain the welcome third. Nothing can be more charmingly easy and conversational than the style of these volumes. We have all experienced that "who writes about amusing books must himself be amusing," is as far from being an axiom as Johnson's immortal parody, "Who drives fat oxen must himself be fat;" and that a work on the belles lettres may be as drowsy as one on weights and measures. But M. Saint-Marc Girardin is one of those writers who make a graceful subject still more graceful; he enhance the beauty of the flowers he gathers by the tasteful way in which he weaves them together. Qualities which make him delightful as a critic are his ready appreciation of beauty, even when that beauty is mingled with much quaintness and absurdity, and his lively sensibility to every trait of genuine feeling. He has at once chastity and largeness of thought--not a common conjunction anywhere, and perhaps especially uncommon in France; he is liberal without being lax, and pure without the least soupçon of prudery.

In the latter part of his second volume he examined the three grand influences which have modified the character of Love, and made us differ so widely from the ancients in our conception and presentation of that passion, namely, Christianity, chivalry, and the doctrine of Platonic love. In the present volume he pursues the subject of Love, and traces its modifications in the sixteenth and seventeenth century, by analysing, or rather graphically sketching the three typical romances. The Amadis, which represents chivalrous love in its more softened and effeminate stage; the Astrée, which mingles Platonic with chivalrous love, under the name of pastoral love; and the Clélia, which is the code of la galanterie honnête, and "marks the apogee of woman's preponderance in the world and in literature." We recommend readers who would like to be told, in the pleasantest way, something about those antediluvian romances, to turn to this volume of M. Saint-Marc Girardin's. He will show them matter for admiration, even in D'Urfé and Mlle. Scudéry, and it is always worth while to widen our circle of admiration. After surveying the general expression of Love under the varying conditions of

society, from antiquity down to the seventeenth century, M.
Girardin enters on an examination of the particular expression
given to this passion in the drama, the romance, and the pastoral,
and it is this part of his work which is most attractive. He
opens for us one book after another, perhaps lying dusty on our
shelves, points out beautiful passages and significant traits,
makes Theocritus appear the most tempting author in the world,
and pastorals in general seem readable--which we humbly confess
we have rarely found them--shows a fine appreciation of Shakespeare, and winds up by charming his reader's interest to Madame
Deshoulières, who ought to be held in grateful recollection, if
for nothing else, at least for having written those incisive lines--

> Nul n'est content de sa fortune,
> Ni mécontent de son esprit--[1]

an epigram to which La Rochefoucauld has given a new dress in his
Maximes.

It is of course impossible for us to follow him through this
lengthy survey, so, by way of selection, we turn to his observations on Romeo and Juliet, in which he compares Shakspeare's
tragedy with the novel of Luigi da Porto. In the novel it is
Juliet who makes the first advance to Romeo; at the first glance
they exchange, the young maiden feels that her heart is no longer
her own, and when the progress of the dance brings Romeo near to
her, she says, "Welcome to my side, Messer Romeo." M. Girardin
observes that this treatment of the subject is entirely in the
spirit of ancient poetry, and he proceeds:--"Why, in ancient
poetry and in the Italian novel, which is here in entire unison
with ancient poetry, why do the women love before being loved?
why do they feel the passion before inspiring it? and why, in
modern poetry and romance, do we find the contrary? Dido loves
Eneas before we know whether she was loved in return, and we may
even doubt whether she was ever loved. Medea loves Jason before
being loved by him. Is it that the love-smitten heroines of
antiquity had less modesty than the love-smitten heroines of
modern times? or is it that the modern poets and romancers are
more refined and reserved in the pictures they give of woman's
sentiments? The manners of antiquity may explain why, in ancient
poetry, woman wants that reserve in feeling, and yet more in
words, which is her rule in modern times. Shut up in the gyneceum,
and never mixing in the society of men, who themselves found objects of love elsewhere, women were compelled, when love took
possession of their hearts, to proffer the avowal of their passion; they must themselves reveal their secret, or let it remain
for ever unknown. . . . The less free woman is made by laws and
conventionalities, the freer does she become through passion when
she yields herself up to it. Thus, the women whose passion made
them famous in antiquity were compelled to forget at once the
first and last proprieties of their sex. In order to be loved,
they were forced to say that they loved; and hence ancient poetry
was accustomed to represent its heroines as making the first
avowals of love."

M. Girardin then goes on to say that Shakspeare, "who is altogether a modern," differs in his treatment from the Italian
novelist, in assigning the first movement and expression of love
to Romeo; as if he meant to imply that Shakspeare is an example
of the antithesis he has just been stating between ancient and
modern love, or rather love-making. He could hardly have made a
more unfortunate selection of a case in point, for--inconvenient

as the fact may be for those whose creed includes at once the doctrine of Shakspeare's infallibility and the doctrines of modern
propriety--Shakspeare's women have no more decided characteristic
than the frankness with which they avow their love, not only to
themselves, but to the men they love. If Romeo opens the duct of
love with a few notes solo, Juliet soon strikes in and keeps it
up in as impassioned a strain as he. Sweet Desdemona, "a maiden
never bold," encourages Othello, not only by a "world of sighs,"
but by the broadest possible hint that he has won her heart.
Rosalind, in her first interview with Orlando, tells him that he
has "overthrown more than his enemies;" Portia is eloquent in
assurances of her love before the casket is opened--

> One half of me is yours, the other half yours--
> Mine own, I would say, but if mine, then yours,
> And so all yours!

And this frankness towards the lover is generally followed up by
the most impassioned soliloquies or confessions to confidants.
Then there are the women who love without being loved in return,
and some of whom even sue for love. Helena in All's Well that
Ends Well, the Helena in the Midsummer Night's Dream, the
shepherdess Sylvia, Viola, and Olivia, who wooes so prettily that
the action justifies itself. Curious it is to contrast these
Shakspearean heroines with some of Walter Scott's painfully dis-
creet young ladies--the Edith Bellendens, Alice Bridgworths, and
Miss Wardours! Whatever may be the respectability of these modern
heroines, it is clear that little could be made of them dramatically; they are like trees trained in right lines by dint of wall
and hammer. But we are wandering from the point we had undertaken to prove, namely, that Shakspeare cannot properly be con-
trasted with the ancients in the expression he gives to woman's
love. If so--if this feminine frankness is not peculiar to the
ancients, the cause of it in them must lie deeper than the
restraints of the gyneceum, to which M. Girardin attributes it:
it must be simply a natural manifestation which has only been
gradually and partially repressed by the complex influences of
modern civilisation.
   In his criticism of Shakspeare, M. Girardin sometimes reminds us of the Germans by his discovery of profound philosophical
intentions where Shakspeare had probably nothing more than poetical and dramatic intentions. For example, Caliban, he tells us,
is meant in the first instance to typify the inevitable brutality
of human nature in the savage state, in opposition to the marvellous stories of voyagers in Shakspeare's days; and in the
second instance, when he "tastes of civilisation"--that is, of
Trinculo's wine--Caliban is meant as a caveat to the hasty
panegyrists of civilised life. But, unlike the Germans, M.
Girardin touches lightly on such subjects--just dips his wings
in the mare magnum of philosophical interpretation, but generally
floats along in the lighter medium of tasteful criticism and quotation. He promises us, at some future time, a fourth volume on
the dramatic treatment of religious enthusiasm, a volume which
will come to us recommended by the memory of much pleasure due to
its predecessors.

Note

1. No one is satisfied with his income
    Or dissatisfied with his wit.

HEINE'S POEMS

Leader, 6 (1 September 1855), 843-4

George Eliot's review of Charles G. Leland's translation of Heine's Reisebilder --Pictures of Travel (London: Trübner, 1855)--anticipates her magisterial essay "German Wit: Heinrich Heine," which appeared in the Westminster in January 1856 (see Essays, pp. 216-54). But in this review for the Leader her style has an epigrammatic point to it that eludes her discussion of wit and humor in the longer essay. In addition, Heine's "supreme lyrical genius," which she extols and illustrates through Leland's translations, penetrated memorably into her sensibility and left its mark on her fiction, as two of the stanzas she quotes illustrate. The rapping "on the window" appears in a slight variation, along with the "dead father," in Adam Bede where "a smart rap, as if with a willow wand, was given at the house door, and Gyp . . . gave a loud howl," and Adam shuddered as "he remembered how often his mother had told him of just such a sound coming as a sign when some one was dying" (ch. 4). When Adam next sees his father Thias, he is dead. And the Lorelei, the "wondrous lovely maiden" who combs "her golden hair," appears in "The Lifted Veil" as Bertha Grant: "The pale-green dress, and the green leaves that seemed to form a border about her pale blond hair, made me think of a Water-Nixie,--for my mind was full of German lyrics, and this pale, fatal-eyed woman, with the green weeds, looked like a birth from some cold sedgy stream, the daughter of an aged river" (ch. 1). GE quotes Heine's poetry in entry 14.

Nature one day resolved to make a witty German. But as this supreme paradox was not to be achieved all at once, it happened that in the ardour of a great purpose she mistook Hebrew blood for German, and while she was busy adding the wit, allowed the best moral qualities of the German to slip out of her hands. So, instead of the witty Teuton she intended, she would have produced merely a Voltairian Jew speaking the German language, if she had not, perceiving her mistake before it was too late, superadded, as some compensation for the want of morale, a passionate heart blending its emotions with the most delicate and imaginative sensibility to the beauties of earth and sky, and a supreme lyrical genius, which could weave the wit, and the passion, and the imagination into songs light and lovely as the rainbows on the spray of the summer torrent.

    Thus it came to pass that we have that wonderful human compound Heinrich Heine, a writer who is master of a German prose as light and subtle and needle-pointed as Voltaire's French, and of a poetical style as crystalline, as graceful, and as musical as that of Goethe's best lyrics; but a writer who is destitute of the distinct moral conviction which often inspired Voltaire, and still more utterly destitute of the profound wisdom and the depth of love and reverence which roll like a deep river under the sparkling, dimpling surface of Goethe's song. Indeed, we know nothing more likely to impress a reader with the grander elements of Goethe's mind than a comparison of his lyrics with Heine's, for the very reason that Heine quite equals Goethe in all the charms of mere song, and has one quality mingling itself with his lyrical power which Goethe has not--namely, wit; or rather, to express it more specifically, French esprit. For, alien as this quality might seem to passionate love-songs and thrilling legendary pictures, such as form the majority of Heine's poems, it is, nevertheless, almost everywhere present, giving your rising tears the accompaniment of a laugh, and, before you have lost the cold

shudder at his spectral visions, appealing irresistibly to your
sense of fun. We cannot agree with his very clever American
translator that Humour is Heine's grand characteristic. He certainly has humour--perhaps even enough to set up an inferior
genius as a humourist--but we think it will be found that his
greatest effects in prose, and most of the contrasts that startle
us in his poetry, arise from a Mephistophelean wit, a verneinender
Geist, rather than from humour which affirms all that is genuinely
human instead of denying it, and is, in fact, an exuberant sympathy acting in company with a sense of the ludicrous, while wit
is the critical intellect acting in company with that same sense.
Nevertheless, it must be admitted that there are many passages of
Sterne-like humour in Heine, and herein he is least akin to the
French, and most nearly allied to the broader and deeper German
nature, which atones for the want of esprit by something which
esprit will never supersede--loving earnestness.

But it is time to turn from such rambling remarks to the object that suggested them--namely, the translation of Heine's
Reisebilder, by a very gifted American. Of Heine, more even than
the majority of poets, we must say that he is untranslatably
felicitous. Many of his lyrics are mere gossamer webs--touch
them, try to transfer them, and all their qualities disappear.
Hence, when we praise Mr. Leland's translation--and we do so very
sincerely--we must not be understood to mean that it will give
the English reader a true conception of Heine's genius. Mr.
Leland has that grand requisite of a translator, rigorous faithfulness; he has also poetical sensibility, command of language,
and an evidently acute perception of wit; in short, he spoils
Heine's poems perhaps as little as it is possible to spoil them
in a translation. This may not seem to be high praise, but we
firmly believe it is the very highest praise that can ever be
given to a translation of Heine's poems, and we recommend the
reader who is hopeless of knowing these poems in the original to
make his acquaintance with them through Mr. Leland's version. He,
of course, succeeds best in the poems which are legendary and
ballad-like rather than purely lyrical. We give one of these,
which has again and again made the blood creep in our veins as we
have read it:--

                    The pale half-moon is floating
                        Like a boat 'mid cloudy waves,
                    Lone lies the pastor's cottage
                        Amid the silent graves.

                    The mother reads in the Bible,
                        The son seems weary and weak;
                    The eldest daughter is drowsy,
                        While the youngest begins to speak.

                    "Ah me!--how every minute
                        Rolls by so drearily;
                    Only when some one is buried,
                        Have we anything here to see!"

                    The mother murmured while reading,
                        "Thou'rt wrong--they've brought but four
                    Since thy poor father was buried
                        Out there by the churchyard door."

    The eldest daughter says, gaping,
       "No more will I hunger by you;
    I'll go to the Baron, to-morrow,
       He's wealthy, and fond of me too."

    The son bursts out into laughter,
       "Three hunters carouse in the Sun;
    They all can make gold, and gladly
       Will show me how it is done."

    The mother holds the Bible
       To his pale face in grief;
    "And wilt thou--wicked fellow--
       Become a highway thief?"

    A rapping is heard on the window,
       There trembles a warning hand;
    Without, in his black, church garments,
       They see their dead father stand.

The following is a very happy specimen of translation; it is easy and musical as an original:--

    I know not what sorrow is o'er me,
       What spell is upon my heart;
    But a tale of old times is before me--
       A legend that will not depart.

    Night falls as I linger, dreaming,
       And calmly flows the Rhine;
    The peaks of the hills are gleaming
       In the golden sunset shine.

    A wondrous lovely maiden
       Sits high in glory there;
    Her robe with gems is laden,
       And she combeth her golden hair.

    And she spreads out the golden treasure,
       Still singing in harmony;
    And the song hath a mystical measure,
       And a wonderful melody.

    The boatman, when once she hath bound him
       Is lost in a wild sad love:
    He sees not the black rocks around him,
       He sees but the beauty above.

    Till he drowns amid mad waves ringing,
       And sinks with the facing sun;
    And that, with her magical singing,
       The witch of the Lurley hath done.

The next is more injured in the rendering, but we give it as a specimen of the most exquisite kind of pathos that Heine ever attains:--

    In dreams I saw the loved one,
       A sorrowing, wearied form;

Her beauty blanched and withered
    By many a dreary storm.

A little babe she carried,
    Another child she led,
And poverty and trouble
    In glance and garb I read.

She trembled through the market,
    And face to face we met;
And I calmly said, while sadly
    Her eyes on mine were set:

"Come to my house, I pray thee,
    For thou art pale and thin;
And for thee, by my labour,
    Thy meat and drink I'll win.

"And to thy little children
    I'll be a father mild:
But most of all thy parent,
    Thou poor unhappy child."

Nor will I ever tell thee
    That once I held thee dear;
And if thou diest, then I
    Will weep upon thy bier.

"Belles Lettres," <u>Westminster Review</u>,
64 (October 1855), USA ed. 315

[MILTON AND EDUCATION]

When in August 1855 George Eliot reviewed Thomas Keightley's <u>An Account of the
Life</u>, <u>Opinions</u>, <u>and Writings of John Milton</u>, <u>with an Introduction to Paradise
Lost</u> (London: Chapman and Hall, 1855) for the <u>Leader</u>, she dwelt on Milton's
doctrine of divorce (see <u>Essays</u>, pp. 154-7). In this review for the <u>West-
minster</u> her primary interest is his tract on education. She corrects Keightley
and defends Milton, whom she once called "my demigod" (<u>Letters</u>, V, 238); nevertheless, she finds some of Milton's theories impracticable too. Her defense
of science in the curriculum and her detestation of a debased classical education made themselves felt in <u>The Mill on the Floss</u>: "Mr. Stelling had a
fixed opinion that all boys with any capacity could learn what it was the only
regular thing to teach: if they were slow, the thumb-screw must be tightened
--the exercises must be insisted on with severity, and a page of Virgil be
awarded as a penalty, to encourage and stimulate a too languid inclination to
Latin verse" (II.iv). GE quotes Milton's "Of Education" in entries 32[a] and
33.

The magnificent impossibility put forth by Milton as a scheme of
education in his famous Tractate,--according to which boys were
in nine years to become masters of knowledge, all accomplishments,
and "fraught with a universal insight into things,"--includes a
higher range of classical writers than any admitted into the curriculum he adopted in his own school. To his hypothetical pupils
he gives, in one state of their studies, "the choice historians,
heroic poems, and Attic tragedies of stateliest and most regal
argument, with all the famous political orations;" but to his
actual pupils, according to the testimony of his nephew Philips,
he was less liberal, confining them, with a few exceptions, to
the driest of classical diet. "In Latin, the Four Scriptores Rei
Rusticae, Cato, Varro, Palladius, and Columella; great part of
Pliny's Natural History, the medical work of Celsus, Vitruvius,
and the Stratagems of Frontinus: to these prose works were added
the philosophic poets Lucretius and Manilius. Such was the Latin
course; the Greek was, from its very nature, somewhat better. It
consisted of Hesiod (probably on the Works and Days), Aratus,
Dionysius' Periegesis, Oppian, Quintus Smyrnaeus, and Appollonius
Rhodius in poetry; while the prose course contained Plutarch's
Placita Philosophorum, and on the Education of Children, Xeno-
phon's Cyropaedia and Anabasis; AElian's Tactics, and the Stratagems
of Polyaenus." We think we see a double reason why this selection
was less preposterous and unaccountable than Mr. Keightley pronounces it. Milton's true principle in education, that the reason
must be cultivated as well as the imagination and memory, and that
it must be cultivated by applying it to the sciences which are of
immediate practical value in life, led him into what may seem an
erroneous plan, simply because the conditions for carrying out
that principle were not yet ripe. Modern science had but lately
been born, and how limited was the progress it had made even
among first-rate minds, may be judged from the fact that Milton
himself held fast to the Ptolemaic system. So in default of the
"Principia," he gives his pupils De Sacro Bosco "De Sphaera;" in
default of Linnaeus and Cuvier, he gave them Pliny; in default of
Johnstone's "Physical Atlas," he gave them Dionysius' "Periegesis."
And perhaps precisely because Milton was a great poet, he shrank

from grinding down the fine gold of his favourite poets into
lessons of syntax and prosody: he could better endure the man-
gling of Apollonius Rhodius than of Homer and AEschylus. As to
the formation of pure and correct taste by placing first-rate
authors in the hands of boys, we think that result is quite an
exceptional one; the ordinary effect is rather that of vulgariz-
ing the finest products of genius by premature familiarity. Too
early an intimacy with the highest, in any department, deadens
the sensibility and robs the mature mind of its proper enjoyments.
A child who has been taken to see the Alps at ten years of age is
pitiable; he will never know the rush of thought and feeling which
would have made the sight an epoch for his manhood.

LIFE OF GOETHE

Leader, 6 (3 November 1855), 1058-61

George Eliot's review of George Henry Lewes's Life and Works of Goethe, 2
vols. (London: David Nutt, 1855) is one of the longest she wrote for the
Leader. Her immersion in Goethe is evident from the quotations from him in
the notebook (see entries 11, 12, 13, 15, 18, 19, 24, 111, 112). The closeness of her thinking about him to Lewes's is reflected in their mutual interest
in the same passages from his work, in her elaboration of Lewes's ideas on
Goethe in essays like "The Morality of Wilhelm Meister" (Leader, 6 [21 July
1855], 703, and "The Shaving of Shagpat," Leader, 7 [5 January 1856], 15-17),
and her use of Goethe's ideas in her fiction (see notes to entries 11, 13,
15, 18, and 24). The excerpts from George Eliot's review of Lewes's Life of
Goethe that are given here can be used to supplement the Prelude of Middlemarch where George Eliot indicates that once an era of epos has passed there
remains "no coherent social faith and order which" can "perform the function
of knowledge for the ardently willing soul."

But the part of the youthful life which gains most in fullness
and distinctness is the Wetzlar, or, rather the Werther period--
thanks to the timely publication last year of the volume called
Goethe and Werther, containing letters of Goethe, and illustrative
documents, which bring into clear daylight his relation to Charlotte Buff, the heroine of Werther, and to her husband, Kestner,
and show us, as by a daguerrotype, what the young Goethe of those
days actually was--how ardent, ingenious, loving, and loveable.
This was the period of the famous Sturm und Drang tendency, by
which Goethe was just so far intoxicated as to be inspired with
the greatest work that tendency produced--Götz von Berlichingen.
Germany had not yet recovered from its astonishment at the bold
innovation of this drama, when a new and yet stronger sensation
was excited by the appearance of Werther. Mr. Lewes thus sketches
the characteristics of the period, of which Götz and Werther are
the intensest expression:--

. . . .

It was, indeed, a strange epoch; the unrest was the unrest of disease, and its extravagances were morbid symptoms. In the letters,
memoirs, and novels, which still remain to testify to the fol-
lies of the age, may be read a self-questioning and sentimental
retrospection, enough to create in healthy minds a distaste both
for sentiment and self-questioning. A factitious air is carried
even by the most respectable sentiments; and many not respectable
array themselves in rose-pink. Nature is seldom spoken of but
in hysterical enthusiasm. Tears and caresses are prodigally
scattered, and upon the slightest provocations. In Coburg an
Order of Mercy and Expiation is instituted by sensitive noodles.
Leuchsenring, whom Goethe satirized in Paty Brey, as a profes-
sional sentimentalist, gets up a secret society, and calls it
the Order of Sentiment, to which tender souls think it a privilege to belong. Friendship is fantastically deified; brotherly
love draws trembling souls together, not on the solid grounds of
affection and mutual service, but on entirely imaginary grounds
of "spiritual communion;" whence arose, as Jean Paul wittily
says, "an universal love for all men and beasts--except reviewers."
It was a sceptical epoch, in which everything established came
into question. Marriage, of course, came badly off among a set

of men who made the first commandment of genius to consist in loving your neighbour <u>and</u> your neighbour's wife.

These were symptoms of disease; the social organization was out of order; a crisis, evidently imminent, was heralded by extravagances in literature, as elsewhere. The cause of the disease was want of faith. In religion, in philosophy, in politics, in morals, this eighteenth century was ostentatious of its disquiet and disbelief. The old faith, which for so long had made European Life an organic unity, and which in its tottering weakness had received a mortal blow from Luther, was no longer universal, living, active, dominant; its place of universal directing power was vacant; a new faith had not arisen. The French Revolution was another crisis of that organic disturbance which had previously shown itself in another order of ideas,--in the Reformation. Beside this awful crisis, other minor crises are noticeable. Everywhere the same Protestant spirit breaks through traditions in morals, in literature, and in education. Whatever is established, whatever rests on tradition, is questioned. The classics are no longer believed in; men begin to maintain the doctrine of Progress, and the superiority of the moderns. Art is pronounced to be in its nature progressive. Education is no longer permitted to pursue its broad traditional path; the methods which were excellent for the past no longer suffice for the present; everywhere new methods rise up to ameliorate the old. The divine right of institutions ceases to gain credence. The individual claimed and proclaimed his freedom; freedom of thought and freedom of act. Freedom is the watchward of the eighteenth century.

THE SHAVING OF SHAGPAT

Leader, 7 (5 January 1856), 15-17

George Eliot wrote to Sara Hennell on 18 January 1856, saying, "If you want some idle reading, get 'The Shaving of Shagpat,' which I think you will say deserves all the praise I gave it in the Leader" (Letters, II, 226). The review begins with the amplification of the idea she records in entry 26 (from Stahr's Torso) that the progress of civilization is from East to West. A principal passage also carries an echo from Lewes's Life of Goethe where he speaks of the West-östlicher Divan as "West-Eastern: the images are Eastern; the feeling Western" (see entry 24, n. 1). Lewes returned to this idea in his own review of Shagpat: "It is more Eastern than Goethe's West-östlicher Divan, less directly imitative than Rückert's Oriental poems" (Saturday Review, 1 [19 January 1856], 216). Both Eliot and Lewes are careful to indicate that Meredith's book is original, not imitative; and this points to an important distinction between "imitation" and "emulation" which Lewes made in an earlier review, "Arnold's Poems": "If Homer lived in our days he would not write like Homer's imitators. In fact the mistake of all imitation is that it naturally fastens on the fleeting modes, and not on the eternal spirit" (Leader, 4 [3 December 1853], 1171). "Such being our critical faith, instead of imitation we counsel Emulation" (p. 1170). In spite of the echoes that are evident here, a reading of the two Shagpat reviews shows that Eliot and Lewes emulated, and did not imitate, each other's review. This essay was reprinted once in Essays and Uncollected Papers, vol. 22 of The Writings of George Eliot, Large Paper Edition, 25 vols. (Boston and New York: Houghton, Mifflin, 1908).

No art of religious symbolism has a deeper root in nature than that of turning with reverence towards the East. For almost all our good things--our most precious vegetables, our noblest animals, our loveliest flowers, our arts, our religious and philosophical ideas, our very nursery tales and romances, have travelled to us from the East. In an historical as well as in a physical sense, the East is the Land of the Morning. Perhaps the simple reason of this may be, that when the earth first began to move on her axis her Asiatic side was towards the sun--her Eastern cheek first blushed under his rays. And so this priority of sunshine, like the first move in chess, gave the East the precedence though not the pre-eminence in all things; just as the garden slope that fronts the morning sun yields the earliest seedlings, though those seedlings may attain a hardier and more luxuriant growth by being transplanted. But we leave this question to wiser heads--

"Felix qui potuit rerum cognoscere causas."[1]

(Excuse the novelty of the quotation.) We have not carried our reader's thoughts to the East that we may discuss the reason why we owe it so many good things, but that we may introduce him to a new pleasure, due, at least indirectly, to that elder region of the earth. We mean "The Shaving of Shagpat" which is indeed an original fiction just produced in this western island, but which is so intensely Oriental in its conception and execution, that the author has done wisely to guard against the supposition of its being a translation, by prefixing the statement that it is derived from no Eastern source, but is altogether his own.
     "The Shaving of Shagpat," is a work of genius, and of poetical genius. It has none of the tameness which belongs to mere imitations manufactured with servile effort or thrown off

with simious facility. It is no patchwork of borrowed incidents.
Mr. Meredith has not simply imitated Arabian fictions, he has
been inspired by them; he has used Oriental forms, but only as an
Oriental genius would have used them who had been "to the manner
born." Goethe, when he wrote an immortal work under the inspiration of Oriental studies, very properly called it West-östliche--
West-eastern--because it was thoroughly Western in spirit, though
Eastern in its forms. But this double epithet would not give a
true idea of Mr. Meredith's work, for we do not remember that
throughout our reading we were once struck by an incongruity between the thought and the form, once startled by the intrusion of
the chill north into the land of the desert and the palm. Perhaps
more lynx-eyed critics, and more learned Orientalists, than we,
may detect discrepancies to which we are blind, but our experience
will at least indicate what is likely to be the average impression. In one particular, indeed, Mr. Meredith differs widely from
his models, but that difference is a high merit: it lies in the
exquisite delicacy of his love incidents and love scenes. In
every other characteristic--in exuberance of imagery, in picturesque wildness of incident, in significant humour, in aphoristic wisdom, the "Shaving of Shagpat" is a new Arabian Night. To
two thirds of the reading world this is sufficient recommendation.

     According to Oriental custom the main story of the book--The
Shaving of Shagpat--forms the setting to several minor tales,
which are told, on pretexts more or less plausible, by the
various dramatis personae. We will not forestall the reader's
pleasure by telling him who Shagpat was, or what were the wondrous
adventures through which Shibli Bagarag, the wandering barber, became Master of the Event and the destroyer of illusions, by shaving from Shagpat the mysterious identical [sic] which had held
men in subjection to him. There is plenty of deep meaning in the
tale for those who cannot be satisfied without deep meanings, but
there is no didactic thrusting forward of moral lessons, and our
imagination is never chilled by a sense of allegorical intention
predominating over poetic creation. Nothing can be more vivid and
concrete than the narrative and description, nothing fresher and
more vigorous than the imagery. Are we reading how horsemen pursued their journey? We are told that they "flourished their
lances with cries, and jerked their heels into the flanks of
their steeds, and stretched forward till their beards were mixed
with the tossing manes, and the dust rose after them crimson in
the sun." Is it a maiden's eyes that we are to see? They are
"dark, under a low arch of darker lashes, like stars on the
skirts of storm." Sometimes the images are exquisitely poetical,
as when Bhanavar looks forth "on the stars that were above the
purple heights and the blushes of inner heaven that streamed up
the sky"; sometimes ingenious and pithy: for example, "she
clenched her hands an instant with that feeling which knocketh
a nail in the coffin of a desire not dead." Indeed, one of the
rarest charms of the book is the constant alternation of passion
and wild imaginativeness with humour and pithy, practical sense.
Mr. Meredith is very happy in his imitation of the lyrical fragments which the Eastern tale-tellers weave into their narrative,
either for the sake of giving emphasis to their sententiousness,
or for the sake of giving a more intense utterance to passion, a
loftier tone to description. We will quote a specimen of the
latter kind from the story of Bhanavar the Beautiful. This story
is the brightest gem among the minor tales, and perhaps in the
whole book. It is admirably constructed and thoroughly poetic in

its outline and texture.

Bhanavar gazed on her beloved, and the bridal dew overflowed her
underlids, and she loosed her hair to let it flow, part over her
shoulders, part over his, and in sighs that were the measure of
music she sang:

> "I thought not to love again!
> But now I love as I loved not before;
> I love not: I adore!
> O my beloved, kiss, kiss me! waste thy kisses like a rain.
> Are not thy red lips fain?
> Oh, and so softly they greet!
> Am I not sweet?
> Sweet must I be for thee, or sweet in vain:
> Sweet to thee only, my dear love!
> The lamps and censers sink, but cannot cheat
> Those eyes of thine that shoot above,
> Trembling lustres of the dove
> A darkness drowns all lustres: still I see
> Thee, my love, thee!
> Thee, my glory of gold, from head to feet!
> Oh, how the lids of the world close quite when our lips meet!"

Almeryl strained her to him and responded:
> "My life was midnight on the mountain side;
> Cold stars were on the heights
> There, in my darkness, I had lived and died,
> Content with little lights.
> Sudden I saw the heavens flush with a beam,
> And I ascended soon,
> And evermore over mankind supreme
> Stood silver in the moon."

And he fell playfully into a new metre, singing:

> "Who will paint my beloved
> In musical word or colour?
> Earth with an envy is moved:
> Sea-shells and roses she brings,
> Gems from the green ocean-springs,
> Fruits with the fairy bloom-dews,
> Feathers of Paradise hues,
> Waters with jewel-bright falls,
> Ore from the Genii-halls:
> All in their splendour approved;
> All; but match'd with my beloved,
> Darker, denser, and duller."

Then she kissed him for that song, and sang:
> "Once to be beautiful was my pride,
> And I blush'd in love with my own bright brow
> Once, when a wooer was by my side,
> I worship'd the object that had his vow:
> Different, different, different now,
> Different now is my beauty to me:
> Different, different, different now!
> For I prize it alone because prized by thee."

Almeryl stretched his arm to the lattice, and drew it open, letting in the soft night wind, and the sound of the fountain, and the bulbul and the beam of the stars, and versed to her in the languor of deep love:

"Whether we die or we live
   Matters it now no more;
Life has nought further to give:
   Love is its crown and its core.
Come to us either, we're rife,--
   Death or life!

"Death can take not away,
   Darkness and light are the same:
We are beyond the pale ray,
   Wrapt in a rosier flame;
Welcome which will to our breath,--
   Life or death!"

An example of Mr. Meredith's skill in humorous apologue is the Punishment of Khipil the Builder. . . . [The long passage which George Eliot quotes is here omitted.]
   We hope we have said, if not enough to do justice to "The Shaving of Shagpat," enough to make our readers desire to see it. They will find it, compared with the other fictions which the season has provided, to use its own Oriental style, "as the apple tree among the trees of the wood."[2]

Notes

1. Happy is he who can know the causes of things. Virgil, Georgics ii. 490.
2. Song of Solomon ii.3.

HEINE'S BOOK OF SONGS

Saturday Review, 1 (26 April 1856), 523-4

Commenting on George Eliot's article "Translations and Translators" (Leader,
6 [20 October 1855], 1014-15), Thomas Pinney remarks, "As the translator of
Strauss's Life of Jesus, Feuerbach's Essence of Christianity, and Spinoza's
Ethics, George Eliot could speak with special authority on the subject of this
article" (Essays, p. 207). In that essay she drew a series of comparisons between translations and originals: a Jew's harp is not a piano, an illustrated
newspaper portrait is not a living face, a slow unwieldy post-horse is not an
Arabian war-horse. What she says here in "Heine's Book of Songs" is that a
Wallis is not a Heine. Like George Henry Lewes she believed that the Germans
translated English better than the English translated German (Essays, p. 210).
But she is not nearly as severe with Wallis as Lewes was eleven years earlier
with Thomas Francklin, a translator of Sophocles: "Sophocles was one of the
most astonishing poets, and Francklin one of the most astonishing blockheads
in the records of poetry; the one the flower of Greek art, the other the
quintessence of the Dunciad" ("German and English Translations from the Greek,"
Foreign Quarterly Review, 33 [1844], USA ed. 250). Heinrich Heine's Book of
Songs, a translation, by John E. Wallis was published in London by Chapman and
Hall in 1856. George Eliot quotes Heine's Buch der Lieder in entry 14.

Heine's Book of Songs, like Tennyson's In Memoriam, draws its inspiration from a single theme. But the English poet, while adher-
ing to the same poetic form, and revolving round the same central
emotion, takes a wide sweep of thought--the German poet, on the
contrary, keeps within a narrow circle of ideas and feelings, but
perpetually varies his poetic form. Unhappy love is the almost
unvarying theme of the Book of Songs; but we have read them
seriatim, again and again, without any disagreeable sense of
monotony--so ever changing, ever charming, are the melodies of
Heine's verse, so inexhaustibly diversified are the modes in which
his imagination presents the same feeling. He gives it us in
eerie dreams, in ballads, in idyls, in sonnets, and most of all
in delicious little lyrics, which he seems to find as easy as
sighing; and everywhere there is the same wonderful grace--every-
where there is that completeness of expression without effort,
which reminds us of nothing so much as of the rapid revelations of
feeling which may be read in a beautiful and expressive human
face. There is no awkward inversion--no far-fetched combination
of epithets--no betrayal of art. Song seems as natural to Heine
as to the thrush and the nightingale, and, while you are reading
him, it is prose that appears artificial.
    Here is the reason why his poems are so difficult to be
translated--or rather, so utterly untranslatable by any one who is
only a versifier and not a poet. Rhythm and rhyme are no fetters
to Heine--they are rather the wings on the sandals of the God,
that help him to float through ether with all the more buoyancy.
To be simple, idiomatic, and poetic is with him the same thing;
but with the generality of translators it is quite another affair.
Instead of floating through ether, they toil heavily along the
ground. They may make a meritorious effort to be faithful--to
say just what Heine says; but there is much the same likeness
between their verses and his as between the phrase "I love you,"
which no one can hear quite unmoved, and the phrase "I feel a
tender passion for you," which probably would not greatly move
any one; or as between the ever-to-be-quoted lines--

>   I could not love thee, dear, so well,
>   Loved I not honour more; --

and the never-to-be-quoted paraphrase--

>   My love would be inferior, dear,
>   Were honour not supreme.

In translation, something might be done by patient labour towards compensating for the want of the original _afflatus_; but, unfortunately, translators have usually either too little patience or too low an ideal. They are too easily tired, or too easily satisfied, or they give their patience to the production of quantity rather than quality. A few of Heine's poems finely translated would make the English reader better acquainted with the poet than a feeble English version of the whole. But the American translator, Mr. Leland, undertakes to translate all the poems as well as all the prose--so that, notwithstanding his ability, he necessarily achieves a much larger amount of failure than of success; and Mr. Wallis now presents us with the whole _Book of Songs_, when we should probably have been able to thank him much more for a small selection. This might have been one of the cases in which a part is greater than the whole.

Mr. Wallis writes very modestly in his preface. He has not thrust his translations on the public hastily, but had long withheld them because they fell below his own requirements; and he was only encouraged to publish them at last by the fact that other translations of Heine, perhaps not superior to his own, have been favourably received. He is clearly a very competent German scholar, and his rendering is generally a close one. With some exceptions, he reproduces faithfully the meaning of the original; but, alas! he fails to reproduce their charm. The scent of the violet is gone; the living song has become mechanical verse; and very often the line-for-line rendering only makes the contrast more striking.

Every reader of Heine remembers the little lyric--

>   Herz, mein Herz, sei nicht beklommen,
>   Und ertrage dein Geschick,
>   Neuer Frühling giebt zurück,
>   Was der Winter dir genommen.
>   Und wie viel ist dir geblieben!
>   Und wie schön ist noch die Welt!
>   Und, mein Herz, was dir gefällt,
>   Alles, Alles darfst du lieben!

The English reader will understand the charm of this little lyric, when we tell him that it resembles that of Burns's more pathetic songs. The following is Mr. Wallis's version:--

>   Heart, my heart, oh, be not troubled!
>   Bear thy lot, though hard it be;
>   Spring will give thee back redoubled
>   All that winter took from thee.
>
>   Think how lovely is creation!
>   Think what joys await thy call!
>   All things bring thee consolation,
>   Thou art free to love them all!

This assuredly does not resemble Burns. "Think how lovely is
creation!" sounds very much like a quotation from a Unitarian
Hymn-book. We are amazed that a mind so evidently accomplished
as Mr. Wallis's could allow such a miserable platitude to stand.
    In another lyric of the same class, he seems to have missed
Heine's meaning entirely, and turns a bit of imaginative pathos
into a flat prosaism:--

>   They both of them loved, but neither
>   The truth to the other would say;
>   They met so proudly and coldly,
>   While both were pining away.
>
>   They parted at length, and in future
>   Encounter'd in dreams alone;
>   They died long since, and to neither
>   The fate of the other was known.

The last two lines in the original are:

>   Sie waren längst gestorben
>   Und wussten es selber kaum--

meaning that the state of separation from each other was so like
death, that death was hardly a change.
    Again, Mr. Wallis entirely loses the point of Sonnet III.
He renders the concluding lines thus:--

>   For when fair Fortune's gifts are from us reft,
>   And broken by the hand of destiny;
>   And when the fragments at our feet are flung;
>   And when the heart within our breast is wrung,
>   Wrung, rent, and wounded irrecoverably,--
>   A bitter laugh is all that we have left.

In the original the last line is

>   Dann bleibt uns <u>doch</u> das schöne gelle Lachen.

This does not mean--nothing is left to us but laughter. It means--
laughter is still left to us. And Heine valued that residuum considerably.
    We were bound to indicate the deficiencies in Mr. Wallis's
book, and to warn the reader that it will not in the least qualify
him to pronounce on Heine's merits as a poet. But there is no
need to dwell longer on those deficiencies, and we may now do
what is more agreeable--give a specimen of Mr. Wallis's more
successful efforts as a translator. Here is a little poem which
he has rendered at once closely and poetically:--

>   My love, we sat together,
>   Alone in our fragile bark.
>   The night was still, and we floated
>   Over the waters dark.
>
>   The spirit Isle, the lovely,
>   Lay dim in moonlight trance;
>   Sweet sounded magic music,
>   And waved the misty dance.

The music grew sweeter and sweeter
The dance waved to and fro;
But we, on the wide, wide ocean,
Floated in silent woe.

"Art and Belles Lettres," <u>Westminster Review</u>,
65 (April 1856), USA ed. 343-4

[MODERN PAINTERS III]

In reviewing <u>Stones</u> <u>of</u> <u>Venice</u>, Volume II, <u>The</u> <u>Sea</u> <u>Stories</u>, for the <u>Leader</u> (4
[17 September 1853], 905), George Henry Lewes indicts Ruskin's "iconoclastic
assertions," "sweeping generalizations," "wilful and capricious outbreaks,"
and "inordinate degree of coxcombry" and then chooses not to discuss these
things: "But after all--having made the most liberal allowance for drawbacks
and demerits--we must welcome every work he produces, more than we welcome the
works of any other writer on Art." The same attitude pervades George Eliot's
review of <u>Modern</u> <u>Painters</u> III, and it is a practical expression of Ruskin's
esthetic concept of "Naturalist Idealism, which accepts the weaknesses, faults,
and wrongnesses in all things that it sees, but so places them that they form
a noble whole, in which the imperfection of each several part is not only
harmless, but absolutely essential, and yet in which whatever is good in each
several part shall be completely displayed" (p. 346). George Eliot
emphasizes Ruskin's "positive excellences" and in doing so reveals her own
esthetic principles. Like Ruskin, she believes in a connection between art
and morality; she suggests in this review that the function of criticism is
to identify and explore that nexus. Such criticism must therefore be open to
what is best in an author at the expense of what is worst. And what is best
in Ruskin is his doctrine of realism and the prophetic voice in which he utters
it. This doctrine when taught to be heard widens our sympathy and deepens the
basis of our tolerance and charity. George Eliot recites Ruskin's lesson in
the voice of the author of "The Sad Fortunes of the Reverend Amos Barton":
"My only merit must lie in the truth with which I represent to you the humble
experience of ordinary fellow-mortals. I wish to stir your sympathy with commonplace troubles--to win your tears for real sorrow" (ch. 5). Thomas Noble
indirectly suggests Ruskin's influence on Eliot when he summarizes her
"artistic credo" as a beginning novelist: "Art has a moral purpose; the purpose is to widen human sympathy; this purpose can be achieved only by giving a
true picture of life" (<u>George</u> <u>Eliot's</u> <u>Scenes</u> <u>of</u> <u>Clerical</u> <u>Life</u> [New Haven and
London: Yale Univ. Press, 1965], p. 38.) For further remarks on Eliot's re-
lation to Ruskin, see the headnote to "Ruskin's Lectures" (p. 238) and entry
89, n. 1. Only a portion of the review of <u>Modern</u> <u>Painters</u> III is reproduced
below.

Our table this time does not, according to the favourite metaphor,
"groan under the light literature of the quarter," for the quarter
has not been very productive; but, in compensation, we ourselves
groan under it rather more than usual, for the harvest is principally of straw, and few grains of precious corn remain after
the winnowing. We accept one book, however, which is a rich
sheaf in itself, and will serve as bread, and seed-corn too, for
many days. We mean the new volume of Mr. Ruskin's "Modern
Painters," to which he appropriately gives the subordinate title,
"Of Many Things." It may be taken up with equal pleasure whether
the reader be acquainted or not with the previous volumes, and
no special artistic culture is necessary in order to enjoy its
excellences or profit by its suggestions. Every one who cares
about nature, or poetry, or the story of human development--every
one who has a tinge of literature or philosophy, will find something that is for him and that will "gravitate to him," in this
volume. Since its predecessors appeared, Mr. Ruskin has devoted
ten years to the loving study of his great subject--the principles
of art; which, like all other great subjects, carries the student

into many fields. The critic of art, as he tells us, "has to take some note of optics, geometry, geology, botany, and anatomy; he must acquaint himself with the works of all great artists, and with the temper and history of the times in which they lived; he must be a fair metaphysician, and a careful observer of the phenomena of natural scenery." And when a writer like Mr. Ruskin brings these varied studies to bear on one great purpose, when he has to trace their common relation to a grand phase of human activity, it is obvious that he will have a great deal to say which is of interest and importance to others besides painters. The fundamental principles of all just thought and beautiful action or creation are the same, and in making clear to ourselves what is best and noblest in art, we are making clear to ourselves what is best and noblest in morals; in learning how to estimate the artistic products of a particular age according to the mental attitude and external life of that age, we are widening our sympathy and deepening the basis of our tolerance and charity.

Of course, this treatise "Of many things" presents certain old characteristics and new paradoxes which will furnish a fresh text to antagonistic critics; but, happily for us, and happily for our readers, who probably care more to know what Mr. Ruskin says than what other people think he ought to say, we are not among those who are more irritated by his faults than charmed and subdued by his merits. When he announces to the world in his Preface, that he is incapable of falling into an illogical deduction--that whatever other mistakes he may commit, he cannot possibly draw an inconsequent conclusion, we are not indignant, but amused, and do not in the least feel ourselves under the necessity of picking holes in his arguments in order to prove that he is not a logical Pope. We value a writer not in proportion to his freedom from faults, but in proportion to his positive excellences--to the variety of thought he contributes and suggests, to the amount of gladdening and energizing emotions he excites. Of what comparative importance is it that Mr. Ruskin undervalues this painter, or overvalues the other, that he sometimes glides from a just argument into a fallacious one, that he is a little absurd here, and not a little arrogant there, if, with all these collateral mistakes, he teaches truth of infinite value, and so teaches it that men will listen? The truth of infinite value that he teaches is realism--the doctrine that all truth and beauty are to be attained by a humble and faithful study of nature, and not by substituting vague forms, bred by imagination on the mists of feeling, in place of definite, substantial reality. The thorough acceptance of this doctrine would remould our life; and he who teaches its application to any one department of human activity with such power as Mr. Ruskin's, is a prophet for his generation. It is not enough simply to teach truth; that may be done, as we all know, to empty walls, and within the covers of unsaleable books; we want it to be so taught as to compel men's attention and sympathy. Very correct singing of very fine music will avail little without a voice that can thrill the audience and take possession of their souls. Now, Mr. Ruskin has a voice, and one of such power, that whatever error he may mix with his truth, he will make more converts to that truth than less erring advocates who are hoarse and feeble. Considered merely as a writer, he is in the very highest rank of English stylists. The vigour and splendour of his eloquence are not more remarkable than its precision, and the delicate truthfulness of his ephithets. The fine largo of his sentences reminds us more of De Quincy than of any other writer, and his tendency to

digressiveness is another and less admirable point of resemblance
to the English Opium-eater. Yet we are not surprised to find
that he does not mention De Quincy among the favourite writers
who have influenced him, for Mr. Ruskin's style is evidently due
far more to innate faculty than to modifying influences; and
though he himself thinks that his constant study of Carlyle must
have impressed itself on his language as well as his thought, we
rarely detect this. In the point of view from which he looks at
a subject, in the correctness of his descriptions, and in a certain rough flavour of humour, he constantly reminds us of Carlyle,
but in the mere tissue of his style, scarcely ever.

"Art and Belles Lettres," Westminster Review,
65 (April 1856), USA ed. 347-8

[STAHR'S TORSO II]

Volume II of Stahr's Torso (see above for the Leader review of volume I) was
to furnish George Eliot with an idea and an image that find their way into
Middlemarch. She records her distaste for connoisseurship--a distaste cultivated by Ruskin's doctrine of realism--in this review by quoting the philosopher Arcesilas's bitter words on those who neglect life for art. Dorothea
phrases a similar criticism in Middlemarch, ch. 39, when she tells her uncle,
Arthur Brooke, why she does not like his collection of paintings: "I used to
come from the village with all that dirt and coarse ugliness like a pain within
me, and the simpering pictures in the drawing-room seemed to me like a wicked
attempt to find delight in what is false, while we don't mind how hard the
truth is for the neighbours outside our walls." The image of the torso of
Hercules (see fig. 2), which gave Stahr the title of his book, gave George
Eliot an element of a memorable scene in Middlemarch, ch. 19. Ladislaw has
just "turned his back on the Belvedere Torso in the Vatican" when his attention is called to Dorothea, who is standing before the Sleeping Ariadne.

Another writer on art, who knows how to make his subject interesting to the uninitiated, is Adolf Stahr, the author of that very
agreeable work on ancient art, "Torso," the first volume of which
we noticed a year ago.[1] The second volume is now before us, and
completes, in moderate compass, a survey of Greek sculptural art
from its earliest dawn to what may be called its faint afterglow
under the Emperor Hadrian--a survey which we commend to all readers who are not already too well-informed on the subject to be
glad of a guide learned enough, if he chose, to make an immense
display of pedantry, but tasteful enough to choose the very opposite course, and not be pedantic at all. Perhaps, indeed, the
majority of his readers would have liked him more frequently to
interrupt the easy flow of his narrative and description by a
definite citation, and by a precise statement of the grounds on
which he has adopted a very decided opinion; but a thirst for full
and accurate knowledge can be satisfied elsewhere, when once the
thirst has been created, and for this last purpose few books can
be better adapted than Professor Stahr's "Torso." German critics
will tell you that he is too enthusiastic and general in his admiration; but for our own part, since an author must be fallible,
we prefer that his fallibility should lie in this direction, and
that he should betray us into feeling too much rather than too
little pleasure in the works of our fellow men. The second volume
is not equal in interest to the first, but this diminution of interest lies in the nature of the subject; for, as the first volume
carries us to the period of Alexander, and includes an account of
the sculptures which owe their fundamental conception to the two
great schools of Phidias and Praxiteles, a continuation necessarily implies a declension. Still, if we consider that, with
the exception of the Parthenon sculptures, almost all the great
works which enable us to form a conception of Greek art as it was
in the days of Greek glory, must be referred to the kindred genius
or the reproductive skill of artists who lived in the period when
Greek art was revived under Roman patronage, we shall hardly be
indifferent to the fragmentary records which remain to us of
artistic life and production in this period, and shall only regret
that our knowledge of the atelier, where statues were wrought, is

so much more scanty than our knowledge of the palace for which
statues were ordered.

The second volume of "Torso" opens with a survey of the
Macedonian period in its relation to art. Under Alexander had already begun the era of connoisseurship. "Most men," says Arcesilas,
a philosopher of that day, quoted by Plutarch, "think it an indispensable requisite to inquire closely into the composition and
value of works of art, which are quite foreign to them, such as
pictures and statues, and to contemplate them carefully both with
their eyes and mind, while they neglect their own life, which
offers to them a fruitful subject of meditation." With Alexander
too began that splendid royal patronage through which art was
made chiefly subservient to the glory of the individual, and thus
determined to the production of portrait and of historical monuments. The Phidias of this new era in art was Lysippus, but his
skill in portrait formed only one direction of his genius. He is
supposed to have completed the Hercules ideal, both as resting
momentarily from his labours, as in the Farnese Hercules, or as
reposing for ever from his toils at the table of the gods, according to the conception indicated by the Torso of the Vatican, which,
if legend may be trusted, was found by Michael Angelo in the workshop of a shoemaker who used it as a block on which to cut out
his last! Lysippus was also famous as a sculptor of animals:
Petronius says of him, that he "lent speech to the souls of animals through the forms he gave to their bodies." He was especially great in horses, so that we may with some probability take
the Horses of the Sun at Venice as an indication of his power in
this way. The wanderings of these famous horses are curiously
indicative of European political vicissitudes. Originally produced by a Greek artist as an offering to some temple of Apollo,
they were first carried from Greece to Rome; then from Rome to
Constantinople; from thence, on the conquest of the city by the
Latins, they were carried as a trophy to Venice; five hundred
years later they were transported by Napoleon to Paris, where
they adorned the triumphal arch of the Tuileries until, after
Napoleon's fall, they were restored to Venice. A favourite occupation of art under the successors of Alexander was the symbolical representation of countries, cities, nations, and rivers as
human individuals. The ideals of the gods were exhausted; hence
the artists were urged to seek new subjects for ideal forms, and
they found them in this kind of personification. Such productions
formed suitable ornaments for the triumphal processions of the
royal personages whose courts now became the centres of Greek art,
while the ancient schools of Greece sank into insignificance.

"Athens, Sicyon, and Argos," says Professor Stahr, "almost
vanished out of the history of art; and although the traditional
forms of art were still practised, and in Athens especially, the
important commissions given by the kings of Egypt, Syria, and
Pergamos, gave very various employment to artists, there had
nevertheless begun a time in which neither the illustrious artists nor the great works produced by them exercised a substantial influence on the further development of plastic art. This
is the period which Pliny marks out as lying between the years
290 and 152 before Christ. At its close commences the revival
of genuine Greek art in Athens, coinciding with the epoch at
which it attained predominance in Rome. Shortly before the beginning of this period, in the time of Alexander the Great, we
see the historical study of earlier art beginning to exhibit

itself in a literary form. Books of travel appeared containing
descriptions of cities and countries which were peculiarly rich
in works of art. Lists were made of the most celebrated works
of art, the merits of great artists were compared, and particular species of art were criticised in systematic and historical
works. And, for the most part, it was not laymen, but artists,
and among them masters of reputation, who in this way sought to
exercise an influence on the taste and judgment of their contemporaries, as well as on the practice of art. In consequence of
this, the earlier creative spontaneity of the artist gave way
more and more to conscious reflection and calculated purpose.
By the great political revolution which had taken place, Art was
removed further and further from its position as a necessary
member of a political and religious organism; its connexion with
the common national life as developed in the organic communities
of the various races and republics of Greece being dissolved, it
became with poetry and literature, principally the affair of the
rich and cultivated."

After Alexander's death, Rhodes and the Greek cities of Asia Minor
rose into celebrity as centres of art. To the school of Rhodes
we are indebted for the Laocoon, the date of which has been so
hotly disputed by the critics. Stahr adopts the opinion that refers it to the period of the early emperors. The school of
Pergamos contributed the Dying Gladiator, Byron's description of
which makes those who are more imaginative than critical unwilling to adopt the interpretation now sanctioned by the best critics,
namely, that it does not represent a gladiator, but is a figure
once forming part of a group of barbarians intended to celebrate
the triumph of Attalus, king of Pergamos, over the Gauls who infested the Macedonian states after the death of Alexander, and
that it was transported to Rome at the time of the Roman conquest
of Pergamos. These statues of barbarians mark an interesting
change in Greek art. We see by the Œginetan sculptures that
early art, as might be expected, attempted no distinction of race
otherwise than by costume. The Trojans resemble the Greeks to a
hair in all but their armour. Of course it was the same in early
painting. When Polygnotus had to paint at Delphos the Ethiopian
King, Memnon, he did not give him the form and complexion of an
Ethiopian, but symbolized his nationality by the embroidery of
his dress, and by placing a Moorish boy at his feet.

"First with Alexander the Great, who by his world-conquering
expeditions opened to the Greeks a close acquaintance with
numerous foreign nations, began also to arise in art the sense
for historical representation in the characteristic style. Hence
followed a radical revolution in plastic art. A totally new
study of nature was necessary to the artist, and the hitherto
exclusive regard to beauty of form necessarily gave way to the
striving after characterization. The artists who received the
commission to commemorate the victory of Attalus over the Gauls,
had to perform the task in the presence of actual reality. These
savage Gauls were well-known figures; hundreds of thousands had
beheld them with terror. The artist who should represent them
was thus not in the position of the Œginetan sculptor, from whom
the barbaric Trojans, represented by him after the Homeric
legend, were removed by many hundred years. Artists like
Pyromachus and his colleagues must undertake an individual
representation of a national type, if they would be understood

by their contemporaries. They must study the Gallic type in
real models--which could not be wanting--in order to represent
it so as to meet the requirements of their age. And this they
did, as we see by their works; but they have also ennobled this
barbaric type, and made it beautiful in its kind."

We have next a sketch of Etruscan art, and the Roman art that
grew out of it in the early times of the Republic, of which we
have perhaps a characteristic relic in the She-Wolf of the Capi-
tol. This prepares the way for an account of that restoration of
Greek art alluded to in a previous quotation as having commenced,
after a century and a half of enfeeblement, in the second century
before Christ, that is, after the close of the second Punic War,
when the Romans began to cultivate art as an exotic. The school
of Athens began to revive, and found a market for its productions
in Rome; Greek artists began to take up their residence in the
world-metropolis; in fact, Rome began to bear something of the
same relation to Greek art that London bears to Italian music.
The conquest of Greece, and the transportation of its art-
treasures to Rome, heightened the appetite for such things as objects of luxury and dilettantism, and it is a significant trait,
that the Romans in this period originated that application of the
word "taste" to art, which rouses Mr. Ruskin's indignation. Professor Stahr illustrates the Roman point of view on this subject
in an interesting chapter on "Cicero and his Relation to Art,"
and in a short discussion of the Roman art-robberies, which he
traces from their germ in the religious belief that to deprive a
state of its divine images was to deprive it of the aid of its
gods, he indicates the advantages we have derived from this
felony on a large scale, which, like so many other misdemeanours,
we at once denounce and practise. In fact, but for Roman blunder
and Roman patronage we should have known little of Greek art; for
in spite of the terrible conflagrations which have again and
again laid the greater part of Rome in ruins, those ruins have
proved our best storehouse; they have preserved to us precious
copies, while the ruins of Greece have yielded few originals.

     The remainder of the volume is occupied with the history of
art under the emperors, from Augustus to Hadrian. The conception
of Bacchus as the Care-Dispeller was a favourite one with the artists of this period, and among the statues which were inspired by
this ideal is the wonderful Barberini Faun, who is sleeping off
the influence of the god. It was found in the moat of the Castle
of St. Angelo, from the battlements of which it was thrown down
by the garrison, in the time of Belisarius, on the heads of the
besieging Goths! To the early part of this period belongs, in
all probability, the Apollo Belvedere, which was found in
Raphael's time among the ruins of the summer-palace of Antium, a
favourite residence of the early emperors, especially of Nero.
The relation which later works of supreme excellence, like this
Apollo, have to the ideals of the earlier Greek artists, may suggest an interesting comparison with certain recent accusations of
plagiarism directed against Longfellow.

"The artists who flourished on Italian ground in the period of
the restoration of Greek art, could hope to place themselves on
a level with their great predecessors only by endeavouring to
complete and ennoble the characteristic types and ideal forms of
the Gods created by the old masters. In this position, at once
of freedom and subordination, which renounced the dangerous

glory of novel invention, lay, as the great Visconti remarks,
one of the secrets which secured the success of later art. Thus
Praxiteles' Venus of Cnidos grew into the Venus de Medici of
Cleomenes, and the Hercules-ideal of Lysippus into the Farnese
Hercules of Glycon. Thus artists of whom history has not preserved to us as much as their names, because they lived later
than those Greek writers on art from whom Pliny drew his information, left behind works like the Torso and the Barberini Faun,
like the Colossi of Monte Cavallo, and the Antinous Braschi,
like the Nile and the Tiber--'Masterpieces which induce us to
believe that the artists whose chisel created them have sur-
passed the old masters. <u>For</u> <u>they</u> <u>did</u> <u>not</u> <u>shrink</u> <u>from</u> <u>being</u> <u>imi-</u>
<u>tators,</u> <u>if</u> <u>only</u> <u>their</u> <u>imitations</u> <u>cast</u> <u>the</u> <u>old</u> <u>originals</u> <u>into</u> <u>the</u>
<u>shade.</u>'--Visconti, Œuvres divers."

Under the magnificent patronage of Hadrian, art rallied before
its final death-struggle, and bequeathed to us the melancholy
beauty of the Antinous. The group of San Ildefonso, which Lessing interpreted as Sleep and Death, is now explained, by the
troublesome acumen of many critics, to represent Antinous being
led by the Genius of Hadrian to the realm of shades. The second
brief division of the volume is occupied with an account of the
portraits of the Roman emperors and their families, which are
preserved to us among the relics of ancient sculpture, and with
considerations on the colossal in plastic art.

Professor Stahr, as we have intimated, aims rather at making
his subject agreeable, and at giving general conceptions, than at
furnishing detailed and systematic information; and besides he
treats almost exclusively of sculpture, his title, which implies
that he treats of ancient art generally, being too comprehensive.
On closing his book, the reader, who was not well instructed be-
forehand will probably want to know precisely what may be learned
from the remains of ancient literature concerning Greek artists
and their works.

Note

1. See <u>Westminster</u> <u>Review</u>, 64 (April 1855), USA ed. 319-20; in the opinion
of Gordon S. Haight this review was not written by George Eliot and her use of
"we" refers to the periodical, not herself.

THE ART AND ARTISTS OF GREECE

Saturday Review, 2 (31 May 1856), 109-10

In this review of Torso I and II, George Eliot treats Stahr's volumes as a unit. Her enthusiasm is considerably muted here as compared to her notice of volume I in the Leader. Though it repeats with some variation what she said in her previous two reviews, her use of humorous anecdotes describing the meetings of artists and emperors adds a touch of freshness to the essay. She transcribed the German text for her translation of the passage on Phidias and Praxiteles in entry 27.

Probably many readers will be glad to hear of a German work which tells the history of Greek Art neither in the bald fashion of an introductory manual nor with the elaborate pedantry of a German Dryasdust, but with that agreeable combination of philosophic insight, picturesque narration, and poetic enthusiasm, to be found only in minds that have prepared themselves for a special study by thorough general culture. Such a work is Torso, by Adolph Stahr, a writer whose Jahr in Italien--two volumes of Italian travel, exhibiting rare artistic feeling as well as knowledge-- prepared its readers to welcome from him a book more exclusively dedicated to art. It is a book not written to settle vexed questions, or to present any new results of independent research, but simply to give such a view of Greek art as will enable ordinarily cultivated persons to understand its organic relation to human development, and to have an intelligent and appreciatory enjoyment of its remains. Critics of a more negative disposition, and possibly of greater technical acquirement than Professor Stahr, will assail him for his too admiring attitude towards ancient art; and a certain tendency towards the oracular in his manner of writing will probably provoke them to detect many errors of statement or of judgment. But the "general reader"--by whom, we imagine, is usually meant a reader of no particular information--is likely to find Torso an acceptable book, which will conduct him through a pleasant region of knowledge without causing him the least weariness in the journey. German writers have too often the uneasy pace of the camel--they take us to many remote quarters which we could hardly reach without their aid, but they cause us much aching and grumbling in the process. Stahr, however, has a style as agreeable as the canter of a well-trained horse. If it ever divides our attention with his subject, it also divides our admiration.

Was Greek art a purely indigenous growth, or only a transplantation from the East? This question of genealogy, of course, presents itself in the first place to the historian, and with especial urgency to the German historian, who, of all others, feels constrained to commencer par le commencement.[1] Winckelmann pronounced against the supposition of an Oriental origin; and German critics, more coerced by his authority than by arguments from facts and analogy, went on maintaining the same opinion long after it had been renounced by the best foreign critics. When at length Ludwig Ross returned from his travels in the Levantine countries, and brought evidence for the filiation of Oriental and Greek art, gathered from a careful investigation of art-remains, he was derided as a "Tourist"--a superficial man, who allowed his opinions to be modified by observation, instead of spinning them, as a philosophic spider should, from a theory-secreting sac

provided for the purpose! However, since then, there have been
plenty of German critics who have not only accepted the newer
idea, but have been its most laborious and valuable illustrators.
Stahr follows in their track, treating the question in a rapid
and popular way. The reference of Greek art to an Oriental
source brings it, he observes, under a generalization which is
more and more confirmed by the discoveries of science and schol-
arship--namely, that

   the process of development in culture and art is the same as
   that of natural products and their cultivation by man. Modern
   botanical research has proved that almost everything which is
   necessary, useful, and agreeable to us in the vegetable kingdom,
   came in a gradual procession from Asia, until it was arrested at
   the western coast of Europe. And now that after a short rest it
   has sprung across the Atlantic, this propagation pursues its
   course through America towards the West. But the West receives
   the gifts of the East only to refine the rude, to develop the imperfect, to ennoble the common.

In the AEginetan sculptures we see Greek art beginning to emanci-
pate itself from Oriental and Egyptian symbolism, and advancing
towards naturalism. But still, though the artist gave a high degree of finish to the limbs, he was incompetent or indifferent to
the rendering of expression or character in the face. Athene is
like the Trojans, and the Trojans are like the Greeks. In this
respect the AEginetan sculptures present an interesting point of
contrast with the works of Giotto, which hold a corresponding
position in the development of Italian painting. Giotto and his
immediate successors, in opposition to the early Greek artists,
threw all their power into the face, and seemed to regard the
body as an insignificant appendage to it. This difference in the
order of artistic progress corresponds with the fundamental difference between Greek and Christian conceptions. To the Greek, a
fine body was the primary condition of a fine mind; but to the
spiritualism of the fourteenth century the body was but the
transient and unworthy dwelling of the immortal soul, which
flourished in proportion as the body was emaciated. Its canon of
art was--

          Give us no more of body than shows soul.

It seems a great leap to pass from the AEginetan sculptures to
those of the Parthenon, in which we see art at its highest point
of development as an essentially religious and political out-
growth. Yet we have no knowledge to fill up the chasm, and to
show us how far the immense advance was due to the individual
genius of Phidias, how far it was prepared by his predecessors.
The age of Phidias, being the period of supreme interest in the
history of Greek art, is naturally also the most delightful part
of Professor Stahr's book. From inference, from historic details, and also from mythical anecdotes, which always have their
historic significance, he forms as vivid a picture as can be obtained of Phidias in his position as an artist; he reconstructs
the Parthenon, and enables us to imagine it as it stood in its
glory; he tells the sad story of its destruction, and describes
with very fine discrimination the fragments which remain to us,--
the only works we possess that come immediately and indisputably
from the genius of Phidias. Among the sculptures which may with

probability be regarded as copies from his originals, is one of
the famous Colossi on the Monte Cavallo, and we single it out
from the rest for the sake of giving a legend admirably characteristic of the mode in which the mediaeval mind explained the
relics of classic antiquity. The reader probably remembers that
the Colossi just mentioned are two groups, each representing a
man controlling a restive horse, one of them being inscribed with
the name of Phidias, the other with that of Praxiteles. The
legend we are going to quote is contained in an Explanation of
the Wonders of Rome, written in monkish Latin of the Twelfth
century:--

In the time of the Emperor Tiberius (says the mediaeval Winckelmann) there appeared in Rome two young philosophers, Phidias and
Praxiteles, who showed themselves openly without any clothing.
When the Emperor was informed of this, he summoned them before
him, and asked them, Why they went about naked? They answered:
"Because everything lies naked and open before our eyes, and because we regard the world as naught--therefore we go about naked
and possess nothing." On account of this wisdom of theirs, the
Emperor raised them high in his palace. But they boasted of
such science that they knew everything the Emperor did, even
when out of their presence, by day and by night, and could tell
it to him to a word; so they said to him: "We will tell thee
everything thou hast spoken when away from us, by night in thy
chamber." "If you do that," answered the Emperor, "I will give
you whatever you desire." Thereupon they said: "We desire no
money, but only a monument." The next morning they related to
the Emperor, in order, the counsel he had held with himself in
the preceding night, and the Emperor, as he had promised,
founded for them the desired monument, namely, naked horses
which tread the earth beneath their hoofs, that is, which tram-
ple on the powerful of this world who rule over men. But, as a
sign that the mighty king will come, who will mount these horses,
two half-naked figures of men, who, with uplifted arm and
clenched fist, announce what will then come to pass. And as
they are themselves naked, so does all earthly knowledge lie
naked before them.

The works of Polykletos and Myron, the great contemporaries of
Phidias, with those of Praxiteles and Scopas in the succeeding
age, are subjects wide enough to carry us nearly to the end of
the first volume--leaving room, however, for a long chapter on
the Social Position of the Artist in Greece, and a discussion of
the colouring and nudity of Greek statues. Apropos of Scopas,
who was the most fertile originator of grotesque ideal beings as
attendants on the deities, Stahr observes that, when the Greeks
conceived combinations of the human with the brute form, they
made the upper part human and the lower part bestial, as in the
centaurs, satyrs, mermaids, &c., while we see the reverse in the
symbolism of the Egyptians. Like many other ingenious distinctions, however, this will not bear a very rigid examination. The
sphinx, at least, might have occurred to him as a sufficiently
remarkable exception.
     Lysippus, whose history opens the second volume, was the
first great master of portrait sculpture. But in all cases of
origination or discovery, it is "the hour and the man," and not
the man alone, that accomplishes the transition from the old to
the new. Lysippus was the contemporary of Alexander, and with

the Macedonian conquests began a new political relation for art.
The glory of the individual was no longer checked by democratic
jealousy--the days of royal patronage began, and art glorified
royalty in return. An amusing indication of the change that had
come over the spirit of art is the story told by Plutarch of the
sculptor Stasikrates. This artist went to Alexander, and proposed to him to fashion Mount Athos into an imperishable statue
of the conqueror of the world, which should touch the sea with
its foot and the clouds with its head, holding in one hand a
populous city, and with the other pouring a perpetual mountain
torrent into the sea. Alexander was wise enough to bid him leave
Mount Athos alone.

Note

1. To begin at the beginning.

"Belles Lettres," Westminster Review
66 (October 1856), USA ed. 311

[LESSING'S LAOKOON]

George Eliot first read Lessing's Laokoon in November 1854 while she was in
Berlin, and she called it "the most un-German of all . . . German books." Her
admiration for Lessing is in the same vein as George Henry Lewes's, who wrote
of him: "His mind is of a quality eminently British. Of all Germans, he is
the least German; yet he created German literature and is the idol of his
country" ("Lessing," Edinburgh Review, 82 [1845], 453). The esthetic debate
in the Laokoon, between the advocates of the plastic arts and those of poetry,
is renewed in Middlemarch, ch. 19, when Naumann claims he can do justice to
Dorothea by painting her and Ladislaw disputes this, saying, "Language gives
a fuller image." And shortly after, Will calls Dorothea "a poem" (ch. 22).
For Lessing's influence on George Eliot, see entry 8a, n. 2; 9, n. 2; and 10,
n. 1.

Every reader of Lessing's "Laokoon" remembers his masterly distinction between the methods of presentation in poetry and the plastic
arts--the acumen and the aptness of illustration with which he
shows how the difference in the materials wherewith the poet and
the painter or sculptor respectively work, and the difference in
their mode of appeal to the mind, properly involve a difference
in their treatment of a given subject. Virgil adds to the effect
of his description by making this Laokoon shriek with agony; the
words, clamores horrendos ad sidera tollit,[1] do not suggest a distorted mouth, but simply intensify in our imagination the conception of suffering. But the sculptor did not attempt to render
this detail, because he could have given us nothing else than the
distorted mouth, which would merely have been rigid ugliness, ex-
citing in us no tragic emotion. And the same fine instinct which
has here guided the sculptor to a different method of treatment
from that of the epic poet, is needed in the dramatist. "It is
one thing," says Lessing, "to be told that some one shrieked, and
another to hear the shriek itself." The narrative is a suggestion, and addresses the imagination only; but the dramatic representation attacks the sense. On the other hand, the poet would
be under an equal mistake if he adopted all the symbolism and detail of the painter and sculptor, since he has at his command the
media of speech and action, and it is the absence of these which
their symbolism is intended to supply.

Note

1. He lifts his horrible cries to the heavens. Aeneid ii.22.

EX ORIENTE LUX

"Ex Oriente Lux" is a good illustration of the way that a particularly satisfying idea could germinate in George Eliot's imagination over a period of years. The idea behind the poem comes from Stahr's Torso, and she recorded it in her notebook at entry 26. She used it in "The Art of the Ancients," "The Shaving of Shagpat," and "Art and Artists of Greece," reviews which are reprinted above. Finally, in 1866, she turned it into a poem. "Ex Oriente Lux" forms part of a MS. labeled "Poetry" (Beinecke Rare Book and Manuscript Library, Yale University); it was previously published in Bernard J. Paris, "George Eliot's Unpublished Poetry," Studies in Philology, 56 (1959), 542-3.

When first the earth broke from her parent ring
Trembling an instant ere her separate life
Had found the unfailing pulse of night & day,
Her inner half that met the effusive Sun
Had earlier largesse of his rays & thrilled
To the celestial music of the dawn
While yet the western half was cold & sad,
Shivering beneath the whisper of the stars.
So Asia was the earliest home of light,:
The little seeds first germinated there,
Birds first made bridals, & the year first knew
Autumnal ripeness. Ever wandering sound
That dumbly throbbed within the homeless vast
Took sweet imprisonment in song & speech--
Like light more beauteous for shattering,
Parted melodious in the trembling throat
Of the first matin bird; made utterance
From the full-rounded lips of that young race
Who moved by the omnipresent Energy
Dividing towards sublimer union,
Clove sense & image subtilly in twain,
Then wedded them, till heavenly Thought was born.

VERSIFICATION (1869)

George Eliot's essay "Versification (1869)" is a further specification of her essay "Notes on Form in Art (1868)" in which she writes: "Poetic Form was not begotten by thinking it out or framing it as a shell which should hold emotional expression, any more than the shell of an animal arises before the living creature; but emotion, by its tendency to repetition, i.e. rhythmic persistence in proportion as diversifying thought is absent, creates a form by the recurrence of its elements in adjustment with certain given conditions of sound, language, action, or environment" (Essays, p. 435). In Eliot's literary theory the function of poetry is to "move men's souls"; therefore, it must be powerful, for "power over the minds of men is . . . the measure of perfection." Such "fine writing demands a fine writer" and the poetry of such a writer is governed more by "natural selection" than by "unbroken observance of a rule." This essay promotes an organic theory of poetry in which "rhythmic and tonic relations" are adjusted to "the bias of passionate experience," and it eschews all rules imposed "for the mere pleasure of bondage." Its hero is Samuel Daniel and its villain Thomas Campion.

The sourcebook for the historical portion of the essay is volume II of Joseph Haslewood's collection Ancient Critical Essays upon English Poets and Poësy, 2 vols. (London: Robert Triphook, 1815). Entries 284-93 show that George Eliot copied long passages from Samuel Daniel's "A Defence of Ryme" (1603) and Thomas Campion's "Observations in the Art of English Poesie" (1602) into her notebook, as well as passages from George Gascoigne, King James, Edmund Spenser, and William Webbe. The theoretical opening paragraph of the essay draws on James J. Sylvester, The Laws of Verse; or, Principles of Versification (London: Longmans, Green, 1870). It borrows a musical terminology from a passage that Eliot quoted from Sylvester in the Folger Middlemarch notebook (see Pratt and Neufeldt, pp. 87-88). This indebtedness indicates that "Versification" in its extant form is, if the date is accurate, a later version of an essay first drafted in 1869. The passages of poetry used to illustrate prosodic principles are drawn in part from a third source: Edwin Guest, A History of English Rhythms, 2 vols. (London: W. Pickering, 1838). Guest, whom Eliot read in August 1868, is also quoted extensively in the Folger Middlemarch notebook (see Pratt and Neufeldt, pp. 8, 74-76). George Eliot's spirited comments on blank verse, Shakespeare, and Fletcher seem to have been inspired by her reading of J. A. Symonds, "Blank Verse," Cornhill Magazine, 15 (1867), 620-40, which she referred to as a "good article" (Diary, 30 May 1867).

"Versification (1869)" forms part of the MS. labeled "Poetry" (Beinecke Rare Book and Manuscript Library, Yale University); paging from the back of the MS. this essay is found on pages 8-15; it is preceded by "Notes on Form in Art (1868)," pages 1-7. The MS. also contains several of Eliot's poems as well as the epigraphs (or "mottoes") she wrote for Felix Holt, Middlemarch, and Daniel Deronda. The poetry and prose in the MS. show George Eliot bringing together in one place both her poetry and her reflections on the art of poetry.

"Versification (1869)" was first printed in 1980 in a limited, hand-set edition by The Halfpenny Press, Madison, Wisconsin.

The rule that English blank verse should consist of five iambi may be compared with the rule that a bar of common time must consist of four crotchets or eight quavers. A poem of any length made up of verses invariably presenting five regular iambi would be about as high a style of composition as a sonata of which every bar presented eight quavers, without rests, without an appoggiatura, without any notes of diverse value. Nothing higher than a jig or

a 'patter' song can be constructed on this homogeneous plan.
High musical expression depends not only on the succession of
tonic intervals; it depends equally on the adjustment of varying
quantities given to the successive notes comprised within a certain number of beats constituting a bar or series of bars. In
any high order of music, & even in rude music which gives voice
to any passion deeper than childish merriment, a large proportion
of these beats are perceived by the inward sense only, & are not
represented in sounds that strike the tympanum.

Though the rhythmic elements of fine verse cannot throughout
their whole range be paralleled with the structure of fine music,
because language is another & a more complex medium than notes;
yet, in their fundamental principles they are analogous. In both
verse & music rhythmic & tonic relations are used as a means of
moving men's souls by the adjustment of those relations to the
bias of passionate experience, i.e. to the accumulated associations of certain modes of sound with ease & struggle, consent or
resistance, joy or sorrow, awe or triumph, calmness or rage. But
in every art that reaches a high degree of practice, the use of
the medium discloses new & newer relations in that medium, so
that the artist in his turn confers fresh associations & enriches
that sensibility of the multitude which originally made all the
wealth of his art.

Our English blank verse having had the good fortune to be
written by poets & not by carpenters ("scit tendere versum non
secus, ac si oculo rubricam dirigat uno,"[1] Persius, Sat. I. 67)
the ten syllable, five iambi rule was never regarded as an absolute type; & even in the sense of five beats or accents it was
departed from by the best writers in some of their most effective
passages. The five-iambi theory was always a background for
licences. Campion, a contemporary of Shakespeare--"Sweet Master
Campion" he was called in 1595, but in 1675 he had sunk into "a
writer of no extraordinary fame"[2]--undertaking to lay down rules
for the writing of English blank verse, begins by allowing to the
"licentiate iambic" a spondee in the first or second place, forbidding it in the third & fifth; & in the second & fourth place
allowing a tribrach or dactyl, or even by way of exception an
anapest. But he presently relaxes all these exceptions to a
still greater freedom:--sees no reason why a trochee should not
come in the first place, so that it be not followed by an iambus,
which, "beginning with a single short syllable, & the other ending before with the like, would too much drink up the verse if
they came immediately together." Therefore, says he, let your
initial trochee be followed by a spondee, a dactyl or a tribrach.
And finally he shows examples where what he mistakenly calls a
tribrach "may be very formally taken" even in the fifth place.

But while "Sweet Master Campion" was giving poor verses of
his own to illustrate these kind indulgences, Master Shakespeare
& Master Fletcher were asking leave of no authority but their own
ears & their own sensibility to pregnant speech, while they produced "licentiate iambics" which the world still accepts as types
of excellence in blank verse. If then we want to know what elements this form of verse must or may consist of, the surest way
will be to examine the best passages of the best masters--to inquire what the great poets have done rather than what small gentlemen have said that poets ought to do.

Careful study will discover that there are certain conditions which are never departed from in a passage of thoroughly
fine blank verse: conditions which cannot be departed from without

a loss of power; & power over the minds of men is in this case
the measure of perfection. "Whatsoever form of words," says that
virile writer Samuel Daniel, "whatsoever form of words doth move,
delight & sway the affections of men, in what Scythian sort soever it be disposed or uttered, that is true number, measure,
eloquence, & the perfection of speech: which . . . . . . hath
as many shapes as there be tongues & nations in the world, nor
can with all the tyrannical rules of Idle Rhetoric be governed
otherwise than custom & present observation will allow."

But these conditions of power are such as can least be fulfilled by the carpenter measurement, & in the greater part are
such as cannot be well stated in the form of rules. There are no
rules that will cover all the requirements of fine writing except
the one rule, that fine writing demands a fine writer.

The most rigorous conditions of fine blank verse are such as
conciliate the rhythmical movement with the demands of forcible
declamation, pregnant expression, fully marked meaning. Time, accent, melodic utterance, have to be so inwrought with the emphasis, the tones, the gradations of rapidity which belong to the
passionate or intellectual intention of the verse, that the versification shall be to the meaning as the mythical wings to the
strong quadruped.

All valid rules--all rules not voluntarily assumed for the
mere pleasure of bondage--must have a psychological or physical
basis. They must be founded either on physical necessities or
on an organic bias which habit has made a necessity, or on a
firmly established sense of relations which is not natural merely
but permanently human. Many have given themselves trouble to
write poems after the shape of wings, arrows, hearts or flowers,
but posterity has not greatly thanked them, any more than it has
thanked the confectioners who shaped the sugar & pastry of our
ancestors into castles & armed knights, into shepherds, shepherd-
esses & their flocks, or other mimicries that pleased the fancy of
the time. Every irregularity is good if it can be shown to be
the secret of a higher pleasure than the unbroken observance of
a rule. Fortunate irregularities are discoveries in art: They
are the stages of its developments, & go on living according to
a natural selection.

But there are certain conditions of blank verse which may
be safely taken as rules having an organic or psychological
validity. The accented syllable in the last foot must never be
so mean as to mar the effect of the delicate pause or hiatus
which should be felt at the end of every verse. There should be
no ending which throws the impetus of the whole verse on some
understrapper, some 'of' or 'for' having no more than the ordinary value of a preposition, & no ending which causes the hiatus
to occur after any word depending for its value on the word that
follows it--related to it as the handle to the blade. Take as
examples to be avoided these verses from Byron's 'Cain':

                    "I look
         Around me on a world where I seem nothing <u>with</u>
         Thoughts which arise within me as if <u>they</u>
         Could conquer all things."[3]
or,

         "I lean no more on superhuman aid.
         It hath no power upon the past, & <u>for</u>
         The future, till the past be gulfed in darkness----"[4]

If Shakespeare in one of his best moods had been writing these
last three lines--which are vigorous & poetic enough in expression, though spoiled by the feebleness of the second ending, they
would probably have come from his pen in this way:

> "I lean no more on superhuman aid.
> It hath no power on the past, & for the future,
> Until the past be gulfed in darkness--"

leaving the third verse shorter than rule would make it, but not
therefore unmelodious, because it is simply a curtailed verse &
carries the ear musically to a pause--just as the curtailed verses
in the lines--

> "Light thickens; & the crow
> Makes wing to the rooky wood;
> Good things of day begin to droop & drowse;
> While night's black agents to their prey do rouse."[5]

Here we are not obliged to Steevens[6] or any other verse-carpenter
who will nail two more feet to the second line. In those verses
of Byron's, we cannot help thinking that if the poet had been
Shakespeare he would have felt a longish pause after "future"
which would have pushed on the feet of the following line, & made
it complete to his inward ear. Again, in Lear we have a thoroughly grand piece of declamation with curtailed verses:

> "It may be so, my Lord.--
> Hear, Nature, hear; dear Goddess, hear!
> Suspend thy purpose, if thou didst intend
> To make this creature fruitful!
> Dry up in her the organs of increase;
> And from her derogate body never spring
> A babe to honour her!"[7]

Not but that Shakespeare himself in his bad, careless moods,
wrote verses with feeble endings enough to give him in this
matter too his usual supremacy.
   It is not needful that all endings should be of equal weight:
on the contrary this would not be tolerable in a poem of much
length, & variety in this respect is often a source of greater
enjoyment. But the declamatory grandeur of weighty endings is
heard in such passages as this from Samson Agonistes:

> "Nothing is here for tears; nothing to wail
> Or knock the breast; no weakness, no contempt,
> Dispraise or blame; nothing but well & fair
> And what may quiet us in a death so noble!"[8]

Where a light syllable at the end of a verse produces a fine effect, it usually belongs to a trisyllable of weight & beauty. In
any case, it must be a word--or a syllable belonging to a word--
which can carry well an occasionally conferred dignity.
   The pauses must be so used as to subserve at once musical
variety & force of meaning. <u>This</u> <u>concurrence</u> <u>being</u> <u>secured</u>,
there is no point in the verse where the pause may not sometimes
occur--the effect of certain pauses which should be kept infre-
quent, gaining by that very infrequency. Thus, in the last place:

>   "Rich conceit
>   Taught thee to make vast Neptune weep for aye
>   On thy low grave on faults forgiven. <u>Dead</u>
>   Is noble Timon."[9]

>   "Loud as from numbers without number, <u>sweet</u>
>   As from blest voices uttering joy."[10]

In the first place: when also weight in the foot marked off by
the pause is essential--in this case the foot which precedes, not
follows, the pause:

>   "His heart
>   Distends with pride, & hardening in his strength
>   <u>Glories</u>; for never since created man
>   Met such embodied force."[11]

Notes

1. "Our poet knows how to draw his lines straight as if he were direct-
ing a ruddle cord with one eye shut," <u>Juvenal</u> <u>and</u> <u>Persius</u>, ed. and trans.
G. G. Ramsay, Loeb Classical Library (1918; Cambridge, Mass.: Harvard Univ.
Press, and London: William Heinemann, 1969), p. 323.

2. George Eliot takes these phrases from Haslewood's commentary, vol.
2, pp. vi and xiii.

3. <u>Cain</u>, I.i.175-78.

4. <u>Manfred</u>, I.265.

5. <u>Macbeth</u>, III.ii.50-53.

6. George Steevens (1736-1800) a well-known editor of Shakespeare.

7. <u>King</u> <u>Lear</u>, I.iv.275-81.

8. Lines 1721-24. George Eliot uses these lines to conclude <u>Daniel</u>
<u>Deronda</u>.

9. <u>Timon</u> <u>of</u> <u>Athens</u>, V.iv.77-80.

10. <u>Paradise</u> <u>Lost</u>, III.346-7.

11. <u>Paradise</u> <u>Lost</u>, I.571-4.

Index

Index

courtesans, 142; manly soul of, 11, 149
Wordsworth, William, 29, 162

Yonge, Charlotte, _History of_

Christian _Names_, xxxvi
Young, Arthur, _A Six Months Tour
through the North of England_, 20,
29, 156, 161